THE DECISIVE BATTLES OF THE WESTERN WORLD

jor-General J.F.C. Fuller C.B., C.B.E., D.S.O.

of the Western World

and their influence upon history

Volume Two

edited by John Terraine

Paladin

Granada Publishing Limited
Published in 1970 by Paladin
3 Upper James Street, London WIR 4BP
Reprinted 1972 (twice)

First published in Great Britain by
Eyre & Spottiswoode (Publishers) Ltd
1954, in the complete edition
Complete edition copyright ©
J.F.C. Fuller 1954
This specially abridged and
revised edition copyright ©
Granada Publishing Limited 1970
Made and printed in Great Britain by
Compton Printing Limited, Aylesbury, Bucks.
Set in 9 on 10pt Baskerville

Contents

Maps and Diagrams

Editor's Preface

Major-General J. F. C. Fuller, C.B., C.B.E., D.S.O. – "Boney" Fuller to all who knew him – died in 1966 at the age of 87, by which time he had become probably the most prolific soldier-writer in our language. He published his autobiography, *Memoirs Of An Unconventional Soldier*, in 1936; that was his twenty-fifth book. The final score was over forty. Much of this output was, of course, strictly professional. Fuller was a preacher; he applied his highly active mind to his soldiering; a stream of ideas poured forth, and as they did so Fuller promptly nailed them into books and articles. Inevitably, since he wrote with excitement to expound his doctrines, sparing none, much of what he wrote provoked deep opposition, particularly in military "establishment" circles. As Liddell Hart once wrote to him, "they now suffer a sort of prickly affection of the skin whenever a book of yours appears in sight."

Fuller's writing falls into two categories: professional-polemical, and historical. His reputation as a writer was first founded on the polemics – the very sharp polemics which surrounded the beginnings of armoured, mechanized warfare. He joined the newly formed Headquarters of the Tank Corps – then known as the Heavy Branch of the Machine Gun Corps – on December 26th 1916; as he wrote later, "though I did not realise it at the time, only now was my career as an unconventional soldier to begin." Repelled, like many others, by the costly static warfare of the Western Front – what he called the war of "cattle-wire and spade" – he was quick to see and develop the potentialities of the new Arm. He was able to look beyond the very limited mobility conferred by the Tanks of 1916-1918[1] to a future of fast-moving mechanized war which, he believed,.

would produce its results more quickly and at less human cost than the war of massed artillery and infantry masses. It is ironical that the war which, in due course, came closest to the fulfilment of Fuller's vision proved, in fact, to be much longer and vastly more destructive of human life than the one which so appalled him.

Having received his vision, Fuller evolved his message and advocated it with all the considerable power of his tongue and pen. This brought him into conflict with all in the Army that was hidebound and somnolent, and also with vested interests – the horse cavalry faction above all. For the military teacher, as for the commander, the study of past wars is a valuable exercise, but for both it can be dangerous. Fuller began by using history to fortify his arguments and illustrate his ideas. This is where the danger lies: in the case of the war in which he himself had taken part, and in which the Tanks had struggled, at times painfully, to find their role, Fuller's judgment was not at first entirely to be accepted. He made a bogy of the High Command, unnecessarily; he was never able to understand that his beloved Tanks had no stauncher supporter in that war than the Commander-in-Chief himself, Field-Marshal Sir Douglas Haig. But Fuller's analytical brain was too good to go on missing main points; if he never was able to bring himself to write kindly about Haig, Haig's strategic principles found handsome vindication in one of Fuller's profoundest treatises, *The Conduct Of War 1789-1961*, published in 1961.

Fuller's army career ended in 1933, on a sour note. He felt strongly the frustration of his attempts to instil what he considered to be the correct principles of mechanized warfare; he thought himself insulted by the offer of command of the Bombay District, and sent in his papers. His friends and brother officers who shared his forward-looking ideas deeply regretted this act, but later generations will take another view. It meant that he was able to free himself more and more for the writing of history, and more and more history itself took possession of him, rather than being a tool which he found convenient for other purposes. Few will dispute that the most magnificent flowering of this pursuit of history is *The Decisive Battles Of The Western World*. This great work, in three volumes, began to appear in 1954; Volume II emerged in 1955, and Volume III in 1956. All three went to a third impression. The complete book has now for fourteen years been a standard work of reference for military historians. It will go on being so, and nothing would be more desirable than for it to become a work of reference for historians in other fields as well. The full title is *The Decisive Battles Of The Western World And Their Influence Upon History*. It is precisely in tracing that influence that Fuller is at his most stimulating and revealing.

It has been my task here to edit Fuller's three volumes down to a more manageable two; this was not easy, because his approach to his subject was consecutive and compendious. It was difficult simply to omit sections without damaging the argument of the whole. I had to make a hard decision – to concentrate on Europe and cut out Fuller's narrative of campaigns outside Europe; no matter how important these might be (e.g. the war against Japan, 1941-1945). But in order to preserve the essential continuity, and to illustrate developments in society and war which would be essential for the understanding of later passages (e.g. the American Civil War) I have had to substitute for Fuller's detailed analyses much shorter statements of my own, in which I have at all times tried to preserve the flavour and penetration of Fuller's own material. I hope that I have succeeded; one thing I know, that merely to attempt such a task is to enlarge one's own knowledge and understanding. But Fuller always was a bracing teacher.

John Terraine

---

[1] In my book *The Western Front* I wrote:

... useful as the 1916-1918 tanks were for breaking into enemy positions and saving infantry lives, they were not weapons of exploitation such as we saw in World War 2. Their 'mobility' over rough ground was often reduced to 1 or 1½ miles per hour: the maximum speed of a Mark 4 (1917) was 3.7 m.p.h., of a Mark 5 (1918) 5 m.p.h., and of a 'Whippet' 7 m.p.h.. Partly because of this, but for other reasons too, they were extremely vulnerable. . . .

WHILE Frederick the Great was laying, in Europe, the foundations of a new power-structure, Britain was in process of building a new empire overseas, and very shortly afterwards of losing one also. Thanks to a naval supremacy which, though often sharply challenged, did not fail to assert itself in the long term, Britain was able to profit from the wars of Europe as others were not. The Seven Years' War proved to be the trigger of both her gain and her subsequent loss.

The British presence in India dated from the first decade of the 17th Century; but the prosperity which alone could sustain the impetus of a trading company – the Honourable East India Company – begins with the acquisition of Bombay in 1662. This was still the India of the Mogul Empire, and it would have been hard to foresee, at that time, that a company of English merchants would become the heirs of the descendants of Tamerlane. Yet, in less than a hundred years, this outcome became inevitable. The key moment was when the British moved from their "factories" in southern India and the tiny enclave of Fort William (Calcutta) into Bengal.

The decisive event was the Battle of Plassey, on 23 June 1757. The trigger of the campaign which culminated in Clive's famous victory, and the conquest of Bengal, was the reoccupation of Calcutta by the Nawab Siraj-ud-daulah the previous year, and the lamentable fate of a number of the surrendered garrison in the Black Hole. This provided, for generations of British historians, a sufficient moral base to justify all that followed; phrases like "base treachery" were considerably overworked down the years. But the truth is that, if the brutality of the Black Hole provided the trigger (as the Sarajevo assassination did for the Great War), the underlying cause of the British conquest of Bengal lay elsewhere: as usual, it lay in the conflict between British and French interests in India, and the defeat of France has to be reckoned as a result of the victory at least as significant as the overthrow of Siraj-ud-daulah. Modern research, incidentally, all tends to exonerate the Nawab from responsibility for the Black Hole atrocity, which would seem to have been an accident, not a calculated act.

The sheer military glitter of the Battle of Plassey, the astonishing improbability of a victory gained by an army of 3,000 (less than one-third of them European) with ten guns over an army of 50,000 with fifty-three guns, have tended to draw attention to the occasion itself, and leave it at that. And, indeed, the powerful personality of Clive, the wild splendour of a Mogul army, the completeness of its overthrow (at a cost to the victors of only eighteen men killed), the great treasure which the English seized after their victory, and the size of the province which they acquired, all add up to a strong enough story. But Fuller is not content to rest with that:

' What did this small battle, little more than a skirmish, accomplish? A world change in its way unparalleled since on October 31, 331 B.C., Alexander the Great overthrew Darius on the field of Arbela. Colonel Malleson, a sober writer says: "There never was a battle in which the consequences were so vast, so immediate and so permanent."[1] And in his *Lord Clive* he writes: "The work of Clive was, all things considered, as great as that of Alexander."[2] This is true; for Clive realized that the path of dominion lay open. "It is scarcely hyperbole to say," he wrote, "that tomorrow the whole Moghul empire is in our power."[3]

' Yet this victory, on the shifting banks of the Bhagirathi, produced deeper changes still. From the opening of the eighteenth century, the western world had been big with ideas, and the most world-changing was that of the use of steam as power. Savery, Papin and Newcomen all struggled with the embryo of this monster, which one day was to breathe power over the entire world. All that was lacking was gold to fertilize it, and it was Clive who undammed the yellow stream.

' "As to Clive," writes Macaulay, "there was no limit to his acquisitions but his own moderation. The treasury of Bengal was thrown open to him. There was piled up, after the usage of Indian princes, immense masses of coin, among which might not seldom be detected the florins, and byzants with which, before any European ship had turned the Cape of Good Hope, the Venetians purchased the stuffs and spices of the East. Clive walked between

---

[1] *The Decisive Battles of India* (1883), p. 68.   [2] *Ibid.* p. 495.
[3] Quoted from *The Cambridge Modern History*, vol. VI, p. 564.

heaps of gold and silver, crowned with rubies and diamonds, and was at liberty to help himself."[1]

'India, the great reservoir and sink of precious metals, was thus opened, and from 1757 enormous fortunes were made in the East, to be brought home to England to finance the rising industrial age, to supply it with its life blood, and through it to create a new and Titanic world. As Alexander had unleashed the hoarded gold of Persia, and the Roman proconsuls had seized upon the spoil of Greece and Pontus, and the Conquistadores the silver of Peru, so now did the English nabobs, merchant princes and adventurers, followers and imitators of the Seths and the Omichands, unthaw the frozen treasure of Hindustan and pour it into England. "It is not too much to say," writes Brooks Adams, "that the destiny of Europe hinged upon the conquest of Bengal."[2]

'The effect was immediate and miraculous. Before 1757 the machinery for spinning cotton[3] in England was almost as primitive as in India, and the iron industry was in a decline. Suddenly all changed. In 1760 the flying shuttle appeared; in 1764 Hargreaves' spinning-jenny; in 1768 Cartwright's power-loom. "But though these machines served as outlets for the accelerating movement of the time, they did not cause that acceleration. In themselves inventions are passive, many of the most important having lain dormant for centuries, waiting for a sufficient store of force to have accumulated to set them working. That store must always take the shape of money, not hoarded, but, in motion."[4]

'Further, after 1760 "a complex system of credit sprang up, based on a metallic treasure".[5] In 1750 Burke[6] informs us that there were not "twelve Bankers shops" in the provinces, while in 1796 they were to be found "in almost every market town". In 1756 the national debt stood at £74,575,000, and in 1815 at £861,000,000, and though between 1710 and 1760 only 335,000 acres of common land were enclosed, between 1760 and 1843 7,000,000 acres were. So the story lengthens out, profit heaped upon profit. "Possibly since the world began," writes Brooks Adams, "no investment has ever yielded the profit reaped from

[1] *Essay on Clive* (edit. 1903), p. 53.
[2] *The Law of Civilization and Decay*, Brooks Adams (edit. 1921), p. 305.
[3] *History of the Cotton Manufacture*, Sir Edward Baines (1835), p. 115.
[4] *The Law of Civilization and Decay*, Brooks Adams, p. 314.
[5] *Ibid.*, p. 317.
[6] *Two Letters on the Proposals for Peace with the Regicide Directory of France*, Edmund Burke (1796), Letter 1, p. 80.

the Indian plunder, because for nearly fifty years Great Britain stood without a competitor."[1]

' Thus it came about that out of the field of Plassey and the victors' 18 dead there sprouted forth the power of the nineteenth century. Mammon now strode into supremacy to become the unchallenged god of the western world. Once in the lands of the rising sun western man had sought the Holy Sepulchre. That sun had long set, and now in those spiritually arid regions he found the almighty sovereign. What the Cross had failed to achieve, in a few blood-red years the trinity of piston, sword, and coin accomplished: the subjection of the East and for a span of nearly 200 years the economic serfdom of the Oriental world.'

Only two years after Plassey, another great triumph electrified the British people. In North America, as in India, the rivalry of France and Britain was long-standing, with violent eruptions when the European wars cast their long shadows across the sea. The difference was that in North America, unlike India, colonization produced new populations of European stock who inherited the feuds of the parent countries. Alike in this respect, the French and British colonies differed in practically every other. The French colonial effort was activated by the State and the Church; the royal and religious influences remained dominant. The British effort was activated by commerce, and by the "mass" emigration of religious and political groups deliberately escaping from the authority of State and Church at home. The result was that, although the French presence in Canada and the British presence along the eastern seaboard of what became the United States began practically simultaneously (in the first decade of the 17th Century), by 1748 "the French in Canada numbered 80,000 and the white inhabitants of the English colonies a million".

It is a tribute to the vigour of the French, their adaptability and general address, that despite this overwhelming disparity in numbers, they succeeded in keeping the British colonies (at least in the north) under permanent threat. The most menacing outward expression of this threat was the construction, in 1720, of the great fortress of Louisbourg on Cape Breton Island, on the flank of the sea-approach to New England. But Louisbourg was only part of a grand design, which found further expression, in the same year, in the foundation of New Orleans at the mouth of the Mississipi (the French province of Louisiana) and Fort

---

[1] *The Law of Civilization and Decay*, p. 317.

Niagara, facing the inland flank of New England. During the next three decades the French pursued their plan with amazing persistence; it was nothing less than the encirclement of the English colonies by a ring of forts pushed down from Canada along the Ohio River and from New Orleans up the Mississipi, until the whole hinterland linking Canada and Louisiana became a French preserve. This scheme, no matter how far-fetched it may seem with our hind-sight, was rapidly pushed forward, "occupying with brilliant strategic insight what have proved to be the sites of the cities of the Middle West".[1]

The War of the Austrian Succession (1740–48) brought mixed fortune to both sides. In 1745 (the year of Fontenoy and the Jacobite Rebellion) the French grand design in America suffered a setback with the loss of Louisbourg to a British force whose land component consisted of New England volunteers. But the war itself ended with exhaustion and no particular advantage to either side; Louisbourg was returned to France by the Treaty of Aix-la-Chapelle in 1748, in exchange for Madras, which they had captured in 1746. This result infuriated and alarmed many in New England, yet under the eye of history takes on a more statesmanlike look than its performers probably deserved.

Peace in Europe did not extend its writ to the American frontier. The French ambition revived; new forts were built in the interior, culminating in the establishment of Fort Duquesne (Pittsburg) on the Ohio in 1753. A British attempt under General Braddock to throw the French out of Fort Duquesne met with complete disaster on the Monongahela River, the only real credit on the British side going to a young Virginian, Major George Washington, who extracted the remains of the defeated column and brought them home. This was the high peak of French ascendancy. Three years later came the Seven Years' War and the destruction of all their hopes.

Under the firm hand of the elder Pitt, British military policy displayed a clarity of purpose and efficiency of execution which was all too rare in the 18th Century – or, indeed, at any time. The decision to break French power in Canada once and for all was implemented with careful planning: the campaign of 1758 was the first stage – the reduction of the three "bastions" of French power, Louisbourg, Fort Ticonderoga ("the Gibraltar of America") and Fort Duquesne. Louisbourg, re-fortified and

[1] C. E. Carrington, *The British Overseas*, Cambridge, 1950.

strengthened, held out for nearly two months, but was forced to capitulate at the end of July; a conspicuous part in its capture was played by a young Brigadier, James Wolfe. Fort Duquesne was evacuated and burnt by the French of their own accord. The attack on Ticonderoga was badly handled and ended in disaster. Nevertheless, enough of the British strategic intention had been fulfilled to warrant pressing on with the next stage in 1759: the assault on Quebec.

Once again, sheer military glitter has tended to put an event in false perspective. Founded in 1608, Quebec, the centre and citadel of French power, was a natural fortress of great strength, improved by the work of skilful engineers. In 1759 it also enjoyed the asset of a Commander-in-Chief of great talent, the Marquis de Montcalm. Against this, the French forces were undoubtedly weak for the task of protecting such a vast area as Eastern Canada against multiple attack, and the corruption of the civil administration went far to nullify Montcalm's best efforts. Nevertheless, the enterprise against such a *place d'armes* was one to stir the imagination.

Other factors were also at work in the same direction. The commander of the British force was Wolfe, whom Fuller describes as "an ardent and highly educated soldier". His General Orders display "the care and trouble he took to form his small army into as perfect an instrument of war as time and circumstances would permit". Wolfe himself was only 32 years old; two of his three brigadiers were under 30: as Julian Corbett wrote, "it was a boy's campaign." But it was also a Combined Operation, and would stand or fall on the quality of cooperation between the Fleet and the Army. In this respect, it became a classic; Admiral Saunders, the naval C.-in-C., was, in the words of Horace Walpole, "a pattern of most sturdy bravery, united with the most unaffected modesty. No man said less, or deserved more. Simplicity in his manners, generosity, and good nature, adorned his genuine love of his country." To Wolfe he proved to be an unfailing and invaluable support; admiral and general, sailors and soldiers worked in complete unity.

The romance, however, which in British eyes at least has always surrounded the capture of Quebec, lies in the occasion itself. Drama was never lacking: the long battle of wits between Wolfe and Montcalm, whose whole object was to gain time until the Canadian winter came to his recue; the success of Wolfe's final deception plan; the silent boats drifting down the St Lawrence River to Wolfe's Cove; the sentry's challenge in the night, and the reply in French; the climb up the cliffs; the brief blast of British musketry, which settled the issue in less than fifteen minutes; Wolfe's death in the moment of victory; his last words, "Now God be praised, I will die in peace"; Montcalm's mortal wound, and death on that same evening; the capitulation of the great fortress. It was one of those moments when history seems to write itself for literature.

As usual, with such moments, certain important aspects tend to be obscured. Quebec was the centrepiece of French dominion, but Quebec was not Canada. It took another year to complete the defeat of France in North America, and this was the work of Amherst. It is frequently forgotten that Wolfe's campaign itself was only a part – though certainly the most important – of a wider plan of operations under Amherst's commander-in-chief. In 1760, he brought this to its final fruition with a brilliantly coordinated series of movements which united three well-separated columns before the walls of Montreal. It was the capitulation of that city two days later (8 September) that gave Britain Canada. Sir John Fortescue says of Amherst: "He was the greatest military administrator produced by England since the death of Marlborough, and remained the greatest until the rise of Wellington."

The peace treaty which ended the Seven Years' War in 1763 did not repeat the old pattern of exchanging and returning conquests. This time the result was final. Fuller writes:

' The treaty secured not only the maritime supremacy of England but also the prestige of Prussia: a greater empire was born and a greater kingdom was founded; the former to control the oceans, the latter to perplex the lands. France not only lost her colonial empire and her navy, but was left in that financial ruin out of which emerged the French Revolution. "Thus then has France disappeared from North America," exclaims Chateaubriand, "like those Indian tribes with which she sympathized."[2] And "All, and more than all, that France had lost," writes Parkman, "England had won. Now, for the first time, she was beyond dispute the greatest of maritime and Colonial Powers."[3]

' Nevertheless, the most important immediate result of Wolfe's victory was the removal of the fear of France from the minds of the colonists of New England, of Virginia, of Pennsylvania, and the other colonies. It was a result realized by many at the time, including the Duke of Bedford, who, on May 9, 1761, had written as follows to Newcastle: "Indeed, my lord, I don't know whether the neighbourhood of the French to our North American colonies was not the greatest security for their dependence on the mother country, which I feel will be slighted by them when their apprehension of the French is removed."[1] '

Historical hindsight now confirms what only a handful of perceptive people appreciated at the time – that the conquest of Canada was only a phase of a larger transaction; that the apparent absolute victory in fact planted the seed of an even more absolute defeat, which was not long delayed. Fuller continues:

'By doubling British colonial responsibilities, the exclusion of the French from north America brought to the fore the problem of imperial control. Thus far, the empire had been a commercial undertaking run on mercantile lines, in which the colonies contributed to the wealth of Great Britain. But now, unseen by king and parliament, the vast acquisitions gained during the Seven Years War introduced a transition from commercial to territorial imperialism, and although, according to the former, the colonies were little more than oversea investments of the homeland, according to the latter, they were potential homelands of their own. The result was that, while king and parliament continued to think in terms of trade, the American colonists began to think in those of liberty, and where the one talked of duties, the other talked of rights. What the motherland looked for was not the servitude of her colonial children, but their obedience, and what the children aspired to was not complete independence, but what to-day is called "Dominion status". Thus, in 1774, when this new idea had become rooted, we find James Wilson of Pennsylvania stating: "All the different

[1] Indeed prophetic words. Quoted from Corbett, vol. II, p. 173. Edward Channing, (*History of the United States*, 1920, vol. II, p. 603) quotes two remarkable forecasts, the one by Choiseul in 1761, and the other by M. de Vergennes, early in 1763. The first expressed his wonder that "our great Pitt should be so attached to the cession of Canada; for the inferiority of its population, he observed, would never suffer it to be dangerous in the hands of France; and being in the hands of France, to us it would always be of service, to keep our Colonies in that dependence which they would not fail to shake off the moment Canada should be ceded." The second said: "Delivered from a neighbour whom they always feared, your other colonies will soon discover, that they stand no longer in need of your protection. You will call on them to contribute towards supporting the burthen which they have helped to bring on you, they will answer you by shaking off all dependence." Another interesting prediction, highly satirical, is to be found in *The Gentleman's Magazine*, 1759, p. 620. It reads: "Canada ought to be restored in order that England may have another war; that the French and Indians may keep on scalping the colonists, and thereby stint their growth; for otherwise the children will be as tall as their mother. . . ."

members of the British Empire are distinct States, independent of each other, but connected together under the same sovereign in right of the same Crown."

'Unfortunately, this new conception of empire, which meant, as one writer has said, that "the colonies could not forever remain half in, half out of the Empire, professing allegiance while refusing obedience", was as incomprehensible to the home government, as government without a king had been during the days of the Great Rebellion. Yet what was appreciated was that, although the war had disposed of the French menace, the Indian menace remained, and that it was a very real one, the Pontiac Conspiracy, which immediately followed the ratification of the Treaty of Paris, made tragically clear. Except for Detroit and Pittsburgh, every western fort was captured by the Red Indians, hundreds of families were brutally massacred, and the frontier from Niagara to Virginia was ravaged. But the most conspicuous fact in this upheaval was that it was the British red-coats and not the colonists who quelled the rising. The latter, who possessed no central government, were unable to combine in their own defence; therefore their protection devolved on the British Government, and its provision carried with it the question of revenue to pay for it.'

The significance of the argument which now developed between the British Government and the American colonists may be judged by the fact that while, in 1748, the cost of military establishments in America had been £70,000 a year, by 1763 the figure had risen to £350,000 – five times as much. With the National Debt standing at £130,000,000, it is not surprising that the Government should have tried to meet some of its colonial expenditure out of the pockets of the colonists whom it was defending. What *is* surprising is, on the one hand, the total failure to appreciate the frame of mind of the colonies, and on the other, the speed with which the quarrel broke into open violence and rebellion.

The sequence of events was as follows: only two years after the Seven Years' War (1765) Parliament passed the Stamp Act – an attempt to raise revenue in America; the reaction there was vigorous and immediate and the Act was repealed the next year. Linked to the repeal, however, was the Declaratory Act, which asserted the right of the King and Parliament to pass laws which would be binding on the colonies. The response to this was a steady increase in violent agitation, which produced four years later (1770) the "Boston Massacre", a riot in which four citizens were killed and seven wounded by British troops. This further inflamed the violence, until three years later (1773) it broke out again in open disorder: the "Boston Tea Party", when a band of men threw tea-chests into Boston harbour in protest against Customs duties. In the same year, the Quebec Act defined the boundaries of Canada and confirmed the French population in their rights to their own laws and religion; both of these results angered the Protestants of New England. The cumulative effect of all these factors was the achievement of what had always appeared impossible, no matter how grave the dangers which might threaten: colonial unity. A "Continental Congress" assembled at Philadelphia in 1774, and passed an Act of Association. This, to the British Government, spelt a "state of rebellion", only to be met by military force.

So, in a space of only twelve years, the British Empire moved from a position of absolute victory over its chief rival in North America, to a War of Independence against its own colonists. The shooting began, at Lexington, in 1775; it continued for eight years, ending in the complete defeat of Britain. For this result, military ineptitude must take a large part of the blame. The higher direction of the war, both by the Secretary of State in London, Lord George Germaine, and by the Commander-in-Chief in America, Sir William Howe, was feeble and inept. The British Army itself was seriously under strength and at a low ebb of efficiency. Even so, such was the weakness of the colonies, their inability to combine effectively, the aversion to serving in regular forces, that for two years the British were able to hold their own without grave difficulty. It was the unswerving determination of Washington which alone, at times, kept the rebellion alive.

What might have been accomplished under better leadership was briefly and tantalizingly glimpsed in the campaign of 1777. An American invasion of Canada had failed disastrously the previous year. The British now planned a pincer movement against New England (the "hot-bed" of the rebellion), the northern arm of the pincer coming down from Montreal, and the southern coming up from the loyal stronghold of New York. The northern force was commanded by Lieutenant-general Sir John Burgoyne, an able, active and intelligent officer; his force was admirably trained and equipped for its task – showing what could have been done with these soldiers by other generals, if they had been so minded. One of the officers wrote, as the campaign opened: "As to our army, I can only say if good discipline, joined to health and spirit among the men at being led by General Burgoyne, who is universally esteemed and respected, can ensure success, it may be expected."

The expectation was utterly dashed, despite a brilliant beginning, through the failure of Germaine in London and Howe in New York to coordinate the operations of the British columns. Instead of bending all his energies to supporting and uniting with Burgoyne, Howe allowed himself to be drawn into divergent operations southward against Pennsylvania. Burgoyne himself made mistakes, but these need not have been fatal if he had received the support he had counted on. Instead, he was left weakened and isolated in the face of an overwhelming superiority of numbers, and forced to capitulate on 17 October at Saratoga. This disaster was the turning point of the war – not because of the surrender of 3,500 British soldiers (all that were left of some 8,000 who had set out from Montreal in June) in America, a loss which could have been repaired, but because of the implications of the event in Europe. Saratoga turned the War of American Independence into a world war: in 1778 France declared war on Britain; in 1779 Spain followed suit; and in 1780 Britain herself multiplied her enemies by declaring war on Holland.

After Saratoga there is a certain inevitability about succeeding events, though they continued to throw up their surprises. One thing had been clear from the start of the rebellion, and that was the immense advantage that Britain possessed through command of the sea. War against her three chief naval rivals and competitors all at once naturally put this at hazard. Off the coasts of America, in the West Indies, and in home waters, the Royal Navy was stretched to its limits. The Great Siege of Gibraltar (1779-82), although a triumph, was also a continuing drain on naval resources. Good seamanship and hard fighting staved off the worst consequences: there was no outright heavy defeat of a British fleet, no Trafalgar in reverse, but there was a falling away of capacity, a mounting failure to use the instrument of sea-power to force decisions. It was precisely this that was seen on 5 September 1781 in Chesapeake Bay.

The war on the American mainland was, at this stage, hanging in balance. In New England the British had made no headway; on the other hand, much as he desired to do so, and despite French help, Washington was unable to dislodge them from New York. In the southern colonies, after successful campaigns in the Carolinas, a British force under Lord Cornwallis had invaded Virginia, and based itself at Yorktown, near the mouth of Chesapeake Bay. But everything depended on command of the sea; by this, and this alone, could British operations be co-ordinated and reinforced; equally, by this the French would be able to pour in sufficient fresh forces to tilt the balance. It was now that the British naval weakness was seen; badly outnumbered in American waters, the British squadrons failed to prevent the landing of French reinforcements which enabled Washington to concentrate in decisive strength against Cornwallis. Worse still, catching the main French fleet at a distinct disadvantage, the British failed to grip their opportunity of destroying it; the battle on 5 September was a straggling, indecisive affair, with only some 500 casualties on both sides, but as Fuller says, it "led to the doom of Cornwallis, and consequently must take its place among the decisive battles of the world." After Chesapeake Bay, it was no longer possible either to evacuate or support Cornwallis by sea, and on 19 October his army was forced to lay down its arms at Yorktown. The British troops marched out to the tune of "The World Turned Upside Down" – which was a good deal more appropriate than they knew. Fuller writes:

'Thus ended the crowning campaign of the war, which after prolonged negotiations was brought to its conclusion by the Treaty of Versailles, signed on November 3, 1783. By its terms the independence of the United States of America was established and the 13 colonies granted unlimited power to expand westward. A new nation, in potentials rivalling all the nations of Europe combined, was added to the western world, and a great empire, possessed of a new imperialism, was born, which in a little over a century was to take its place among the world's great powers, and half a century later still, in wealth and might exceed them all.

'More immediately important, the War of American Independence brought to a close the Age of the Reformation. What Luther and Calvin had created, and what the Thirty Years War and the Puritan Rebellion in England had developed was brought to its final expression in the Declaration of Independence, drafted by Thomas Jefferson, the disciple of John Locke. In this epoch-shattering document may be read:

' "We hold these truths to be self-evident, that all men are created equal, that they are endowed by their Creator with certain inalienable rights, that among these are life, liberty, and the pursuit of happiness. That to secure these rights governments are instituted among men, deriving their just powers from the consent of the governed. That whenever any form of government becomes destructive to these ends, it is the right of the people to alter or abolish it, and to institute new government, laying its foundations on such principles and organizing its powers in such form, as to them shall seem most likely to effect their safety and happiness."

'This was a challenge not only to the government of the King of England, but to absolutism throughout the western world. Thus it came about that when, on December 6, 1777, Louis XVI wrote "approved" on Vergenne's proposals for an American alliance, he signed his death warrant, and when Spain entered the war, she abrogated her colonial empire.

' It was not in France but in America that the French Revolution sprang to life. It was from America that the French soldiers brought home with them the seed of liberty, equality and fraternity. Summing up his impressions of the war, the youthful Saint-Simon exclaimed:

' "I felt that the American Revolution marked the beginning of a new political era; that this revolution would necessarily set moving an important progress in general civilization, and that it would, before long, occasion great changes in the social order then existing in Europe."[1]

'And Mathieu Dumas wrote:

'"We listened with avidity to 'Doctor Cooper', who, while applauding our enthusiasm for liberty said to us: 'Take care, take care, young men, that the triumph of the cause on this virgin soil does not influence overmuch your hopes; you will carry away with you the germ of these generous sentiments, but if you attempt to fecund them on your native soil, after so many centuries of corruption, you will have to surmount many more obstacles; it cost us much blood to conquer liberty; but you will shed torrents before you establish it in your old Europe'."[2]

[1] _Œuvres de Saint-Simon_ (1865–1878), vol. i, p. 12.
[2] _Souvenirs du Lieutenant-Général Comte Mathieu Dumas_ (1839), vol. i, p. 108. In his _Memoirs_ the Chevalier de Pontgibaud, aide-de-camp to Lafayette, writes: "When

we think of the false notions of government and philanthropy which these youths acquired in America, and propagated in France with so much enthusiasm, and such deplorable success – for this mania of imitation powerfully aided the French Revolution, though it was not the sole cause of it, – we are bound to confess that it would have been better, both for themselves and us, if these young philosophers in red-heeled shoes had stayed at home. . . ." (Quoted by Trevelyan in his *George the Third and Charles Fox*, 1912, vol. II, pp. 401–402.)

The coming of the French Revolution

Although it was the American Revolution that set the French Revolution vibrating, no two countries could have been less alike than the United States and France in 1789. The one was a vast, undeveloped land that offered boundless opportunities to a free and democratically-minded people; the other an ancient, monarchial state shackled by traditions and privileges. In America, taxation–the cause of the rebellion of 1775–was decided by representation, in France it was determined by the king and paid by the Third Estate–that is, by everybody except the nobility and clergy. The grievances caused by this lack of equity were stimulated instead of mitigated by the rising prosperity of France, because every increase in wealth was at once cancelled out by increased debt and additional taxation. It was not the poverty-stricken proletariat, but the well-to-do middle classes–the wealth producers–who were hardest hit, and it was their demands for social justice and a place in the direction of national affairs which resulted in the revolution.

To pay for the part played by France in the War of the American Independence, Louis XVI (1774-1792) had summoned to his counsels the Genevese banker Jacques Necker, and he, to avoid increased taxation, had adopted the expedient of financing the war on loans, until interest on them could no longer be paid without increased taxation. It was debt which precipitated the flood predicted by Louis's grandfather, Louis XV, when he is reputed to have exclaimed: *"Après moi le déluge."*

In 1781 Necker was dismissed, and soon after was replaced by Charles Alexandre de Calonne who, to stay the crisis, persuaded Louis to assemble the *Notables* (deputies of the nobility and clergy). They met in 1787, but when they found that Calonne's financial reforms struck at their privileges, they refused to sanction them. Next, on August 8, 1788, Louis, with much trepidation, was persuaded by the *Parlement* of Paris[1] to summon the States General for the following year. They had not met since 1614.

---

[1] The *Parlements* (Municipal Councils) had been abolished by Louis XV, and were recalled by Louis XVI on his accession.

What the people wanted was a constitutional monarchy, under which their representatives would meet periodically and grant supplies, and it was with these ideas in mind that the States General assembled in Versailles and held their first session on May 5, 1789.

The representatives of the Third Estate refused to sit as a separate order, and invited the deputies of the nobility and clergy to deliberate with them, and because few were willing to do so, on June 10, the representatives declared themselves a National Assembly. Ten days later, in the famous Tennis Court, they took an oath that they would not separate until they had decided upon a new constitution. To appease them, Louis ordered all deputies of the privileged orders to join the Commons, but simultaneously, to forestall trouble, he instructed the Duc de Broglie to form a camp of Swiss and German troops at Versailles, and he dismissed Necker, whom he had called back some time before.

This thinly disguised threat put the Paris mob, the tool of the capitalists, who held that Necker was the only man who could effect a recovery, in a frenzy. The outcome was that, on July 14, the rabble stormed the Bastille and massacred its garrison. When the news was brought to Louis he exclaimed: "This is a great revolt." The Duc de Liancourt replied: "No, Sire, it is a great revolution."

The immediate effects of this outbreak were the recall of Necker and the formation of the National Guard under the Marquis de Lafayette.

In order to reassure the people, on August 26 the National Assembly issued a declaration known as "The Rights of Man", which closely resembled the American "Declaration of Independence". As Louis hesitated to ratify it, on October 5, Lafayette, with a detachment of the National Guard, followed by a howling mob, brought the royal family from Versailles to the capital. Thereon the King's youngest brother, the Comte d'Artois, fled the country with the first wave of *émigrés*, who at once began to plot the overthrow of the Revolution. Their intrigues with foreign powers were one of the main causes of eventual war.

As the country was bankrupt, on the suggestion of the Bishop of Autun (Talleyrand)–lover of Necker's daughter Madame de Staël–the Assembly set out to reform the Church in order to appropriate its vast estates. It declared that the bishops and clergy should henceforth be elected by the representatives of the people. Next, Mirabeau urged that money in the form of *assignats* be issued against the confiscated Church lands. But Necker out-jockeyed him and obtained vast tracts of ecclesiastical property as security for his promises to pay in gold and silver; but as neither existed his notes were refused and a run on the exchanges followed. Necker then fled the country, and under Mirabeau's influence the land-money was issued.

This anti-religious legislation cut Louis to the quick. "I had rather be King of Metz," he exclaimed, "than rule over France on such terms." The result was that, shortly after it had come into force, he began to contemplate flight, not to loyal Normandy or Brittany, as Mirabeau had suggested, but to the *émigrés* at Metz. In this he was ardently supported by the Queen – Marie Antoinette – daughter of Maria Theresa and sister of the Austrian Emperor Leopold II (1790–1792).

On the night of June 20–21, Louis and his family gave their guardians the slip and set out on the road to Montmédy, but they were recognized and arrested at Varennes, and sent back to Paris. When the news reached Leopold, he declared that the King's arrest "compromised directly the honour of all sovereigns and the security of every government". On August 27, in con-junction with Frederick William II of Prussia (1786–1797), he issued the "Declaration of Pilnitz", in which the two monarchs stated that they were ready to join other European rulers should they support Louis. Leopold's aims were far from disinterested, for shortly before the declaration was issued he had concerted a plan with Frederick William to partition France: Austria was to take Alsace and Lorraine and Prussia the duchies of Jülich and Berg and be given a share in the contemplated partition of Poland.

On September 14, the National Assembly, which had decided on a new constitution, dissolved itself and was replaced by the Legislative Assembly provided for by the Constitution. It held its first session on October 1, 1791.

Its leadership passed into the hands of a group of young middle-class enthusiasts, known as the Girondins, because many came from the Gironde. They were violently opposed to the *émigrés*, Leopold and Marie Antoinette. Fearful of, and insulted by, the assembly of small *émigré* armies on the eastern frontiers of France, they argued that war with Austria would unite the nation and compel Louis to show his hand.

In December, this enthusiasm for war led to the organization of the troops along the eastern frontier of France into three armies: the Army of the North under Rochambeau, the Army of the Centre under Lafayette, both of whom had served in America, and the Army of the Rhine, under Marshal Nicolaus Luckner, an old German hussar. These were the first armies of the Revolution.

Increasingly, the Paris press stimulated the warlike passion of the people, and at the Jacobins[1] and in the Assembly Brissot excited enmity toward the court and belief in the necessity of war. War was required not only to consolidate the people and keep them subservient to the will of the Assembly, but also because, as Hérault de Sechelles said, "in time of war measures can be taken that would appear too stern in time of peace" – a forecast of the approaching Terror.

When the Bastille was stormed there was no idea in Europe of a crusade against France. The problem which then held the attention of the courts was Poland and not the Revolution. With the death of Leopold on March 1, 1792, a change rapidly set in; for his son Francis – Francis II and last of the Holy Roman Emperors (1792–1835) – took up the challenge of the Girondins and was eager to vindicate the honour of his aunt. At the same time, Frederick William looked upon France as easy prey and saw in the Revolution an excuse to extend his realm, while Catherine II of Russia (1762–1796) sought to entangle both Vienna and Berlin in the affairs of France, so that she might gain elbow-room in Poland, which was on the verge of its second partition. Finally, the monarchial party in France saw in an Austrian irruption and the scattering of the French levies the sole means of saving Louis. Such was the situation when on April 20, 1792, under a Girondin Ministry, Louis XVI, its captive, proposed to his captors a declaration of war against Austria, in order that they might be overthrown and himself released.

France was quite unprepared for war: her treasury was empty, her army chaotic and her people hysterical. On July 11 a general call to arms was made and a rabble of volunteers enrolled. A fortnight later, Prussia declared war on her, and the Duke of Brunswick, who had been appointed to the command of the

---

[1] When the Assembly moved to Paris, certain representatives of the Third Estate rented a large room in the monastery of the Jacobins, hence the name of the most famous of the revolutionary clubs.

Prussian army, issued an ill-advised manifesto, concocted by the *émigrés*, which threw Paris into a frenzy. On August 10, the Tuileries was stormed, and a decree issued that abolished the Constitution of 1791 deprived Louis of all his powers and established universal suffrage. The Legislative Assembly was succeeded by the Convention.

In the midst of this chaos, the gravest peril came from the army, 82,000 strong, excluding frontier garrisons. On the left, the Army of the North, now under Lafayette, covered the frontier from Dunkirk to Malmédy, and was split into two groups, one (24,000) in camps on the Flemish border, and the other (19,000), known as the Army of the Ardennes, near Sedan. On its right stretched the Army of the Centre–also called the Army of Metz–(17,000) from Montmédy to the Vosges, under Marshal Luckner. And on his right lay the Army of the Rhine (22,000) from the Vosges to Basle, under General Biron (formerly the Duc de Lauzun). In the rear, around Soissons, there was also a rabble of unorganized and insubordinate volunteers, known as the Reserve Army.

When, on August 11, Lafayette, then at Sedan, learnt of the decree of the day before, he at once ordered General Arthur Dillon, at Pont-sur-Sambre, and General Dumouriez, at the Camp of Maulde, to march on Paris. Though the former–a Royalist–agreed, the latter–a friend of the Girondins–refused to do so. The Assembly learnt of the mutiny and sent commissaries to Sedan, who were seized by Lafayette and imprisoned. Others were then sent, and on August 18 they placed Dumouriez in command of the Army of the North. The next day, when he found that his army had lost confidence in him, Lafayette and many of his officers crossed the Luxemburg border and surrendered to the Austrians. At the same time, Luckner at Metz–a friend of Lafayette–refused to accept the decree and was replaced by General François Christophe Kellermann and sent to Châlons to command second line troops. Nearly all Luckner's principal officers were dismissed, and in the Army of the Rhine, Biron alone among its generals full-heartedly accepted the decree. Such was the state of the army when Dumouriez succeeded Lafayette.

CHAPTER I

The Cannonade of Valmy, 1792

The Cannonade of Valmy was more than a military event; it drew a sharp line between the form war had taken since 1648 and the form it was to assume after 1792. In the earlier period, as previously related, war became more and more limited both politically and militarily. With a few notable exceptions, campaigns were methodical, leisurely, and punctuated by an accepted etiquette. Writing in 1677, the Earl of Orrery observes that "we make war more like Foxes than Lyons, and you have twenty sieges for one Battel".[1] Some 20 years later we find Daniel Defoe writing: "Now it is frequent to have armies of fifty thousand men of a side stand at bay within view of one another, and spend a whole campaign in dodging, or, as it is genteely called, observing one another, and then march off into winter quarters."[2] A hundred years later it is much the same. Lazare Carnot notes that, "What was taught in the military schools was no longer the art of defending strong places, but that of surrendering them honourably, after certain conventional formalities."[3]

At the siege of Pizzighetone, in 1733, we are offered a perfect example of idyllic war. A truce had been arranged and, we read:

"A bridge thrown over the breach afforded a communication between the besiegers and the besieged: tables were spread in every quarter, and the officers entertained one another by turns: within and without, under tents and arbours, there was nothing but balls, entertainments and concerts. All the people of the environs flocked there on foot, on horse back, and in carriages: provisions arrived from every quarter, abundance was seen in a moment, and there was no want of stage doctors and tumblers. It was a charming fair, a delightful rendezvous."[4]

A hundred years after Carnot's observation, and when the new form of war approached its zenith, Marshal Foch castigated these

[1] *A Treatise of the Art of War, etc.* (1677), p. 15.
[2] "An Enquiry upon Projects" in *The Earlier Life and Chief Earlier Works of Daniel Defoe*, Henry Morley (1889), p. 135.
[3] *De la defense des places fortes* (1812), p. xiii.
[4] *Memoirs of Goldoni*, trans. John Black (1814), vol. 1, p. 207.

"antiquated methods . . . in which there is no decisive solution, nothing but a limited end . . .", and poured scorn on Maurice de Saxe (1696–1750) for having said: "I am not in favour of giving battle, especially at the outset of a war. I am even convinced that a clever general can wage war his whole life without being compelled to do so."[1]

Nevertheless, the reasons for these "antiquated methods" were ignored by Foch. They were not only abhorrence of the unlimited barbarities of the Thirty Years War and the realization that wars between gentlemen are preferable to wars between cads, but also the growing cost of regular, standing armies coupled with the deficiencies of their commissariat and the slowness of supply by requisitioning. These restrictions led to the avoidance of battles, which at the close musket range of this period were extremely costly in life, and also to the frequency of sieges, in order to establish supply depôts at intervals along the lines of march. Basically, the pace-maker was cost–that is, money–and this was realized by Guibert as early as 1770. He considered that wars of punctilious courtesies, of bloodless manoeuvres and honourable surrenders were only superficially cheap because they led to no grand political solutions. In their place he suggested a very different kind of conflict.

"But let us suppose," he writes, "that a vigorous people were to arise in Europe: a people of genius, of resources and of political understanding: a people who united with these stirling virtues and with a national militia a fixed plan of aggrandizement, and never lost sight of it: a people who knows how to make war cheaply and sustain itself on its victories. Such a people would not be compelled to limit its fighting by financial calculations. One would see this people subjugate its neighbours, and overthrow our feeble Constitutions, like the north wind bends the frail reeds."[2]

Valmy was the herald of the type of war Guibert had in mind, and one year after its cannonade had thundered and two years after Guibert was dead, in order to assure the "permanent requisition of all Frenchmen for the defence of the country", on

[1] *The Principles of War*, trans. Hilaire Belloc (1918), pp. 27–28. Well may it be asked: if wars are to be, are not limited ends preferable to unlimited ones? Is not the behaviour at Pizzighetone wiser and more rational than the behaviour at the Battle of the Somme in 1916, or at the bombing of Hiroshima in 1945?

[2] In "Discours Préliminaire" of his *Essai Général de Tactique*, 1770. (See *Oeuvres Militaires de Guibert*, 1803, vol. I, pp. 15–16.) A point to note here is the introduction of the idea of amorality into war; force becomes the dominant factor.

August 23, 1793, the National Convention passed a law whereby unlimited warfare became the order of the day.

"The young men shall fight", we read; "the married men shall forge weapons and transport supplies; the women will make tents and clothes and will serve in the hospitals; the children will make up old linen into lint; the old men will have themselves carried in to the public squares and rouse the courage of the fighting men, to preach hatred against kings and the unity of the Republic.

"The public buildings shall be turned into barracks, the public squares into munition factories. ... All fire-arms of suitable calibre shall be turned over to the troops: the interior shall be policed with shot guns and cold steel. All saddle horses shall be seized for the cavalry; all draft horses not employed in cultivation will draw the artillery and supply wagons."[1]

Such was the birth-cry of total war.

It was these two forms of war—the limited and unlimited—which were brought into clinch during the French Revolution, and both are well exemplified by the leaders in the initial clash—Charles William Ferdinand Duke of Brunswick on the one hand, and Charles François Dumouriez on the other.

Brunswick was born in 1735 and Dumouriez in 1739; they were therefore approximately of the same age, which was their sole common link. The one was a *grand seigneur* and a nephew of Frederick the Great; the other an astute political and military adventurer, son of a French commissary. In 1792, Brunswick was held to be the greatest soldier in Europe; Dumouriez believed himself to be such. He had an unbounded confidence in himself, saw in the Revolution a career exactly suited to his talents, and instinctively felt that to make the most of its fanatical spirit, audacity was the highest prudence; of principles he had none, other than opportunism. On one occasion he proposed a plan to save the monarchy. It was simple and audacious. In order to defeat the Jacobins, he said, all that was necessary was to become one. "Think as they do, adopt their spirit and language, and then turn upon them."[2] In the field he was completely fearless, made light of difficulties, showed an indefatigable activity and possessed that most precious gift—ability to electrify his men. He was

---

[1] Quoted from *Mémoires sur Lazare Carnot*, Lazare Hippolyte Carnot (1907), vol. i, p. 379.
[2] *Valmy*, Arthur Chuquet (n.d.), p. 12.

a brilliant and talented military gambler, imaginative, quick-witted, foreseeing and as optimistic as Candide.

Brunswick was a learned, highly cultivated pedant, cautious, painstaking, and apt to examine every problem in such minute detail that the problem itself vanished from sight. His reputation was founded largely on his 1787 campaign in Holland. It was so completely bloodless that in the eyes of his contemporaries it appeared to be an example of perfect generalship. And so it actually was, for within the narrow limits of methodical warfare, Brunswick, like an expert chess player, could foresee every move, as long as his opponent observed every rule. He invariably magnified his own difficulties and seldom considered those of his adversary, and usually was as loth to express an opinion of his own, as under pressure he was yielding to the opinions of others. Unfortunately for him, Frederick William—an impulsive and shallow-minded man—tried to play the part of Frederick the Great, and Brunswick, who considered that the first duty of a Prussian field-marshal was to obey his prince, against his better judgment complied with his wishes. Further, Brunswick intensely disliked the Austrians; looked upon France as Prussia's true ally, and held the *émigrés* in abhorrence. So highly was he thought of by both the Girondins and Jacobins that, early in 1792, the Revolutionary Government offered him the supreme command of the French army,[1] which, had he accepted it, would have made Dumouriez his collaborator instead of his opponent.

The armies commanded by these two men were also very different. The Prussian and Austrian were the obedient tools of their respective monarchs. The French, though still largely composed of the soldiers of the old Royal Army, was a national army animated by a national spirit. Under leaders who knew how to exploit its spirit, it could display wonderful *élan*, and under those who could not, it was subject to panics and mutinies. Though lamentably deficient of officers, more especially in the infantry and cavalry, for thousands had become *émigrés*, thanks to its magnificent corps of long service non-commissioned officers, officers could readily be promoted. At the time of Valmy, we find, either in command or in the ranks, many of the famous names of the Empire, names such as Jourdan, Lecourbe, Oudinot, Victor, Macdonald, Davout, Gouvion-Saint Cyr, Mortier, Soult,

[1] See *Charles William Ferdinand, Duke of Brunswick*, Lord Edmond Fitzmaurice (1901), pp. 45–49.

Leclerc, Lannes, Masséna, Berthier, Bessières, Suchet, Laharpe, Friant, Lefebvre and Kellermann (the elder).

The French artillery was the best in Europe, for though the father of modern gunnery was an Englishman, Benjamin Robins, who in his *New Principles of Gunnery* (1742) advocated the breech-loading rifled gun and placed gunnery on a scientific footing, the greatest progress in artillery was made in France under the direction of Gribeauval. In 1776, when appointed Inspector-General of Artillery, he reorganized the French artillery from top to bottom. He restricted field artillery to 4-pounder regimental guns, and for the reserve (divisional artillery) to 8- and 12-pounder guns and 6-in. howitzers. For garrison and siege work he adopted 16- and 12-pounder guns, 8-in. howitzers and 10-in. mortars. He introduced limber-boxes and had gun-carriages constructed on a uniform model, their parts, as far as possible, were interchangeable.

These improvements[1] influenced artillery as radically as the introduction of the bayonet had influenced infantry a century earlier, and led to the increasing dominance of the cannon over the musket. Two effects are to be noted. The first was that the increasing use of artillery involved an increase in the number of horses and wagons, and therefore to the lengthening of columns on the line of march, and to the necessity of protecting them by light troops–*chasseurs à pied* and *à cheval*. The second was the rise in the cost of armies and the ever-increasing demands put upon industry for standardized arms and equipment.

Though in the Prussian army the infantry and cavalry were excellent, the artillery was indifferent and the commissariat antiquated. Many of the generals were old, and not a few of the younger officers favoured the Revolution. But the weakest link was its command, for between Frederick William and Brunswick there was no unity of thought. The latter detested the *émigrés*; the former was subservient to them. They exaggerated the monarchial sentiments of the French people and boasted of their good understanding with the French officers. " 'I', said Bouillé, 'can answer for the taking of fortresses, for I have the keys of all of them in my

---

[1] Two notable inventions of this period–both English–were Mercier's "operative gun shell", a 5.5-in. mortar shell fired from a 24-pounder gun, first used at the siege of Gibraltar (1779–1783), and Henry Shrapnel's "spherical case" ("shrapnel shell"), invented in 1784, but not adopted by the British army until 1803. The one was destined to render obsolete the wooden battleship, and the other to revolutionize artillery tactics.

pocket'."[1] These claims led Frederick William to believe that all he had do was to march straight on Paris, and there be received with plaudits by its loyal citizens.

Brunswick thought not, for he not only distrusted the *émigrés* but was opposed to the war. His idea was to limit the first campaign to the capture of the fortresses of Longwy, Montmédy, and Sedan; next, to establish depôts at them, outmanœuvre any French army which might come to their relief, and lastly go into winter quarters and prepare for next year's campaign. To wage an autumn campaign in France, with uncaptured fortresses in his rear and in a country which might prove hostile, terrified him. Further, he knew that his commissariat prohibited a rapid advance, and in this he was right, for as Massenbach, one of his staff officers, later said: "The question of supply hung like a dead weight on our legs."[2]

The plan finally decided upon was to invade Lorraine with three armies: (1) Brunswick with 42,000 Prussians, 5,500 Hessians, and 4,500 *émigrés* was to move from Coblenz into Lorraine between Kellermann's army at Metz and Dumouriez's at Sedan; (2) 15,000 Austrians, under Clerfayt, based on Belgium, were to advance southward on the Prussian right flank; and (3), an equal number, under Prince Hohenlohe-Kirchberg, based on the Palatinate, was to move on the Prussian left flank. When the three armies joined in Lorraine, the Meuse was to be crossed and the road to Paris gained.

The Prussians took 20 days to march from Coblenz to the French frontier and it was not until August 23 that they arrived before the border fortress of Longwy, and, after a short bombardment, forced its capitulation.

Dumouriez was then urging Servan, the French Minister of War, to invade the Netherlands. His plan was that while Dillon at Sedan and Kellermann at Metz held back the Prussians, from Valenciennes he would deal with the Austrians under Clerfayt. This was an *idée fixe* with Dumouriez, and he likened himself to Agathocles and Scipio. "It is thus", he wrote in a letter to the Assembly, "that the Roman people carried their war into Africa, when Hannibal was at the gates of Rome."[3]

[1] Quoted from *History of the French Revolution*, Heinrich von Sybel (1867), vol. II, p. 112. The Marquis de Bouillé was the French general Louis XVI hoped to join in his flight to Varennes.
[2] Quoted by Fitzmaurice in his *Duke of Brunswick*, p. 67.
[3] Quoted in *Valmy*, p. 25.

Strategically, he may have been right, for he had measured Brunswick's worth pretty accurately. But politically he was wrong, because, had he marched north, the citizens of Paris would have imagined the eastern roads to the capital unbarred, and would at once have cried "treason!" Fully aware of this, on August 22, Servan urged Dumouriez to cooperate with Kellermann, then falling back before Hohenlohe. And when, on August 24, Paris was thrown into consternation by the news that Longwy was invested, he ordered Dumouriez to proceed to Sedan.

Dumouriez arrived at Sedan on August 28 to find, as he writes, "an army without generals or senior officers, and divided into factions. More than half the soldiers regretted a chief [Lafayette] they had loved, and looked upon his successor as his personal enemy and the author of his ruin."[1]

Next day, when he paraded his men, instead of the customary cheers, he was met by silence and scowls. At length a grenadier cried out: "*C'est ce b . . . là qui a fait declarer la guerre!*" "Do you think", replied Dumouriez, "that liberty can be won without fighting?" When another soldier shouted "*A bas le général!*" Dumouriez drew his sword and challenged him to fight, and when the culprit slunk back, suddenly Dumouriez realized that his unconventional behaviour had won over his men to him.[2]

Next, when he learnt that Verdun was threatened, he sent Lieutenant-Colonel Galbaud and two battalions to reinforce its garrison. They failed to reach the fortress and retired on St. Ménehould. That night he wrote as follows to Servan: "The army is in the most deplorable state. If we retire, I fear it will disband itself, and if we advance, as it appears to wish to do, we shall certainly be beaten . . . it has neither clothing, nor shoes, nor hats . . . and is short of many muskets."[3]

Still obsessed by his Netherlands plan, on August 30 he summoned a council of war which, in spite of what he writes in his *Mémoires*,[4] approved of it. But in Paris, Servan, who thought that Dumouriez had dropped it, on September 1 wrote to urge him to fall back on the Argonne and at the same time informed him that Kellermann was under orders to march to his support. On the following day, while in Paris the tocsin rang in the

[1] *La Vie et les Mémoires du Général Dumouriez* (1822), vol. II, p. 385.
[2] *Ibid.*, vol. II, p. 383, and *Valmy*, pp. 36–37.
[3] Quoted from *L'Europe et la Révolution Française*, Albert Sorel (1891), vol. III, p. 29.
[4] See vol. II, pp. 387–391.

September Massacres, and Danton thundered, "*il nous faut de l'audace, et encore de l'audace, et toujours de l'audace, et la France est sauvée*", Servan wrote to Dumouriez again: "In the name of the fatherland . . . lead your army to between the Meuse and the Marne. Move to St. Ménehould or its vicinity, or even on Châlons. . . ."[1]

In the meantime, on August 31 – that is, before either of these letters had been written – Dumouriez, at Bazeilles, heard gunfire from the direction of Verdun[2] and at the same time learnt that Clerfayt with 15,000 to 18,000 men was about to cross the Meuse at Stenay, and at length saw that his invasion plan was impossible, for his right flank was threatened and Sedan was therefore no longer tenable. "Never", he wrote to Servan, "has the danger to France been so great in any war. . . . To avoid greater evils I shall perhaps be compelled to leave Montmédy and Verdun to their garrisons; abandon the whole length of the Meuse and by the shortest road retire . . . to the river Aire and defend the gap of Autry."[3]

This meant falling back on the Forest of the Argonne, which skirts the right bank of the upper Aisne. It consists of low hills, thickly wooded, and cut up by streams and marshes. In 1792, it was a more difficult country for troops to operate in than it is to-day, for the roads were then unkept and in rainy weather the soft clay soil over which they ran was rapidly churned into mud. For an army followed by an artillery and a supply train, the forest could be crossed only by five roads that ran through the following five defiles: (1) Les Islettes, the Verdun-Clermont-St. Ménehould-Châlons-Paris road; (2) La Chalade, the Verdun-Rheims Road; (3) Grandpré, the Varennes-Vouziers Road; (4) Croix-aux-Bois, the Stenay-Vouziers Road; and (5) Chesne-Populeux, the Sedan-Rethel Road.

For Dumouriez who, at Sedan, was farther away from the two main defiles of Grandpré and Les Islettes than were Clerfayt at Stenay and Brunswick at Verdun, haste was imperative. He

---

[1] Quoted in *Valmy*, p. 36.

[2] Writing on August 31, Goethe mentions the use of rockets in the bombardment of Verdun. He writes: "These tailed fire-meteors, we had only to observe quite quietly gliding through the air, and shortly afterwards a part of the town was seen in flames." (*Campaign in France in the Year 1792*, trans. Robert Farie (1859), p. 31.)

[3] Sorel, vol. III, p. 30. It would appear that the idea of retiring to the Argonne was first suggested by General Money at the council of war on August 30. Money was an English soldier who had fought in the Seven Years War and had served under General Burgoyne in America. (See *The History of the Campaign of 1792, etc.*, J. Money, 1794, pp. 38–41.) He has already been mentioned in the Saratoga campaign, chap. 9.

realized that he had not sufficient troops to hold all five defiles in strength and ordered Duval with 6,000 men[1] at the camp of

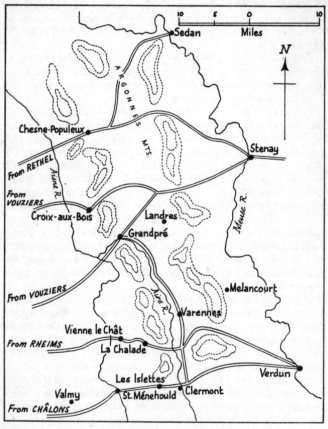

I. THE ARGONNE, 1792

Pont-sur-Sambre and Beurnonville with 10,000 at the camp of Maulde, to march with all speed to Rethel, the former to arrive there on September 7 and the latter on September 13.

[1] Dumouriez's *Mémoires*, vol. II, p. 394. Chuquet (*Valmy*, p. 98) says 3,050.

Dumouriez left Chesne-Populeux and Croix-aux-Bois for the time being unguarded, and on September 1 he sent Dillon forward with the advanced guard (6,000) to take over Les Islettes and La Chalade, and with the main body (13,000) he followed the shortest road, marched across Clerfayt's front, and arrived at Grandpré on September 4. Dillon arrived at Les Islettes on the following day.

From Grandpré, on September 5, Dumouriez sent the following heroic dispatch to Servan: "Verdun is taken, I await the Prussians. The Camps of Grandpré and les Islettes are Thermopylaes, but I shall be more fortunate than Leonidas."[1]

But what of Brunswick? On September 2 Verdun capitulated, but instead of pushing on he remained in camp there until September 11. True, the weather was appalling, and heavy rain had fallen ever since the allies had crossed the frontier. On August 28, Goethe jotted down in his journal "frightful weather"; on September 6, "everything was sunk into bottomless mud", and on September 12, "it rained incessantly".[2] Also hundreds of men were dying of dysentery in the Prussian camp.[3] Though, as Goethe points out on September 4: "Mention was often made of the Islettes, the important pass between Verdun and St. Méne-hould. Nobody could understand why it was not taken possession of, and why it had not been occupied before."[4] The reason was that Brunswick and Frederick William were unable to agree upon what next to do.

With Verdun taken, Brunswick's plan was to occupy Sedan, to go into winter quarters around Montmédy, Mézières and Givet, and to establish a solid base for the next year's campaign. But the King would not listen to this, and not only was he supported by the *émigrés*, but also by several of Brunswick's officers. What the King and his supporters saw, was that at bottom the war was a political rather than a strategical operation, and that they were confronted by a revolutionary and not a normal army. Therefore the idea of establishing magazines at Verdun and Longwy and of going into winter quarters, was quite unsuitable. Instead, they urged, what was needed was to burst into Champagne like a torrent and submerge the French in one

---

[1] Dumouriez's *Mémoires*, vol. III, p. 2.
[2] *Campaign in France*, pp. 17, 49 and 53.
[3] An eyewitness states that the whole front of the camp was covered with excrement (*Valmy*, p. 76).
[4] *Campaign in France*, p. 47.

great battle, the winning of which was assured by the superior discipline of the Prussians. Only thus could a decisive political victory be won in time to save Louis XVI and Marie Antoinette.

Though so unconventional a procedure shocked Brunswick, because of the state of his army, of the roads, and of his commissariat, he knew that a rapid advance could not be made. Nevertheless, obediently he abandoned his own plan for the King's; yet he did not order an immediate advance, but wasted his time in detailed preparations. At length, on September 7, he and the King rode forward to Clermont and reconnoitred Les Islettes. Brunswick saw many enemy troops among the woods, and when he learnt from a peasant that the French were entrenched, he feared that a frontal attack would prove too costly and suggested a turning movement. Ultimately it was agreed to force one of the five defiles, and to do so the following distribution was decided on. Les Islettes to be masked by Hohenlohe's Austrians and the Hessians, while the Prussian army marched on Grandpré. The cavalry and corps of *émigrés* were to move on Chesne-Populeux, and Clerfayt, supported by Kalkreuth, was to secure the defile of Croix-aux-Bois.

At length, on September 10, Brunswick issued his orders to advance, and on the following morning, in pouring rain, the Prussians marched out of their sodden camp and took the road to Melancourt. There they halted for the night, and on September 12 marched on to Landres; on the way they were much perturbed to find the countryside deserted, for this made subsistence still more difficult. To fight the French army was one thing, but to fight it in a deserted country was another, and this depressed the allies, as also did the indescribable condition of the camp at Landres, which became known as the *Drecklager* ("filth camp"). On the left, Hohenlohe's Austrians and the Hessians masked the eastern side of Les Islettes, and on the right, Clerfayt's army from Stenay faced the defile of Croix-aux-Bois.

Croix-aux-Bois was held by two battalions, a squadron and four guns under Colonel Colomb, a veteran of the American war. On September 11 he informed Dumouriez that his position was impregnable, and in consequence the latter, who considered that the main enemy effort would be made against Grandpré, ordered him to leave 100 men under a captain to hold the defile, and bring the remainder to Grandpré.[1]

[1] Dumouriez's *Mémoires*, vol. III, pp. 19–20.

Unfortunately for Dumouriez, Clerfayt learnt of the withdrawal from a peasant and on September 12 sent out a detachment of chasseurs and hussars which rushed the defile and captured it, and because its loss threatened the southern flank of Chesne-Populeux, its commander, Colonel Dubouquet, withdrew its garrison. At 5 p.m., the arrival of fugitives at Grandpré was the first intimation Dumouriez received of the disaster, and as he realized how serious was the loss of Croix-aux-Bois, he ordered General Chazot with eight battalions, five squadrons and four guns to march from Grandpré by way of Vouziers and retake the defile on September 13. The road was in so bad a condition that Chazot only reached Vouziers at nightfall. He set out again the next morning and retook the defile, but shortly after was driven out of it by an Austrian counter-attack, and returned to Vouziers. The astonishing thing about this action was that he was not pursued. As Jomini points out,[1] had Clerfayt pushed on, and had Brunswick simultaneously attacked Grandpré, Dumouriez's army would in all probability have been destroyed.

The situation of the French was at its worst; Dumouriez was at his best. He reckoned on the slowness of the Prussians, as well as on the execrable weather to add to their delay,[2] and at once decided, while holding fast to Les Islettes and La Chalade, to pull out of Grandpré, fall back on St. Ménehould, and place his army in a position facing the rear of his enemy once he had advanced through the abandoned defiles. It was a stroke of genius, and in order to trap his sluggish opponent, aides and messengers were sent galloping in all directions. First a detachment was sent out to mask Croix-aux-Bois, then Chazot was ordered to move from Vouziers at midnight and rejoin the main body on the plain of Montcheutin. Beurnonville and his 10,000 men at Rethel were ordered up to St. Ménehould, and an aide was sent to Kellermann, then near Bar-le-Duc, to hasten his march northward. Instructions were sent to Dillon at Les Islettes to resist the Austrians to the death, and urgent requests were made to General Sparre at Châlons to send forward reinforcements, and to General d'Harville to collect all remaining troops at Rheims, Epernay, and Soissons.[3]

Brunswick, astonished to find the Argonne still held, decided to

[1] *Histoire Critique et Militaire des Guerres de la Révolution*, Jomini (1820), vol. II, pp. 119-120. See also Dumouriez's *Mémoires*, vol. III, p. 25.
[2] Dumouriez's *Mémoires*, vol. III, p. 27.
[3] *Ibid.*, vol. III, pp. 24-25.

enter into negotiations with Dumouriez, and to effect this he sent out Colonel Massenbach to arrange an interview. From the French outposts Massenbach was taken to General Duval's headquarters, but Dumouriez refused to see him. While with Duval, Massenbach had noticed great activity in his camp, and on his return he informed Brunswick that, in his opinion, the French were preparing to retire. Brunswick was overjoyed, for it meant that his manœuvre had succeeded, and according to his code of war, a successful manœuvre was equivalent to a victory. Immediately after, Massenbach met the King, and when the latter learnt that the French were on the point of retiring, he flew into a violent rage, for he wanted a victory and not a manœuvre. He galloped away, cursing, toward Grandpré.

Massenbach was right, Dumouriez did intend to withdraw, but not to the river Marne as Massenbach suspected, but to St. Ménehould, and this Dumouriez set out to do at 3 a.m. on September 15. At 8 a.m. Autry on the Aisne was reached, from where the main body marched on to Dommartin-sous-Hans on the Bionne.

In accordance with his instructions, Chazot should have set out from Vouziers at midnight September 14, in order to reach the plain of Montcheutin ahead of the main body and under cover of its rear guard. But his men were so exhausted by their exertions of the morning and afternoon, that he did not set out until dawn September 15, and when some hours later his corps debouched into the plain of Montcheutin it was attacked by a body of 1,500 Prussian hussars. Though at first his men beat off their enemy, suddenly some of them were seized by panic and scattered in all directions, shouting: "*Sauve qui peut! Nous sommes trahis! Nous sommes coupés.*" Next Chazot's whole corps – 10,000 strong – disbanded itself, and, as Dumouriez informs us, more than 2,000 of them fled as far as Rethel, Rheims, Châlons, and Vitry, where they proclaimed that the army had been annihilated and that Dumouriez and all his generals had gone over to the enemy.[1] In their headlong flight they met reinforcements on their way up from Châlons, which at once turned tail and fled back to that town.

When the panic occurred, Dumouriez was tracing out his camp at Dommartin-sous-Hans, when again, as in the Croix-aux-Bois mishap, the first news of the disaster was brought to

[1] *Ibid.*, vol. III, pp. 31–32.

him by fugitives yelling: "All is lost! The Army is in rout! The enemy is at our heels!"[1] He galloped forward and met General Miranda,[2] who was rallying the infantry. A few hours later, on returning to Dommartin and when about to sit down to dinner, for no accountable reason a second panic suddenly exploded, this time in his own camp, and which, after causing inextricable confusion, was only stayed by his energetic action.[3] Much of the following day–September 16–was spent in disentangling the disorder.

To the west of St. Ménehould and to the north of the Châlons Road rises a plateau which extends from the latter to the village of Neuville-au-Pont on the Aisne. On this plateau Dumouriez encamped his troops, their right about Maffrecourt, their centre west of Chaude Fontaine, and their left on the Châlons Road, in part protected by a marsh called L'Etang-le-Roi. Westward of the camp, at Braux-St. Cohière, he posted an advanced guard under General Stengel, with outposts on the Tourbe stream, which runs north of, and parallel to, the Bionne. In front of his camp he drew up his batteries to sweep the low ground, and along the right bank of the Aisne he threw out a line of strong posts to link his right with Dillon's left at La Chalade. Lastly, he selected St. Ménehould as his headquarters, because it lay half way between his camp and Dillon's.[4]

That he was able to do this was entirely due to the slowness of his enemy, for had the Prussians attacked him between September 16 and 18–that is, immediately after the panic and before he was reinforced–his army would most certainly have been routed. Even as things were, his situation was critical, for Beurnonville, who had arrived at Rethel on September 13, on September 16 approached the village of Auve and heard of the panic. Afraid of finding himself in the midst of the enemy, at once he withdrew to Châlons. There he received an urgent call from Dumouriez, and he set out again on September 18 to arrive at St. Ménehould the following day.

A somewhat similar incident delayed the arrival of Kellermann. On September 12 his army had reached Bar-le-Duc, but when, on the following day, he received Dumouriez's dispatch informing him of the loss of Croix-aux-Bois, he did not wish to get

---

[1] *Valmy*, p. 139.
[2] Spanish-American adventurer in the French service. (See footnote Dumouriez's *Mémoires*, vol. III, pp. 10–11.)
[3] *Ibid.*, vol. III, p. 30.   [4] *Ibid.*, vol. III, pp. 35–36.

involved in a defeat and instead of hurrying on to support Dumouriez, he switched his march westward to Vitry-le-François. Not until September 15, when he received a peremptory order from Marshal Luckner[1] to proceed by forced marches to St. Méne-hould, did he again set out. On September 18 he reached Dampierre-sur-Auve, and the following day crossed the river Auve and went into camp on the Châlons Road at Dommartin-la-Planchette. He brought with him 17 battalions and 30 squadrons; in all, 16,000 men.

Brunswick had missed two opportunities to destroy his enemy: the first at Croix-aux-Bois, and the second on September 15 when he sent forward only 1,500 hussars instead of the whole of his advanced guard. Now he missed a third, for though he occupied Grandpré on September 16, instead of advancing his main body, still in the camp at Landres, he kept it there until September 18. The reason for this was that he could not move it until his supply train had brought bread from Verdun. "The indifferent arrangement that had been made for subsistence," says Nassau-Siegen, "compelled us to halt and lose time at Grandpré as at Verdun."[2]

At length, on September 18, the bread had come up and Brunswick began to contemplate a plan of action. Again it was by means of an envelopment to turn the enemy out of his position and force him to withdraw. Late that day he and Massenbach rode forward to reconnoitre, and afterward, Brunswick decided to march the Prussians by way of Grandpré against the western side of the La Chalade and Les Islettes position, while the Austrians pressed its eastern side. This, he considered, would force Dumouriez to abandon his camp. "Our left wing," he said to Massenbach, "will advance, we must hunt the enemy out of the Argonne. We will take les Islettes and without much bloodshed. As you know we must economize our men, for we are not over numerous."[3]

The following morning the Prussian army set out, but at noon, as the King was about to eat, a messenger arrived with the news that the French were evacuating St. Ménehould. Assuming that Dumouriez was about to retire, Frederick William in a rage turned to Massenbach, and though Brunswick was present, he did not even consult him, but ordered the army to move directly toward

---

[1] Kellermann was an independent commander, and not under Dumouriez.
[2] Quoted from *Valmy*, pp. 169–170.
[3] *Ibid.*, p. 173. See also Sybel, vol. II, p. 134.

the Châlons Road, and by cutting the French line of retreat bring the enemy to battle. Though this completely upset Brunswick's grand manœuvre, he raised no objection. Soon after, another message was received to cancel the previous one; nevertheless, the King adhered to his order, and therefore must bear full responsibility for the ultimate fiasco.

"Thus," writes Chuquet, " . . . the Prussians with heads down, moved straight forward toward the French, without carrying out a single reconnaissance, without sending forward a single officer to examine the ground and without a plan of battle."[1]

That night the Prussians bivouacked along the road leading from Suippes to Valmy, with their main body about Somme-Tourbe on the Tourbe, south of which ran the Bionne stream.

South of the Bionne lay the battlefield of Valmy, bordered on its eastern flank by the river Aisne and on its southern by the river Auve. North of the latter ran the St. Ménehould-Châlons highway, passing through Dumouriez's left flank at L'Etang-le-Roi and also through Dommartin-la-Planchette, where Kellermann was now encamped. About a mile and a half west of Dommartin was the posting-house of Orbeval, from where westward the highway rose to a tavern named La Lune, at which a branch road from Somme-Bionne joined it. East of the branch road rose a ridge, the northern part of which was called Mont Yron (or Hyron) and the southern the *butte* or *tertre* (mound or hillock) of Valmy. On the mound stood a windmill—where the monument now stands—and a little to the north of it lay the village of Valmy. From La Lune, Orbeval, Dommartin, and the mound of Valmy could clearly be seen, and east of them in the distance the high ground of the Argonne.

No sooner had Kellermann encamped at Dommartin-la-Planchette than he rode over to St. Ménehould and told Dumouriez that he considered his position insecure because the swampy Auve ran immediately in the rear of it, and that therefore on the following morning he intended to recross the Auve and occupy the villages of Dampièrre and Voilement. Dumouriez suggested that it would be better to occupy La Lune and the high ground about Valmy; but Kellermann disagreed and the withdrawal was decided upon. In order to cover his camp during the night, Kellermann instructed his advanced guard, under General Deprez-Crassier, to move forward toward the Bionne,

[1] *Valmy*, p. 180.

order to support Deprez-Crassier, Kellermann had sent forward
to the tavern his reserve corps under General Valence.

He had done this because at 7 a.m. news had been received of
the Prussian advance, and as he realized that he would not have
sufficient time to cross the Auve before the Prussians fell upon him,
he counter-ordered the withdrawal and substituted for it Dumouriez's suggestion of the evening before. He hastily fell in his men,
and under cover of the fog and Deprez-Crassier's and Valence's
guns, ordered his second line and 18 guns, under Muratel, to
advance and occupy the mound of Valmy and take over its
defence from Stengel. Next, not being able, because of the fog,
to judge the extent of the high ground, which was restricted, he
ordered his first line, with another 18 guns, to follow the second,
and then, for some reason unknown, instead of keeping his
cavalry on the low ground about Orbeval, he ordered it to follow
the first line. The result was that in the fog his infantry, cavalry,
and artillery were jammed together in a confused mass around
the windmill. Fortunately for Kellermann the fog obscured the
confusion from the Prussians, and equally fortunate, at that
time Valence's guns at La Lune put to flight three Prussian
squadrons, which in the fog had ridden into them. After this
repulse Hohenlohe halted his advanced guard until some batteries
could be brought forward to fire on La Lune, which gained for
Kellermann time to straighten his army.

When Hohenlohe's guns opened fire, Deprez-Crassier and
Valence fell back to a position close to Orbeval, in order to protect
the left flank of the Valmy position and fill in the gap between it
and the strong detachments posted by Kellermann in the Château
of Maupertius and the village of Gizaucourt on the Auve.

Thus it came about that the French line of battle, which
stretched from Mt. Yron to Maupertius, assumed a semicircular
form. On the right stood Stengel's advanced guard on Mt. Yron;
in the centre the mass of Kellermann's army on the mound, and on
the left, from below the windmill to Orbeval, the troops of
Deprez-Crassier and Valence, with the detachments at Maupertius and Gizaucourt on their left and south of the Châlons Road.

Thus it also came about that, instead of Kellermann's army
prolonging Dumouriez's left and covering his communications
with Vitry-le-François, it was isolated in front of its left centre,
which meant that, were it attacked, it would receive the full
shock of the enemy's assault. In order to mitigate this, Dumouriez

ordered Stengel to move forward to the western edge of Mt. Yron, and to support him he brought up in rear of him 16 battalions under Beurnonville. To strengthen Kellermann's left, he sent forward nine battalions and several squadrons to reinforce Valence and drew up 12 battalions and six squadrons on the Châlons Road east of Orbeval as a reserve.

Though the French had been caught unprepared and were forced on the defensive, Dumouriez had no intention of abandoning the offensive altogether. He decided on two audacious manœuvres. Firstly, he instructed General le Veneur, with 12 battalions and eight squadrons, to cross the Aisne above Neuville-au-Pont, advance on Berzieux and Virginy, and fall upon the rear of the Prussians and Austrians. Secondly, he ordered Duval, at Vienne-le-Château, also to cross the Aisne and attack the Prussian baggage train, then drawn up in wagon-laager (*Wagenburg*)[1] at Maison-de-Champagne.

When Valence fell back and the fog in places began to lift, Massenbach, accompanied by Brunswick's natural son the Count of Forstenburg, rode forward from the advanced guard to La Lune. At once they recognized its tactical importance, for from it the highroad to Orbeval could be swept by gunfire and the mound of Valmy taken in flank, and galloped back and informed Brunswick, who ordered forward a battery to La Lune. About the same time, Dumouriez, who also had recognized its importance, ordered General Chazot to occupy it; but when he approached it he found it too strongly held to attack and withdrew.

While La Lune was occupied by Hohenlohe, the Prussian main body came up in two columns, which slowly formed face toward Mt. Yron and Valmy, their right rested on La Lune and their left on the Bionne. At noon, while the deployment was completed, the fog thinned, and to their surprise, Frederick William, Brunswick, and Goethe, at La Lune, saw before them, not as they had expected an enemy in precipitate retreat, but an army drawn up in ordered line of battle. Nor were they encouraged, when Kellermann, at the windmill, saw them, raised his hat, decorated with a tricolor plume, on his sword, and cried out, "*Vive la nation!*" To which a roar of "*Vive la nation! Vive la France! Vive notre général!*" swept down the French ranks.[2]

When this incident occurred, the Prussian artillery—58 guns—

---

[1] See *Valmy*, p. 177. [2] *Valmy*, p. 207.

commanded by General Tempelhoff, had been drawn up in battery position from La Lune northward, and faced Kellermann's 40 pieces, under General d'Aboville, on the Valmy ridge. The range was about 1,300 yards.

Suddenly a strong wind began to blow, the fog dissipated, and the sun shone out brightly. "Now", writes Goethe, "commenced the cannonade of which so much has been spoken, but the violence of which at the time it is impossible to describe."[1] Money says it "was heavier than I ever heard".[2] It reached its height at 1 p.m., and, according to Goethe, the whole battlefield trembled.[3] Yet, in spite of the intensity of the fire–Dumouriez says that each side expended more than 20,000 shot[4]–casualties were slight. Not only was 1,300 yards a long range for cannon of that day, but the clayey soil was so sodden that most of the shot buried itself in it instead of ricochetting.

Though the cannonade had not produced the effect Brunswick's staff had expected, it was agreed that there was only one thing now to do, that was, to assault the Valmy position.

While this question was discussed, Brunswick carefully examined his enemy through a telescope. He had marched 30 odd miles to avoid attacking Les Islettes, and now, ironically, he was faced with an attack on Valmy. This, certainly, did not fit in with his strategy; nevertheless he ordered the attack to be made.

At once the Prussian infantry, under cover of the smoke of their batteries, began to form up into two lines of attack. But no sooner had they begun to advance than the whole of Kellermann's artillery was turned upon them and some of the battalions wavered and lost their dressing. Brunswick, who though he had ordered the attack was at heart opposed to it, found sufficient excuse in this to halt it before it had covered more than 200 paces. At the time this order was given, Dumouriez rode up to Kellermann at the windmill, and the enemy's sudden halt made him certain that Brunswick would not attempt an assault.

At about 2 p.m. a Prussian shell blew up three ammunition wagons behind Kellermann's line, the noise of the explosion resounded over the battlefield. A thick cloud of smoke enveloped the French gunners, who ceased firing, as also did the Prussian gunners, whose target was obscured. Two French regiments broke back, at once to be rallied by Kellermann, but the artillery

[1] *Campaign in France*, pp. 72–73.   [2] *The History of the Campaign of 1792*, p. 88.
[3] *Campaign in France*, p. 77.   [4] Dumouriez's *Mémoires*, vol. III, p. 44.

wagoners, who were undisciplined civilians, in flight streamed toward the rear: it was a critical moment.

Massenbach, then at La Lune, saw the commotion around the windmill, thought that the battle was as good as won, and rode to the King and Brunswick to urge them to reinforce the right of the halted attack and carry the mound of Valmy by storm.

No sooner had he spoken than the cannonade began again, and it was seen that the French had recovered their ranks. Impressed by the steadiness of the French infantry, and noticing that in the plain between Orbeval and the Auve the French troopers stood to their horses, Brunswick turned to those around him and said: "Gentlemen, you see by what kind of troops we are faced. Those Frenchmen are only waiting for us to advance before mounting their horses and charging us."[1] Then he paused, as if turning over in his mind whether to resume the attack or await the arrival of Clerfayt, whom he had ordered with all speed to join him. He glanced again at the French, then summoned a council of war, at which the King and a few senior officers were present. For the first time in the campaign he assumed the full authority of a commander-in-chief, and as the guns thundered, he pronounced his decision: "*Hier schlagen wir nicht*" ("We do not fight here"). Hohenlohe, Manstein (the King's A.D.C.) and General Grawert agreed with him, and when Brunswick declared that the assault would fail, and even should it succeed, no good could come of it, the King gave way.[2]

In the meantime, on the left, Kalkreuth bombarded Mt. Yron, on which, as Chuquet points out, the resistance put up by Stengel, which prevented Kellermann's right being turned, was not the least of the factors which contributed to French success.[3]

The assault was called off and at 4 p.m. the Prussians moved across the highway to cut off their enemy from Châlons and Paris. The cannonade ceased, and as evening closed in a drenching storm of rain swept over the battlefield. A few hours later, Kellermann, under cover of night, withdrew his army to Dampièrre and Voilement, in order to cover the Vitry-le-François Road.

Thus ended the Battle of Valmy, in which 34,000 Prussians

---

[1] *Valmy*, p. 215.
[2] In *Dumouriez and the Defence of England against Invasion* (1909), p. 129, J. Holland Rose and A. M. Broadly suggest that Duval's raid on the Prussian baggage train may have contributed to Brunswick's decision to call off the battle.
[3] *Valmy*, p. 217.

faced 52,000 Frenchmen, of whom 36,000 of the latter were engaged. The casualties were insignificant; the French lost about 300 officers and men and the Prussians 184. Many of the wounded died on the battlefield.

There can be little doubt that, though Brunswick's generalship, emasculated as it was by the interferences of Frederick William, was beneath contempt, his decision not to fight was a wise one. His army was reduced by dysentery; winter was approaching and the roads would increasingly become worse. His line of communications was insecure, and his commissariat was so inefficient that a rapid march on Paris was out of the question. Even were it reached, by then his army would have become so weak and worn that it would have risked annihilation. The aim of the campaign had become unattainable and the campaign itself had been reduced to an absurdity, a condition Brunswick had foreseen from the start. But the overruling reason which led to his decision was that, in spite of its panics and its mutinies, he felt—though he would never have acknowledged it—that the French generals and their men were superior to him and his slow-moving unthinking troops.

"The enemy", wrote Lombard, the King's private secretary, "had disappointed our hopes. Dumouriez and Kellermann had proved themselves generals not to be despised. They had chosen excellent positions; they had under their orders all that remained of the old French troops of the line; the volunteers helped by their numbers, and were in a position to render real service when attached to the veteran troops; their light cavalry was excellent and quite fresh. Their army lacked nothing, and we—we lacked everything. They were well fortified in their positions, both front and rear, and their artillery was at least equal to ours. This is what prevented a decisive blow being struck."[1]

The writer of this illuminating *aperçu* played an important part in bringing the campaign to its end. On September 30 he was captured by General le Veneur in his daring raid on the rear of the Prussian army, and at the particular request of Frederick William, Dumouriez released him, and took the opportunity to send by means of him a memorandum[2] to the King setting forth his reasons why the war should be terminated. Also, as he heard that the King was without coffee and sugar, as a gift he sent him 12 lb.[3]

---

[1] Quoted from *Ibid.*, pp. 242–243.
[2] See Dumouriez's *Mémoires*, vol. III, Appendix A. 　　　　[3] *Ibid.*, vol. III, p. 66.

Brunswick with eagerness seized upon the idea, and was supported by the King who had just received perturbing news from Poland. A week of negotiations followed, and on September 27 Dumouriez sent a second memorandum in which the separation of Prussia from Austria was his sole theme. The King indignantly refused to consider it, and though this brought the truce to an end, on September 29 Dumouriez urged upon Lebrun, Minister of Foreign Affairs in Paris, the need of moderation, because, as he wrote, "a general peace, which we might obtain on glorious conditions, would be better for us than the dangers of a long war. . . ."[1] But the Revolutionary Government would not listen to this, and defiantly declared that: "The Republic does not discuss terms until its territory is evacuated."

On the night of September 30–October 1, Brunswick struck camp at La Lune and skilfully withdrew his army to the right bank of the Meuse. Dumouriez, who on September 27 had been appointed Commander-in-Chief of the French armies, then returned to his plan of invading the Netherlands. He took over command of the Army of the North at Valenciennes, marched into Belgium, and on November 6, to the consternation of Europe, defeated Albert Duke of Saxe-Teschen and Clerfayt at Jemappes.

Valmy was the Marathon of the French Revolutionary and Napoleonic Wars. Faced by the most formidable armies in Europe, led by the most noted general of the day, the French under Dumouriez and Kellermann had repulsed the one and discredited the other. "After Valmy", writes Chuquet, "every Frenchman who held sword or musket in hand, looked upon himself as the champion of a cause which was destined to triumph."[2] Valmy was the deathbed of the Old Régime and, spiritually, the cradle of the New Republic which, in the fond dreams of Camille Desmoulins and others, was to carry liberty, equality, and fraternity into the enslaved countries, in order that kings might perish and paradise be realized on earth.

Though this alluring dream was soon to give way to a nightmare, some at the time sensed that the thunder of the cannonade heralded a portent. Massenbach wrote: "You will see how those little cocks will raise themselves on their spurs. They have undergone their baptism of fire. . . . We have lost more than a battle. The 20th September has changed the course of history. It is the

---

[1] Quoted from Sybel, vol. II, p. 173.   [2] *Valmy*, p. 232.

The maritime struggle between France and England

After the battle of Valmy, two ideas directed the foreign policy of the Revolution: that of the visionaries and that of the realists. The former were Alexandrian in outlook and offered to the world a new dispensation based on the brotherhood of man. The latter were Caesarians who sought in the conquest of neighbouring countries, not only a means to consolidate France, but also to mend her shattered finances. Both ideas urged the Revolution outward, the one to share with other peoples the freedom France had won, and the other to plunder them and lay them under tribute.

Whether Dumouriez was aware of it or not, both these causes of expansion lay at the bottom of his *idée fixe*, for the Austrian Netherlands was both a rich country and one eager to cast off Austrian rule. Further, could the mouth of the Scheldt be brought under French control, in time Antwerp might rival, if not oust London as the centre of world trade. That, at least in part, this was realized is supported by the fact that, immediately after Dumouriez's victory at Jemappes, the National Convention declared that the Scheldt was open to commerce, and also that military aid would be accorded to all peoples striving after liberty. This threat to the Low Countries, which had brought England into war during the previous hundred years, coupled with the thinly veiled declaration of war on all monarchies was, on January 21, 1793, sealed by the execution of Louis XVI. It made the meaning of the Revolution unmistakable, and so shocked the government of England that two days later, the Marquis de Chauvelin, the French envoy in London, was given eight days' notice to leave the kingdom. His peremptory dismissal so infuriated the Convention that the day after his departure it declared war on Great Britain and Holland, and a month later hurled an ultimatum at Spain. Thus was opened a war which, except for one short spell, was to last for 22 years.

Though the proportions of this conflict were vast – it eventually was to embrace most of Europe—for France its central problem was how to force England to terms, either directly by gaining command of the English Channel, or indirectly by strangling England's continental and colonial trade. But it was not until the First Coalition against France collapsed in 1795, and until in the following year the National Convention gave way to the Directory, that events began to reveal it.

The five Directors resolved that a continuation of the war would consolidate their power and they pressed on with it. Under their pilotage the year 1796 witnessed a series of French triumphs which, in 1797, culminated in Bonaparte's conquest of northern Italy and the acceptance by Austria of the Treaty of Campo Formio, which ceded Lombardy and the Austrian Netherlands to France. In the meantime, in June, 1796, the Directors had turned their attention to an oversea attack on Great Britain and Ireland, which in December resulted in an abortive invasion of the latter, and in February, 1797, in Colonel Tate's farcical landing in Wales.

One of the most critical moments in British history followed. On April 15, the Channel Fleet at Spithead mutinied, and on May 2, Admiral Duncan's North Sea Fleet at the Nore followed suit. At this time the Dutch fleet, under French control, expected to find the main British fleet drawn toward Ireland and was preparing to sail with 42 transports to invade England, and Duncan, then lying off Yarmouth, was ordered to blockade the Dutch or bring them to battle. Because of the mutiny, he was able to induce only two of his ships to put to sea. Nevertheless, with them he proceeded to blockade the Texel, and thus matters stood until June 21, on which date the Directory urged the Dutch to carry 20,000 men to Ireland, while another fleet carried 6,000 more from Brest.

Nothing happened until October 9, when Duncan, who learned that the Dutch had sailed with the intention of disembarking a force in the Clyde in order to draw British troops from Ireland, on October 11 brought 16 Dutch ships to action off Camperdown and captured nine of them. Immediately after this defeat, the Directory appointed General Bonaparte to command the army designated to invade England.

Bonaparte reached Dunkirk on February 11, 1798, and at once inspected the coastal establishments, issued orders for the building of a flotilla of flat-bottomed boats, and on February 23 reported to the Directors: "Make what effort we will, we shall not for many years gain naval supremacy. To make a descent on England, without being master of the sea, is the boldest and most difficult task imaginable." Always ready with an alternative, he suggested that, until naval preparations were adequate, the correct course to take was to strike at England's eastern trade by seizing Malta, occupying Egypt, and invading India. This proposal was accepted.

Fired by the exploits of Alexander the Great, on May 19 Bonaparte set out from Toulon with 13 sail of the line, 300 transports, and upward of 35,000 troops and 15,000 sailors and civilians. In chief naval command was Admiral Brueys, accompanied by Admirals Ganteaume, Villeneuve, and Decrès. Malta was occupied on June 12; the army landed at Alexandria on July 2, and on July 21 the Battle of the Pyramids was won. Then, as Bonaparte organized his conquests, suddenly he learnt that on August 1–2 Nelson had destroyed his fleet in Aboukir Bay and won the Battle of the Nile.

The news of this decisive victory brought into being the Second Coalition, a combination of England, Naples, Austria, Russia, and Turkey, and while Bonaparte warred in Syria its members took the offensive. The Franco-Italian republics were overrun by Suvarov, Holland was assailed by a joint British-Russian army, and Switzerland was invaded by a joint Russian-Austrian one. So critical was the French situation that the Directory recalled Bonaparte. He handed over his army to Kléber, and on the night of August 22–23 he set sail from Alexandria, eluded the English ships, and on October 9 landed in France at Fréjus. Meanwhile, Suvarov had been driven out of Switzerland and the British and Russians out of Holland.

When Bonaparte arrived in Paris, he was at once placed in command of its garrison, and as he sensed that the Army and the people were behind him, with the aid of his brother Lucien, then President of the Council of Five Hundred, and one of the Directors, the Abbé Sieyès, he carried out the *coup d'état* of the 18th Brumaire (November 9). The Directory was abolished and a new constitution voted which made him the first of three consuls appointed to rule France for 10 years. On December 15, the new constitution was promulgated and shortly after confirmed by a plebiscite of 3,011,007 votes to 1,562. Thus ended the democratic revolution, henceforward the drill-sergeant was to govern France.

Bonaparte had made himself all but dictator and was ready to face the forces of the Second Coalition. Craftily, in order to justify his intentions in the eyes of the people, he appealed to George III and the Emperor Francis to end the war. Nothing came of this and on May 6, 1800, he left Paris for Geneva; crossed the Alps at the Great St. Bernard, and on June 14 fell upon the rear of the Austrians under Melas in Piedmont and routed them at Marengo. Routed again on December 2 by Moreau at Hohenlinden, the war of the Second Coalition collapsed and the Austrians accepted the Peace of Lunéville on February 9, 1801.

Freed from Austria, Bonaparte at once returned to his project of striking at England. Already, on December 12, 1800, he had persuaded Russia, Prussia, Denmark, and Sweden to form, on the lines adopted by Catherine II in 1780, a League of Armed Neutrality against England, but soon after it was brought to ruin by the assassination of Paul I of Russia, and by Nelson's decisive victory on April 2, 1801, over the Danish fleet at Copenhagen.

It was when the above maritime alliance was being formed that Bonaparte began to grapple in earnest with the problem of subduing England. In February he addressed a letter to Talleyrand in which he outlined a vast programme of naval expeditions to be undertaken by the fleets of France, Spain, and Holland, supported by Russia and Denmark. The central idea was to decoy the main British fleet to Egypt; for the French navy was too weak to dispute with England the mastery of the seas. A return was made therefore to the idea of slipping a force across the English Channel, once the English fleet had been inveigled away. To effect this, Admiral Decrès was made Minister of Marine, and, as planned, the army of invasion was to number 114,554 officers and men carried in more than 2,000 small craft.

But the collapse of the Armed Neutrality, coupled with the formation of the Addington Ministry in England, in October led to the preliminaries of peace which culminated in the signing of the Treaty of Amiens on March 27, 1802. Peace was proclaimed between France, Spain, and the Batavian Republic (Holland) on the one part, and by Great Britain and Ireland on the other. Its main terms were that England was to retain Ceylon and Trinidad and restore all other colonies taken from France and her allies, and that Malta was to be evacuated by the English, and France was to withdraw her troops from Taranto and the States of the Church.

The Peace of Amiens left France arbiter of Europe, and the gratitude of the people toward Bonaparte was shown when, on May 10, the Council of State put to the nation the following question: "Is Napoleon Bonaparte to be made Consul for Life?" It was answered by a plebiscite of 3,568,885 "ayes" to 8,374 "nays". Bonaparte became "Napoleon" to France and to history.

The peace was no more than a truce which neither side strictly observed. Causes of friction at once arose and the main ones were the protectionist policy of Napoleon, which crippled English trade; the refusal of England to evacuate Malta; and the refusal of Napoleon to withdraw his garrison from Holland. After a year of contentious wrangling, on May 2, 1803, Lord Whitworth, British Ambassador in Paris, sent for his passports; on May 17 he crossed the Strait of Dover, and the next day England declared war on France.

The French navy, which had never recovered from the shock of the Revolution, then consisted of 23 ships of the line, 25 frigates and 107 corvettes, etc., ready for service; also 167 small craft belonging to the invasion flotilla of 1800. Forty-five sail of the line were under construction, and in addition, France had at her call the Batavian fleet of 15 sail of the line, of which only five were fit for service.

Facing these two fleets was the English, commanded by men who had scored victory after victory. In January, 1803, it comprised 34 sail of the line in commission, supported by 86 50-gun ships and frigates, and behind it in reserve were 77 sail of the line and 49 50-gun ships and frigates. On the declaration of war, Earl St. Vincent, First Lord of the Admiralty, at once ordered the blockade of the main French naval ports. Nelson was chosen for the Mediterranean command, Lord Keith to watch the North Sea and Strait of Dover, and Corwallis to blockade Brest .

With so great a disparity between the French and English naval forces, and with most of the French fleet bottled-up, Napoleon was left with the flotilla project as his sole hope. He rightly realized that the strategical centre of gravity of every continental war in which England was engaged lay in the English Channel, and it was not long before he appreciated that a flotilla of *prames*, *chaloups* and *cannonières*, which had already gained for him the soubriquet of "*Don Quixote de la Manche*", was not in itself sufficient to master it. But that this project, as some suppose, was from first to last only a bluff to cover the raising of armies against Austria and Russia, has little support.[1] That eventually the Army of England was used against Austria in no way sustains the hoax theory, for Napoleon never worked to a fixed plan, but always had one or more alternatives up his strategical sleeve.

That the threat of invasion roused England is proved by the immense effort made to raise regular and volunteer troops. The official returns of December 9, 1803, show that by then, 463,000 men had been enrolled, and those of January 1, 1805, that this figure had been increased to 590,000, a tremendous effort for a country of some ten million inhabitants.

In the autumn of 1803 the Russian Government had made overtures to Great Britain and Austria with reference to French designs on Turkey, and after William Pitt was returned to office in May, 1804, this proposal was actively considered. Pitt realized that it was impossible for Great Britain single-handed to wage a successful offensive against Napoleon and he saw in the overtures a means to establish yet another coalition against France, but as Russia wanted to dismember Turkey in Europe, in order to annex Moldavia and Constantinople, and split up the rest into separate states under Russian protection, as well as obtain Malta, the outcome was a prolonged diplomatic wrangle which ended on April 11, 1805, in a treaty between Great Britain and Russia. According to this it was agreed to form a European league for the restoration of peace and the balance of power. A little before this treaty was signed, Pitt decided to send a force under Sir James Craig to garrison Malta, and thereby set free some 8,000 seasoned troops to occupy Sicily, who, with the assistance of Nelson, were to prevent it falling into French hands.

No fighting occurred in 1803, nor during the opening months of 1804. Both England and France prepared for a contest to the death, and to add to French prestige, exactly a year after the declaration of war, the *Senatus Consultum* of the 28th Floréal, year XII (May 18, 1804,) awarded to Napoleon the title of Emperor of the French. In Notre Dame, on December 2, he gently waved aside Pope Pius VII, and with his own hands crowned himself to the chant of *Vivat in aerternum semper Augustus*.

[1] In January, 1805, according to Miot de Mélito (*Memoirs*, vol. II, p. 244), Napoleon told his Council that his preparations for the invasion of England were only a pretext to cover the assembly of a great army with which to invade Austria. What would seem more likely is, that this information was vouched his Council in order to mislead his enemies.

The Battle of Trafalgar, 1805

The renewal of the war found England in the weakest position she had held since 1781. Not only was she now faced with the combined fleets of France and Holland, but the alliance of Spain was guaranteed to France by treaty. This meant that Napoleon had at his call all the ports from the Texel to Genoa for shipbuilding and refuge. Further, it was clearly apparent that he had every intention to invade England, for the ports of France rang with the blows of the shipwright's hammer.[1] Nor was his assertion that he intended gradually to create a French navy of 130 sail of the line, supported by 60 Spanish, 20 Dutch, and 15 Genoese ships, altogether an empty one; for, in spite of his numerous campaigns from 1805 onward, by 1815 the French fleet had grown to 103 sail of the line and 55 frigates.[2]

The English naval problem was, therefore, not merely one of meeting the allied fleet in the Channel, but also of preventing allied ships–then existing and as they were built–from leaving their ports and putting to sea. This meant blockade carried out in such a way that the escape of any one impounded squadron would not lead to a chain-reaction–that is, to the releasing of the other squadrons–a problem which became still more difficult to solve when, on December 12, 1804, Spain declared war on England.

The allied ships of the line were then distributed as follows: Toulon–11; Cartagena–5; Cadiz–10; Ferrol–9; Rochefort–5; Brest–21; and at the Texel–6. The first two were blockaded by Nelson with 12 sail of the line; the third by Sir John Orde with five; the forth, fifth, and sixth by Cornwallis and his subordinates with 37 off Ushant and in the Bay of Biscay, and the seventh by Lord Keith with nine off the Downs and in the North Sea. Besides these ships there were five of the line in British ports and 12 in the East and West Indies. In European waters therefore, British numerical superiority over that of the allies was slight.

This lack of strength was more than made good by the British

[1] By August, 1805, 2,343 landing craft had been built (*Napoleon and the Invasion of England*, H. F. B. Wheeler and A. M. Broadley, 1908, vol. II, p. 233).
[2] *Mémoires pour servir à l'historie de Napoléon 1er*. Claude François Méneval (1894), vol. I, p. 366. By 1814 the British Navy numbered 240 of the line, 317 frigates and 611 smaller craft (*The Cambridge Modern History*, vol. IX, p. 243).

Admiralty's adherence to England's traditional naval policy of holding in force the western mouth of the Channel. As long as a powerful fleet rode off Ushant, no flotilla invasion was possible in face of Keith at the Downs. Therefore it was laid down by the Admiralty as an inflexible principle that, should a blockaded squadron escape and should the blockading fleet be unable to bring it to battle, the latter was at once to rally off Ushant and thereby increase the strength of the fleet stationed there.[1] Ushant, therefore, was the centre of gravity of British naval defence, and, in consequence, Cornwallis's fleet excelled all others in importance. Were he defeated, Keith would be uncovered, and should Keith be defeated, except for the weather, there was next to nothing to prevent the Boulogne flotilla from fulfilling its purpose. Napoleon understood this full well, and though he had little grasp of naval tactics and paid scant respect to wind and tide, as a naval strategist he had nothing to learn because the principles of strategy are universal.

Though the campaign which culminated in the battle of Trafalgar sprang from Napoleon's instructions of March 2, 1805,[2] given to Vice-Admiral Ganteaume at Brest and Vice-Admiral Villeneuve at Toulon, in order to clarify events it is as well to return to December 12, 1804, the day Spain declared war on England.

On that day Napoleon ordered Villeneuve to break out of Toulon, sail for the West Indies and at Martinique link up with Admiral Missiessy, who was to break out of Rochefort and join him. Next, after a stay of 60 days, in which he was to do all possible damage to British possessions, Villeneuve was to sail for Ferrol, free Captain Gourdon's (or Gordon) squadron of five of the line and two frigates blockaded there, and then proceed to Rochefort.[3]

On January 11, Missiessy escaped from Rochefort with five of the line and four frigates and sailed for Martinique. A week later, when Nelson had taken his squadron to Maddalena Islands, in the Strait of Bonifacio, Villeneuve, with 11 sail of the line and nine frigates, stood out from Toulon. When he learnt of his escape, "regardless of probabilities,"[4] Nelson concluded that Villeneuve

[1] See *La Campagne Maritime de 1805, Trafalgar*, Edouard Desbrière (1907), pp. 3 and 79.
[2] *Correspondance de Napoléon Ier*, Nos. 8379 and 8381, vol. x, pp. 182, 185.
[3] *Ibid.*, Nos. 8206 and 8231, vol. x, pp. 63 and 78.
[4] See *Nelson the Sailor*, Captain Russell Grenfell (1949), p. 172.

was bound for Malta or Egypt, and forthwith sailed eastward to arrive at Alexandria on February 7. When he found nothing there, he set sail for Malta, where he learnt that Villeneuve had been forced back to Toulon by a storm. Still convinced that Villeneuve's goal was Egypt, on March 26, in order to intercept Villeneuve the next time he set out, Nelson anchored his squadron off the south of Sardinia. Four days later he received the news that Villeneuve had put to sea again, for unknown to Nelson Villeneuve was carrying out Napoleon's instructions of March 2.

The aim of these instructions was to assemble a fleet of over 40 sail of the line at Martinique, the main contingents to be Ganteaume's Brest squadron of 21 sail of the line and six frigates and Villeneuve's Toulon squadron of 11 and six respectively. On the way out, the former was to release Gourdon's squadron of four of the line and two frigates at Ferrol, and the latter the Cadiz squadron, under the Spanish Admiral Gravina, of about seven of the line. At Martinique, Missiessy, with five of the line and four frigates, was to join them, and once this union was effected Ganteaume was to take over the supreme command of the combined fleets, sail for Ushant, attack the English fleet there, and make for Boulogne. Villeneuve was instructed that should he reach Martinique ahead of Ganteaume, he was to wait 40 days for him, and if by then he had not arrived, he was to sail to Cadiz, where orders would await him.

Here it is convenient, before the tussle that was to lead to Trafalgar began, briefly to measure the characters of the two men who were to play the major parts in it–Villeneuve and Nelson.

Villeneuve, who was five years younger than Nelson–the one born in 1763 and the other in 1758–was of the French *noblesse*, and one of the few well-born French naval officers to survive the Revolution, hence his rapid promotion. He was an educated and studious sailor, who might have done good work at the French Admiralty, but was unfitted for command. Though he in no way lacked personal courage, by temperament he was a defeatist. He did not believe in Napoleon's project of invading England; he had no confidence either in his subordinates or his allies, and worst of all he had none in himself. At the battle of the Nile he had commanded the *Guillaume Tell*, one of the two French ships of the line which had escaped, and from then on *le souvenir d'Aboukir* paralysed him; ever after he was haunted by the spectre of Nelson.

Nelson stood at the opposite pole. He was a bold and imaginative tactician, independent in outlook, ambitious, sensitive of his reputation, at times vainglorious and frequently violent in his dislikes. His moral courage was extraordinary, as his action when he left the line and single-handedly attacked the Spanish van at the battle of St. Vincent shows. Captain Grenfell says of it that it was "a piece of individual initiative . . . unsurpassed in naval history . . . an act of supreme valour,"[1] His pugnacity at the Nile, Copenhagen, and Trafalgar has seldom been equalled; nevertheless he was an indifferent strategist because he failed to realize that strategy is a science, and though not an exact one, one at least based on facts and not on intuitions. In 1804–1805, the uppermost strategical fact was Napoleon's naval threat to England; yet in Nelson's dispatches and letters of these years the word "invasion" occurs but once, and then incidentally and after Napoleon had abandoned his project.[2] The reason was that his gaze was always fixed on the Mediterranean, and because of this, unwittingly Villeneuve succeeded in outwitting him. What Nelson failed to grasp was that in 1804–1805 the strategical centre of gravity lay in the English Channel and not off Sardinia or at the mouth of the Nile. Nevertheless, in spite of this defect, he was the greatest fighting admiral England has ever had.

On March 10 Nelson, with his squadron, was in the Gulf of Palmas, at the south-western corner of Sardinia, and when he learnt that Villeneuve was embarking his troops, he set sail for Toulon. He found there every appearance that Villeneuve was about to put to sea and jumped to the conclusion that his most probable destination was Egypt, and in consequence returned to Palmas, from where he could cover Naples and Sicily, block the main seaway to Egypt, and be well placed to strike westward, should Villeneuve's aim be to make for the Atlantic. There he was when, on March 30, in accordance with Napoleon's instructions, Villeneuve stood out from Toulon for Cadiz to pick up Gravina's squadron before sailing for the West Indies.

The first news Nelson received of his departure was on April 4, when from one of his frigates he learnt that, on March 31, she had sighted Villeneuve's squadron some 60 miles south by west of Toulon–that is, some 300 miles west of Palmas. This news Nelson sent by dispatch to the Admiralty, saying "I shall push

[1] See *Nelson the Sailor*, p. 66.
[2] *The Dispatches and Letters of Vice-Admiral Lord Viscount Nelson*, Sir Nicholas Harris Nicholas (1856), vol. VII, p. 87.

for Egypt."[1] Next, with Egypt still in mind, believing that Ville-neuve would make for the island of Galita–off Bizerta–and attempt to reach Alexandria by hugging the African coast, he took up position with his squadron between Sardinia and Galita. But no sooner had he done so than, afraid that Villeneuve would round the north of Sardinia, he shifted his position to the island of Ustica, 50 miles north of Palermo, and arrived there on April 7.

On the same day Villeneuve was off Cartagena, and Sir John Orde, who was blockading Gravina in Cadiz, was warned by Sir Richard Strachan, who had been sent by Nelson to escort a homeward-bound convoy past Algeciras, that on April 8 he had seen Villeneuve coming out of the Strait. As Orde had but four of the line with him, this news placed him in a most perplexing situation. Should he stay where he was and await Nelson, or should he close in on Ushant? This question was decided when Strachan informed him that Nelson was occupied with Egypt. Orde left his frigates to keep touch with Villeneuve, and after sending a dispatch to the Admiralty, stood out for the north.

His dispatch is illuminating, for it shows that he–the man Nelson traduced in violent terms[2]–had a far clearer appreciation of the strategical situation than Nelson. This dispatch reads: "I am persuaded the enemy will not remain long in Cadiz, and I think the chances are great in favour of their destination being westward where by a sudden concentration of several detach-ments, Bonaparte may hope to gain a temporary superiority in the Channel, and availing himself of it to strike his enemy a mortal blow."[3] This was exactly what Napoleon intended, and when he penetrated his enemy's scheme, Orde set out to reinforce the centre of gravity–Ushant.

On April 9 Villeneuve anchored outside Cadiz and signalled Gravina to come out. But his fear that Nelson was on his tracks was so great that, at 1 p.m. he waited no longer for Gravina, but weighed anchor and left the Spaniards to straggle after him.

Soon after this, as Villeneuve did not appear in the Tyrrhenian Sea, Nelson shifted his position from Ustica to Toro, a small island

---

[1] *The Dispatches and Letters of Vice-Admiral Lord Viscount Nelson*, Sir Nicholas Harris Nicholas (1856), vol. VI, p. 397.
[2] Due to an old quarrel which started in 1798, and was accentuated when, in 1804, Orde was appointed to blockade Cadiz, a profitable command because of prize money, and one which Nelson coveted.
[3] Quoted by Corbett in his *Trafalgar*, p. 64.

near the Gulf of Palmas, and on April 18, when he learnt that Villeneuve's squadron had been sighted off Gibraltar on April 8, he informed the Admiralty that because of his "vigilance" the enemy had found "it impossible to undertake any Expedition in the Mediterranean,"[1] and the next day he sent another dispatch in which he stated that, as he was satisfied that Villeneuve was not bound for the West Indies, but more likely for Ireland and Brest, he was proceeding off the Scilly Islands.[2] Though late in the day, this was strictly in accordance with the Admiralty principle already defined.

Delayed by foul weather, Nelson did not reach Gibraltar until May 6. There he fell in with Rear-Admiral Donald Campbell, then in the Portuguese service, who informed him that Villeneuve was on his way to the West Indies. Nelson, always impulsive and pugnacious, made up his mind, and on May 10, with his 10 sail of the line and three frigates, set out to cross the Atlantic.

Commenting on this, Captain Russell Grenfell remarks:

"It is a debatable point whether Nelson's decision to make for the West Indies was a sound one. With the 'Army of England' making its noisy preparations at Boulogne, there was an inescapable possibility that Villeneuve's movements were connected with the transport of that army across the Channel. Wherever Villeneuve had gone, he was a month ahead of Nelson, and if, as it was both reasonable and prudent to assume, the Franco-Spanish fleet was engaged in a feint designed to draw British squadrons away from the Channel, it could well be thought likely that a decoy fleet which had disappeared westward or south-westward that length of time before might now be on its way back towards its final and decisive destination. There was therefore a considerable risk that by starting off for the West Indies so long after Villeneuve had vanished, Nelson was but playing into the enemy's hand. It can be plausibly argued that, on a broad survey of the whole strategical field, Nelson should have steered for Brest, to be on the safe side of a very uncertain and precarious situation."[3]

There was another reason, as Captain Grenfell points out, why Nelson should have joined Cornwallis. It was that by May 10 his dispatch of April 19, which notified his intention to sail for the Scilly Islands, would have been received by the Admiralty, who, should they have learned of Villeneuve's true movements, might

---

[1] *Nelson's Dispatches and Letters*, vol. VI, p. 407.
[2] *Ibid.*, vol. VI, p. 411.   [3] *Nelson the Sailor*, p. 180.

well have made their own arrangements to follow him up. In these circumstances, were Nelson to sail for the West Indies, two squadrons instead of one would be in pursuit. This is what very nearly happened, for when the Admiralty learnt from Orde (on April 30) as well as from agents that Villeneuve was bound for the West Indies, Lord Barham, First Lord of the Admiralty, ordered 11 of the line under Vice-Admiral Collingwood to proceed there, and only by accident,[1] when he was on his way, did he learn that Nelson was already in pursuit. Had this accident not occurred, 21 battleships would have gone on a wild-goose chase.

On June 4, after a rapid voyage, Nelson put in at Barbados, where he was joined by Rear-Admiral Cochrane and two sail of the line. There he was wrongly informed that the French fleet had been seen to windward of St. Lucia, and the result was that he missed his enemy. Villeneuve had reached Martinique on May 14 to find that Missiessy had returned to Rochefort and that Ganteaume had not arrived. The latter was still blockaded at Brest, and Napoleon, brooking no further delay, had, on April 29, sent off Rear-Admiral Magnon and two of the line with orders to Villeneuve instructing him to remain in the West Indies for 35 days after their receipt, and if by then Ganteaume had not joined him, he was to sail for Ferrol, pick up the 15 ships blockaded there, next release the 21 at Brest, and lastly, "*avec cette armée navale*", enter the English Channel and appear before Boulogne.[2]

Magnon arrived on June 4, and on June 7 the news was received that Nelson was in the West Indies. It so unnerved Villeneuve that, regardless of his new orders, on June 10[3] with all haste he stood out for Europe. Two days later Nelson reached Antigua, and rightly guessed that Villeneuve was returning to Europe – either to Cadiz or Toulon, more probably the latter, because, as he wrote at the time, "They may fancy they will get to Egypt without any interruption"[4] – and he decided to return to Gibraltar.

[1] At Gibraltar, Nelson had detached Sir Richard Bickerton in the *Royal Sovereign* to assist in covering General Craig's passage to Malta. Next, an Admiralty Order instructed Bickerton to reinforce Calder at Ferrol. On May 17 Bickerton sailed north, and 10 days later, as he neared Finisterre, he met Collingwood coming down, and informed him that Nelson with 10 of the line was already in pursuit.

[2] *Correspondance*, No. 8583, vol. x, p. 321.

[3] *The Campaign of Trafalgar*. Julian S. Corbett (1910), p. 167. Desbrière (*Trafalgar*, p. 42) says June 11 and Captain Grenfell (*Nelson the Sailor*, p. 183) says June 8.

[4] *Dispatches and Letters*, vol. vi, p. 454. Napoleon seems to have been aware of Nelson's obsession. On April 20 (No. 8603) he wrote to Decrès, "Nelson will probably make a second voyage to Egypt," and again on April 23 (No. 8617), "Publish in the Dutch papers that a French squadron has disembarked 10,000 men in Egypt, and that the French admiral has skilfully manœuvred to deceive Nelson."

Before he set out, Nelson sent back to England the brig *Curieux* commanded by Captain Bettesworth, to notify the Admiralty of his return, and during her voyage home, on June 19, the French fleet was sighted on a course well to the north of the Mediterranean. This could only mean that Villeneuve was making for the Bay of Biscay and not, as Nelson supposed, for the Strait of Gibraltar. On July 7 the *Curieux* arrived at Plymouth, and on July 19 Nelson cast anchor at Gibraltar.

On July 18, when off Cape Spartel, Nelson had communicated with Collingwood, then blockading Cadiz, and had received from him a reply which should have enlightened him on the strategical situation. What Collingwood said was, that he believed Napoleon's aim to be Ireland, and that Villeneuve's fleet would "now liberate the Ferrol Squadron . . . make the round of the Bay, and, taking the Rochefort people with them, appear off Ushant, perhaps with thirty-four sail, there to be joined by twenty more. . . . The French Government", he added, "never aim at little things while great objects are in view. . . . Their flight to the West Indies was to take off the naval force, which proved the great impediment to their undertaking. This summer is big with events."[1]

On July 20 Nelson went ashore (at Gibraltar) "for the first time since 16th June, 1803,"[2] and in a letter of the same date to Lord Barham he says that, unless Russian frigates replaced Collingwood's, now withdrawn "from the upper part of the Mediterranean . . . the French will, whenever they please, convey an Army to Sardinia, Sicily, the Morea, or Egypt . . . for which service I have repeatedly applied for many, many more Frigates and Sloops of War".[3] The mention of these places shows that even Collingwood's illuminating letter of July 18 had not altered Nelson's ideas. On August 3 he was ordered to sail to Ushant to join Cornwallis.[4]

In the meantime important political events had taken place which were profoundly to influence Napoleon's project. On May 12, 1804, Pitt had returned to office, and his controlling idea was to build up another coalition. In part his project was based on Dumouriez's "General Reflections of the Defence of England" of

---

[1] *Dispatches and Letters*, vol. VI, p. 472, and *Public and Private Correspondence of Vice-Admiral Lord Collingwood*, G. L. Newnham Collingwood (1829), pp. 107–108. In the former the letter is dated July 18 and in the latter July 21. The two versions differ in places.

[2] *Dispatches and Letters*, vol. VI, p. 475.   [3] *Ibid.*, vol. VI, p. 476.

[4] Corbett's *Trafalgar*, p. 230.

1804.[1] The members were to be England, Russia, Austria, Sweden, and Naples, and after a year's negotiations, on April 11, 1805, a treaty between England and Russia was signed, to be followed, on August 9, by another between Russia and Austria. Prussia was also approached, but refused to become a partner. These treaties provided that Russia would put into the field 180,000 men, Austria 315,000 and Sweden 12,000, and that England would pay an annual subsidy of £1,250,000 for each 100,000 soldiers, up to a total of 400,000, employed by her allies against France and Spain.

When the *Curieux* arrived at Plymouth, Captain Bettesworth posted to London, and reported to Lord Barham on July 9. The latter at once appreciated the importance of Bettesworth's information and forthwith sent a dispatch to Cornwallis instructing him to order Rear-Admiral Stirling to raise the Rochefort blockade and reinforce Sir Robert Calder off Ferrol. Also Cornwallis was to instruct Calder, once he had been reinforced, "to proceed without loss of time off Cape Finisterre, from whence he is to cruise for the enemy to the distance of 30 or 40 leagues to the westwards for the space of six or seven days".[2] Thus, in the middle of July, 1805, Napoleon's strategical aim was more than half attained. Except for Brest and Cadiz, all the French and Spanish ports were free from blockade.

Villeneuve had passed the Azores on July 2, and on July 22 approached Cape Finisterre in a dense fog. Had it continued, he might have sailed past Calder's 15 sail unobserved, and have effected a junction with Ganteaume at Brest. But at noon the fog lifted, one of Calder's look-out frigates reported the French fleet in sight, and at 5 p.m. an indecisive engagement was fought, in which two of Villeneuve's ships struck their colours. Though on July 23 the two fleets kept in sight, they did not re-engage, and the following day when Calder bore northward to join Cornwallis, Villeneuve crowded on sail and made for Vigo Bay, where he arrived on July 28. From there he sailed for Ferrol, which he reached on August 1.

The moral effect of this action was decisive, for the little faith Villeneuve had in his fleet now oozed out of the soles of his shoes. On August 6 he wrote: "In the fog our captains, without ex-

---

[1] See *Dumouriez and the Defence of England against Napoleon*, J. Holland Rose and A. M. Broadley (1909), pp. 240–261, particularly pp. 260–261.
[2] Quoted from Corbett's *Trafalgar*, p. 184.

perience of an action or of fleet tactics, had no better idea than to follow their second ahead, and here we are the laughing-stock of Europe."[1] The action palsied him.

At Ferrol Villeneuve received Napoleon's dispatch of July 16, in which he was ordered to raise the blockade of Ferrol, and "manœuvre in such a way as to render us masters of the Strait of Dover, either by uniting with the Rochefort and Brest squadrons or by uniting with the Brest squadron alone, or the Rochefort squadron alone, and then with this fleet double Ireland and Scotland in order to join up with the Dutch squadron at the Texel". Further, if, because of battle or some other cause Villeneuve was unable to accomplish this task, on no account was he to enter the port of Ferrol, but instead proceed to Cadiz.[2]

With a man of Villeneuve's disposition, this last injunction was a fatal error on the part of Napoleon; for to get to Cadiz—as far away as possible from Brest—was the master thought in Villeneuve's mind. Forbidden to enter Ferrol, he left three damaged ships there, then put in at Coruña, where he was strengthened by 14 sail of the line.

When Admiral Stirling withdrew from Rochefort in order to reinforce Calder, on July 17 Rear-Admiral Allemand, who had replaced Missiessy, slipped out of Rochefort under orders to unite with Villeneuve on August 13. But because Decrès omitted to notify Villeneuve of this,[3] an extraordinary sequence of misadventures followed, which culminated in fiasco on August 13.

That day Villeneuve put to sea, and when he sighted some frigates he assumed them to be English and altered course southward to avoid them. They belonged to Allemand's squadron, which was searching for him. Had Villeneuve united with Allemand, he would have brought his fleet up to 34 sail, and had he then borne north instead of south, fortune might have favoured him, for on August 16 Cornwallis had split his fleet of 35 sail into two, and had sent one of these (18 sail) under Calder to Ferrol. Therefore, had Villeneuve, in accordance with his orders, sailed northward, and had he by good fortune eluded Calder, he might have raised the Brest blockade.

"What a chance Villeneuve has missed!" wrote Napoleon. "By coming down upon Brest from the open he might have played

[1] *Projets et Tentatives de Débarquement aux Îles Britanniques.* E. Desbrière (1900–1902) vol. v, p. 776.
[2] *Correspondance*, No. 8985, vol. xi, p. 18.
[3] Desbrière's *Projets et Tentatives*, vol. v, pp. 727–728.

prisoners' base with Calder's squadron and fallen upon Cornwallis; or with his thirty of the line have beaten the English
twenty, and obtained a decisive superiority."[1] Though, theoretic-
ally, this may be correct,[2] actually it is extremely doubtful, for
Cornwallis had retained with him 10 three-deckers, and, according
to the computation of that day, one three-decker was equivalent
to two two-deckers in fighting value.

Villeneuve continued southward, and on August 20 entered
Cadiz, and there was blockaded by Collingwood's three sail of the
line. On August 22 Collingwood was reinforced by Sir Richard
Bickerton's four of the line, and on August 30 by Calder and
his 18.

On August 3 Napoleon arrived at Boulogne. Time pressed, for
already there were indications that a coalition was forming in
his rear: Austria was massing troops in Venetia and the Tyrol,
and a levy en masse of the Neapolitan militia was reported by St.
Cyr. On August 13, having by then heard of Villeneuve's action
with Calder, on which he congratulated him, Napoleon instructed
him to unite with Allemand, sweep everything before him,
intermingle his French and Spanish ships, and come to the
Channel.[3] Also he wrote to Decrès to complain of Villeneuve's
slowness,[4] and on August 22 to Ganteaume to state that Villeneuve was on his way to join him, and that on his arrival not a
day was to be lost in setting sail up the Channel, in order that
six centuries of England's insults might be avenged.[5] This same
day he wrote again to Villeneuve, addressing his letter to Brest:
"I trust you are now at Brest. Sail, do not lose a moment, and with
my squadrons reunited enter the Channel. England is ours. We
are ready and embarked. Appear for forty-eight hours, and all
will be ended."[6]

Next day, still ignorant that Villeneuve was at Cadiz, he wrote
to Talleyrand: "The more I reflect on the situation of Europe, the
more I see how urgent it is to take a decisive step." If Villeneuve
with his 34 ships "follows my instructions and unites with the
Brest squadron and enters the Channel, there is still time: I am
master of England. Otherwise I shall raise my camp at Boulogne

---

[1] Correspondance, No. 9160, vol. xi, p. 161.
[2] Whereas Mahan (The Influence of Sea Power upon the French Revolution and Empire,
vol. ii, p. 576) stigmatizes it a blunder, Corbett (The Campaign of Trafalgar, pp. 246–
254) considers it a masterstroke.
[3] Correspondance, No. 9073, vol. xi, 87.   [4] Ibid., No. 9071, vol. xi, p. 85.
[5] Ibid., Nos. 9113 and 9114, vol. xi, p. 115.   [6] Ibid., No. 9115, vol. xi, p. 115.

and march on Vienna."[1] At last, on August 26 he made up his mind and instructed Berthier to prepare to move the army at Boulogne against Austria,[2] and on August 31 to Duroc he wrote: "The army is in full movement . . . I shall be ready on 27th September. I have given the Army of Italy to Masséna. Austria is very insolent, she is redoubling her preparations. My squadron has entered Cadiz. Keep this secret, it is for you alone. Collect all the maps you can of the Danube, the Main and Bohemia, and let me have the organization of the Austrian and Russian armies."[3] On September 2 he left Boulogne. Thus the Army of England became the Grand Army, and instead of crossing the Channel it set out to cross the Rhine.

It was related earlier that Nelson on August 3 was sailing northward to Ushant, off which, on August 15, when he had saluted Cornwallis's flag, he received a signal to proceed with the *Victory* to Portsmouth, where he cast anchor on August 18. In England he spent his time between London and Merton, and on September 2, news was brought by Captain Blackwood of the frigate *Euryalus* that Villeneuve had entered Cadiz and Nelson's brief holiday was cut short. On September 5 he sent his heavy baggage to Portsmouth, and on September 14 arrived there himself. The next day the *Victory*, accompanied by the *Euryalus*, set sail, and when he joined Collingwood on September 28, Nelson took over command of his fleet.

The following day was his forty-seventh birthday, and in a letter to some unknown friend he wrote: "The reception I met with on joining the Fleet caused the sweetest sensation of my life. The officers who came on board to welcome my return, forgot my rank as Commander-in-Chief in the enthusiasm with which they greeted me."[4] Nelson assembled his Captains and explained to them the plan of battle he had worked out when at Merton,[5] contained in what is usually called his "Secret Memorandum".

Before we turn to it, it is as well to glance at an earlier plan, which he had thought out on his way to the West Indies, because of the two it more clearly reveals the factor which, as a fighting admiral, differentiates Nelson from the admirals of his day.

The essence of the earlier memorandum is that in a "close and decisive battle"—always Nelson's aim—subordinates must not

[1] *Correspondance*, No. 9117, vol. XI, p. 117.
[2] *Ibid.*, No. 9137, vol. XI, p. 141.
[3] *Ibid.*, No. 9155, vol. XI, p. 157.
[4] *Dispatches and Letters*, vol. VII, pp. 66–67.
[5] *Ibid.*, vol. VII, p. 241.

wait for signals, but act on their own initiative, and to enable them to do so without risk of upsetting the battle, they must be fully acquainted with the commander-in-chief's "mode" of attack.[1] Nelson did not fight in order to carry out a plan, instead he planned in order to carry out a fight, and between the two there is a vast difference.

The novelty in this memorandum does not lie in the "modes" of attack, of which two are mentioned, for of necessity they vary according to circumstances, but in the liberty of action delegated to subordinates to carry them out. Nelson, as a subordinate, had displayed the highest initiative at the battle of St. Vincent, and he expected his captains to model themselves upon him. Unlike Napoleon, who seldom tolerated initiative on the part of his marshals, Nelson wanted his captains to be Nelsonically-minded. Coupled with his pugnacity, it was not only his own initiative but also the initiative of his subordinates, though the latter ran counter to the rigid naval discipline of the day, which made Nelson England's supreme fighting admiral.

The Secret Memorandum, first discussed with Admiral Sir Richard Keats, when Nelson was at Merton,[2] is based on the supposition that Nelson's fleet numbered 40 sail of the line and Villeneuve's 46, and that it is almost impossible to bring 40 ships into line of battle without much loss of time. Therefore, in order to save time, the fleet was to be organized into two lines of 16 sail each, and an "Advanced Squadron", or reserve line, of eight ships. Again, to save time, the order of sailing was to be the order of battle, and to make the most of opportunities, the two lines were to act independently. One was to be under Nelson and the other under Collingwood, who was to "have the entire direction of his line".

The "mode" of attack was that, while Collingwood attacked the 12 rear ships of the enemy's line, Nelson was to attack the enemy's centre in order to prevent it attacking Collingwood, and at the same time interpose his ships between the enemy's centre and van before the latter could wear about and come to the assistance of the enemy's rear. Meanwhile the Advanced Squadron was to cut in, two or three or four ships ahead of the enemy's centre, "so as to ensure getting at their Commander-in-Chief, on whom every effort must be made to capture", presumably because he was the directing organ and moral centre of

---

[1] *Dispatches and Lettters*, vol. VI, pp. 443-445.   [2] *Ibid.*, vol. VII, p. 241.

his fleet. "Something must be left to chance," writes Nelson, "nothing is sure in a Sea Fight beyond all others. Shot will carry away the masts and yards of friends as well as foes; but I look with confidence to a victory before the van of the enemy could succour their Rear, and then the British Fleet would most of them be ready to receive their twenty Sail of the Line, or to pursue them, should they endeavour to make off."[1]

Nelson's idea is reminiscent of Epaminondas's at Leuctra. In that battle the Theban right wing by threatening the Spartan left wing and centre held them to their ground while the Theban left wing destroyed the Spartan right wing. At Trafalgar, Nelson held back the centre and van of the Franco-Spanish fleet, not by threatening but by attacking, while Collingwood destroyed the enemy's left wing–his rear. Because the tactical idea was, in fact, an ancient one, it in no way detracts from the credit due to Frederick at Leuthen or to Nelson at Trafalgar. In war fundamental ideas are always reborn–they transmigrate from generation to generation.

Of the conference he had with his captains, Nelson wrote to Lady Hamilton: " . . . when I came to explain to them the '*Nelson Touch*', it was like an electric shock. Some shed tears, all approved–'It was new–it was singular–it was simple!'; and, from Admirals downwards, it was repeated–'It must succeed, if ever they will allow us to get at them! You are, my Lord surrounded by friends whom you inspire with confidence'."[2] On October 9 or 10 the Secret Memorandum was circulated in writing.

At Cadiz, Villeneuve found himself in worse straits than ever. His treasure-chest was empty; sea-stores, provisions, even handspikes were difficult to obtain, and besides being 2,000 men short of establishments, he had 1,731 sick. Equally bad, there was constant quarrelling between his French and Spanish officers and men. On September 2 he poured out his grievances to Decrès. Nevertheless, on September 24 he was able to report that he had shipped six months' supplies and was ready to sail.

Napoleon, all idea of invading England abandoned, had devised for Villeneuve–"*un misérable*", as he called him[3]–a new and fatal scheme. From St. Cloud, on September 14, he sent him the following instructions:

[1] For the Memorandum as originally written and subsequently amended see *Admiralty Committee Report* (Cd. 7120 of 1913), pp. 64–65.
[2] *Dispatches and Letters*, vol. VII, p. 60.
[3] *Correspondance*, No. 9174, vol. XI, pp. 176–177.

"Having resolved to make a powerful diversion by directing into the Mediterranean our naval forces concentrated at the port of Cadiz ... we would have you know that our intention is that ... you will seize the first opportunity of sailing with the Combined Fleet and proceeding into that sea.

"You will first make for Cartagena to join the Spanish squadron which is in that port.

"You will then proceed to Naples and disembark on some point of the coast the troops you carry on board to join the army under the orders of General St. Cyr. . . .

"The fleet under your command will remain off the Neapolitan shores as long as you may judge necessary, in order to do the utmost harm to the enemy as well as intercept a convoy which they intend to send to Malta.

"After this expedition, the fleet will sail to Toulon to revictual and repair.

"Our intention is that wherever you meet the enemy in inferior force you will attack them without hesitation and obtain a decision against them.

"It will not escape you that the success of these operations depends essentially on the promptness of your leaving Cadiz."[1]

Two days later the Emperor sent instructions to Decrès to replace Villeneuve by Admiral Rosily;[2] but out of consideration for Villeneuve's feelings, Decrès did not communicate this to him. Rosily arrived in Madrid on October 10.

On October 1 Villeneuve began his final preparations, intending to put to sea on October 7, but the wind changed and for 10 days he was kept in port. On October 8 he held a council of war at which he explained to his captains how he proposed to fight the coming battle. He intended, he said, to divide his fleet of 33 sail of the line into two divisions, a *corps de bataille* of 21 ships, under his personal command, and a *corps de reserve* of 12 ships under Admiral Gravina, which would be stationed to windward of the former.[3] With extraordinary accuracy, he next outlined his enemy's probable tactics. "The British Fleet", he said, "will not be formed in a line of battle parallel with the

---

[1] *Correspondance*, No. 9210, vol. XI, p. 195. [2] *Ibid.*, No. 9220, vol. XI, p. 204.
[3] On October 16 the final order of battle was decided upon. The *corps de bataille* was to consist of three squadrons, each of seven ships: 2nd Squadron (Van) under Vice-Admiral Alava, flagship the *Santa Ana*; 1st Squadron (Centre) under Villeneuve, flagship the *Bucentaure*, and 3rd Squadron (Rear) under Rear-Admiral Dumanoir, flagship the *Duguay Trouin. Corps de reserve*, Admiral Gravina, flagship the *Principe de Asturias*.

Combined Fleet ... Nelson ... will seek to break our line, envelop our rear, and overpower with groups of his ships as many of ours as he can isolate and cut off."[1] Of how best to meet this attack he said nothing, apparently because he knew that his captains were only capable of forming line ahead. All he added was, that if the Combined Fleet was to windward, it would bear down on the enemy and engage ship to ship; and if to leeward, it would form a close line ahead and await attack, each captain looking out for himself.

The French and Spanish ships were to be mingled, as Napoleon had ordered him to do. They comprised one four-decker, the *Santissima Trinadad* of 131 guns, then the largest ship afloat; three three-deckers (two of 112 guns and one of 100); six 80-gun ships; twenty-two 74's, one 64 and seven frigates and corvettes. Eighteen of the ships of the line were French and 15 Spanish. They mounted 2,626 broadside guns, exclusive of carronades, and carried 21,580 officers and men. The regiments embarked were drawn from the Cadiz garrison, and among them were the Regimento de Africa (formerly Tercio de Sicilia) and the Regimento de Soria (formerly Tercio de Soria) both of which had fought in the Spanish Armada.

The British fleet should also have numbered 33 sail of the line, but shortly after Nelson took over its command, Rear-Admiral Thomas Louis and his squadron of six of the line had been ordered away with a convoy bound for Malta; hence Nelson found himself with 27 of the line. Of these ships, seven were three-deckers—three of 100 guns and four of 98—and 20 were two-deckers—one of 80 guns, sixteen of 74 and three of 64. Also he had four frigates, a schooner, and a cutter. The fleet was manned by 16,820 officers and men, and, exclusive of carronades, it mounted 2,148 broadside guns.

Because of the absence of Louis's squadron, Nelson dropped his original idea of forming his fleet into three lines, and substituted two, a van or weather column of 12 of the line, under his personal command in the *Victory*, and a rear or lee column of 15 under Collingwood in the *Royal Sovereign*. This was his first deviation from the Secret Memorandum, and as others followed, which since have given rise to much pedantic explanation, it is as well to set down what we believe Nelson had in mind when Trafalgar was fought.

His aim was to gain a decisive victory, to capture or sink

[1] Quoted from *The Enemy at Trafalgar*, Edward Fraser (1906), p. 54.

20 of the enemy ships; for, as he said when he was dying: "I bargained for twenty."[1] He realized, as the Secret Memorandum infers, that the old engagements of line ahead in parallel order were generally indecisive because they were so slow and prohibited the concentration of strength against weakness. He looked upon them, we may assume, as contests between two one-armed boxers, and, so far as he was concerned, he intended to fight with two arms. His fleet was to have a left punch and a right punch. The weather column was to protect the right, and the lee column was to knock out the enemy's rear. He selected the rear in preference to the van, because, in order to support the rear, the enemy's van would have to wear about, which would take a long time, whereas had he selected the van, in order to support it, all the enemy's rear would need to have done was to continue on its course.

To give both his punches the maximum of momentum, he did not adhere either to a formal line ahead or abreast. Instead, he substituted for them two groups of ships in order of sailing—that is, coveys and not lines of ships. Of this there can be no doubt, for when he explained his tactics to Admiral Keats at Merton, he said: "It will bring forward a pell-mell Battle, and that is what I want."[2] In support of this, in a letter written two months after Trafalgar, Collingwood says: "Lord Nelson determined to substitute for an exact order an impetuous attack in two distinct divisions. . . . It was executed well, and succeeded admirably; probably its novelty was favourable to us, for the Enemy looked for a time when we should form something like a line."[3] This is what Nelson had foreseen, for at Merton he suddenly turned to Keats and said: "But I'll tell you what I think of it. I think it will surprise and confound the Enemy. They won't know what I am about."[4] Surprise was to add to concentration as much as superior gunnery.

The differences between the Secret Memorandum and what occurred are those between idea in mind and idea in action. The tactical aim remained the same, but the means of attaining it varied according to the moment. No pedantry can explain this.

[1] *Dispatches and Letters*, vol. VII, p. 251.
[2] *Ibid.*, vol. VII, p. 241.   [3] *Ibid.*, vol. VII, p. 242.
[4] *Ibid.*, vol. VII, p. 241. Lieutenant B. Clement of the *Tonnant* said: "We went down in no order but every Man to take his Bird." (Quoted from Newbolt's *The Year of Trafalgar*, p. 101.)

On October 15 Villeneuve received news from Bayonne that Admiral Rosily was on his way to Cadiz, and as he knew that Rosily had not been at sea for over 12 years, he concluded that he was on an administrative mission. Next, news came from Madrid that Rosily was to supersede him, and feeling that his honour was impugned, Villeneuve decided to slip out of Cadiz before his arrival. On October 17 this intention was fortified when he learnt–very belatedly–that Admiral Louis's squadron had been detached from Nelson's fleet. The wind was favourable, and after a conference with Gravina he ordered the captain of his flagship to signal "Prepare to sail." No sooner had he done so than the wind dropped and soon died away altogether.

The next day Nelson wrote in his diary: "Fine weather, wind Easterly; the Combined Fleet cannot have finer weather to put to sea."[1] Nevertheless, Villeneuve hesitated, and it was not until 6 a.m. on October 19 that he signalled his fleet to "Make sail and proceed."

Two and a half hours later, when lying some 50 miles to the west-south-west of Cadiz, Nelson received the signal from one of his inshore frigates that the enemy was coming out of port. At once he signalled "General chase",[2] as his aim was to cut off the Combined Fleet from the Mediterranean. Next came the signal, "Enemy's fleet at sea." This was incorrect, for on October 19 only Admiral Magnon's division got out of Cadiz, and it was not until noon October 20 that Villeneuve had the whole of his fleet under way.

By daylight on October 20, when close to the Strait of Gibraltar, Nelson had seen nothing of his enemy and wore his fleet and made to the north-west. At 7 a.m. Villeneuve's fleet was sighted, and at noon was reported to be sailing westward. An hour later the *Victory* hove to, and Collingwood came on board to receive final instructions. Later Nelson learnt that Villeneuve had changed direction to the south-east, and before sunset he ordered his frigates to keep sight of the enemy during the night.[3]

At daybreak on Monday, October 21, when the British fleet was still in no precise order or formation, the enemy in close line of battle, bearing east by south, was seen 10 to 12 miles away. As it was still too dark for flags to be distinguished, it was not until 6.10 a.m. that Nelson made the general signal "Form the order

[1] *Dispatches and Letters*, vol. VII, p. 126.
[2] *Ibid.*, vol. VII, p. 133.   [3] *Ibid.*, vol. VII, p. 136.

of sailing in two columns," which brought Collingwood's column to the starboard of the van. Immediately after, the signal "Bear up and sail large of E.N.E. course" was run up, and at 6.22 a.m. was followed by "Prepare for battle."[1]

Villeneuve was headed for the Strait of Gibraltar, and when he realized that because of the lightness of the wind it would not be possible to avoid battle, at 8 a.m. he signalled his whole fleet to go about, so that he should have Cadiz harbour under the lee as a refuge for crippled ships. It was an unfortunate last minute change of plan, for not only did it look like a retreat, and therefore was discouraging for his crews, but the wearing about took over two hours and resulted in the formation of a confused line of battle. It was crowded in some places and had gaps in others, its centre sagged to leeward, and the whole line formed an irregular crescent about three miles long. The wearing placed Gravina's squadron behind, instead of to windward of, the line, and Dumanoir's squadron became the van. Once the change of direction was completed, the Combined Fleet moved slowly ahead on a northerly course at the rate of a knot or a little more.

When the Combined Fleet went about, the British in two columns, or rather, groups of ships—the Weather Line under Nelson and the Lee Line under Collingwood—slowly bore down on it under full sail. The wind, from the north-west, was very slight; there was a heavy westwardly ground swell, and the rate of advance, at first estimated at three knots, soon fell to one and a half. As Nelson did not shorten sail, there was no possibility of the two columns forming regular line. Further, like two school-boys, he and Collingwood set out to race each other; the former steered, not for the van of the enemy centre, as originally decided, but for the centre of his van, while Collingwood steered for the van of his rear.

The reasons for Nelson's change of direction would appear to have been that when he saw the enemy wear about, he jumped to the conclusion that Villeneuve was trying to escape to Cadiz. This is borne out by the fact that, shortly before 11.40 a.m.—the time the message was received—he telegraphed Collingwood: "I intend to pass [push] or go through [the end of] the enemy's line to prevent them [from] getting into Cadiz."[2] In other words, to head off their van. Next, at 11.48 a.m., he sent out his famous

---

[1] For signals see *Admiralty Committee* (Cd. 7120) Appx. V.
[2] *Ibid.*, see Signals, p. 102.

general signal: "England expects that every man will do his duty."[1]

When this signal was sent, Collingwood closed in on the enemy's rear, for already at 11.30 a.m. Villeneuve had run up the signal "Open fire!", to be followed at 12.15 p.m. by another: "*Tout capitaine qui n'est pas dans le feu n'est pas à son poste.*"[2] At 11.45 a.m. the first shot was fired by the *Fougueux*, next astern of the *Santa Ana*, and was aimed at the *Royal Sovereign*, then rather more than a quarter of a mile away. Thereon in unison the ships of the two fleets hoisted their colours, "the drums and fifes playing and the soldiers presenting arms" in the French and Spanish ships.[3]

The battle then opened, and may be divided into three distinct actions: Collingwood's attack, Nelson's attack, and Dumanoir's abortive counter-attack. We will follow these in turn.

When the *Fougueux* opened fire on the *Royal Sovereign*, Collingwood's division sailed on the larboard line of bearing,[4] at approximately two cables (about one quarter mile) interval between ships. It was, therefore, in a diagonal, though irregular, line abreast formation which, because of the curvature of the enemy's line, brought it almost parallel with it.

For five to 10 minutes after the *Fougueux* opened the battle, the *Royal Sovereign* held on her course while the *Santa Ana* discharged a broadside at her. Then she closed in and broke through the enemy's line, astern of the *Santa Ana* and ahead of the *Fougueux*, or, as Collingwood says in his dispatch, "about the twelvth [ship] from the rear."[5] When she passed under the stern of the *Santa Ana*, she raked her with a double-shotted broadside, which did her tremendous damage. Next, she fired her starboard broadside at the *Fougueux*, and then sheered up on the starboard quarter of the *Santa Ana* and engaged her at the gun-muzzle.

Collingwood soon found himself surrounded by enemy ships, and within 40 minutes of opening fire the *Royal Sovereign* was

---

[1] *Admiralty Committee* (Cd. 7120) Appx. V, p. 102.
[2] *The Enemy at Trafalgar*, Edward Fraser, p. 114.
[3] *Ibid.*, p. 114. The plan of the battle on page 87 is based on Desbrière's. No two plans, whether contemporary or subsequent, agree, and not a few are fantastic.
[4] "He [Collingwood] changed the formation of his division from an irregular line ahead to an irregular line of bearing. In his *Journal* he writes: 'made the signal for the Lee Division to form the larboard line of bearing and make more sail'. " (*Admiralty Committee*, Cd. 7120, p. xii.)
[5] Collingwood's *Correspondence*, p. 120. Actually it was the fifteenth, because three allied ships were to leeward of the enemy's line and were unseen by Collingwood or mistaken as frigates. (*Admiralty Committee*, Cd. 7120, p. xiii.)

Eight minutes after the *Royal Sovereign* engaged, the *Belleisle* came into action and cut through the enemy's line, astern of the *Fougueux*. Like the *Royal Sovereign* she was at once engaged by several of the enemy's ships, and for a time was unable to fire a gun because of the wreckage of her masts. Nevertheless she kept her ensign flying by nailing it to the stump of her mizen-mast. Later she was relieved by the *Polyphemus*, *Defiance*, and *Swiftsure*.

A quarter of an hour after the *Belleisle*, the *Mars* came into action, and after her, in rapid succession, the *Tonnant*, *Bellerophon*, *Colossus*, and *Achille*. Ship after ship came up, and as they broke through the enemy's line in all parts, each closed with the first enemy ship encountered and engaged her yard-arm to yard-arm. Next, each ship sailed on to leave the pounding of the enemy to ships astern. This resulted in a continuous concentration of fire on the enemy's ships.

Of Collingwood's rear ships, the *Dreadnought* did not engage until an hour after the *Royal Sovereign*, and a quarter of an hour later was followed by the *Defiance*. The *Defence* did not come up until an hour later still, and the last ship of Collingwood's division to enter the battle was the *Prince*, which did not engage until 3 p.m.

When the action of the Lee Column ended, Collingwood's victory was complete. Of the 15 French and Spanish ships he fought, 10 were captured, one–the *Achille*–blew up, and only the *Principe de Asturias*, carrying Admiral Gravina, mortally wounded, the *Algésiras*, *Montañés*, and *Aigle* escaped.

Twenty-five minutes after Collingwood's division engaged, Nelson's went into action. Unlike the former, it retained its irregular line ahead formation, and according to the "Private Log" of Thomas Atkinson, Master of the *Victory*, it was "still standing for the enemy's van."[1] Also in accordance with Atkinson, "At 11.50 [actually 12.10 p.m.] the Enemy began to fire upon us, and at 4 minutes past 12 [12.24 p.m.] open'd our Larboard guns at Enemy's van."[2]

From north to south, the five leading ships of Dumanoir's van were probably the *Neptuno*, *Scipion*, *Intrépide*, *Formidable*, and *Duguay-Trouin*, and, according to Dumanoir, Nelson's leading three three-deckers moved on the centre of his van, and

---

[1] Though no time is given for this entry, according to *Admiralty Committee*, Cd. 7120, pp. xiii and 63, it refers to the period immediately preceding Collingwood's attack.
[2] *Ibid.*, p. 63.

at 12.15 p.m. became engaged with it, and after a cannonade of 40 minutes wore to starboard.[1]

As far as Nelson's three leading ships were concerned, the cannonade was far shorter than Dumanoir states, for immediately after the *Formidable* opened fire, the *Victory* and *Téméraire* wore to starboard, which is mentioned by Lieutenant Conor of the *Héros*, who adds: "Whereas the other ships of the same column kept on the port tack threatening our van."[2] Nelson searched for Villeneuve's flagship, for his overmastering desire was to lay his own ship alongside her. "Although," says James, "every glass on board the *Victory* was out in requisition to discover the flag of the French Commander-in-Chief, all the answers to Nelson's repeated questions on the subject ended in disappointment."[3] The *Victory*, therefore, made for the *Santissima Trinidad* to seek Villeneuve[4] in the largest ship of the enemy's fleet, and, according to the Master of the *Spartiate*, at 12.57 p.m., when the *Victory* bore down on her, to her stern was seen the French Admiral's flag "at the Fore" of a French two-decker (the *Bucentaure*).[5] Raked by the enemy's guns, the *Victory* shortly after passed under the stern of the *Bucentaure* and fired her forecastle carronade – a 68-pdr. – loaded with a round shot and a keg of 500 musket balls, as well as a double-shotted broadside, into her cabin windows, and did her tremendous damage. Next, as the *Neptune* (Br.) and *Conqueror* closed on the *Bucentaure*, the *Victory* put her helm hard to starboard and ran alongside the *Redoubtable*, commanded by Captain Lucas.

At once their rigging became entangled and the two ships were locked together. Both crews then prepared to board, but the Frenchmen were prevented from doing so by the *Victory's* starboard carronade and a broadside from the *Téméraire*, which cut them down in scores. About an hour later, the two ships still interlocked, Nelson was hit by a musket shot aimed from the mizen-top of the *Redoubtable* while he was walking with Captain Hardy on the quarter-deck. The ball struck the epaulette on his left shoulder, penetrated his chest and lodged in his spine. He fell on his face, and when raised from the deck gasped: "They

[1] Desbrière's *Trafalgar*, p. 150. Captain Berrenger of the *Scipion* in his "Journal" states that the *Formidable* opened fire at 12.35 p.m.; he also mentions that the head of Nelson's column moved on the centre of the van (*ibid.*, pp. 155–156).
[2] *Ibid.*, p. 168.
[3] *Naval History of Great Britain, 1793–1820* (1886), vol. III, p. 32.
[4] Actually, Nelson believed that Decrès was in command.
[5] *Admiralty Committee* (Cd. 7120), "Log of *Spartiate*", p. 53.

have done for me at last, Hardy . . . my backbone is shot through."[1] He was carried down to the cockpit of his ship, and at 4.30 p.m., in the knowledge that the battle had been won, died.

When the *Victory* engaged the *Redoubtable*, the *Téméraire* steered clear of the former and opened fire on the *Santissima Trinadad*, and next on the *Neptuno* (Fr.) and *Redoubtable*. Shortly after, the *Fougueux*, which after engaging the *Belleisle* crossed the space between the allied rear and centre, bore up to assist the *Redoubtable*, and was grappled by the *Téméraire*. The latter poured into her a full broadside at point-blank range, and immediately caught her fore-rigging and lashed it to her spare anchor. No sooner were the two ships interlocked, than the *Redoubtable's* "main yard and all the wreck fell on the *Téméraire's* poop, which entirely encumbered the after part of the ship". Then, "with a prize lashed on each side and the greater part of her batteries out of action", the *Téméraire* raked the *Santissima Trinadad* for half an hour with her foremost guns.[2]

Ten minutes after the *Victory* broke the enemy's line the *Neptune* (Br.), fired her first broadside into the *Bucentaure*, passed on to the *Santissima Trinadad*, and an hour and a half later, with 254 of her crew killed and 173 wounded, the great four-decker struck her colours. The scene in her, as described by Midshipman Badcock of the *Neptune* (Br.) gives some idea of what early nineteenth century naval fighting was like. "I was on board our prize the Trinidada," he writes, "getting the prisoners out of her. She had between three and four hundred killed and wounded, her beams were covered with Blood, Brains and pieces of Flesh, and the after part of her Decks with wounded, some without legs and some without an Arm."[3]

The *Britannia* next came up, followed by the *Leviathan* and *Conqueror*. The last two came alongside the *Bucentaure*, and at 2.5 p.m. Villeneuve hauled down his flag. The scene on board her is described by Captain Atcherley of the *Conqueror's* marines. "The dead, thrown back as they fell," he writes, "lay along the middle of the decks in heaps, and the shot passing through these, had frightfully mangled the bodies. . . . More than four hundred had been killed and wounded, of whom an extraordinary proportion had lost their heads."[4]

---

[1] *Dispatches and Letters*, vol. VII, p. 244.
[2] Quoted by Newbolt in *The Year of Trafalgar*, p. 140.
[3] Quoted by Fraser in *The Enemy at Trafalgar*, p. 272.   [4] *Ibid.*, p. 142.

The *Ajax* came into action 40 minutes after the *Victory*, and the *Agamemnon* later still. The *Africa*, a sixty-four and the smallest battleship on either side, had an unusual adventure. During the night of October 20–21 she lost sight of the fleet, and at daybreak was several miles north of it. Directly she discovered its position, she headed for the *Victory*, and a few minutes after the *Royal Sovereign* opened the battle she came within range of the enemy's van. According to her log,[1] at 11.40 she engaged the headmost ship and then ran down the whole of the van and fired at each ship she passed, after which she bore down to assist the *Neptune* (Br.), engaged the *Santissima Trinadad*, and later fought the *Intrépide*.

The *Orion* also played a singular part, for when he saw the enemy ships of the central division more than outmatched by Nelson's, Codrington, her Captain, sailed south to help the *Royal Sovereign*. Next she passed the *Mars*, *Colossus*, and *Tonnant* and then turned north toward the *Victory*. The last two ships of Nelson's division, the *Minotaur* and *Spartiate*, had not engaged when Villeneuve struck.

We come now to Dumanoir's counter-attack, if so it can be called.

At 12.30 p.m., when Nelson bore down on the allied centre, Villeneuve made a general signal to instruct all his ships not then engaged to get into action. To this Dumanoir made no response and Villeneuve took no notice of it. Half an hour later, Dumanoir still bore north and, in consequence, opened up a gap between the van and the centre. Instead of acting on his own initiative, he asked for orders. Nevertheless, Villeneuve sent no reply until 1.50 p.m., when he ordered him to come to the help of the hardly pressed centre.

The wind was very light and Dumanoir had considerable difficulty in going about, and instead of keeping his squadron intact, so that he might hit with full force, he split it into halves.[2] So slow was his manœuvre that it was not until between 3.15 p.m. and 3.30 p.m. that Captain Hardy in the *Victory* noticed that the nearer five of Dumanoir's 10 ships were drawing southward. At once he signalled Nelson's division to make ready to receive them.

---

[1] *Admiralty Committee* (Cd. 7120), p. 6.
[2] Or what seems more probable is that the first five ships which got about sailed on in advance of the other five, or that half the ships disobeyed orders.

The five ships Hardy saw were the *Héros*, *Intrépide*, *San Augustin*, *San Francisco de Asis*, and the *Rayo*, and soon after he had signalled they bore down on the *Conqueror*, *Ajax*, *Agamemnon*, and *Leviathan*. A little later the *San Augustin* struck; the *Héros* broke away and made for Cadiz, and the *San Francisco de Asis* and *Rayo* escaped, the one to be wrecked and the other to surrender to the *Leviathan* on October 23. The *Intrépide*, commanded by Captain Infernet, was gallantly attacked by the *Africa*, and then engaged by the *Ajax*, *Agamemnon*, and *Orion*, and after a tremendous fight surrendered to Captain Codrington.

In the meantime Dumanoir's remaining five ships got about: the *Formidable* and two others had to be towed round by boats. They hauled to wind and came down the line, the *Formidable* in the lead, followed by the *Scipion*, *Mont Blanc*, *Duguay-Trouin*, and *Neptuno*. They opened fire on the *Conqueror*, and then passed on and poured their broadsides into the *Victory*, *Téméraire*, and *Royal Sovereign*. Soon, the *Minotaur* and *Spartiate*–not yet engaged– closed in on them, and cut out the *Neptuno*, which later struck her colours. In the meantime Dumanoir's remaining four ships disappeared to the south, and on November 4 were rounded up and captured by Sir Richard Strachan's squadron.

When, at 4.30 p.m., the battle neared its end, of Villeneuve's 33 ships, nine were on their way to Cadiz; four were flying for the Strait; and of the remaining 20, 17 were totally disabled, 13 in possession of prize crews, and one in flames. As night closed in, the storm which had threatened since the morning broke and blew for four days, and during it many of the damaged ships foundered, including all the British prizes except four. Yet, throughout the battle and storm not a single British ship was lost.

The casualties in life and limb are variously given. According to the *London Gazette* of November 27 and December 3, 1805, the British lost 449 killed and 1,214 wounded. The French and Spanish losses, given by Fraser,[1] are as follows: French, 3,373 killed and drowned and 1,155 wounded; Spanish, 1,022 killed, 1,383 wounded and between 3,000 and 4,000 prisoners. As the French loss in prisoners must, at least, have equalled the Spanish, the total allied losses probably amounted to some 14,000 officers and men. Though a high figure, it was nevertheless small when compared with the losses suffered at the battle of Lepanto.

[1] *The Enemy at Trafalgar*, p. 374.

On both sides the battle was remarkable for its gallantry, the French and Spaniards, though from the first at a heavy discount, fought as stubbornly as the British. Also, when compared with present-day battles and their aftermath, it was remarkable for the chivalry displayed during it and the courtesies meted out after it. For instance, when a prisoner of war, Captain Lucas of the *Redoubtable* was lionized by London society; Captain Infernet of the *Intrépide* paid his compliments to Mrs. Codrington, wife of his captor; and Admiral Villeneuve and Captain Magendie were given permission to attend Nelson's funeral. In spite of the Revolution, war was still the occupation of gentlemen, as the following incident illustrates.

After the battle, Captain Codrington of the *Orion*, in a letter written home gives the following description of life at Gibraltar: "Whilst the Governor of Algeziras (old Gibraltar) is dining with the Governor of the Rock (new Gibraltar), or whilst the Governor of the Rock, with one-half of the officers and many of the private soldiers, is at a horserace in Spain, the Algeziras gunboats are making an attack on a convoy coming in with supplies for the garrison. I was actually, when last here, standing with one of General Fox's aides-de-camp in the Spanish lines observing the Spanish fire at the 'Beagle' sloop of war which happened to come within range of their shot, with the same apparent indifference as would have attended me on seeing them attack a nation hostile to England."[1]

Collingwood's dispatch on the battle was sent home on October 27 in the schooner *Pickle*, commanded by Lieutenant Lapenotière. On November 4, Lapenotière arrived at Falmouth, from where within half an hour he posted to London. He changed horses 19 times on the way and drew up at the gates of the Admiralty at one o'clock on the morning of November 6.[2] A few minutes later he was met by the First Secretary, and the first words he said to him were: "Sir, we have gained a great victory, but we have lost Lord Nelson!"

Nelson's pre-eminence as an admiral largely rests on his break away from the theory of the parallel order of battle, and though he was by no means the first to do so, more clearly than his

---

[1] Quoted by Fraser in *The Enemy at Trafalgar*, pp. 381–382.
[2] Napoleon received the news of Villeneuve's defeat when at Znaym on his march to Austerlitz (*Correspondance*, No. 9507, vol. XI, p. 424). A few months later he paid Nelson the remarkable tribute by directing that "*La France compte que chacun fera son devoir,*" should be painted prominently on board every man-of-war.

predecessors he saw that it was based on a purely defensive idea. According to this, a line of battleships could bring so great a superiority of fire to bear against an enemy approaching in line ahead formation, that it was suicidal for him to attempt to do so. But Nelson saw the flaw in this theory, he saw that because of the restricted range and inaccuracy of the guns of his day, the danger of being blasted out of action by a wall of converging fire was limited to the last few hundred yards of the approach. Further, he saw that once contact was gained, superiority of gunnery, far more than numerical superiority or linear formation, was the decisive factor. It was in this respect that the British crews completely outclassed their antagonists, for not only was their fire more accurate, but twice as rapid, and, therefore, more than twice as destructive, as a comparison between the casualties proves. In part, at least, this was because the French and Spaniards had been unable to practise during the blockade, whereas the English could.

When Collingwood commanded the *Dreadnought*, we read that the sailors were so constantly practised "in the exercise of the great guns . . . that few ships companies could equal them in rapidity and precision of firing." And that Collingwood was accustomed to tell them that, "if they could fire three well-directed broadsides in five minutes, no vessel could resist them; and from constant practice, they were enabled to do so in three minutes and a half."[1] What this meant was that, once closely engaged, a ship which could fire twice as rapidly as her opponent was in fire power equivalent to two ships. Therefore, the tactical problem, as Nelson saw it, was to close with the enemy *coûte qu'il coûte*. It was what, to-day, in journalese would be described as "*blitzkrieg* at sea".

In every respect, Trafalgar was a memorable battle and its influence upon history was profound. It shattered for ever Napoleon's dream of an invasion of England. It brought to an end the 100 years struggle between her and France for the lordship of the seas. It gave England the Empire of the Oceans, which was to endure for over a century and make possible the *Pax Britannica*. More immediately important, it showed the world of 1805 that Napoleon was not invincible, and it compelled him to fall back on his Continental System, to seek to establish a universal empire which economically would strangle England,

[1] Collingwood's *Correspondence*, pp. 124–125.

and which instead ended by his own political strangulation. Without Trafalgar there could have been no Peninsular War, and without the Peninsular War it is hard to believe that there would ever have been a Waterloo. Therefore Mr. H. W. Wilson does not exaggerate the importance of this greatest of naval victories when he writes: "Trafalgar was the really decisive battle of the Napoleonic War."[1]

[1] *Cambridge Modern History*, vol. ix, p. 243.

The continental struggle between France and England

Phase I

Though Napoleon's direct attack on England had to be abandoned, the indirect approach remained open, and as the solution of the former hinged on the command of the Channel, that of the latter depended on the command of the coastal ports of Europe. Could he gain control of them, England's foreign trade, the source of her financial power, would be strangled, and without a heavy purse it would be impossible for the English Government to subsidize their continental allies, without whom they could not hope to defeat Napoleon. Therefore, as Mr. Paul H. Emden states in his *Money-Power of Europe in the Nineteenth and Twentieth Centuries*, "The strongest of all the powers allied against Napoleon was the power of British finance."

This was apparent to Charles James Fox and Count Andréossy, the French Ambassador in London. The former, when he urged the evacuation of Malta, had said: "Must we then, to gratify the ambition of our merchants, spill torrents of British blood? . . . I had rather blood should flow for romantic expeditions like that of Alexander, than for the gross cupidity of a few merchants greedy after gold." And the latter, a few weeks before the outbreak of war in 1803, had written to the First Consul to say: "In a country where the main interest is business, and where the merchant class is so prosperous, the Government had to appeal to the merchants for extraordinary funds, and they have the right to insist that their interests should be considered in the policy which is adopted." Because the French embargo on English goods was the cause of an ever-growing trade depression in England, the one thing the merchant-bankers wanted was freer trade.

But Napoleon would not consider this, because he held that free trade would make France become the debtor of England. His economic ideas were those of Rousseau, according to whom, "the perfect state was one that sufficed for all its needs and could do without foreign trade." It was in pursuance of this autarchic idea that, in the autumn of 1793, the Convention had excluded all British goods not carried in French bottoms, and three years later, in order to stimulate French industry, had prohibited the import of all enemy manufactured products.

Not only did Napoleon refuse to modify this policy, but he began to elaborate it into his Continental System—his trade war with England. Two months before the rupture of the Peace o Amiens, in a conversation with Lord Whitworth he had said: "Do you suppose that I want to risk my power and renown in a desperate struggle? If I have a war with Austria, I shall contrive to find my way to Vienna. If I have a war with you, I shall take from you every ally on the Continent; I shall cut you off from all access to it, from the Baltic to the Gulf of Taranto. You will blockade us, but I will blockade you in my turn."

This was not an idle boast, for when the war was renewed in May, one of Napoleon's first acts was to seize Hanover, in order to control the mouth of the Elbe, and to send St. Cyr with a body of troops to occupy Taranto and other ports in the kingdom of Naples, in order to gain a footing in the central Mediterranean. Nevertheless, as we have seen, it was not until August, 1805, when the threat of the Third Coalition matured, that he was compelled to abandon his attempt to invade England.

The forces then assembled against him, though immense, were scattered: 84,000 men in Italy under the Archduke Charles; 34,000 in Tyrol; 58,000 on the Danube under the Archduke Ferdinand and General Mack; and 55,000 Russians under Kutusov, who were expected on the Inn by the middle of October, three weeks before it was reckoned that Napoleon could reach the Danube. Kutusov was to be followed by two armies, one under Bennigsen and the other under Buxhöwden, and in addition 50,000 Russians, Swedes, Danes, Hanoverians and English were to recover Hanover and invade Holland, and 50,000 Russians, English, and Neapolitans were to drive the French out of southern Italy.

Though the allies had observed great secrecy, Napoleon was well aware of their intentions, and in order to prevent Prussia from joining the Coalition, he offered Hanover to Frederick William, and on August 24 sent General Duroc to Berlin with powers to sign a treaty. At the same time he informed Frederick William that he had warned Austria that if her troops were not withdrawn into their peacetime cantonments, he would enter Bavaria at the head of more than 100,000 men.

On September 3 this ultimatum was rejected, and when, on September 8, the Austrian troops crossed the Inn, the Elector of Bavaria withdrew his army to Würzburg and Bamberg to await the French. On September 26 the Grand Army began to cross the Rhine, from where at top speed it set out to fall upon the Austrians, under Ferdinand and Mack, before Kutusov could come to their support.

On October 6 Napoleon reached the Danube, and, on October 17, he repeated his Marengo manœuvre and forced the capitulation of Mack and 15,000 men at Ulm, and at the same time rounded up 13,000 more under General Werneck.

While Frederick William considered whether to accept the offer of Hanover, Bernadotte's corps violated Prussian neutrality by passing through Ansbach. The Tsar was then pressing the king to join the Coalition, and Bernadotte's affront so annoyed the latter that, on November 3, he received Alexander at Potsdam, and in return for Russian support pledged himself to declare war on France if Napoleon did not withdraw from Austrian territory within four weeks of the arrival of his envoy, Count Haugwitz, who, as he was against Prussia's entry into the war, delayed his departure until November 14.

The day before this, Napoleon had entered Vienna, from where, because Francis refused to make peace, he decided to press on. On November 19 Kutusov and Buxhöwden united their armies at Olmütz, and the next day, at the head of 40,000 men – rapidly reinforced to 65,000 – Napoleon entered Brunn. His position there was critical, for not only was the bulk of his army still scattered, but at Olmütz, 40 miles to his north-east, he was faced by 82,500 Russians and Austrians, under Alexander and Francis, and by the middle of December their forces would be doubled by the arrival of the armies of Bennigsen and the Archduke Charles. Further, by then 180,000 Prussians might also be in the field.

Fortunately for Napoleon, supplies at Olmütz were short, and in spite of Kutusov's protests, Alexander decided not to wait for Bennigsen, but to attack Napoleon before he could gather in the rest of his army. The result was the battle of Austerlitz, fought on December 2. Lured by Napoleon into a false position, the allied army was cut in two and its left wing annihilated. The allies lost 12,000 men killed and wounded, 15,000 captured, and 180 guns. The French casualties were 6,800. Austerlitz was Napoleon's masterpiece, and of all his battles the one of which he was most proud. Nothing comparable with it had been seen since the days of Frederick.

Morally the allied disaster was so overwhelming that Francis immediately asked for an armistice, which was agreed to on condition that the Russians would withdraw from Austria and the Prussians would be prohibited from entering it. At first, Napoleon was willing to leave Austria intact, if Russia would agree to exclude British goods from the Continent; but as Alexander would not consider this, negotiations were opened and a treaty of peace signed at Pressburg on December 26. For Austria its terms were shattering: Venetia, Istria and Dalmatia were ceded to Napoleon as King of Italy; the Emperor renounced his feudal rights over Bavaria, Würtemberg and Baden; Bavaria and Würtemberg became kingdoms; Augsburg, Nuremberg, Brixen, Trent, Tyrol and Vorarlberg were ceded to Bavaria; Austria received nothing, except Salzburg and Berchtesgaden, and had to pay an indemnity of 40,000,000 francs.

Throughout, Talleyrand was opposed to these severe measures, for he held that Austria should be maintained as a great power because she was "a needful bulwark against the barbarians, the Russians". But Napoleon would not listen to this, for Austria – virtually a landlocked country – was of little importance in his Continental System, and as his aim was to exclude British shipping from the Baltic, his eyes were fixed on Prussia and Russia.

His problem became this. How was he to separate Prussia and Russia and isolate England? Though he had no exact knowledge of the Potsdam compact, his suspicions had been aroused, and in order to gain time, when Haugwitz arrived he had had him kept waiting until after Austerlitz was fought. Then, at Vienna, on December 15, Haugwitz, instead of presenting Frederick William's ultimatum, was compelled to agree to a treaty whereby France and Prussia would enter upon an offensive and defensive alliance, the latter to cede Cleves, Neuchâtel and Ansbach in return for Hanover. Two months later this treaty was superseded by the Treaty of Paris, according to which the alliance was to be wholly defensive, and Prussia was forthwith to annex Hanover and close the mouths of the Ems, Weser and Elbe to England. This treaty was ratified at Berlin on February 24, 1806, and immediately after this England seized 300 Prussian ships and blockaded the Prussian North Sea ports.

Napoleon considered these were satisfactory terms with Prussia, and next set out to establish his dynasty and consolidate his gains. In March he made his brother Joseph, King of the Two Sicilies and his brother Louis, King of Holland. Further, he created a new aristocracy, Berthier, Talleyrand and Bernadotte became princes of Neuchâtel, Benevento, and Ponte Corvo, and other honours were showered on his leading generals. At the same time he dissolved the Empire and founded a league of states to be known as the Confederation of the Rhine. Its more important members were Bavaria, Würtemberg, Baden, Berg and Nassau. Later it was enlarged to include all the territory west of the Elbe and Bohemia (less Baireuth and Hanover) as well as Mecklenburg, east of the Elbe.

The treaty constituting this confederation was ratified at Saint Cloud on July 19 and Napoleon was declared its Protector. On August 1, the Emperor Francis II absolved all electors and princes from allegiance to him, and declared himself Francis I, Emperor of Austria. Thus, after a thousand years, the Holy Roman Empire came to an end.

While Napoleon formed this confederation he also intrigued with Russia and England. From the one he wanted Alexander's recognition of Joseph as King of The two Sicilies, in order to strengthen his position in the Mediterranean and obtain Sicily, then in English hands. To the other he offered to restore Hanover, Prussia to receive compensation in its stead.

The news of these proposals leaked out, and on August 9 Frederick William, under pressure by the Prussian war party – headed by Queen Louise and Prince Louis Ferdinand – ordered a partial mobilization of his army. Next, an incident occurred which detonated war.

In July a Nuremberg bookseller named Palm had circulated an anonymous pamphlet entitled *Germany in her Deep Humiliation*. Napoleon took offence and ordered his arrest, and on August 25 Palm was court-martialled, condemned, and shot. This high-handed act so profoundly stirred Prussia that, on September 6, the king reopened the North Sea ports to British ships. On September 21 the king left Berlin for his army headquarters at Naumburg, and five days later sent an ultimatum to Paris demanding the withdrawal by October 8 of the French armies still cantoned in southern Germany to beyond the Rhine.

"Among the world's great autocrats and conquerors," says Fuller, "Napoleon has but two compeers – Alexander the Great and Augustus."

' The warrior spirit of the one he shared to the full, as he did the administrative abilities of the other, and though he failed to establish a universal empire, he so completely uprooted the last vestiges of the medieval conception of commonwealth that ever since his day the nations have groped after his dream of unification.

He was fortunate in the year of his birth,[1] for in 1769 a thousand years of European civilization was about to dissolve. The Industrial Revolution was in its cradle; that year James Watt in England patented his steam engine and in France Cugnot drove the first steam-propelled wagon; the American Revolution was simmering, and out of it was to boil the greater revolution in France. A new age was in precipitation, and it awaited a man of genius to seize hold of it and mould it to his will.

'Possibly, in 1779, Guibert sensed this when he wrote: "A man will arise, perhaps hitherto lost in the obscurity of the crowd; a man who has not made his name either by speech or writing. A man who has meditated silently; a man, in fact, who has perhaps ignored his own talent and has been only conscious of his power while actually exercising it, one who has studied very little. This man will seize hold of opinions, of circumstances, of chance, and will say to the great theoretician what the practical architect said to the orator: 'All that my rival tells you, I will carry out'."[2]

'Such a man was Napoleon, the supreme egoist and architect, the entirely isolated and self-centred man who relied on himself alone and centralized everything. Méneval says of him: "He took not only the initiative in thought, but also attended personally to the detail of every piece of business . . . his genius, superhuman in its activity, carried him away: he felt he possessed the *means* and

[1] At Ajaccio on August 15, 1769.
[2] *Oeuvres de Guibert* (1803), vol. IV, p. 74.

the *time* to manage everything . . . in reality it was he who did everything."[1]'

Despite the splendour of the "sun of Austerlitz", it was the campaign against Prussia in 1806 which displayed the Napoleonic style of war at its most dramatic. The following year saw him at the very height of his imperial powers. But the outward sheen of military achievement can only be properly assessed in terms of the political purposes which Napoleon was trying to fulfil:

' The first was to make France orderly, prosperous, and above all glorious, and the second—its derivative induced by the opposition of England—to establish a universal empire in the form of a league of kingdoms under the aegis of France. The foundations of the first were laid when he became First Consul and during the Peace of Amiens, when, in order to consolidate his gains, undertake great public works, initiate great legal and social reforms, and stimulate science, art and industry—in short, close the abyss created by the Revolution—he earnestly wished for peace. Yet, as we have seen, the clash between his protectionist policy and England's need for free trading made peace impossible.

' The struggle which then began was not between right and wrong, but between two survival values that arose out of the early Industrial Revolution. To remain prosperous and powerful, England had to export her manufactured goods, and to become prosperous and powerful France had to protect her infant industries. As Metternich said: "Everyone knew that England could not give way on this question [the maritime problem], which to her was a matter of life and death."[2] And it was because Napoleon realized this that he relied on his Continental System to strangle England's trade and thereby undermine her credit, without which she could not continue to raise enemies against him.[3]

' "The power of the English", he said, ". . . rests only upon the monopoly they exercise over other nations, and can be maintained only by that. Why should they alone reap the benefits which millions of others could reap as well?"[4] And again:"The good of that Europe which seems to envelop her with goodwill counts for

---

[1] *Mémoires pour servir a l'histoire de Napoléon 1er* (1894), vol. III, p. 50.

[2] *Memoirs of General de Caulaincourt Duke of Vicenza*, trans. Hamish Miles (1935), vol. II, p. 10.

[3] *Ibid.*, vol. I, p. 521.

[4] *Ibid.*, vol. I, pp. 10

nothing with the merchants of London. They would sacrifice every state in Europe, even the whole world, to further one of their speculations. If their debt were not so large they might be more reasonable. It is the necessity of paying this, of maintaining their credit, that drives them on. . . ." [1]

' In his struggle with England, he saw "the basic solution of all the questions" that were "agitating the world and even individuals".[2] Therefore, as he told Caulaincourt, England was his sole enemy: "He was working against the English alone," and "since their trade had ramifications everywhere he had to pursue them everywhere".[3] It was out of this pursuit that the idea of a universal empire arose. From a weapon with which to destroy England, the Continental System became an instrument whereby a new world conception could be realized: a veritable Alexandrian vision – Europe united in Concord.'

"Whatever we may think of this gradiose scheme," continues Fuller, "it was anathema to England, because she could not hope to survive as the dominant maritime power were Europe federated. Therefore, the clash between her and France was to the death. . ." In 1806 the talent of Napoleon suggested that in this struggle it would not be France that went down. This is accordingly a convenient moment to examine the personal qualities, the instrument and the methods by which he was able to dazzle the world.

'As a general in the field, his activity was phenomenal. During an advance, he generally remained in rear, but when near the enemy he went forward. He saw everything for himself, for as he said: "A general who has to see things through other people's eyes will never be able to command an army as it should be commanded.'[4] Time to him was everything, day for seeing and night for working. "The Emperor", writes Caulaincourt, "always arose at eleven o'clock at night, or at the latest, midnight, when the first dispatches from the army corps came to hand," and after working on them for two or three hours, he issued his orders for the next day.[5] He adopted this method so that the troops should receive orders based on the latest information by reveille. "The loss of time," he once said, "was irreparable in war; reasons alleged for it were always bad, for operations only fail through delays." [6]

[1] *Memoirs of General de Caulaincourt Duke of Vicenza*, trans. Hamish Miles (1935), vol. I, p. 424.

[2] *Ibid.*, vol. I, p. 529.   [3] *Ibid.*, vol. I, p. 429.

[4] *Napoleon in Exile*, B. E. O'Meara (1822), vol. II, p. 377.

[5] Caulaincourt's *Memoirs*, vol. I, p. 599.

[6] *Correspondance*, No. 9997, vol. XII, p. 203.

'As a soldier, Napoleon was doubly fortunate in the year of his birth, for between the end of the Seven Years War and the close of the century, French military organization and, consequently, tactics, were profoundly modified. Though the flintlock was little improved,[1] as we have seen, gunnery was greatly advanced by Gribeauval, and Napoleon was pre-eminently a gunner, who as a youth had studied Benjamin Robins's *New Principles of Gunnery*.[2] In the battles of this period, because of the short effective range of the musket, field artillery could gallop within 350 yards of an enemy and batter his battalions to pieces. Yet, strange to say, the full meaning of this was not completely grasped until late in the Napoleonic Wars.

'In 1759, thanks to the experiments of Maurice de Saxe, Marshal de Broglie had introduced the divisional system, which, in 1804, became the basis of Napoleon's army corps—completely self-contained bodies of troops. But the greatest innovation of all was the introduction of conscription, which was finally established by General Jourdan and the Council of Five Hundred in 1798. Though there was nothing new in the idea of compulsory enlistment, under the Directory it was placed on a national footing, every able-bodied male citizen from his twentieth to his twenty-fifth year was by law compelled to serve his country. Not only did conscription render Napoleon's policy of conquest possible, but it radically changed infantry tactics by increasing the average intelligence of the ranks.

'Although the training of the French conscripts was negligible, their tactics were individual and elastic, based on man and musket more than on mechanical volley firing. The skirmishers were, Sir Robert Wilson said, "as sharp-sighted as ferrets and as active as squirrels".[3] And the Duke of York's aide-de-damp wrote: "No mobbed fox was ever more put to it to make his escape than we were, being at times nearly surrounded."[4] Of the conscripts, a Prussian officer said: "In the woods, when the soldiers break rank and have no drill movements to carry out, but only to fire

---

[1] "With the French flint-musket one misfire might be expected in every nine shots, and one hang-fire in every eighteen. The flint had to be changed every thirty shots." ("Mémoire sur le fusil de guerre", *Oeuvres du Marquis de Chambray*, 1840, vol, v, p. 292.)

[2] See *The Growth of Napoleon,* Norwood Young (1910), p. 166.

[3] *Life of Sir Robert Wilson,* H. Randolph (1862), vol. I, p. 86.

[4] *Journals and Correspondence of Sir Henry Calvert* (1853), p. 220.

under the cover of the trees, they are not only equal but superior to us. Our men, accustomed to fight shoulder to shoulder in the open field, found it difficult to adopt that seeming disorder which was yet necessary if they were not to be targets for the enemy." [1] Equally important, the French soldier lived on the enemy's country, and therefore the French trains needed but a fraction of the animals to be found in the Prussian supply columns. This added enormously to French mobility.

'Such was the army Napoleon inherited–active, mobile, intelligent and fanatical, but in discipline weak. "He was ready to grant," says Caulaincourt of the Emperor, "that his system of warfare could not admit of severe discipline, as the troops were forced to subsist without any proper rationing."[2] Nevertheless, it was a dangerous principle to work on; after Eylau there were 60,000 marauders, [3] and before Wagram thousands of men were drunk. [4] Yet in moral force the spirit of the army remained firm. It was an army inspired rather than trained, and quite unlike the Austrian, Prussian, Russian, and British. Of the last, Gourgaud informs us: "His Majesty finds English discipline rather too rigorous; it doesn't leave sufficient to one's honour." [5]

'As a strategist, Napoleon has never been excelled, and in this the age in which he lived also favoured him, for roads were being improved by men such as Thésaguet in France and McAdam in England. Increasing prosperity demanded better roads, and, when built, the regions they traversed grew more prosperous and in consequence enabled armies more easily to live on the land they marched through, and therefore to dispense with the old magazine and depôt system that dated from the days of Marlborough and Turenne.

'Napoleon, himself a master road-builder, fully appreciated this change and largely founded his strategy upon it. In the Ulm campaign his men said: "The Emperor has discovered a new way of waging war, he makes use of our legs instead of our bayonets." [6]

---

[1] Quoted from *Les Guerres de la Révolution*, A. Chuquet, vol. ii, p. 96.
[2] *Memoirs*, vol. i, pp. 592–593.
[3] *Souvenirs militaires de 1804 à 1814*, Duc de Fézensac (1863), p. 163.
[4] *Étude sur l'armée révolutionaire*, Pierre Cantal, p. 118.
[5] *The St. Helena Journal of General Baron Gourgaud*, edit. Norman Edwards (1932), p. 51.
[6] *Correspondance*, No. 9392, vol. xi, p. 336. In the Jena Campaign a day's march in the Prussian army seldom exceeded 12½ to 15 miles. In the French, some of the marches were phenomenal. On one occasion Lannes's corps covered 65 miles in 50 hours, and on another Bernadotte's corps marched 75 miles in 69 hours. Much of Napoleon's success was due to rapid marching.

Or, as he himself expressed it: "In the art of war, as in mechanics, time is the grand element between weight and force." [1]

' If rapidity be looked upon as the soul of strategy, planning may be likened to its body. Napoleon always had a plan—a strategical, but not necessarily a tactical one—worked out on what he intended to do, and which bore little or no reference to the enemy's probable intentions. In 1807 he said to Soult: "One should never try to guess what the enemy can do. My intention is always the same," [2] which meant that his initiative was to be given free play. His plan was invariably offensive. "It is an axiom in strategy," he wrote as early as 1793 in *Le Souper de Beaucaire*, "that he who remains behind his entrenchments is beaten; experience and theory are at one on this point." Also in St. Helena he said: "In short, I think like Frederick, one must always be the first to attack." [3]

' His tactics were as offensive as his strategy. In all his many campaigns there is only one example of a wholly defensive battle, that of Leipzig on October 18, 1813. One reason for this was his aggressive temperament, another, as he said: "The change from a defensive to an offensive attitude is one of the most delicate of operations."

'As a tactician he possessed a wonderful eye. "The fate of a battle," he said, "is a question of a single moment, a single thought . . . the decisive moment arrives, the moral spark is kindled, and the smallest reserve force settles the matter." [4] And again: "There is a moment in engagements when the least manœuvre is decisive and gives victory; it is the one drop of water which makes the vessel run over." [5] As a tactician, Caulaincourt writes of him: "Even when chasing the enemy helter-skelter before him, or in the heat of one of his greatest victories, no matter how weary the Emperor was he always had an eye for ground that could be held in the event of a reverse. In this respect he had an astonishing memory for localities. The topography of a country seemed to be modelled in relief in his head. Never did a man combine such a memory with a more creative genius. He seemed to extract men, horses and guns from the very bowels of the earth." [6]

---

[1] *Ibid.*, No. 14707, vol. XVIII, p. 218.   [2] *Ibid.*, No. 11939, vol. XIV, p. 380.
[3] *Journal de Sainte Hélène*, Genl. G. Gourgaud (1899), vol. II, p. 336.
[4] *Journal*, Las Casas, vol. I, Pt. ii, p. 6.
[5] *Correspondance*, "Précis des guerres de J. César," vol. XXXII, p. 104.
[6] *Memoirs*, vol. I, p. 600.

'As his wars lengthened, his infantry deteriorated, and though he said that "it is not sufficient that the soldier should shoot, he must shoot well," [1] he was not much interested in musketry. For instance, in 1800, on the day before crossing the St. Bernard, we find Berthier ordering that all conscripts should fire a few rounds in order "that they may know which eye to aim with and how to load their muskets." [2] Not until 1811 do we hear of Napoleon approving target practice for recruits, and then only if inferior powder were fired. [3] The truth is that throughout he relied more upon gun than musket. "In siege warfare, as in the open field," he said, "it is the gun which plays the chief part; it has effected a complete revolution . . . it is with artillery that war is made." [4] The following figures support this statement: At the battle of Malplaquet the French fired 11,000 cannon shot; at Wagram– 71,000; and at Leipzig–175,000; and whereas, under Henry IV, the French cannon numbered 400, under Louis XIV–7,192; under Louis XV–8,683; under Louis XVI–10,007; in 1815 under Napoleon they numbered 27,976. [5]

'Strange as it may seem, though Napoleon was a gunner by training, he only slowly evolved his artillery tactics. As late as the battles of Eylau (1807), Friedland (1807) and Aspern (1809) his infantry dashed themselves to pieces against the enemy guns. After Aspern he massed his artillery against the point of attack, and at Wagram (1809) and Borodino (1812) he blew great holes in his enemy's lines and columns. "In every case where the services of the artillery, because of the want of this weapon, failed, Napoleon was obliged to have recourse to a series of successive efforts, which cost him infinite forces and time." [6]'

The Prussian Army, against which Napoleon marched in 1806, was the legacy of Frederick the Great, formidable in numbers (over 200,000) and reputation. But, as Fuller says, for practical purposes it was "a museum piece", incapable of coping with French tactics, and its High Command was divided and inept. There is therefore something undoubtedly spurious about the great triumph commemorated to this day by the magnificent

---

[1] *Correspondance*, No. 11390, vol. xiv, p. 35.
[2] *Le Maréchal Berthier*, V. B. Derrécagaix (1904), vol. i, p. 399.
[3] *Correspondance*, No. 18219, vol. xxii, p. 540.
[4] *Ibid.*, "Diplomatie-Guerre", vol. xxx, p. 447.
[5] *Des Changemens survenus dans l'art de la guerre 1700–1815*, Marquis de Chambray 1830), p. 23.
[6] *The Influence of Firearms upon Tactics*, Anonymous (English edit., 1876), p. 83.

Pont de Jena across the Seine. Closer examination of the event confirms this: while Napoleon's main force was winning its battle at Jena on 14 October, the Emperor himself was acting under a delusion. He believed that he had the Prussian main body in front of him, whereas in fact it was thirteen miles away at Auerstädt. It was there encountered by Marshal Davout, with his III Army Corps of 26,000 men and forty-four guns – against 60,000 Prussians with 230 guns. As Fuller comments: "While Napoleon fought at Jena a battle which, because of his numerical superiority, he could not lose . . . Davout had been engaged in another which, by all the rules of war, he could not win." And yet he *did* win – a brilliant feat of arms which has always tended to be obliterated by the propaganda acclamations of the Emperor. Nevertheless, the fact remains that the double victory of Jena-Auerstädt was decisive, and what immediately followed does Napoleon's military reputation more credit than his actual battle:

'On the morning of October 15, there began one of the most famous pursuits in history: Murat, Soult, Ney and Bernadotte set out to follow up the fragments of the beaten armies and annihilate resistance, while Napoleon with Davout, Augereau, Lannes and the Guard took the road to Berlin. Further, Louis and Mortier were ordered to advance into Hesse.

'On October 27, Napoleon entered Berlin in triumph, and though conditions of peace were discussed and decided, the King received a dispatch from St. Petersburg to inform him that if he stood by his alliance with Russia, the Tsar would come to his assistance with 140,000 men, and refused to ratify them. In the meantime fortress after fortress surrendered – Erfurt, Prenzlau, Spandau, Stettin, Küstrin, Magdeburg and Hameln, and on November 7 Blücher capitulated at Lübeck. Thus, in 24 days, the entire military might of Prussia and Saxony was destroyed: 25,000 men had been killed and wounded, 100,000 had been made prisoners, and the remainder had disbanded themselves and dispersed. The immense booty included 4,000 cannon, 20,000 horses and 100,000 muskets taken in Berlin alone.

'Strategically and tactically, few victories have been so decisive as those of Jena and Auerstädt; nevertheless, politically, Napoleon failed to attain his aim. The defeat of Prussia did not bring with it the withdrawal of England from the war, and it was because of this that the influence of these two battles on history was to be so profound. They did not bring peace, and in the warring years which followed them Europe became so exhausted that, when finally Napoleon was overthrown, the field was clear for England to become the workshop and the banker of the world, the very thing Napoleon had sought to prevent.'

The overthrow of Prussia enabled Napoleon to make his next move against his chief foe – England. On 21 November 1806 he issued his famous Berlin Decree, Article 1 of which read:

"The British Islands are declared in a state of blockade." The object of the Decree was to strike a fatal blow at British trade; Fuller writes:

'This decree became the cornerstone of Napoleonic policy. Whatever nation accepted it was the friend of France; whatever nation did not was her enemy.

'England's counter-attack was immediate. On January 7, 1807, an Order in Council was promulgated that forbade neutrals to trade between any two ports in possession of France or her allies under pain of confiscation of ship and cargo. In answer, on January 27 Napoleon decreed the seizure in the Hanse towns of English goods and colonial produce. Thus the real battle was waged.

'But Russia was still in the field, and as Alexander, the Continental champion of the British credit system, refused to come to terms, Napoleon determined to smash him.

'Bennigsen lay at Warsaw with 60,000 Russians, and Buxhöwden with 40,000 more would be ready in a month. On November 25 Napoleon had left Berlin for Posen; Murat entered Warsaw on November 28, followed by the Emperor on December 18. By then the two Russian armies had been united under the command of Kamenskoi, and on February 8, 1807, in a blinding snow-storm Napoleon attacked him at Prüssisch-Eylau. A most bloody battle resulted, but with no definite French gain, for the Russians withdrew in good order. For the first time Napoleon had failed in a pitched battle, and on April 26 Russia and Prussia signed the Convention of Bartenstein, by which the Tsar and Frederick William bound themselves to drive the French out of Germany, and were supported by Great Britain, who undertook to pay Prussia a subsidy of £1,000,000, and to send 20,000 troops to Stralsund to reinforce 16,000 Swedes under Gustavus IV.

'Next, Napoleon laid siege to Danzig, and immediately after its capitulation Bennigsen foolishly assumed the offensive. On

June 14 he was routed by the French at the battle of Friedland. It was a decisive victory, and the Tsar not only asked for peace, but proposed an alliance with his conqueror.

'On June 25 the two emperors met on a raft moored in the middle of the river Niemen, and for three hours discussed terms of peace, while in the rain on the river bank Frederick William awaited their decisions. What, above all, Napoleon desired, was a return to the League of Armed Neutrality of Paul I, which meant the closing of the Baltic to English ships. This was agreed, and on July 7 peace between France and Russia was signed. Two days later peace between France and Prussia was signed at Tilsit, according to the terms of which the latter was deprived of her territory west of the Elbe, of her Polish provinces annexed in 1793, and of the southern part of west Prussia acquired in 1772, and Kottbus was assigned to Saxony. Danzig was made a free city, and Prussia, reduced to half her former size, undertook to take common actions with France and Russia against England. Napoleon's triumph seemed complete.

The continental struggle between France and England

Phase II

Though Napoleon had reached the zenith of his power, his task was far from completed, for England still refused to make peace, and until she did there could be no peace for Europe. Therefore, immediately he returned to Paris he extended the radius of his Continental System. On July 19, 1807, he warned Portugal that it would be to her advantage to close her ports to British shipping by September 1, and on July 31 he sent a somewhat similar warning to Denmark, to be followed on August 16 by a demand that the Danish fleet was to cooperate with the French. But England had set her eyes upon this fleet, and already, on July 26, Admiral Gambier and a powerful expeditionary force had been sent to the Sound to demand its surrender. As the Danes refused to comply, on September 2, and without a declaration of war, Copenhagen was bombarded, and when it capitulated on September 7, 18 sail of the line and 52 other vessels of war were seized. After this high-handed act Denmark joined France and declared war on England.

With the spectacle of Copenhagen before them, the Portuguese refused to close their ports, and to compel them to do so Napoleon made a convention with Spain for a joint invasion of Portugal, and sent General Junot and 28,000 troops through Spain to march on Lisbon. Thus originated the War of the Spanish Peninsula, which in its accumulative effects was to prove as decisive a factor in the eventual overthrow of Napoleon as his disastrous Russian campaign. The Portuguese fleet escaped him, for the Regent, under British persuasion, reluctantly sought refuge in the flagship of Sir Sidney Smith's squadron in the Tagus, and with the Portuguese fleet set sail for Brazil. Annoyed by this rebuff, Napoleon determined to secure the Spanish ports, and particularly Cadiz.

In March, 1808, Charles IV of Spain abdicated in favour of his son Ferdinand VII (1808–1833). Napoleon refused to recognize the latter, enforced his abdication, and in his stead set Joseph Bonaparte, then King of Naples, on the Spanish throne. The appointment was as unwise as it was unfortunate, for Spain was already in insurrection, and Joseph was not the man to suppress revolt, though, besides Junot's army in Portugal, he had some 90,000 French troops in Spain. Napoleon believed the insurrection to be no more than an affair of banditti and instructed his brother to send out flying columns to disperse them. This Joseph did, and ordered the largest, 22,000 strong, under General Dupont, to quell the revolt in Seville and Cadiz. At Baylen, on July 19, 1808, Dupont ran into difficulties, and four days later he disgracefully capitulated to General Castaños.

Baylen was the greatest disaster French arms had suffered since, in 1801, Belliard and Menou capitulated in Egypt, and compared with the latter it was more portentous, for it initiated a revolt, not of the kings, but of the common people against Napoleon's despotism, and without popular support, whatever else might happen, his cause was doomed. The immediate result of Baylen was the evacuation of Madrid on August 1, to be followed two days later by the landing of a British expeditionary force under Sir Arthur Wellesley in Portugal and the defeat of Junot at Vimiero on August 21. In the meantime, Napoleon had ordered three veteran corps under Victor, Mortier, and Ney to march for Spain. Nothing came of a letter jointly signed by himself and the Tsar and addressed to George III, begging him to consider a general peace, and on October 30 the Emperor left Paris, placed himself at the head of 200,000 men, and invaded Spain. He was before Madrid on December 2 – the anniversary of Austerlitz.

In the meantime, on October 6, the command of the British forces in Portugal had devolved on Sir John Moore, and he, to draw away Napoleon from the ports of southern Spain, set out to cut the French communications at Burgos. When, on December 23, he reached Sahagun and learnt that Napoleon had left Madrid and was advancing against him, he set out to retire on Vigo and Coruña. The Emperor pursued him as far as Astorga, and there he handed over the army to Soult and hastened back to Paris. The reason for this sudden departure was that he had learnt that Talleyrand, Fouché, and Murat were intriguing with Count Metternich, the Austrian ambassador in Paris, and secretly encouraging Austria to oppose him, and that Josephine was implicated. In this he saw what he called the "invisible hand", his implacable foes, the London and Amsterdam bankers and merchants. Certain that another great conflagration was in preparation, he set about to raise 800,000 men, and in March, when Austria declared war, he had available 300,000 in Spain, 100,000 in France, 200,000 drawn from the Rhenish territories, and 60,000 in Italy. The Austrian field army numbered 265,000.

On April 10, 1809, the Austrians, under the Archduke Charles, crossed the Bavarian frontier, and on April 22 were beaten at Eckmühl and lost nearly 40,000 men. On May 13 Napoleon entered Vienna, and nine days later the sanguinary battle of Aspern-Essling was fought, in which Marshal Lannes was killed. It was a near defeat for Napoleon, and it sent a thrill of hope throughout Europe. On July 5–6 came the stubbornly fought battle of Wagram, in which Charles was defeated. It led to the signing of the peace treaty of Schönbrunn on October 15, by the terms of which Austria ceded large districts to Bavaria, France, Russia, and Saxony; was limited to an army of 150,000 men; and compelled to pay an indemnity of 75,000,000 francs. In January, 1810, a treaty was signed between France and Sweden; and during that month Napoleon divorced Josephine. On March 11 he married Marie Louise, daughter of Francis I, in order to obtain an heir as well as to strengthen his position *vis-à-vis* Russia. In order to tighten the blockade, on July 9, by Imperial edict, Holland was annexed to France, and a month later the Swedish Diet recognized Bernadotte, Prince of Ponte Corvo, heir to the Swedish throne, and in October Sweden declared war on England.

Thus far the war between the French and English "systems" had gone well for Napoleon, and particularly so the annexation of Holland, which led to a severe slump in British trade and to a financial crisis aggravated by the failure of the English harvests in 1809 and 1810. By allowing, subject to heavy duty, the import of corn into England, coupled with the cost of maintaining Wellington's army in Spain, the stores of bullion in London were rapidly depleted, and so pronounced became the drain that France alone had stores of bullion in the bank. As something had to be done to break Napoleon's grip on the City of London, Sir Francis Baring, regarded as the first merchant in Europe, and his friends saw that, unless Alexander could be persuaded to break away from the Continental System, England would be bankrupted into submission.

Napoleon did not want war, he wanted peace, but peace on his own terms, which were the destruction of the English System. Above all, he did not want war with Russia, for the Tsar was not only his ally, but the king-pin in his Continental System.

In 1810, Alexander had begun to weaken and accept English goods. Next, he allowed 600 English merchantmen, which had been chased from the Baltic ports, to land their cargoes in Russia. In retaliation and to tighten the blockade, Napoleon annexed the Duchy of Oldenburg, an action which deeply offended the Tsar, because the Grand Duke was his brother-in-law. The situation then deteriorated so rapidly that Napoleon remarked: "War will occur in spite of me, in spite of the Emperor Alexander, in spite of the interests of France and the interests of Russia. I have so often seen this that it is my experience of the past which unveils the future to me. . . . It is all a scene of the opera and the English control the machinery." When at St. Helena he said to Las Casas: "Russia was the last resource of England. The peace of the whole world rested with Russia. Alas! English gold proved more powerful than my plans."

At length the crisis came. On January 12, 1812, in secret treaty with England, Alexander sent Napoleon an ultimatum to demand that all French troops be withdrawn west of the Oder, a demand which Napoleon could not accept.

Napoleon was well prepared to meet the challenge, for he had raised an immense army of 680,000 men, approximately 500,000 infantry, 100,000 cavalry, and nearly 1,400 field and siege guns. Early in May he assembled 450,000 men on the Vistula. Opposed to him were two Russian armies, the one under Barclay de Tolly and the other under Bagration. The former numbered 127,000 men and was extended on an immense frontage – Schavli – Vilna – Prushany. The latter, entirely separated from the former, was at Lutzk, south of the upper Pripet, and numbered 66,000.

Napoleon's idea, rather than plan, was to advance on Vilna, break through the right wing of Barclay's army; next, fall upon the communications of his centre and left wing, and lastly separate him from Bagration. In the small hours of June 24, 1812, the Grand Army began to cross the Niemen at Kovno, Pilona, and Grodno, and Barclay fell back. On June 28 the French entered Vilna and remained there until July 16. This delay, caused by the breakdown of the supply columns, was fatal, because it enabled the two Russian armies to unite at Smolensk on August 1. Again, at Vitebsk, Napoleon decided to halt for a fortnight, this time in order to rally stragglers and establish magazines. Next, on August 16, 17, and 18 he attacked his enemy, but his failure to cut the Moscow Road enabled the Russians again to withdraw.

It is generally held that at Smolensk Napoleon should have gone into winter-quarters and have reopened the campaign in the following spring. This was not practicable because he could not supply his army there, and also because Bernadotte had joined Russia and was well placed with English assistance to fall upon his rear. Only one of two courses were open to him; either to abandon the campaign or continue it. The former course meant victory for England; the latter was to gamble that the occupation of Moscow would force the Tsar to terms. Here for the first time Napoleon allowed politics to intrude on strategy – the occupation of a geographical point instead of the destruction of his enemy's army became his aim.

Napoleon knew that his enemy was demoralized by constant retreat and that the fiery Kutusov had replaced Barclay, which meant a fight, and he accepted the throw of the dice. On September 7 he fought the bloody and indecisive battle of Borodino (Moskowa), in which he lost 28,000 men killed and wounded and the Russians 45,000. Kutusov fell back through Moscow and abandoned the city, which Napoleon entered and occupied on September 14.

The rest of the story may be written in one word – ruin. Between September 15 and 19 three-quarters of Moscow was burnt, probably accidentally. A formidable guerrilla war had already been launched against the French communications, and as the Tsar would not come to terms, to remain in Moscow was impossible. On October 19 the city was abandoned, and at the head of 108,000 men and 569 guns Napoleon began his return to Smolensk. The next day the first frost set in, and on November 4 it began to snow. On November 28 and 29 was fought the battle of the Beresina, in which 25,000 Frenchmen were killed and wounded. "There," writes the Marquis de Chambray in his *Histoire de l'expédition de Russie,* "ended the career of the Grand Army, which had made Europe tremble; it ceased to exist in a military sense, its only safety now lay in headlong flight." On December 5, at Smorgoni, Napoleon handed over the supreme command to Murat, and accompanied by Caulaincourt and a few others he set out for Paris. On the road, always the invincible optimist, he said to Caulaincourt: "The Russians should be viewed by everyone as a scourge. The war against Russia is a war which is wholly in the interests—if those interests are rightly judged—of the older Europe and of civilization. . . . The reverses that France has just suffered will put an end to all jealousies and quiet all the anxieties that may have sprung from her power or influence. Europe should think of only one enemy. And that enemy is the colossus of Russia."

On the night of December 18, at full gallop the Emperor's carriage bore him through the Arc de Triomphe, and as the clock struck the last quarter before midnight he alighted safe and sound at the central entrance of the Tuileries.

CHAPTER 3

The Battle of Leipzig, 1813

With Napoleon's retreat from Moscow the whole character of the war changed. Except in Spain, hitherto he had been opposed by monarchies, henceforth he was to be opposed by peoples possessed with the spirit of self-reliance which in his youth the French Revolution had awakened in France, and which in 1792 had swept the Duke of Brunswick out of Champagne. Now, in 1813, that same spirit was to hurl back the man who, by raising France to as privileged a position among the nations as the *ancien régime* had held *vis à vis* the French people, had sown revolt throughout his conquered lands. The flames of Moscow spiritually set fire to the entire Continent, hence the struggle on the plains of Leipzig has rightly been called "The Battle of the Nations"—a battle out of which a new Europe was to emerge.

This profound change was little realized by Napoleon, and in consequence the situation which faced him on his return to Paris, though complex, appeared to him by no means desperate. Though his prestige had suffered, his military power was only temporarily crippled. Behind him stood France, war-worn yet loyal. Italy, Illyria, the Netherlands, and all Germany, except Prussia, were still his, and both Prussia and Austria were in alliance with him. England and Russia alone were his enemies; the one held his forces in Spain, the other was bankrupt and divided between Kutusov's peace party, which urged that the war should end on the Prussian frontier, and the Tsar's war party, the aim of which was the annihilation of Napoleon. Yet Alexander knew that single-handed he could not carry Russia with him.

For Napoleon, the two doubtful quantities were Prussia and Austria. But the former was militarily so weak that were she to desert him—which appeared probable—he felt confident that he could crush her and Russia combined. The latter posed a more serious problem, for were Austria to join Russia and Prussia he would be faced either by a war on two fronts, or by an overwhelming combination on one. Therefore, on his return to Paris, in order to make certain of Austrian neutrality, he at once opened negotiations with his father-in-law.

England also was then in negotiation with Austria; this Napoleon learnt through Count Otto, his minister in Vienna.[1] But Austria played a double game: she did not want the barbaric Russian hordes to enter and pillage her territories, but she did want to be quit of French tutelage. She was as yet unready for war, therefore her policy was to play for time.

In the meantime, on the Niemen, an event occurred which proved decisive. On December 30, General Yorck von Warten-berg, in command of 30,000 Prussians—half Marshal Mac-donald's rearguard—concluded with the Russians the convention of Tauroggen, according to the terms of which his corps was declared neutral.

The results of this unexpected desertion were twofold. Firstly, Murat, still in command of the remnants of the Grand Army, was compelled to fall back, and on January 16, three days after the main Russian army crossed the Niemen, he handed over his command[2] to Prince Eugène, Viceroy of Italy, an incapable palace general. Secondly, Yorck's defection was the signal for a great popular rising in Prussia which, on February 26, induced Frederick William to conclude with Russia an offensive and defensive alliance at Kalisch. By its terms, Russia undertook to provide 150,000 men and Prussia to contribute 80,000. On March 13 the treaty was published and Prussia declared war on France. Thus the aim of the Russian war party was secured.

In Prussia the declaration of war was followed by wild en-thusiasm. A *levée en masse* was proclaimed. Every man not in the regular army or *Landwehr* was to support the army by acting against the enemy's communications and rear. The people were to fight to the death and with every means in their power. The enemy was to be harassed, his supplies cut off and his stragglers mas-sacred. No uniforms were to be worn, and on the enemy's ap-proach, after all food stocks had been destroyed, and mills, bridges and boats burnt, the villages were to be abandoned and refuge sought in the woods and the hills. "Such", writes Fain, "are the new means that the . . . enemies of Napoleon propose to employ against him."[3] It was to be a repetition of 1792.

In the meantime, on January 18, the Russians crossed the

---

[1] *Manuscrit de Mil Huit Cent Treize*, Baron Fain (1824), vol. i, p. 39. Fain was Secretary of Napoleon's Cabinet.

[2] About 100,000 men. Out of the 600,000 who had entered Russia, some 200,000 were French, therefore the loss to France was not as great as is often assumed.

[3] Fain, vol. i, p. 108.

Vistula, and on February 7 entered Warsaw. Eugène left garrisons in Danzig, Graudenz, Thorn, Modlin, and other fortresses—54,000 men in all, of whom 33,000 were French—and early in March, fearful of the popular risings and the approaching Russians, he abandoned the line of the Oder and fell back on the Elbe. There he was ordered by Napoleon to evacuate Dresden and concentrate his forces at Magdeburg. On March 12, distance obliged Eugène to abandon Hamburg, which was entered by Tettenborn and his Cossacks amid the rejoicings of its citizens.

Napoleon was busily engaged upon one of his most remarkable feats, the creation of a new army in four months. "France was one vast workshop", writes Caulaincourt, ". . . the entire French nation overlooked his reverse and men vied with one another in showing their zeal and devotion. It was as glorious an example of the French character as it was a personal triumph for the Emperor, who with amazing energy directed all the resources of which his genius was capable into the organization and guidance of this great national endeavour. Things seemed to come into existence by enchantment."[1]

Napoleon's aim was to raise 656,000 men. In the previous November he had ordered a new conscription for 1813, which was reckoned to bring in 137,000 recruits. Earlier still, when on the road to Moscow, in order to add to home security, he had ordered "cohorts" of the National Guard, 80,000 men, to be raised; these he now placed on a foreign service footing. Further, he called out the whole of the 1814 contingent (200,000) as well as the contingents of 1808, 1809 and 1810, which had escaped previous drafting (100,000); drew many veterans and four regiments of the Guard from the 270,000 men he had in Spain;[2] raised 40,000 veteran gunners from the Navy;[3] 3,000 cavalry officers and n.c.o.'s from the Gendarmerie; and ordered Italy to supply a corps (30,000) under General Bertrand. Largely because of desertion these figures were never fully realized.

On the whole, the new infantry would appear to have been good, though Caulaincourt says they were "but an organized mob".[4] But with all deference to Caulaincourt, one cannot but agree with D'Odeleben that, when it came to fighting, "it would be almost impossible to find elsewhere soldiers who braved death

---

[1] *Memoirs of Général Caulaincourt* (1938), vol. II, pp. 611-12. See also *Relation Circonstanciée de La Campagne de 1813 en Saxe*, Baron D'Odeleben (French edit., 1817), vol. I, p. 62.
[2] Fain, vol. I, p. 33.   [3] *Ibid.*, vol. I, p. 35.   [4] *Memoirs*, vol. II, p. 620.

with so much intrepidity and courage, and who, in the midst of all difficulties and dangers, could have shown themselves more devoted to their chief and their service".[1] As before, the artillery was excellent, but the cavalry was insufficient and inefficient, and by April numbered no more than 15,000, of which half was fit for service. The reasons were that practically the whole of the old cavalry had perished in Russia; sufficient suitable chargers were not to be found in France; the younger cavalry officers lacked training, and the new saddles and harness as well as poor horsemastership put many horses out of service. Napoleon's lack of efficient cavalry hampered him throughout the campaign.

By a decree, issued from the Trianon on March 12,[2] the provisional composition of the new army was laid down as follows: Ist Corps, Marshal Davout (Prince of Eckmühl); IInd Corps, Marshal Victor (Duke of Belluno); IIIrd Corps, Marshal Ney (Prince of Moskova); IVth Corps, General Bertrand; Vth Corps, General Lauriston; VIth Corps, Marshal Marmont (Duke of Ragusa); VIIth Corps, General Reynier; VIIIth Corps, Prince Poniatowski; IXth Corps, Marshal Augereau (Duke of Castiglione); Xth Corps, General Rapp (in Danzig); XIth Corps, Marshal Macdonald (Duke of Taranto); and XIIth Corps, Marshal Oudinot (Duke of Reggio). Besides these there were various German contingents.

By the middle of April, when Napoleon was ready to take the field, he had at his disposal 226,000 officers and men and 457 guns organized in two armies: the Army of the Main, under himself, consisting of the IIIrd, IVth, VIth and XIIth corps, the Guard and the Guard Cavalry; and the Army of the Elbe, under Eugène, comprising the Vth and XIth corps, portions of the Ist, IInd and VIIth corps and the 1st Cavalry Corps.[3]

To raise and equip in so short a time nearly a quarter of a million men and assemble behind them an equivalent number in reserve was a unique effort, and had Napoleon's future depended solely upon physical force, it is highly probable that before the next four months had elapsed he would more than have cancelled out the debt he incurred in Russia. Why he failed to do so is to be attributed, not to lack of physical means, but to the system of command which hitherto had led him from victory to victory.

[1] Vol. I, pp. 210–211. Baron D'Odeleben was a Saxon officer attached to Napoleon's headquarters as an interpreter. He is an exceedingly impartial eyewitness.

[2] *Correspondance*, No. 19,698, vol. xxv, p. 63, with slight modification.

[3] See Lanrezac's *La Manœuvre de Lützen*, p. 116. Lanrezac's total strength is 202,000.

Conditions had changed since Wagram. Armies had grown in size, and theatres of operations had become so extended that it was no longer practicable for a single commander, even when operating on interior lines, to direct all troop movements. This was true, not only strategically, but also tactically; for at the battle of Leipzig numbers were too great and the situation too complex for Napoleon's personal system of command.

Equally important, hitherto he had always acted on the offensive and used his army like a thunderbolt. But in 1813 he was compelled to act on the defensive, and, be it noted, in a theatre of war in which the inhabitants were violently hostile. Their hostility not only forced him to employ more troops on his lines of communication and entrench depôts and bridgeheads, but it made the gathering of information most difficult, a difficulty increased by his lack of light cavalry. On this question D'Odeleben says, that ". . . all the efforts of Napoleon's generals were useless, either because of the hostility of the inhabitants . . ., who had been ill-treated [by the French], or because of the raids of the Cossacks, who were everywhere to be found. The little that was learnt was almost exclusively based on the reports of prisoners, which in number were few and undetailed. In short, we only knew what was happening in the districts the enemy had withdrawn from. Though, in offensive warfare, suchlike information may suffice, it is worthless when a defensive war is in question."[1]

Another important factor was that his previous successes had rendered him more and more dictatorial. He considered himself to be invincible and the only general in the world fit to command a great army. This led him to despise his enemy, and, like Charles XII, to believe that no obstacle was insurmountable. Listen to Fézensac: "His orders had to be executed whatever the means at command. This habit of undertaking everything with insufficient means, this determination not to recognize any impossibilities, this boundless assurance of success, which in the beginning were the causes of our triumphs, in the end became fatal to us."[2]

Several historians, when considering the last years of Napoleon's generalship, have jumped to the conclusion that his lack of success is to be explained either by ill-health or physical degeneracy caused by indulgence and increasing bodily weight. There is

[1] D'Odeleben, vol. I, p. 167.
[2] *Souvenirs Militaires de 1804 à 1814* (1863), pp. 118-119.

little to support this contention and much to refute it.[1] During his 1812 campaign in Russia many instances of his ceaseless activity are noted by Caulaincourt, such as: "The Emperor showed incredible activity during his stay at Wilna. Twenty-four hours did not give him a long enough day. . . ." "He spent the day in the saddle, reconnoitred the terrain in every direction, even at a considerable distance, and returned to his tent very late, having actually seen and checked everything for himself. . . ." "He worked all day and part of the night. France was administered, Germany and Poland felt the impulse of his mind, just as if he had been at the Tuileries."[2] In 1813, the same activity is remarked upon by D'Odeleben.[3]

The truth is, that it was his activity, not his lethargy, which was as much the cause of his fall as of his rise, for it led him to believe that in his person he could combine the duties of commander-in-chief and chief of staff, and the result was that, when the army had grown so large that skilled staff officers were needed, they were not to be found. Again, listen to Caulaincourt. In 1812 he informs us that "The staff foresaw nothing, but on the other hand, as the Emperor wanted to do everything himself, and to give every order, no one, not even the general staff, dared to assume the responsibility of giving the most trifling order."[4] Though, in 1812, Napoleon had written to Berthier: "The General Staff is organized in such a manner that it cannot be relied upon for anything",[5] in 1813 we find D'Odeleben writing: "It appears that in this campaign the officers of Berthier's headquarter staff were not so skilful or so experienced as those who had formerly surrounded him. . . . As a whole, the army in this campaign was a too complicated and imperfect machine to allow of coordination being established. Promotions, reforms, the replenishment of supplies; in a word, the multiplicity of movements which later on took place, gave birth to difficulties which all the authority of Napoleon could not always surmount."[6]

Napoleon's marshals had not been brought up to command, but solely to obey, they were followers and not leaders, vassal

[1] Before setting out on the Leipzig campaign, Napoleon, as reported by D'Odeleben, said: "I shall carry out this campaign as General Bonaparte and not as Emperor", and in greater part he did.
[2] *Memoirs*, vol. I, pp. 135, 141 and 245. In 1809, though an indifferent horseman, Napoleon rode from Valladolid to Burgos, a distance of 77 miles, in five hours.
[3] See, notably, vol. I, p. 224.
[4] *Memoirs*, vol. I, p. 155.   [5] *Correspondance*, No. 18,884, vol. XXIV, p. 7.
[6] D'Odeleben, vol. II, pp. 363-364.

princes many of whom had been raised in rank for dynastic, political and personal reasons. Many were of humble origin. Thus Masséna was the son of a publican, as was Murat; Ney, of a cooper; Lefebvre, of a miller; Lannes, of a groom; and Augereau of a mason, and *folie de grandeur* went to their heads. The Emperor heaped wealth and rank on these men, gave them incomes up to a million francs, and made them dukes and princes. After his fall and just before he left France for Elba, he told Caulaincourt that: "He found fault with himself for having made so much use of the marshals in these latter days, since they had become too rich, too much the *grands seigneurs*, and had grown war-weary. Things, according to him, would have been in a much better state if he had placed good generals of division, with their batons yet to win, in command."[1]

Opposed to the new French army were the armies of Russia and Prussia. The former numbered about 110,000 men, of whom 30,000 were cavalry and Cossacks. The latter were undisciplined horsemen, the terror not only of the French rear services but also of the German peasantry; among them were many Baskirs and Tartars still armed with bow and arrow.[2]

The Prussian army was the offspring of the degradation following the battle of Jena, which transformed Prussia from a feudal into a semi-liberal State. On October 9, 1807, serfdom was abolished by the Edict of Emancipation; the semi-feudal organization of the army was scrapped and civil patriotism inculcated as the moral basis of military service. Though by the Convention of Paris of September 8, 1808, Napoleon had, on a 10 years' enlistment, limited the strength of the Prussian army to 42,000 officers and men, by means of the *Krümpersystem*, introduced by Scharnhorst, recruits were rapidly and secretly passed through the line into the reserve. Throughout, Scharnhorst's aim was to create a true national army, but actually this did not take place until 1814.

At the time of Yorck's defection, there were no more than 38,000 soldiers left in Prussia; but before this, in order to make good the wastage incurred in Russia, Napoleon had instructed Frederick William to raise an additional 30,000. Next, by a decree issued on February 9, 1813, the *Landwehr*–a conscript militia–was created, and volunteer *Jäger* units were raised as well as a number of "free companies", largely recruited from

---

[1] *Memoirs*, vol. II, pp. 363-364.   [2] Fain, vol. II, p. 361.

foreigners. By the middle of April, when Napoleon was ready to take the field, the Prussian army numbered 80,000 men.

On March 11, the Emperor explained his first plan of operations to Eugène,[1] and though it was never implemented, it is of considerable interest, for throughout the campaign it was never entirely forgotten. It was to cross the Elbe at Havelberg, carry 300,000 men to Stettin, and next relieve Danzig. This would gain an additional 30,000 men. But there was far more in it than that, for a campaign in the north would carry war into the heart of Prussia, would place Berlin at Napoleon's mercy, and would completely upset Prussian recruiting. Further, by threatening from the north the Russian communications through Poland, it would draw both the Prussian and Russian armies northward – that is, away from Austria and thus isolate her. Further still, were Napoleon to out-march his enemies, which was probable, by coming down on their rear he might create an opportunity to fight another Jena, this time with his front facing France. As Count Yorck von Wartenberg says, it was a plan which "need not fear comparison with his best, either in point of boldness or of brilliancy".[2]

It was never carried out because by May, when the movement was contemplated, Napoleon had barely two-thirds of the 300,000 men he required, and none to pin down his enemy within the Dresden area while he moved on Havelberg and Stettin. Also by then it had become apparent to him that the growing unrest in the States of the Rhenish Confederation prohibited a move so far away from them. Already the rising spirit of nationalism throughout Germany began to limit his strategy.

Napoleon's second plan was to advance directly on Leipzig and thence on Dresden, and thereby compel his enemies either to accept battle or fall back behind the Elbe.[3] Because his weakness in cavalry prevented him from screening his movements and adequately protecting his base and lines of communication, as an alternative he was compelled to rely on defended river lines. Should the allies, of whose whereabouts he was by no means certain, decide to advance against him, Eugène was to strike at their right flank; but should they advance against Eugène, he himself would fall upon their left. As we shall see, Plan 2 was not

---

[1] *Correspondance*, No. 19697, vol. xxv, pp. 61–63.
[2] *Napoleon as a General* (1902), vol. ii, p. 242.
[3] See *Correspondance*, No. 19902, vol. xxv, pp. 225–226.

so much an alternative as a preliminary step toward accomplishing Plan 1; the need to seize Berlin and operate in the north remained Napoleon's controlling idea. But to realize it demanded first a decisive victory in the south which would re-establish his prestige throughout Germany.

On April 15 Napoleon left St. Cloud for Mayence, where he arrived in two days. On April 25 he pushed on to Erfurt, the point of assembly for all but Bertrand's corps, and according to D'Odeleben "he appeared very uneasy,"[1] apparently because his lack of cavalry prevented him from discovering what the enemy was doing.[2] He moved on to Eckartsberg, and on April 28 we read that the grooms with the led horses were long delayed by "the swarms of the enemy's light horse which infested the road"[3] – an ominous opening of the campaign.

On the evening of April 30 the Army of the Elbe (62,000) was in position around Merseburg, and the bulk of the Army of the Main was in the neighbourhood of Naumburg and west of it. In the meantime the allied forces – 64,000 infantry, 24,000 cavalry, and 552 guns – under the command of the Russian Field-Marshal Prince Wittgenstein (Kutusov had died on April 28) were assembled in the area Zwenkau–Altenburg, south of the Naumburg–Leipzig Road. Napoleon could immediately oppose to them 145,000 men and 372 guns, but only 7,500 of these were cavalry. He badly needed a quick and decisive victory, not only to blood his young troops, but to reinstate his prestige.

On May 1, the Army of the Elbe was ordered to advance from Merseburg to Schladebach, and the corps of the Army of the Main to move as follows: the IIIrd (Ney) with the cavalry of the Guard from Weissenfels toward Lützen, with the VIth (Marmont) in support; the Guard to move to Weissenfels; and the IVth (Bertrand) and XIIth (Oudinot) to march on Naumburg. This day Marshal Bessières was killed by a cannon shot, and on its close Napoleon entered Lützen.

On May 2 Ney was ordered to stand fast at Lützen and hold in strength the villages of Klein and Gross Görschen, Rahna and Kaja, south of Lützen, in order to cover the advance of the Army of the Elbe on Leipzig and the rear elements of the Army of the Main as they closed on Lützen. In case of an attack from the

[1] D'Odeleben, vol. I, p. 34.
[2] See *Correspondance*, No. 19873, vol. xxv, pp. 204–205.
[3] D'Odeleben, vol. I, p. 35.

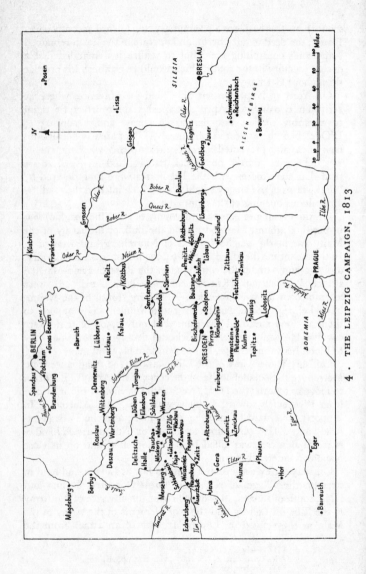

4 . THE LEIPZIG CAMPAIGN, 1813

direction of Zwenkau, Ney's flank guard was to become an advanced guard, which, when it fixed the enemy, would gain time for the remainder of the army to manœuvre around it.

Meanwhile the Russian cavalry had reported to Allied Headquarters that the French were spread out in column of march from Weissenfels to Leipzig, with a weak flank guard at Kaja. This was correct, because Ney had neglected to reconnoitre in the direction of Peggau and Zwenkau, which at 4 a.m. he had been ordered to do,[1] and instead of concentrating the bulk of his corps in the Kaja area, had left three of his five divisions at Lützen. Further, his outposts were so inert that they failed to discover the enemy, who was only two miles distant from them. When he received the cavalry report, Wittgenstein decided to destroy the French flank guard, cut his enemy in half, and drive all east of Lützen into the swamps of the Elster.

Napoleon did not expect to be attacked on May 2,[2] and at about 9 a.m. he left Lützen and rode forward to join Lauriston, who had been ordered to drive Kleist out of Lindenau and occupy Leipzig. When at 11 a.m., accompanied by Eugène and Ney, he was approaching Leipzig, suddenly a violent cannonade was heard in the direction of Kaja.[3] At once Ney galloped back to his corps, and the Emperor, after he had ordered all troops on the Leipzig Road to turn about and march on Kaja, and Marmont and Bertrand, still west of Lützen, to do the same, returned to Lützen.

In the meantime desperate fighting took place in Rahna and Gross and Klein Görschen, and when, at 2.30 p.m., Napoleon galloped up he found the IIIrd Corps in a critical situation, but as always his presence had a magical effect on his men. From all sides there rang out the cry of *"Vive l'Empereur!"* "Hardly a wounded man passed before Bonaparte", writes D'Odeleben, "without saluting him with the accustomed *'vivat'*. Even those who had lost a limb, who in a few hours would be the prey of death, rendered him this homage."[4] The Emperor encouraged Ney's men and led them forward. "This is probably the day of all his career," writes Marmont, "on which Napoleon incurred the greatest personal danger on the battlefield. . . . He exposed himself constantly, leading back to the charge the defeated troops of

---

[1] *Correspondance*, No. 19942, vol. xxv, p. 254.

[2] D'Odeleben, vol. I, p. 49, and *Mémoires du Maréchal Marmont Duc de Raguse* (1865), vol. v, p. 15.

[3] Fain, vol. I, p. 348.   [4] Vol. I, p. 51.

the IIIrd Corps."[1] In the desperate fighting that followed General Scharnhorst was mortally wounded.

At about 5.30 p.m., while Macdonald was closed in on the right of the allied Army and Bertrand[2] and Marmont on its left, Napoleon ordered Drouot to form a battery of 80 guns a little to the south-west of Kaja.[3] Next he drew up the Young Guard in four columns, supported by the Old Guard and Guard Cavalry, and at 6.30 p.m. the order rang out, "*La garde au feu!*" Thereupon Rahna, Gross and Klein Görschen were carried by storm, and with the fall of night the battle ended. The allies learnt that Kleist had been driven out of Leipzig, and afraid that their line of retreat would be cut, they decided to fall back, which they did in perfect order, carrying away their wounded and covered by their cavalry.

The victory won by the French was in no way decisive. With two more hours of daylight it would certainly have been so, for nothing short of a miracle could have prevented the allies from being driven into the Elster and annihilated. There was no pursuit, for the French cavalry was incapable of facing the Russian. The victory was a costly one; the French lost 18,000 in killed, wounded and prisoners, of whom 12,000 were accountable to Ney's corps, and the allies lost 11,500.

At 3 a.m. on May 3 Napoleon ordered Ney to rest his corps at Lützen for 24 hours, and then march by way of Wittenberg on Berlin, while the Army of the Elbe pursued the allies, who were now in full retreat on Dresden. Bülow was left with some 30,000 Prussians to protect Berlin, and after much quarrelling and argument the Russians and Prussians withdrew by way of Dresden on Bautzen, where they were reinforced by 13,000 Russians under Barclay.

On May 8 Napoleon entered Dresden, where he decided to establish his main advanced depôt. His line of communications ran from Mayence to Weimar and thence bifurcated by way of Jena and Altenburg to Dresden, and by Naumburg to Leipzig. Next, as reinforcements steadily arrived, he began to reorganize his army in such a way that it could simultaneously operate against Berlin and Bautzen. He sent the incapable Eugène to Italy, first

---

[1] *Mémoires*, vol. v, p. 26.
[2] At 1 p.m. Bertrand's leading division was less than four miles from Kaja, but instead of marching on the cannon he halted until 3 p.m. to await further orders. This is typical of the lack of initiative on the part of Napoleon's generals.
[3] At Lützen the French fired 39,000 cannon shot (Fain, vol. 1, p. 367).

amalgamated the Armies of the Elbe and Main, and then split the total into two separate armies, the one under Ney and the other under himself. The first comprised the IIIrd (Ney), Vth (Lauriston), VIIth (Reynier) and IInd (Victor) corps, a light cavalry division and the 2nd Cavalry Corps (79,500 infantry and 4,800 cavalry); and the second the IVth (Bertrand), VIth (Marmont), XIth (Macdonald) and XIIth (Oudinot) corps, the Guard, Guard Cavalry and 1st Cavalry Corps (107,000 infantry and 12,000 cavalry).

When thus engaged, he learnt that the Austrians had been negotiating with the Russians and Prussians, but because of the allied defeat at Lützen were now marking time.[1] He saw in this an opening leading toward his dominant aim, the establishment of a general peace, and on May 17 he instructed Caulaincourt to proceed to the enemy's outposts and request to be presented to the Tsar, to whom he was to propose an armistice as a preliminary to the assembly of a peace conference at Prague.[2] Simultaneously and in order to force the pace, convinced that the allies would accept battle at Bautzen, he ordered the XIth, VIth and IVth corps, supported by the XIIth, to advance on that town, and at the same time instructed Ney, while advancing with the IIIrd and Vth by way of Hoyerswerda on Bautzen, to move the VIIth and IIIrd on Berlin. Shortly after this he cancelled the last movement and directed Ney to march his whole army on Bautzen. Unfortunately, Ney had already halted Reynier and sent Victor off, and, in spite of the counter-order, this meant that the IInd Corps and probably also the VIIth would be kept out of the forthcoming battle. Berlin, at best, was but a secondary objective, for were the allies decisively beaten at Bautzen, the fall of Berlin must inevitably have followed. It is strange that Napoleon failed to see this when he issued his first order to Ney. Had he done so, instead of being a second Lützen, the battle of Bautzen might have gained for him the peace he so ardently desired.

On May 19, after he had reconnoitred the allied position at Bautzen, which lay on the eastern bank of the Spree and was held by 64,000 Russians and 32,000 Prussians under the nominal command of Wittgenstein, Napoleon decided to fix his enemies by a frontal attack on May 20, and the following day, bring Ney's army down from the north to fall upon their rear, sever their communications,

[1] Fain, vol. 1, pp. 388–390.
[2] See *Correspondance*, Nos. 20017 and 20031, vol. xxv, pp. 299 and 390.

131

and drive them against the Bohemian mountains. Were this done, Austria, still unready, would not dare to move, and without Austrian assistance the shattered Russians and Prussians would be forced to accept a dictated peace.

On May 20 the battle went entirely in Napoleon's favour, for the Tsar, who invariably ignored his commanding generals, believed that his enemy's intention was to turn the allied left and drive it northward away from Austria and played straight into Napoleon's hands by insisting on reinforcing the left to the detriment of the centre and right. In the meantime Ney's army advanced by forced marches, and on the evening of May 20 reached the following places: IIIrd Corps, Sdier; Vth, Särchen; VIIth, Hoyerswerda; and IInd, Senftenberg. The first two were close to the Spree, the third was 35 miles distant from it and the last more than 50.

At 4 a.m. on May 21 Ney received an order to march on Weissenberg and halt at Preititz at 11 a.m., where he was to be prepared to fall upon the allied rear when, at that hour, Napoleon launched his final and general assault. The IIIrd and Vth Corps left their bivouacs between 4 and 5 a.m., crossed the Spree at Klix, and reached Preititz at 10 a.m. There Ney halted them and awaited the general assault. But it did not develop until 3 p.m., and when it did, instead of pressing on toward Weissenberg, Ney got involved with the enemy's right wing. Had Ney had the whole of his army up, this would not have mattered, for then he could have directed the IInd and VIIth corps on Weissenberg.

The allies realized the danger they were in and at 4 p.m. broke off the battle and, covered by their powerful cavalry, fell back in good order on Görlitz. Nevertheless, their condition was critical, for they had lost faith in each other, violent dissensions had broken out between them, and had Napoleon been in a position to carry out a powerful cavalry pursuit, it would seem nearly certain that they would rapidly have disintegrated.

The failure by the French to gain a decisive victory must be shared between Napoleon and Ney. The fatal initial order of the one deprived the other of Victor's corps, and led to the arrival of Reynier's only as the battle ended. And the obtuseness of Ney, who never in his whole career grasped the meaning of Napoleonic strategy, led to the muddle at Preititz. Well may it be asked, since Ney was to deliver the decisive blow, should not Napoleon on the morning of May 21 have ridden over to Klix–eight to nine miles from Bautzen—and personally have superintended Ney's attack?

The French and allied losses are variously given, probably they amounted to about 20,000 on each side. At such a price the French gain was meagre. Like Lützen, Bautzen was another Pyrrhic victory, and Napoleon recognized it as such, for as he watched his enemies retire, he remarked: *"Comment! après une telle boucherie aucun resultat! point de prisonniers! Ces gens-là ne me laisseront pas un clou!"*[1] A few minutes later, Marshal Duroc, who had been with him when he uttered these words, was mortally wounded by a cannon ball. The shock of his death so profoundly affected the Emperor that he ordered the cease-fire to be sounded.

On May 22, when the pursuit was taken up, Oudinot was left behind to gather in his corps and then march on Berlin. On May 27 he reached Hoyerswerda, and on the same day the main army crossed the Katzbach and the allies fell back on Silesia in order to keep touch with Austria. Two days later Davout and Vandamme reoccupied Hamburg, and on June 1, with the allies withdrawn to Schweidnitz, Napoleon entered Breslau.

Although on May 19 the Tsar had refused to grant Caulaincourt an interview,[2] on June 1 an armistice was agreed to by all three belligerents, which at Pläswitz, on June 6, was extended to July 20 and later to August 16, in order to enable peace terms to be discussed at Prague.

Although Lord Burghersh, who was the British representative accredited to allied headquarters, considered that the armistice was greatly in Napoleon's favour,[3] Jomini[4] believed that it was the greatest blunder in Napoleon's career, and since then, with the notable exception of Colonel F. N. Maude, nearly every historian of the campaign has thought the same.

Should the strategical situation alone be considered, undoubtedly they are right, for had the allies at Schweidnitz accepted battle, which unknown to Napoleon they had resolved to do, all he need to have done was to hold them in front, turn their right flank and drive them pell-mell into the Riesen Gebirge. What, then, were Napoleon's reasons for this astonishing cessation of hostilities? They are given in a letter dated June 2 and addressed to General Clarke in Paris. "I decided for it [the armistice]", he

---

[1] Fain, vol. I, pp. 421–422. [2] *Ibid.*, vol. I, p. 402.
[3] *Memoir of the Operations of the Allied Armies, 1813–1814* (1822), p. 2.
[4] Jomini had been Ney's chief of Staff at Lützen, but shortly after had deserted to the allies.

said, "on two grounds. First, because of my want of cavalry, which prevented me dealing great blows, and secondly, because of the assumption of a hostile attitude on the part of Austria."[1] When quoting this passage, Yorck von Wartenberg adds: "We doubt whether these two reasons fully explain this surprising act."[2] They do not, and of the many students of this campaign, Colonel Maude is one of the very few who has troubled to examine them. What he points out is this: Because at the time 90,000 of Napoleon's men were on the sick list,[3] and because his losses to date had exceeded those of his opponents by 25,000 men, he had not sufficient forces left to fight another battle, and a defeat would at once have brought Austria into the war. Further, a powerful and efficient force of cavalry was indispensable for Napoleon's method of waging war. "His artillery", writes Maude, "might tear out gaps in the enemy's line with case fire, but in the face of the enemy's superior cavalry, his infantry could only avail themselves of the lanes of death thus formed by marching in dense columns, ready to form square at a moment's notice. This, he knew, meant delay, which the enemy utilized to break off the fighting." Without cavalry, there could be no decision. Equally important, " . . . he had left Dresden with only ammunition enough for '*un jour de bataille*,' and his march had been so rapid that his trains could not overtake the troops."[4] Further still, his lines of communication were infested with Cossacks and partisans. On May 25, Halle had been raided, and though on June 1 Napoleon did not yet know of it, on May 30 an artillery convoy, escorted by 1,600 troops, had been intercepted and captured near Halberstadt. Therefore, the truth would appear to be that, in spite of the deplorable strategical position of the allies, Napoleon's momentum was exhausted, and like Pyrrhus he had to abandon his campaign.

On June 10 Napoleon returned to Dresden, and as he held the crossings of the Elbe between Hamburg and Dresden, he decided to make that river his supply base.[5] "What is important," he wrote later to St. Cyr, "is not to be cut off from Dresden and the Elbe. I care little whether I am cut off from France."[6]

[1] *Correspondance*, No. 20070, vol. I, p. 346.
[2] *Napoleon as a General*, vol. II, p. 268.
[3] *The Cambridge Modern History*, vol. IX, p. 521, says 30,000.
[4] *The Leipzig Campaign 1813*, Col. F. N. Maude (1908), pp. 142–143.
[5] See *Correspondance*, No. 20142, vol. XXV, pp. 393–397.
[6] *Ibid.*, No. 20398, vol. XXVI, p. 78.

In the meantime his enemies were not idle. On June 15, England by treaty granted Russia and Prussia a subsidy of £2,000,000 and offered Austria £500,000 should she join them. On July 7, Bernadotte, Crown Prince of Sweden, was won over to the allied cause, and on July 19, at Reichenbach, Austria also. There, by treaty, it was agreed that under no circumstance was any one of the allied powers to incur the risk of a single-handed battle with Napoleon in person. Whichever army met him was at once to retire until all forces in the field could be united against him. Shortly after, Austria offered France peace on the following terms: that the Grand Duchy of Warsaw and the Confederation of the Rhine be abolished; that the Illyrian provinces be restored to Austria; and Prussia replaced in the position she held in 1805. As these terms were unacceptable to Napoleon, on August 10 the armistice was renounced by Russia and Prussia, and two days later Austria declared war on France.[1]

On August 15 – the last day of the armistice – D'Odeleben informs us that Napoleon was "extremely grave and pensive".[2] He certainly had every reason to be, for the forces gathering were enormous. By then he had assembled 442,000 men, of whom over 40,000 were cavalry. They were marshalled in 559 battalions, and 395 squadrons, and were supported by 1,284 guns. In addition Napoleon had 26,000 men garrisoning the fortresses of the Elbe; 55,000 holding those in Poland and Prussia, and 43,000 men in second line. Opposed to him were the field forces of Russia, 184,000; of Prussia, 162,000; of Austria, 127,000; and of Sweden, 39,000; as well as an Anglo-German contingent 9,000 strong, which included a British rocket battery commanded by Captain Bogue. The four field forces comprised 556 battalions, 572 squadrons, 68 regiments of Cossacks and 1,380 guns. Behind them were available reserves and besieging forces numbering 143,000 men, and 112,000 more garrisoning the fortresses in Prussia and Bohemia. The allied field forces were divided into three armies: the Army of Bohemia, under Prince Schwarzenberg; the Army of Silesia, commanded by Prince Blücher and the Army of the North under Bernadotte.

These strengths were unknown to Napoleon who, at Dresden on August 12, believed that the main enemy army, 200,000 strong under the Tsar and King of Prussia, was in Silesia, and that, because Austria would have to watch the French forces on the

---

[1] See *Correspondance*, No. 20300, vol. xxvi, p. 34.   [2] Vol. i, p. 231.

Inn and Izonzo, she was unlikely to mass more than 100,000 in Bohemia. In order to meet this problematical distribution, he decided on two operations, a defensive in the south based on Dresden and an offensive in the north based on Hamburg. The first was to comprise the Ist Corps (Vandamme) to arrive at Dresden on August 17, the IInd Corps (Victor) at Rothenburg; the IIIrd Corps (Ney) at Liegnitz; the Vth Corps (Lauriston) at Goldberg; the VIth Corps (Marmont) at Bunzlau; the XIth Corps (Macdonald) at Löwenberg; the XIVth Corps (Gouvion-St. Cyr) at Pirna; the Guard at Dresden, and the 1st, 2nd, 4th and 5th Cavalry Corps. The first task of this force was to flank the lines of march of the Army of Silesia leading northward to Berlin and southward towards Bohemia.

The offensive operation, under Oudinot, was to be directed against Berlin and supported by Davout operating from Hamburg. The former was given the IVth Corps (Bertrand) at Peitz; the VIIth Corps (Reynier) at Kalau; the XIIth Corps (Oudinot) at Baruth and the 3rd Cavalry Corps; and the latter the XIIIth Corps (Davout) near Hamburg, with Girard's division.[1]

Marshal St. Cyr was opposed to an offensive on Berlin, as also was Marshal Marmont. The former pointed out to Napoleon that he had greatly underestimated the strength and fighting value of Bernadotte's army,[2] and the latter, prophetically, said to him: "I fear greatly lest on the day on which your Majesty has gained a victory, and believe you have won a decisive battle, you may learn that you have lost two."[3] In his *Memoirs*[4] Marmont tells us that it was passion which prompted Napoleon to act quickly against Prussia; yet a better reason would appear to be that, as in his project of March 11, a move on Berlin might draw the Prussians and Russians northward, and therefore away from Austria.

On August 15 Napoleon and the Guard left Dresden for Bautzen, where, on August 17, news was received that a considerable force of Russians had been detached from Blücher's army and was *en route* for Bohemia. Forthwith Napoleon decided to move against Blücher, and, once he had beaten him, to turn against the armies of Bohemia and the North and destroy them in detail.[5] To help in this, he ordered up Vandamme to Bautzen,

[1] See *Correspondance*, Nos. 20357, 20360 and 20365, vol. XXVI, pp. 32, 34 and 37.
[2] *Mémoires pour servir à l'Histoire, etc.* (1831), vol. IV, p. 59.
[3] *Mémoires du Maréchal Marmont* (1851), vol. V, pp. 140, 207.
[4] *Ibid.*, vol. V, p. 139.   [5] *Correspondance*, No. 20398, vol. XXVI, pp. 77-78.

intending either to move him to Zittau, or, should the enemy meanwhile threaten Dresden, to send him there to support St. Cyr. To the latter he allotted the following task: "to gain time, dispute the ground and hold Dresden, and keep up secure and active communications with Vandamme and General Headquarters."[1]

At Görlitz, on August 18, when he received confirmation that 40,000 Russians were on their way from Silesia to Bohemia, Napoleon decided to go to Zittau and attack them in flank when on the line of march. However, on August 20, he learnt that Blücher was advancing on the IIIrd, Vth and VIth corps, and set this project aside, turned against him, and crossed the Bober on August 21. But immediately Blücher learnt of his presence, in accordance with the Reichenbach plan, he at once fell back. Apparently Napoleon failed to realize that this was a planned strategical manœuvre.

On August 22 Napoleon was at Löwenberg, and from there he sent a letter to Maret in Paris in which the following illuminating words occur: "The worst feature, generally speaking, of our situation is the little confidence my generals have in themselves. Whenever I am not present, they exaggerate the enemy's strength."[2] Possibly this referred to a message he had received from Dresden in which St. Cyr informed him that the Army of Bohemia was approaching and that Dresden was in danger. Be this as it may, Napoleon at once handed over the chief command in Silesia to Macdonald, and ordered him to push back Blücher to Jauer and then occupy a defensive position on the Bober, in order to flank Blücher should he attempt to march either on Berlin or Dresden. Next, he committed an error which was to cost him the campaign. Suddenly he saw, as if in a vision, the possibility of a tremendous manœuvre, and overlooking St. Cyr's precarious position, instead of sending Vandamme to his support, he ordered him to carry his corps to Stolpen.[3]

What was this grand manœuvre? It was to concentrate the Guard, the 1st Cavalry Corps and the Ist, IInd and VIth corps at Stolpen on August 25, and on the following night advance 100,000 men over the Elbe at Königstein, occupy Pirna, fall upon the rear of the Army of Bohemia, annihilate it, and then march on Prague and force Austria out of the war.[4]

[1] *Correspondance*, No. 20398, vol. XXVI, pp. 77–78.
[2] *Ibid.*, No. 20437, vol. XXVI, pp. 112–113.
[3] *Ibid.*, No. 20446, vol. XXVI, p. 119. See also Fain, vol. II, p. 234.
[4] *Ibid.*, No. 20449, vol. XXVI, pp. 121–122.

At 1 a.m. on August 25 Napoleon set out for Stolpen, from where he sent General Gourgaud to Dresden to ascertain St. Cyr's situation. In the afternoon he received a rumour that, on August 23, Oudinot had been defeated by Bernadotte and Bülow at Gross Beeren, a few miles south of Berlin, and was retiring on Wittenberg. At 11 p.m. Gourgaud returned and reported that the situation at Dresden was critical. As he did not dare to risk the loss of Dresden[1]—his main supply depôt—he forthwith decided to march direct on the Saxon capital, and at 1 a.m. on August 26 he issued orders to that effect: the Guard and 1st Cavalry Corps were to start at 4 a.m., while Vandamme continued in the direction of Pirna,[2] and on their arrival at Stolpen, Marmont and Victor were immediately to follow the Guard. Then, as D'Odeleben writes, "the army advanced like a torrent".[3] At 9 a.m. Napoleon rode into Dresden to the frantic cries of "*Vive l'Empereur!*" At 10 a.m. the Guard began to arrive—they had marched 120 miles in the past four days—and during the night came Victor and Marmont.

When we review these rapid changes, there can be little doubt that had Napoleon reinforced St. Cyr with Vandamme's corps, as was his original intention, the high probability is that the two together would have been able to hold fast to Dresden until August 28, and that, in consequence, there would have been no need to whittle down the Pirna manœuvre, which under Napoleon's personal direction must have led to the destruction of the Army of Bohemia. But, as we shall see, though by marching direct on Dresden he made certain of saving his main depôt, by sending Vandamme single-handed to Pirna he lost the campaign. Had he but reinforced Vandamme with either Victor's or Marmont's corps, he might well have won a second Jena, and again have been master of Europe. This possibility shows that the armistice was not such a blunder on his part as so many historians have supposed.

When Napoleon turned against Blücher, Schwarzenberg set out to strike at Leipzig, in order to sever the French communications, which erroneously he believed to be vital to Napoleon. But, on August 20, when he heard that the Emperor was at Zittau, and afraid that he was about to march on Prague, he

---

[1] See Fain, vol. II, pp. 258–259.
[2] *Correspondance*, No. 20472, vol. XXVI, p. 139, and Fain, vol. II, p. 258.
[3] Vol. I, p. 250.

Q

wheeled his army toward Dresden and arrived before that city on August 25.

The next day he decided to attack it at 4 p.m. – the signal for which was to be three cannon shot. On the morning of August 26 the three monarchs (Francis, Frederick William, and Alexander) rode out to watch his preparations, and at 9 o'clock to their consternation through the mist came a great cheer of "*Vive l'Empereur!*" – Napoleon had arrived! At once a council of war was assembled which, after a prolonged argument, decided on a retreat, when someone fired the signal guns, and without further orders the attack launched itself.

Though Napoleon had 70,000 men to face his enemy's 150,000, he easily repulsed them,[1] and shortly after the fighting ended at 9 p.m. Marmont and Victor began to arrive. Meanwhile Vandamme had crossed the Elbe at Königstein and had driven an allied detachment, commanded by Prince Eugene of Würtemberg, back in Peterswalde.

For August 27, Napoleon's plan was to hold the enemy's centre, attack both his wings and drive him into the mountains while Vandamme marched on Teplitz and blocked his line of retreat.

At 6 a.m. the battle reopened in torrents of rain.[2] The allied left wing was practically annihilated, over 13,000 prisoners were taken, and at 4 p.m. the allies began to withdraw. Drenched to the skin,[3] Napoleon returned to Dresden in the belief that the battle would be continued on the next day.[4] That night he wrote the following three lines to Cambacérès in Paris: "I am so tired and busy that I cannot write to you at length. The Duke of Bassano [Maret] will do so. Things here are going very well."[5] This clearly explains what historians have called "his lethargy".

Early on August 28 the French took up the pursuit and Napoleon rode forward. Abandoned arms and other signs of a precipitated withdrawal convinced him that the enemy was badly beaten, and feeling unwell he got into his coach and returned to Dresden; the pursuit was left in the hands of his corps commanders.[6] This also explains his inaction on August 28,

---

[1] Commenting on this action, Yorck von Wartenberg writes: "I know of no example in war which furnishes clearer evidence, that the numbers and *moral* of troops, important factors as these are, may be over-matched by the weight of one person of genius." (*Napoleon as a General*, vol. II, p. 246.)

[2] Fain, vol. II, pp. 277.   [3] D'Odeleben, vol. I, p. 261.

[4] *Correspondance*, No. 20480, vol. XXVI, p. 144.

[5] *Ibid.*, No. 20482, vol. XXVI, p. 147.   [6] Fain, vol. II, p. 297.

which has been so severely criticized. At 4 p.m. he ordered Vandamme, then at Hellendorf, to press on to Tetschen, Aussig, and Teplitz and strike at the enemy's rear. At 8.30 p.m. he received the news that Macdonald had been routed by Blücher on the Katzbach and had lost 15,000 men captured and over 100 guns. In addition, the rumour of Oudinot's defeat was confirmed, he had lost 3,000 men.

On August 29, when Napoleon was still at Dresden, Vandamme advanced to Kulm, and there at 8 a.m. on August 30, when he tried to push back a Russian corps, through a fortuitous accident he was attacked in rear and his corps dispersed at a loss of some 13,000 prisoners, including Vandamme. The news of this defeat was received by Napoleon at 2 a.m. on August 31. "Thoughtfully," writes Fain, "he again gazed at the map, and idly picking up a pair of dividers, audibly repeated these lines which came back to mind:

> *J'ai servi, commandé, vaincu quarante années;*
> *Du monde entre mes mains j'ai vu les destinées;*
> *Et j'ai toujours connu qu'en chaque événement*
> *Le destin des états dépendent d'un moment.*[1]

"The battle of Kulm", wrote Colonel Butturlin, the Tsar's aide-de-camp, "changed into a cry of joy the despair which was spreading through the valleys of Bohemia."[2] This was indeed true, for following as this battle did on the heels of Grossbeeren and Katzbach, not only did it thrill all Germany, but it also confirmed the allegiance of Austria to the Triple Alliance.

Strange as it may seem, this succession of defeats did not induce Napoleon to set aside his project to occupy Berlin, which had played so important a part in distracting his strategy. Eager to arrest the Army of the North from marching on the Elbe, he replaced Oudinot by Ney, and on September 2 ordered the latter to march on Baruth by September 6, on which day he would be at Luckau to support him, and next from Baruth to advance on Berlin and occupy it on September 9 or 10.[3] But the following day Napoleon was compelled to abandon his part in the joint project, for he received an urgent appeal from Macdonald, who was hard pressed on the Bober.

On September 3, he set out from Dresden to Bautzen, and

---

[1] Fain, vol. II, p. 320.   [2] *Ibid.*, vol. II, p. 321.
[3] *Correspondance*, No. 20502, vol. XXVI, p. 162.

headed Macdonald's shattered army in an advance to Hochkirch. Blücher judged from the impetuosity of the French attack that Napoleon was again in command, and at once retired. This, writes D'Odeleben, put Napoleon in a very bad temper.[1]

On September 6, an alarmist report from St. Cyr brought him back to Dresden, and there on September 8 he learnt that Ney on September 6 had met with a catastrophic defeat at Dennewitz, and had lost 22,000 men, of whom 13,000 were captured. Nevertheless, says St. Cyr, he discussed it "with all the coolness he could have brought to a discussion of events in China. . . ."[2]

Dennewitz, following the other allied victories, led to Tyrol declaring for Austria, and to Bavaria's decision to desert. In the meantime Cossacks were active in Hanover, Hartz, and Westphalia: Tettenborn seized Bremen; Dornburg surprised a French division near Hamburg; and Czernichev penetrated into Brunswick. Wherever the Cossacks went, insurrections followed.[3] The whole of Germany was rising against Napoleon.

By September 5, when Napoleon pressed back Blücher, the Army of Bohemia had sufficiently recovered for Schwarzenberg again to advance on Dresden. But no sooner had he set out than he learnt that the Emperor had returned, and forthwith fell back to Teplitz. On September 10 Napoleon advanced against him, but he found his position too strong to attack, and he left St. Cyr to mask it and went back to Dresden.

Four days later Schwarzenberg advanced again, whereon Napoleon went to Pirna and reconnoitred the allied positions on September 17 and 18. When thus engaged, he received from Ney a premature report that Bernadotte had crossed 80,000 men over the Elbe at Rosslau. He returned to Dresden on September 21, and on the following day with the Guard he joined Macdonald and drove Blücher back to a strong position he had prepared near Bautzen. Next, as he faced him there, he received a second premature report from Ney that Bernadotte had bridged the Elbe at Wartenberg. Thereon he decided to abandon all territory east of the Elbe, except the bridgeheads, and ordered Macdonald to retire to the left bank. This step was forced upon him by the state of his army. Since August 16 he had lost 150,000 men and 300 guns; 50,000 were sick and many of the remainder half-starved. On September 23 he wrote a long, detailed letter on the

---

[1] D'Odeleben, vol. I, p. 270.   [2] Mémoires, vol. IV, p. 148.
[3] Fain, vol. II, pp. 353–356.

question of supplies to Count Daru, Director of Administration, and in it said: "The army is not nourished. It would be an illusion to regard matters otherwise."[1] Nevertheless, by the end of September he was still able to put 256,000 men and 784 guns into the field; but many of his men were raw, untrained conscripts.

Bernadotte, who had reached the Elbe, bridged it at Rosslau and below Wittenberg, and on September 24 appeared in full force before Wartenberg. Blücher then decided on a momentous move, to march north and join him, and at the same time Schwarzenberg made up his mind to cease operations against Dresden and to advance on Leipzig. On October 3, Blücher, at the head of some 60,000 men, beat Bertrand with 15,000 at Wartenberg, and the following day crossed the Elbe. Bernadotte, with 76,000 men, crossed it that day at Rosslau and Berby and marched up the Mulde. This compelled Ney to fall back on Delitzsch.

Napoleon could mass his 250,000 men against either Blücher and Bernadotte's 140,000 in the north or against Schwarzenberg's 180,000 in the south, and, placed as he was on interior lines, he had every hope of destroying each in turn. He was in no way the hunted animal he has been depicted to be: strategically, he was still master of the situation. On October 2 he handed over to Murat, the IInd (Victor, 16,000); Vth (Lauriston, 14,000) and VIIIth (Poniatowski, 7,000) Corps, as well as the 5th Cavalry Corps, and instructed him, while St. Cyr (XIVth, 28,000) and Lobau (Ist, 12,500) held Dresden, to oppose the advance of the Army of Bohemia on Leipzig. Meanwhile he would march with the main army against Blücher and Bernadotte and destroy them before Schwarzenberg could reach Leipzig.

We now come to the strangest incident of the whole campaign. On the afternoon of October 6, in a long interview with St. Cyr, Napoleon impressed upon him the importance of defending Dresden. Next, at midnight, he sent for him and told him that he had decided to abandon the city and take him and Lobau north. St. Cyr asserts that he said: "I am certainly going to have a battle; if I win it, I shall regret not having all my troops under my hand; if, on the contrary, I suffer a reverse, in leaving you here you will be of no service to me in the battle, and you are hopelessly lost. Moreover, what is Dresden worth to-day?"[2] In consequence, at

[1] *Correspondance*, No. 20619, vol. XXVI, pp. 236–238.
[2] *Mémoires*, vol. IV, p. 185.

1 a.m. on October 7 orders were sent to St. Cyr to withdraw from Dresden on October 8 and 9.[1] However, 12 hours later Napoleon again changed his mind, and, in violation of the Napoleonic principle of concentration, he ordered St. Cyr to remain at Dresden.[2] Why? We hazard to suggest that it may have been he feared that were Dresden abandoned, Saxony would declare for the allies.

On October 8, Napoleon concentrated 150,000 men at Wurzen, east of Leipzig; Bertrand at Schildau formed his right wing, and Marmont, with Latour-Maubourg, at Taucha, his left. He rightly believed that Blücher was at Düben and Bernadotte at Dessau, though he underestimated their forces, and on October 9 he set out to attack the former; but when his advanced troops entered Düben, they found that Blücher had again slipped away. Actually, on October 10, and unknown to Napoleon, Blücher linked up with Bernadotte near Halle.

Furious at having the same old trick played on him again, what could he do? He could not indefinitely continue to march northward, because he knew that Schwarzenberg was approaching Leipzig and that Murat could not for long block his way. Should he move rapidly against Schwarzenberg, Schwarzenberg would almost certainly withdraw. Obviously the correct thing to do was to let him advance, and once he was involved with Murat descend upon him like a thunderbolt. In the writer's opinion, Napoleon's alleged lethargy at Düben has been completely misunderstood by all historians. Napoleon pitched his headquarters at Eilenburg, a little to the south of Düben, and remained there until October 14. D'Odeleben says that he saw the Emperor in his room sitting idly on a sofa covering a sheet of paper with large letters,[3] and Fain says that he remained almost constantly shut up in his room consulting his generals.[4] These things may be true, but the fact remains that between October 10 and October 13 he dictated 62 letters, which cover 42 pages of the *Correspondance*, and in the meantime heard that Bavaria had gone over to his enemies. On October 12 he abandoned the idea of a pursuit of Blücher and Bernadotte and informed Marmont that he had decided to march on Leipzig and concentrate 200,000 men there on October 14;[5] also he wrote to Maret to the same effect.[6] At 3 a.m. on October

[1] *Correspondance*, No. 20711, vol. xxvi, pp. 299–300.
[2] *Ibid.*, No. 20719, vol. xxvi, p. 304.   [3] Vol. ii, p. 9.
[4] Vol. ii, pp. 272–273.   [5] *Correspondance*, No. 20775, vol. xxvi, p. 339.
[6] *Ibid.*, No. 20776. See also 20771 and 20772, vol. xxvi, pp. 336–338.

14 orders were issued for the move,[1] and at 7 p.m. he wrote to Macdonald, "There can be no doubt that tomorrow, 15th, we shall be attacked by the Army of Bohemia and by the Army of Silesia."[2]

At noon, October 14, Napoleon arrived at Leipzig, from where he heard Murat's guns thunder in the south. That day at Liebertwolkwitz the greatest cavalry battle of the campaign was fought, but with no decisive result. On the morning of October 15, accompanied by Murat, the Emperor reconnoitred the whole field, and by nightfall the French were posted as follows:

IVth (Bertrand) at Entritzsch; VIth (Marmont) at Lindenthal; VIIIth (Poniatowski) at Markkleeberg and Dösen; IInd (Victor) at Wachau; Vth (Lauriston) at Liebertwolkwitz; IXth (Augereau) at Zuckelhausen; IIIrd (Souham) at Mokau and Düben; XIth (Macdonald) at Taucha; and VIIth (Reynier) at Düben. The Guards were in general reserve at Reudnitz and Crottendorf; the 5th Cavalry Corps (L'Héritier) on the right of the southern front, the 1st and 4th (Latour-Maubourg and Kellermann) behind its centre, and the 2nd (Sebastiani) on its left.

Strange things happened in the allied camps. Blücher was at Halle and Bernadotte some 15 miles to the north of him. The former wanted to close on Napoleon from the north directly the Army of Bohemia began to do so from the south. The latter, who dreaded Napoleon, wished to avoid him, and instead proposed to protect his line of communications with Berlin. The outcome was that Blücher marched off on his own, and later Bernadotte reluctantly followed, to arrive too late for the vital battle on October 16.

Schwarzenberg, with 160,000 men, had set out on September 26, but marched so slowly that he did not reach Altenburg until October 14, 17 days to cover 70 miles. He also wanted to avoid a direct clash with Napoleon, preferring manœuvre to battle, but on October 13, when he received the following message from Blücher, "The three armies are now so close together that a simultaneous attack, on the point where the enemy has concentrated his forces, might be undertaken", the Tsar intervened, and Wittgenstein with a large force of cavalry was sent out to make a reconnaissance in force. This led to the great cavalry battle with Murat. October 15 was devoted by the allies to

---

[1] *Correspondance*, No. 20799, vol. XXVI, pp. 356–357.
[2] *Ibid.*, No. 20801, vol. XXVI, p. 358.

preparations for battle the following day, and Blücher was ordered to hasten his march and effect a junction with the Army of Bohemia at Markranstädt, nine miles south-west of Leipzig.

In 1813, Leipzig, then a city of some 30,000 inhabitants, was surrounded by antiquated fortifications, beyond which lay many suburbs. On its western side it was skirted by the rivers Pleisse and Elster, which ran through a network of channels spanned by bridges; the main one was at Lindenau, whence roads ran to Merseburg and Weissenfels. On its northern side flowed the Partha, which joined the Pleisse at the village of Paffendorf. To the south lay a succession of low ridges, the highest of which was the Galgenberg, a little to the west of Liebertwolkwitz.

The allied plan of attack, as devised by Schwarzenberg and amended by the Tsar, was that while Blücher and 54,000 men advanced on the north-western side of Leipzig, three separate forces were to advance upon the city from the west and south. Gyulai with 19,000 was to attack Lindenau and cut the French communications; Meerveldt with 28,000 was to advance from Zwenkau northward between the Pleisse and the Elster; and Wittgenstein with 96,000, with his left on the Pleisse, was to attack the position Murat had taken up on October 14, the centre of which lay at Wachau. This wide distribution led to four separate engagements, those of Möckern and Lindenau in the north, and of Dölitz and Wachau in the south.

As regards the first, Napoleon, in spite of his message to Macdonald, did not believe that Blücher would engage in battle on October 16. Throughout the campaign he never credited him with the energy and pugnacity he possessed, and this occurred again in 1815. At 10 p.m. on October 15 he wrote to Marmont, then at Lindenthal, that Bernadotte was reported to be at Merseburg, and that many camp fires were to be seen at Markranstädt, "which makes me believe", he added, "that the enemy will not advance by the Halle Road, but by that of Weissenfels, in order to unite with the Army of Bohemia at Zwenkau or Peggu."[1] He assumed that this was so and at 7 a.m. on October 16 he instructed Marmont to move his corps to a position halfway between Leipzig and Liebertwolkwitz, from where he could either move on Lindenau, should it be attacked – "which seems to me to be absurd" – or move south when called upon to do so.[2] The reason

[1] *Correspondance*, No. 20812, vol. XXVI, p. 362.
[2] *Ibid.*, No. 20814, vol. XXVI, pp. 364–365.

for the second move was that Napoleon had decided to turn the right flank of the allies on the Wachau front with Macdonald's corps; therefore, in order to make certain of this flank attack, he wanted Marmont to support Macdonald.

Unfortunately for Napoleon, his assumption was wrong, and though on the night of October 15-16, from the church tower at Lindenthal Marmont had clearly seen the glow of Blücher's camp fires in the distance, on receipt of the above order he reluctantly set out to comply with it. Barely had he begun to move than Blücher's advanced guard drove the French posts out of Radefeld, Stahmeln and Wahren. Marmont realized that it was now impossible to carry out the order and turned about and took up a defensive position between Möckern and the Elster. He then appealed to Ney, who was in supreme command of the northern front. Next, at about 10 a.m. Ney directed Bertrand with the IVth Corps to take Marmont's place and proceed to the half-way *rendez-vous*. This Bertrand set out to do, but when on the way he received an urgent call for help from Arrighi at Lindenau, as he was being violently attacked by superior forces under Gyulai. Bertrand knew how vital the Lindenau bridge was to the whole army and immediately complied. He advanced on Gyulai and drove him back. Later, when Souham's IIIrd Corps came up from Düben, Ney sent one of his divisions to support Marmont, and the remaining two to carry out Bertrand's original task. They set out, but when near Macdonald, Marmont's situation became so critical that one aide after another was sent at a gallop to call them back. As Fain says, the result was that during the whole of the day they wandered between the two battlefields without firing a shot on either. "In the eyes of the Emperor," he adds, "this was the calamity of the day."[1]

At Möckern, Marmont was fiercely attacked by Yorck's corps; again and again the village changed hands, but at length at 5 p.m., after he had lost a third of his men, Yorck established himself in it and Marmont fell back to Gohlis and Eutritzsch.

Sometime after daybreak, Napoleon and Murat again rode out to the Galgenberg. The morning was cold and rainy, and a thick mist covered the ground. At nine o'clock, as it began to clear, "three cannon shot fired at regular intervals announced the opening of the allied attack. . . . Next, followed a terrific cannonade on both sides, which continued without break for five hours."[2]

[1] Fain, vol. II, p. 404. [2] D'Odeleben, vol. II, pp. 19-20.

Under cover of their cannon, the allies moved forward in four columns on a wide frontage, a faulty distribution because they

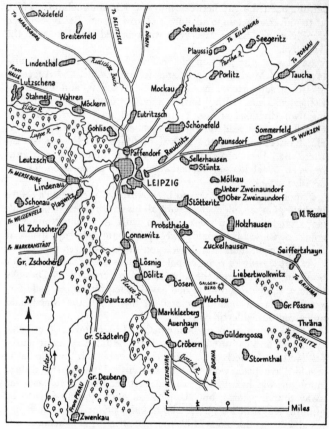

5. THE BATTLEFIELD OF LEIPZIG, 1813

could not see each other, and, therefore, could not coordinate their attacks. Eugene of Würtemberg advanced on Wachau, where furious hand-to-hand fighting took place until 11 a.m. Finally, his men were driven out of the village. On Eugene's left,

Kleist stormed Markkleeberg, but was pinned down there by the French artillery; and on Eugene's right, Gortchakov advanced on Liebertwolkwitz, to be driven back by blasts of gunfire. This repulse opened a gap between him and Klenau's columns, which at 10 a.m. had begun to advance on Gross Pössna. Lastly, between the Pleisse and Elster, Meerveldt was repulsed and thrown on the defensive.

At 11 a.m. the position of the French was as follows: Poniatowski held Markkleeberg, Connewitz and Dölitz, and Augereau at Dösen supported him. Victor held Wachau, and Lauriston, Liebertwolkwitz, with Mortier and Oudinot, each commanding two divisions of the Young Guard, in reserve. The Old Guard was in rear of the Galgenberg, and Macdonald, at Holzhausen, awaited the arrival of Marmont. Drouot, meanwhile, had been ordered to mass a great battery of 150 guns between Wachau and Liebertwolkwitz in preparation for the decisive attack.

Napoleon's intention was to break through the enemy's centre in the region of Güldengossa with all his cavalry, less Sebastiani's corps, and follow up the confusion with an infantry attack in columns, while Macdonald, directly Souham came up, struck at the allied right flank and drove it on to the shattered centre.

At a little before 2 p.m., Napoleon was no longer able to wait for Souham, and ordered the advance, when, covered by Drouot's battery, some 10,000 to 12,000 cavalry, led by Murat, rode forward, while the infantry massed in their rear and Macdonald advanced on Seiffertshayn.

At first Murat swept all before him and rode down two infantry battalions and captured 26 guns. Had the infantry immediately followed on the heels of his horse, the probability is that the battle would have been won. But at the critical moment a distant rumbling was heard in the north. Berthier thought it was a far away thunder storm, but Napoleon at once recognized it to be gunfire. He turned his horse about and rode for Möckern, hence his absence at the moment he was most needed at Wachau.

By the time Murat had penetrated to well south of Güldengossa, Victor had stormed and taken the sheep farm of Auenhayn; Oudinot was advancing on Cröbern, Mortier on the University Wood, Lauriston on Güldengossa, and Macdonald on Seiffertshayn. But in the meantime the allies had called up their reserves, and Murat, whose horses were now blown, was violently attacked in flank by 13 squadrons of Russian cuirassiers and with Lauriston's Corps was driven pell-mell back to Drouot's battery. On the French side, the confusion became general: Victor was compelled to abandon the sheep farm and Oudinot was forced out of Seiffertshayn, while on the French right, Meerveldt, who had crossed the Pleisse and got into Dölitz, was ejected and himself captured.

When the fighting was over, Napoleon ordered his headquarters tents to be pitched in a dried-up pond at Stötteritz,[1] where as usual he was surrounded by the Old Guard. He then sent for General Meerveldt, with whom he was acquainted, and from him he learnt that the Bavarian General Wrede had joined the Austrians on the Inn, and intended to march against the French communications at Mayence and Frankfort. This convinced him that retreat was inevitable, and, in order to gain time, he decided to send Meerveldt back to allied headquarters with a proposal to open negotiations.[2] Nothing, of course, came of this.

That Napoleon decided to retire, seems to us to be beyond dispute, because at 7 p.m. he ordered Bertrand with the IVth Corps to be prepared to set out and secure the passages of the Saale and Unstrut at Merseburg, Freiberg, Weissenfels and Kösen; Mortier with two divisions of the Young Guard to replace him at Lindenau. But, so it would seem, through personal pique he did not intend to do so until October 18. This was a fatal blunder, for he still could muster 160,000 men, and if, on October 17, he had set out for the Rhine, though it would have meant the abandonment of Germany, there is little doubt that he would have been able to secure the eastern frontier of France and have been in an incomparably better situation than he eventually found himself in in 1814.

On October 17 very little fighting took place, both sides spent the day in preparing for the morrow. At 2 a.m. on October 18, rain still fell and, the French pulled out of their bivouacs and withdrew to the line Connewitz-Dölitz-Probstheida-Zuckelhausen-Holzhausen-Zweinaundorf-Paunsdorf-Schönefeld, and thence along the Partha to Paffendorf and Gohlis. Reynier's corps arrived during the day.

Like the French, the allies remained where they were on

[1] D'Odeleben, vol. II, p. 23.
[2] See Fain, vol. II, pp. 409–411, and for Meerveldt's report, Burghersh, Appendix III, pp. 349–353.

October 17 awaiting the arrival of Colloredo, Bernadotte, and Bennigsen, who brought the allied strength up to 295,000 men and 1,466 guns. Schwarzenberg's plan for October 18 was to attack in six columns: the Prince of Hessen-Homburg on Lösnig; Barclay on Probstheida; Bennigsen on Zuckelhausen-Holzhausen; Blücher north-east of Leipzig; Gyulai on Lindenau, and Bernadotte between him and Blücher.

At 11 p.m. on October 17 Napoleon ordered his headquarters to be moved to the tobacco mill at Stötteritz, and three hours later he drove to Probstheida and from there to Reudnitz to see Marshal Ney. At Reudnitz he remained until 5 a.m., and then went on to Lindenau, where, according to Baron Fain, he gave orders for additional bridges to be built.[1] At 8 a.m. he was in Stötteritz, and while at breakfast the enemy's guns began to fire. At once he sent Bertrand his final orders to set out for the Saale.

Up to 2 p.m. the French advanced posts were slowly driven back; the allied forces advanced with caution. Only the allied left column, under Hessen-Homburg, experienced severe fighting at Dölitz and Dösen, which were taken. Next he advanced on Connewitz, but was repulsed by Poniatowski's Poles. Barclay, on Hessen-Homburg's right, advanced on Probstheida, but suffered heavy losses from the French batteries and halted to await Bennigsen who, still far in rear, made his way slowly on Zweinaundorf. But there were as yet no signs of Bernadotte's approach. Meanwhile at Lindenau Bertrand completely defeated Gyulai, and then pushed on to Weissenfels.

At 2 p.m. fierce fighting broke out around Lösnig, but Augereau and Poniatowski held fast to Connewitz, while at Probstheida, Victor's corps, supported by Lauriston's, repeatedly hurled back Barclay's columns. Assault on assault was made, until Schwarzenberg ordered Barclay to go on the defensive. Meanwhile Bennigsen, who was vastly superior to Macdonald, after desperate fighting, occupied Holzhausen and Zuckelhausen. He pushed on and took Zweinaundorf, but at Stötteritz was repulsed. Bernadotte had at last come up on his right, and together, at 3 p.m., they stormed Mölkau. Next, supported by tremendous gun fire and by Captain Bogue's rocket battery, an advance was made on Paunsdorf, which was also stormed. Shortly after, Napoleon retook it with the Young and Old Guard, but he found it untenable, and Ney withdrew his

[1] Fain, vol. II, pp. 415 and 440. See also D'Odeleben, vol. II, p. 40.

right wing to Schönefeld, Sellerhausen and Stüntz. While this withdrawal was under way, two of Reynier's Saxon brigades and a Saxon field battery, which had been posted in front of Sellerhausen, deserted to the enemy,[1] and the French cavalry, who thought that they were advancing to the attack, cheered them as they passed by.

Though Connewitz, Probstheida and Stötteritz held firm, as evening set in, at other points the French had been forced back on to the outskirts of Leipzig. Marmont had been driven out of Schönefeld and had fallen back on Reudnitz, and at 4 p.m. Ney and Souham had been wounded. By then Napoleon recognized that his position was no longer tenable, and, as night closed in, at a camp fire, "with his usual precision",[2] he dictated his orders for the retreat. These orders have since been lost, but the order of march set down in them was that the Old Guard, followed by Oudinot's two divisions of the Young Guard, the 4th Cavalry Corps, and IXth and IInd Corps, and lastly the 2nd Cavalry Corps, should at once begin to retreat by Lindenau, under cover of the rest of the army. Until 8 p.m. Napoleon remained at his bivouac, and then rode to the Rossplatz in Leipzig and put up at the Hotel de Prusse. There he worked with the Duke of Bassano (Maret) far into the night.[3]

Blücher learnt that evening that Bertrand was on his way to the Saale, and at once ordered Yorck with his corps to set out and occupy Merseburg and Halle.

When fighting ended on October 18, no decision had been reached. The French line held firm from Connewitz to Probstheida, Stötteritz, Crottendoft, Reudnitz to the north of Leipzig, and to the west Napoleon's line of retreat was still open. The scene that night is graphically described by Danilewski:

"Night fell; the sky glowed red, Stötteritz, Schönefeld, Dölitz, and one of the suburbs of Leipzig were in flames. Whilst with us (the allies) all were intoxicated with joy, and messengers of victory sped in every direction, indescribable confusion reigned in the enemy's army. Their baggage, their artillery, their broken regiments, the soldiers of which had been for days without food, were stopped for want of bridges over the streams round Leipzig. In the narrow streets resounded the cries of innumerable wounded, as our shot and shell fell upon them. Over the battlefield, so recently

---

[1] See *Correspondance*, No. 20830, vol. xxvi, pp. 274–279.
[2] D'Odeleben, vol. ii, p. 34.   [3] *Ibid.*, vol. ii, p. 37.

filled with the thunder of 2,000 guns there reigned the stillness of the grave. The silence ensuing after a battle has something terrible in it which inspires the soul with an unspeakable feeling."[1]

On the evening of October 18, Schwarzenberg issued his orders for the following day. As usual, there was to be a wholly line abreast attack; for, like all his previous attack orders, no attempt was made to concentrate against any one point. Further, except for the step Blücher had already taken, nothing was done to cut the French line of retreat or prepare for a pursuit.

At 2 a.m. on October 19, the French left outposts and camp-fires burning at Connewitz, Probstheida and Stötteritz, and withdrew from those villages, and Macdonald with the VIIth, VIIIth and XIth Corps–30,000 men in all–was ordered to cover the retreat by holding Leipzig. Orders were also sent to St. Cyr to effect his escape if he could.

At 7 a.m. on October 19 the allies renewed their advance, and shortly after, a pause occurred in order to negotiate for the surrender of the city, because the Tsar wished to spare it batter and storm. At the same hour Napoleon heard that Bertrand had successfully established himself at Weissenfels. At nine o'clock he bade farewell to his ally the King of Saxony, and then rode to the Lindenau bridge through a scene of anarchy, thus described by D'Odeleben: "Ammunition wagons, vivandiers, gendarmes, cannon, cows and sheep, women, grenadiers, post chaises, soldiers –unharmed, wounded and dying–pell-mell struggled together in so great a confusion that it was all but impossible to continue on the march, and much less to defend oneself."[2]

In this confusion General Château met, not far from the bridge, "a man of peculiar dress and with only a small retinue; he was whistling the air of 'Malbrook s'en va-t-en guerre', although he was deeply lost in thought. Château thought he was a burgher and was on the point of approaching him to ask a question. . . . It was the Emperor, who, with his usual phlegm, seemed to be perfectly callous to the scenes of destruction which surrounded him."[3]

Napoleon crossed the bridge at 11 a.m., dismounted at the Lindenau mill, and after dictating orders, fell asleep. In the meantime the Tsar's negotiations had come to nothing and

---

[1] Quoted by Petre in *Napoleon's Last Campaign in Germany 1813* (1912), p. 369, from Danilewski's *Denkwürdigkeiten aus dem Kriege 1813* (1837), pp. 259–260.

[2] Vol. II, p. 39.

[3] *Précis politique et militaire des campagnes de 1812 à 1814*, Jomini (1886), vol. II, p. 207.

fighting broke out in Leipzig, where the French and Poles fought with the ferocity of despair.

A little before one o'clock, while Napoleon was asleep, undisturbed by the thunder of the guns, suddenly he was awakened by a terrific explosion. It was the premature blowing up of the Lindenau bridge by a sapper corporal, whose colonel had ridden forward to ascertain which corps would be the last to cross. To what remained of the French rearguard it was a cruel blow, for the sole supplementary bridge which had been built had already collapsed. Macdonald, Poniatowski, and other officers, as well as many men, plunged into the river. Macdonald succeeded in reaching its western bank, but Poniatowski, who the day before had been promoted Marshal of France on the field of honour, was drowned. Soon after, on the eastern side of the Elster, the fighting ended in a general surrender.

On October 20 the main body of the defeated army crossed the Saale at Weissenfels. On October 23 it entered Erfurt and remained there until October 26 to replenish its supplies. When there, Napoleon found his line of retreat blocked at Hanau by Prince von Wrede and 40,000 Bavarians. He advanced against him, and between October 28 and 31 severely defeated him at a loss of over 9,000 men. The Emperor pushed on through Frankfort and reached Mayence on November 2. There he halted until November 7, when he left for Paris and arrived at St. Cloud on November 9. Two days later, St. Cyr in Dresden capitulated. Thus ended the campaign.

The casualties suffered on October 18 are not known exactly; probably they amounted to about 25,000 on each side. Between October 16 and 19 it has been estimated that the allies lost 54,000 in killed and wounded and the French 38,000, or with prisoners, sick in hospital, and deserters, nearly twice this figure. The trophies captured by the allies were immense, including 28 flags and eagles, 325 guns, 900 ammunition wagons and 40,000 muskets. Of the leading French generals, six were killed in battle and 12 wounded; 36 generals were captured, including Lauriston and Reynier. Further, Fain informs us that on October 18 the French fired 95,000 cannon shots, and between October 16 and 19 more than 200,000. On October 19 only 16,000 rounds remained in the artillery reserve.[1]

"For the first time in his life," as D'Odeleben writes, "the

[1] Vol. ii, pp. 428–429.

leader of the French had been beaten under the eyes and in the centre of civilized Europe. . . . In one word, he had lost a decisive battle."[1] This time there could be no excuses, no Polish mud or Russian winter. He had lost a second Trafalgar, this time on land: his initiative was gone.

Though he bore the shock heroically, it was a mortal blow from which he could never recover; for the victory of the allied powers lit a new candle in European history. Nothing was to be exactly what it had been before this victory was won. The joy that swept the continent was as ecstatic as it had been after Lepanto. The sluice gates of invective were opened, and, like a corrosive acid, a deluge of vitriolic propaganda swept the nations, a presage of the degradation of wars to come. "London was illuminated, and every town and village lit its bonfire and burnt Napoleon in effigy as Guy Fawkes, whilst the Press vomited forth a cacophony never as yet heard. . . . 'The First and Last, by the Wrath of Heaven, Emperor of Jacobins, Protector of the Confederation of Rogues, Mediator of the Hellish League, Grand Cross of the Legion of Horror, etc.'." According to General Dupont's statements, "he (Napoleon) commenced his career of murder at the age of sixteen, by poisoning a young woman, at Brienne, who was with child by him, etc."[2]

Yet the influences of the Battle of the Nations—to-day commemorated by a colossal and barbaric monument—were more notable than these ravings: they were the victory of the English System, the rise of modern Prussia and the decay of France. Further, they predicted that the struggles between individual powers were increasingly to become a thing of the past, and that the time was approaching when these politically primitive conflicts would give way to wars of world dimensions.

Napoleon's strategy failed, not only because his means were inadequate, or because his presumption was inordinate, but because his policy was out of tune with the spirit of his age. He had aimed at establishing a universal empire and had followed in the footsteps of the great conquerors of the past. But times had changed. No longer was Europe a conglomeration of tribes and peoples, but instead a mass of crystallizing nations, each seeking its separate path towards the illusive pinnacle of a new presumption—its personal deification.

[1] Vol. II, pp. 36–37.
[2] *Napoleon in Caricature 1795-1821*, A. M. Broadley (1909), vol. II, pp. 246–248.

At Jena, Napoleon destroyed not only a feudal army, but the last vestiges of the feudal idea, and out of the ashes arose a national army, which at Leipzig destroyed him. On the corpse-strewn fields by the Elster, present-day Europe writhed out of its medieval shell.

The campaign of 1814

Although England had played an insignificant part in the 1813 campaign, had it not been for her war in Spain, which since 1808 had placed Napoleon between two hostile fronts, the crowning battle of Leipzig would never have been won, nor would it have been won without the assistance of her subsidies. Towering above her allies, she was both the permanent and dominant factor in Napoleon's overthrow, and had been ever since Trafalgar. Throughout, her aim had been commercial as much as political, and with peace in sight, her statesmen—who never forgot that for England all the greater continental powers are potential enemies—set out to attain that aim by re-establishing the balance of power. It did not demand the partition or debilitation of France, but instead a return to her geographical frontiers— the Rhine, the Alps, and the Pyrenees.

This policy was favoured by Austria, who feared the growing power of Russia and Prussia, and though it was opposed by the Tsar, who was eager to wash out Napoleon's affront to Moscow by dictating peace in Paris, on November 16, 1813, England's policy was tentatively accepted and its terms communicated to Napoleon. But, as his reply was evasive, they were at once withdrawn and a declaration substituted that the allied powers would invade France and overthrow Napoleon, but that they hoped "to find peace before touching her soil". This proclamation did not win over the war-weary French people, instead its sole effect was to reawaken the spirit of 1792. The sacred soil was in danger; France sprang to arms.

The position of France was desperate, for under Macdonald in the north and Marmont in the south, there were only 53,000 soldiers available to hold 300 miles of the Rhine. Five armies faced France: in the north Bernadotte's and Blücher's, respectively 102,000 and 82,000 strong; in the centre Schwarzenberg, with 200,000 men; and in the south an Austro-Italian army of 55,000, and in Gascony, Wellington, with 80,000.

Napoleon had calculated that his enemies would not move forward until the spring of 1814. In this he was in error, and no sooner had the new year opened than one disaster followed another. On January 11, Murat, King of Naples, deserted to the allies, and three days later Frederick VI of Denmark followed suit. Worse still, in the north and east the allies began to advance with unexpected speed: Bülow and Graham (Lord Lynedoch) overran Holland; Schwarzenberg and the main allied army moved forward through Basle and Belfort on Langres, while Blücher with the Army of Silesia advanced into Lorraine and drove Victor out of Nancy. On January 25 Schwarzenberg, with 150,000 men, was between Langres and Bar-sur-Aube, and Blücher, who had crossed the Marne at St. Dizier, was near Brienne, then held by Victor and Macdonald.

On this same day the Emperor left Paris for Châlons-sur-Marne, to open a campaign which in brilliance was to equal any he had so far fought. He had 42,000 men near St. Dizier, Macdonald was approaching with 10,000, and Mortier was at Troyes with 20,000. At once he scattered an enemy division near St. Dizier, and then, on January 29, fell upon Blücher in the hope that he would prevent him linking up with Schwarzenberg. In this he failed; Blücher withdrew to Bar-sur-Aube, and, on February 1, severely repulsed Napoleon at La Rothière and the latter withdrew to Troyes. The allies believed that Napoleon's power was now shattered and they looked upon the war as won, but though they invited each other to dinner at the Palais Royal in a week's time, their rickety combination was at breaking point.

While Napoleon fell back on Troyes, the allies held a council of war at which they decided that, while Blücher with 50,000 men advanced from the north-west on Paris, Schwarzenberg with 150,000 would approach the capital from the south-west by way of Sens. The reason for this unstrategic division of forces was political. Austria was gravely alarmed by Russian ambitions; like England, she did not want an emasculated France. But the Tsar wanted a weak France in order to tilt the balance of power in his favour, because his aim was to gain the whole of Poland, and to indemnify Prussia for the loss of her Polish lands by giving her Saxony.

Lord Castlereagh, the British Foreign Minister, who was then at allied headquarters, vigorously opposed the Russian policy, for he saw that the only sure pledge of a lasting peace was the establishment of a moderately strong France, preferably under the rule of her old dynasty. Metternich supported Castlereagh, but the Tsar, who did not trust Metternich, decided to push on to Paris, but agreed to leave the French free to select their future ruler.

Nothing could better have suited Napoleon than this division of forces, for as he was operating on interior lines, it enabled his small army to deal with his enemies in detail, an operation rendered still more inviting because Blücher, whose forces were now mainly Russian, was advancing in three separated columns. To achieve their overthrow, on February 7 the Emperor ordered Marmont to occupy Sézanne, and on February 9 he set out to support him. The next day Marmont and Ney fell upon Alsusiev's corps at Champaubert, and virtually annihilated it, and on the following day with 20,000 men Napoleon struck at Sacken's corps at Montmirail, defeated it and drove it northward over the Marne at Château-Thierry. Mortier was left to pursue Sacken, and on the night of February 13 Napoleon set out to reinforce Marmont at Vauchamps, then hard pressed by Blücher's third column. He fell upon it and after a stubborn fight drove it back on Bergères. Thus, in four days and with less than 30,000 men, he had scattered Blücher's 50,000 and inflicted upon him 15,000 casualties. The effect of these victories was electric: Paris recovered her nerve and the peasants rose against the invaders, cut off their foragers and ambushed their patrols.

No sooner had Blücher been dealt with, than Napoleon learnt that Schwarzenberg was advancing in two columns, one by Bray-sur-Seine and the other on Fontainebleau. Furious because he had to abandon his pursuit of Blücher, he turned southward and, on February 18, fell upon Eugene of Würtemberg at Montereau, drove him back, and retook the vital bridge over the Seine.

Pride ruined his splendid strategy. Aware that Alexander's ambitions excited alarm, he sought to detach Austria from the Coalition, but because he refused to surrender Belgium and the Rhine frontier, negotiations failed, and on March 1, at Chaumont, the allies bound themselves not to treat with him singly, and to continue the war until France accepted her old frontiers. In these negotiations England's main part was to grant her allies a further subsidy of £5,000,000.

In the meantime Blücher resumed his advance, and when on February 25 Napoleon, at Troyes, learnt of this, he set out against him, but on his approach the former skilfully withdrew northward and, delayed for 36 hours at La Ferté-sous-Jouarre by a broken bridge, Napoleon was unable to catch up with him until March 7, when he attacked him at Craonne, and drove him back on Laon. There, on the night of March 9 and 10, Blücher surprised Marmont and routed him, whereon Napoleon withdrew to Soissons, and on March 17 learnt that to the south of him Schwarzenberg was again advancing on Paris. He marched against him, and on March 20 the desperate and bloody battle of Arcis-sur-Aube was fought between 23,000 Frenchmen and 60,000 Austrians. It ended when the Emperor had to withdraw to Sézanne.

Napoleon did not possess force enough to head Schwarzenberg off from Paris, and he decided to move into Lorraine, rally its fortress garrisons, and then, by falling on Schwarzenberg's rear and communications, force him to turn about. It was a desperate gamble. At St. Dizier he proclaimed a *levée en masse* and ordered the Lorraine garrisons to cut their way out and join him. But on March 23, one of his couriers, who carried to Paris a letter to the Empress, was captured by a Cossack patrol, and when the Tsar learnt from it what Napoleon had in mind, he persuaded Schwarzenberg–already in retreat–to turn about, abandon for the time being his communications, link up with Blücher, and with him advance on Paris. Thus, instead of compelling the Austrians to fall back, all Napoleon's manœuvre accomplished was to unbar the road to Paris.

On March 25, Schwarzenberg set out, while Blücher marched parallel with him from Châlons. On that day Marmont's and Mortier's corps were routed at La Fère-Champenoise, and near there General Pacthod's division of National Guards, 4,500 strong, after an epic fight, the most heroic in this remarkable campaign, was all but annihilated. Nothing remained but the wreck of Marmont's and Mortier's corps to defend Paris, which under the weak leadership of the Emperor's brother Joseph was in a state of panic.

At the foot of Montmartre the two marshals drew up their forces, and there, on March 30, the last battle of the campaign was fought. When Joseph and his brother Jérôme saw from the heights above that it was lost, they directed Marmont and Mortier to treat with the enemy. An armistice was agreed upon, and Paris was granted honourable terms of surrender.

Napoleon was at Vitry, and when he learnt that Paris was in danger, he hastened ahead of his troops to Fontainebleau. There he learnt that Marmont had gone over to the enemy, and as his marshals refused to follow him, on April 11 he abdicated. On April 20 he bade farewell to his Guard, and on the night of April 28, at Fréjus, accompanied by Bertrand and Drouot, he embarked in the British frigate *Undaunted*, which bore him to Elba.

On May 30, a series of treaties, collectively known as the First Treaty of Paris, was signed, which fixed the frontiers of France as they stood on November 1, 1792. According to one of its terms, a congress of all belligerents was to be held in Vienna to determine a general peace settlement. In September the Congress assembled and soon brought the allies to the brink of war; the Tsar demanded the whole of Poland. Castlereagh, supported by Metternich and Talleyrand, led the opposition. England, Austria, and France, distrusted the growing strength of Russia, and considered, should her boundaries be pushed westward into Germany, the balance of power would be completely upset, so on January 3, 1815, they formed a secret compact to raise 450,000 men to wage war on Russia. The Congress was still sitting when, on March 4, news was received that Napoleon had escaped from Elba.

While the Congress was in session, Napoleon had been kept well informed of its quarrels, and when, on February 13, he learnt that Fouché was plotting the overthrow of Louis XVIII, he decided to hazard his fortune by a return to France. On the night of Sunday February 26, at Porto Ferrajo, with 1,050 officers and men of his bodyguard he embarked in the brig *l'Inconstant* and six small craft, eluded the French guard ship and landed in the Bay of St. Juan on March 1.

On March 7, near Grenoble, he found the defile of Laffrey held by the 5th Regiment, and as he approached it a Royalist officer called out: "There he is: fire on him!" Napoleon turned to Colonel Mallet, in command of his bodyguard, and said: "Order the soldiers to put their muskets under their left arms, muzzles down". Then he stepped forward and said: "Soldiers of the 5th, do you know me? Here is your Emperor. Who will may shoot." A shout of "*Vive l'Empereur!*" burst forth. The first round of the Waterloo campaign was won. On March 20, he was back again in Paris; it was the birthday of his son.

CHAPTER 4

The Battle of Waterloo, 1815

The Waterloo campaign has been so thoroughly investigated and criticized that the errors committed in it are apt to appear exceptional and glaring. They were not, they were the usual errors to be found in most campaigns. But what was exceptional is that the two most noted captains of their age met in clinch for the first time in a war of 22 years' duration, and that both were outstanding generals. Thus far, except for the Archduke Charles, Napoleon had faced and fought leaders of only moderate abilities, and, in his turn, so had Wellington. Now the two great protagonists were to meet face to face, and in consequence the errors they and their subordinates committed have been spotlighted by their personal renown and exceptional abilities.

That the greater of the two went down before the lesser has given rise to the myth that Napoleon's genius was on the wane, and that he was either a sick man or had grown lethargic. Such evidence that has been raked up in support of these contentions is as forced as it is distorted; for he was no better or worse than he had been at Marengo, Austerlitz, Jena, and Leipzig; a man so mastered by his genius that at times he lived in a land of illusions.[1] So convinced was he of his own powers and good fortune that, as Caulaincourt once said: "He had a wholly incalculable antipathy for any thoughts or ideas about what he disliked."[2] When, on June 21, after his defeat at Waterloo, he alighted at the Elysée, he said to Caulaincourt: "Well, Caulaincourt, here is a pretty to-do! A battle lost! How will the country bear this reverse? All the material is lost. It is a frightful disaster. The day was won. The army had performed prodigies; the enemy was beaten at every point; only the English centre still held. Just as all was over the army was seized with panic. It is inexplicable. . . ."[3] It was nothing of the sort; it was the logical end of his illusions that personally he could control and do everything, and that a perfect

---

[1] "Once he had an idea implanted in his head, the Emperor was carried away by his own illusion. He cherished it, caressed it, became obsessed with it. . . . " (*The Memoirs of Caulaincourt*, 1935, vol. I, p. 93.)

[2] *Ibid.*, vol. I, p. 602. [3] *Ibid.*, vol. II, p. 423.

plan, irrespective of the means at hand, could not fail to lead to a perfect solution.

In Wellington he met a soldier very different from himself and a general whose armies had been small and compact, and in which command could be centralized; obedience and not initiative was required of subordinates. Though as autocratic and dictatorial as Napoleon, because Wellington possessed the faculty of combining foresight with common sense, his imagination seldom ran away with his reason. His armies usually were numerically inferior to his opponent's, he was compelled to be prudent. Yet it is a great mistake to assume, as many have done and as Napoleon himself did, that he was no more than a cautious general. Though a master of defensive warfare, he could, when conditions were favourable, be audacious in the extreme, as he was at Assaye and Argaum in 1803, in the Vimiero and Talavera campaigns, and in the storming of Ciudad Rodrigo and Badajoz. His Fabian tactics were common sense: when conditions demanded prudence, he was prudent, and when they did not, he could strike like a thunderbolt.

Few generals of his age understood the ingredients of tactics so thoroughly as he did. He grasped the limitations of the musket of his day, that it was a deadly weapon at point-blank range, but nearly useless at a distance. He realized that the dominant characteristics of the English soldier were steadiness and stolidity, and that the French soldier did not possess them. Therefore he welcomed meeting column by two-deep line, which meant that he could multiply his fire power at least fourfold. In order to protect his men as well as to mystify his enemy, he seldom failed to make the fullest use of cover by ground. Because of this, at Vimiero, Junôt was completely deceived, and at Busaco, Masséna mistook the British centre for its right. At Salamanca it was the same, and also at Waterloo.

In the main his grand tactics were of a defensive-offensive order; that is to say, he encouraged the enemy to attack, and when he was in confusion, under cover of the smoke of his muskets, he attacked him in turn. He seldom massed his guns, not only because he seldom had a sufficiency of them, but because his line tactics demanded artillery dispersion and not concentration. Also, he seldom pursued a beaten foe, because generally his cavalry was weak and indifferent. One other fact must be mentioned, for, combined with his use of ground, it raised him to the position of supreme tactical artist. It was that he saw everything for himself and only when it was impossible to do so did he rely upon secondhand information. As he once said: "The real reason why I succeeded . . . is because I was always on the spot–I saw everything, and did everything myself." Like Napoleon, he combined the duties of chief of staff with those of commander-in-chief, and because of this his command was, in fact, Napoleonic. But had he been called upon to command a large army, split into several independent or semi-independent bodies, it goes without saying that his centralized system would have proved as defective as Napoleon's increasingly did after Austerlitz.

Once back in Paris, Napoleon set to work on his Herculean task of raising his last great army. Men were plentiful, for France was thronged with disbanded veterans and returned prisoners of war; but muskets, equipment, horses, and ammunition were lamentably deficient, and the Royal Army, about 100,000 strong, was decrepit. But his main problem was the selection of his principal officers, for many of his marshals and generals, including Soult, Berthier, Macdonald, St. Cyr, Suchet, Augereau, and Ney, had sworn allegiance to Louis XVIII, and not a few of those who rejoined him had little confidence in the triumph of his cause. Equally bad, there was mutual suspicion between those who had or had not served Louis.[1]

For the effective execution of his grand tactics, he needed at least four men who thoroughly understood his *bataillon carré* system: a chief of staff who could express his ideas clearly in written orders; a cavalry general who could handle masses of horsemen; and two wing commanders who, when he was not present, could carry out his aim. Hitherto he had relied on Berthier as his chief of staff, and though that able head clerk was willing to return to him, on June 1 he met with a fatal accident. In his place, Napoleon selected Soult. It was a thoroughly bad choice, for though an able commander, Soult had never held the office of chief of staff of any army or even of a corps, and the campaign was lost largely through bad staff work.

Napoleon refused to take back Murat as his cavalry leader, and chose Grouchy. But no sooner had the campaign opened than he appointed the latter to the command of his right wing. This

[1] See the report of the Chevalier d'Artez of May 6, 1815, on conditions in France (Wellington's *Supplementary Despatches*, 1863, vol. x, pp. 247–256). It is, however, so exaggerated that, instead of helping Wellington, it probably misled him.

again was a bad choice, for though Grouchy was a skilful cavalry general, he had never commanded a corps, let alone an army wing. Equally bad, he gave the command of his left wing to Ney, of whom, in 1808, he had said that he was as ignorant of his projects "as the last-joined drummer boy".[1]

These four appointments were the most fatal of all the errors Napoleon committed during the Hundred Days, and it is no exaggeration to say that they were the chief cause of his defeat. At St. Helena he realized this, for he told Las Casas that, had he had Murat with him, victory would have been his,[2] and he told Gourgaud that Soult did not serve him well,[3] that "it was a great mistake to employ Ney",[4] and that he ought to have given the command of the right wing to Suchet and not to Grouchy.[5]

One man he did not mention, and that was Davout, probably the most skilful officer he ever had. He left him at Paris as Governor because, as he said to him, he could not entrust the capital to anyone else. Yet surely Davout was right when he replied: "But, sire, if you are the victor, Paris will be yours, and if you are beaten, neither I nor any one else can do anything for you."[6]

What the French marshals lacked in ardour was in no way made good by the wild enthusiasm of the regimental officers and men. A spy, writing to Wellington, compared them with the soldiers of 1792, and Houssaye, summing up the disposition of the Army of 1815, writes that it was "impressionable, critical, without discipline, and without confidence in its leaders, haunted by the dread of treason, and on that account, perhaps, liable to sudden fits of panic . . . it was capable of heroic efforts and furious impulses. . . . Napoleon had never before handled an instrument of war, which was at once so formidable, and so fragile.[7]

In spite of all difficulties, by the end of May Napoleon had raised the strength of the active army to 284,000 men, supported by an auxiliary army of 222,000 strong;[8] but in both many men were no more than figures borne on the registers. Of the former,

---

[1] *Lettres Inédites de Napoléon Ier*, Léon Lecestre (1897), vol. I, No. 217, p. 142.
[2] *Mémorial de Sainte Hélène* (1923), vol. II, p. 276.
[3] *Sainte-Hélène, Journal inédit* (1899), vol. I, p. 505.
[4] *Ibid.*, vol. II, p. 276.   [5] *Ibid.*, vol. I, p. 502 and vol. II, p. 424.
[6] *Histoire de la Vie Militaire, etc., du Maréchal Davout*, L. J. Gabriel de Chenier (1866), p. 540.
[7] *1815 Waterloo*, Henry Houssaye (English edit. 1900), p. 48. (See also Wellington's *Supplementary Despatches*, vol. x, pp. 364–366.)
[8] See Houssaye's *1815 Waterloo*, pp. 21 and 310–311.

124,500 were formed into the Army of the North under his personal command; the remainder was split between the Armies of the Rhine, Loire, Alps and Pyrenees, as well as other formations, depôts and fortresses.

The Army of the North was organized into five infantry corps, the Imperial Guard, and reserve cavalry. The first comprised the Ist Corps (d'Erlon) 19,939 men; the IInd (Reille) 24,361; the IIIrd (Vandamme) 19,160; the IVth (Gérard) 15,995; and the VIth (Lobau) 10,465. The second consisted of the Old Guard (*grenadiers*) under Friant; the Middle Guard (*chasseurs*) under Morand; and the Young Guard (*voltigeurs*) under Duhesme, which, with Guyot's and the Lefebvre-Desnouettes's divisions of Guard Cavalry, numbered in all 20,884 officers and men. The Reserve Cavalry, under Grouchy, was divided into four divisions: 1st (Pajol) 3,046 men; 2nd (Exelmans) 3,515; 3rd (Kellermann) 3,679; and 4th (Milhaud) 3,544. In all, the army consisted of 89,415 infantry, 23,595 cavalry, and 11,578 artillery with 344 guns.[1]

In Vienna, the allies, who had formed the Seventh Coalition, were engaged upon raising five armies: an Anglo-Dutch Army (93,000 men under Wellington) and a Prussian Army (117,000 men under Blücher) in Belgium; an Austrian Army (210,000 men under Schwarzenberg) on the Upper Rhine; a Russian Army (150,000 men under Barclay de Tolly) on the Middle Rhine; and an Austro-Italian Army (75,000 men under Frimont) in northern Italy.

In brief, their plan, as devised by Gneisenau, was to crush Napoleon by force of numbers. Wellington, Blücher, and Schwarzenberg were to march straight on Paris, and should one of them be beaten or forced to retire, Barclay was to come to his help while the remaining two continued their advance.[2] Frimont's army was to move on Lyons and not on Paris; Wellington was to command all forces in Belgium; and the French frontier was to be crossed simultaneously by all armies between June 27 and July 1.

Early in April, Wellington set out from Vienna for Brussels, and on May 3 he met Blücher at Tirlemont. Though neither believed that Napoleon would assume the offensive, it would seem they

---

[1] These figures are taken from *Histoire de la Campagne de 1815*, Lt.-Colonel Charras (5me edit.), vol. i, pp. 65–68.
[2] See Wellington's *Supplementary Despatches*, vol. x, pp. 196–197.

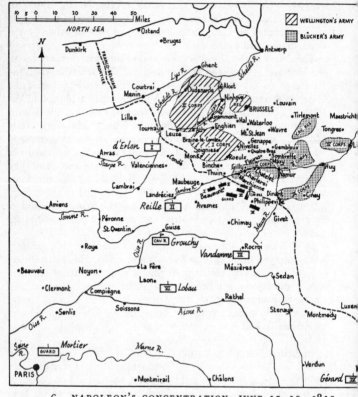

6. NAPOLEON'S CONCENTRATION, JUNE 15-19, 1815

agreed that, should he do so, they would concentrate their armies on the line Quatre-Bras-Sombreffe. Whether this was so or not, on the following day Blücher moved his headquarters from Liège to Namur, and ordered his four corps forward; the Ist (32,692 men under Ziethen) to Fleurus; the IInd (32,704 under Pirch) to Namur; the IIIrd (24,456 under Thielemann) to Huy; and the IVth (31,102 under Bülow) to Liège. Blücher's army contained 99,715 infantry, 11,879 cavalry, and 9,360 artillery with 312 guns.[1]

Wellington's army was a heterogeneous body of troops and consisted of 31,253 British; 6,387 men of the King's German Legion; 15,935 Hanoverians; 29,214 Dutch-Belgians; 6,808 Brunswickers; 2,880 Nassauers; and 1,240 engineers, etc. In all he had 69,829 infantry, 14,482 cavalry, 8,166 artillery with 196 guns, and 1,240 engineers, etc. Nominally, his infantry was organized into two corps and a reserve: the Ist Corps (25,233 men) under the Prince of Orange; the IInd (24,033 men) under Lord Hill; and the Reserve (20,563) under Wellington's direct command.[2] By the end of May the Ist Corps occupied Mons, Roeulx, Frasnes, Seneffe, Nivelles, Genappe, Soignies, Enghien, and Braine-le-Comte, and the IInd Corps occupied Leuze, Ath, Grammont, Ghent, Alost, and Oudenarde. The cavalry, under Lord Uxbridge, was encamped along the Dender, and the Reserve was cantoned around Brussels, where Wellington had established his headquarters.

Fully aware of the over-extended distribution of the allies in Belgium, and rightly judging that they would not be ready to advance before July 1, Napoleon decided to seize the initiative, enter Belgium and beat in turn the English and Prussians before they could unite their forces. After this, he reckoned, the Belgians –pro-French at heart–would rise in his favour and the English Ministry would fall and be replaced by one more friendly to France. Should the destruction of the Anglo-Prussian armies not end the war, he would next unite with the Army of the Rhine (23,000 men under Rapp) in Alsace, and fall upon the Austrians and Russians.[3] As in 1814, he planned to make the most of his central position, and what he desired above all things was a startling and glorious victory at the very outset of the war in order to consolidate France and demoralize her enemies.

[1] For strengths see Charras, vol. I, pp. 81–82.
[2] For strengths see Siborne's *History of the War in France and Belgium in 1815* (1844), vol. I, pp. 28–29.
[3] *Commentaires de Napoléon Ier* (1867), vol. v, pp. 116–117.

Early in June, the Army of the North was ordered to concentrate in the area Maubeuge-Avesnes-Rocroi-Chimay, and on June 12, at 3.30 a.m., when its corps approached their destinations, Napoleon set out for Avesnes. There he was joined by Marshal Ney, who three months earlier had boasted that he would deliver the Emperor to Louis in an iron cage. At Avesnes he issued a stirring Order of the Day, which opened: "Soldiers, to-day is the anniversary of Marengo and Friedland", and which ended–"the moment has come to conquer or perish!"[1] On June 14 he moved his headquarters to Beaumont, and by nightfall, except for the IVth Corps, the concentration was virtually completed.

While the French massed, oblivious of what was in progress the English and Prussians lay scattered in their cantonments. Not until the night of June 13–14, when Ziethen's outposts on the Sambre reported to him that many bivouac fires were to be seen around Beaumont, did he suspect what was happening.[2] He forwarded the news to Blücher, who on the evening of June 14– presumably depending on the Tirlemont agreement that Wellington would come to his support–ordered his IInd, IIIrd and IVth Corps to concentrate at Sombreffe. He also instructed Ziethen to cover their concentration by a stubborn resistance, and if pushed back to retire on Fleurus. Strategically, this forward concentration within striking distance of the enemy was a most foolhardy undertaking, for it presented Napoleon with a grand opportunity victoriously to end the campaign within 48 hours of its opening. Though Blücher was working in the dark, on June 15 his eyes were opened, for early that day General de Bourmont, who commanded the leading division of Gérard's corps, deserted to Ziethen and revealed to him Napoleon's orders and strength. But Blücher, who deemed himself invincible, remained blind, and sped from Namur to Sombreffe where he arrived at 4 p.m., determined to accept battle.

At 3 a.m.[3] on June 15 Napoleon mounted his horse, and at noon rode into Charleroi amid scenes of frantic excitement. There, a little after 3 p.m., he was rejoined by Ney, who through lack of horses had been delayed at Avesnes. The Emperor greeted him in a friendly way and forthwith gave him command of the Ist and IInd corps as well as Lefebvre-Desnouettes's cavalry division, and

---

[1] *Correspondance de Napoléon 1er*, No. 22052, vol. XXVII, p. 281.
[2] Certain rumours had been received earlier, see *Supplementary Despatches*, vol. x, pp. 470–471.
[3] *Correspondance*, No. 22055, vol. XXVIII, p. 286.

ordered him to "Go and pursue the enemy".[1] There can be little doubt that he must have said more than this, and, according to Gourgaud, he instructed him to sweep the enemy off the Charleroi-Brussels Road and occupy Quatre-Bras.[2] The probability of the last injunction is supported by the statement in the Bulletin of June 15 that "The Emperor has given the command of the left to the Prince of Moskova, who this evening established his head-quarters at Quatre-Chemins on the Brussels Road".[3] Though Ney did not do so, this statement indicates that Napoleon intended that he should.

As Ney rode away to take over his command, Grouchy appeared upon the scene, and shortly after was given command of the IIIrd and IVth Corps as well as Pajol's and Exelmans's divisions. Napoleon ordered him to push back the Prussians toward Sombreffe, but Grouchy was so dilatory that, at 5.30 p.m., Napoleon grew uneasy and rode forward to urge him on. A vigorous attack followed, and the bulk of Ziethen's corps was driven back to Fleurus. In the meantime Ney drove a Prussian detachment out of Gosselies, but then he ceased to be the Ney of Jena, yielded to prudence, and halted Reille's corps and sent forward Lefebvre-Desnouettes unsupported. At 6.30 p.m. the latter came under fire of a detachment of Dutch-Belgians of Prince Bernard of Saxe-Weimar's Nassau Brigade at Frasnes, which withdrew to Quatre-Bras. Lefebvre followed it up but found it too strongly posted to attack with cavalry alone and fell back to Frasnes.

That night, in three columns, the French Army bivouacked in a square of ten miles by ten, and, says Napoleon, "was disposed in such a way that it could manœuvre with equal facility against the Prussian Army or against the Anglo-Dutch Army, for it was already placed between them".[4] In the square the three columns were located as follows: *Ney's*—Lefebvre-Desnouettes's cavalry division at Frasnes; Reille's IInd Corps between Gosselies and Frasnes with Girard's division pushed out on the Fleurus Road, and d'Erlon's Ist Corps between Marchienne and Gosselies. *Grouchy's*—Pajol's and Exelmans's cavalry divisions around Lambusart (south of Fleurus); Vandamme's IIIrd Corps and Reserve Cavalry between Charleroi and Fleurus, and Gérard's IVth Corps astride the Sambre at Châtelet. *Reserves*—Guards

[1] Colonel Heymès "Relation", *Documents Inédits sur la Campagne de 1815*, duc d'Elchingen (1840), p. 4. Heymès was Ney's first A.D.C.
[2] *Campagne de Dix-Huit Cent Quinze* (1818), pp. 46–47.
[3] *Commentaires*, vol. v, p. 136.
[4] *Ibid.*, vol. v, p. 136.

between Charleroi and Gilly, and Lobau's VIth Corps south of
Charleroi.

At 9 p.m. Napoleon returned to his headquarters at Charleroi

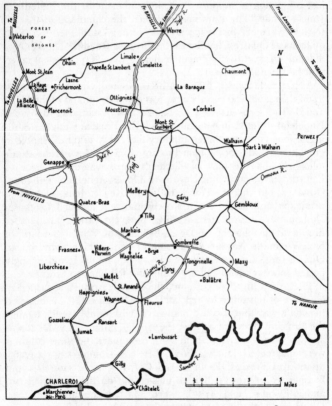

7. AREA OF OPERATIONS, JUNE 15–19, 1815

exhausted–he had been in the saddle since 3 a.m.–and at once
lay down to rest.[1] At midnight he was aroused by the arrival of
Ney, who stayed with him until 2 a.m. on June 16. Of this interview Colonel Heymès writes: "The Emperor made him stay to

[1] *Correspondance*, No. 22055, vol. XXVIII, p. 286.

R

supper, gave him his orders" and "unfolded to him his projects and his hopes for the day of the 16th. . . ."[1] Therefore, it goes without saying that Ney must have told the Emperor why he had not occupied Quatre-Bras, and that the latter must have instructed him to occupy it early on June 16. This is common sense, for should Wellington come to the support of Blücher, it was vital to Napoleon's project of dealing with one hostile army at the time that the Nivelles-Namur Road should be blocked. To assume otherwise is to write Napoleon down as a strategic dunce.

In the meantime, what was Wellington doing? Though his actions have been minutely analysed by all competent historians of the campaign, the only certain fact which has emerged is that he was totally unprepared to face the situation. He did not believe that Napoleon would assume the offensive,[2] and, it would seem, had become so involved in the gay life of Brussels that, on June 13, a rumour that Napoleon was at Maubeuge so little disturbed him that "he took Lady Jane Lennox to Enghien for a cricket match and brought her back at night, apparently having gone for no other object but to amuse her".[3] Though further rumours reached him on June 14, it was not until 3 p.m. the following day that a definite report was received to announce that the Prussian outposts near Thuin had been attacked. Possessed by the idea that Napoleon's intention was to advance by way of Mons and fall upon the Anglo-Dutch communications,[4] between 5 and 7 p.m.,[5] Wellington ordered his divisions to concentrate at the points already designated for them and hold themselves in readiness to march at the shortest notice.[6] According to this order, the Prince of Orange was to collect his 2nd and 3rd Divisions (Perponcher and Chassé) at Nivelles.

Next, in the evening, a dispatch came in from Blücher to announce the concentration of his army at Sombreffe.[7] Thereon, at 10 p.m., the Duke issued a second set of orders, according to which the 3rd Division (Alten) was to move from Braine-le-

---

[1] Heymès "Relation," p. 6.
[2] See his letter to Lord Lynedoch on June 13 (*The Dispatches of the Duke of Wellington.* Gurwood, 1838, vol. XII, p. 462).
[3] Quoted from a letter written at Brussels, on June 13, by the Rev. Spencer Madan, tutor to the young Lennoxes (*The Life of Wellington*, Sir Herbert Maxwell (1900), vol. II, p. 10).
[4] An extraordinary misconception of Napoleonic strategy, because such a move would have driven Wellington and Blücher not apart but together.
[5] *Supplementary Despatches*, vol. x, p. 509.   [6] *Dispatches*, vol. xii, pp. 472-473.
[7] See *Passages from my Life*, etc., Baron von Müffling (1853), p. 229. Müffling was Blücher's liaison officer attached to Wellington's headquarters.

Comte to Nivelles; the 1st (Cooke) from Enghien to Braine-le-Comte; the 2nd (Clinton) and 4th (Colville) from Ath and Oudenarde to Enghien; and the cavalry, under Lord Uxbridge, from Ninhove to Enghien.[1] This meant a concentration away from Blücher and was clearly intended to cover the roads leading from Mons and Ath to Brussels, and not in order to cooperate with him.

Immediately after these orders had been sent, the Duke went to the Duchess of Richmond's ball and remained there until 2 a.m. Toward midnight he received a report from General Dörnberg at Mons to inform him that Napoleon had moved with all his forces on Charleroi and that there was nothing in front of Mons. At length Wellington's fears for his right were laid at rest, and in his official report he informs us that he then directed "the whole army to march upon Les Quatre Bras".[2]

This decision is corroborated by Captain (later General Sir George) Bowles. He says that at supper time Wellington and the Duke of Richmond left the table and went into the study to examine a map. Closing the door, Wellington said: "Napoleon has humbugged me, by G—! he has gained twenty-four hours march on me." When Richmond asked what he intended to do, he replied: " 'I have [? will] ordered the army to concentrate at Quatre-Bras; but we shall not stop him there, and if so, I must fight him *here*' (at the same time passing his thumb-nail over the position of Waterloo)."[3] Immediately after this Wellington left, and at 7.30 a.m. set out for Quatre-Bras.

Should the experiences of Captain Mercer be typical, then the forward concentration of the Anglo-Dutch Army, distracted as it was by orders and counter-orders, was carried out in extreme confusion. Some units received no orders at all, others defective ones; some officers were still in ballroom dress, and many had no idea of what was happening. At Nivelles, writes Mercer, "The

[1] *Dispatches*, vol. XII, p. 474.
[2] *Dispatches*, vol. XII, p. 479. See also Müffling's *Passages*, p. 230, and *Supplementary Despatches*, vol. X, p. 510. Some time after 2 a.m. June 16.
[3] See *Letters of the First Earl of Malmesbury* (1870), vol. II, p. 445. Bowles says that the Duke of Richmond repeated this conversation to him two minutes after it had taken place. With reference to it, and when combined with Wellington's social proclivities, it is illuminating to read that, at 3 a.m. on June 18—a few hours before the battle of Waterloo opened—the Duke wrote to Lady Frances Webster—"A very pretty woman"—that she should be prepared "to remove from Bruxelles to Antwerp in case such a measure should be necessary" (*Supplementary Despatches*, vol. X, p. 501), and that at 8.30 a.m. on June 19 he wrote to her again that she could "remain in Bruxelles in perfect security". (*Ibid.*, vol. X, p. 531.) Well may it be asked, was it Napoleon who had done the humbugging?

road was covered with soldiers, many of them wounded but also many apparently untouched. The numbers thus leaving the field appeared extraordinary. Many of the wounded had six, eight, ten and even more, attendants. When questioned about the battle and why they left it, the answer was invariably, 'Monsieur, tout est perdu! les Anglais sont abimés, en déroute, abimés, tous, tous, tous!' "[1] The battle of Quatre-Bras had begun.

When Wellington was on his way to Quatre-Bras, 25 miles to the South of Brussels, Ziethen's corps occupied a salient along the Ligny brook, its right at Wagnelée, its centre at St. Amand and its left at Ligny. There it remained unsupported until noon, when the IInd Corps, under Pirch, and the IIIrd, under Thielemann began to arrive. The former was posted immediately in rear of Ziethen's Corps and the latter was deployed on its left between Sombreffe and Mazy with a strong covering force alongthe Ligny, brook. Bülow's IVth Corps was far behind, therefore Blücher was only able to concentrate 84,000 men on the field of Ligny.

In the meantime, assuming that the allies would behave according to the rules of war–that is, fall back in order to secure their concentration–Napoleon jumped to the conclusion that Wellington would withdraw on Brussels. He therefore decided to advance on that city and fight Wellington should he stand, or drive him on to Antwerp–that is, away from Blücher, who was based on Liège. But before this could be done, it was necessary to push Ziethen back beyond Gembloux, in order to deny Blücher the use of the Namur-Wavre-Brussels Road. With this in mind, at about 6 a.m. Napoleon dictated two letters, one for Ney and the other for Grouchy, to explain his intentions.[2]

In his letter to Grouchy he wrote that, should the Prussians be at Sombreffe or Gembloux, he would attack them, and once he had occupied Gembloux he would next swing his reserves over to Ney and operate against Wellington. He restated this in his letter to Ney and instructed him to be ready to march on Brussels directly the reserves joined him, and that meanwhile he was to push one division five miles north of Quatre-Bras, hold six at Quatre-Bras, and send one to Marbais to link up with Grouchy's left. Also he told him that Kellermann's division would replace Lefebvre-Desnouettes's. Then, so it would seem, he remembered

---

[1] *Journal of the Waterloo Campaign*, General Cavalie Mercer (1870), vol. i, chapter xi, and p. 250.
[2] See *Correspondance*, Nos. 22058 and 22059, vol. xxviii, pp. 289–292.

how thick-headed was Ney and explained to him the method of his manœuvre. "I have adopted for this campaign," he wrote, "the following general principle, to divide my army into two wings and a reserve. . . . The Guard will form the reserve, and I shall bring it into action on either wing as circumstances may dictate. . . . Also, according to circumstances, I shall draw troops from one wing to strengthen my reserve."

Shortly after these letters were dispatched (about 8 a.m.) Napoleon received a message from Grouchy to inform him that strong columns had been seen to approach Sombreffe from the direction of Namur. This pointed to the probability that the whole, or most, of the Prussian army would assemble at Sombreffe, and therefore to the further probability that the Anglo-Dutch army would come to the support of Blücher. As this disrupted Napoleon's plan, he refused to believe it, modified nothing, and set out from Charleroi and arrived at Fleurus shortly before 11 a.m. There he found Vandamme's corps in line facing St. Amand—the western side of Ziethen's salient—and learnt that Gérard's was still far in rear, due, it would appear, to faulty staff work. At once Napoleon reconnoitred the enemy position, and though he could see only Ziethen's corps, its dispositions convinced him that it was no rear guard, but instead a force covering a general advance, as well as one securing the Sombreffe-Quatre-Bras Road—that is, the only main road by which Wellington could approach.[1] In an instant all was clear; in spite of his fixed idea and the rules of war, it was apparent that the allies were concentrating forward, and, therefore intended to unite. But until Gérard's corps came up, which it began to do at 1 p.m., Napoleon did not feel strong enough to attack. Meanwhile Pirch and Thielemann deployed, and overjoyed when he saw that he had to deal with more than one corps, he decided to settle accounts with Blücher that afternoon.

His plan—a truly brilliant one—was first to contain Blücher's left (Thielemann's corps) with Pajol's and Exelmans's cavalry, and secondly to annihilate his right and centre (Ziethen and Pirch). The latter operation he intended to carry out by engaging the Prussian centre and right frontally, so as to compel Blücher to exhaust his reserves, and meanwhile to call in Ney from Quatre-Bras to fall upon the rear of Blücher's right wing while the Guard smashed through his centre. By these means he expected to destroy

[1] Gourgaud, *Campagne de 1815*, pp. 55–56.

two-thirds of Blücher's army and compel the remaining third to fall back on Liège–that is, away from Wellington.

At 2 p.m. he instructed Soult to inform Ney that Grouchy would attack the enemy between Sombreffe and Brye at 2.30 p.m. Next, we read: "His Majesty's intention is that you also will attack whatever force is in front of you, and after having vigorously pushed it back, you will turn in our direction, so as to bring about the envelopment of that body of the enemy's troops whom I have just mentioned to you. If the latter is overthrown first, then His Majesty will manœuvre in your direction, so as to assist your operation in a similar way."[1]

Then he turned to Gérard, whose corps was deploying against Ligny–the southern face of Ziethen's salient–and said: "It is possible that three hours hence the fate of the war may be decided. If Ney carries out his orders thoroughly, not a gun of the Prussian Army will get away: it is taken in the very act (*prise en flagrant délit*)."[2]

At 2.30 p.m., while Grouchy's cavalry contained Thielemann, Vandamme and Girard[3] vigorously attacked St. Amand while Gérard assaulted Ligny. But the Prussian resistance was so stubborn that, at 3.15 p.m., Napoleon instructed Soult to send the following message to Ney:

"His Majesty desires me to tell you that you are to manœuvre immediately in such a manner as to envelop the enemy's right and fall upon his rear; the army in our front is lost if you act with energy. The fate of France is in your hands.

"Thus do not hesitate even for a moment to carry out the manœuvre . . . and direct your advance on the heights of Brye and St. Amand so as to co-operate in a victory that may well turn out to be decisive. . . ."[4]

Immediately after its dispatch, Napoleon heard from Lobau, at Charleroi, that Ney was confronted by a force 20,000 strong. He feared that the 3.15 p.m. order might not be sufficiently explicit, and assuming that, with Reille's corps alone, Ney should be able to hold the enemy back, Napoleon sent by Count de la Bédoyère his celebrated "pencil note"[5] to him. As circumstances prevented Ney advancing with his whole army on Brye, he in-

---

[1] *Documents Inédits*, duc d'Elchingen, No. XIII, p: 40.

[2] *Commentaires*, vol. v, pp. 140–141.

[3] On the night of June 15–16 Girard's division of Reille's corps, as we have seen, bivouacked on the Fleurus Road. On June 16 it was attached to Vandamme's corps.

[4] *Documents Inédits*, duc d'Elchingen, No. XIV, p. 42.

[5] This note has since been lost.

structed him to order d'Erlon's corps alone to march against the Prussian rear. At the same time he sent an order to Lobau to advance his corps to Fleurus.

This last order introduces Napoleon's crucial blunder on June 16. When, at about 10 a.m., he set out from Charleroi for Fleurus, he should, at the same time, have ordered Lobau forward. Had he done so, and had Lobau started at, say, noon, since Fleurus is eight miles from Charleroi, the head of his corps would have reached Fleurus by 3.30 p.m.; in which case there would have been no need to send the "pencil note" to Ney. Should it be suggested that, at 10 a.m., Napoleon could not tell where he might need to employ Lobau, then he should have ordered him to Mellet, near the junction of the Roman and Charleroi-Brussels roads, where he would have been far better placed than at Charleroi either to assist Ney or himself. Actually, Lobau reached Fleurus at 7.30 p.m., and as Fleurus is more than four miles from Wagnelée, it was then too late for him to move against Blücher's right rear. The eventual wanderings of d'Erlon's corps were a serious but not an unusual incident, somewhat similar mishaps occurred at Jena and Leipzig. But on the morning of June 16 to leave Lobau at Charleroi was an inexcusable blunder.

In the meantime, the battle continued furiously; Girard was killed assaulting St. Amand, and Gérard stormed into Ligny. So hard pressed was the Prussian right that Blücher was compelled repeatedly to draw on his reserves, until at 5 p.m. they were nearly exhausted. By then, out of the 68,000 troops which Napoleon had brought on to the field, he had used no more than 58,000, and with them had fixed Blücher's 84,000. The time, therefore, had come to strike the decisive blow, and calculating that, at 6 p.m. he would hear the roar of d'Erlon's guns in rear of the Prussian right wing, he prepared to launch the Guard against the enemy centre at Ligny; smash through it, cut off Blücher's right from Sombreffe and annihilate Ziethen and Pirch.

While the Guards prepared for their grand assault, suddenly Vandamme rode up to the Emperor with alarming news. Two and a half miles to the rear, he said, an enemy column, 20,000 to 30,000 strong, had been sighted approaching Fleurus. Was it Ney? Was it d'Erlon? Vandamme was positive that it was hostile.[1]

---

[1] Vandamme had sent out an officer to reconnoitre the column, but he merely approached it, and then galloped back exclaiming: "They are enemies." It is strange that d'Erlon did not send forward a galloper announcing his arrival.

Napoleon was perplexed, for he expected d'Erlon to move to Brye by the Roman Road and not on Fleurus, which lay to the south of the Prussian centre. At once he suspended the movements of the Guard, made dispositions to meet the advancing column, and sent Duhesme's division of the Young Guard to support Vandamme, whose men bordered on panic. At the same time he sent an aide-de-camp to ascertain to whom the column belonged. At 6.30 p.m. the aide-de-camp returned,[1] and reported it to be d'Erlon's. Forthwith, so it would seem, another aide-de-camp was sent galloping to d'Erlon with orders to press on to Wagnelée, but when he arrived he found that, except for his leading division (Durutte's), the rest of his corps was in full retreat—in compliance with orders sent by Ney. To send out yet another aide to order d'Erlon to counter-march was useless, for nearly three hours would be required to bring him to Wagnelée, and by then it would be dark.

Too frequently it has gone unrecognized that d'Erlon's expected approach in the least expected of directions nearly cost Napoleon the battle. It so completely unhinged the morale of Vandamme's corps that General Lefol, one of his divisional commanders, in order to arrest the flight of his men, turned his cannon on the fugitives.[2] The Prussians took advantage of the French disorder and vigorously assaulted St. Amand, and had it not been for the arrival of the Young Guard, who counter-attacked with superb *élan*, it is probable that the whole of Vandamme's corps would have taken to flight. The net result of the d'Erlon fiasco was that, once the situation again was stabilized, Napoleon was left with so little time[3] that, even should the final assault of the Guard on Ligny prove successful, it was improbable that it would prove decisive. This is what happened, for not until 7.30 p.m. was Napoleon again ready to launch his final assault.

Though the sun was still high above the horizon, great, rolling storm clouds now shrouded the battlefield in blackness. Then, as the storm broke, and the thunder drowned the roar of the cannonade, in sheets of rain and with cries of "*Vive l'Empereur!*" the Guard advanced at the charge, for the deluge rendered firing impossible; like an avalanche of steel they swept the Prussians out of Ligny.

---

[1] Gourgaud, *Campagne de 1815*, p. 59.
[2] See Houssaye's *1815 Waterloo*, pp. 99–100, quoting Lefol's *Souvenirs*.
[3] The sun set at 8.20 p.m., and the battle ended in the dark at 9.30 p.m.

When the rain ceased and the last rays of the setting sun gleamed between the scattering clouds, at full gallop Blücher arrived on the field. He counted on Röder's cavalry – 32 squadrons in all – to repel the French, placed himself at their head, and ordered them to charge the squares of the Guard, then slowly advancing toward the mill of Bussy (south of Brye). In the resulting mêlée Blücher's horse was struck by a bullet and rolled over its rider. His aide-de-camp, Nostiz, sprang from his horse and came to Blücher's help. Though surrounded by the 9th Regiment of Cuirassiers, under cover of the increasing gloom and the confusion of innumerable fugitives, he dragged the 73-year-old field-marshal, bruised and half-conscious, to safety. Had he not done so, Waterloo would never have been fought.

Though Blücher's centre was completely shattered and his right wing severed from his left, under cover of night the broken Ist and IInd corps fell back in disorder to between Sombreffe and the Roman Road. Had d'Erlon been in their rear, they would have been destroyed. But what is equally probable is, with two hours more daylight the Guard alone would have accomplished as much. Captain Becke in no way exaggerates what this would have led to when he writes: "The news of such a victory . . . would have shaken Europe to its foundations, and at the same time have raised France to a pitch of enthusiasm that must have carried Napoleon on to ultimate victory."[1] Nevertheless, Ligny was a great victory and it presented Napoleon with the opportunity to attack Wellington on the next day without fear of Prussian interference.

Toward 11 p.m. the Emperor returned to Fleurus, and under cover of its outposts the whole French Army bivouacked on the left bank of the Ligny brook. As usual, the casualties are variously given, but it would appear that those of the Prussians in killed, wounded and prisoners amounted to about 16,000, and of the French to between 11,000 and 12,000. To the Prussian losses must be added between 8,000 and 10,000 men who during the night abandoned their colours and fled toward Liège.[2] This flight had an extraordinary repercussion on June 17, and was worth to Blücher at least an additional army corps.

In the meantime, what had taken place at Quatre-Bras? At

[1] *Napoleon at Waterloo* (1914), vol. I, p. 270.
[2] According to Ropes (*The Campaign of Waterloo*, 1910, p. 159), quoting Gneisenau, "These men belonged to provinces which had formerly been part of the French Empire, and their sympathies were with Napoleon."

10 a.m., when Wellington arrived there, he found Saxe-Weimar's and Bylandt's brigades holding the cross-roads and hamlet. Though this concentration of Perponcher's Division contravened Wellington's 5 p.m. order of June 15, it was fortunate for the Duke, for had his order been obeyed it is highly unlikely that he would ever have reached Quatre-Bras. What had happened was this:

When the Prince of Orange left Nivelles to attend the Duchess of Richmond's ball, General Rebecque, his Chief of Staff, heard that Saxe-Weimar's brigade had been attacked and had fallen back on Quatre-Bras and ordered Perponcher with his remaining brigade—Bylandt's—to support him. Next, at 11 p.m., when Wellington's 5 p.m. order was received by Rebecque, he passed it on to Perponcher without comment, and on his own initiative the latter set it aside, and instead of concentrating his division at Nivelles, concentrated it at Quatre-Bras. Little suspected by him at the time, this act of intelligent disobedience saved Blücher; for had he complied with the order Ney would have found Quatre-Bras unheld, and therefore would have been able to carry out the Emperor's 6 a.m. instruction to the letter, and later those contained in Soult's 2 p.m. dispatch.

Wellington found little in front of him and at 10.30 a.m. wrote to Blücher[1] to inform him of his troop movements. These appear to have been based on a memorandum[2] which had been handed to him before leaving Brussels by Colonel De Lancey, his Chief of Staff. It was a thoroughly slipshod document, for several of the units mentioned in it were nowhere near the positions assigned to them, therefore their arrival at Genappe and Quatre-Bras could not be correctly timed. Some time after this letter was sent, all remained quiet, Wellington rode over to Brye and at 1 p.m. met Blücher at the Bussy windmill.

What took place during the interview is uncertain, but, according to Müffling,[3] Wellington agreed to come to Blücher's support provided he himself was not attacked. What he thought of Blücher's dispositions is made clear in the reply to a question posed to him by Sir Henry Hardinge, his military attaché at Blücher's headquarters. When the latter asked him what he thought of Blücher's deployment, the Duke replied: "If they fight here they will be damnably mauled."[4]

[1] See *The Campaign of Waterloo*, Ropes, p. 106.
[2] *Supplementary Despatches*, vol. x, p. 496.   [3] *Passages*, p. 237.
[4] *Notes of Conversations with the Duke of Wellington, 1831–1851*. Philip Henry, 5th Earl of Stanhope (1886), p. 109.

Some time after 2 p.m. Wellington set out on his return, and when at three o'clock he was back at Quatre-Bras, because of the De Lancey memorandum he found his own dispositions even more damnable than Blücher's. Actually, he was lucky ever to have got back there, which he most certainly would not have done had Ney lived up to his reputation.

When, after his midnight interview with the Emperor, Ney returned to Gosselies, instead of ordering Reille, whom he actually visited, to concentrate his corps as soon as possible after dawn at Frasnes—at the time held by Bachelu's Division and Piré's cavalry—and at the same time sending instructions to d'Erlon to close up on Gosselies, he waited until 11 a.m. before doing so. This quite unnecessary delay of five or six hours was the root cause of all his subsequent predicaments, and it contrasts glaringly with Perponcher's bold initiative.

At 11.45 a.m. Reille set out, and at two o'clock was ordered by Ney to clear the enemy out of the woods south of Quatre-Bras. Reille feared what he called a "Spanish battle"—that is, that the English were hidden away and would only appear at the critical moment—and advanced with extreme caution. He had in all 19,000 men backed by 3,000 cavalry within call and 60 guns, and in rear, d'Erlon with 20,000 more, though still distant, was approaching. Actually, though Reille was unaware of it, the Prince of Orange then had only 7,800 infantry, supported by 50 horsemen and 14 guns. Therefore, had Reille or Ney displayed but usual boldness, nothing could have saved Quatre-Bras. As it was, when Wellington returned there at 3 p.m., he found the situation critical. The hamlet of Quatre-Bras was nearly lost and would have fallen had not Picton's Division come up by the Brussels Road and van Merlen's cavalry brigade from Nivelles. Immediately after, the Duke of Brunswick's Corps arrived and Reille was slightly outnumbered.

Shortly before 4 p.m., Ney received Soult's 2 p.m. letter ordering him to press the enemy back and then move against Blücher's right rear. At last Ney realized the importance of gaining Quatre-Bras and ordered a general forward movement, during which the Duke of Brunswick was mortally wounded, as his father had been at Auerstädt.

Ney, who counted on d'Erlon to support Reille, impatiently awaited his arrival, and long before this he would have been at hand had he set out earlier. Actually, the head of d'Erlon's column

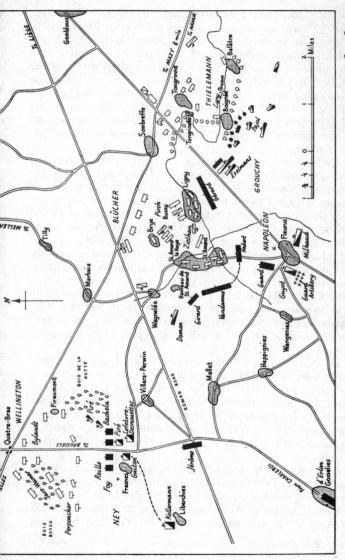

8. BATTLES OF QUATRE-BRAS AND LIGNY BETWEEN 2.0 P.M. AND 2.30 P.M., JUNE 16, 1815

was not far away, for between four and a quarter past four o'clock, half his corps was already north of the Roman Road, and he himself had ridden forward to reconnoitre Quatre-Bras. It was while he was away that General de la Bédoyère galloped up with the "pencil note" for Ney, and instead of warning the commander of the van of its purport, and then taking the note on to Ney, on his own initiative he "ordered the column to move in the direction of Ligny".[1] The "pencil note", it would seem, was an all but illegible scrawl, and de la Bédoyère read it incorrectly and instead of directing the column on Wagnelée, instructed it to march on St. Amand.

On his return, d'Erlon learnt of this change of direction and at once sent his Chief of Staff, General Delacombre, to inform Ney what had happened. Ney, who increasingly was outnumbered, relied on d'Erlon to win his battle, and when he was acquainted with what had transpired he flew into a violent passion which was raised to still higher pitch when a few minutes later the officer carrying Soult's 3.15 p.m. dispatch—"the fate of France is in your hands"—arrived. To make matters worse, at this moment the van of Alten's division debouched from Quatre-Bras and, maddened by the sight and blinded with rage, Ney cast the Emperor's orders aside. He did not for a moment consider that tactically d'Erlon's corps was now beyond profitable recall, and sent Delacambre back with an imperative order to d'Erlon to countermarch his corps. This the latter did and rejoined Ney after nightfall.

For Ney, the irony of this fiasco was that, had not d'Erlon's corps been diverted, in all probability Wellington would have suffered a severe defeat. And for Napoleon that, had the "pencil note" been legible, there would have been no alarm, and Blücher would not have gained a breathing-space in which to prepare to meet Napoleon's final assault, which would have been launched two hours earlier, and therefore would have permitted a pursuit to follow.

Both these lost chances were due to failures to concentrate in time: Gérard's IVth Corps was at least three hours late in arriving at Fleurus, and Reille's IInd Corps over five hours late in concentrating at Frasnes. As it happened, of all the corps commanders engaged in the two battles, d'Erlon was the least to blame,

[1] *Le Maréchal Drouet, Comte d'Erlon* (1844), pp. 95–96. Also *Documents Inédits*, duc d'Elchingen, pp. 95–96.

though when Delacombre caught up with him near Villers Perwin, he should have disobeyed Ney's frantic order, because lack of time did not permit it profitably to be carried out.

Deprived of d'Erlon, Ney not only lost his temper, but also his judgment. He called up Kellermann and ordered him with a single brigade of cuirassiers to charge Wellington's infantry squares and trample them under foot. This Kellermann most gallantly set out to do, and after he had scattered Halkett's 69th Regiment and had driven his 33rd into the woods, though repulsed by the 30th and 73rd[1] he nevertheless succeeded in penetrating as far as the cross roads.[2]

When this heroic[3] though fruitless charge was under way, Major Badus, who had been sent by the Emperor with a verbal message to Ney, came up. The message was that, whatever Ney's circumstances might be, the order to d'Erlon must be executed absolutely.[4] Maddened with rage, Ney abruptly turned from him, rushed into the midst of his routed infantry, and succeeded in rallying them.

At nine o'clock the battle ended in a draw, both armies retook the positions they had held in the morning. Even by the close of the day, thanks to his delays on June 15 and the De Lancey memorandum, Wellington had succeeded only in concentrating less than half his infantry, a third of his artillery, and only one-seventh of his cavalry, in all 31,000 men. Nevertheless, Ney had done no better, for out of the 43,000 men entrusted to him he assembled only 22,000. The casualties were about equal, between 4,000 and 5,000 on either side.

Thus far Napoleon's plan had worked well enough. He had beaten Blücher, therefore all that remained was to beat Wellington. How to defeat his army now became the problem, consequently on his return to Fleurus at 11 p.m., as he had heard nothing from Ney throughout the day,[5] he should have sent an

---

[1] See *Waterloo Letters*, Major-General H. T. Siborne (1891), pp. 318–337.

[2] Mercer (*Journal of the Waterloo Campaign*, vol. 1, p. 263) writes: "Just in front of the farm of Quatre Bras there was a fearful scene of slaughter–Highlanders and cuirassiers lying thickly strewn about. . . ."

[3] In *Letters of Colonel Sir Augustus Simon Frazer, K.C.B.* (1859), p. 540, Frazer writes: "The enemy's lancers and cuirassiers are the finest fellows I ever saw;–they made several bold charges, and repeatedly advanced in the very teeth of our infantry."

[4] See Houssaye's *1815 Waterloo*, p. 122.

[5] In Soult's 2 p.m. letter Ney was instructed to inform the Emperor of his dispositions and what happened on his front. This he did not do until 10 p.m., when he sent in a report on Quatre-Bras which was so meagre as to be valueless. (See *Napoleon and Waterloo*, Captain A. F. Becke, vol. II, Appx. II, p. 287.)

officer to Frasnes to obtain for him a report on Ney's situation, also he should have instructed Ney to keep him hourly informed of Wellington's movements. That he did not do so may have been because of complete exhaustion,[1] in which case Soult, on his own initiative, should have acted for him, or what is equally possible, he assumed that Blücher would fall back on his base at Liège and that Wellington would retire from Quatre-Bras during the night, as he should have done, but apparently delayed doing because he had so little cavalry and artillery at hand to cover his retreat.

The first of these illusions was strengthened when, at 7 a.m. on June 17, he learnt that at 2.30 a.m. Grouchy had sent out Pajol's cavalry, which at 4 a.m. had reported that the enemy was in full retreat on Liège. Actually what Pajol's squadrons had come up against were the thousands of deserters who had fled the field of Ligny. This news was received when the Emperor was at breakfast, and at the same time General Flahaut, an aide who had carried a dispatch to Ney on the previous day, returned from Frasnes with news of the battle of Quatre-Bras and that Wellington was still in position there. At once Soult wrote to Ney to inform him of Blücher's defeat and retreat. Next, he wrote:

"The Emperor is going to the mill of Brye, where the highway leading from Namur to Quatre-Bras passes. This makes it impossible that the English Army should act in front of you. In the latter event, the Emperor would march directly on it by the Quatre-Bras road, while you would attack it from the front, and this army would be destroyed in an instant. . . .

"His Majesty's wishes are, that you should take up your position at Quatre-Bras; but if this is impossible . . . send information immediately with full details, and the Emperor will act there as I have told you. If, on the contrary, there is only a rearguard, attack it and seize the position.

"To-day it is necessary to end this operation, and complete the military stores, to rally scattered soldiers and summon back all detachments."[2]

[1] On June 15 Napoleon rose at 3 a.m., rested at Charleroi between 9 p.m. and midnight, interviewed Ney from midnight to 2 a.m. June 16, and presumably rested between 2 a.m. and 4 a.m. (Houssaye, p. 346, footnote 7). At 10 a.m. he left Charleroi for Fleurus, returned to Fleurus at 11 p.m. and rested until about 6.30 a.m. on June 17. Therefore, between 3 a.m. on June 15 and 6.30 a.m. on June 17, in all 51½ hours, he rested for 12½. This was not excessive for a man who, as Caulaincourt says, "needed much sleep" (Memoirs, vol. 1, p. 599). Fain (Mémoires, 1908, p. 290) says, "It was his habit to sleep about seven hours out of the twenty-four; but it was always in several naps."

[2] Documents Inédits, duc d'Elchingen, No. XVII, pp. 45-47.

This is an extraordinary document, for it shows that, though Napoleon was uncertain whether the whole of Wellington's army was still at Quatre-Bras, he was in no way certain that it was not. Therefore, knowing that Blücher was retreating, whether Wellington's army were retiring or not, he should forthwith have ordered Ney to attack whatever was in front of him and simultaneously have carried the VIth Corps and the Guard to his support. Instead he ordered Lobau to assist Pajol on the Namur Road, and sent out a cavalry reconnaissance to Quatre-Bras to make certain whether the English were still there. After this he got into his coach, drove to Grouchy's headquarters, visited the wounded and reviewed his troops. While thus engaged, between 10 and 11 a.m., the officer in command of the reconnaissance returned and reported that the English were still at Quatre-Bras,[1] and at the same time Pajol reported that the Prussians were massing at Gembloux. At last Napoleon awoke from his trance, made up his mind, and sent orders to Lobau and Drouot to march the VIth Corps and Guard to Marbais in order to support Ney's attack on Quatre-Bras. Next, he dictated two letters, one for Grouchy, to whom he had already given verbal orders, and the other for Ney. In the first, we read: "Proceed to Gembloux with the cavalry . . . and the IIIrd and IVth corps of infantry . . . You will explore in the directions of Namur and Maestricht [i.e. south-east and north-east of Sombreffe] and you will pursue the enemy. Explore his march, and instruct me respecting his manœuvres, so that I may be able to penetrate what he is intending to do. . . . It is important to penetrate what the enemy is intending to do; whether they are separating themselves from the English, or whether they are intending still to unite, to cover Brussels or Liège, in trying the fate of another battle. . . ."[2]

The letter to Ney, which is timed midday, reads:

"The Emperor has just ordered a corps of infantry and the Imperial Guard to Marbais. His Majesty has directed me to inform you that his intention is that you are to attack the enemy at Quatre-Bras and drive him from his position and that the force which is at Marbais will second your operations. His Majesty is about to proceed to Marbais, and awaits your reports with impatience."[3]

[1] Gourgaud, *Campagne de 1815*, p. 74.
[2] See Ropes, *The Campaign of Waterloo*, pp. 209–210 and 358.
[3] *Documents Inédits*, duc d'Elchingen, No. XVI, pp. 44–45.

When Blücher was incapacitated, Gneisenau had ordered the Prussian Army to retire on Tilly and Wavre, not in order to keep contact with Wellington, but because most of the army had been driven north of the Nivelles-Namur Road, and therefore it was safer to fall back on Louvain and from there reopen communication with Liège than to attempt a direct withdrawal on Liège. Later, when Blücher had been carried to Mellery–a mile or two north of Tilly–and had sufficiently recovered, he discussed the next move with Gneisenau, his Chief of Staff, and Grölmann, his Quarter Master General. Gneisenau, who did not trust Wellington and considered him to be a knave, urged that the army should fall back on Liège, but Blücher, still full of fire and supported by Grölmann, disagreed, and it was decided to maintain contact with the English.[1]

When this decisive argument took place, Wellington was at Genappe, and as he had heard nothing from Blücher since 2 p.m., at 2 a.m. on June 17 he sent Colonel Gordon and a troop of cavalry to discover what had happened. Gordon returned at 7.30 a.m. and reported that he had contacted Ziethen and had learnt that the Prussians had been beaten and were retiring on Wavre. Wellington then decided that he must also retire. Next, at 9 a.m., when his army was prepared to do so, an officer arrived from Blücher to confirm what Gordon had said. Further, he informed Wellington that the Field-Marshal was anxious to know his intentions. The Duke replied that he was falling back on Mont St. Jean, and there would offer Napoleon battle if Blücher would support him with one army corps.[2] At 10 a.m., covered by Lord Uxbridge's cavalry, the retreat on Mont St. Jean began.

That Wellington was able to retire unmolested was entirely because of Ney's inactivity. Though the latter had been ordered to attack, he did nothing, and at noon, when his enemy was in full retreat, his men sat about preparing their mid-day meal.[3]

While they were thus peacefully engaged, the Emperor set out from Brye and reached Marbais at about one o'clock. Because he did not hear a cannonade at Quatre-Bras he was much perturbed, and when he pressed on with his cavalry and debouched on the Brussels Road he was astonished to find Ney's army still in bivouac.[4] At once he ordered all troops to fall in, but it was not

---

[1] See Stanhope's *Conversations*, pp. 108–110.   [2] Müffling, *Passages*, p. 241.
[3] *Waterloo Letters*, No. 75, p. 166.   [4] Gourgaud, *Campagne de 1815*, p. 77.

until two o'clock that the head of d'Erlon's Corps came up. Napoleon realized the magnitude of his lost opportunity and said to d'Erlon: "France has been ruined; go, my dear General, and place yourself at the head of the cavalry, and press the English rearguard vigorously."[1] Next, when he saw Milhaud's horsemen drawn up alongside the road, the Emperor led them forward at breakneck speed toward Genappe.

When the French pursuit began, "The sky", writes Mercer, "had become overcast since the morning, and at this moment ... large isolated masses of thundercloud, of the deepest, almost inky black ... hung suspended over us, involving our position and everything on it in deep and gloomy obscurity; whilst the distant hill lately occupied by the French army still lay bathed in brilliant sunshine." Next, he says:

"Lord Uxbridge was yet speaking when a single horseman [Napoleon] immediately followed by several others, mounted the plateau I had left at a gallop, their dark figures thrown forward in strong relief from the illuminated distance, making them appear much nearer to us than they really were. For an instant they pulled up and regarded us, when several squadrons, coming up rapidly on the plateau, Lord Uxbridge cried out, 'Fire!–fire!' ... The first gun that was fired seemed to burst the clouds overhead, for its report was instantly followed by an awful clap of thunder, and lightning that almost blinded us, whilst the rain came down as if a water-spout had broken over us."[2]

In part, at least, this terrific storm of rain saved Wellington, for it so drenched the ground that the French were unable to advance across country, and were, in consequence, tied to the Brussels Road.[3] Had they been able, as was Napoleon's wont, to advance in extended order, it is probable that, in spite of the late start, the Emperor would have caught up with his enemy by five or six o'clock. Had he done so, and had he attacked Wellington and fixed him to his position when not fully deployed, it is also possible that he might have beaten him during the next morning, or what is more likely, have forced him to retire during the night.

---

[1] *Le Maréchal Drouet, Comte d'Erlon*, p. 96.

[2] Mercer's *Journal*, vol. I, pp. 268-270. The rain at once extinguished every slow-match in the brigade.

[3] Captain W. B. Ingliby, R.H.A. writes: "The road and ground became so quickly deluged with the heavy rain . . . that it became impracticable for the French Cavalry to press our columns in any force. In fact, out of the road in the track of our own Cavalry, the ground was poached into a complete puddle." (*Waterloo Letters*, No. 81, p. 196.)

From Quatre-Bras, the pursuit and retreat resembled a "fox-hunt". "Lord Uxbridge urging us on", writes Mercer, "and crying 'Make haste!—make haste! for God's sake, gallop or you will be taken' . . . away we went, helter-skelter—guns, gun-detachments, and hussars mixed pêle-mêle, going like mad."[1] Genappe with its single narrow bridge was reached, the rain stopped, and toward 6.30 p.m. Napoleon with the van of his cavalry rode on to the heights of La Belle Alliance,[2] which were separated by a shallow valley from a parallel range of heights, behind which, unseen to Napoleon, Wellington's army lay. At once the Emperor ordered up four horse batteries and under cover of their fire Milhaud's cuirassiers charged up the slope to discover that the whole of the Anglo-Dutch Army was in position. Napoleon pointed to the sun and exclaimed: "What would I not give to-day to have had Joshua's power to have slowed down the enemy's march by two hours."[3] Though he himself was by no means free of blame, had Ney attacked his enemy early in the morning those two hours, and more, would have been gained.

Napoleon turned about and rode to his headquarters, which had been established in the farm of Le Caillou, a mile and a half south of La Belle Alliance, and about 9 p.m. he received a report from Milhaud that one of his patrols had sighted a Prussian column retiring from Géry toward Wavre. This did not perturb him, for he could not bring himself to believe that, in face of Grouchy's 33,000 men, Blücher would dare to attempt a flank march across his front in order to join Wellington.

After resting for an hour or two, at 1 a.m. on June 18 Napoleon set out in torrents of rain to ride round his outposts. He returned to his headquarters at dawn to find that at 2 a.m. a dispatch, timed 10 p.m. June 17, had come in from Grouchy. It informed him that the Prussians appeared to be withdrawing in two columns, one on Wavre and the other on Perwez, and it added: "Perhaps it may be inferred that one portion is going to join Wellington, whilst the centre, under Blücher, retires on Liège; another column, accompanied by guns, has already retreated to Namur. This evening General Exelmans is pushing six squadrons of cavalry towards Sart-à-Walhain, and three to Perwez. When their reports are at hand, then if I find the mass of the Prussians is retiring on

---

[1] Mercer's *Journal*, vol. 1, pp. 270–274.
[2] Gourgaud, *Câmpagne de 1815*, p. 79. The leading French infantry were still several miles in rear.
[3] *Commentaires*, vol. v, p. 200.

Wavre I shall follow them, so as to prevent them gaining Brussels and to separate them from Wellington."[1]

Coupled with Milhaud's report, this dispatch should at once have been answered.[2] Yet it was not until 10 a.m. that a reply was sent off to inform Grouchy "that at this moment His Majesty is going to attack the English Army, which has taken up its position at Waterloo. His Majesty desires that you will head for Wavre in order to draw near to us, and to place yourself in touch with our operations and to keep up your communications with us, pushing before you those portions of the Prussian Army which have taken this direction, and which have halted at Wavre; this place you ought to reach as soon as possible."[3]

For a man of Grouchy's limited intelligence, it was a badly worded message. All that was necessary was: "Draw near to us and prevent the Prussians marching to Wellington's assistance", and had Soult accepted the responsibility of sending it out at 3 a.m., it would have reached Grouchy at Gembloux by 8 a.m. at latest. Even had Napoleon sent it out between 4 and 5 a.m., Grouchy would have received it when, as will be related, he was at Walhain. In which case, at most, only one Prussian corps could have come to Wellington's assistance.

At the identical hour that Grouchy's message was delivered at Imperial Headquarters, Wellington received an answer to his 10 a.m. message to Blücher. It informed him that, at daybreak June 18, Bülow's corps would march to his aid, immediately followed by Pirch's, and that the Ist and IIIrd Corps would hold themselves in readiness to follow Pirch. This was indeed more than Wellington had expected, and he at once determined to accept battle and await Bülow's arrival.

It is time now to return to Grouchy, who at 1 p.m. had received his orders to pursue Blücher. An hour later he set out, but advanced with such incredible slowness that he only reached Gembloux at nightfall. There he collected the information given in his 10 p.m. dispatch to the Emperor, and an hour later, when he learnt from his cavalry that the Prussians were marching on

---

[1] See Becke's *Napoleon and Waterloo*, vol. II, Appx. II, No. 28, p. 292.
[2] Gourgaud says that at 10 p.m. an officer was sent to inform Grouchy that a great battle, south of the Forest of Soignes, would be fought on the following day, and that, should the Prussians remain at Wavre, Grouchy was to move on St. Lambert and join the right of the French Army. Further, that when Grouchy's dispatch was received at 2 a.m., it was answered at 3 a.m., a duplicate of the 10 p.m. dispatch being sent. (*Campagne de 1815*, pp. 82–83.) Neither of these dispatches is traceable.
[3] See Becke's *Napoleon and Waterloo*, vol. II, Appx. II, No. 29, p. 293.

Wavre,[1] he jumped to the conclusion that they only intended to assemble there and then push on to Brussels. Next, instead of deciding to pursue them in flank, by way of Géry and Moustier on Wavre, he determined to follow up their rearguard by advancing on Sart-à-Walhain.[2] Worse, instead of moving off at dawn on June 18, he ordered Vandamme to march at 6 a.m. and Gérard at 8 a.m. Actually they moved off at eight and nine o'clock.

Grouchy left Gembloux between 8 and 9 a.m., and at 10 a.m. caught up with the head of the IIIrd Corps at Walhain. There he entered the house of the local notary, a M. Hollert, in order to write a note to the Emperor to inform him that it appeared that the Prussians intended to concentrate at Chyse, 10 miles south of Louvain, "to give battle to their pursuers, or finally to join hands with Wellington", and therefore, that he would mass his troops at Wavre in order to interpose them "between the Prussian Army and Wellington".[3]

He sent this message off, then sat down to breakfast, and at 11.30 a.m., when strolling with Gérard in the garden, the roar of cannon was heard in the direction of Mont St. Jean. At once Gérard exclaimed: "I think we ought to march on the cannon." This Grouchy refused to consider, as he believed it to be merely a rearguard affair. A violent altercation followed, in which finally Gérard urged that he and his corps be sent off alone. Grouchy would not hear of this, but said that he must obey the Emperor's orders, which from start to finish he utterly failed to understand.[4]

What was the Prussian position at the time? Bülow's van had reached Chapelle-St. Lambert, but the rear of his corps was so far behind that it did not close up until 3 p.m. Pirch was to start in half an hour, so was Ziethen, who was to advance on Ohain, and Thielemann's corps was in position at Wavre. Therefore, at 11.30 a.m. three-quarters of the Prussian army was still at, or near, Wavre. Consequently, had Grouchy acted on Gérard's suggestion and at noon set out for Moustier and Ottignies on the Dyle, both eight miles away, in spite of the bad roads, he would have reached them between 4 and 5 p.m. and have placed himself on Blücher's left flank and rear. Instead, in a single column he

---

[1] See Houssaye's *1815 Waterloo*, p. 164.
[2] Whether it was Sart-à-Walhain or Walhain is disputed. (See Houssaye's *1815 Waterloo*, pp. 396–398.)
[3] See Becke's *Napoleon and Waterloo*, vol. II, Appx. II, No. 32, p. 295.
[4] For this conversation, see Houssaye's *1815 Waterloo*, pp. 167–170.

continued his march by way of Corbaix on Wavre, and at 2 p.m. reached La Baraque–three and a half miles east of Moustier and Ottignies, where the bridges were still standing and unguarded. From La Baraque, or near by, the Prussians were seen marching toward the field of Waterloo, and, as Ropes points out, had Grouchy even then masked Thielemann at Wavre with his cavalry, he could have moved his two corps on the Dyle bridges, and had he done so "he would have certainly arrested the march of Bülow and Pirch", though not of Ziethen.[1] With such subordinates as Grouchy and Ney, Michael and all his angels would have lost the campaign.

Between 4 and 5 a.m. orders were issued by Soult for all troops to be in position to attack at 9 a.m. precisely,[2] but because of the rain, preparations were so much delayed that this was found to be impracticable. Between 7 and 8 a.m. the rain ceased, and when the Emperor sat down to breakfast, Soult, who since the evening before had been perturbed about Grouchy, suggested to Napoleon that at least part of Grouchy's command should at once be re-called. This advice was rudely brushed aside, and when Jérôme remarked that at supper the night before, the waiter who served him, and who had served Wellington that morning, informed him that one of the Duke's aides had spoken of a junction between the English and Prussians, the sole answer Napoleon vouchsafed was "nonsense!"[3] Nothing would shift the fixed ideas which possessed him, that after Ligny the Prussians were incapable of intervention, and that Wellington's polyglot army could be smashed by a single blow.

Breakfast at an end, the Emperor called for his horses, and with Drouot set out to examine the ground and the enemy. When thus engaged, Drouot, an experienced artillery officer, advised him to postpone the attack for two or three hours, because, he urged, the ground was as yet too wet for rapid artillery movements.[4] Napoleon, also an expert artillerist, agreed to this, and postponed the attack until 1 p.m. This, Houssaye states, was his most fateful blunder during the campaign, for had he not agreed, "the English army would have been routed before the arrival of the Prussians."[5]

[1] The Campaign of Waterloo, p. 261.
[2] See Becke's Napoleon and Waterloo, vol. II, Appx. II, No. 33, pp. 296–297.
[3] Houssaye, 1815 Waterloo, p. 180.
[4] Besides, it should be remembered that round-shot buried themselves in the soft ground instead of richochetting. (See The Diary of a Cavalry Officer, Lieut.-Col. Tomkinson (1895), pp. 297–298.)
[5] 1815 Waterloo, p. 288.

At 10 a.m., when at Rossomme Farm, Napoleon suddenly remembered Grouchy and instructed Soult to reply to his last dispatch, and a few minutes later, as if he half-consciously sensed danger from the east, he ordered Colonel Marbot to take up his position with the 7th Hussars at Frichermont, and send patrols to the bridges of Moustier and Ottignies,[1] apparently to get in touch with Grouchy and send back prompt notice of his approach. After this, when the troops were in their battle positions, Napoleon reviewed his army to frenzied shouts of "*Vive l'Empereur!*"

At 11 a.m. he dictated his very brief attack order,[2] and as his aim was the same as at Ligny—to break his enemy's centre and exploit the penetration—he instructed Ney at 1 p.m. or soon after, on the heels of an intense preliminary artillery bombardment, to advance d'Erlon's corps on the village of Mont St. Jean with Reille's abreast of it on its left flank. A few minutes after, to distract Wellington and cause him to weaken his centre by reinforcing his right, he ordered Reille immediately to send a division against Hougoumont to carry out a powerful demonstration. Meanwhile, a great battery of 80 guns was brought into position in front of, and to the right of, La Belle Alliance, to open fire at noon.[3]

Even for battles of this period, the field of Waterloo was restricted, for its depth from Mont St. Jean to Rossomme was no more than two and a quarter miles, and its extreme width from Braine l'Alleud to the Paris Wood—four miles. Roughly, it was cut into halves by the Charleroi-Brussels Road, and was flanked on the south by a low irregular ridge on both sides of La Belle Alliance, and on the north by another low ridge along which ran the Braine l'Alleud-Wavre Road. The two ridges were separated by a shallow valley, about 45 ft. lower than themselves.

Wellington's main line ran along the second of these ridges, three-quarters of a mile south of the village of Mont St. Jean, and extended for about a mile and a quarter east of the Brussels Road and for nearly a third of a mile west of it. On his left front, from four to eight hundred yards in advance of it, lay the hamlets of Smohain, La Haye and Papelotte; immediately south of his centre stood the farm of La Haye Sainte as well as an extensive

---

[1] *Mémoires* (*1799–1854*), le General Baron de Marbot (1891), vol. III, p. 403.

[2] *Correspondance*, No. 22060, vol. XXVIII, p. 392.

[3] Gourgaud, *Campagne de 1815*, p. 92. Kennedy (p. 107) says 74 guns about "600 yards from the Anglo-Allied position."

sandpit, and in advance of his right flank rose the Château of Hougoumont, surrounded by orchards and gardens. Facing Wellington, Napoleon's line ran from a point a mile and three-quarters south of Mont St. Jean on the Mont St. Jean-Nivelles Road across the southern face of Hougoumont to the Château of Frichermont, which faced Papelotte, La Haye and Smohain.

The general distribution of the two armies at 1 p.m. is shown on the diagram, and, according to Siborne,[1] Wellington's army numbered 49,608 infantry, 12,408 cavalry, and 5,645 artillery with 156 guns—67,661 men; and Napoleon's: 48,950 infantry, 15,765 cavalry, and 7,232 artillery with 246 guns—71,947 men. In part compensating Grouchy's detachment, Wellington, still fearful of being turned by way of the Mons-Brussels Road, left at Hal and Tubize 17,000 men and 30 guns under Prince Frederick of the Netherlands. When one considers that, on the morning before, the Duke had asked for the assistance of only one Prussian corps, to leave this strong detachment eight to nine miles away during the whole of June 18 was a blunder of the first magnitude. Without the assistance of Blücher, it might have saved the Anglo-Dutch Army by manœuvring against Napoleon's left flank, and even had it not rained in torrents, with it Wellington would surely have been strong enough to hold his own until Blücher arrived. As it was, these 17,000 men—one-fifth of his whole force—were utterly wasted, and, as Kennedy remarks, it would be "difficult to comprehend how any French force could have got to Tubize and Hal without its advance being previously known".[2]

At half-past eleven o'clock the French batteries opened fire, and Jérôme's division of Reille's Corps advanced against Hougoumont. But instead of restricting his attack to a demonstration, Jérôme at once got involved in an all-out attempt to occupy the *château*. This was the first tactical blunder of several made by the French; for it led to exactly the opposite result Napoleon had intended. Instead of drawing in the English, it drew in the French. Soon a brigade of Foy's division was sent forward to support Jérôme who, instead of destroying the solid buildings with howitzer fire, ordered attack after attack, until "the trees in advance of the *château* were cut to pieces by musketry".[3]

[1] *History of the War in France and Belgium in 1815*, vol. i, pp. 460–461.
[2] *Notes on the Battle of Waterloo*, p. 69.
[3] *The Diary of a Cavalry Officer in the Peninsular and Waterloo Campaigns*, Lieut.-Col. W. Tomkinson (1895), p. 318.

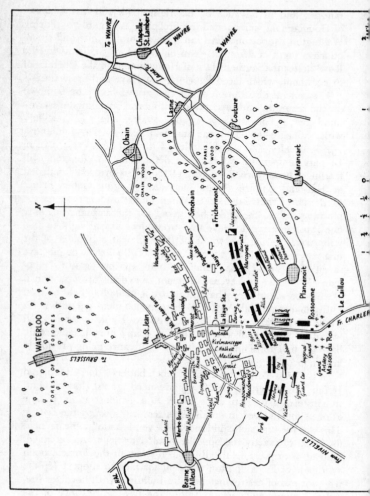

9. BATTLE OF WATERLOO, 1815

While this misplaced operation was in full swing, the Emperor busily prepared d'Erlon's assault on Wellington's centre, and close upon one o'clock, when all was ready, he glanced round the field and noticed in the distance, about four to five miles to the north-east, what looked like a "dark cloud" emerging from the woods of Chapelle-St. Lambert. At once all glasses were turned upon it. Soult said that he could plainly see troops, and at once it was thought that they must be Grouchy's. A moment later the mystery was solved, some of Marbot's Hussars appeared with a captured Prussian dispatch rider, and from his dispatch it was learnt that the "dark cloud" was Bülow's advanced guard.[1] Though this was somewhat of a shock for the Emperor's fixed idea, he was in no way perturbed: to him it was a complication and nothing more. Not for a moment did he doubt that he could ruin Wellington long before Bülow could arrive. Nevertheless the new danger had to be met, and to a letter he had just dictated in reply to one of Grouchy's, he bade Soult add the following postscript:

"A letter which has just been intercepted tells us that General Bülow is to attack our right flank. We believe we can perceive this corps on the heights of Chapelle-Saint Lambert. Therefore do not lose a minute to draw nearer to us and to join us and crush Bülow, whom you will catch in the very act."[2]

According to Gourgaud, the officer sent with this letter could deliver it in less than two hours. This was quite impossible, and the letter did not reach Grouchy until about five o'clock, when he was fully engaged at Wavre with Thielemann. Had the summons been sent early that morning, then Napoleon's complaisance would have been fully justified.

Next, the Emperor ordered the light cavalry divisions of Domont and Subervie to move toward Chapelle-St. Lambert, and under their cover he instructed Lobau to follow them with his corps and hold Bülow in check.[3] With these steps to secure his right flank taken, it was now about half-past one o'clock and he ordered Ney to attack.

In the French army since 1792, in order that the ground might rapidly be crossed without confusion, the approach phase of the attack usually was carried out in column formations. Next, when the enemy was neared, so that the maximum fire power might be

---

[1] *Campagne de 1815*, Gourgaud, p. 89.   [2] See Houssaye's *1815 Waterloo*, p. 192.
[3] *Campagne de 1815*, Gourgaud, p. 90.

developed, the columns deployed into line. To facilitate deployment, columns were usually of battalion strength at half or full deploying intervals: they were handy, favoured rapid deployment and, in the event of meeting cavalry, could quickly be formed into square. The attack was based on the following principles: (1) While the columns advanced, the artillery compelled the enemy to remain in line – that is, in the least vulnerable formation to case and round shot fire; (2) just before they deployed, the cavalry, by threatening the enemy, compelled him to form from line into squares – that is, not only in the securest formations in which to meet cavalry, but also in a very vulnerable one in which to meet infantry and artillery fire; (3) next, under cover of the cavalry, the columns deployed in order to bring to bear on the squares a heavier fire than the squares themselves could deliver, which was supplemented by case shot fire from the regimental guns; and (4) lastly, when once the squares were thrown into confusion, the assault with the bayonet was made, and the cavalry finished off the enemy by annihilating the fugitives.

In the present case, for some reason which has never been explained, three of d'Erlon's four attacking divisions, instead of being drawn up in battalion columns, advanced in divisional columns on a battalion frontage – that is, each battalion extended in three ranks,[1] one behind the other. As each of the three divisions which adopted this clumsy formation consisted of eight or nine battalions, each column had a frontage of some 200 men and was from 24 to 27 ranks deep. Not only did these heavy columns make rapid deployment impossible, but their size rendered them peculiarly vulnerable to the enemy's case and round shot fire.

Unfortunately for Ney and d'Erlon, they were faced by a general who understood the French tactics, and in part, at least, knew how to neutralize them. Instead of lining the ridge along which the Braine l'Alleud-Wavre Road ran, Wellington drew up the bulk of his forces in rear of it, where they were sheltered from the shot and shell of the enemy's great battery which, as it was composed of guns and not howitzers, could not search the rear slope. The result was that his men suffered little from the preliminary bombardment. All they had to do was to lie down in ranks behind the ridge, and when the enemy's columns approached its summit,

---

[1] The French maintained the old three ranks system, whereas under Wellington the English always deployed in two ranks, and thereby increased their fire power by one-third.

rise, advance a few paces and deliver a crashing volley on their heads before they could deploy. These tactics did not modify the problem of meeting cavalry, which remained that of forming into squares. Throughout the battle, as we shall see, it was the indifferent cooperation between the French cavalry and infantry, even more than the faulty column formation, that wrecked the French assaults.

These brief tactical comments should make clear why d'Erlon's assault failed. It was made in four columns in *échelon*, the left division (Donzelot) led on La Haye Sainte with Traver's brigade of cuirassiers on its left, while the right column (Durutte) advanced on Papelotte, and Allix's and Marcognet's were in between.[1] Papelotte was stormed without great difficulty, but Donzelot failed to take La Haye Sainte, which was most gallantly held by a battalion of the King's German Legion under Major Baring. Meanwhile, in the centre, Allix's and Marcognet's Divisions came under heavy fire as they climbed the ridge. They came up against Bylandt's Dutch-Belgian brigade, the only body of troops Wellington had deployed on the forward slopes of the ridge, and which, in consequence, had already suffered severely from French artillery fire, and drove it back in rout, and at about the same time the three companies of the 95th Rifles, who held the sandpit, found their position untenable and fell back, and the engagement became general. Meanwhile Wellington watched the attack from the post he had taken up at the foot of an old elm tree which stood at the junction of the Braine l'Alleud-Wavre and Charleroi-Brussels roads, while Napoleon at Rossomme was similarly engaged: to the latter and his staff it looked as if d'Erlon's success was certain.

Seldom has a mirage proved more illusory, for the faulty arrangement of d'Erlon's columns, which had already slowed down the approach, now led to disaster. They had become mere masses of men which, when they neared the top of the ridge, were incapable of deploying in any semblance of order, and, as they tried to do so, Picton brought his division (4,000 men) forward. Whereon, when it topped the ridge, Kempt's brigade, at 40 paces distance, poured a crashing volley into the advancing French, while Pack's rushed out from behind the hedge which skirted the Wavre Road and with bayonets fixed charged into the seething masses. A moment later, Picton was shot dead.

[1] Some accounts place Allix on the left and Donzelot next to him. (See Houssaye, pp. 194-195.)

The crisis was reached, and Uxbridge seized it. He launched Somerset's and Ponsonby's cavalry brigades into the battle.[1] First, they scattered Traver's brigade of cuirassiers, which had accompanied d'Erlon, and next they charged d'Erlon's disordered infantry and drove them pell-mell down the slope; they captured 3,000 prisoners and two eagles. Borne on by their horses, the English cavalry crossed the valley at full speed, passed through the French outposts and up the opposite slope. In vain Uxbridge sounded the retreat, but nothing could stop them. On they pressed, and were near the great battery when they were charged in flank by Martigue's lancers, and Ponsonby was killed. Next, Farine's brigade of cuirassiers was thrown in, and after they had left over a third of their number on the field, Somerset's and Ponsonby's brigades were driven back in complete disorder. Meanwhile the attack on Hougoumont continued to the steady exhaustion of Reille.

At 3 o'clock the battle died down, and though d'Erlon's attack had failed, Wellington's position was approaching a critical stage: Bylandt's brigade (some 4,000 men) was *hors de combat*, and because of Somerset's and Ponsonby's inconsiderate charge, 2,500 of Wellington's best horsemen had been lost to him. Everything depended on the arrival of Blücher, whose advance was painfully slow.

Napoleon's position was no less anxious, for he had just received Grouchy's 11.30 a.m. dispatch from Walhain, which must have made it clear to him that no help could be expected from that quarter. Though he might have saved his army by retiring,[2] it would have meant not only the loss of the campaign but a political upheaval; therefore he took advantage of Bülow's slowness, and decided to crush Wellington before the Prussians could come into line. At 3.30 p.m., by when d'Erlon had rallied some of his battalions, he ordered Ney to occupy La Haye Sainte, as he contemplated using it as the base from which to launch a grand assault with d'Erlon's and Reille's corps, followed by the bulk of the cavalry and the infantry of the Guard.

The cannonade was intensified, but because of the disorganized state of d'Erlon's corps and the difficulty Reille had in disengaging troops from before Hougoumont, Ney was only able to attack with

[1] See Kennedy's *Notes on the Battle of Waterloo*, pp. 110–111.
[2] It is probable that the moral state of his army prohibited a successful retreat. Further, retreats were not Napoleon's strong point. (See Caulaincourt's *Memoirs*, vol. 1, p. 601.)

two brigades. Though they were repulsed, he saw between the drifting clouds of smoke numbers of enemy ammunition wagons streaming to the rear–actually they were engaged upon carrying back wounded–and he jumped to the conclusion that his enemy was in retreat. He did not wait for the Emperor's authority to launch the cavalry, but ordered Milhaud and his two divisions forward. As they moved off, Lefebvre-Desnouettes, whose division was in rear of Milhaud, on his own initiative conformed with the movement. Thus some 5,000 horsemen were thrown into the fray *before* La Haye Sainte had been taken, and why Napoleon did not stop this unsound movement was because his attention was then riveted on his right flank. What was happening there?

Though Bülow had reached Chapelle-St. Lambert at one o'clock, it was not until four o'clock that the heads of his columns debouched from the Paris Wood. As they did so, they were checked by Domon's squadrons, which then fell back and un-masked Lobau's infantry. Though outnumbered by three to one, Lobau forthwith attacked the heads of Bülow's two leading divisions, and then fell back on Plancenoit. There, attacked on three sides, he was driven out of the village, and from it the Prussian batteries opened fire on the Brussels Road. Because the loss of Plancenoit threatened the French line of retreat, Napoleon ordered Duhesme to retake it with the Young Guard. This he did, Lobau with the VIth Corps extended to their left to link up with the right of the Ist Corps.

It was while the Emperor was thus occupied that Ney, "carried away by an excess of ardour",[1] between four and a quarter past four o'clock, had placed himself at the head of Milhaud's cuiras-siers and led them forward against Wellington, who had no thought of retiring, for his sole aim was to hold on to his position until the Prussians arrived. Though the allies expected that some time during the day a great cavalry attack would be made on them, to launch it against unbroken infantry came to them as a surprise.[2] At once the allied infantry formed squares and the gunners were ordered to remain in front with their pieces until the last moment, and then with their horses to seek refuge in the squares.

The French cavalry advanced, says Kennedy, "in lines of columns", and filled nearly the whole space between La Haye Sainte and Hougoumont.[3] They came on at a slow canter up the

[1] Gourgaud, *Campagne de 1815*, pp. 96–97.
[2] See Kennedy, *Notes on the Battle of Waterloo*, p. 114.   [3] *Ibid.*, p. 116.

slope, and as the supporting French batteries ceased firing the allied batteries opened, their pieces loaded with double-shotted charges.[1] The "Charge" was then sounded, and with cries of "*Vive l'Empereur!*" the 5,000 horsemen surged through the allied batteries. Though all were captured, no preparations had been made to render them ineffective. There were no horses at hand to drag the guns away and no spikes to render them useless. Nothing was done, and it did not even occur to a single officer to have the sponge-staves broken. Had the guns been spiked, which could have been done with headless nails and hammers, the next great cavalry assault would almost certainly have succeeded, for it was more from case and grape shot than from musketry that cavalry suffered in the attack.

Cuirassiers, chasseurs, and lancers charged the squares and surged round them, until the whole plateau was flooded with horsemen. Of this action, Frazer writes: ". . . the French cavalry made some of the boldest charges I ever saw: they sounded the whole extent of our line. . . . Never did cavalry behave so nobly, or was received by infantry so firmly."[2]

Uxbridge, who watched the mêlée, and still had in hand two-thirds of his cavalry fresh, suddenly hurled against the French Dörnberg's, Arenschild's, Brunsvick's, van Merlen's and Ghigny's brigades, in all some 5,000 horsemen. As they swept the French back, the allied gunners rushed out from the squares, manned their pieces and poured grape and case shot into the retiring enemy. Undaunted, at the bottom of the slope, Milhaud and Lefebvre-Desnouettes re-formed their squadrons, and again cantered up the slope, only to be volleyed upon by the allied batteries and again driven back.

Though, at Rossomme, those with the Emperor were elated by what they saw, Napoleon was far from being so. Impatiently he turned to Soult and exclaimed: "This is a premature movement, which may well lead to fatal results." Soult replied: "He [Ney] is compromising us as he did at Jena."[3] Nevertheless, in spite of its prematurity, afraid that the repulse of his cavalry might unnerve the army and lead to panic, Napoleon sent General Flahaut to Kellermann to order him to support Ney. Kellermann, who also considered the action premature, expostulated, but while he did so General L'Heritier, who commanded his 1st

---

[1] A round shot with case over it.   [2] Frazer's *Letters*, p. 547.
[3] Gourgaud, *Campagne de 1815*, p. 97.

Division, without awaiting orders set off at a trot; whereon Kellermann followed with Roussel's 2nd Division. Next, Guyot, like Lefebvre-Desnouettes, either without orders or on a wrongly given one, with his division of Guard Cavalry, followed Kellermann. This was a fatal move, for not only did it deprive the Emperor of his last cavalry reserve, but it so completely overcrowded the field with horsemen that to manœuvre became impossible. No wonder, as Kennedy remarks, the allies were amazed to see some 12,000 horsemen[1] massing for an attack on the 1,000 yards frontage between Hougoumont and La Haye Sainte, of which "these horsemen could advance on a front of only 500 yards, as they were obliged to keep at some distance from the enclosures of both Hougoumont and La Haye Sainte".[2]

The advance of Kellermann and Guyot, followed by the now exhausted horsemen of Milhaud, took place at 5.30 p.m., and was unsupported by infantry and badly supported by artillery, for only one battery was brought up in rear of the horsemen to breach the allied squares. Undoubtedly, the heavy, churned-up ground made artillery movement difficult; nevertheless, had but two or three horse artillery batteries been advanced to within case-shot range, nothing could have saved Wellington's army.

Although the second grand assault met with the fate of the first, the stresses and strains it set up in the allied line were severe, and by now Wellington had used up most of his cavalry and most of his infantry reserves. What would he not have given to have in hand the 17,000 men he had left at Hal and Tubize?

But Ney could not take advantage of his enemy's critical situation because the whole of his tactics was at fault—instead of combining his arms, he used them separately. Had he, as he had been ordered, first occupied La Haye Sainte, and next established his batteries in advance of it, he could have riddled his enemy's squares. Further, had he supported his cavalry with infantry, success would have been assured to him. As it was, one French battery, writes Mercer, "established itself on a knoll somewhat higher than the ground we stood on, and only about 400 to 500 yards a little in advance of our left flank. The rapidity and precision of this fire was quite appalling. Every shot took effect, and I certainly expected we should be annihilated . . . the whole livelong day had cost us nothing like this."[3]

[1] Actually 9,000 to 10,000. [2] Kennedy, *Notes on the Battle of Waterloo*, p. 118.
[3] Mercer's *Journal*, vol. I, pp. 325–326.

Ney had not only forgotten his objective – La Haye Sainte – but also his infantry, and only after Kellermann's fourth charge did he think of using his 6,000 bayonets. At 6 p.m. he advanced Foy's and Bachelu's divisions of Reille's corps, but unsupported by cavalry, they were met, as Foy describes it, by such a "hail of death" that in a few minutes they lost some 1,500 men and were repulsed.

When this attack took place, Napoleon rode along the entire battle front to steady his men, and at the same time he sent an order to Ney to take La Haye Sainte whatever it might cost. This Ney did with part of Donzelot's division; he succeeded very largely because Baring's detachment ran out of ammunition. The sandpit was also lost by the allies.

This time Ney made immediate use of his success; he brought a battery into action near La Haye Sainte and within 300 yards of the allied position, and pushed forward the remnants of Allix's, Donzelot's and Marcognet's divisions and gained a footing on the Wavre Road. But by then his men were too exhausted to advance farther, and in order to support them he sent Colonel Heymès to the Emperor to ask for reinforcements.

"Troops!" cried Napoleon, "Where do you expect me to get them? Do you expect me to make them?"[1] But Ney was right, the decisive moment, which faulty tactics had so long delayed, had been reached. Napoleon, though hard pressed, was not altogether lacking reserves, but apparently he did not realize how desperately critical Wellington's position then was.

In regard to this, Kennedy writes:

"La Haye Sainte was in the hands of the enemy. . . . Ompteda's brigade was nearly annihilated, and Kielmansegge's so thinned, that those two brigades could not hold their position. That part of the field of battle, therefore, which was between Halkett's left and Kempt's right, was unprotected; and being the very centre of the Duke's line of battle, was consequently that point, above all others, which the enemy wished to gain. The danger was imminent; and at no other period of the action was the result so precarious as at this moment. Most fortunately Napoleon did not support the advantage his troops had gained at this point, by bringing forward his reserve. . . .

"Of such gravity did Wellington consider this great gap in the very centre of his line of battle, that he not only ordered the

[1] *Documents Inédits*, duc d'Elchingen, p. 18.

Brunswick troops there, but put himself at their head, and it was even then with the greatest difficulty that the ground could be held. . . .

"In no other part of the action was the Duke of Wellington exposed to so much personal risk as on this occasion . . . at no other period of the day were his great qualities as a commander so strongly brought out, for it was the moment of his greatest peril as to the result of the action. . . ."[1]

Napoleon still had in hand eight battalions of the Old Guard and six of the Middle, and had he sent to Ney but half this force, Wellington's centre must inevitably have been overwhelmed; for all it needed was the appearance of a comparatively small force of fresh troops to throw the allies into a panic. But Napoleon's situation was then as critical as Wellington's. The Young Guard had been thrown out of Plancenoit, and overpowered on his right flank, the Emperor was now threatened by an eruption on his rear. Instead of reinforcing Ney, he formed 11 battalions of the Guard into as many squares, and posted them facing Plancenoit from La Belle Alliance to Rossomme; one battalion he kept at Le Caillou, and two he sent under Morand and Pelet to retake Plancenoit.

With drums beating the 1st Battalion of the 2nd Grenadiers and the 1st Battalion of the 2nd Chasseurs advanced on the village, and without deigning to fire a shot, with bayonets fixed, in 20 minutes they swept the Prussians out of it; after which the Young Guard reoccupied Plancenoit.

It was now past seven o'clock, and with Plancenoit again in French hands Napoleon decided to support Ney and strike his final blow before the sun set. He ordered Drouot to bring forward eight battalions[2] of the Guard under Friant, and on their arrival he placed himself at their head, led them forward in advance of La Belle Alliance, and handed them over to Marshal Ney. At the same time he ordered the batteries to intensify their fire, sent instructions to Reille and d'Erlon as well as to the cavalry to support Ney's assault, and, in order to restore his troops' morale,

---

[1] *Notes on the Battle of Waterloo*, pp. 127–129.

[2] There has been much controversy over the number of battalions actually employed. Ropes (pp. 316–317) favours eight or six, and Houssaye (pp. 223 and 428) – five. Napoleon (*Correspondance*, vol. XXXI, p. 198) says that Friant had four battalions, and Gourgaud (pp. 101–102) says four battalions of the Middle Guard. Ney, who is not likely to have exaggerated the number, in his letter of June 26 to the Duke of Otranto (Fouché) says "four regiments of the Middle Guard" – that is, eight battalions. (See Becke, vol. II, pp. 301–306.)

sent General de la Bédoyère down the front to announce the arrival of Grouchy, whose guns could be heard thundering in the distance. As the Guard formed up under cover of dense clouds of smoke, a cavalry officer deserted to the enemy, and through him Wellington learnt what was in progress.[1]

Actually, the decisive moment had passed, for since Heymès had begged reinforcements of the Emperor, Donzelot's, Allix's and Marcognet's men had been pushed off the plateau, and Wellington, who had regained his former position and who knew that Ziethen's advanced guard had reached Ohain at six o'clock, drew Vandeleur's and Vivian's cavalry brigades from his left to his centre and brought up Chassé's 3rd Dutch Belgian Division from Braine l'Alleud in rear of Maitland's Guards Brigade and Adam's Light Brigade, which, on Wellington's right centre, sheltered behind the banks of the Wavre Road, west of the sand-pit.

Though accounts differ, it would appear that the Guard was marshalled in one column with its battalions formed in close column of grand divisions – that is, on a frontage of two companies, each in the usual three ranks. Because each battalion numbered about 500 men and had four companies, the frontage of the column was 75 to 80 men; the battalions were accompanied by two batteries of horse artillery of six pieces each, which fired as the infantry advanced.

Instead of marching up the Brussels Road, the embankments of which would to some extent have sheltered his men from fire, Ney moved diagonally over the slope between Hougoumont and La Haye Sainte towards his enemy's right centre. The attack was, however, carried out not in one column but in two,[2] and though the reasons for this are obscure, it would seem that either, because the start was hurried,[3] the leading four battalions (grenadiers of the Old Guard) advanced ahead of the four in rear (chasseurs of the Middle Guard), or – as frequently happens – the head of the column stepped out more rapidly than the rear and got ahead of it, with the result that the column broke into two columns, and the rear one inclined to the left rear of the forward one.[4] This is borne

---

[1] Frazer's *Letters*, p. 552.
[2] Possibly three, see *Waterloo Letters*, No. 128, p. 302.
[3] The sun was sinking.
[4] It must be remembered that, in the days of black powder, smoke was frequently so dense that soldiers could not see clearly for more than a few yards. In these circumstances it would be easy for the rear half to diverge from the forward one.

out by General Maitland who says: "As the attacking force moved forward it separated, the Chasseurs inclined to their left. The Grenadiers ascended the acclivity towards our position in a more direct course, leaving La Haye Sainte on their right, and moving towards that part of the eminence occupied by the 1st Brigade of Guards."[1]

As is common in nearly all eyewitnesses' descriptions, they vary in accordance with the position of the observer, and when pieced together, as Houssaye has done, detail is apt to obscure the decisive moments. There were two; the destruction of the leading column by Maitland's Guards and of the rear column by Adam's Light Brigade. As regards the first, Captain Powell of the 1st Foot Guards says that before the assault the English Guards sheltered themselves during the cannonade in the ditch and behind the bank along the Wavre Road, and "without the protection of this bank every creature must have perished".[2] Next, he continues:

". . . suddenly the firing ceased, and as the smoke cleared away a superb sight opened on us. A close column of Grenadiers (about seventy in front) . . . were seen ascending the rise *au pas de charge* shouting '*Vive l'Empereur!*' They continued to advance till within fifty or sixty paces of our front, when the Brigade were ordered to stand up. Whether it was from the sudden and unexpected appearance of a Corps so near them, which must have seemed as starting out of the ground, or the tremendous heavy fire we threw into them, *La Garde*, who had never before failed in an attack, *suddenly* stopped."[3]

Maitland's account reads:

"The Brigade suffered by the Enemy's Artillery, but it withheld its fire for the nearer approach of the Column. The latter, after advancing steadily up the slope, halted about twenty paces from the front rank of the Brigade.

"The diminished range of the Enemy's Artillery was now felt most severely in our ranks; the men fell in great numbers before the discharges of grape shot, and the fire of the musketry distributed among the Guns.

"The smoke of the Artillery happily did not envelop the hostile Column, or serve to conceal it from our aim.

---

[1] *Waterloo Letters*, No. 105, p. 244.
[2] In spite of the assault being carried out with eight battalions of Guard, instead of the normal 24, Wellington's position was nevertheless critical. Frazer says of it, "this last struggle was nearly fatal to us". (*Letters*, p. 552.)
[3] *Waterloo Letters*, No. 109, pp. 254–255.

"With what view the Enemy halted in a situation so perilous, and in a position so comparatively helpless, he was not given time to evince.

"The fire of the Brigade opened with terrible effect.

"The Enemy's Column, crippled and broken, retreated with the utmost rapidity, leaving only a heap of dead and dying men to mark the ground which it had occupied."[1]

Had the Grenadiers of the Guard been supported by cavalry it is highly probable that Maitland would have been overwhelmed, for then he would have had to form into squares and his brigade would have been badly mauled by the French horse artillery and musketry.

Meanwhile, in rear and probably obscured by the smoke, the chasseurs of the Middle Guard moved on and came up on the right of Maitland's brigade, some 10 to 15 minutes after the grenadiers were repulsed, to find Adam's Light Brigade deployed on their left front. As they neared the top of the ridge, Colonel Sir John Colborne (later Lord Seaton), ordered his regiment, the 52nd, supported by the 95th, to wheel to the left. This change of front placed it "nearly parallel with the moving Column of the French Imperial Guards". Next, he ordered forward one company in extended order to fire into the column; whereon the column halted, "formed a line facing towards the 52nd", opened fire and caused many casualties in the extended company. At this moment the Duke rode up and ordered Colborne to press forward up a slight rise toward the chasseurs. "At the time," writes Colborne, "the 71st formed on our right flank, and I ordered the bugles to sound the advance, and the whole line charged up the hill; and on our arriving at the edge of the deep road, the opposite side of which the Imperial Guards had occupied, the 52nd fired, at least most of the Companies. . . ."[2]

Next, according to the account given by Lieutenant ·Gawler of the 52nd:

"The enemy was pressing on with shouts, which rose above the noise of the firing, and his fire was so intense that, with but half the ordinary length of front, *at least* 150 of the 52nd fell in less than four minutes. . . . When the 52nd was nearly parallel to the Enemy's flank, Sir J. Colborne gave the word, 'Charge', 'charge'. It was answered from the Regiment by a loud steady cheer and a hurried dash to the front. In the next ten seconds the Imperial

[1] *Waterloo Letters*, No. 105, pp. 244-245.   [2] *Ibid.*, No. 123, pp. 284-286.

Guard, broken into the wildest confusion, and scarcely firing a shot to cover its retreat, was rushing towards the hollow road in the rear of La Haye Sainte, near to which, according to La Coste's account, Napoleon himself was then standing."[1]

Again, as with the grenadiers, had the chasseurs been supported with cavalry, Adam would have had to throw his brigade into squares, and in consequence this famous counter-attack would never have taken place. It was lack of cavalry, and more particularly Guyot's heavy cavalry of the Guard, that deprived Napoleon of his last chance of victory.

When the final French attack was under way, Ziethen had at last come up on Wellington's left flank to link it to Bülow's corps near Frichermont, and when the two columns of the Guard were repulsed, his troops drove Durutte's and Marcognet's divisions out of La Haye and Papelotte. Lobau then fell back toward Plancenoit, and Wellington, watching his enemy's rapidly increasing confusion, decided to finish the day. He spurred his horse forward to the edge of the plateau, took off his hat and waved it in the air. At once this signal was understood, and a general advance from the left to the right began; 40,000 men gradually poured down the slope with Vivian's hussars and Vandeleur's dragoons in the van.

"I have seen nothing like that moment," writes Frazer, "the sky literally darkened with smoke, the sun just going down, and which till then had not for some hours broken through the gloom of the day, the indescribable shouts of thousands, where it was impossible to distinguish between friend and foe. Every man's arm seemed to be raised against that of every other. Suddenly, after the mingled mass had ebbed and flowed, the enemy began to yield; and cheerings and English huzzas announced that the day must be ours."[2]

Meanwhile, Napoleon, near La Haye Sainte, formed up such troops as he could in order to support the Guard, when suddenly he saw the whole French front give way. At once he formed the shattered and retreating column of the Old Guard into three squares with its right on the Brussels Road, from where it fell back before the advance of Adam's Light Brigade. As Colborne and the 52nd came up, "the Duke of Wellington rode forward", writes Kennedy, "and ordered Colborne to attack them [the squares], remarking that they would not stand. Colborne then

---

[1] *Waterloo Letters*, No. 124, p. 293. [2] *Letters*, p. 553.

advanced ... routed and dispersed them",[1] and the survivors joined in with the fugitives who poured down the Charleroi Road.

To the south, near de Coster's house, the two battalions of the 1st Grenadiers of the Guard, *élite* of the *élite*, under General Petit, had formed squares, and in that of the 1st Battalion the Emperor sought refuge. Slowly they fell back on each side of the road, and from time to time halted to arrest their pursuers. During one of these halts the Emperor pushed on to Le Caillou, and from there with the 1st Battalion of the 1st Chasseurs he took the road to Charleroi.

At a little after nine o'clock, when the 1st Grenadiers were still close by de Coster's house, Blücher met Wellington at or near La Belle Alliance, and after they had greeted each other it was decided that the Prussians should take over the pursuit.

In spite of the darkness of night, the pursuit was pressed with the utmost vigour, and at Genappe, as at Lindenau in 1813, dammed by the single narrow bridge over the Dyle, the French retreat piled up into a struggling confusion of men, horses, guns and vehicles.

From Genappe, with Soult, Drouot, and Bertrand, Napoleon pushed on to Quatre-Bras, which he reached toward one o'clock on the morning of June 19. He halted for a short spell, and instructed Soult to send a message to Grouchy to fall back on the Sambre. This the latter did most skilfully and carried his army to Givet. Had he during his advance displayed a fraction of the resolution he showed in his retreat, the outcome of the campaign would have been very different.

The Emperor pressed on from Quatre-Bras and reached Charleroi at five o'clock, and Philippeville at nine. There he wrote his last Bulletin,[2] a most revealing document which describes the events of June 16, 17 and 18, and next rode on to Laon where he spent the night. On June 20 he left Laon and the following day was in Paris. Urged by his brother Lucien to collect the few remaining troops in the capital and disperse the Chamber, he refused to do so. He knew that his star had set and the idea of precipitating a civil war was hateful to him: never had he been a leader of the rabble. The next day he abdicated in favour of his son, the King of Rome, and on June 25 retired to Malmaison.

Meanwhile Blücher's army pressed on and ravaged the country

[1] *Notes*, p. 145.   [2] *Correspondance*, No. 22061, vol. XXVIII, pp. 293–299.

it passed through. On July 3 it marched into Versailles, Wellington's followed more leisurely in rear, and on July 7 together the allied armies triumphantly entered Paris. Louis XVIII followed on July 8 with their baggage trains.

The casualties of this memorable battle were heavy. "The face of the hill near La Haye Sainte and from thence to Hougoumont", writes Tomkinson on the morning of June 19, "has more the appearance of a breach carried by assault than an extended field of battle",[1] and Kincaid says that "the 27th Regiment (Inniskillings) were lying literally dead in square".[2] The total losses in killed and wounded, so far as can be estimated, for those of the French are only approximately known, were: Wellington's Army, 15,100; Blücher's 7,000; and Napoleon's 25,000, to which must be added some 8,000 captured and 220 guns.[3]

These figures speak for themselves, and Wellington was never under any illusion how close defeat had been, and in spite of Ney's inept tactics. On the night of the battle he said to Lord Fitzroy: "I have never fought such a battle, and I trust I shall never fight such another",[4] and to his brother he wrote: "In all my life I have not experienced such anxiety, for I must confess I have never before been so close to defeat."[5]

Had Napoleon won, and it is as startling as it is ironical that, in spite of his mistakes and those of his Marshals, a few pounds weight of nails and two dozen hammers would have cancelled out one and all, it is almost certain that the Seventh Coalition would have collapsed. Nevertheless it is equally probable that an eighth and possibly a ninth would have followed, and that in the end France would have been overwhelmed.

Though the allied triumph at Leipzig was the strategical climax of the long war, because it left France too exhausted to achieve ultimate victory, Waterloo, its epilogue, was a battle of profound economic and political significance. Where the one led to the triumph of European nationalism over French militarism and hegemony, the other resulted in the triumph of the English System—as Napoleon called it—not only over France, but over Europe and most of the world. For England, Waterloo was the copestone of Trafalgar: the latter assured her command of the sea, the former opened to her the markets of the world. For two

[1] *The Diary of a Cavalry Officer*, p. 317.
[2] *Adventures in the Rifle Brigade* (1909 edit.), p. 170.
[3] Becke's *Napoleon and Waterloo*, vol. II, pp. 134–135.
[4] Frazer's *Letters*, p. 560.   [5] Quoted from Becke, vol. II, p. 136.

generations and more she was to be the world's workshop and banker.

The Second Treaty of Paris, signed on November 20, 1815, redrew the map of Europe. It left France virtually as she had been in 1792, and strong enough to play a part in maintaining the balance of European power, which was essential to England's security. It pushed Prussia westward as a counter-poise to France; but by allotting Finland, and, above all, the greater part of Poland to Russia, like a wedge it thrust Muscovite power between Prussia and Austria–the eastern European bastions which faced "the barbarians of the North". Further, in order to fill the gap created by the dissolution of the Holy Roman Empire, it established a Germanic confederation of 38 sovereign States, and by doing so prepared the future for Sadowa and Sedan.

As her share of the spoils, England gained Malta, the Cape of Good Hope, Mauritius, and Ceylon. But of even greater importance than these, the war left her mistress absolute of the oceans and the seas. "So impressive was the aggrandizement of England beyond the seas," writes Professor H. A. L. Fisher, "that some writers have regarded the augmentation of the British Empire as the most important result of Napoleon's career."[1]

Out of sea power, steam power, money power and the prestige with which Waterloo had crowned England, emerged the *Pax Britannica*, which was destined to survive as long as British sea power and British credit retained their dominance. Actually they did so for a hundred years and controlled extra-European events and localized European wars. During this century, though revolutions were frequent and at times violent, Europe enjoyed the most stable and prosperous peace she had known since the days of the Antonines.

Quoted in Vol. I, Chronicle 8, was the panegyric of the Greek Sophist Aelius Aristides, addressed by him to the Emperor Marcus Aurelius, in which he sang the praises of the *Pax Romana*. Forty-five years after Waterloo, when the *Pax Britannica* had reached its zenith, Mr. Horsman, member for Stroud, in the House of Commons, gave voice to it in the following words:

"We seem to forget that there are great moral as well as material considerations involved in our security . . . the safety of England, in the estimation of every reflecting person in Europe, is the preservation of all that is valuable to the peace and progress of man-

[1] *The Cambridge Modern History*, vol. IX, p. 770.

kind . . . the security of England means the security of the only moderating and tranquillizing Power that exists in Europe. They (foreigners) know that if England should vanish out of existence the whole of the continent of Europe would probably pass under the domination of despotism. If England fell, how long would the nationality of Belgium endure? How long would the independence of Germany remain? How long would Italian unity be anything but a dream? No: the moral influence of England abroad is irresistible in exact proportion to her impregnability at home. Our greatness does not consist merely in our wealth, our commerce, our institutions, our military renown, but in those tributary elements that constitute a gigantic moral force, of which freedom is the animating principle and peace the holy mission. There is not a friend to freedom of thought who does not turn to England as its supporter. . . . Every man who is the friend of his species, looks upon England as the great depository of political truth, her safety as their pride, and the peril of England as their despair. With such considerations, while I value the safety of England as regards the security of our coasts, I value it also for the responsibilities and duties imposed upon us in our relations to humanity at large."[1]

Yet, when these memorable words were spoken, in Europe, in North America and in Asia, rumblings were to be heard of changes to come, which, in a little over half a century, were to put an end to the *Pax Britannica* and blast the entire world with war.

[1] *Parliamentary Debates (Hansard)*, vol. 160, 3rd series, col. 566, for August 2, 1860.

The industrial revolution

While the French Revolutionary and Napoleonic wars ploughed up the remnants of European feudalism, the greatest revolution the world had so far seen sowed the seeds of a new dispensation – a way of life based on coal, steam and machinery. After the outburst of nationalism awakened by the American and French Revolutions, in the century subsequent to Waterloo Cyclopean forces were unleashed which were to change the face of the world and to raise war from the cockpit of gladiatorial armies to the grand amphitheatre of contending continents. Even as early as 1825 – that is, only 10 years after Napoleon's final defeat – we find Stendhal in his *Racine et Shakespeare* writing: "What a change from 1785 to 1824! In the two thousand years of recorded world history, so sharp a revolution in customs, ideas and beliefs has perhaps never occurred before."

Before Stendhal's 1785, the Industrial Revolution, so far as it was fostered by steam power, had been nearly a century in gestation. It may be said to have been begotten by Thomas Savery's steam pumping engine of 1698, and Thomas Newcomen's atmospheric engine of 1705. But it was not until 1769 – the birth year of Napoleon and Wellington – that James Watt, a Glasgow instrument maker, matured the steam pumping engine, and in 1782 invented the double-acting engine. Also in 1769 Cugnot, in France, built and drove the first steam-propelled road carriage, and in 1785 came Edmund Cartwright's power-loom, and with this invention we reach Stendhal's initial date.

From 1785, because of the development of steam power and the introduction of the "puddling" process in the manufacture of bar iron, England strode ahead, and during the Napoleonic wars established a virtual monopoly of industrial manufactures. Admiral Lord Cochrane (later tenth Earl of Dundonald) on June 2, 1818, pointed out in the House of Commons that England would have been brought "to total ruin", but "for the timely intervention of the use of machinery."

As the discovery that gunpowder could be used as a propellant had led to an outburst of inventiveness which changed the technics of war, so did the use of steam power as a source of energy revolutionize armies; it made possible their movements and supply by steamship and railway. Further, it enabled vast improvements in armaments to be made, as well as their mass production.

The two outstanding military inventions of the first half of the nineteenth century were the percussion cap and the cylindro-conoidal bullet. The first was made possible by the discovery of fulminate of mercury in 1800. Seven years later the Rev. A. Forsyth patented a percussion powder for priming, and in 1816 Thomas Shaw, of Philadelphia, invented the copper percussion cap. The next improvement came in 1823, when Captain Norton, of the British 34th Regiment, designed a cylindro-conoidal bullet with a hollow base, so that when fired it would automatically expand and seal the bore. Though rejected by the British Government it was later taken up in France, and in 1849 M. Minié designed the Minié bullet which was adopted by the British Army, and rifles of the Minié pattern were issued to it in 1851. These two inventions revolutionized infantry tactics. The former made the musket serviceable in all weathers, and vastly reduced misfires; the latter made the rifle the most deadly weapon of the century.

The percussion cap made possible the expansive cartridge case, which in its turn rendered practicable the breech-loading system. This case revolutionized gunnery by preventing the escape of gases at the breech. First came the pin-fire cartridge in 1847; next the rim-fire, and lastly, in 1861, the central-fire cartridge. While other nations argued over the merits and demerits of flint and percussion lock muzzle-loaders, in 1841 Prussia took a bold step and issued to certain regiments the Dreyse breech-loading rifle, better known as the needle gun, a bolt-operated weapon firing a paper cartridge. Though, because of escape of gas at the breech, its effective range was considerably less than that of the Minié rifle, seven shots a minute could be fired with it instead of a maximum of two. But its main advantage was not its rapidity of loading; it was that a breech-operated rifle can easily be loaded in the prone position – that is, when the rifleman is lying down.

The development of artillery was slower, for although breech-loading and rifled cannon had long been known, it was not until 1845 that these two characteristics were combined in an effective breech-loading rifled cannon. But its cost was so great that no country would face its adoption until the outbreak of war in the Crimea, when some cast-iron muzzle-loading smooth-bore 68-pdrs. and 8-in. guns were converted into rifled pieces. Their greater range and accuracy made the bombardment of Sebastopol "a very hideous thing", and after the war all the Powers began to experiment with breech-loading rifled ordnance.

Another weapon which was developed at the opening of the nineteenth century was the war rocket, actually the oldest of all explosively propelled projectiles. For centuries it had been extensively used in Asia as an anti-cavalry weapon, and it was the rocket employed by Tipu Sultan at the siege of Seringapatam in 1799 that gave Colonel Sir William Congreve, an inventor of note, the idea of improving upon it. He informs us that he made rockets weighing from two ounces – "a species of self-moving musket-balls" – to three hundredweight. In 1806 his rocket was successfully tested in an attack on Boulogne, and he predicted: "The rocket is, in truth, an arm by which the whole system of military tactics is destined to be changed"; a prophecy which was to be fulfilled in the Second World War.

While these changes were under way, steam propulsion in the form of the marine engine and the locomotive laid the foundations of a totally new type of warship and opened to armies the possibility of adding vastly to their size. Although the paddle-wheel dated from Roman times and was the most obvious mechanical means for water propulsion, one of the earliest types of steamboat, constructed by James Rumsey, a Virginian, in 1775, was driven by water-jet propulsion: a steam pump sucked in water at her bow and ejected it at her stern. But he and other early steamboat designers were eclipsed by a young American, Robert Fulton, a man of extraordinary inventive genius. In 1797 he submitted to the Directory the plans of a "plunging boat" called the *Nautilus*, and tests with this early submarine[1] were carried out in Brest harbour in 1801, when she remained under water for about an hour. In 1803, Fulton experimented with a steamboat[2] on the Seine, the value of which was appreciated by Bonaparte. On July 21, 1804, he wrote that the project of moving ships by steam "is

[1] In 1776 David Bushnell invented a turtle-shaped submarine in which, during the American War of Independence, he dived beneath the British warship *Eagle* and tried to screw a "torpedo" into her bottom. Through an error of judgment he failed.
[2] The first practical steamboat was the *Charlotte Dundas*, tried out in the Forth in 1802. The first to cross the Atlantic was the American built *Savannah* in 1819.

one that may change the face of the world. . . . A great truth, a physical, palpable truth, is before my eyes."

Fulton returned to America in 1807 and built an improved steamship, the *Clermont*, which travelled the 150 miles from New York to Albany, in under 32 hours. Earlier he had invented a torpedo, which was tried by Lord Keith against the French flotilla outside Boulogne in September, 1804, and in 1813 he built the first steam-driven warship, the *Demologos* (later renamed the *Fulton*). She was of twin-hull construction with a central paddle-wheel between the hulls, and was protected by a belt of timber 58 in. thick. This monstrous vessel clearly showed that two things were required: a less vulnerable system of propulsion than the paddle-wheel and a less clumsy means of protection.

The first problem was solved by the introduction of the screw propeller, patented by Captain John Ericsson, of the Swedish army, in 1836, and the second by the substitution of iron for wooden armour, first proposed by Congreve in 1805. But it was not until the war in the Crimea that the Emperor Louis Napoleon ordered the construction of a flotilla of floating armoured batteries which could resist solid shot and explosive shell. Five were built, protected by 4 in. iron plate. They mounted 56-pdr. shell guns and were equipped with auxiliary steam machinery. Their success was complete. Not only was the need to armour ships proved beyond all doubt, but also that armour would necessitate the introduction of more powerful ordnance. This, by degrees, led to the general adoption of rifled ship cannon.

Soon after the Crimean war, France and Great Britain laid down the first two armoured steam warships, *La Gloire* and the *Warrior*. The latter was 380 ft. in length, of 8,830 tons displacement, her engines developed 6,000 initial h.p. and her speed was $14\frac{1}{2}$ knots. Her armament consisted of 28 7-in. guns, and her armour belt was $4\frac{1}{2}$ in. thick.

When we turn from sea to land, we find that the first practicable locomotive was designed by Richard Trevithick in England in 1801, and the first true railway was built by George Stephenson between Stockton and Darlington in 1825. Although the locomotive was wholly of British origin, it is no coincidence that the nation which produced Clausewitz was the first to grasp the supreme importance of the railway in war. Thus, in 1833, F. W. Harkort pointed out that a railway between Cologne and Minden and another between Mainz and Wesel would add enormously to the defence of the Rhineland, and C. E. Pönitz urged the general building of railways to protect Prussia against France, Austria, and Russia. Simultaneously, Friedrich List, an economist of unique genius, pointed out that from the position of a secondary military Power, whose weakness was that she was centrally placed between powerful potential enemies, Prussia could be raised by the railway into a formidable State. "She could be made into a defensive bastion in the very heart of Europe. Speed of mobilization, the rapidity with which troops could be moved from the centre of the country to its periphery, and the other obvious advantages of 'interior lines' of rail transport would be of greater relative advantage to Germany than to any other European country."

In 1833, before a single rail had been laid, this remarkable man projected a network of railways for Germany which is substantially that of to-day, and 13 years later, the year of his death, the first extensive troop movement by rail was made by a Prussian army corps 12,000 strong with horses and guns to Cracow. After this experiment the Prussian General Staff made a comprehensive survey of the military value of railways. Although during the revolutionary troubles of 1848–1850 Prussia gained further experience in rail movements, as also did Austria and Russia, it was not until the Franco-Italian War of 1859 that troop movements by rail may be said to have become fully established. Thus it came about that the genius of George Stephenson gave life to the Clausewitzian theory of the nation in arms, for without the railway the mass-armies of the second half of the nineteenth century could not have been supplied.

When Jomini[1] reviewed these changes, so far as they had advanced by 1836, he was of opinion that war would become "a bloody and most unreasonable struggle between great masses equipped with the weapons of unimaginable power. We might see again wars of peoples like those of the fourth century; we might be forced to live again through the centuries of the Huns, the Vandals and the Tartars." Further, he pointed out that unless governments combined to proscribe inventions of destruction, infantry would be obliged "to resume its armour of the Middle Ages, without which a battalion will be destroyed before engaging the enemy. We may then see again the famous men-at-arms all

---

[1] Baron Henri Jomini, Swiss military writer. Served under Napoleon as colonel and was aide to Marshal Ney. After 1813 was lieut.-gen. in Russian service and aide to the Tsar.

covered with armour, and horses also will require the same protection."

Yet out of the Industrial Revolution came changes deeper than Jomini could foresee. The ancient foundations of manual labour were fast uprooted; workers were torn from their homes and villages and regimented in factories, the power-houses of national wealth and the barracks of social revolution.

Widespread misery caused vast emigration; a veritable *Völkerwanderung* occurred between 1831 and 1852, when over three million people left Great Britain and Ireland for the United States, and many of those who were unable to do so turned towards Socialism, the new cult to which the Industrial Revolution had given birth.

The spiritual moulders of this age of power were the three Charles – Clausewitz, Marx, and Darwin. The first, in his *On War* (1832), expounded a return to Spartanism, which turned the State into a military machine; the second, in his *Communist Manifesto* (1848), based his social theorem on class antagonism; and the third, in his *Origin of Species* (1859), brought the whole apocalyptic vision to its summit in his hypothesis of the survival of the fittest through never ending conflict. All three were prophets of the mass-struggle – in war, in social life, and in biology.

Although, when the Machine Age was in its youth, the consensus was that it heralded an age of peace, sharp differences between one country and another caused discord and contributed to the intensification of nationalism, and as countries outside Europe became industrialized, the problem became world-wide. The road led from limited to total war and totalitarianism became the hidden philosophy of the age.

In 1861 the American Civil War broke out between the Northern (Federal) and Southern (Confederate) States. This was, says Fuller, "the first of the unlimited industrialized wars . . . the first great conflict of the steam age, and the aim of the Northern . . . states was unconditional surrender – that is, total victory. Its character was, therefore, that of a crusade, and because of this, as well as because it put to the test the military developments of the Industrial Revolution, it opened a radically new chapter in the history of war."

What, [asks Fuller] were the strategical considerations which faced the contenders? In themselves they were exceedingly simple: to re-establish the Union the North must conquer the South, and to maintain the Confederacy and all that it stood for the South must resist invasion. On the one side the attitude was offensive, on the other defensive. To conquer the North was out of the question; therefore the Southern attitude resolved itself into inducing Europe to intervene and exhausting the North so as to compel the Union to abandon the contest. Since it was uncertain what Europe would do, the latter consideration was the more important; consequently, of equal importance was the question of how long Southern resources could stand the strain, since the South depended on the industries of both the North and Europe.

In the event, the surprising feature of the American Civil War was its duration: in theory, the industrial North, with its much greater population, should have been able to overwhelm the South in short order. "Of the 31,443,321 inhabitants of the United States in 1860 the eleven states forming the Confederacy contained approximately nine million, of whom over three and half million were slaves . . . Furthermore, the North was strengthened militarily by the immigration of young men from Europe, so that it had 4,010,000 white males between the ages of fifteen and forty at the time of the Civil War while the South had only 1,140,000 such males." [1] Fuller tells us that on the outbreak of war "there were fewer than 200,000 muskets in the Confederate arsenals, which were equipped with no machinery 'above the grade of a foot-lathe.'" Yet the war continued for 48 months – only three months less than the duration of the First World War; this fact is another important reason why the two events may be compared. It is clear that, as between 1914 and 1918, a balance of strength was somehow struck between outwardly very unequal forces. The reasons for this are still difficult to define with exactitude.

One element in the balance of force was the fighting quality of the Confederate soldier. "Except for his lack of discipline," says Fuller, "the Southern solder was probably the finest individual fighter of his day." And he adds: "In brief, the Federal soldier was semi-regular and the Confederate semi-guerilla. The one strove after discipline, the other unleashed initiative." This analysis requires a little questioning; in some respects the Confederates became more "regular" than the Federals – their military system at least permitted the evolution of veteran units, whereas the Union continued, to the end, to field newly-raised, raw regiments, while battle-hardened formations withered away. The real difference in quality between the soldiers of the two armies would seem to lie in the fact that the majority of Confederates were countrymen, with developed field instincts, while the majority of Federals were not. But the difference was always marginal; there were very good and very bad performances by both sides; and, as one historian has said, "Actually, Northern troops proved to be as brave, dependable and heroic in combat as Southern solders." [2]

A more obvious advantage to the South may be discerned in the quality of officers, particularly general officers. This was not a matter of training or military education; the professional background was the same for both sides: "Most of the able officers on both sides were trained at West Point, and many had fought in the Mexican War. There were three hundred and four West Point graduates in the Confederate Army, including one hundred and forty-eight generals. The Union Army had approximately

[1] Clement Eaton, *A History Of The Southern Confederacy*, Free Press, New York, 1954.

[2] Eaton.

twice that number of generals who were West Point graduates."
The South's advantage lies in the selection made for high
command; President Jefferson Davis was less compelled than
President Lincoln by political pressures; he was also less inclined
to chop and change, so that Southern officers were able to develop
their expertise by continuity of experience. As Fuller has said
elsewhere: "Regardless of seniority, Davis chose as officers men
he considered capable and energetic, and on the whole he made
few mistakes."[1] One Confederate officer who deserves mention
(and very rarely receives his due) was General Josiah Gorgas,
the Chief of Ordnance, whose duty was to keep the Confederates
supplied with arms and ammunition. The fact that they were
able to remain in the field for four years was largely due to his
amazing ability to create a munitions industry out of nothing,
and maintain an effective overseas trade (blockade-running) in
the face of overwhelming Union naval superiority.

As Fuller says, the war itself was profoundly marked by changes
in weapons which had been taking place during the previous two
decades, and these changes on the whole probably benefited the
Confederates more than the Union.

In the Napoleonic wars the flintlock musket, which possessed
an effective range of less than one hundred yards, was considerably outranged by cannon firing grape or canister;
therefore the gun was the superior weapon. But in 1861 the
musket had given way to the muzzle-loading percussion-
capped rifle, a weapon with an effective range of five hundred
yards, which could outrange grape and canister fired either by
smooth-bore or rifled guns. The whole of fire tactics underwent
a profound change. The gun had to fall back behind the
infantry and become a support weapon, and the infantry
fire-fight opened at four hundred yards' range instead of fifty
to one hundred yards. The result of this long-range fire-fighting
was that the bayonet assault died out; individual good shooting
became more effective than volley firing, and for full effective-
ness it demanded initiative and loose order. Therefore the
percussion-cap rifle well fitted Confederate tactics and the
character of the Southern soldier.

So we see that it was out of an agglomeration of larger and

[1] Fuller, *The Generalship Of Ulysses S. Grant*, John Murray, 1929.

smaller causes, rather than the operation of any one grand factor, that the South was able to offset the North's advantages for so long. Yet, short of some unforeseeable event – political collapse in the North, or European intervention – the ultimate outcome could hardly be doubted. By the end of 1862, the possibility of European support for the Confederacy was ruled out. The decisive event was the Battle of Antietam (17 September). The battle itself was the outcome of the first of two invasions of the North by General Robert E. Lee's Army of Northern Virginia. Attacked by greatly superior Federal forces of the Army of the Potomac under General George B. McClellan, the Confederates held their own through the long day of "the bloodiest one-day battle of the entire war".[4] But on the night of 18 September Lee's army slipped quietly away under the noses of their enemies, recrossed the Potomac, and evacuated Northern territory.

> Who won at Antietam? Tactically, Lee did. McClellan, repulsed in his assault, had dared make no further attack, as the Southerners contemptuously held their positions on 18 September. Strategically, since Lee's invasion of the North had been ended, and the Army of Northern Virginia then retired from the field, it was a Union victory, with far-reaching effects. President Lincoln used it as a spring-board for his preliminary Emancipation Proclamation, long-delayed for just such an opportunity. England, faced now by the fact that any official pro-Southern move would *ipso facto* infer a pro-slavery bias, would decline Napoleon III's later suggestion that Europe force an armistice between North and South. The war became America's business only, and Confederate hopes for European intervention went by the board.[4]

It was the following year, 1863, which marked the inevitable doom of the Confederacy. The month of July was the fatal month. Once more Lee had boldly carried the war into the North; this time the decisive confrontation took place at Gettysburg in Pennsylvania. In a three-day battle, which did not display Lee's tactical abilities to their best advantage, the splendid Army of Northern Virginia wasted itself in uncoordinated assaults on the Federal positions. On 3 July Lee shot his last bolt – and failed. But once more (as at Antietam) his opponent, General George G. Meade, lacked the self-confidence and drive to smash the

---

[1] *The Compact History Of The Civil War* by Col. R. E. Depuy & Col. T. N. Dupuy; Hawthorn Books (N.Y.), 1960.

Confederates by counter-attack. Once more Lee stood his ground for a day, out-facing his enemies, and then slipped away; but once more the outcome was unquestioned strategic defeat, at a cost which the Confederacy could no longer afford.

It was on the very day – the Fourth of July, 1863 – that Lee stood contemplating the ruins of his hopes and the gloomy prospects of retreat, that, far away on the Mississipi, a whole Confederate army of 31,000 men laid down its arms. This was the triumphant result of brilliant operations by General Ulysses S. Grant against the fortress of Vicksburg. Grant's star was now in the ascendant, and five months later, in the central theatre of war, Tennessee, he made sure that it would remain so with another success at Chattanooga. Fuller writes:

> Grant's victories at Vicksburg and Chattanooga sealed the eventual doom of the Confederacy. The one severed the States east of the Mississipi from those to the west of it, and the other blocked the main approach northward into Tennessee and opened the road to Atlanta – the back door of Lee's army in Virigina.
>
> On 3 March 1864, Lincoln, who at length had found the type of general he had been seeking, called Grant to Washington and made him commander-in-chief. He arrived there on 9 March and at once set to work out the plan which was to bring the war to an end. This was to hold Lee in Virginia by relentless attacks while from Chattanooga Sherman seized Atlanta and then operated against Lee's rear. In brief, to open a two front attack on what remained of the Confederacy and pinch it out of existence.

The plan was sound, its execution inexorable. Yet, against the skill of the Southern generals – Lee in the east and Joseph E. Johnston in the west – it took the Union a further year to bring it to fruition. During that year the last great hazard, political crisis in the North, was overcome; 1864 was a Presidential Election year, and in the prevailing condition of war-weariness of the North there was no certainty that Lincoln would win again. Grant's strategy was as much designed to fortify the President with successes in the field as to defeat the Confederate armies. His two chief instruments of success were General William T. Sherman's march through Georgia, into the very heart of the Confederacy, and General

Philip H. Sheridan's operations in the Shenandoah Valley, which finally liberated Washington from the fear of Southern attack. In his biography of Grant, Fuller wrote:

> Then came 8 November, a dull rainy day in Washington, and Lincoln was re-elected, receiving two hundred and twelve electoral votes, whilst twenty-two went to McClellan. Though this event 'was a greater triumph over the principles of the rebellion than any military victory could be', it must not be overlooked that it was mainly the effect of military causes, the most important of which were the occupation of Atlanta and Sheridan's success in the Valley; a success so close to the physical Washington that the moral Washington was re-vitalised as if by magic. [1]

The combination of Lincoln's political victory and Grant's steady military progress was irresistible; on 9 April 1865, Lee surrendered the remnants of the Army of Northern Virginia to Grant at Appomattox – "7,872 infantry with arms, 2,100 cavalry, sixty-three guns, and not a single ration". [2] The Confederacy was destroyed. Fuller sums up:

'After four years of fratricidal war the Union was affirmed and a mighty empire born, which, moated by the Atlantic and Pacific Oceans, was virtually unattackable. Linking as it did Europe in the east with Asia in the west it held in its hands the eventual balance of world power.

'Although the war brought ruin and chaos to the South, and although its ills were aggravated by the vengeance of the years of reconstruction, to the North it brought victory and unprecedented prosperity. "Never before," write Morison and Commager, "had the American people exhibited greater vitality, never since has their vitality been accompanied by more reckless irresponsibility. To the generation that had saved the Union everything seemed possible: there were no worlds, except the worlds of the spirit, that could not be conquered. Men hurled themselves upon the continent with ruthless abandon as if to ravish it of its wealth." [3]

'The resources of the new empire were all but inexhaustible: iron, coal, oil, labour and individual energy abounded. Inventions

[1] *The Generalship Of Ulysses S. Grant.*
[2] *Decisive Battles.*
[3] *The Growth of the American Republic* (1942), vol. II, p. 9.

flowed from drawing boards, goods from the factories and wheat from the fields, while hundreds of thousands of emigrants poured into the cities and over the land. Whereas, in 1865, there were 35,000 miles of railways in the United States, by 1900 there were 200,000, a mileage greater than that of all Europe.

'It has been estimated that the war cost the belligerents twenty billion dollars, and as Marx has pointed out it "left behind it a colossal national debt, with the consequent increased pressure of taxation, the creation of a financial aristocracy of the meanest kind, the handing over of an enormous proportion of the public lands to speculative companies for exploitation by means of railways,[1] mines, etc. – in a word, the centralization of capital at a headlong pace."[2]

'Within two generations from the ending of the war the United States became the greatest capitalist as well as the greatest industrial power in the world. Stephen Vincent Benét calls it, "The great metallic beast," and depicts its emergence from the Titanic struggle of the Civil War in these tremendous lines:

> Out of John Brown's strong sinews the tall skyscrapers grow,
> Out of his heart the chanting buildings rise,
> Rivet and girder, motor and dynamo,
> Pillar of smoke by day and fire by night,
> The steel-faced cities reaching at the skies,
> The whole enormous and rotating cage
> Hung with hard jewels of electric light,
> Smoky with sorrow, black with splendor, dyed
> Whiter than damask for a crystal bride
> With metal suns, the engine-handed Age,
> The genie we have raised to rule the earth. . . .[3]

'The reverse of this urge and power to produce in peacetime is the urge and power to destroy in wartime, and because of this – to revert to a point already touched upon – for the first time in modern history the aim of war became not only the destruction of the enemy's armed forces, but also of their foundations – his entire political, social and economic order. Lee, as Rhodes says,[4] in all essential characteristics resembled Washington, and resembling him mentally he belonged to the eighteenth century – to the agricultural age of history. Sherman, and to a lesser extent Grant, Sheridan, and other Northern generals, spiritually and morally

---

[1] "Altogether the Federal Government gave to the railroads 158,293,377 acres – almost the area of Texas" (*ibid.*, vol. II, p. 112).
[2] *Capital* (Everyman's Lib.), vol. II, pp. 857–858.   [3] *John Brown's Body*, p. 376.
[4] *History of the United States*, vol. III, p. 413.

belonged to the age of the Industrial Revolution. Their guiding principle was that of the machine which was fashioning them – namely, efficiency. And as efficiency is governed by a single law – that every means is justified by the end – no moral or spiritual conceptions or traditional behaviour must stand in its way. Sherman must rank as the first of the modern totalitarian generals. He made war universal, waged it on his enemy's people and not only on armed men, and made terror the linchpin of his strategy. To him more than to any other man must be attributed the hatred that grew out of the Civil War.

' In tactics, because the rifle made the defensive the stronger form of war, the offensive became more and more difficult and costly. This is noted by Colonel Theodore Lyman, who says: "Put a man in a hole, and a good battery on a hill behind him, and he will beat off three times his number, even if he is not a very good soldier."[1] And Frank Wilkeson wrote: "Before we left North Anna I discovered that our infantry were tired of charging earthworks. The ordinary enlisted men assert that one good man behind an earthwork was equal to three good men outside it."[2] This gave rise to a progressive increase in the strength of armies.

' Other changes – and many for years after the war remained unnoticed – were that the cavalry charge had become impotent; that the rifled-cannon was coming more and more to the fore, and that the dethronement of the bayonet was complete. "I don't think a single man of them was bayonetted,"[3] writes one eye-witness. General John B. Gordon says: "The bristling points and the glitter of the bayonets were fearful to look upon as they were levelled in front of a charging line; but they were rarely reddened with blood. The day of the bayonet is past."[4] And Surgeon-Major G. Hart writes that he saw few bayonet wounds "except accidental ones. . . . I think half-a-dozen would include all the wounds of this nature that I ever dressed."[5]

' It is easy to criticize the tactical ability of Grant, Lee, and other generals of this war, but it should be remembered that they had few precedents to guide them. To all intents and purposes the rifle was a new weapon. When we do criticize we should remember that in 1914 – 50 years after the Civil War – seven out of eight

---

[1] *Meade's Headquarters*, 1863–1865 (1922), p. 224.
[2] *The Soldier in Battle, or Life in the Ranks of the Army of the Potomac* (1896), p. 99.
[3] *Life in the Confederate Army*, William Watson, p. 217.
[4] *Reminiscences of the Civil War* (1904), pp. 5 and 6. See also *Memoirs of the Confederate War of Independence*, Heros von Borcke (1886), vol. I, p. 63, and vol. II, p. 50.
[5] *M.H.S.M.*, vol. XIII, p. 265.

professional soldiers still believed in the bayonet.

The war fought by Grant and Lee, Sherman and Johnston, and others closely resembled the first of the World Wars. No other war, not even the Russo-Japanese War of 1904–1905, offers so exact a parallel. It was a war of rifle bullets and trenches, of slashings, abattis, and even of wire entanglements – an obstacle the Confederates called "a devilish contrivance which none but a Yankee could devise" because at Drewry's Bluff they had been trapped in them and "slaughtered like partridges."[1] It was a war astonishing in its modernity, with wooden wire-bound mortars, hand and winged grenades, rockets, and many forms of booby traps. Magazine rifles and Requa's machine gun were introduced and balloons were used by both sides, although the Confederates did not think much of them.[2] Explosive bullets are mentioned[3] and also a flame projector,[4] and in June, 1864, General Pendleton asked the chief ordnance officer at Richmond whether he could supply him with "stink-shells" which would give off "offensive gases" and cause "suffocating effect." The answer he got was: "stink-shells, none on hand; don't keep them; will make if ordered."[5] Nor did modernity end there; armoured ships, armoured trains, land mines and torpedoes[6] were used, together with lamp and flag signalling and the field telegraph. A submarine was built by Horace L. Huntly at Mobile. It was 20 ft. long, 5 ft. deep, and $3\frac{1}{2}$ ft. wide and was "propelled by a screw worked from inside by seven or eight men."[7] On February 17, 1864, she sank the U.S.S. *Housatonic* off Charleston and went down with her.

'Had the nations of Europe studied the lessons of the Civil War and taken them to heart they could not in 1914–1918 have perpetrated the enormous tactical blunders of which that war bears record.'

---

[1] *Battles and Leaders*, vol. IV, p. 212.
[2] *The Times* Special Correspondent, January 1, 1863.
[3] *Campaigns and Battles of the Army of Northern Virginia*, George Wise (1916), p. 160.
[4] *Meade's Headquarters*, Colonel Theodore Lyman, p. 284.
[5] *W.R.*, vol. LXIX, pp. 888–889. [6] *Battles and Leaders*, vol. II, p. 636.
[7] *M.H.S.M.*, vol. XIV, pp. 450, 453.

The expansion of Prussia

While the semi-independent American states were being fused by friction into a federal empire, central Europe became the scene of another gestation. It arose out of the void created by the dissolution of the Holy Roman Empire, which the Congress of Vienna, in 1815, had hoped to fill by calling into being a Germanic Confederation of 38 sovereign States. Its object was to guarantee the external and internal peace of Germany and its organ was a Diet, permanently established at Frankfort-on-Main, in which each State was represented. Actually, the Diet remained impotent because it was a Senate without a House of Representatives – a conference and not a parliament.

More important than the Germanic Confederation was the creation of the Prussian *Zollverein* or Customs' union. In idea it originated with Friederich List, who saw that until the tariff barriers which separated the various States were removed British goods must continue to inundate Germany, whose own restrictions would prevent her from becoming industrialized. In order to put an end to this absurd situation all customs duties within Prussia, of which there were 67 affecting nearly 3,000 different articles, were abolished in 1818, and in October the following year the first tariff treaty was signed between Prussia and the small sovereign State of Schwarzburg-Sonderhausen. This soon gave birth to two Customs' unions, a northern and a southern, which in 1829 agreed to suspend all duties on the mutual exchange of products until 1841. In that year the *Zollverein* was reaffirmed, and three years later it included the whole of Germany less the Austrian dominions. Inevitably commercial unity led in the direction of political control, and therefore towards mutual military security.

Although we hear much of the *Pax Europa*, the 40 years after Waterloo was a period of nightmares and delirium in which reaction and revolution chased each other. No sooner was Louis XVIII re-established in Paris than reaction climbed back into the saddle. In France the *Tricolore* was abolished and so was divorce; in Spain the Church demanded and obtained the restoration of the Inquisition; in Austria the Emperor would go neither backward nor forward, and Prince Metternich, his chief Minister, looked upon the unification of Germany as an "infamous object." In England Whig and Tory, oblivious of the onrush of the Industrial Revolution, demanded protection for the agricultural interests and close trade within the Empire; and at the same time Alexander of Russia, a religious fanatic, persuaded the Emperor of Austria and the King of Prussia to sign with him in the name of "The Indivisible Trinity" a treaty called "The Holy Alliance," which was well suited to provide occasions for further Russian expansion. Later, all the leading monarchs, except the Prince Regent of England, subscribed to this treaty, and the only potentates not asked to do so were the Sultan and the Pope.

Although the 20 years which followed this "loud-sounding nothingness," as Metternich called it, witnessed no single great battle, the surge of nationalism against reaction made them some of the most bloody in Western history. The Spanish-American colonies revolted against Spain and Brazil against Portugal; Spain and Portugal were swept by revolution, and in the name of the Holy Alliance France invaded Spain. The Greeks revolted against the Turks, and in Russia the Decembrist Revolt followed the death of Alexander. In 1827 England, France and Russia intervened on behalf of the Greeks and on October 20 annihilated the Turkish fleet at Navarino. Russia invaded Persia and in 1828 declared war on the Porte and invaded Bulgaria. At length, in 1830, came the reckoning. Paris was rocked by revolution, Charles X was dethroned and Louis Philippe called to power; Belgium revolted against Holland; Poland against Russia; Hanover and Hesse Cassel boiled over in turmoil, and disturbances rent Austria, Hungary, Switzerland and Italy. In 1831 the Poles were defeated at Ostrolenka and their constitution abolished, and the Papal states, which revolted against Austria, were crushed. In 1832 the French laid siege to Antwerp; in 1833 Sir Charles Napier, with extraordinary audacity, destroyed Don Miguel's fleet off Cape St. Vincent, and in 1834 the Carlist War opened in Spain and for seven years drenched the Peninsula with blood. At length, in 1837, with the accession of Queen Victoria to the throne of England, a period of relative quietude set in for 10 years.

The next revolutionary outburst occurred in 1848. Its aim was no longer to change the form of government but the national structure, in the bottom strata of which living conditions had steadily worsened as industrialism deepened. In 1847 the Communist League was founded in London under Marx and Engels, and from its inauguration the *Marseillaise* passed to the bourgeoisie and a more formidable battle-song – the *Internationale* – vibrated from the throats of the workers:

> *Debout! les damnés de la terre!*
> *Debout! les forçats de la faim!*
>
> . . . .
>
> *Le raison tonne en son cratère,*
> *C'est l'éruption de la fin.*
> *Du passé faisons table rase,*
> *Foule esclave, debout, debout!*
> *Le monde va changer de base:*
> *Nous ne sommes rien, soyons tout!*

On February 22, 1848, Louis Philippe and his Queen slipped out of a back door of the Tuileries and fled to England as Mr. and Mrs. Smith.

Seldom had a revolution started with so little bloodshed. The right to work was established as the leading principle of reform, and to guarantee it the National Guard was suppressed and the workers were armed. In June General Cavaignac was appointed dictator; he led the west-end of Paris against the industrial east-end under Pujol and crushed the revolt with his cannon. "The combatants," writes Mr. C. A. Fyffe, "fought not for a political principle or form of government, but for the preservation or overthrow of society based on the institution of private property." Nevertheless France was so badly shaken that the Duke of Wellington wrote: "France needs a Napoleon! I cannot yet see him. . . . Where is he?"

In England there was much excitement, but the Chartists' demonstrations fizzled out. In 1849 the Corn Laws were repealed and Great Britain slid into free trade. Meanwhile revolution broke out in Vienna and was followed by a general upheaval throughout the Empire. Charles Albert of Piedmont with all Italy, except the Pope, behind him and urged on by Cavour decided on war to his cost. Defeated at Santa Lucia and Custozza, on March 23, 1849, he was finally crushed at Novara and compelled to abdicate in favour of his son Victor Emmanuel (1849–1878). Hungary in the meantime burst into flames; the Czechs rose in Bohemia and the Serbs and Croats took up arms. These revolts led to a recurrence of revolution in Vienna and to the abdication of Ferdinand I in favour of his nephew Francis Joseph (1848–1916), a boy of 18. Nevertheless, Hungary refused to acknowledge him, and since the Austrian Government was unable to suppress the revolt, Russia was called in, in the name of the expiring Holy Alliance, and on August 9, 1849, the Hungarians were routed at Temesvár and the rebellion ruthlessly suppressed.

Although in Germany the workers, who followed the lead set by the French, clamoured for a greater share in the profits of their masters, rebellion took on a national rather than a social form. In February, 1847, Frederick William IV (1840–1861) had been compelled to summon a united Prussian Diet, which at once suspended the old Diet of 1815 and authorized the assembly of a German National Parliament at Frankfort in order to construct a new Germany out of the States. In the middle of its debates Schleswig and Holstein revolted against the Danish Crown and a Prussian army was sent to support the Holsteiners. Russia supported the Danes and Frederick William, taking fright, flouted the National Parliament by agreeing to an armistice. In spite of this setback the National Parliament next offered to make him Emperor of Germany, and with Austria in turmoil had Frederick William accepted the offer it would probably have been unopposed. But as he loathed the democratic policy of the National Parliament he declined it unless the sanction of the Princes and free cities was first obtained. This was a death-blow to the hopes of the German patriots.

To offset this blunder Frederick William concluded a treaty with the Kings of Hanover and Saxony so as to agree on a new constitution. The suggestion was that, instead of an Emperor, a supreme chief aided by a College of Princes should be established. The proposal was accepted and assumed the name of "The Union." But unfortunately for Frederick William the propitious moment had passed, for Austria had now recovered and, on her detaching Saxony and Hanover from the Union, Germany was split into two hostile parties – one supporting Prussia and the other Austria. A disturbance in Hesse Cassel brought them to the verge of war; but as Frederick William was in no way prepared to wage one, on November 29, 1850, at Olmütz, he yielded virtually everything to Austria; the Union was dissolved and Prussia was compelled to recognize the old Frankfort Diet. Never since the black day of Jena had Prussia suffered such an eclipse.

Meanwhile in France, after the "June Days," Cavaignac

reigned as dictator, but because he failed to establish a stable government he was defeated on December 10, 1848, by Louis Napoleon in the presidential elections. At length there had appeared the man for whom less than a year before Wellington had looked vainly.

He was the third son of Louis Bonaparte and Hortense Beauharnais, daughter of Josephine, and therefore nephew and stepgrandson of Napoleon I. Because he was an astute opportunist politician he had every intention of investing in the glory of his great uncle. When in May, 1850, the Assembly blindly reduced the number of electors from nine million to six – a highly unpopular act – Louis Napoleon saw his opportunity. Although a year or two before he had posed as a vindicator of universal suffrage, he now sided with the Assembly in order to precipitate its ruin. When a friend said to him: "But you will perish with it," he replied: "On the contrary, when the Assembly is hanging over the precipice, I shall cut the rope."

After he had discredited the Assembly he flattered the clergy, promised prosperity to the bourgeoisie and wealth to the workers, and distributed cigars and sausages to the soldiers, until in the eyes of the people from a simple *citoyen* he became *notre prince*. Once he had carefully prepared everything, he overthrew the government on December 2, 1851, and a year later was elected by popular vote Emperor of the French with the title of Napoleon III.

While he was scheming the Great Exhibition was held in London. "It seemed," writes Mr. Fyffe, "the emblem and harbinger of a new epoch in the history of mankind, in which war should cease. . . . Yet the epoch on which Europe was then about to embark proved to be pre-eminently an epoch of war. In the next quarter of a century there was not one of the great Powers which was not engaged in an armed struggle with its rivals."

The first of these conflicts was the war in the Crimea, and although the pretext for its outbreak was Louis Napoleon's revival of the claims of France to the guardianship of the holy places in Palestine, the hidden cause was the expansionist policy of Russia and the craving by Nicholas I (1825–1855) to obtain control of the Dardanelles. Once she felt assured of the support of the western Powers, Turkey declared war on Russia in October, 1853, and early in 1854 was joined by France and Great Britain, and later by Sardinia.

This war ended the 40 years peace which followed Waterloo and its results were fatal to the peace of Europe. From 1856 to 1878 Europe was afflicted with five great wars, all of which found their roots in the Crimean conflict.

Immediately after the Crimean War, when Russia was helpless and Great Britain had her hands full with the Indian Mutiny, a plot to assassinate Louis Napoleon was hatched in London by the revolutionist Felice Orsini. This not only caused acute friction between France and Great Britain, but so terrified the Emperor that he persuaded himself that, unless he took up arms in favour of the liberation of Italy, other attempts on his life would follow. The result was the Franco-Austrian War in 1859, which, after the French victory of Solferino, terminated on November 10 with the Treaty of Villafranca. By its terms France gained Savoy and Nice, and with the exception of Venetia and Rome, all Italy was united under Victor Emmanuel.

In these two wars the following military developments are of interest. In the Crimea, chloroform was first used; the Press began to exert a decisive influence and for the first time newspaper correspondents accompanied armies. James Cowen, a philanthropist, proposed the use of armoured traction engines fitted with scythes to mow lanes through the enemy infantry; Bauer, a German, built a submarine – the *Diable Marin* – for Russia, and Lord Dundonald revived his project of 1812 to use burning sulphur to suffocate the garrisons of naval fortresses. Although his scheme was not tried out, he predicted that poison gas as a weapon "would ultimately become a recognized means of warfare." In 1859 for the first time in war the railway was extensively used; rifled-cannon were employed in numbers, and on account of the sufferings of the wounded at Solferino, the first Geneva Convention came into being in 1864.

Since her humiliating surrender at Olmütz Prussia had been recuperating, and a rapid revival followed the accession of William I (1861–1888) on January 2, 1861.

William was born in 1797 and in 1814 had taken part in the battle of Arcis-sur-Aube. He was a soldier by instinct and education, and in his first speech from the throne proclaimed: "The Prussian Army will, in the future, also be the Prussian Nation in Arms" – words which were to change the destiny of Europe, and with it that of the world. He at once set about reorganizing the Prussian army with the aim of creating an effective war force of

371,000 men, backed by a reserve of 126,000, and a *Landwehr* of 163,000. He appointed Count von Roon as Minister of War, Count von Moltke as Chief of the General Staff, and in 1862 he made Otto von Bismarck his President-Minister.

Bismarck's policy was simple and direct – to drive Austria out of Germany – and because Russia had not recovered from the Crimean War and France, though formidable, was engaged in a wild-goose chase in Mexico, his road was clear, and he determined to travel along it at the first opportunity. It came in 1863, when on the accession of Charles IX to the Danish throne, Saxon and Hanoverian troops marched into Holstein. On the pretext of restoring peace, Bismarck persuaded Austria to join Prussia. In 1864 came the Schleswig-Holstein War, and in October it was concluded by the Treaty of Vienna, which put the two duchies under the joint control of Austria and Prussia.

Bismarck calculated correctly that Schleswig-Holstein would become a bone of contention and lead to war with Austria. Therefore, in order to isolate her, he promised Louis Napoleon a free hand in Belgium or part of the Rhinish Provinces if in his turn he would persuade Austria to sell Venetia to Italy. This he knew Austria would refuse to do. At the same time, in order to annoy Austria, he reopened the question of German federation. As Austria would not part with Venetia, an offensive and defensive treaty of alliance was signed by Italy and Prussia on April 8, 1866; and Louis Napoleon, who was watching the gathering storm and who believed that the time was opportune to erase the treaties of 1815, offered to join Prussia with 300,000 men in return for the Rhinish Provinces. Bismarck, however, had no intention of parting with them, and now that Italy was in the Prussian knapsack, he ordered troops into Holstein to precipitate the conflict. On June 12 Austria broke off diplomatic relations.

The war which was now fought was not a war of aggression in the common meaning of the word, nor a war of conquest, but a war of diplomacy – of rectification. The aim of Prussia was not to humiliate Austria or even to weaken her, but to persuade her that nationalism in Germany was a living, growing force which demanded unity. On no account did Bismarck want to make Austria a vindictive enemy, because he knew that one day Germany would have to contend with France for the hegemony of Europe, and when that day came he wanted a neutral Austria.

When he learnt that the Austrians were concentrating in

Moravia in order to advance into Bohemia, Moltke decided to invade the latter with two armies, the First, under Prince Frederick Charles, and the Second under the Crown Prince. One was to advance on Müchengrätz and the other on Trautenau-Nachod, from where they would move forward and unite at Gitschin. When Prince Frederick Charles neared Müchengrätz, the Austrians, under Clam-Gallas, fell back on Gitschin, and when the Crown Prince defeated Ramming at Nachod and Skalitz, Field-Marshal Benedek, the Austrian commander-in-chief, ordered a general withdrawal on Sadowa. On June 30 the two Prussian armies were sufficiently close to unite at short notice, and on July 3 the battle of Königgrätz (also called Sadowa) was fought. The First Army engaged the Austrians during the morning, and in the afternoon the Second fell upon their right flank and crumpled it up. Although the victory was decisive – the Austrians lost nearly 45,000 men in killed, wounded and prisoners – Benedek with some 150,000 got away, because the two Prussian armies were in such a state of confusion that pursuit was out of the question. On July 18 Moltke issued orders for an advance on Wagram, 10 miles north-east of Vienna, and on the 21st the Austrians asked for an armistice, which was conceded.

On the Austrian defeat at Königgrätz the Emperor Francis Joseph telegraphed to Louis Napoleon to intervene. But his escapade in Mexico made him unwilling to embark on a war, and moreover the rapid Prussian victories were entirely contrary to his expectations. Peace with Prussia had to be made, and in accordance with the treaties of Prague, Berlin and Vienna, although the integrity of the Austrian monarchy was respected, Italy received Venetia and Prussia Hanover, Schleswig-Holstein, Hesse, Nassau and the free city of Frankfurt-am-Main. Saxony was left intact and the States north of the Main were formed into a North German Confederation under Prussia, and those to the south into a separate Southern Union.

To placate liberal sentiment, William, on his triumphal return to Berlin, established a Federal Parliament, and a new party called the National Liberals was formed with the main object of securing a union between southern and northern Germany. Such a fusion, in spite of the Customs Parliament (*Zollparlament*) now agreed upon by the two groups of States, would have taken a long time to effect had not the French Emperor brought such pressure to bear on the whole of Germany as to make it inevitable. He did what Bismarck calculated he would do. Even before the Treaty of Prague was signed he had claimed the left bank of the Rhine in compensation for Prussia's gain in power, and he now claimed it again. Fear of France threw the Southern Union into the arms of the Northern Confederation, and a secret offensive and defensive alliance under the King of Prussia was agreed. All that was now required was a common war against a common enemy in order to weld together the severed halves of Germany, and for this Bismarck steadily prepared.

CHAPTER 5

The Battle of Sedan, 1870

The causes of the Franco-Prussian War were, on the one hand the determination of Prussia to unite all Germany under her leadership, and on the other the determination of France to prevent this union. Added to these was the age-old animosity between Gaul and Teuton. Few nations have had so bad a neighbour as Germany has had in France. Between 1675 and 1813 she had invaded her on no fewer than 14 occasions – on the average once every 10 years. Besides, France for centuries had been *la grande nation*, the dominant power in Europe, and the secret fear that her glory was fading awoke in her a touchy and irascible temper. Ever since 1789 the political foundations of Europe had been in flux; power was passing from kings and courts to demagogues and parliaments to become the shuttle-cock of Press and people and the battledore of the great financial and industrial interests.

The immediate cause – the spark which exploded these well-tamped animosities – was little more than an extraneous accident; nevertheless, it is of sufficient interest to be described in some detail because it is a classic example of how wars are detonated in the democratic age.

In September, 1868, a mutiny in the Spanish fleet led to the expulsion of Queen Isabella II and the appointment of Marshal Prim as regent. Because the mass of the people did not favour a republic Prim offered the Spanish crown to one foreign prince after another, but with no success. At length in February, 1870, he entered into secret negotiations with Bismarck, who suggested as a possible candidate Prince Leopold of Hohenzollern-Sigmaringen, a distant relative of the Prussian royal house. Prim communicated with the Prince, who welcomed the suggestion provided the consent of Louis Napoleon and the King of Prussia could first be obtained. Prim then wrote to William, who was profoundly surprised by his letter, for he had no knowledge of the secret negotiations. He strongly opposed the suggestion and informed Prim accordingly. Further negotiations between Prim and

Bismarck followed, and suddenly, on July 3, 1870, the secret was revealed by the Spanish newspaper *Epoca*. Even more surprised than William was Louis Napoleon, who at once dispatched strongly worded protests to Spain and Prussia. The Paris newspapers published violent articles and talked of the revival of the Empire of Charles V. So hysterical did Paris become that on July 5 Edouard Vaillant (a French politician) wrote in his diary: "It seems to me that this is war, or very nearly so." The next day the French Emperor summoned his Council of State; mobilization was discussed, and on the suggestion of the Duke of Gramont, the French Foreign Minister, it was decided to instruct Count Benedetti, the French ambassador at Berlin, to go to Ems, where the King of Prussia was taking the waters, and request him to persuade Leopold to withdraw his candidature.

On July 9 William saw Benedetti and told him that he had no intention of encouraging Leopold and that the question concerned Madrid alone. As this did not satisfy Louis Napoleon, Gramont telegraphed Benedetti: "We demand that the King forbids the Prince to persist in his candidature." When he was informed of this William was exceedingly annoyed; nevertheless, he gave Benedetti permission to telegraph to Leopold direct. At the time Leopold was in Switzerland and the telegram was received by his father, who at once replied that he withdrew the candidature in the name of his son. This he had every right to do as head of his princely house. When he heard of this William was delighted and considered the matter closed. Not so the French Emperor, who told Gramont to instruct Benedetti to see the King again and obtain his personal assurance that he would forbid Leopold to revive his candidature at a later date.

On July 13 at 9 a.m. Benedetti met William in the park at Ems and was cordially greeted by him. The King said that he was delighted to see that Leopold's renunciation had been published in the German Press. Benedetti then put forward Louis Napoleon's new demand, on which William replied: "My cousins are honourable people; as they have withdrawn the candidature it is not with the intention of reviving it later." He then broke off the conversation.

When he learnt what had taken place, Bismarck, through his representative at Ems, begged the King to cease these irregular personal interviews and revert to the normal procedure of negotiating through ambassadors and ministers. The King agreed, but

Benedetti, urged on by Gramont, asked for another audience. William refused to see him, sent Bismarck a report on what had taken place, and left it to him to decide whether it should be communicated to the embassies and the Press.

Bismarck received the King's dispatch on the evening of July 13, took advantage of the King's permission to publish it, and reduced it to a précis which read: "Because the French ambassador has requested the King at Ems to authorize the dispatch of a telegram to Paris stating that he pledges himself never to allow a revival of the candidature, his Majesty has refused to see the ambassador again, and through an aide-de-camp has informed him that he has nothing further to communicate to him."

That Bismarck falsified the "Ems telegram" is a pure invention. What he did was to condense the King's dispatch into telegraphic form; in any case the original was not meant for publication as it stood. He knew that the French were bent on war, and as he said later: "It is essential that we should be attacked. . . . If I communicate this draft to the Press and telegraph it to the embassies it will soon be known in Paris . . . and its effect on the Gallic bull will be that of a red rag."[1]

No sooner was this telegram published in Paris than the Emperor assembled his Council, and while it was deliberating a dispatch from Benedetti was handed in. It was more moderate than Bismarck's; Gramont, in order to avoid war, proposed that a European Conference should be called to forbid reigning families to permit their members to accept foreign crowns. Although the Emperor approved of this proposal the Empress did not; it was laid aside, and no alternative was suggested. Next, the mob in Paris took charge; the *Marseillaise*, hitherto forbidden, was sung, and "*Vive la guerre, à Berlin!*" was shouted. In spite of the warnings of Thiers and Gambetta the French Assembly lost all balance and, urged on by the popular outcry, rapidly slid into war, which officially was declared on July 19.

France had hoped to have Austria and Italy as her allies, and in 1869 approaches had been made to both, but only vague replies were received. Not until the storm was about to break did Louis Napoleon send a personal representative to Vienna to discuss an alliance, and on July 20 – the day after war was declared – back came the answer – "neutrality!" Denmark also decided to remain

[1] The above account of the "Ems incident" is taken from *Histoire de France Contemporaine* (edit. Ernest Lavisse, 1921), vol. VII, pp. 209–219.

neutral, and England, who all along had been opposed to war, was in no way encouraged to support France, especially when, on July 25, Bismarck had a letter published in *The Times* divulging the French Emperor's project of 1866 to annex Belgium.

Thus France stood alone. Worse still, since 1815 she had been living spiritually on the Napoleonic legend of French invincibility. This illusive dream obscured from the public view what actually existed – a divided, profit-seeking people, a *bric-à-brac* government, "a corpse upon which, like vultures, a swarm of contractors gathered to divide between themselves the budget."[1] "While the soldier held firm to his ancient courage, innate among the French, in the government, the administration, the command, direction, preparations, science, artillery and the furnishing of the arsenals all had been degraded and neglected. . . . *Voilà le matérialisme. Il raille la terre et blasphème le ciel!*"[2] General Trochu says much the same: each revolution since 1815 had "excited ambitions, provoked competitions, confused in the mind of the masses the idea of the true and the false, of the just and the unjust, and had substituted for patriotism and public interest self-profit."[3]

That the Emperor and his councillors should have been living in such a fool's paradise is all but incomprehensible, for they had been kept fully informed by Lieutenant-Colonel Baron Stoffel, the exceptionally observant French Military Attaché in Berlin, of conditions in Prussia, and he had not been afraid to compare them with those prevalent in France. His reports are so illuminating that they warrant quoting at some length.

May 26, 1868. "During divine service it is upon the King and the army the minister calls down, before all others, the blessing of the Most High. The great bodies of the State are only named afterwards. . . . What a contrast with the position filled by the army in France, where it is but a mass of men, the outcasts of fortune, who lose every day more and more discipline and military spirit."

August 12, 1869. "The principal points that I seek to make are clear:

"(1) War is inevitable, and *at the mercy of an accident*.

"(2) Prussia has no intention of attacking France; she does not seek war, and will do all she can to avoid it.

---

[1] *Un Ministère de la guerre de vingt-quatre jours*, le Général Cousin de Montauban, Cte de Palikao (1871), p. 78.

[2] *Les Deux Abimes*, le Comte Alfred de la Guéronnière (1871), pp. 19, 25.

[3] *Une page d'histoire contemporaine devant l'Assemblée Nationale*, Général Trochu (1871), p. 18.

"(3) But Prussia is far-sighted enough to see that the war she does not wish will assuredly break out, and she is, therefore, doing all she can to avoid being surprised when the fatal accident occurs.

"(4) France, by her carelessness and levity, and above all by her ignorance of the state of affairs, has not the same foresight as Prussia.

. . . .

"What, on the contrary, do we see in France? A Chamber that boasts itself as representing the people and which is its reflection, so far as levity and inconsistency are concerned . . . whose patriotism consists of spiteful recrimination or premeditated malice; who hide their incapacity and impotence under flowers of rhetoric, who pretend that they alone are anxious for the well-being of the country, and who, to gain a factious popularity, dispute with the Government over one soldier, one franc . . . they seek to weaken France, they betray her into the hands of her most formidable enemy . . . a Press always vain and empty, whose leading journals descant on the most important subjects without in the least comprehending them, seeking to serve parties, not France. . . . France has laughed at everything; the most venerable things are no longer respected; virtue, family ties, love of country, honour, religion, are all offered as fit subjects of ridicule to a frivolous and sceptical generation. . . . Are not these things palpable signs of real decay?"[1]

Such was the state of the French nation, depicted not by foreigners but by Frenchmen, and this state was reflected by the army, which in Algeria, the Crimea, China, Italy and Mexico had learnt to despise its officers and to hypnotize itself into believing that the *élan* of the French soldier would prove irresistible. In 1859 the saying "*C'est le général soldat qui a gagné la bataille de Solferino*" implied that generals were of little account, and its spirit was fostered by the democratic Press.[2]

Conditions in Prussia were totally different. The army was aristocratic and not democratic, and since William's accession it had become what he had determined it should become – the Prussian Nation in Arms. Since the humiliating Convention of

[1] *Military Reports*, Lieut.-Colonel Baron Stoffel, French Military Attaché in Prussia, 1866–1870 (English edit., 1872), pp. 93, 142.
[2] *Tactical Deductions from the War of* 1870–71, A. von Boguslawski (English edit., 1872), p. 8.

Olmütz, the General Staff had accepted Clausewitz's *On War* as its military gospel, and because from 1866 onward it profoundly influenced the theory and practice of war, we shall here summarize its leading doctrines:

"War is only a continuation of State policy by other means" . . . "War is not merely a political act, but also a real political instrument, a continuation of political commerce" . . . "War is only a part of political intercourse, therefore by no means an independent thing in itself" . . . "Is not war merely another kind of writing and language for political thought?" . . . "If war belongs to policy, it will naturally take its character from thence. If policy is grand and powerful, so will also be the war."

Secondly, as to the nature of war:

"War is nothing but a duel on an extensive scale" . . . "Let us not hear of Generals who conquer without bloodshed" . . . "War is an act of violence pushed to its utmost bounds" . . . "Our aim is directed upon the destruction of the enemy's power" . . . "Destruction of the enemy's military forces is in reality the object of all combats" . . . "The more is war in earnest, the more is it a venting of animosity and hostility."

This leads, thirdly, to the offensive:

"There is only one form of war – to wit, the attack of the enemy" . . . "The combat is the single activity in war."

Which, fourthly, demands numerical superiority:

"The best strategy is always to be strong" . . . "A war" should be "waged with the whole weight of the national power" . . . "A people's war in civilized Europe is a phenomenon of the nineteenth century."

And, fifthly, war demands moral and intellectual superiority:

"Courage is the highest of virtues" . . . "The chief qualities are the talents of the Commander; the military virtue of the army; its national feeling" . . . "There is nothing in war which is of greater importance than obedience."

Sixthly, as regards tactics:

"The destructive principle of fire in the wars of the present time is plainly beyond measure the most effective" . . . "The defensive form of war is in itself stronger than the offensive . . . but has a negative object" . . . "The attack is the positive intention, the defence the negative" . . . "Only great and general battles can produce great results."

Lastly, organization:

"War is divided into preparation and action" . . . "Everything is very simple in war, but the simplest thing is difficult" . . . "War belongs not to the province of Arts and Sciences, but to the province of social life."[1]

Although Moltke was saturated with Clauzewitz's ideas he did not blindly follow him, but adapted his theories to the conditions of his own day, which were very different from those of Napoleon, on whose campaigns *On War* had been based. The railway was now revolutionizing logistics, and with it armies were growing in size, which demanded more and more a highly trained General Staff. Besides, the chaos of Königgräts had terrified Moltke as much as the success of the great flank attack had electrified him. As early as 1861 he had considered that infantry were frontally unassailable, and he had compared an open plain to a wet ditch which cannot be rushed. After 1866 he realized that a man who shoots at rest has the advantage over a man who fires when advancing; and therefore that the Napoleonic principle of concentration before battle could be supplemented by that of concentration during battle. Further, that the Napoleonic grand tactics of penetration must give way to that of the decisive flank attack.

In 1869 he issued a series of *Instructions for Superior Commanders of Troops*, in which we read:

"Very large concentrations of troops are in themselves a calamity. The army which is concentrated at one point is difficult to supply and can never be billeted; it cannot march, it cannot operate, it cannot exist at all for any length of time; it can only fight.

"To remain separated as long as possible while operating and to be concentrated in good time for the decisive battle, that is the task of the leader of large masses of troops. . . . Little success can be expected from *mere frontal* attack, but very likely a great deal of loss. *We must therefore turn towards the flanks of the enemy's position.*"[2]

One serious matter which Moltke never tackled was the provision of the Prussian infantry with a more effective rifle than the Dreyse needle gun, which, although improved, had been retained

[1] *On War*, Carl von Clausewitz (English edit., 1908). The quotations in order will be found in: Vol. I, p. 33; vol. I, p. 23; vol. III, p. 121; vol. III, p. 122; vol. III, p. 123; vol. I, p. 1; vol. II, p. 288; vol. I, p. 4; vol. I, p. 42; vol. I, p. 253; vol. I, p. 16; vol. I, p. 40; vol. I, p. 207; vol. I, p. 231; vol. II, p. 341; vol. I, pp. 20–21; vol. I, p. 179; vol. I, p. 187; vol. II, p. 9; vol. II, p. 135; vol. III, p. 254; vol. I, p. 285; vol. I, p. 93; vol. I, p. 77, and vol. I, p. 121.

[2] Quoted from *The Development of Strategical Science during the 19th Century*, Lieut.-General von Cämmerer (English edit., 1905), p. 214.

since 1841. In the 1866 war it had been badly outranged by the Austrian muzzle-loading Lorenz rifle, but because of its quicker loading in the prone position it had proved itself the superior weapon. Nevertheless, much of its superiority could have been discounted had the Austrians made better use of the rifled field gun they had adopted in 1863, for it had an effective case shot range of 500 yards, which was as great as the effective range of the needle gun. This was appreciated by Moltke, and as he knew that the French infantry were armed with the *Chassepot* breech-loading rifle, which was sighted to 1,200 m., that is twice the sighting of the needle gun, he hoped to make good the deficiency of the latter by means of the superiority of the Prussian iron breech-loading field gun over the French bronze muzzle-loader. The latter had been retained by the French because they had a secret weapon up their tactical sleeve. It was Reffeye's *mitrailleuse*, a machine gun of 25 barrels, axis grouped, which was sighted to 1,200 m., and could fire 125 rounds a minute. It was planned to use it to replace case shot, but it was kept so secret that it was not issued to the army until a few days before the outbreak of war, and according to Reffeye was then used "in a perfectly idiotic fashion."

The main weakness and strength of the two armies lay not in their armaments, but in their respective General Staffs. In the French, as we have seen, the lack of an efficient General Staff was one of the main causes of Napoleon I's ultimate ruin. This was little appreciated in France after 1815, and when war broke out in 1870 we find that the officers of the General Staff of the Second Empire were mere popinjays and clerks, either young "bloods" out of touch with the army or greybeards overwhelmed by the minutiae of routine. So far did Marshal Bazaine distrust his General Staff that he forbade its officers to appear on the battlefield, and instead of them he used his Personal Staff, as Napoleon had done 60 years before. And this in spite of the fact that, on February 25, 1868, Stoffel had reported:

"But of all the elements of superiority which Prussia, in case war broke out, would possess, the greatest and the most undeniable will be that she will obtain from the composition of her corps of staff officers . . . ours cannot be compared with it. . . . The composition of the Prussian staff will, in the next war, constitute the most formidable element of superiority in favour of the Prussian Army."[1]

[1] *Military Reports*, pp. 48, 56.

Since the days when Scharnhorst and Massenbach first organized an intelligence staff and systematized staff duties, the Prussian General Staff had developed so rapidly that by 1866 its authority had become paramount. Thus in 1870 we find that, in order of responsibilities, Moltke, the Chief of the General Staff, took precedence over the Commander-in-Chief – the King. From this it followed that, as the supreme command became less personal, more and more initiative was transferred from the Commander-in-Chief to the subordinate army and corps commanders, with the result that unity of doctrine became all-important in order to harmonize the actions of these subordinate officers. In brief, the art of war became mechanical and doctrinaire.

The routine character of staff command is explained as follows by General von Verdy du Vernois.[1] Every morning, under the chairmanship of the Chief-of-Staff, a staff conference was held at which the situation was discussed and decisions were made. These were then taken to the King and, if approved by him, were dispatched to the subordinate commanders concerned.

This clockwork system of command had an important defect: it took little or no account of the unexpected; it left local decisions in the hands of those on the spot, which at times was apt to throw the general plan out of gear.

The Prussian General Staff plan of war was first prepared in 1867, since when it had been constantly revised. It was in character highly offensive and in idea simplicity itself – general direction, Paris; objective, the enemy wherever met. Three armies were to be employed:

First Army, General von Steinmetz, the VIIth and VIIIth Corps and one cavalry division; 60,000 men.

Second Army, Prince Frederick Charles, the IIIrd, IVth and Xth Corps, Guards and two divisions of cavalry; 131,000.

Third Army, Crown Prince of Prussia, the Vth and XIth Prussian and Ist and IInd Bavarian Corps, the Württemberg and Baden Divisions, and one cavalry division; 130,000.

Reserve, under the King of Prussia, the IXth Corps and XIIth Saxon Corps; 60,000 at Mainz.

Besides these, the Ist, IInd and IVth Corps, one Regular

[1] See *With the Royal Headquarters in 1870–1871*, J. von Verdy du Vernois (English edit., 1897), vol. I, pp. 30–31. A full account of the Prussian General Staff is given in *The German General Staff*, Walter Görlitz (English edit., 1953).

division and four *Landwehr* divisions were held back to watch the Danish coast and the Austrian frontier.

Moltke reckoned correctly that the French would not be able to bring into the field more than 250,000 men against his 381,000, and that, because of railway communications, they would be compelled to assemble their forces about Metz and Strasbourg, which meant that they would be separated by the Vosges. He decided therefore to assemble his three armies behind the fortresses of the middle Rhine; the First about Wittlich, the Third near Landau and Rastatt, and the Second between Homburg and Neuenkirchen to act as a connecting link between the First and Third. Then, should the French attempt an *attaque brusquée* before they were completely mobilized, which he suspected they would do, he reckoned that, because their two army groups would be separated by the Vosges, he would be in a position to reinforce either his centre or flanks more rapidly than these two groups could be brought together either in Lorraine or in Alsace. Of his intention he says:

"But above all the plan of war was based on the resolve to attack the enemy at once, wherever found, and keep the German forces so compact that a superior force could always be brought into the field. By whatever special means these plans were to be accomplished was left to the decision of the hour; the advance to the frontiers alone was pre-ordained in every detail."[1]

Opposed to this plan was the French Emperor's, which may be described as bastard Napoleonic, for though it looked well on paper it was so highly speculative as to be in fact suicidal. Marshal Leboeuf, Minister of War, had calculated – or rather guessed – that on the ninth day of mobilization 150,000 men could be assembled in Lorraine and 100,000 in Alsace, and that this total could rapidly be brought up to 300,000. Because the Emperor knew that the Prussian army would outnumber him by approximately 100,000, he decided on an *attaque brusquée* before his own mobilization was completed. Fixed in his mind was the idea that a sudden attack eastward would force the south German States to desert Prussia and would bring Austria and possibly also Italy to his support. He decided therefore to assemble 150,000 men at Metz, 100,000 at Strasbourg and 50,000 at Châlons, move forward the first two, unite them, cross the Rhine, force neutrality upon

---

[1] *The Franco-German War of 1870-71*, Field-Marshal Count Helmuth von Moltke (English edit., 1891), pp. 10–11.

the south German States, link up with Austria, and then move *via* Jena on Berlin, while his fleet threatened the Elbe and the Baltic.

This grandiose scheme obviously demanded the most careful preparation and timing; yet directly war was declared complete chaos reigned while Prussian mobilization worked like a well-regulated clock. Nothing had been arranged; camps were not pitched because no one knew where the tents were; railway time tables had not been made out; some formations had no guns, others no transport, still others no ambulances; magazines were found unstocked and fortresses unsupplied. On August 10, the day Count Palikao was called to Paris to be Minister of War,[1] he received a letter from a general at the front informing him:

"In the supply depôts no camp-kettles, dishes or stoves; no canteens for the ambulances and no pack-saddles; in short no ambulances either for divisions or corps. Up to the 7th it was all but impossible to obtain a mule-litter for the wounded. That day thousands of wounded men were left in the hands of the enemy; no preparations had been made to get them away. . . . If for four days our soldiers lived on the charity of the inhabitants, if our roads are littered with stragglers dying of hunger, it is the administration which is to blame. . . . On the 6th an order was given to blow up a bridge, no powder could be found in the whole army corps, nor with the engineers, nor with the gunners!"[2]

As confusion became worse confounded the idea of invading southern Germany was abandoned and the fleet sailed for the Elbe without troops. The scattered state of the corps[3] finally persuaded the Emperor to form them into two armies – the Ist Corps and a division of the VIIth, 35,000 men under Marshal MacMahon about Strasbourg; and the IInd, IIIrd, IVth, and Vth with the Guard, 128,000 men known as the Army of the Rhine, about Metz under his own control. The VIth Corps, of 35,000 men, under Marshal Canrobert, was to remain in reserve at Châlons, and the remainder of the VIIth was left at Belfort to watch the exits of the Black Forest. When, on July 28, the Emperor took over the supreme command, not a single corps was ready to take the field.

---

[1] Marshal Lebœuf had gone forward with the Emperor.

[2] *Un ministère de la guerre de 24 jours*, Palikao, pp. 57–59.

[3] There were nominally seven army corps and the Guard, but the VIth and VIIth Corps were never united. They were Ist (MacMahon) at Strasbourg; IInd (Frossard) at Forbach; IIIrd (Bazaine) at St. Avold; IVth (Palikao) at Lyons; Vth (de Failly) at Bitche; VIth (Canrobert) at Châlons; VIIth (Félix Douay) at Belfort and Colmar; and the Guard (Boubaki) at Metz.

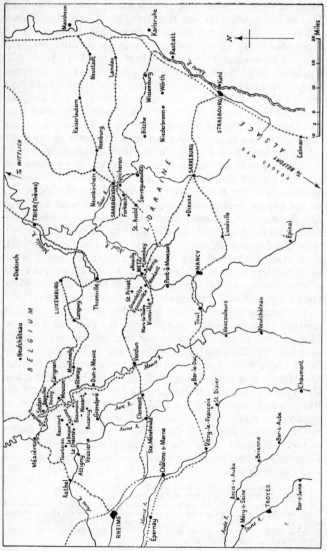

10. THE FRANCO-PRUSSIAN WAR, 1870–1871

Hesitation at once handed strategy over to the Paris mob. The boulevards were thronged, and shouts were raised demanding the instant invasion of Germany. This clamour forced the Emperor's hand, and on August 1 he initiated a movement on the Saar, which was entrusted to Marshal Bazaine. Besides his own corps, the IIIrd, Bazaine had under his orders the IInd and Vth. He pushed the Vth (de Failly) forward, and on August 2, when it came up against a detachment of the VIIIth Corps of the First Prussian Army at Saarbrücken, the latter fell back. Thereupon Moltke instructed Steinmetz to concentrate his army toward the Second Army, and at the same time he ordered the Third Army to cross the frontier and prevent the French from transferring troops from Alsace to Lorraine.

On August 3, Marshal MacMahon occupied Weissemburg with one division under Abel Douay who, unconscious of the approach of the Third Prussian Army, was surprised on the following day while in bivouac. Douay was killed, and his division fell back to join MacMahon near Wörth, where MacMahon was able to assemble some 32,000 infantry and 4,500 cavalry. On the 5th, the Third Army, with 72,000 infantry and 4,500 cavalry, came up with him. Vaguely informed of his enemy's strength, MacMahon planned an advance on the 7th, and the Crown Prince, whose army was scattered, decided to postpone his attack until he had concentrated his corps. This was not to be, for a clash between outposts early on August 6 involved the IInd Bavarian and Vth Prussian Corps and precipitated the battle of Wörth. It was the first major engagement of the war, and although the German attacks were disjointed, the French, after they had displayed their traditional valour, were unable to withstand the superiority of numbers brought against them, were forced back, and hurriedly withdrew through the Vosges to Neufchâteau, which they reached on August 14. From there by rail MacMahon's group was sent to Châlons, where it arrived on August 19. In this unlooked for battle each side lost between 10,000 and 11,000 in killed and wounded, and the Third Army was so unprepared to fight it that there was no pursuit.

Before the battle of Wörth was fought, Moltke's intention was that the First and Second Armies should concentrate behind the Saar on August 6 and pause there until the Third Army had secured the passages of the Vosges. But when he learnt of the action at Saarbrücken, the impetuous Steinmetz pushed ahead

towards it, as also did the leading troops of Prince Frederick
Charles's Second Army. At the time Saarbrücken was occupied by
Frossard's IInd Corps, but when Frossard learnt of Douay's disaster at Weissemburg he considered his position too exposed and,
on August 5, fell back to the heights of Spicheren, a few miles to
the south-west. Early on August 6 the advanced cavalry of the
Second Army drew fire from Frossard's outposts, and shortly afterwards General von Kameke's 14th Division came up. As Kameke
felt sure of support and believed that he was faced by no more
than a rearguard, he did not wait for orders but sent a single
brigade forward to storm the Rotherberg in the centre of Frossard's
position. This it did and, again as at Wörth, the battle started
before the Prussians were ready. Nevertheless, as successive bodies
of troops arrived on the field, Kameke was able to hold fast to the
Rotherberg and Frossard, who believed that he was outnumbered
– which he was not – ordered a retreat. Again there was no pursuit, because the Prussian cavalry were far behind. Spicheren cost
the French nearly 4,000 killed and wounded and the Prussians
about 5,000.

These two disasters, Spicheren and Wörth, threw the Imperial
headquarters at Metz into panic, and an order was issued to fall
back on Châlons. When this became known in Paris the Government, under the regency of the Empress, declared that, should the
army retire, the capital would revolt. Accordingly, on August 9
the plan was changed, and all troops east of Metz were ordered
to halt, while Metz was to be held at all costs. This caused a
separation of forces, for whereas Bazaine halted, MacMahon was
in the process of falling back.

The same day the Ollivier Ministry fell and the Imperialist
Party, headed by the Empress, handed over the Government to
General Count Palikao, who at the outbreak of the war had been
in command of the IVth Army Corps at Lyons. On the following
day, August 10, he took over the direction of the war, and from
then onward strategy became the creature of politics. His
"Apology", published in 1871, is illuminating, for it shows the
total incapacity of a weakly led democratic assembly to conduct
a war. For instance, he tells us that each morning at eight o'clock
a Council of Ministers was held at which interminable discussions
took place. On August 9 it was agreed to raise 500,000 soldiers in
eight days, and on the 10th fear was expressed that, should they
be armed, they might prove more dangerous than the Prussians.

On the 11th a resolution was passed to sacrifice the last *écu* and the last man, and on the 18th and 23rd M. Jules Favre was still shouting: "It is weapons we need!" Whereupon the Left yelled: "Arms! Arms!" for their sole aim was to overthrow the Government.[1] Such was the political instrument directing operations.

On August 12 the Emperor, although he remained with the army, handed over the supreme command to Marshal Bazaine. This change was made at a critical moment, because on the 13th Steinmetz's First Army, on the Prussian right, reached the river Nied, east of Metz; Frederick Charles's Second Army secured a bridgehead over the Moselle at Pont-à-Mousson, and the advanced guards of the Crown Prince's Third Army were approaching Nancy and Lunéville. All three armies were converging on Bazaine from the east and south, and although he was far from fully aware of this, he decided, when he learnt that Metz was badly provisioned, to abandon the line of the Moselle and fall back to the Meuse about Verdun.

To facilitate this withdrawal he ordered bridges to be thrown over the Moselle, but unfortunately for him heavy rain flooded the river and swept away several, with the result that on August 14 the greater part of his army was still east of Metz. There it was attacked at Colombey and Borny by Steinmetz's VIIth Corps, but under cover of night it succeeded in crossing the Moselle and in taking up a position astride the Metz-Verdun road facing south-west. This meant that, unless the Prussians were defeated, the withdrawal to Verdun would have to be abandoned and that the only line of retreat left open would be by way of the Metz-Briey-Montmédy road, which led either to Rethel or to Sedan. The truth is that Bazaine was already more than half cornered, although at the time he was unaware of it; he could not continue his withdrawal without a fight and to attempt to withdraw by the Metz-Montmédy road, which would entail a flank march in face of a victorious enemy, was to say the least a most hazardous operation.

While Bazaine marshalled his army, the 5th Cavalry Division of Frederick Charles's Second Army crossed the Moselle at Pont-à-Mousson and on August 15 came into contact with French cavalry near Vionville and Rezonville. By nightfall the Xth Corps was also across the Moselle at Pont-à-Mousson and the IIIrd Corps at Novéant. On the following day at 9 a.m. a violent

[1] *Ibid.*, pp. 68, 138, 141, 142, and 144.

attack by von Alvensleben's IIIrd Corps precipitated the battle of Vionville, also called Mars-la-Tour. It was a desperately fought engagement, in which at times the Prussians were hard pressed, and though it ended in a draw it was for Moltke strategically

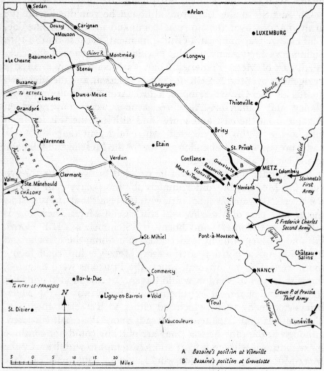

II. BATTLES OF VIONVILLE AND GRAVELOTTE, ·1870

decisive, because it compelled Bazaine to abandon all further idea of withdrawing to the Meuse. Instead, he ordered his army to fall back on a strong position between St. Privat and Gravelotte, to the north-west and west of Metz. The losses in the battle were about 16,000 on either side.

On August 17 Bazaine's withdrawal was carried out without interference. Moltke was engaged in bringing up the whole of his

First and Second Armies, less the IVth Corps, which was on its way towards Toul to form a connecting link with the Third Army. On the next day the great battle of Gravelotte, also called St. Privat, was fought between 200,000 Prussians and 140,000 French. As at Valmy in 1792 each army faced its base, which meant disaster for the defeated. The action was hotly contested, but in the late afternoon the Prussians succeeded in turning the French right by storming St. Privat and Bazaine was forced to retire within the fortifications of Metz. He thus separated his army from Paris and MacMahon who, on the 16th, had been joined by the Emperor. Gravelotte was the most bloody battle of the war; the Prussians lost more than 20,000 in killed and wounded, and the French about 13,000 besides 5,000 prisoners.

The original Prussian plan of campaign had not provided for the withdrawal of the main French army to Metz, only the invest-ment of the fortress by a number of *Landwehr* divisions. As this unexpected withdrawal demanded the formation of an army of investment, the whole of the First Army and the bulk of the Second, 150,000 troops in all, were placed under the command of Prince Frederick Charles, who was instructed to pin Bazaine down to his fortifications.

The Third Army, now 85,000 strong, remained under the Crown Prince of Prussia; and the Guard, IVth and XIIth (Saxons) Corps, of 138,000 men, were formed into the Army of the Meuse under command of the Crown Prince of Saxony. On August 20 the latter, on a broad front between Briey and Com-mercy, advanced on Verdun and the advanced guards of the former crossed the Meuse at Void and pushed forward toward Ligny-en-Barrois and Bar-le-Duc. Both were moving on Paris in order to compel the French to accept battle east of their capital. On the 23rd the Army of the Meuse reached the right bank of the Meuse about Verdun, failed to seize that fortress by a *coup-de-main*, and pushed out its advanced cavalry to Clermont and Ste. Ménehould.

Meanwhile at Châlons Marshal MacMahon was instructed to form a new army, to be known as the Army of Châlons, and this he did on August 18–20. It was a heterogeneous force consisting of the Ist Corps (Ducrot) 32,000 men; the Vth (de Failly) 22,000; the VIIth (Félix Douay) 22,000; the XIIth (Lebrun) 41,000, and two divisions of cavalry. Besides these there were some newly formed infantry divisions, a corps of marines, refugees from Wörth

5

and a number of Parisian *Gardes Mobiles*, then in a state of mutiny. In all this army comprised 166 battalions, 100 squadrons and 380 guns and totalled 130,000 men. Many of its units were so untrained that General Lebrun informs us he allotted five rounds to each of his men to enable the officers and non-commissioned officers to show them how to load and sight their rifles.[1]

At Châlons MacMahon decided to fall back on Paris, and in this he was supported by General Trochu, who arrived there on August 16 to take over command of the XIIIth Corps, then forming. On August 10 Trochu had written to a confidant of the Emperor that Bazaine's army ought to fall back on Paris, and although the Emperor agreed, Palikao had cancelled the movement.[2] On the 17th, the day after the Emperor arrived from Metz, a conference was held at which it was decided that, as he had handed over the supreme command to Bazaine, he should return to Paris and take charge of the government. This he agreed to do, and appointed Trochu Governor of Paris. Next he ordered him to return to the capital and announce his own arrival, while MacMahon fell back on Paris. Trochu then set out on his return journey.[3]

He arrived in Paris on the night of August 18 and was at once received by the Empress who, when she had learnt the import of his mission, exclaimed: "General, only the enemies of the Emperor can have counselled him to return to Paris; he will not enter the Tuileries alive. . . . No, General, the Emperor must not enter Paris, he must remain at Châlons . . . and you will defend Paris; you will fulfil your mission without the Emperor."[4]

After some hesitation Trochu agreed. He presented himself to Palikao, but was badly received. He was informed that his strategical ideas were absurd, and that under no consideration would Palikao agree to MacMahon retiring on Paris.[5] From then on every obstacle was placed in Trochu's way.

While Trochu was on his mission, MacMahon prepared to withdraw, and on August 21 fell back to Rheims, his men straggling over the countryside and antagonizing the inhabitants. On the 22nd the army remained at Rheims, and during the halt M. Rouher, President of the Senate and an envoy of Palikao's,

---

[1] *Bazeilles-Sedan*, le Général Lebrun (1884), p. 9.
[2] *Une page d'histoire contemporaine*, Trochu (1871), pp. 28–29.
[3] *Ibid.*, pp. 31–33. See also *Bazeilles-Sedan*, Lebrun, pp. 3–4.
[4] *Une page d'histoire contemporaine*, Trochu, pp. 34–35.
[5] *Ibid.*, pp. 36–37 and 42–45.

arrived at Imperial Headquarters to persuade the Emperor not to return to Paris and to urge him to instruct MacMahon to move on Metz. When this became known to MacMahon he telegraphed Paris: "How can I move towards Bazaine when I am in complete ignorance of his situation, and when I know nothing of his intentions?"[1]

As ill fortune would have it, no sooner had this message been dispatched than two telegrams came in. One, from Bazaine, said that he expected to retire in a northerly direction; the other, from the Regency Council, addressed to the Emperor, read: "Unanimous decision, more pressing than ever. . . . Not to support Bazaine will have the most deplorable consequences in Paris. Faced by this disaster, it is doubtful whether the capital can be defended." To this the Emperor replied: "Tomorrow we leave for Montmédy."[2] Therefore on August 23 the army moved to Bethiniville, its men scouring the countryside for supplies, and on the 24th to Rethel, where it remained over the 25th. On August 26 MacMahon advanced to Tourteron, and the next day to le-Chesne-Populeux, where he received information that the Crown Prince of Saxony had crossed the Vosges, advanced on Nancy and turned north-west. MacMahon ordered the following movements for the 28th: the XIIth Corps on La Becase, the Vth on Nouart or Buzancy, the VIIth on Stonne and the Ist on Raucourt.

While MacMahon was making his wide detour eastwards in order to slip past the right flank of his enemy and join hands with Bazaine, the Army of the Meuse and the Third Army advanced westward under orders to reach the line Vitry-St. Ménehould on August 26. The Prussian cavalry scoured the countryside in front of them and on August 24 entered Châlons to discover that it had been evacuated. Letters were picked up intimating that MacMahon was about to relieve Metz and that he was at Rheims with 150,000 men. This news surprised Moltke because he could not believe that his adversary would commit so flagrant an error as to uncover Paris and march across a hostile front with the Belgian frontier close to his left flank. But the next day the information was corroborated by a telegram from London, as well as by the Paris newspapers – particularly *Temps*, which kept nothing secret,[3] and on the 26th orders were issued to both armies to wheel northward. The same day the Prussian General Headquarters

[1] *Bazeilles-Sedan*, Lebrun, p. 39.   [2] Lavisse, vol. VII, p. 238.
[3] See *The Franco-German War*, Moltke, vol. I, p. 95.

moved from Bar-le-Duc to Clermont, and on the 27th the fore-most corps, the XIIth (Saxons) of the Army of the Meuse was directed on Stenay and adopted a non-offensive attitude until the Third Army arrived. Two days later a French staff officer was captured while carrying MacMahon's orders to two of his corps. These furnished the Prussian Headquarters "with a complete confirmation of the movements of the French Army as they had been conjectured."[1] The four corps of the Third Army had now closed up; the 5th Cavalry Division was pushed forward to Attigny across the enemy's lines of communication, while the 6th followed on the heels of the French. The royal headquarters were moved to Grandpré and the decision was taken to attack the French the following day before they could cross the Meuse.[2] The Army of the Meuse was directed on Beaumont and the Third Army to between Beaumont and Le Chesne.

When he learnt that Bazaine had not moved from Metz and that two enemy armies were moving towards his communications, MacMahon abandoned his advance and ordered his army to withdraw to Mézières. On August 28 another urgent dispatch from Paris persuaded him to resume his march on Montmédy. By now these orders and counter-orders had completely demoralized his men. On the 30th, when contact was established with the enemy, de Failly's Vth Corps was surprised at Beaumont by the Prussian IVth Corps as its men were drawing their rations and its artillery horses were at water.[3] This surprise cost MacMahon some 5,000 men and 42 guns. He felt that he could no longer make headway and between eight and nine o'clock in the evening he ordered Lebrun to move his XIIth Corps to Sedan. He said to him: "This has been an unfortunate day . . . nevertheless the situation is not desperate. The German army which is before us numbers at most from sixty to seventy thousand men. If we are attacked so much the better, I expect to be able to drive them into the Meuse."[4] This miscalculation of his enemy's strength was to lead to his ruin.

That night Moltke issued the following orders:

"The forward movement is . . . to be continued tomorrow as early as possible, and the enemy to be vigorously attacked wherever he stands on this side [west] of the Meuse; he is to be squeezed

[1] See *With the Royal Headquarters*, Verdy du Vernois, vol. 1, p. 116.
[2] *The Franco-German War*, Moltke, vol. 1, p. 102.
[3] See *Bazeilles-Sedan*, Lebrun, p. 62.   [4] *Ibid.*, p. 74.

into the narrowest possible space between that river and the Belgian frontier.

"The army detachment of H.R.H. the Crown Prince of Saxony has the special task of preventing the enemy's left wing from escaping to the east. For this purpose it is advisable that, if possible, two corps should push forward on the right bank of the Meuse and attack in flank and rear any enemy posted opposite Mouzon.

"In the same way the Third Army is to deal with the enemy's front and flank. Artillery positions as strong as possible are to be taken on this bank so as to disturb the marching and encamping of enemy columns in the valley plain on the right bank from Mouzon downwards.

"If the enemy should pass on to Belgian territory without being at once disarmed he must be pursued thither without more ado."[1]

Meanwhile, in Algeria, Fate had placed her finger on the man destined to seal the French downfall.

At 8.35 p.m. on August 22 General de Wimpffen, in command of the troops at Oran, received a telegram from Palikao ordering him forthwith to Paris. He left by boat on August 24, disembarked at Marseilles on the 27th, and the next day at 8 p.m. arrived in the capital. He found Palikao engaged until midnight and did not see him until 1 p.m. the following day, when he was informed that Bazaine was attacking Prince Frederick Charles in front, while MacMahon had fallen on his rear![2] Palikao suggested that, as General Trochu "*cherche trop à grandir sa personnalité*,"[3] he wished de Wimpffen to replace him. De Wimpffen refused and instead was appointed to succeed de Failly in command of the Vth Corps. He was then handed a roll of maps of the wrong locality and, on the morning of August 29, as he was about to enter his railway carriage and leave for the front, a messenger rushed up and thrust into his hand the following letter signed by Palikao:

"In the event of Marshal MacMahon being incapacitated, you will take over the command of the troops actually placed under his orders. I will send you an official letter regulating this, which you will make use of as occasion demands."[4]

General de Wimpffen arrived at Rheims at midday. At Rethel, as the line was unsafe, he left for Mézière by carriage at 7 p.m.

[1] Moltke's *Military Correspondence*, Précis by Spenser Wilkinson (1923), p. 122.
[2] *Sedan*, le Général de Wimpffen (1871), p. 121.
[3] *Ibid.*, p. 122.   [4] *Ibid.*, p. 124.

and arrived there at 8 a.m. on August 30. From Mézières he took a train to Bazeilles, where complete chaos reigned. At 9 p.m. he heard that MacMahon was falling back on Sedan. At 1 a.m. on the 31st he entered Sedan to find it blocked with transport, and at 9 a.m. reported to MacMahon, who received him coldly. There followed a fracas with de Failly, who had heard nothing about his demission. De Wimpffen took over the command of his corps, but made no mention of the all-important letter.

As the two Prussian armies pushed on in accordance with the instructions already quoted, the Army of Châlons straggled into Sedan. The Emperor had arrived there the previous evening and, without consulting MacMahon, had fortunately counter-ordered the advance of the newly formed XIIIth Corps from Mézières to Sedan. When MacMahon's corps entered the fortress the XIIth (Lebrun) was instructed to hold Bazeilles and the hills facing La Moncelle and Daigny, with the Ist (Ducrot) on its left, facing Givonne; while the VIIth (Félix Douay) occupied Illy and the Vth (de Failly) was held in reserve.

Sedan was badly supplied. There were no more than 200,000 rations in store and a train which brought in 800,000 more encountered shell fire and was ordered back to Mézières before it could be unloaded.[1] The truth would appear to be that only MacMahon imagined that the Army would remain in Sedan, for as Lebrun says, it was a "*nid à bombes*." Verdy du Vernois describes it as follows:

"The town itself lay before us as on a tray, so that we could even look into its streets. Several very large buildings and churches gave it quite an important look, while the clearly defined lines of the fortifications around it enclosed the whole as in a frame. Behind the town there rose gradually from the plain a line of hills, on the slopes of which a large French encampment was visible, in which there was much stir; on its crest, which descended to the left of the plain, was a wood. The lines of the distant hills beyond formed part of the neighbouring state."[2]

On the morning of August 31 Bavarian troops of the Third Army, imbued with the spirit of the offensive, crossed the Meuse by a pontoon as well as by the railway bridge south of Bazeilles, but were driven back by Lebrun's XIIth Corps. The second of

---

[1] *Histoire de la Guerre de 1870–1871*, Pierre Lehautcourt (Palat) (1907), vol. VI, p. 492.
[2] *With the Royal Headquarters*, Verdy du Vernois, vol. I, p. 127.

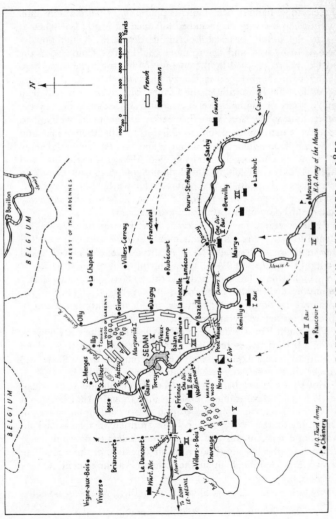

12 · BATTLE OF SEDAN, SEPTEMBER 1, 1870

these bridges had not been blown, apparently because MacMahon intended to use it in his proposed advance on Metz; but when at 5 p.m. he finally ordered Lebrun to demolish it, the powder proved to be wet, and before more could arrive from Sedan the bridge was reoccupied by the enemy.[1] Much the same thing happened with the bridges at Douzy and Donchéry. Orders were issued for the demolition of the former, but no one carried them out; a party of engineers were sent out from Sedan to destroy the latter, but while 'they were inspecting it the train which had brought them steamed off to Mézières with their tools and powder![2] Everywhere confusion reigned. When General Douay set about to entrench his position, MacMahon stopped him and said: "What, entrenching! But I do not intend to shut myself up as in Metz, I mean to manœuvre." To which Douay replied: "Will they give you time to do so?"[3] MacMahon then rode away and spent hours on inspections and routine.

Little wonder that that evening Ducrot was in despair. He turned to Dr. Sarazin and exclaimed: "*Nous sommes dans un pot de chambre et nous y serons emmerdés.*"[4] At 8 p.m. General Douay asked General Doutrelaine: "Well, what do you think of the situation?" To which Doutrelaine replied: "I think, General, we are lost." Douay was silent for a moment, then rejoined: "That is my opinion . . . nothing now remains, my dear Doutrelaine, but to do our best before we are overwhelmed."[5]

That night Paul Déroulède, a private soldier in the 3rd Zouaves, wrote a brief pencil note to his mother: "Sedan, August 31, 1870. A battle will be fought tomorrow. Eve of Jena, or eve of Waterloo, which? God alone knows. I kiss and love you, Paul."[6]

Moltke could not believe that MacMahon intended to accept battle in so unfavourable a position and thought that he would either fall back on Mézières during the night, or advance on Carignan, or retire over the Belgian frontier. Yet he issued no orders and left it to his two army commanders to continue their advance on the lines laid down in his directive of the 30th. The Crown Prince decided upon the following arrangements for his Third Army:

[1] *Bazeilles-Sedan*, Lebrun, pp. 88–89. See also *Belfort, Reims, Sedan*, le Prince Bibesco, p. 128.
[2] *Histoire de la Guerre de 1870–1871*, Palat, vol. VI, p. 484.
[3] *Ibid.*, p. 496.
[4] *Récits sur la dernière guerre franco-allemande*, Docteur Sarazin (1887), p. 115.
[5] *Belfort, Reims, Sedan*, Bibesco, p. 132.
[6] *1870-Feuilles de Route*, Paul Déroulède, pp. 175–176.

XIth and Vth Corps to move at dawn *via* Donchéry on Vrigne-aux-Bois.

The Württemberg Division to cross the Meuse at Dom-la-Mesnil and come into reserve.

The IInd Bavarian Corps to advance one division to the south of Douzy and the other to between Frénois and Wadlincourt.

The Ist Bavarian Corps to remain at Remilly and cooperate with the left of the Army of the Meuse.

The Crown Prince of Saxony's orders for the Army of the Meuse were:

One division of the Guard to move on Villers-Cernay and the other on Francheval.

The XIIth Corps to move by Lamécourt on la Moncelle.

The IVth Corps to send one division to Remilly to cooperate with the Ist Bavarian Corps, and the other to be held in reserve at Mairy.[1]

The Army of Châlons had by now fully occupied the triangle between the rivers Meuse, Floing and Givonne. The XIIth Corps (right wing) occupied Balan, Bazeilles, la Moncelle and la Platinerie; the VIIth Corps (left wing) stretched from Floing to Illy; and the Ist Corps (centre) linked these two wings together, while the Vth was held in reserve at Vieux-Camp. Unfortunately for the French, during the night of August 31, and contrary to orders, the outposts of the XIIth Corps had fallen back from the Meuse and Bazeilles. This enabled General von der Tann, commander of the Ist Bavarian Corps, to cross by the railway bridge at 4 a.m. on September 1, under cover of a dense fog, and penetrate as far as Bazeilles.[2] There the French gallantly counter-attacked and his Bavarians were driven back. Meanwhile, the Saxons advanced on la Moncelle, only to be checked by the French skirmishers, and at 8 a.m. the Saxon artillery, by then reinforced, silenced their opponents' batteries.

At about 7 a.m.,[3] as this action was being fought, Marshal MacMahon was so severely wounded by a shell fragment while visiting the XIIth Corps that he relinquished his command and appointed General Ducrot to succeed him. About 8 a.m. Ducrot received this information, and as he knew nothing of MacMahon's plan, nor had received any instructions from him, he at once took

---

[1] See *The Franco-German War, 1870–1871* (German Official Account, English trans. 1881–1884), vol. II, part I, pp. 307–309.

[2] *Ibid.*, p. 312.   [3] *Bazeilles-Sedan*, Lebrun, p. 100.

action. From the first he had been opposed to accepting battle in so unfavourable a position, and when the news of his appointment reached him he was watching strong enemy columns moving north-west to turn the left flank of his corps. He turned to his Staff and exclaimed: "Gentlemen, I have been placed in supreme command. We have not a moment to lose. We must at once withdraw to the plateau of Illy. When we are there our retreat will be assured, and we can then make up our minds what to do."[1] His chief of staff suggested that the Emperor should first be informed of this change, whereupon Ducrot turned on him and shouted: "*Que l'Empereur aille se faire f—— ou il voudra*, it is he who has put us in this mess."[2]

At once he sent orders to his own corps, the Ist, and to Lebrun's, the XIIth, to disengage and fall back on Illy, preparatory to a withdrawal on Mézières. Lebrun at first demurred, and then, at 9 a.m., began to evacuate Bazeilles. By 10 a.m. the Bavarian advance was eased, and before 11 o'clock the village was in their hands.

Now took place an event rare in history. The Army of Châlons had had two commanders-in-chief within three hours of the opening of the battle; now it was about to have a third – General de Wimpffen, at the time in command of the Vth Corps at Vieux-Camp. At 7.15 a.m. he had heard that Marshal MacMahon was wounded[3] and a little over an hour later that Ducrot was in command;[4] yet he had made no use of Palikao's letter. At about 8.30 a.m. he visited General Lebrun, and as he believed that the repulse of the Bavarians meant a French victory he was furious to learn soon after that Ducrot had ordered a withdrawal. Pulling out his letter of commission he proclaimed himself commander-in-chief, turned to Lebrun and exclaimed: "Stop forthwith the movement General Ducrot has ordered you to carry out. . . . I will not have a retirement on Mézières. If the army is to retire it is to be on Carignan and not on Mézières."[5] He then wrote a hasty note to Ducrot informing him that he was superseded.[6]

---

[1] *Sedan*, Ernest Picard (1912), p. 33 (Déposition Ducrot). In *La Journée de Sedan*, Ducrot (1871), a slightly different version is given.

[2] *La Guerre de 1870–71* (French Official History, 1901), vol. III, p. 55.

[3] *Sedan*, Wimpffen, p. 158.

[4] *La Guerre de 1870–71* (French Official History), vol. III, p. 66, and *Bazeilles-Sedan*, p. 110.

[5] *Bazeilles-Sedan*, Lebrun, pp. 111–112.

[6] See *La Journée de Sedan*, Ducrot, pp. 28–29, and *Sedan*, Wimpffen, p. 162. The latter is unreliable, several words in the original document are changed.

Ducrot, on receipt of it, galloped to de Wimpffen's corps and in conversation with him discovered his ignorance of the field of battle to be so profound that he did not know what Illy was.[1] De Wimpffen counter-ordered the withdrawal and at 10.30 a.m. met the Emperor who, when informed of its cancellation, became greatly agitated. "Your Majesty need have no fears," said de Wimpffen. "Within two hours from now we shall have thrust the enemy into the Meuse."[2]

The Crown Prince of Saxony was engaged on the Givonne. At 7.30 a.m. King William and his Staff rode over to the small hill south-west of Frénois to watch the advance of the Third Army, which had marched out of its bivouacs at 3 a.m. The XIth Corps had crossed the Meuse at Donchéry and was marching on the sound of the guns. The road was good and its advanced guard, meeting no opposition, passed through the defile of St. Albert and occupied St. Menges. At 10 a.m. seven of its battalions began to form front against Illy and these were soon supported by 62 guns from the rise of Hattoy. So devastating was their fire that General Marguerite ordered General Galliffet to charge the enemy infantry then approaching Illy. He most gallantly did so, and was driven back at great loss.

When this advance was reported to General de Wimpffen he began to realize his danger, but worse was to follow. The Crown Prince's Vth Corps, which had advanced close on the heels of the XIth, brought up 60 guns to the wood of Hattoy to support the 84 of the XIth Corps then in action. The fire of these two groups crossed that of the guns of the Army of the Meuse and demolished the French batteries. Half an hour later the left of the Third Army and the right of the Army of the Meuse made contact near Illy and the French forces were surrounded.

The King, Bismarck, Moltke, Roon, princes, dukes, gunners and aides-de-camp now gathered on the hill by Frénois. They were joined by Colonel Walker, the British military plenipotentiary, and General Sheridan of Five Forks fame.

"About 11 o'clock," writes Moritz Busch, "there rises from the fortress, which, by the way, is not firing, a black, grey pillar of smoke, edged with yellow. Beyond it the French are firing furiously, and above the wood of the gorge rise unceasingly a

[1] *La Journée de Sedan*, Ducrot, pp. 30–31.
[2] *Ibid.*, p. 32. See also *Histoire de la Guerre de 1870–71*, Palat, vol. VI, p. 546, for a slightly different version.

number of little white clouds from bombs, whether German or French we know not; sometimes also the cracking and snarling of a *mitrailleuse*."[1]

While the Third Army was enveloping the French left, the Prussian Guard, who had entered Villers-Cernay at 8 a.m., moved round the left of the French Ist Corps and brought into action 120 guns on the enemy batteries west of the Givonne. Once again this concentration of fire proved overwhelming; it drove the French infantry into the wood of Garenne, already crowded with fugitives. At 10 a.m. the Saxons carried Daigny and brought up 29 batteries at the gallop. At this phase of the battle, writes Prince Hohenlohe, "the effect of their combined fire at such a short range was truly terrible. . . . The spectacle of the carnage was horrible; the fearful cries of the victims of our shells reached as far as where we stood . . . our superiority over the enemy was so overwhelming that we suffered no loss at all. The batteries fired as if at practice."[2]

"It was now one o'clock," continues Busch. "Our line of fire by this time swept the larger half of the enemy's position on the heights on the other side of the town. . . . Between two and three o'clock by my watch, the King came close past the place where I was standing, and said to the people about him, after looking for some time through a glass towards the suburb: 'They are pushing great masses forward there to the left – that, I think, must be an attempt to break through'."[3]

He was right: General Marguerite's cavalry division was preparing to attack Floing. At about 2 p.m. Ducrot, who realized that the position was desperate, rode over to Marguerite and implored him to blaze a trail through the enemy for his infantry to follow. He at once agreed but was mortally wounded while reconnoitring. Galliffet took over command and three charges were made. In spite of the heroism shown, each failed, but Galliffet, accompanied by a few officers and chasseurs, penetrated to the enemy reserves. On their return, when they were within pistol-shot of a Prussian battalion, its commander was so filled with admiration that he ordered the cease fire. The French troopers shouted *"Vive l'Empereur!"* at which the German officers saluted as they galloped past.[4]

[1] *Bismarck in the Franco-German War*, J. H. M. Busch (1879), vol. I, p. 97.
[2] *Letters on Artillery*, Prince Kraft zu Hohenlohe-Ingelfingen (English edit., 1890), pp. 93, 94.
[3] *Bismarck in the Franco-German War*, vol. I, pp. 98–99.
[4] See *Sedan*, Ernest Picard, pp. 108–109.

Although the doom of the Army of Châlons was now sealed, General de Wimpffen seemed oblivious of the true situation; at the moment when the enemy was storming the Calvaire d'Illy he sent the following message to General Douay:

"I have decided to smash my way through the enemy and reach Carignan in order to gain Montmédy. You are to cover the retreat. Rally around you all troops now in the wood [of Garenne]."[1]

The situation confronting Douay's VIIth Corps is described by Prince Bibesco as follows:

"The wrack of the rout is rolling towards the moats of Sedan, which are to swallow up the débris of our unfortunate army, consisting of fractions of all corps and all arms. From every point on the horizon shells are being fired which smite the maddened masses in front, in flank and in rear. Amidst shouts of fear mingled with groans, on our right an ambulance bursts into flames and is pulverized by shells. Around us artillery limbers explode to add to the number of the victims. Everywhere one can see singly and grouped together the riderless horses of our heroic cavalry – exhausted and bleeding."[2]

Between noon and 1 p.m. Lebrun's XIIth Corps held its own and the Bavarians failed to push beyond Bazeilles. In order to cut his way to Carignan, de Wimpffen decided to throw in the Vth Corps and hurl the enemy into the Meuse. To cover this desperate attempt he had sent his order to Douay and at the same time had instructed Ducrot to assemble his corps and march by way of la Moncelle on Bazeilles. At 1.30 p.m. he sent the following note to the Emperor:

"Sire, I have decided to force the line facing General Lebrun and General Ducrot rather than be taken prisoner in Sedan.

"I beg your Majesty to place yourself in the midst of your soldiers, so that they may have the honour of opening a way for your retreat."[3]

Louis Napoleon was in Sedan when this note was handed to him; he read it and rightly set the proposal aside. Instead, he considered reassuming the supreme command and capitulating.

While he pondered this last act of his reign Ducrot's corps dissolved and huddled in and around Sedan. As Ducrot entered the moat of the citadel an officer shouted: "The white flag is hoisted!"

[1] *Belfort–Reims–Sedan*, Bibesco, p. 154.
[2] *Ibid.*, p. 155.   [3] *Sedan*, Wimpffen, p. 170.

At that moment Ducrot received de Wimpffen's orders. He writes:

"Within Sedan the situation was indescribable: streets, open places and entrances were blocked with wagons, carts, cannon and and all the impedimenta and débris of a routed army. Bands of soldiers without rifles or equipment rushed here and there seeking refuge in the houses and the churches, while at the gates of the town they crushed each other to death. Athwart this rabble galloped troopers *ventre à terre*, and gunners on limbers lashed their way through the maddened mob. Such as were not completely insane had set to work to pillage, and others shouted: 'We have been betrayed, we have been sold by traitors and cowards!'"[1]

Ducrot presented himself to the Emperor, who exclaimed: "Why is the firing going on? I have hoisted the white flag." He bade Ducrot write a note ordering all fire to cease. Ducrot did so, but refused to sign it as de Wimpffen was commander-in-chief, and General Faure, chief of staff, also refused to sign.[2] The Emperor dictated another letter, this time for de Wimpffen, and gave it to Lebrun to take to him,[3] but the commander-in-chief refused to read it. Lebrun pointed out that the white flag had been hoisted. "No! No!" cried de Wimpffen, "I will have no capitulation. Haul the flag down. I intend to continue the battle."[4]

De Wimpffen hurried to Sedan, not to see the Emperor but to collect such men as he could for his counter-attack. With the idea of rousing the terror-stricken fugitives he shouted: "Bazaine approaches! Bazaine approaches!"[5] but although a few rallied round him, many skulked away. At length, when he had gathered some 1,200 men and two guns he headed them for Balan. It was the act of a madman. The band of heroic or demented men met a hail of bullets from both sides and ran howling back to the fortress. Whereupon de Wimpffen exclaimed to Lebrun: "I resign my appointment as general-in-chief; you will take my place!"[6]

Naturally Lebrun refused the honour, and at 6 p.m. the Emperor informed General Ducrot that he wished him to take over command. He refused, and so did General Douay. Thereupon de Wimpffen, wildly gesticulating, shouted: "Sire, if I have lost the battle, if I have been beaten, it is because my orders have not been carried out, it is because your generals have refused to obey me."[7]

---

[1] *La Journée de Sedan*, p. 46.
[2] *La Journée de Sedan*, Ducrot, p. 48–51.
[3] *Bazeilles-Sedan*, Lebrun, p. 133.
[4] *Ibid.*, p. 135.
[5] See *Sedan*, Picard, p. 147.
[6] *Bazeille–Sedan*, Lebrun, p. 141.
[7] *La Journée de Sedan*, Ducrot, p. 52.

Ducrot sprang to his feet and contradicted him and a wordy dispute followed. At length de Wimpffen accepted the inevitable and agreed to proceed to the enemy's headquarters and surrender the army.

Some time before this scene a Bavarian officer galloped up the hill of Frénois, where the royal headquarters were still established, and informed the King that the French had decided to capitulate. "About half past six, a guard of honour of cuirassiers appeared a little way off, and the French General, Reille, the bearer of Napoleon's flag of truce, rode slowly up the hill. He dismounted 10 paces from the King and went up to him, took off his cap and presented him with a letter bearing a large red seal."[1] The King opened it and read:

> *Monsieur mon Frère,*
>
> *N'ayant pu mourir au milieu de mes troupes, il ne me reste qu'à remettre mon epée entre les mains de Votre Majesté.*
>
> > *Je suis de Votre Majesté,*
> > *le bon Frère,*
> > *Napoléon.*
>
> *Sédan, le 1er Septembre, 1870.*

He conferred with his Chancellor, and then wrote a reply. General Reille, accompanied by an officer, and a Uhlan trumpeter carrying a white flag, then rode back to Sedan in the twilight. "The town was still blazing in three places, and the red lights flashing in the pillar of smoke rising over Bazeilles showed that the conflagration there was still raging. But for these signs the tragedy of Sedan was played out, and the curtain of night fell on the scene."[2]

The next morning, at about six o'clock, a voice called out in the passage of Doctor Jeanjot's house in Donchéry: "Your Excellency! Your Excellency! there is a French general [Reille] down here at the door; I don't understand what he wants." Bismarck leapt out of bed, hastily dressed and rode to Sedan. As soon as he could, Dr. Busch followed him to a solitary house, some 800 paces from the bridge over the Meuse at Donchéry: "a one-storied house, painted yellow, with four windows in front, white shutters on the ground floor, and on the first floor white venetian blinds." Busch then writes: "Soon afterwards a little thick-set man came

---

[1] *Bismarck in the Franco-German War*, Busch, vol. I, p. 101.
[2] *Ibid.*, vol. I, p. 102.

forward, behind the house, who wore a red cap with a gold border, a black patelot lined with red, with a hood, and red trousers. He spoke, first to the Frenchmen, some of whom were sitting on the bank near the potatoes. He wore white kid gloves, and was smoking a cigarette."[1]

It was the Emperor. He had surrendered himself to Prussia, but the capitulation of his army was left to General de Wimpffen. After a lengthy argument this resulted in an all but unconditional surrender.[2]

The losses in the two German armies were about 460 officers and 8,500 men killed and wounded,[3] and the French lost 3,000 killed, 14,000 wounded, and 21,000 prisoners;[4] which with 83,000 prisoners at the capitulation and 3,000 disarmed in Belgium made a total of 124,000. Also one eagle and two colours, 419 field guns and *mitrailleuses*, 139 garrison guns, 1,072 carriages and 6,000 serviceable horses were surrendered.

"The victory of Sedan," writes the German official historian, "crowns the united efforts of the German leaders and their men with a success almost unprecedented in history." These words are not exaggerated. He continues:

"With the defeat of an entire army the Napoleonic dynasty in France crumbles for the third time to the dust. Instantaneously as the lightning's flash, the startling intelligence spreads throughout the realms of Germany and through the whole of Europe, where it is received partly with sparkling enthusiasm and partly with incredulous astonishment. The German Army, however, in ignorance at first of the *political* consequences of the victory, casts, with the captive adversary at its feet, an anxious glance towards the French Capital."[5]

What went on in Paris on that fateful day?

At 10.35 a.m. the commander of the 1st Division of the XIIIth Corps at Mézières telegraphed to Palikao: "I am informed at this very instant that King William and his son, who slept last night at Clermont in Argonne, are in full retreat." Later came in a dispatch from Brussels, timed 7.25 p.m.: "MacMahon has this morning defeated the Prussians; this morning Bazaine was pur-

---

[1] *Ibid.*, vol. I, pp. 103–104.

[2] For the capitulation see *The German Official History* (1881–1884), vol. II, part I, pp. 402–409, and *The French Official History*, vol. III, pp. 242–273.

[3] For detail see *The German Official History*, Appendix I.

[4] *Ibid.*, vol. III, part I, p. 408. The official French figures are 799 officers killed and wounded, and 23,689 men killed, wounded and disappeared.

[5] *German Official History*, vol. II, part I, p. 416.

suing them towards Sedan"; which report was confirmed from London at 12.30 a.m. on September 2.[1]

Apparently the exchanges were busy rigging the stock-markets. Then came de Wimpffen's letter to Palikao, beginning: "*Mon général*, – I can say: I came, I saw and I was defeated. . . ."[2] which threw Paris into revolution. On September 4 the Assembly was stormed by a rabble shouting "*Vive la sociale!*" Palikao fell, and Trochu, whom he had persistently frustrated, replaced him as head of the Government: the last lap and the longest of the war was now entered.

By the end of September Paris was surrounded, and while Metz, Belfort, Strasbourg, Toul, Verdun and Mézières held out, the Defense Nationale raised new armies. Then all the fortresses fell one by one, except Belfort, and on December 17 the bombardment of Paris was opened. On January 29, 1871, Paris capitulated. For over 200 years it had been the centre of European politics, Berlin took its place until 1918.

An event which preceded the capitulation by 11 days was equally important. On January 18, 1871, in the Hall of Mirrors in the Palace of Versailles, in the centre of which is painted "*Le Roi Gouverne Par Lui-Même*," William I of Prussia was proclaimed Emperor of Germany. Thus did Wallenstein's dream of 240 years before come true. Equally historic, when the French garrison in Rome was withdrawn during the war, the Papal mercenaries laid down their arms before Victor Emmanuel. Thus was the national union of Italy accomplished, a task urged by Machiavelli upon the Italian princes three and a half centuries earlier.

Disorder followed on the surrender of Paris, and on March 18 came the Commune, in which 30,000 men, women and children perished in fratricidal strife. Finally, on May 10, the treaty of Frankfort was signed, and ratified by the National Assembly on the 18th. Its terms were moderate and in no way vindictive.[3]

---

[1] *Un Ministère de la Guerre*, etc., Palikao, pp. 74–75.   [2] *Ibid.*, p. 121.

[3] When in September, 1870, the *National Zeitung* complained of the considerate treatment accorded to the captive French Emperor, Bismarck by no means shared this view. "Popular feeling, public opinion," he said, "always take that line. People insist that, in conflicts between States, the conqueror should sit in judgment upon the conquered, moral code in hand, and inflict punishment upon him for what he has done, not only to the victor himself, but to third parties as well. This is an altogether unreasonable demand. Punishment and revenge have nothing to do with policy. Policy must not meddle with the calling of Nemesis, or aspire to exercise the judge's office. . . . In such a case as the one referred to, the question would be, 'Which of the two will be most useful to us – a badly-used Napoleon or a well-used Napoleon?' It is by no means impossible that he may one day rise to the surface again" (*Our Chancellor*, Moritz Busch, English edit., 1884, vol. 1, pp. 98–99).

(*1*) The payment of an indemnity of £200,000,000.

(*2*) The right of Germany to be treated by France as the most favoured nation.

(*3*) The annexation of Alsace and Eastern Lorraine.

Although Leopold von Ranke and most Germans at the time justified the annexation of Alsace – an essentially German province – and of Eastern Lorraine – mainly French – it would have been wiser for Prussia to have foregone their strategical advantages and to have considered the political implications of their seizure. It not only humiliated a proud nation, but mortgaged the future, because from the Peace of Frankfort onward every foreign enemy of the German Empire would be able to count upon France as a potential if not an actual ally. Thus the annexation of Alsace-Lorraine became a festering sore in the peace of Europe.

What were the influences of this war on history?

The first was that, by humbling France – a humiliation from which she never recovered – it made Germany "Queen of the Continent."[1] The second was her upsurge of strength unhinged the balance of power in Europe and directly challenged the *Pax Britannica*, which had prevented the war from developing into a general European conflict. The third was that Britain was compelled to bring to an end her centuries old quarrel with France in order to re-establish the balance of power in regard to Germany. The fourth was that, when after the war Germany set out to become a leading industrial country, a quarrel with Great Britain over the markets of the world became inevitable. Henceforth there were to be only two really great military and commercial Powers in Europe proper, Britain who commanded the sea, and Germany who commanded the land, and, as in the days of Napoleon, although there was room enough in Europe for half-a-dozen great Powers to live in concord, there was insufficient room for two although neither desired war with the other. This ineluctable fact, which has dogged European history since the fall of Rome, established a general fear which through industrialization led to the militarization of Europe, until before the end of the nineteenth century all her continental nations, in varying degrees of efficiency, had become nations in arms. And because henceforth the words "military" and "political" were to become interchangeable, it is of no little importance briefly to consider the influences of the Franco-Prussian conflict on the art of war.

[1] Thomas Carlyle in a letter to *The Times*, November 11, 1870.

The first is the growing preponderance of artillery over infantry, which is seen throughout the war, and is well expressed by a French officer taken prisoner at Sedan, when he ascribed the German success to "five kilometres of artillery."[1] The preponderance of the cannon and all the technical requirements which followed in its wake gave a tremendous stimulus to science and industry, which began to become the material bases of war. As the cavalry age in war had given way to the infantry, so now was the infantry age giving way to that of artillery. War was to become more and more industrialized and industrial civilization demanded its military counterpart.

The second is the increasing influence of railways on military organization, and because of them the rapid development of mass-armies. Though the idea of the nation in arms dates back to Guibert and was expanded by Clausewitz, it was unrealizable until railways were built. It was the locomotive which regimented the nations, democratized their armies, and made peace a preparatory period for war.

The third is the increasing importance of the Staff system (business management). In so complex an instrument as a modern army its advantages are obvious; yet its dangers and defects were not appreciated, or at most very superficially so, once the war was at an end.

Guglielmo Ferrero in his essay *The Problem of Peace* points out that, between 1870 and 1914, war-making power and peace-making power, which formerly had been in the same hands, became separated; the one became the exclusive province of the General Staff and the other of civilians and diplomats. "But what could civilians and diplomats do," he writes, "when the old rules of the art of making peace were made inoperative by the new methods of making war? The soldiers perfected the technique of war; the diplomats lost the art of making peace. . . . Being unable to make peace, the diplomats in their turn began to prepare the way for war by making and unmaking alliances. Two Powers had signed the armistice of 1871, but when it was repudiated in 1914 it was two formidable groups of Powers that confronted one another, armed to the teeth."[2] In other words, the more perfect the technical side of war grew, the less possible did it become politically to limit

---

[1] Quoted from *Decisive Battles Since Waterloo*, Thomas W. Knox (1889), p. 358.
[2] *Peace and War* (1933), p. 132. To Ferrero the period 1870–1914 was an armistice and not a peace.

its radius, until the whole world became so explosive that a pistol shot in some obscure corner of it was sufficient to detonate a global war. In its turn, this foretold that national wars would give way to wars between coalitions, and that in the future, unless a nation was a partner of a coalition, its resources would prove insufficient to conduct successfully a war single-handed.

This point – the growing power of the Prussian Staff system – introduces the question of generalship and command.

Moltke's famous maxim was "First reckon, then risk," and in this war the risks were not great, yet had he been faced by a normally good general assisted by a normally efficient staff, they might easily have become startling. As it was, the Prussian Staff system displayed many defects, obscured only by the utter rottenness of the French. For instance, the insubordination of General Steinmetz ("the Lion of Nachod"), whom Bismarck called "a blood-spendthrift", and the precipitated way such battles as Spicheren, Wörth, and Colombey were fought. Of the first two, Verdy du Vernois says: "Both battles are peculiar, in so far as they were fought against the will of the Commander-in-Chief"[1] – an extraordinary confession.

Moltke may be described as a general on rails, for his system of war was both direct and rigid. He was a supremely great war organizer, who relied on logic rather than on opportunity. For success his art depended on adherence to a somewhat static doctrine set in motion by *directives* rather than by orders. To him a war of masses was a war of accidents in which genius was subordinate to the offensive spirit. Whereas Napoleon I led and controlled throughout, Moltke brought his armies to their starting points and then abdicated his command and unleashed them. On August 31 and September 1 he never issued an order except for a few suggestions to General Blumenthal, chief of staff of the Third Army. He never foresaw the encirclement of the French, which was due to their stupidity, the initiative of the Prussian army commanders and the superb handling of the Prussian artillery. Moltke is not a general to copy but to study. His reckonings were wonderful, yet his risks against an able opponent might easily have proved damnable; for he was apt to be run away with by his subordinates.

Finally, this war showed, as Thiers said, "that in the great duel of peoples, unless accidents or material means are disproportion-

[1] *With the Royal Headquarters in 1870–71*, vol. I, pp. 56–57.

ate, victory remains with the nation which holds ascendency in science and moral force."[1] The will to win and the means to fight were the pillars of might which only emerged from the fogs and mists of doctrinaire soldiership into clear daylight during the First and Second World Wars.

[1] Quoted from *Les Deux Abimes*, Alfred de la Guéronniere, p. 16.

EDITOR'S NOTE 4

The end of the 19th Century was a period of accelerating technological change, which naturally deeply affected arms and armies. (It also deeply affected navies, and we should note in passing that the last decade of the century saw much profound and justified soul-searching about the reality of the supremacy of the Royal Navy. One able admiral wrote: "I always look on the year 1889 as marking the lowest level of efficiency of material that the British Navy had known since the middle of the 18th century.")[1] On land there were important developments of armaments, the most radical, says Fuller, being the adoption of the small bore magazine rifle and smokeless powder. It fell to the British Army to make the first encounter with these phenomena on a large scale during the South African War of 1899-1902.

In this war the old terror of a visible foe gave way to the paralysing sensation of advancing on an invisible one, which fostered the suspicion that the enemy was everywhere. A universal terror, rather than a localized danger, now enveloped the attacker, while the defender, always ready to protect himself by some rough earth or stone-work, was enabled through the rapidity of rifle-fire to use extensions unheard of in past fighting, and in consequence to overlap every frontal attack. Thus, at the battle of the Modder River, the Boers extended three thousand men on a frontage of seven thousand seven hundred yards; at Magersfontein, five thousand on eleven thousand; and at Colenso, four thousand five hundred on thirteen thousand. Yet in spite of this human thinness, these fronts could not be penetrated. This spelt the end of successful frontal rifle attacks.

The lesson was very soon spelt out again, but unfortunately not heeded by the great military powers. What could not fail to be

[1] Admiral Sir Reginald Bacon, *A Naval Scrap-Book, 1877-1900*, Hutchinson.

heeded, however, was the fact that a new great power had emerged – in Asia. The deliberate isolationism of Japan had been roughly overturned by America and the leading European states in 1854, but the modernisation of Japanese society did not really begin until 1869. European and American capitalists financed the process of industrialization, which went forward at such a pace that, as Fuller says, "by the time the century had run its course Japan had accomplished in a generation what Europe had taken twenty generations to effect. From a feudal polity, such as had existed in the West in the 14th century, she stepped over the threshold of the 20th century a fully equipped industrial, military and naval power." Like others of the same ilk, Japan soon applied her new-found strength to overseas expansion, and the area where this could most readily be performed was, of course, the neighbouring territory of China and Korea.

For the greater part of the 19th Century China had been the prey of other aggressive empires, most notably Russia, which obtained by the Treaty of Aigun in 1858 the cession of no less than 715,000 square miles on the left bank of the Amur, and two years later a further 173,000 square miles – the province of Manchuria. Not satisfied with this, Russian expansionists cast greedy eyes upon Korea. This was alarming to Japan, and as early as 1876 the Japanese began their infiltration of that area. By 1894 Korea had become a Japanese "sphere of influence", and an appeal by the Korean Government to China for help against revolutionaries in that year led immediately to the first Sino-Japanese War. At sea and on land the Japanese won battle after battle, culminating in the capture of Port Arthur at a trifling cost on 21 November. In April 1895 China sued for peace, and by its terms Japan gained the Liao-tung peninsula, Formosa and the Pescadores, and recognition of Korea's "independence".

It was at this point, in the flush of victory, that Japan sustained a rude shock. Combined pressure by Russia, Germany and France compelled her to abandon the Liao-tung peninsula and Port Arthur. Japanese distrust of European motives and dislike of European methods were naturally much enhanced by this event, and its sequel proved just as infuriating. In 1897 Russia secured the lease of the Liao-tung peninsula, and with it permission to construct a railway line connecting Port Arthur with Harbin, on the main Trans-Siberian railway route from Moscow to Vladivostock. At the same time the Germans obtained the lease of Kiao-chow, the French Kwang Cho Wan, and the British, not to be left out, Wei-hai-wei. Sauce for the European geese was evidently not for the Japanese gander. Nevertheless, the Boxer Rising in China in 1900 produced a last flicker of imperialist amity and cooperation: an International Force comprising British, French, German, Russian, Austrian, Italian, American and Japanese contingents. Of these the Japanese contingent was by far the largest; its bravery, and its efficiency were much admired, and its behaviour compared well with that of some European forces.

If Europeans took an interested note of their first close-up view of the Imperial Japanese Army in action, the Japanese took heart from what they observed of the Russians – "an army of un-believable inefficiency."[1] In 1902 there were two important developments: the first was the signature of the Anglo-Japanese Alliance which was to be a large factor in the policies of both countries until 1921. In 1902 it carried the special significance of British recognition of Japanese "interests" in Korea, and the further implication that in the event of war with Russia, Japan could count on British help if any other power (e.g. Russia's ally, France) came in on the Russian side. The second development was that in 1902 war with Russia became virtually certain. In 1903 the Russians tried to claim Korea as their own sphere of influence. The Japanese then "offered to recognize Russia's position in Manchuria, provided that Russia extended similar recognition to Japan's position in Korea, and further they proposed that all nations should be granted equal commercial rights in both countries."[2] But the negotiations came to nothing; signs of bad faith on the Russian side multiplied, and on 5 February 1904 war broke out.

The Russo-Japanese War was dominated by two strategic considerations. The first was the importance to the Japanese of Port Arthur. "In 1894," says Fuller, "Japan had taken Port Arthur and then had been deprived of it because she was too weak to hold it. To regain it would not only justify the war, but above all it would proclaim the superiority of Japan over Russia, and, incidentally, of Asia over Europe. In short, whether strategy demanded it or not, the conquest of Port Arthur was for Japan

[1] Fuller.

[2] Fuller.

the spiritual pivot of the conflict." The second consideration was that the distance from Moscow to Port Arthur is five thousand five hundred miles, and in 1904 the link was a single-track railway with a gap in it of one hundred miles at Lake Baikal. Added to the established shortcomings of the Russian military system, this gave the Japanese a clear advantage.

The course of the war was marked (as in 1894) by an unbroken sequence of Japanese successes on land and sea. Port Arthur fell, after a grim siege, on 4 January 1905; over twenty-four thousand Russians were captured, and a further thirty-one thousand killed, wounded and missing. The Japanese losses were fifty-seven thousand, and in addition thirty-three thousand sick, of whom no less than twenty-one thousand were suffering from beriberi. In February-March the Battle of Mukden was fought on a frontage of forty miles, ending with Japanese victory at a cost of seventy-one thousand casualties, compared with the Russian eighty-five thousand (including prisoners). In May the Russian Baltic Fleet was annihilated in the Battle of Tsushima Strait, and three months later the war ended. By the Treaty of Portsmouth Russia (now threatened with internal revolution) agreed to evacuate Manchuria, ceded the Liao-tung peninsula to Japan, together with half the island of Sakhalin, and recognised Japanese preponderance in Korea. It was a brilliant result for the new island power.

We have already noted a significant tactical change arising from the introduction of the magazine rifle and smokeless powder. Fuller continues:

' Besides the magazine rifle, the crude *mitrailleuse* of 1870 had given way to a number of improved machine-guns – the Gatling, Gardener, Nordenfeldt, Hotchkiss, Colt, and Maxim. The last named was designed by Hiram S. Maxim in 1884, and in the First World War it became the queen of the battlefield. Probably it has killed and wounded more men than any other weapon, yet in its youth it was little considered by soldiers.

' Since the introduction of rifled cannon, the field-gun had steadily forged ahead. In the Russo-Turkish War of 1877–1878 the Russian General Oukanov had said: "Artillery will become the scourge of mankind. . . . The day cannot be much longer delayed when artillery shall raise itself from being an auxiliary to the rank of the principal arm." A decisive step toward this end was taken when the proposals put forward by General Wille in

Germany and Colonel Langlois in France in 1891–1892 a few years later led to the invention of the quick-firing field gun, which by absorbing its recoil on discharge enabled the non-recoiling gun carriage to be introduced; it permitted a bullet-proof shield to be attached to it, and thus reintroduced armour on the battlefield. Until this improvement was made, the magazine rifle was the dominant weapon, but after its introduction it was challenged by the quick-firing gun, which not only outranged it and could be fired with equal rapidity, but which by indirect laying could also be made invisible.

There was a general failure in the world's armies (at any rate in their controlling staffs) to take due note either of the new power of artillery displayed in the Russo-Japanese War – especially the great modern howitzers which had reduced Port Arthur's defences – or of the effect of machine guns in conjunction with wire entanglements and trenches. A crude form of poison gas had even been employed by the Japanese, and this also escaped notice and consideration. All too soon the great powers would have to re-learn the lessons they might have absorbed from Manchuria at a terrible cost. But Fuller goes on:

‘ More important than these tactical changes were the influences of Japan's victory on world affairs. It disrupted Russia by stimulating the virus of revolution which for long had eaten into her bowels. By liberating Germany from fear of war on her eastern flank it freed her to concentrate on her western border, and thereby upset the balance of power in Europe. This caused Great Britain to abandon her policy of isolation, which had been the backbone of the *Pax Britannica*, and, in order to re-establish the balance, it drew her away from Germany toward France. Further, by challenging the supremacy of the white man over the coloured, it awakened Asia and Africa and dealt a deadly moral blow to every colonial empire. Though this was little appreciated at the time, in his treatise *The Problem of National and Colonial Policy and the Third International*, M. Pavlovich points out that "The Russian Revolution of 1905 played the same great part in the life of the Asiatic people as the French Revolution had formerly played in European countries. It gave the impulse in Turkey to the revolutionary activities which led to the fall of Abdul Hamid. It made an overwhelming impression upon Persia, which was the first Asiatic nation to start a simultaneous struggle against its own despots and against the rapacity of European governments. The same is true of China. But everywhere European intervention frustrated the fulfilment of dreams of national liberty."

' In Africa the influence was equally profound. Dicey, an Englishman, who had lived in that continent for 40 years, writes: "Suddenly and unexpectedly, the conviction that native forces, however brave, were bound to be worsted by Europeans, was shaken to its base by the discovery that Russia, which was regarded in the East as the greatest military power in Europe, had been driven from pillar to post by the victorious Japanese, that her armies had been put to flight, her navy destroyed, her fortresses captured by a comparatively diminutive and feeble Power, whose people, whatever else they might be, were certainly not Caucasians or Christians. It may be said with truth that the native Africans . . . knew nothing . . . about Japan. But yet I should doubt whether there was a town or village in the whole of Africa where the inhabitants did not learn directly or indirectly that the Russian invaders of the Far East had been scattered like sheep by an unknown non-European race."

' But it was in India – the pivot of British imperial power – that this world revolution took surest form. There "A stir of excitement passed over" the northern provinces, writes C. F. Andrews. "Even the remote villages talked over the victories of Japan as they sat in their circles and passed round the *huqqa* at night. . . . A Turkish consul of long experience in Western Asia told me that in the interior you could see everywhere the most ignorant peasants 'tingling' with the news. Asia was moved from one end to the other, and the sleep of the centuries was finally broken. . . . A new chapter was being written in the book of the world's history. . . . The old-time glory and greatness of Asia seemed destined to return."

' In corroboration of this, Mr. Pradhan writes: "It is impossible to exaggerate the effects of the Japanese victory on the Indian mind." Indian students began to study the history of Japan to discover what had enabled her to wound so deeply one of the greatest European Powers. They found the answer in Japanese patriotism, self-sacrifice and national unity. Here were miraculous powers beyond the might of armaments. The rise of Japan was looked upon as "a divine dispensation". Indian students flocked to the Rising Sun, and in the years 1907, 1908 and 1909 they returned haloed with knowledge, both true and spurious, to take part in the *Swadeshi* movement, and to help a cause which the

Japanese victories had endowed with a vigour undreamt of before the war.

'All these stupendous happenings were fertilized by this conflict, fought on the far eastern flank of Asia, as over 450 years before an equally great conflict had been fought on the far eastern flank of Europe. The fall of Port Arthur in 1905, like the fall of Constantinople in 1453, rightly may be numbered among the few really great events in history.'

That the awakening of Asia was one of the great events in history is not to be doubted; but it is one of the ironies of history that it was soon overtaken by a series of events of even greater dimensions. In fact, it was in the very year of the fall of Port Arthur, 1905, that the first of the crises occurred which inexorably led to the First World War nine years later.

Fuller leans to the theory that the First World War was above all an "economic war"; he quotes a saying of President Woodrow Wilson in 1919: "This war . . . was a commercial and industrial war. It was not a political war." Fuller also quotes John Maynard Keynes (writing at about the same time): "England had destroyed, as in each preceding century, a trade rival . . ." One wonders whether either Wilson or Keynes would have said the same things quite so categorically in 1929 or 1939.

Certainly, trade rivalry between Germany and Britain had become a serious matter by 1914 – but statistics can be misleading. Fuller, for example gives figures showing that between 1894 and 1904 German merchant shipping tonnage increased by 234 per cent. This may be so, but it is nevertheless a fact that in 1910-12 British merchant shipping tonnage amounted to 11,700,000, while German tonnage was 3,000,000 – which puts a somewhat different gloss on the rivalry. Similarly with world trade; Fuller points to an increase in the value of German trade from £365 million in 1894 to £610 million in 1904. This ignores the fact that Germany was already the second largest exporter of manufactured goods in the world by 1880 – without any talk of "rivalry" or risk of war. It also ignores the facts that in 1913 Germany's share of world trade in manufactures was 21·7 per cent, while Britain's was 27·2 per cent, and that in the same year the value of German exports of manufactured articles was $1,615, while the value of Britain's was $2,029.[1] There is no argument

[1] All my statistics here are from the excellent tables comparing the British and German economies in Appendix I of *The Kaiser And His Times* by Michael Balfour, Cresset Press, 1964.

with the fact that Germany's rapidly expanding population and booming industrialisation during the last decades of the 19th Century had given her formidable economic strength; but there can be no argument, either, with the fact that Britain's lead was still considerable, despite some clear signs that some of her industries had passed their peak and entered a serious decline. But finally there remains the fact that the First World War was not, in the first place, between Britain and Germany at all. It was a war whose timing and form were dictated by the German war plan, and that plan barely considered Britain. It was directed against France and Russia – for political reasons; Woodrow Wilson was wrong – it *was* a political war.

The essence of the German "problem" (as it was often called) lies in geography – Germany's position in the centre of Europe between three great empires. After the defeat of Austria in 1866, Germany had no more to fear from that quarter, and, indeed, her whole policy was to cultivate the closest relations between the two Germanic powers. But there remained Russia in the east and France in the west. France had made an astonishing recovery after the disaster of 1871 – a tribute to her own robust economy – and her desire to reverse the decision of that fatal year became a disturbing factor. It was always a keystone of Bismarck's policy to keep France and Russia apart – which was not too difficult, since one was a Republic and the other a frequently brutal autocracy. But in 1890 the young Kaiser Wilhelm II dismissed Bismarck, and thereafter statesmanship was conspicuously lacking in German policy. By 1893 Russia and France had signed a defensive alliance, and in 1895 the miracle was seen of the Russian Tsar receiving a tremendous ovation from the Parisian crowd during a state visit.

Not content with linking his two most powerful potential continental enemies, the Kaiser (Queen Victoria's favourite grandson) now embarked on a further policy which could not fail to alienate Britain and drive her into the arms of his foes: he began to build a German battle fleet. Fuller is unconvinced that this constituted a real challenge to the British Empire. He quotes figures for expenditure on naval construction between 1909 and 1914 which bring him to the conclusion: "how anyone could say that German naval expansion threatened England is difficult to understand." He suggests that it was not the Imperial German Navy, but the German Merchant Marine which was the real threat. But we have already noted that Germany's Merchant Marine in 1912 was just over a quarter of the size of Britain's, and we now need to note the steady underlying purpose of the building of the Imperial Navy. This was succinctly (though paranoiacally) stated in a "Very Secret" Memorandum of Admiral Tirpitz in 1897: "For Germany the most dangerous naval enemy at the present time is England. It is also the enemy against which we most urgently require a certain measure of naval force *as a political power factor.*" [1]

By 1904 the German naval threat had already done its work: it had drawn Britain and France together in the *Entente Cordiale*. Then came the fatal year, 1905; France's chief ally, Russia, was immersed in military defeat and revolution. Germany decided to profit by these calamities to test the real strength of the Entente. The occasion was supplied by a crisis with France over political and economic influence in Morocco – but to Germany's disgust the Entente stood the test. Instead of falling apart, it drew Britain and France even closer, and at the Algeçiras Conference in 1906 Germany had to make a humiliating climbdown.

The consequences were far-reaching. It was this crisis that brought about the secret Staff Talks between Britain and France which would quietly but remorselessly later become a dominant political factor, and would also go far to give the World War its shape and character. More than that, in 1907, despite the Anglo-Japanese Treaty, Britain was drawn into new close relations with Russia (the Anglo-Russian Agreement), and so the Triple Entente was born, challenging the Triple Alliance of Germany, Austria-Hungary and Italy. These power blocs were designed, at the time, to give all parties to them the security which they could no longer find in isolation. But because of the various "dependencies" which were also involved – inflammable material in the Balkans above all, the blocs, so far from conferring security, actually placed it in greater hazard. A pointer to what they might imply came in 1908, when Austria annexed Bosnia and Herzegovina. Russia's "protectorate" over the Balkan Slavs was clearly menaced; it was no accident that when war came it should be the electricity of that region which caused the flash.

After 1905, the road to war was depressingly smooth and well-

[1] Quoted in *Yesterday's Deterrent* by Jonathan Steinberg, Macdonald, 1965.

signposted. Crisis followed crisis: in 1909 a naval scare in Britain over possible secret German construction which produced a fever of ship-building; in 1911 a fresh crisis in Morocco (Agadir) provoked by German sabre-rattling; in 1912-13 the Balkan Wars, from which the Slav kingdom of Serbia emerged all-too successfully for Austria's liking. And in the event, in 1914, it was conflict between Austria and Serbia which tripped the world into war. Russia backed Serbia, Germany backed Austria, thus aligning herself squarely against one of the Triple Entente powers. For such a contingency, Germany only possessed one remedy: the war plan drawn up by the General Staff under Count von Schlieffen. Schlieffen was dead, and his plan had been somewhat watered down by his successor, but it was still the only plan on which Germany's great army could be mobilised and committed to battle. And the essence of the plan, predicating a two-front war in which Russia ("the steam-roller") would mobilise only slowly, was an immediate attack on France with a view to destroying her military power in forty days. As the Kaiser discovered to his deep dismay, there was only one direction in which the German armies could march – westward, against France; not only that, but in order to outflank the French frontier defences, westward through Belgium. Belgian independence was guaranteed by Britain; whether British public opinion might or might not have recoiled from the Entente at the last moment, it would not recoil from the Belgian guarantee. The circle was complete (except for Italy, already applying the principles of *sacro egoismo*); all the protestations of peace-loving, all the search for security, all the liberal dreams had crashed; in August 1914 the First World War began, and with it the most drastic, swift and terrifying processes of change yet known to Man.

EDITOR'S NOTE 4

CHAPTER 6

The Battles of the Marne and Tannenberg, 1914

The war which leapt out of the Serbo-Austrian brawl rapidly assumed the shape of a world conflict. The reason was that all the greater Powers involved, including Japan and Turkey, who respectively joined the Triple Entente and the Central Powers on August 23 and October 29, and Italy, who joined the former on May 4, 1915,[1] were empires whose frontiers for the most part clashed with each other. Eventually, when on April 6, 1917, the United States declared war on Germany and was followed by some South American and other States, the war became global and not a single greater Power was left free to act as its arbiter.

It is manifestly impossible in so vast a conflict, within the limits of this book, to touch upon circumferential campaigns, although most of them had vast historical consequences. Further, it is considered more to the point to use some of the space which might be devoted to these operations to the pre-war military theories held by the leading belligerents, particularly those of the French and Germans – who set the tactical pace – before the first decisive battle is described. Unless these theories are appreciated, it is impossible clearly to fathom the reasons why, in spite of the disastrous defeat sustained by the Germans within six weeks of the start of the war, the war dragged on until November, 1918; it was the complications arising out of the length of the war which fundamentally changed the course of history.

The 40 years before the war were prolific in military theories, for they were years of advancing industrial development, and if they were not the cradle, they were the nursery of the present scientific age. Among the many military theorists who appeared during these years, one was outstanding, namely I. S. Bloch, because he got down to the roots of the war problem. He was a

---

[1] Later Rumania and Portugal joined the Allies and Bulgaria the Central Powers. Greece tried to remain neutral, but when the Allies occupied Salonica she was forced to join them.

Polish banker and economist. In 1897 he published an elaborate analysis on modern warfare, entitled *The War of the Future in its Technical, Economic and Political Relations*, and in 1899 an abridged edition, edited by W. T. Stead, appeared in English under the title *Is War now Impossible?*

Bloch's thesis was that war is shaped by civilization, and because at the end of the nineteenth century civilization had nearly passed out of its agricultural into its industrial phase, the character of war had changed with it. "What is the use," he wrote, "of talking about the past when you are dealing with an altogether new set of considerations? Consider for a moment what nations were a hundred years ago and what they are to-day. In those days before railways, telegraphs, steam ships, etc., were invented each nation was more or less a homogeneous, self-contained, self-sufficing unit. . . . All this is changed. . . . Every year the interdependence of nations upon each other for the necessaries of life is greater than it ever was before. . . . Hence the first thing that war would do would be to deprive the Powers that made it of all opportunity of benefiting by the products of the nations against whom they were fighting. . . . The soldier is going down and the economist is going up." Therefore war is no longer a profitable court of appeal. The old conception of war as a business is absurd; to-day it is a mad kind of burglary – the plundering of one's own house.

"The outward and visible sign of the end of war," he said, "was the introduction of the magazine rifle. . . . The soldier by natural evolution has so perfected the mechanism of slaughter that he has practically secured his own extinction."

His description of the modern battle is exact, for it is exactly as it was fought 17 years later. And his prediction of the war is no less accurate:

"At first there will be increased slaughter on so terrible a scale as to render it impossible to get troops to push the battle to a decisive issue. They will try to, thinking that they are fighting under the old conditions, and they will learn such a lesson that they will abandon the attempt for ever. . . . The war, instead of being a hand-to-hand contest in which the combatants measure their physical and moral superiority, will become a kind of stalemate, in which neither army being able to get at the other, both armies will be maintained in opposition to each other, threatening each other, but never being able to deliver a final and decisive attack. . . . That is the future of war – not fighting, but famine, not the slaying of men, but the bankruptcy of nations and the break-up of the whole social organization. . . . Everybody will be entrenched in the next war. It will be a great war of entrenchments. The spade will be as indispensable to a soldier as his rifle. . . . All wars will of necessity partake of the character of siege operations . . . soldiers may fight as they please; the ultimate decision is in the hand of *famine*."[1]

He pictured that in a war between the Triple and Dual Alliances 10 million men would take the field; that battle fronts would be so enormous that command would become impossible; that cavalry would be useless; the day of the bayonet gone, and that artillery would be the dominant arm.

Although this picture exactly depicted the next war, Bloch failed to follow his thesis to its logical conclusion. If granted to be correct, then it followed that the sole thing impossible was for warfare to stand still. The validity of his forecast depended on the conditions of his day remaining static, and the turn of the century witnessed an outburst of inventiveness which was destined to revolutionize war even more completely than had the introduction of the horse in the third millennium B.C.

Of the many inventions of this period, the two most fateful for war were the internal combustion engine and wireless telegraphy.[2]

As a commercial proposition the gas engine was first introduced by Dr. N. A. Otto in 1876.[3] Nine years later Gottlieb Daimler improved upon it; he fitted a small petroleum spirit internal combustion motor to a bicycle and produced the first petrol driven vehicle.[4] Next, it was adapted to four-wheeled carriages, and in 1895 the first automobile race was held. It was from Paris to Bordeaux and back, and the winner covered the 744 miles at a mean speed of 15 miles an hour. Lastly came the most revolutionary of its triumphs. On December 17, 1903, at Kill Devil Hill, Kitty Hawk, North Carolina, Orville Wright in a power-driven aeroplane flew for 12 seconds. Six years later Blériot in a monoplane spanned the English Channel in 31 minutes. After 3,000

[1] Quoted from the Preface ("Conversations with the author, by W. T. Stead") of *Is War Impossible?* (1899).
[2] Others were: Bell's electric telephone, 1876; Parson's steam turbine, 1884; Dunlop's pneumatic tyre, 1888; Batter's endless chain track tractor, 1888. Also, at the opening of the present century, Rutherford and Soddy were at work on the nuclear atomic theory, which was to lead to the invention of the atomic bomb.
[3] In idea it was old, and dates from Christian Huygens in 1680.
[4] In the same year (1885) Butler, in England, propelled a tricycle by means of a benzoline engine exploded electrically.

years the legend of Daedalus came true. A power had been born which within half a century was destined to change the face of war.

The second invention – wireless telegraphy – was first given theoretical form in 1887 by Rudolf Hertz. He proved that under certain conditions an electrical spark creates an effect which is propagated into space as an electric wave. This drew the attention of Guglielmo Marconi to the invention of a practical device which could detect these waves, and so successful was he that in 1897 he transmitted a wireless message over a distance of nine miles, and in 1901 over 3,000 miles.

These two inventions introduced warlike possibilities which went far beyond anything as yet accomplished by either gunpowder or steam power. The former not only led to a revolution in road transport, and consequently in land warfare, but as it solved the problem of flight it raised war into the third dimension. The latter virtually raised it into the fourth dimension; for to all intents and purposes the wireless transmission of energy annihilated time as well as space. Thus two new battlefields were created – the sky and the ether.

These changes, as well as others which resulted from scores of less prominent inventions, when coupled with the strides made in the metallurgical, chemical, electrical, biological and other sciences, set in motion forces very different from those released by coal and steam. Mind more than matter, thought more than things, and above all imagination, struggled to gain power. New substances appeared, new sources of energy were tapped and new outlooks on life took form. The world was sloughing its skin – mental, moral and physical – a process destined to transform the industrial revolution into a technical civilization.

Divorced from civil progress, soldiers could not see this. They could not see that as civilization became more technical, military power must inevitably follow suit: that the next war would be as much a clash between factories and technicians as between armies and generals. With the steady advance of science warfare could not stand still. Even the far-sighted M. Bloch failed to see this.

Few soldiers and sailors were as clear-sighted as he, and those who did see clearly, like him, failed to see that industry and science had already placed in their hands weapons of such power that if rightly combined they could prevent a war of pure attrition. Most were hostile to novelty, nevertheless faith in a war of movement abounded, and in this respect most military opinion was in opposition to that of Bloch. For instance, in 1912, a French soldier of distinction wrote: "In a war between France and Germany we do not anticipate a battle of such a nature [*i.e.*, an entrenched battle]. . . . Battles in entrenched camps as occurred at Plevna or Mukden will never take place in a war with the French army."[1]

The godhead of this heresy was formed by General Foch, General Grandmaison, and General Langlois, who established a school of thought rivalled only by the dervishes of the Sudan.[2] Their leading principle was that morale was the infallible answer to the rifle bullet – pure witchcraft. Foch quoted approvingly the words of Joseph de Maistre: "A battle lost is a battle one thinks one had lost; for a battle cannot be lost physically." Foch added: "Therefore it can only be lost morally. But, then, it is also morally that a battle is won, and we may extend the aphorism by saying: 'A battle won is a battle in which one will not confess oneself beaten'."[3]

Coupled with this sophistry, he believed that "any improvement of firearms is ultimately bound to add strength to the offensive." Therefore in battle there is only one principle to follow – namely, attack![4] He appears to have overlooked that to make attack profitable a return must be made to the essence of the Napoleonic offensive, which was – "it is with artillery that war is made."[5]

Count von Schlieffen, Chief of the German General Staff, 1891–1905, partly realized this,[6] and to make the attack superior to the defence he increased the number of the German heavy guns; but

[1] Quoted in *A Critical Study of German Tactics*, Major de Pardieu (1912), p. 117. The outlook of the French on the approaching war is summarized by General Herr in his *L'Artillerie* (1923), pp. 4–5. Among other things he says: "The war will be short and of rapid movements, where manœuvres will play the predominant part; it will be a war of movement. The battle will be primarily a struggle between two infantries . . . the army must be an army of personnel and not of material. The artillery will only be an accessory arm. . . . The necessity for heavy artillery will seldom make itself felt. . . . It will serve no useful purpose to encumber oneself with an over-numerous artillery. . . ."

[2] They drew their inspirations from Colonel Ardant du Picq's *Études sur le combat*, which exaggerated the value of the moral factor in war. His theory was sound enough for the hand-to-hand combat of classical times; moderately sound for musket and bayonet warfare, but most misleading for rifle warfare. After 1871 his book cast a spell on the French army.

[3] *The Principles of War* (English edit., 1918), p. 286.

[4] *Ibid.*, p. 32.

[5] *Correspondance*, vol. xxx, p. 447.

[6] So did Admiral Sir John Fisher in England; hence the laying down of the first *Dreadnought* battleship in 1905.

he did not see that this in itself was insufficient, and that true superiority could only be gained when a new fighting organization was built round the gun. This was the leading tactical problem which faced all armies after the Russo-Japanese War, and it was by no means an obscure one.[1]

Such was the unseen tactical background of the war of 1914–1918; the apparent background was this:

After the Franco-Prussian war the French and German General Staffs periodically revised their training manuals, and after 1905 the tactical doctrines expressed in them were almost exclusively based on the offensive; the bayonet assault remained the accepted goal of the attack. Such differences as existed between them arose mainly out of national and traditional characteristics. Intellectually, the German is heavy and methodical and the Frenchman quick and cautious. The French followed Napoleon, and believed in attack in order to uncover, and then, when information had been gained, to manœuvre against the point selected *during* battle for the decisive blow. The Germans did not. They believed in marching direct upon the enemy once he had been located, and then to attack him *au fond* in front and simultaneously to envelop his flanks. Their system was Spartan, an advancing wall of men without a general reserve; that of the French was Roman, a lighter front supported by a heavy rear. The Germans recognized that fronts were inviolable, but must always be attacked in order to fix them. The French believed that a flank attack can always be anticipated, whereas a frontal one cannot be. In brief, because the Germans were methodical they believed in plan supported by brute force, and because the French were individual they believed in skill adapted to ground. The Germans considered that the French method would lead to disorder, they pinned their faith on the general and his plan; the French, because they believed that the German method would lead to excessive slaughter and blunt the attackers, pinned their faith on the initiative of their private soldiers.

As regards infantry tactics, the German believed in opening an attack with a dense firing line; to advance it until the enemy's fire was felt; then to smother the enemy's position with bullets; next to crawl forward to between 800 and 400 yards of the enemy; to gain fire superiority, and lastly to advance again and at 100 yards assault with the bayonet. Should this last advance prove

[1] See *Memoirs of an Unconventional Soldier*, J. F. C. Fuller (1936), pp. 23–26.

impossible, the final forward movement was to be made by night and the assault carried out at dawn. The French theory was based on the doctrines of Ardant du Picq; to move forward under controlled fire to 400 yards range, at which point it was held that, because aimed fire would become impossible, losses would diminish, and then to advance and take the position with the bayonet.

Both general staffs studied the artillery tactics of the Manchurian war. The French considered the reports on the preponderance of the Japanese artillery exaggerated, and the Germans learnt that the artillery duel and the infantry attack were one and not two separate acts of battle. Both accepted the advantages of indirect laying for all guns not immediately supporting the infantry attack; but on the whole the Germans disliked defiladed fire, and held that, as their artillery was numerically superior to the French, by simultaneously opening fire with all guns from uncovered positions they could more rapidly crush their antagonist. The main difference lay in their respective outlooks on the howitzer. After Plevna the Germans had adopted the light howitzer; after Mukden they adopted the heavy. The French did not like howitzers; they considered their 75 mm. field guns all-sufficient. The heavy howitzer, they said, was a cumbersome weapon unsuited for mobile warfare, and though the Germans acclaimed the tremendous effect on morale of its heavy shells the French answer was: that German troops required to be stimulated by noise, but French troops did not – they were too intelligent.

Such were the theories propounded between 1905 and 1914, and of the two armies it was certainly the German which had learnt most from the Manchurian struggle. But both sides missed its main lesson: the preponderance of the projectile, bullet and shell *in the defensive*, and its logical consequence – field entrenchments. Both failed to see that unless the next war could be won in the first shock, because of the bullet a conflict between millions, instead of hundreds of thousands of men, must become a war of entrenchments, and that a war of entrenchments must result in an enormous increase of artillery and of shell ammunition.

On the outbreak of war the strengths of the belligerent armies were as follows:

	France	Britain	Russia	Belgium	Serbia	Germany	Austria
Inf. Divs.	62	6	114	6	11	87	49
Cav. Divs.	10	2	36	1	1	11	11

Although armaments varied in design, generally speaking they were on the same scale. Almost all transport was still horse-drawn; lorries were only just coming into use, and on the declaration of war the British War Department owned no more than 80 of them. Motor cars, however, were used freely by higher commanders and their staffs. Aircraft was on a very limited scale: the German army had 384 aeroplanes and 30 dirigibles; the French, 123 aeroplanes and 10 dirigibles; and the British 63 aeroplanes; these machines were mainly used for reconnaissance. Compared with armies in the past, probably the most important difference was that those of 1914 had well-organized divisional cable companies for inter-communication, which were also provided with wireless sending and receiving sets.

The French and German plans of campaign had nothing in common except that both were based on the offensive, and as regards that of the French, it is necessary to enter into some extraneous detail, for it is a classic example of how a plan should not be devised.

On June 29, 1911, General Messimy became Minister of War in the Caillaux Government; he was the fourth to hold that appointment within four months. Three days later, for the first time he met General Michel, vice-president of the Supreme War Council (*Conseil Supérieur de la Guerre*) and general-in-chief designate in the event of war, and Colonel de Grandmaison, head of the operations branch of the General Staff (*3e Bureau*). These two did not see eye to eye, and behind Michel's back one of those politico-financial intrigues which are the curse of French democracy was brewing.

General Michel's views were that in the event of a war with Germany the probabilities were that the Germans would do two things: (*1*) simultaneously mobilize their reserve with their active troops, and (*2*) direct their main line of advance through Belgium. Therefore, in his opinion, it was essential that the French reserves should be similarly mobilized and that the plan of war should pivot on frustrating this advance. The distribution he suggested was: 490,000 men between Lille and Avesnes; 280,000 between Hirson and Rethel; 300,000 between Montmédy and Belfort; and a reserve of 220,000 about Paris, which could reinforce any one of these groups directly the German plan was disclosed.[1]

---

[1] For General Michel's scheme in full see *1914 Les erreurs du haut commandement*, Général Percin (1922), pp. 42–49.

For various reasons this project was anathema to the General Staff. The more important one was that to mix reserve with active formations would delay offensive operations; yet it cannot have been overlooked that ever since 1813 the Germans, the originators of the reserve system, had never failed to mix them. Messimy knew of this, also he knew that three members of the Supreme War Council – General Galliéni, General Dubail and General Durand – were hostile to Michel. In order to get rid of the latter, on July 19 he summoned a meeting of the Council, and when the question of reserves was vetoed by a majority of its members, he said to Michel that as his colleagues had lost confidence in him, he must ask for his resignation. Thus it came about that the sole member of the Council who saw clearly what was ahead, and as clearly understood how to meet it, was dismissed. Messimy looked around for a successor.

First he thought of General Galliéni, but as he had voted against Michel he set him aside and asked General Pau, who refused. Then he turned to General Joffre, who had never commanded an army – not even on paper – and who had no knowledge whatever of General Staff work. Joffre accepted, and asked for General Foch to be his chief of staff;[1] but this was not allowed, because Foch was a Catholic. Messimy informs us that he selected Joffre because he possessed "a strong, powerful and lofty personality . . . a clear though slow wit . . . power of decision, though not very quick . . . and imperturbable sang-froid."[2] Be this as it may, because Messimy was only the tool of the General Staff camarilla which controlled the army, it would appear that the truth was that this irresponsible body had pushed Joffre forward because, as General Percin says, he knew nothing about what he would have to do, and that therefore it would be easier to make him do all that the General Staff required.[3] In other words, from the General Staff point of view Joffre would make a good ventriloquist's dummy.

Joffre was the son of a cooper of Rivesaltes, born in 1852. He was a typical French peasant – slim though unimaginative, stubborn, astute, secretive and practical. He knew his own defects and he hid them. He seldom wrote a memorandum or read one. A

---

[1] *The Memoirs of Marshal Joffre* (English edit., 1932), vol. i, p. 12. These Memoirs were not written by Joffre, but by one of his staff officers.
[2] Quoted from *Les lois éternelles de la guerre*, Général Arthur Boucher (1925), vol. ii, pp. 144–145.
[3] *Les erreurs du haut commandement*, p. 121.

man of simple mind, he liked simple solutions and his Staff fed him on simple précis of the subjects he had to deal with. As a general he was a strategical vacuum within which buzzed his General Staff. Nevertheless, as the fighting peasant he saved France, because he did not shirk responsibility, and because he was a man of great courage and also of great brutality. Though before the war he selected his own subordinates, once war was declared and they failed him he dismissed them in droves. In one month – August 2 to September 6 – two army commanders, 10 corps commanders and 38 divisional commanders were retired, that is, about half the superior generals placed under his orders.[1]

The theory of "mass plus velocity", then held by the General Staff, exactly fitted Joffre's bull-like understanding. The offensive became his one and only aim, as it became that of his political master, President Fallières, who, in 1912, had asserted: "We are determined to march straight against the enemy without hesitation. . . . The offensive alone is suited to the temperament of our soldiers."[2] Thus Joffre became the instrument of a school of military occultism, a Bergsonian society, as Pierrefeu calls the General Staff, "whose doctrine was founded on the discredit of intelligence and favoured the cult of the intuitive."[3] These military occultists, backed by the *Comité des Forges de France*, were Joffre's brain, out of which percolated the plan of war. It was of pathetic simplicity, *"reposant"*, as Jean de Pierrefeu says, *"tout entier sur l'idée mystique de l'offensive"*,[4] as well as on the ideas of General Bonnal, who had been responsible for the previous two plans – Nos. XV and XVI.

Bonnal was a profound though blind student of Napoleon; a copyist whose slavish erudition had gained for him the reputation of being the leading strategist of his day. Saturated in Napoleonic lore he failed to equate his knowledge with changed conditions. He thought in "lozenges" of men and in *"battalions carrées"*, but not in railways, magazine rifles and quick-firing artillery. His leading idea was simplicity itself. Because, as he assumed, the Germans would marshal some 10 corps on a frontage of 60 to 80 kilometres between Toul and Épinal, the sole thing necessary was to confront them with a *"battalion carrée"* of 800,000 men – three lines of armies, one in first line, three in second, and one in fourth.

[1] *Mes Souvenirs*, Général Adolphe Marie Messimy (1937), pp. 349–350.
[2] *The Memoirs of Marshal Joffre*, vol. I, p. 30.
[3] *Plutarque a menti*, Jean de Pierrefeu (1922), p. 38.
[4] *Ibid.*, p. 55.

A head-on collision between the first line army and the enemy would then take place, under cover of which the second and third line armies would manœuvre. This was the Jena manœuvre in elephantiasis; yet "Bonnal was convinced that he had discovered the secret of victory."[1]

Joffre's young intellectuals adopted Plan XVI as a foundation, and then set to work to build on to it Plan XVII. It was based on two postulates. The first was that the Germans would not at first bring into line reserve formations as well as active ones; therefore they would not be numerically strong enough simultaneously to advance through Belgium as well as Lorraine. The second was that as the French soldier is irresistible in attack the sole thing to do was to concentrate the French armies between Mézières and Épinal and move forward. Behind this was the insistance of the *Comité des Forges* that the Lorraine iron fields must be protected.

Joffre accepted these ideas blindly, and though he informs us that he was convinced that the Germans would not use their reserve troops[2] or move through Belgium, he nevertheless says in his *Memoirs*: "We were acquainted with their plan of mobilization bearing the date of October 9, 1913; we knew that in this plan it was set down that 'reserve troops will be employed in the same way as active troops'."[3] He further states that he had in his hands a map of an exercise "executed by the German Great General Staff in 1905, in which the movement of the German right wing across Belgium was studied"; also a plan of "a big war-game carried out in 1906" which showed the same move.[4] In order to prove that the General Staff was right, things were carried to such a pitch that, in 1913, Lieutenant-Colonel Buat forged a document, *La Concentration Allemande*, which he pretended he had found in a railway carriage. It showed that the German reservists would *not* be in first line, and that the German advance would be by the *right bank* of the Meuse on Mézières.

In spite of the fact that Joffre & Co. were intent upon playing the rôle of Napoleon, so far as he was concerned it would appear that he never had a plan at all. He says: "there never was any

---

[1] *Les lois éternelles de la guerre*, Boucher, vol. II, p. 126.
[2] *The Memoirs of Marshal Joffre*, vol I, pp. 61 and 64.
[3] *Ibid.*, vol. I, p. 145.
[4] *Ibid.*, vol. I, pp. 63 and 46. It is of interest to note that Jaurès, in his *L'armée nouvelle* (1899), p. 537, predicted that the Germans would use their reserve formations and would move through Belgium

plan of operations set down in writing. . . . I adopted no preconceived idea, other than a full determination to take the offensive with all my forces assembled. . . . I, therefore, decided to limit our studies to a concentration capable of lending itself to any possible plan of operations."[1]

Nevertheless, as we shall see, this is exactly what the concentration he accepted did not do. It was:

(1) *First Army* (Dubail): Charmes – Arches – Darney; headquarters Épinal; five active corps, four divisions and two cavalry divisions: total 256,000 men.

(2) *Second Army* (de Castelnau): Pont St. Vincent – Mirecourt; headquarters Neufchâteau; five active corps, three divisions and two cavalry divisions: total 200,000 men.

(3) *Third Army* (Ruffrey): St. Mihiel – Damvillers; headquarters Verdun; three active corps, three divisions and one cavalry division: total 168,000 men.

(4) *Fourth Army* (de Langle de Cary): Vavincourt – Bar le Duc – Void; headquarters St. Dizier: three active corps and one cavalry division: total 193,000 men.

(5) *Fifth Army* (Lanrézac): Grandpré – Suippes – Chaumont – Porcien; headquarters Rethel: five active corps, five divisions and one cavalry division: total 254,000 men.

(6) *Cavalry Corps* (Sordet): Mézières, three divisions.

(7) *Right Flank Guard:* Vesoul, three divisions.

(8) *Left Flank Guard:* Sissonne, three divisions.

Such was the distribution decided upon by the French General Staff and accepted by Joffre, whose idea, when war was declared, was to advance the First Army on Baccarat – Sarreburg, and the Second Army on Château Salins – Sarreburg, and overwhelm his enemy.

His opponent's plan, though equally offensive, was very different. In 1905 Count von Schlieffen, who as Chief of the General Staff had succeeded von Moltke in 1891, recast the then existing plan by turning it round. Moltke's idea was an offensive against Russia and a defensive against France; but as the defeat of the Russians in the Russo-Japanese War had altered the balance of

[1] *Ibid.*, vol. 1, p. 69. When in 1919 he was called before the Briey Commission and asked, "Who elaborated the war plan?" he replied: "The General Staff", and when pressed to state which officers were concerned, his answer was: "I no longer remember. . . . A plan of operations is an idea carried in one's head and not set down on paper. . . . You ask me a heap of things to which I cannot reply. I know nothing" (*Les erreurs du haut commandement*, see Appendix, pp. 179-278, in which the minutes of the Commission are given in full).

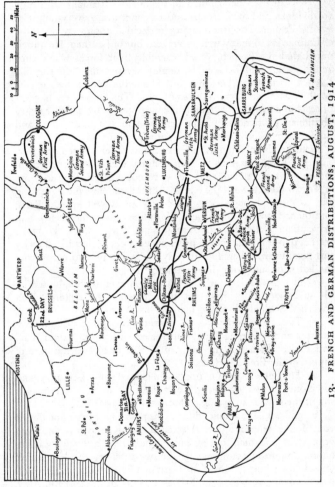

13. FRENCH AND GERMAN DISTRIBUTIONS, AUGUST, 1914

power, Schlieffen determined to oppose the Russians with only 10 divisions and local troops and to concentrate everything else against France. The grand tactics he decided upon were not those of Cannae, as so many writers suggest, but of Leuthen. He anticipated that the French would assemble their forces where they actually did, and decided to deploy seven armies on the line Krefeld–Mulhausen, centred on Thionville–Metz; five to the north of Metz and two to the south of it. The former was to comprise thirty-five and a half corps, supported by seven cavalry divisions, 16 brigades of Landwehr and six Ersatz divisions, and the latter five corps supported by three cavalry divisions.

Next, he planned to advance in oblique order pivoted on Metz. The left wing was first to gain contact with the French main forces, pin them down, or if this were not possible, then to retire and draw them toward the Rhine. At the same time the right wing was to move through Belgium, swing south-west around Paris, and thence move eastward and fall on the rear of the French and drive them pell-mell into Germany and Switzerland. To make certain that this wing should be strong enough, he decided, directly this gigantic wheel was on its way, to withdraw two corps from the left wing and with them reinforce it.

When we consider the plan which was eventually adopted by his successor, it is important to remember the factors which governed Schlieffen's grand tactics:

(1) The right wing was to operate through good offensive country and be strong enough to besiege Antwerp, Namur, etc., and Paris, which was the rail centre of France and the base of supply of the French armies.

(2) The left wing was to operate in good defensive country, and to be only just strong enough to mislead the French and make it worth their while to attack it. Its rôle was *defensive*.

In 1906 Schlieffen handed over this plan to his successor Count von Moltke, who had been selected by the Kaiser to replace him because he imagined that his name would have a terrifying effect on neighbouring countries. In this we discover the key which unlocks the whole system of the German Higher Command, which was as royally rotten as the French was politically corrupt. After 1870, as after 1763, the German army rested on its laurels, and when William II succeeded to the throne he set out to create a parade army, a toy which he loved to play with. Unable to tolerate soldiers of real worth he set them aside and filled the higher army appointments with royal princes – figurehead generals who knew little or nothing of war. General von Moltke was one of his creatures; he had not passed through the Staff College, and most of his service had been spent as aide-de-camp to his uncle and the Kaiser. In 1914 he was 68 years old, out-of-date and soused in the staff ideas of his uncle, which he copied slavishly. To him the army was commanded by the staff, and as commander-in-chief, for that is what he was in all but name, he looked upon his rôle as that of the starter of a race: all he had to do was to lower the flag, and then to leave operations to his generals. He did not believe in executive control, nor even in contact, and his system of communication with his subordinates, as we shall see, was about as defective as it could be.

Though Moltke accepted Schlieffen's plan, he entirely changed its character, notwithstanding that several new corps were raised between 1906 and 1914. On the Russian front he left things much as they were, and allotted to it four active and reserve corps, one reserve division, one cavalry division, and some Landwehr formations; in all about 200,000 men. But on the French front he not only radically altered the proportional strengths of the two wings, but by reinforcing the left he set out to win a Cannae instead of a Leuthen.[1] Colonel Tappen, Chief of Operations, says that this change was forced upon him by technical reasons – railways, etc.[2] This is to be doubted, for the real reason would appear to have been the pressure brought to bear upon him by the royal princes to strengthen their armies.

In 1910 he cancelled the withdrawal of the two corps from the left wing, and concentrated the six Ersatz divisions in the neighbourhood of Metz. Lastly, when nine new divisions became available, he allotted one, as well as one withdrawn from the Russian

---

[1] Sir James Edmonds (*A Short History of World War I*, 1951, p. 16) says that "In 1912, owing to changed conditions and the necessity to cover the Rhineland industrial area, Schlieffen (who in the interval had written a book on Cannae, a battle which he regarded as a model of a battle of annihilation) himself suggested the alteration of his 1905 plan to the one which was put into force. This was revealed in 1934, under the Hitler régime, by the officer who examined the papers of General von Moltke." If this is correct, then Schlieffen's strategical sense must have sadly degenerated in his seventy-ninth year, for the region of the Vosges is some of the best defensive country in Western Europe, and to attempt a rapid envelopment through it would be an act of madness. On this question, Görlitz (*The German General Staff, 1657–1945*, 1953, p. 142) writes: "Even as late as 1912 he [Schlieffen] was still busy with his theoretical planning, and in that year – he had come to recognize the growth of the offensive spirit in France – he began to develop the idea of attacking along the whole front all the way from Belgium to Switzerland. But even in the hour of death, the great plan continued in his thoughts. His last words were: "See you make the right wing strong.""

[2] *Jusqu'à la Marne en 1914*, Général Tappen (French edit.), p. 97.

front, to the right wing, and the remaining eight to the left. The initial distribution of the seven German armies then became:

(*1*) *First Army* (General von Kluck): headquarters Grevenboich; seven corps, three cavalry divisions and three Landwehr brigades. To march on Aix-la-Chapelle and thence on Brussels. Total 320,000 men.

(*2*) *Second Army* (General von Bülow): headquarters Montjoie; six corps, two cavalry divisions and two Landwehr brigades. To capture Liége and thence advance with its right flank on Wavre and its left on Namur. Total 260,000 men.

(*3*) *Third Army* (General von Hausen): headquarters Prüm; four corps and one Landwehr brigade. To march westward with its right on Namur and its left on Givet. Total 180,000 men.

(*4*) *Fourth Army* (Duke of Württemberg): headquarters Trèves; five corps and one Landwehr brigade. To march westward with its right on Framay and its left on Attert, north of Arlon. Total 180,000 men.

(*5*) *Fifth Army* (The Crown Prince): headquarters Saarbrücken; five corps, one division, two cavalry divisions and five Landwehr brigades. To keep its left on Thionville and to move its right on Forenville. Total 200,000 men.

(*6*) *Sixth Army* (Prince Rupprecht of Bavaria): headquarters St. Avold; five corps, three cavalry divisions and four Ersatz divisions. To advance on the Moselle and attack the French and pin them down. Total 220,000 men.

(*7*) *Seventh Army* (General von Heeringen): headquarters Strasbourg; three corps, one division, two Ersatz divisions and four Landwehr brigades. To advance on the Meurthe or to counter-attack in Lorraine. Total 125,000 men.

Although the shadow of the Schlieffen plan remained, its substance was altered completely by the change in balance between the weight of the two wings hinged on Thionville–Metz. The one allotted 59 Active, Reserve and Ersatz divisions to the northern wing and nine Active and Reserve divisions to the southern. In the other, the proportion was 55 Active and Reserve divisions to 23 Active, Reserve and Ersatz divisions. In percentages the Schlieffen plan represented 100:15, and the Moltke plan 100:42. Further, as Schlieffen intended to shift two corps from the left to the right wing directly the French forces in Alsace and Lorraine were entangled, the proportion of 100 : 15 was to fall to 100 : 9 *in order that the southern wing might be pushed back.*

Now we see two offensive wings, of which the southern, instead of enticing the enemy eastward so that the northern wing might the more easily wheel round his rear, pushed him westward – that is, away from the manœuvre against his rear. This was no Cannae, nor Leuthen. To call it either would make Hannibal or Frederick turn in his grave.

While the enormous German phalanx, strong in form yet weak in structure, formed up, and while far away in East Prussia General von Prittwitz with his comparatively minute force made ready to block the onrush of the Russian hordes, futility and discord reigned in Paris. In May, General Messimy had again become Minister of War, and was, so we are told, "constantly at the end of the telephone asking for information or giving meaningless orders and not in the least conscious of the greatness of his task."[1] On July 31 "Nothing was discussed except . . . financial measures. . . ."[2] On August 2 came mobilization and, on the 3rd, Joffre assembled his army commanders. Secretive as usual, he vaguely sketched for them the "broad line of manœuvre" he would "probably execute." This was "a combination of two attacks, one in Lorraine and the other north of the line Verdun–Toul."[3] On the 4th he established his General Headquarters at Vitry-le-François; meanwhile Moltke remained in Berlin, from where he later moved to Coblenz.

The day Joffre assembled his army commanders, the advanced guard of General von der Marwitz's Cavalry Corps crossed the Belgian frontier at Gemmenich, and, on August 5, the surrender of Liége was demanded and refused by General Leman. On the following day the German assault failed. General Ludendorff, Quartermaster-General of the Second Army, then took charge of the attack, and on the 7th his men penetrated between the forts and entered the city. On August 12 some 420 mm. howitzers were brought forward; the forts were pulverized, and, on the 16th, Liége was in German hands.

Meanwhile a detachment of Dubail's First Army had entered

[1] *Britain and the War: A French Indictment*, General Huguet (English edit., 1928), p. 31.
[2] *The Memoirs of Marshal Joffre*, vol. 1, pp. 124–125.
[3] *Ibid.*, vol. 1, p. 135. It is extremely difficult to discover what did happen. In the Briey enquiry Joffre says he never assembled his generals as they all knew exactly what to do. Throughout the war these contradictions occur.

Mulhausen, and on August 7, as five German corps had by then been identified on the Belgian front,[1] Lanrézac informed Joffre that the probability was that the Germans intended to operate along the left bank of the Meuse. The answer he received was, "so much the better."[2] Still convinced that the main German forces were in the Thionville–Metz area, on the 8th Joffre ordered the First and Second Armies to prepare to attack.[3] This meant that one-third of his total forces was to penetrate Lorraine. The attack was launched on August 14, when, according to plan, Prince Rupprecht's Sixth Army fell back.

In the meantime Lanrézac continued to warn Joffre that the main German forces were in Belgium, but with no effect until August 15, when Joffre informs us that "for the first time this hypothesis began to take actual shape."[4] By the 18th he was sufficiently perturbed by it to create a new army, the Army of Lorraine, under General Maunoury, to protect the left flank of the Second Army from "forces which might debouch from the entrenched camp of Metz."[5] The right of the First Army was already protected by the Army of Alsace, under General Pau, which had been formed on August 9.

Although Joffre little realized it, the position of his First and Second Armies was critical, and would have become more so had Rupprecht only continued to fall back. Instead, urged on by his ambitious Chief of Staff, Colonel von Dellmensingen – the real commander of the Sixth Army – he obtained permission to draw in the six Ersatz divisions, and with the Seventh Army, which had already been placed under his command, he counter-attacked the French on August 20; pushed the French First and Second Armies out of the trap they had unwittingly entered, and beat them back to the Grand Couronné of Nancy and the Meurthe. The first nail had been driven into the Schlieffen-Moltke plan and it so unbalanced Moltke that he abandoned the idea that the left wing was a reservoir for the right, and substituted the idea of a double envelopment. Thus it came about that from August 25 to

[1] See: *La préparation de la guerre et la conduite des opérations*, Maréchal Joffre (1920), p. 32, and *The Memoirs of Marshal Joffre*, vol. I, p. 141.
[2] *Historie illustrée de la guerre de 1914*, Gabriel Hanotaux (1920–1927), vol. VIII, p. 246.
[3] See *La préparation de la guerre*, etc., p. 68, and *La conduite de la guerre jusqu'à la bataille de la Marne*, Lieut.-Colonel Grouard, p. 5.
[4] *The Memoirs of Marshal Joffre*, vol. I, p. 159. It would appear that this *hypothesis* took form on the 17th and not the 15th, because on the 16th an official *communiqué* stated: "the *attaque brusquée* by Belgium had lamentably failed" (see Percin, p. 117).
[5] *Ibid.*, vol. I, p. 166.

September 7, the Sixth and Seventh Armies dashed themselves to pieces in the defensive region Schlieffen had warned them against attacking.

While Rupprecht and Dellmensingen emasculated the German plan of war, Joffre "assassinated" his generals. Because the attack had failed, victims had to be found in order to propitiate General Messimy. "*Donnez-moi la guillotine, je vous donnerai la victoire!*"[1] he shouted, and, on August 24, Messimy wrote to Joffre: "I consider that, as in 1793, there are only two punishments, dismissal and death. You want to win; to do so use the most rapid, brutal, energetic and decisive methods."[2] Fortunately for France, on August 27, Messimy was dismissed.

Two days before Rupprecht launched his attack the First, Second, and Third German Armies set out on their advance through Belgium and the bulk of the Belgian forces fell back upon Antwerp. Then the second nail was driven into the Schlieffen-Moltke plan, because General von Kluck was ordered to detach the 3rd Reserve Corps to cover Antwerp, which meant a reduction in strength of some 35,000 men. When Namur was reached the third nail was driven home, because its reduction forced the Second Army to detach the Reserve Corps of the Guard, and the Third Army to detach the XIth Corps as well as one division of the 7th Reserve Corps. On August 21 the Second Army came into contact with the French Fifth Army and Kluck, now under Bülow's orders, was instructed to move south-westerly instead of westerly. Thus was the fourth nail hammered home, because, had he continued on his original course, instead of a head-on collision with the British Expeditionary Force at Mons, he would have outflanked it and quite possibly have annihilated it. On August 22, the river Sambre was reached.

Two days before this happened, Joffre suddenly saw daylight; "the German manœuvre was clear to my eyes," he said.[3] Yet was it? From the action he took he would seem to have had only a hazy idea of the formidable nature of the great German wheel through Belgium. Instead of trying to smash the advancing German right wing he launched the Third and Fourth Armies into the difficult country of the Ardennes to sever it from its base, and ordered the Fifth Army on their left, in cooperation

---

[1] *Mes Souvenirs*, Messimy, p. 350.
[2] *The Memoirs of Marshal Joffre*, vol. 1, p. 184.
[3] *Ibid.*, vol. 1, p. 170.

with the British Expeditionary Force – the last units of which were about to land – to hold back the head of the onrushing flood.

The initial objective given the French Third and Fourth Armies were Arlon and Neufchâteau, and their advance on them led to a head-on collision with the Fourth and Fifth German Armies. The battle of the Ardennes followed, or, as the Germans call it, the battle of Longwy and Neufchâteau, in which the French Fourth Army was severely repulsed and on August 24 the Third forced to retire behind the Meuse. Like the offensive in Lorraine, this attack was a complete failure.

Meanwhile the French Fifth Army, under Lanrézac, advanced on the Sambre. On August 22 it was met in front by Bülow's Second Army and attacked on its right flank by Hausen's Third Army. The outcome was the battle of Charleroi, called by the Germans the battle of Namur, in which Lanrézac was forced back, and Sir John French withdrew on Mons. There, when isolated, he was attacked by Kluck's First Army, and on the 24th forced to continue his retreat. On this day the general situation was that the whole of the French left wing was in retreat, and the whole of the German left wing was battering itself to pieces on the lower Moselle, from Toul to Nancy, and thence to St. Die.

To understand what now followed on the western front it is first necessary to examine events on the eastern front.

The aim of the original Russian plan was to hold back the Germans with the First Army, while the Third, Fourth, Fifth and Eighth, with the Second in reserve at Warsaw, assumed a vigorous offensive against the Austrians, and the Ninth remained at Petrograd to repel a possible German invasion. Immediately after mobilization this plan was changed in order to help the French; the Second Army was moved toward East Prussia to cooperate with the First, and the Ninth took its place as a reserve. Thus two groups of armies were formed, the North-Western, under General Jilinski, consisted of the First Army under General Rennenkampf and the Second under General Samsonov; and the South-Western, under General Ivanov, which included the Third, Fourth, Fifth and Eighth Armies. The whole was under the command of the Grand Duke Nicholas Nikolaievich.

The First and Second Armies were respectively deployed in the Vilna district and on the Narew; the First consisted of the IIIrd, IVth and XXth Corps, supported by five cavalry divisions, and the Second of the IInd, VIth, XIIIth, XVth and XXIIIrd Corps and three cavalry divisions.

Though numerically these two armies – the First Army 200,000 strong and the Second Army 250,000 – were vastly superior to the German Eighth Army, which then held East Prussia, in quality and command they could not compare with it. Further, the German railway system was in every way superior to that of the Russians.

Though improvements had been made since the Russo-Japanese War, the Russian remained what he always had been, a big-hearted child who thought out nothing and was surprised by everything. The generals were incapable, and what made things worse was that they thirsted for a fight. The Staff was grotesquely inefficient, and the worth of that of the Second Army may be judged from the fact that it "had a compass but no maps." General Knox, British Military Attaché with this Army, says that on one occasion "An eccentric youth travelled with me, the son of a chocolate manufacturer of Warsaw, who is on the Staff of the 2nd Army simply because he can draw caricatures."[1]

The original Schlieffen plan had been worked out in 1905 when Russia was weak. It was based on the formation of the Vistula, which describes in its course an immense "S". Its centre is Warsaw, with Danzig at its northern extremity and Cracow at its southern, and at the bends of the "S" are the fortresses of Thorn in the north and Sandomir in the south.

On this skeleton Schlieffen worked out his plan. As he expected that the main Russian forces would assemble between Warsaw and Sandomir, he decided to deploy against them a weak front which rested between two powerful groups: an Austro-Hungarian army in the south, which was to move on Lublin, and a German army in the north which was to move on Pultusk. Because he reckoned that the Russian deployment would take between six and seven weeks he considered he would be able to dispense with the northern army until after he had crushed France, and then, by a rapid transfer of troops from the western theatre of war to build it up and carry out a true Cannae operation.

By 1913 this situation had changed, for the Russians had largely recovered from their defeats in 1904–1905. Further, they had strengthened their western railways. Therefore Moltke rightly

[1] *With the Russian Army, 1914–1917*, Major-General Sir Alfred Knox (1921), vol. I, pp. 78 and 86.

14. BATTLE OF TANNENBERG, AUGUST 26-31, 1914

assumed that their mobilization would take less time and decided that a properly constituted army would be required – namely, the Eighth. He allotted to it the following formations: Ist Corps (General von François), XVIIth Corps (General von Mackensen), XXth Corps (General von Scholtz), Ist Reserve Corps (General Below), 3rd Reserve Division (General von Morgen), 1st Cavalry Division (General Brecht) and three Landwehr brigades as well as all the fortress troops in East Prussia. The whole was commanded by General von Prittwitz, who in the event of an advance of greatly superior Russian forces was instructed to withdraw to the left bank of the Vistula.[1]

Directly war was declared, General Conrad, Chief of the General Staff of the Austro-Hungarian Armies, launched an offensive on Lublin and was driven back upon Lemberg. Meanwhile von Prittwitz deployed his 160,000 men (without counting Landsturm), as follows:

(*1*) From Angerburg to the Baltic, on the river Angerapp and south of the Pregel, he held his front with the Ist Reserve Corps, the XVIIth Corps and the Ist Corps, and to the area north of the Pregel, along the Deime, he allotted the Königsberg garrison.

(*2*) From Johannisburg to Thorn and based on Deutsch-Eylau he deployed the XXth Corps. Its object was to protect the railway which supplied his army. It was supported by the garrisons of Thorn and Graudenz.

When General von Prittwitz held this line, Rennenkampf, in true Russian fashion, did not wait to complete mobilization of his rear services and crossed the frontier on August 17; he drove back the German advanced troops at Stallupönen and defeated the left of the Eighth Army at Gumbinnen. Then his supply system broke down and the gauge of the railway changed from broad to narrow.[2] Four days later Samsonov crossed into East Prussia. He occupied Willenberg on August 22 and Ortelsburg and Neidenburg on the 23rd. His advance was even more chaotic. A German description of it reads:

"Whole army corps advanced from Byelostok without bread or oats, and had to have recourse to their reserve rations. Even before the Narew the march discipline was bad, and from that river to the Prussian frontier the Russian columns had to wade through

[1] See *The War of Lost Opportunities*, General von Hoffmann (English edit., 1924), p. 12.
[2] See *Memoirs and Impressions of the War and Revolution in Russia, 1914–1917*, General Basil Gourko (1918), pp. 31, 62.

sand. Nerves were so shaky that the troops fired at every airman, occasionally even at their own automobiles. The Higher Command was ignorant of the enemy's movements. Corps commanders were only informed of the immediate objectives of the neighbouring corps; they were told nothing, for instance, of the task of Rennenkampf's army. . . ."[1]

There was no cooperation either between the units of the Second Army or between that army and the First. The IInd Corps, which was directed to advance between these two armies, kept contact with neither, and it has been hinted that this lack of solidarity was due to the personal dislike of Samsonov for Rennenkampf. A better reason would appear to be the inherent inefficiency of the Russian cavalry, more especially the Cossacks, who were little more than brigands.

The repulse of the Eighth Army at Gumbinnen, although no more than a tactical incident, led to the most astonishing strategical results. Firstly, Rennenkampf – who very nearly had been defeated – sat down to enjoy his escape, and to show how strange Russian mentality can be, we will quote General Knox, an eye-witness:

"B—— asked the General if he might go to bed, and was told that he might, but that he should not undress. He lay down for an hour and was awakened by Rennenkampf, who stood beside his bed, smiling, and said: 'You can take off your clothes now; the Germans are retiring'."[2]

As Knox remarks, surely it was precisely the time to exert every effort to keep in touch with the retiring Germans, and certainly not the moment to undress.

Secondly, because Samsonov believed the Eighth Army to have been routed, he cast precaution to the winds; lost contact with Rennenkampf, and he pushed on toward Deutsch-Eylau to cut off Prittwitz from his base. Thirdly, Prittwitz, when he learnt of this advance, panicked and ordered a retirement to the Vistula. On the advice of General Grünert and General Hoffmann, he cancelled this order, which was fortunate for the Germans, for the Russian Second Army was nearer to that river than his own. He then decided to attack Samsonov's left wing, and on the evening of August 20 issued the following orders: The XXth Corps to concentrate at Hohenstein; the Ist Corps and 3rd Reserve

---

[1] Quoted from *With the Russian Army*, Knox vol. 1 p. 84.
[2] *Ibid.*, vol. 1, p. 88.

Division to move by rail to the right wing of the XXth; the Königsberg garrison to hold the line Pregel–Deime, and the Ist Reserve Corps and XVIIth Corps to fall back directly west.

Strangely enough the repulse at Gumbinnen, coupled with Prittwitz's nervousness, led to events which were destined to change the whole course of the campaign, not only in the east, but also in the west.

When the news of Gumbinnen was received in Coblenz and was followed by a copy of Prittwitz's order to fall back on the Vistula, which, though according to plan, would, as Ludendorff says, "have spelt ruin,"[1] two changes were decided upon. The first was to find a new commander for the Eighth Army, and the second to reinforce it – which will be dealt with later. A telegram was sent to General Paul von Hindenburg, an old soldier born in 1847 and a veteran of the 1866 and 1870–1871 wars, then in retirement at Hanover, to ask him to take over Prittwitz's appointment. His answer was: "I am ready."[2] On the same day (August 22) a letter was sent to General Ludendorff to appoint him Hindenburg's Chief of Staff. It found him between Wavre and Namur, and when he received it he got into his car and sped to Coblenz. He reported himself to Moltke, who explained to him the situation in the east in detail, after which, at his request, the following instructions were sent to Prittwitz:

"The 1st Reserve Corps, the 17th Army Corps and the Main Reserve of the Königsberg garrison were to call a halt. The 1st A.C. was not to be detrained at Gosslershausen, but near General von Scholtz's position, somewhere east of Deutsch-Eylau. Any available troops from the garrisons at Thorn, Kulm, Graudenz and Marienburg, were to go to Strasburg and Lautenberg. . . . Thus, in the south-west part of East Prussia a strong group was formed which could undertake an offensive, while the northern group either continued its retreat in a south-westerly direction, or could be brought straight south to assist in the action against the Narew (Second Russian) Army."[3]

Unknown to Ludendorff, on the suggestions of General Grünert and General Hoffmann, almost identical moves were being made.

Once these orders had been sent Ludendorff hastened to Hanover; met Hindenburg, and with him went to Marienburg,

---

[1] *My War Memories*, General Ludendorff (English edit., 1920), vol. 1, p. 45.

[2] *Out of my Life*, Marshal von Hindenburg (English edit., 1920), p. 81.

[3] *My War Memories*, Ludendorff, vol. 1, p. 46. See also Hindenburg's *Out of my Life*, pp. 87–88.

where they arrived on the afternoon of August 23. There they learned that "The situation had changed and the decision to retire behind the Vistula had been abandoned."[1] They also learned that Rennenkampf's army was still inactive; that the 37th Division on the left wing of the XXth Corps had been furiously attacked and was in retreat; that Samsonov's order of pursuit, which had been sent out in clear, had been intercepted; and more important still, that Jilinski's plan of operations had been found on a captured Russian officer. "It told us," writes Hindenburg, "that Rennenkampf's Army was to pass the Masurian Lakes on the north and advance against the Insterburg–Angerburg line. It was to attack the German forces presumed to be behind the Angerapp, while the Narew Army was to cross the Lötzen–Prtelsburg line to take the Germans in flank."[2]

Meanwhile Samsonov slowly moved westward on a frontage of some 60 miles. From left to right his distribution was: Ist, XXIIIrd, XVth, XIIIth, and VIth Corps. The IInd' had by now been replaced by the Ist Corps and transferred to the First Army. This widened the gap between the two Armies and this was increased by Samsonov who to ease his supply directed his left on to the Nowo Georgiewsk–Mlawa–Soldau railway, which pulled his right away from Rennenkampf.

Ludendorff's quick eye at once noticed this gap and he determined to turn it to his advantage. He decided to leave a thin screen of troops to amuse Rennenkampf and to concentrate everything else against Samsonov. He writes:

"Gradually during the period from 24th to 26th August, the battle plan took shape in all its details. The great question was whether it would really be possible to withdraw the 1st Reserve Corps and the 17th Army Corps from their position facing Rennenkampf, so as to unite them with other units of the 8th Army, for a blow against the Narew Army. It depended solely on Rennenkampf himself, for if he knew how to make the most of his success of Gumbinnen and advance quickly my plan would be unthinkable. . . .

"We discovered by degrees that Rennenkampf was advancing only slowly. The two Army Corps could therefore be gradually deflected . . . in a sharp southerly direction to Bischofsburg-Neidenburg.

"Next, the 17th A.C., protected by the 1st Cavalry Division

[1] *My War Memories*, Ludendorff, vol. 1, p. 47.   [2] *Out of my Life*, p. 87.

and the 1st R.C., was moved south *via* Schippenbeil to Bischofstein. As soon as it had passed behind the 1st R.C., and on the 26th advanced from Bischofstein to Bischofsburg, the 1st Army Corps itself moved, south of Schippenbeil, in the direction of Seeburg. Only the 1st Cavalry Division remained facing Rennenkampf, near, and to the south of Schippenbeil. Of this division, also on the 26th, the 1st Cavalry Brigade received the order to draw out *via* Rössel on Sensburg. Accordingly from the 27th of August onwards, only two cavalry brigades stood between Lake Maur and the river Pregel, facing twenty-four very strong and several cavalry divisions of Rennenkampf's. . . .

"On this line the two Corps were marching in rear of the Narew Army from Neidenburg to Allenstein. In this way they exposed their rear without adequate protection to Rennenkampf's Army, which was only two or three days' march away. When the battle began in real earnest on the 27th . . . Rennenkampf's formidable host hung like a threatening thunder-cloud to the north-east."[1]

It was a plan of supreme daring and good judgment, which resulted not only in the most brilliant campaign of the war, but in one of the most tactically decisive.

"A general," writes Ludendorff, "has much to bear and needs strong nerves. The civilian is too inclined to think that war is only like the working out of an arithmetical problem with given numbers. It is anything but that. On both sides it is a case of wrestling with powerful, interwoven physical and psychological forces, a struggle which inferiority in numbers makes all the more difficult. It means working with men of varying force of character and with their own views. The only quality that is known and constant is the will of the leader."[2]

These are true words, and they carry with them the great truth that generalship in its highest form is a combination of will and idea, and not merely a matter of calculations.

The battle which was fought on August 26 may be divided into two operations. While half the XXth Corps, supported by General von der Goltz's Landwehr, held back Samsonov's main forces in the centre, (1) the Ist Corps and the remaining half of the XXth attacked the Russian left at Usdau and drove back the Russian Ist Corps; (2) from the north the Ist Reserve Corps with the XVIIth on its left struck at the Russian VIth Corps and drove back one of its divisions on Bischofsburg. The flanks were now

[1] *My War Memories*, vol. i, pp. 47–49.   [2] *Ibid.*, p. 53.

cleared for the envelopment of Samsonov's centre – the XIIIth, XVth, and XXIIIrd Corps.

While these converging movements were made, Samsonov, with the XVth Corps, watched its advance though "Destitute of any information concerning the other troops under his control."[1] He was worried, so General Knox informs us, "because he had not yet received a letter from his wife,"[2] and when he heard of the attack on his Ist Corps he buckled on his sword and set out to see what was happening.

The next day, as Rennenkampf slowly moved toward Königsberg, the attack continued. On Samsonov's left the greatest confusion set in: the troops at Niedenburg panicked, and in his centre many of the men of the XIIIth Corps when they reached Allenstein were under the impression that they had entered Berlin.[3]

That evening, on the German left, the Ist Reserve Corps occupied Wartenburg, some eight miles north-east of Allenstein. The XVIIth Corps on its left approached Bischofsburg, and the XXth, in the centre, much exhausted, held its ground, while on its right, the Ist Corps, still in the neighbourhood of Usdau, prepared to advance on Neidenburg. Samsonov's centre slowly pushed forward between Allenstein and Gilgenburg.

For August 28 Ludendorff's orders were: The Ist Corps to occupy Neidenburg; the Ist Reserve Corps and the XVIIth Corps to abandon the pursuit of the Russian VIth Corps and to move south-west on Passenheim against the right flank of the Russian XIIIth Corps, while the XXth Corps assumed the offensive and Goltz's Landwehr stormed Hohenstein. His idea was that, while the German centre attacked, the two wings, by closing in on Willenburg, would encircle the Russian centre.

Though the morning of August 28 started badly for the Germans, during the afternoon Hohenstein was occupied, and a little later the Ist Reserve Corps reached a position south of Allenstein, while the Ist Corps held the left flank of the Russian centre north of Neidenburg. The next day the Ist Russian Corps again appeared on the field and caused a critical situation on the German right when it launched a rear attack on the German Ist Corps. It was driven back as the double envelopment closed in on Samsonov's doomed centre.

---

[1] *Memories and Impressions*, etc., Gourko, p. 64.
[2] *With the Russian Army, 1914–1917*, vol. I, p. 68.   [3] *Ibid.*, vol. I, p. 84.

The end was near. On August 30 the Russian centre was surrounded and on the 31st, "the day of harvesting", as Hindenburg calls it, Hindenburg sent the following dispatch to the Kaiser:

"I beg most humbly to report to Your Majesty that the ring round the larger part of the Russian Army was closed yesterday. The 13th, 15th, and 18th [XXIIIrd] Army Corps have been destroyed. We have already taken more than 60,000 prisoners, among them the Corps Commanders of the 13th and 15th Corps. The guns are still in the forests and are now being brought in. The booty is immense though it cannot yet be assessed in detail. The Corps outside our ring, the 1st and 6th, have also suffered severely and are now retreating in hot haste through Mlawa and Myszaniec."[1]

While from the German bivouacs scattered among the forest rose the hymn of the Battle of Leuthen, Samsonov accompanied by five staff officers hastened on foot through the darkness toward the Russian frontier. At length, exhausted, he began to lag behind and ultimately disappeared. What his fate was is unknown, but it is believed that he shot himself.[2]

Thus ended this great battle, which Ludendorff named the Battle of Tannenberg after a village which lies to the north of Usdau as an answer to the victory won there by the Poles and Lithuanians over the Teutonic Knights in 1410. Although it had no decisive influence on the war, had the Germans lost it, it would have changed its course completely. As it was, its indirect influence on the western theatre was profound.

In that theatre, of all the days during this war, probably the most fateful for both the French and the Germans was August 25. On that day the French commander-in-chief made a decision, and the German commander had one forced upon him by a subordinate officer – Colonel Tappen, chief of the operations section at Coblenz.

Tappen believed that a great and decisive victory had already been won in the west,[3] and, perturbed by events in East Prussia, he believed that reinforcements should be sent there immediately. This suggestion fitted Moltke's original intention to withdraw six corps from the western front once they could be spared and to

[1] *Out of my Life*, p. 99.
[2] A dramatic account of his last hours is given by Genera Gourko, see *Memories and Impressions*, etc., pp. 65–67.
[3] *Jusqu'à la Marne en 1914*, Général Tappen, p. 112. (See also *Documents Allemands sur la bataille de la Marne*, 1930.)

send them to East Prussia. Two were to be taken from the left wing, two from the centre, and two from the right wing. Urged by Tappen that the moment was now opportune, Moltke approached Rupprecht and the Crown Prince, but both protested so vigorously against the withdrawal that he decided to take only one from the Second Army and one from the Third. Tappen then telephoned Ludendorff and informed him that three (*sic*) army corps and one cavalry division had been ordered to reinforce the Eighth Army. Ludendorff replied that they were not wanted; Tappen answered "that the troops could be spared." The next day he telephoned again and explained "that only the XIth and Reserve Guard Corps [both then besieging Namur] and also the 8th Cavalry Division would come, but that the Vth Army Corps . . . was wanted in the West." Once again General Ludendorff assured him "that the corps would arrive too late for the battle that was then being fought," and therefore it was unnecessary to send them.[1]

It would appear that this conversation was never reported to Moltke, and the result was that the Second Army was ordered to withdraw the Guard Reserve Corps and the Third Army the XIth Corps and the 8th Cavalry Division. There can be little doubt that these armies were selected because their commanders were not royal princes, and in spite of the fact that they already had provided the following detachments: the IIIrd and IXth Reserve Corps to Antwerp and the VIIth to Maubeuge, as well as some minor detachments to watch Givet and Brussels. In all, the decisive right wing was now reduced from 34 to 25 divisions, that is, with casualties added, by a third of its original strength.

While, all unknown to the French, this destruction of the Schlieffen-Moltke plan took shape, the complete breakdown of Plan XVII as well as the successive defeats of the French armies had thrown Paris into panic. Nevertheless, on August 25, when a

---

[1] *The War of Lost Opportunities*, Hoffmann, pp. 34–35. General Hoffmann says the first of these calls took place "On one of the last days of the battle of Tannenberg", Ludendorff says "The telegram announcing the proposed reinforcements arrived just at the commencement of the battle of Tannenberg" (vol. I, p. 58), which is probably correct. Further, he says: "The decision to weaken the forces on the Western Front was premature. . . . But it was particularly fateful that the reinforcements destined for the Eastern Front were drawn from the right wing, which was fighting for a decision" (vol. I, pp. 58–59). And again: "If Moltke had not sent the Guard Reserve Corps and the XI Corps . . . all would have gone well. If he wished to send something, he should have taken the Corps from the left wing" (see *Army Quarterly*, vol. III, p. 50). General von Kluck says the same thing (see *The March on Paris*, English edit., 1920, p. 77).

8

Council of Ministers was assembled, Viviani, its President, made a long discourse on finance, and Doumergue upon Italian-Albanian relationships. In the middle of this fatuous debate Messimy very rightly sprang to his feet and shouted: "*Je me f——de l'Albanie.* What only matters is that within ten days of now the Germans may appear before Paris."[1] It was therefore decided to create an army to cover the capital and to replace General Michel, whom Messimy loathed, by General Galliéni as Governor of Paris. Two days later Messimy was dismissed and was succeeded by Millerand as Minister of War.

Who it was who first thought of creating a defence force for the capital is not easy to decide. Galliéni says he suggested it toward 3 p.m. on August 25,[2] and Joffre says that the order was dated 7 a.m. that day.[3] In all probability the order was dispatched before the meeting of the Council of Ministers, for such councils do not generally meet at so early an hour. The order read:

"If victory does not crown the success of our armies, and if the armies are compelled to retire, an army of at least *three active corps* should be moved to the entrenched camp of Paris, to assure it protection."[4]

This order, it appears, was received at 11.30 a.m.[5]

Meanwhile Joffre, according to his *Memoirs*, thought on somewhat similar lines, for "on the evening of August 25th" he decided to create a new army "outside of the British and in a position to outflank the German right." It was to consist of "the VIIth Army Corps and one division coming from Alsace, two divisions taken from the entrenched camp of Paris, and two divisions withdrawn from the Army of Lorraine." Next, he tells us that at 9 p.m. he received the Minister of War's 7 a.m. order, and "that there was no actual connection between the idea of constituting an army of manœuvre in the region of Amiens, which was my thought, and that of sending three active corps to defend the entrenched camp of Paris, which was what the Ministers' decision amounted to."[6]

---

[1] *Mes Souvenirs*, 368–370.
[2] *Mémoires du Général Galliéni* (1926), p. 21.
[3] *The Memoirs of Marshal Joffre*, vol. I, p. 193.
[4] *Les Armées Françaises dans la Grand Guerre* (French Official History), Tome I, vol. II, Annexes vol. I, Annexe No. 372, p. 263.
[5] *1914 Les erreurs du haut commandement*, Percin, p. 276.
[6] *The Memoirs of Marshal Joffre*, vol. I, pp. 190–193. The writer of Joffre's Memoirs is frequently unreliable. On p. 146 he makes Joffre say that, on August 23, he became aware the Germans were using reserve formations, and, then, on August 25, he writes: "Believing as I still did that the Germans were engaging only active army corps in their offensive operations," etc.

Be this as it may, that evening he issued *"Instruction Générale No. 2"* (it is untimed) and it reads:

"As it is impossible to carry out the offensive manœuvre which had been projected, future operations will have as their objective to form on our left a mass capable of resuming the offensive. This will consist of the Fourth, Fifth and British Armies, together with new forces drawn from the Eastern Front, while the other armies contain the enemy for as long as is necessary.

. . . .

"A new group, comprising formations transported by rail (VIIth Corps, four divisions and perhaps in addition another active corps) will be formed between the 27th August and the 2nd September in front of Amiens, between Domarten–Ponthieu and Corbie, or behind the Somme between Picquigny and Villers-Bretonneux. This group will be in readiness to assume the offensive in the general direction of St. Pol–Arras or Arras–Bapaume."[1]

This army, known as the Sixth Army, was created on the following day and was placed under the command of General Maunoury.[2]

The day this army was created, Kluck attacked the British Army at Le Cateau, drove it from its position, yet failed to pursue. Joffre then realized that were Sir John French's two corps destroyed, the projected manœuvre of the Sixth Army would become impossible, so he ordered Lanrézac's Fifth Army, which on August 27 was immediately south of the river Oise, to relieve the pressure upon the English by launching a counter-attack. Meanwhile Moltke, who still blindly rested in Coblenz – 200 miles from the scene of action – issued the following directive for the 28th:

The French Army is fighting to gain time in order to facilitate the offensive of the Russian Armies. "The objective of the German Army, therefore, must be to advance as rapidly as possible on Paris, not to give the French Army time to recover, to prevent it from forming fresh units, and to take from France as many of her means of defence as possible."

The First Army to advance on the lower Seine, marching west of the Oise.

The Second Army to march on Paris.

---

[1] *Les Armées Françaises*, etc., Tome I, vol. ii, Annex vol. i, Annex 395, pp. 278–280. See also text Tome i, vol. ii, pp. 116 and 580–581.
[2] *Ibid.*, Annexe 619, p. 421.

The Third Army to march on Château-Thierry.

The Fourth Army to march on Épernay.

The Fifth Army to move on Verdun and invest that fortress.

The Sixth and Seventh Armies to oppose an advance of the enemy into Lorraine and Alsace.

"If the enemy puts up a strong resistance on the Aisne and later on the Marne, it may be necessary to abandon the south-western direction of the advance and to wheel south."[1]

Thus the Schlieffen-Moltke plan was retained, but it was inoculated with doubt.

Simultaneously Kluck, when he found that the French left wing was retreating in "a southerly and south-westerly direction", came to the conclusion that it was of decisive importance "to find the flank of this force" and drive it away from Paris. He proposed to Bülow that the Second and the First Armies should "wheel inwards", and no sooner had he done so than Moltke's directive of August 27 arrived, in which it was found that such a move was not excluded.[2] No change, however, was made, and, on the 29th, while the First Army came into contact with General d'Amade's detachment of Territorials on its right flank, and simultaneously learnt of enemy detrainments at Amiens and Moreuil, the battle of Guise-St.. Quentin was fought between Bülow and Lanrézac. It was indecisive; the French slipped back and no pursuit followed. Meanwhile the British Army continued to retire. Joffre met Sir John French but to no good purpose,[3] for General Berthelot, Joffre's Chief of Staff, "even at this hour . . . did not appreciate fully the importance of the German threat to" the French "left flank."[4]

Neither did Kluck appreciate the importance of the French threat from Amiens to his right wing. So certain was he of victory that it seems he never even reported it, and he reverted to his idea of an inward wheel. At 9.30 a.m. on August 30 he prepared to carry it out, and at 5.55 p.m. he heard by wireless from Bülow that he had beaten the French, that they were in retreat and that, on the 31st, the Second Army would rest.

At 6.30 p.m. another message came in from Bülow to ask for the cooperation of the First Army. "To gain the full advantages of

[1] Quoted from *Liaison, 1914*, Brigadier-General E. L. Spears (1932), pp. 533-534. Also see *The Campaign of the Marne, 1914*, Sewell Tyng (1935), pp. 371-374.

[2] *The March on Paris*, von Kluck, pp. 75-76.

[3] See *Memoirs of Marshal Joffre*, vol. 1, pp. 213-214.

[4] *Britain and the War*, Huguet (1928), p. 75.

the victory," it read, "a wheel inwards of the First Army pivoted on Chauny toward the line La Fère–Laon is urgently desired." As this fitted his own ideas, he at once complied, and informed the Supreme Command: "The First Army has wheeled round toward the Oise and will advance on the 31st by Compiègne and Noyon to exploit the success of the Second Army."[1]

Moltke, now established at Luxemburg, agreed to this. His message reads: "The Third Army has converged toward the south against the Aisne . . . and will pursue a southerly direction. The movements undertaken by the First and Second Armies conform to the intention of the High Command."[2] As Bülow points out: "This order was of the highest importance. To all appearances it ignored that since the 29th enemy troops had detrained at Amiens, Moreuil, Montdidier and Roye, and that important forces had already attacked the right wing of the First Army at Villers-Bretonneux east of Amiens."[3]

The fault, therefore, rests with Kluck, who never reported this attack; also with Moltke who, 150 miles away to the north-east, might as well have been in Berlin.

While this vital change was made, which meant the end of the Schlieffen-Moltke plan in shadow as well as in substance, in London Lord Kitchener, who had been appointed Secretary of State for War on August 6, was alarmed to hear from Sir John French that he intended to retire to the south-west of Paris, which was tantamount to an abandonment of the campaign. A telegraphic battle followed which ended when Kitchener hurried over to France. Then, on August 31, the wheel of the German First Army was spotted by a British aeroplane, and its position was confirmed by a captured order. At once Joffre was informed of this momentous news.

It was on the following day, September 1, that the fast approaching series of battles, to become known to history as the Battle of the Marne, finds its origin, and though it is true that if the Sixth Army had not been created it could not have been fought, it is equally true that had Kluck not wheeled eastward, its four divisions – two of the VIIth Corps and the 55th and 56th divisions – would in all probability easily have been swept aside.

On this day Joffre asked the Minister of War to place the

---

[1] *The March on Paris*, von Kluck, pp. 82–83.
[2] *Mon rapport sur la Bataille de la Marne*, von Bülow (French edit., 1920), p. 51.
[3] *Ibid.*, p. 51.

capital directly under his command. He then ordered Maunoury to retire on Paris, moved his headquarters to Bar-sur-Aube, and issued "*Instruction Générale No. 4*", in which he said:

"As soon as the Fifth Army has escaped the menace of envelopment against its left, the Third, Fourth and Fifth Armies will resume the offensive. . . .

"If circumstances permit, parts of the First and Second Armies will be recalled in due course to participate in the offensive. Finally the mobile troops of the fortified camp of Paris may also take part in the general action."[1]

Vague though this order was, it carried with it a definite hint of a counter-attack from Paris, and its vagueness may have in part been due to Joffre's uncertainty about the British, for Sir John French was still in full retreat. Meanwhile, on the German side, though it was known that the French were hurrying troops to Paris,[2] Bülow was instructed by Moltke to move his left wing eastward in order to support the Third Army.[3] This drew him away from the First Army.

The next day, September 2, the British continued their retreat, and Kluck abandoned the pursuit and moved the IIIrd and IXth Corps on Château-Thierry to help Bülow.[4] No sooner had he done so than he received this order from Moltke: "The intention is to drive the French in a south-westerly direction from Paris. The First Army will follow in echelon behind the Second Army and will be responsible for the flank protection of the Armies."[5] Kluck comments in his book: "The Supreme Command, however, seemed to be firmly convinced that the garrison of Paris need not be taken into account for any operations outside the line of forts of the capital,"[6] and instead of halting and assuming his new rôle of flank guard – he was already a day's march ahead of the Second Army – he set Moltke's order aside and pushed on to Château-Thierry – that is, away from Paris.

Meanwhile, while General Maunoury fell back on Paris, Joffre dispatched a secret note to his Army Commanders in which he ordered them to establish themselves on the general line Pont-sur-Yonne – Méry-sur-Seine – Arcis-sur-Aube – Brienne-le-Château – Joinville, and then:

[1] *La préparation de la guerre*, etc., Joffre, pp. 95–96.
[2] *Jusqu'à la Marne en 1914*, Tappen, p. 115.
[3] *Mon rapport sur la Bataille de la Marne*, von Bülow, p. 54.
[4] *The March on Paris*, von Kluck, p. 91.
[5] *Ibid.*, p. 94.   [6] *Ibid.*, p. 95.

"To reinforce the right-hand army by two corps drawn from the armies of Nancy and Épinal.

"At that moment to assume the offensive on the whole front.

"Cover our left wing with all available cavalry between Montereau and Melun.

"Ask the British Army to participate in the manœuvre,

(*1*) – by holding the Seine from Melun to Juvisy,

(*2*) – by debouching from that front when the Fifth Army assumes the offensive.

"Simultaneously the garrison of Paris will act in the direction of Meaux."[1]

The extraordinary point in this order is that a retirement to Joinville meant the abandonment of Verdun, the pivot upon which the whole of the left of the French Army swung. Had that fortress been abandoned, Joffre's front would have been cut in two, and no sortie from Paris could have saved the situation. Fortunately for Joffre, General Sarrail, who on August 30 had replaced Ruffrey, set this order aside, and instead of withdrawing his right he held fast to Verdun and swung back his left some 15 miles until it faced due west. This made a gap between his army and the Fourth Army, into which the Crown Prince entered and was attacked in flank.

It is obvious from the secret note of September 2 that Joffre's mind was befogged. Nevertheless, while Moltke sat in monastic seclusion at Luxemburg, Joffre acted. At least he did something, and thanks to Sarrail it was something worth while, and something which gradually began to clear the mists which surrounded him. It was that, so long as his right held fast to Verdun and his centre was not driven in, might not it be possible to swing his left forward?

Thus it came about that he was attracted toward that flank. Two things next happened: firstly, he replaced General Lanrézac by Franchet D'Espérey – probably the ablest of the French generals – and secondly he began to pay some attention to Galliéni. Strange as it may seem, thus far Joffre had left him in ignorance of his intentions, and for some unexplained reason Galliéni only received his General Instruction No. 4 this day.[2] He then at once considered the problem of advancing Maunoury's army on Meaux.[3] Toward noon, for the first time he learnt of Kluck's

---

[1] Quoted from *Liaison, 1914*, Spears, pp. 365–366.
[2] *Mémoire du Général Galliéni*, p. 77.   [3] *Ibid.*, p. 81.

wheel eastward,[1] and he asked for instructions regarding Maunoury, and suggested that he be moved north of the Marne toward the river Ourcq. Joffre replied that part of his active troops "can be pushed to the north-east at any moment from now on, so as to threaten the right flank of the Germans" and encourage the British.[2] Then, suddenly, the clouds of doubt thicken again and Joffre wrote to Millerand:

"As one of the allied powers our duty is to hold out, gain time and contain the strongest possible German forces. . . . My decision therefore is to wait several days before launching the battle . . . rest our troops and prepare an eventual offensive with the British Army and the mobile garrison of Paris."[3]

This meant a wearing battle followed by an eventual attack at some uncertain future date. Meanwhile General von Kluck plunged on. His order for September 4 reads: "The First Army will continue its march across the Marne tomorrow, so as to force the French away eastwards. If the British offer opposition they are to be driven back."[4] At the same time Bülow believed that the French Fifth Army was in rout.[5]

In spite of this rosy outlook, on the following day nervousness began to show itself at Luxemburg. It was decided to move the headquarters of the Seventh Army and two corps from the left flank to the right.[6] Meanwhile Kluck continued his advance, and such skirmishes as his IVth Corps – on his right flank – had with Maunoury's patrols led him to believe that there was little behind them.

On the Allied side, far from the battle being several days distant, as Joffre supposed, it was imminent, and it emerged chaotically out of a confusion of conferences. Joffre, who still thought in terms of the defensive, created a new army, the Ninth, under General Foch, between his Fourth and Fifth Armies, and then returned to his offensive idea and at 12.45 p.m. telegraphed Sir John French, and asked him whether his army would be ready "to deliver battle tomorrow."[7] Simultaneously he sent an identical message to Franchet d'Espérey.[8]

---

[1] *Ibid.*, pp. 93–94. See also *Les Carnets de Galliéni* (1932), pp. 58–59.
[2] *Memoirs of Marshal Joffre*, vol. I, p. 241.
[3] *Plutarque a menti*, Pierrefeu, pp. 98–99. See also *Liaison*, Spears, pp. 372–373.
[4] *The March on Paris*, p. 100.
[5] *Mon rapport sur la Bataille de la Marne*, p. 56.
[6] *Jusqu'à la Marne en 1914*, Tappen, pp. 100, 116.
[7] *Liaison, 1914*, Spears, p. 399.
[8] *Memoirs of Marshal Joffre*, p. 246.

When Galliéni and Maunoury were told by Joffre to get into touch with Sir John French, they visited his headquarters at Melun at 3 p.m., but as they found him absent they provisionally arranged with Sir Archibald Murray, French's chief of staff, that while on the 5th the Sixth Army was to advance on Meaux, the British Army would fall back to make room for it, and on the 6th or 7th "pivot on its right wing . . . so as to face east, its left joining the Sixth Army." Then both were to attack the right flank of the German First Army while held by the French Fifth Army.[1]

On his return Sir John French approved this plan; but a little later General Sir Henry Wilson, his sub-chief of the General Staff, arrived with a totally different plan. What had happened?

Franchet d'Espérey, who wished to meet Sir John French, set out for Bray-sur-Seine. There, at 3 p.m., he was met by Wilson – Sir John French was out. He explained to Wilson that the First German Army was "in the air", with its communications exposed, and that it was not in contact with the Second Army. He then proposed:

(*1*) On September 5 the Fifth Army should take up the line Sézanne–Provins in readiness to attack on the front Sézanne–Courtaçon.

(*2*) The Sixth Army should advance to the Ourcq and fall on the flank and rear of the First German Army.

(*3*) The British Army should cooperate by filling the gap between the Fifth and Sixth Armies with its axis directed on Montmirail and its right covered by Conneau's Cavalry.

These proposals he at once telegraphed to Joffre, and Wilson took them to Sir John French, who, now quite bewildered, did nothing. When this telegram arrived Joffre was telephoned by Galliéni, who told him that he was ready to move, but that British cooperation was essential. Half an hour later – at 10 p.m. – Joffre issued General Instructions No. 6; according to which an attack was to be launched against the exposed wing of Kluck's Army on September 6. Its main items were:

(*1*) The Sixth Army to cross the Ourcq and move in the direction of Château-Thierry.

(*2*) The British Army, on the front Changis–Coulommiers, facing east, to be ready to attack in the direction of Montmirail.

(*3*) The Fifth Army, on the front Courtaçon–Esterney–Sézanne, to be ready to attack from south to north.

[1] See *Liaison, 1914*, Spears, pp. 406–407, and Galliéni's *Mémoires*, pp. 119–128.

(4) The Ninth Army to cover the right of the Fifth Army and, hold the boundaries of the marshes of St. Gond.

(5) The Fourth Army to stand fast and maintain contact with the Third Army.

(6) The Third Army, while it held back its right, to advance its centre and left and attack the left of the enemy forces marching west of the Argonne.[1]

Strangely enough, in idea this was a Cannae plan. While the French centre – the Fifth, Fourth, and Ninth French Armies – held the Second, Third, and Fourth German Armies in a great pocket, the two French wings – the French Sixth Army and British on the left flank and the Third French Army on the right – were to operate toward Rheims, the one to advance eastward against the German First Army and the other westward against the German Fifth Army.

This night Galliéni ordered Maunoury to be ready to attack directly Sir John French decided to cooperate.[2]

While at the French G.H.Q. all was activity, Moltke, who thus far had rigidly followed the non-interference theory of his uncle, began to doubt its wisdom as report after report was received of French rail movements towards Paris. At length, anxious about the safety of the right flank of his armies, at 7 p.m. on September 4 he ordered Tappen to telegraph the following message:

"The First and Second Armies are to remain facing the eastern front of Paris: The First Army, between the Oise and the Marne, is to occupy the Marne crossing west of Château-Thièrry; the Second Army, between the Marne and the Seine, is to occupy the Seine crossing between Nogent and Méry inclusive."[3]

This order was received by the First Army at 7.15 a.m. on September 5. At 11 a.m., General von Gronau, in command of the IVth Reserve Corps, which acted as flank guard to the First Army, and who was suspicious of enemy concentrations west of him, attacked the heights of Monthyon, surprised the advanced guards of the Sixth French Army, which that morning had moved forward, and drove them back. Thus opened the Battle of the Marne; prematurely so far as the French were concerned because the Allied forces were not yet ready.

A stubborn fight followed, and Gronau, when he found himself

---

[1] *La préparation de la guerre*, etc., Joffre, pp. 108–110.
[2] *Mémoires du Général Galliéni*, p. 112.
[3] *The March on Paris*, Kluck, p. 105.

outnumbered, fell back some six miles, but was not pursued. When he heard of this action, Kluck at once turned about his IInd Corps (General von Linsingen) and hurried it to Gronau's support.

Shortly before this decision was made, Lieutenant-Colonel Hentsch, one of Moltke's staff officers, had arrived at Kluck's headquarters. Kluck was then under the impression that the armies on his left were advancing victoriously and he was amazed to learn that the Fifth, Sixth, and Seventh Armies had been held up, and because the French were moving troops by rail from the east toward Paris[1] a general retirement of the German front might become necessary.

Meanwhile Joffre's anxiety about Sir John French's intentions had become so unbearable that, at 2 p.m. he visited him at Melun; explained to him the vital necessity for British cooperation, and ended by exclaiming: "*Monsieur le Maréchal, c'est la France qui vous supplie.*" Sir John French tried to reply in French, but words failed him and he turned to an English officer and exclaimed: "Damn it, I can't explain. Tell him that all that men can do our fellows will do."[2] Thus at last cooperation was established, and Joffre issued the following proclamation to his troops:

"We are about to engage in a battle on which the fate of our country depends and it is important to remind all ranks that the moment has passed for looking to the rear; all our efforts must be directed to attacking and driving back the enemy. Troops that can advance no farther, must, at any price, hold on to the ground they have conquered and die at the spot rather than give way. Under the circumstances which face us, no act of weakness can be tolerated."[3]

The Battle of the Marne – opened on September 5 by Gronau's surprise attack on the leading troops of General Maunoury's army – was destined for seven days to rage up and down the western front from Verdun to Senlis, and it comprised so many engagements that they will be here restricted to those fought on the vital right flank of the German phalanx. They may be divided into the battle of the Ourcq, the battle of the two Morins, and the "battle" of the Gap.

As regards the battle of the Ourcq, the fighting on September 5 was continued on the following day by Linsingen, who arrived at

[1] *Ibid.*, p. 107.
[2] *Liaison, 1914*, Spears, p. 417. See also *Memoirs of Marshal Joffre*, vol. 1, pp. 253–254.
[3] *The Memoirs of Marshal Joffre*, vol. 1, p. 255.

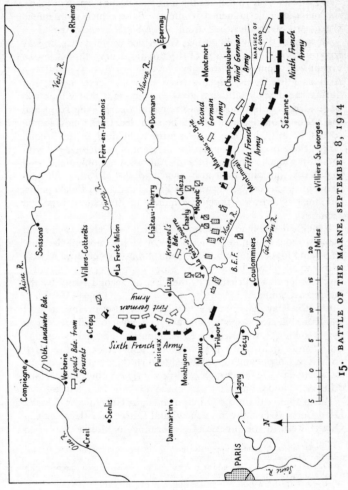

15. BATTLE OF THE MARNE, SEPTEMBER 8, 1914

Trilport at 5 a.m. In spite of the long march his corps had made, six hours later he launched it into the fight, which soon spread northward along the whole front of the Sixth French Army.[1]

In spite of the severe fighting, von Kluck was as yet in no way convinced of the seriousness of the situation; nevertheless, on an urgent call from von Linsingen, he sent forward General von Arnim's IVth Corps, which arrived early on September 7. But during the day the situation grew so precarious that Kluck was persuaded to order back his two remaining corps – the IIIrd and the IXth.[2] This decision, as will be seen, led to the most fateful results, because, in order to secure the right flank of the Second Army, these two corps were at the moment of recall engaged with the Fifth French Army, and their withdrawal not only uncovered that flank, but simultaneously increased the already wide gap between the Second Army and the First. Further, as Bülow points out, their withdrawal raised the morale of Franchet d'Espérey's men.[3]

Kluck's decision to withdraw the IIIrd and IXth Corps was taken without consulting either Bülow or Moltke, not only because he was no longer under Bülow's control, but also because Moltke had lost all power to intervene. From September 5 to 8, not a single order was sent either to the First or Second Army by the Supreme Command.[4]

On this day Maunoury's position was also precarious and Galliéni collected some 1,200 Paris taxi-cabs to rush reinforcements to him.[5] On September 8, Maunoury attempted to outflank his enemy's right, but without success, and Kluck, as the IIIrd and IXth Corps came up, planned to turn the French left on the following day. He felt certain of a speedy victory, but fate decided differently, and on another part of the 300-mile long battle-front.

When the battle of the Ourcq opened, as General von Kluck's IIIrd Corps (General von Lochow) and IXth Corps (General von Quast) were in the process of conforming to Moltke's order to

[1] In all, General Maunoury appears to have had under his command some 150,000 men. See *Mémoires du Général Galliéni*, pp. 110–111.

[2] On the evening of September 6 an order of Joffre's was found on a prisoner which revealed the seriousness of the attack (see *Jusqu'à la Marne in 1914*, Tappen, p. 116).

[3] *Mon rapport sur la bataille de la Marne*, Bülow, p. 68.

[4] In *La direction suprême de l'armée pendant la bataille de la Marne* (Documents Allemands), p. 133, Lieut.-Colonel Muller-Löbnitz writes: "Even during the battle the Supreme Command abstained from all intervention." He informs us that General Tappen said to him: "The Supreme Command considered best to give the Army Commanders a free hand."

[5] See *La véritable histoire des taxis de la Marne*, Commandant Henri Carré (1921).

protect the right flank of the Second Army, suddenly a violent and unexpected bombardment burst on them. All unknown to them the tide of battle had turned. The Fifth French Army, which was considered beaten, was upon them. Lochow and Quast rushed their corps forward and soon all along the front a battle raged between these two corps and the three left-wing corps – the XVIIIth, IIIrd, and Ist – of Franchet d'Espérey's Army, while his Xth Corps was engaged on their right. The French advanced about one mile that day, but by nightfall they were held up and ordered to entrench. The next day their attack was continued in the direction of Montmirail.

Although Bülow had held his own, the situation was sufficiently serious to warrant a retirement behind the Petit Morin; this he carried out during the night of September 7–8, which meant the end of Moltke's order of September 4. Thus it was that not until September 8 did the French regain contact, by when the IIIrd and IXth Corps were on their way to the Ourcq in response to Kluck's urgent call. During the day several French frontal attacks were repulsed, and, on the night of September 8–9 General de Maud'huy, Commander of the XVIIIth Corps, carried Marchais-en-Brie, to the west of Montmirail. This success, as Mr. Tyng points out, was an event of supreme importance, because its capture rendered Montmirail indefensible, and since that town was now completely dominated from the west, "Bülow ordered his VIIth and Xth Reserve Corps to fall back to the line Margny-le-Thoult, a position running from north to south. It was a retreat of ten kilometres towards the east, which left the right wing of the German Second Army facing west instead of south, and it ended all further possibility of closing the breach between Bülow and Kluck."[1]

For the Germans the best chance of victory that remained was to break through the front of Foch's Ninth Army, which extended from Villeneuve to Sommesous along the marshes of St. Gond; to turn the right wing of the Fifth and force it to retire. On September 6, General von Hausen had launched his Third Army against Foch, and on the 8th, at 3 a.m., he surprised his right, drove it back and carried Fère Campenoise, but failed to penetrate. Though it is related that Foch reported to Joffre, "Hard pressed on my right. My centre is yielding. Impossible to manoeuvre. Situation excellent. I am attacking," it is not true; it is true how-

[1] *The Campaign of the Marne, 1914*, Sewell Tyng (1935), p. 251.

ever that he ordered attacks and counter-attacks in rapid succession, but to no avail, for his men had as much as they could do to hold on by the skin of their teeth.

While Maunoury compelled Kluck to draw the whole of his Army to the Ourcq, and Franchet d'Espérey forced Bülow to retire north-eastward, Sir John French and his three corps[1] cautiously crept into the gap between Kluck and Bülow, unwittingly to conjure forth from a situation created for them "the miracle of the Marne", or, as Pierrefeu describes it: "How Sir John French saved the situation without understanding it."[2]

On the morning of September 6 French had set out against what was a near vacuum, because on the night before Kluck had withdrawn his IInd Corps, which early on the 6th was followed by his IVth. All that remained in front of the British Army were two divisions of General von der Marwitz's Cavalry Corps and some Jäger and cyclist battalions. French slowly felt his way as he advanced with the IIIrd Corps (Pulteney) on his left, the IInd (Smith-Dorrien) in the centre, and the Ist (Haig) on his right, and when on the following day Bülow fell back and the IIIrd and IXth Corps of the First German Army were ordered north, the IInd and IIIrd British Corps crossed the Grand Morin while the Ist was delayed near Rozoy. Seldom in the history of war was speed more necessary; yet Sir John French, although a cavalry officer, did little or nothing to urge on his corps. On September 8 the Petit Morin was crossed after some opposition and the advance was continued to the Marne. In three days the British Army had moved forward 25 miles, and because it stood at the entrance of the gap between the First and Second German Armies, all it had to do was to step forward and sever the head of the invading phalanx from its body.

Joffre saw this, and that evening, at 8.7 p.m., he ordered his Sixth Army to hold on to the Germans on the Ourcq, while the British crossed the Marne between Nogent-l'Artaud and la Ferté-sous-Jouarre and advanced against Kluck's left and rear. Also, he instructed the Fifth Army to cover the right flank of the British.

Meanwhile what of Moltke at Luxemburg? With only just sufficient information to fill him with the gravest anxiety, he sent for Lieutenant-Colonel Hentsch and instructed him to visit the

---

[1] The IIIrd Corps, commanded by Lieut.-General Sir W. Pulteney, came into being on August 30.
[2] *Plutarque a menti*, p. 121.

five right-wing armies and ascertain the exact situation. At that moment neither he nor any of his staff dreamt that a general retirement would be necessary;[1] nevertheless the situation was of sufficient importance for written instructions to have been given to Hentsch, but he received only verbal ones. He says: "The Chief of the General Staff empowered me, should it be necessary, to order the five armies to fall back behind the Vesle along the heights north of the Argonne," and "I was given the mission, if it were necessary, to order the retreat of the armies on the line Sainte Ménehould–Rheims–Fismes–Soissons. I was given full powers to give orders in the name of the Supreme Command."[2]

Hentsch, who was no optimist, left Luxemburg at 11 a.m. on September 8. First he visited the Fifth, Fourth, and Third Armies, and arrived at Montmort, the headquarters of the Second Army, at 7.45 p.m. There he found that Bülow believed a retreat of the First Army to be inevitable and that he had decided to withdraw his own army.[3]

At 7 a.m. on September 9, Hentsch set out for Chézy, the First Army headquarters, and although it was no more than 25 miles away, because of troop movements along his road he did not arrive there until noon. Every mile he travelled he witnessed confusion and disorder[4] – conditions no more than normal in rear of a retiring army – which accentuated his pessimism and must have suggested to him that the situation was desperate. As he found Kluck out, he talked the situation over with his chief of staff, General von Kuhl, and while he did so a message came in from the Second Army that Bülow was falling back. Hentsch, who knew that the gap between the First and Second Armies had widened to over 30 miles, and that the British had entered it, then invoked the power given him by Moltke, and ordered the First Army to retire. This was done without the approval of Kluck and in spite of the fact that he was not far off.[5]

That Hentsch was empowered to give the order is undoubted, but it was of such supreme importance that he had no right to give it to anyone other than Kluck himself, and that he did not do so goes to show how far the presumptions of the General Staff had replaced the authority of the commanding generals. It would

[1] *La direction suprême de l'armée*, etc., Muller-Löbnitz, p. 137.
[2] *Ibid.*, pp. 138–139.
[3] *Mon rapport sur la bataille de la Marne*, p. 66.
[4] *La direction suprême de l'armée*, Muller-Löbnitz, p. 161.
[5] See *The March on Paris*, Kluck, p. 137.

appear that Kluck never saw Hentsch, and when he heard of the order he accepted it against his better judgment,[1] probably because of his awe for the Great General Staff. Although he did not know that the French on his right were contemplating retreat, he must have been aware of the inordinately slow and cautious advance of the British in the gap between him and Bülow. Had he ignored Hentsch's verbal order and acted on the principle "when in doubt hit out", not only might he have driven back Maunoury, but by doing so have paralysed the British and carried Bülow along with him. As Görlitz points out, this is what Seydlitz did at Zorndorf, and adds, "but this kind of thing was not in the mode of the era of William II."[2]

Thus the Schlieffen-Moltke plan, created and directed by the staff, was liquidated by the staff, because generalship was bankrupt. On the morning of September 11, for the first time during the campaign Moltke went forward and visited the headquarters of his armies. On his return he was taken seriously ill[3] and soon after was replaced by General von Falkenhayn.

Tannenberg and the Marne were both decisive battles – the one tactically and the other strategically. The former led to no strategical results other than exalting Hindenburg and persuading the German General Staff to assume that a rapid defeat of Russia was a comparatively easy task. Yet, had the battle been won by the Russians, its effects on both Germany and Europe might have been appalling. On the contrary, the latter battle, which was only a partial tactical success, led to such overwhelming strategical results that Sir James Edmonds is unquestionably right when he classes Joffre's victory "as one of the decisive battles of the world."[4] It meant that Germany had lost her one and only chance to defeat France before she engaged Russia *au fond*.

One reason for this was that, as Bloch had foreseen, mobile warfare rapidly degenerated into siege. Under the cover of innumerable entrenchments the initiative passed from the General Staffs to the industrial potentials of the contending nations. Where these potentials were weak, as in Russia, mobile warfare, though attenuated, was still possible; but where they were strong, as they were in France and Great Britain, it ceased altogether. Henceforward decision in the West was more and more sought in

[1] *The German General Staff*, Walter Görlitz (English edit., 1953), p. 162.
[2] *Ibid.*, p. 162.   [3] See *Jusqu'à la Marne en 1914*, Tappen, p. 121.
[4] *History of the Great War, France and Belgium, 1914*, vol. I, p. 295.

factories than in armies, and also in sea power, which could either safeguard or strangle industrial supplies. As Bloch had foretold, the ultimate arbiter was to be famine.

Deeper than this, there was a fundamental misjudgment in the Schlieffen plan, which had it been appreciated might, and probably would, have deterred Germany from going to war unless supported by England or assured of her neutrality. This misjudgment arose out of the composition of the German two-front war. Had it been restricted to a conflict with France and Russia, the probability is that, had the Schlieffen plan been adhered to, France would have been hurled into the dust within six weeks of the start of the war and that a compromise peace with Russia would have followed. But, as things stood in August, 1914, the western front included England as well as France, and though the British Army would, in the circumstances stated, have shared the fate of the French, the integrity of England would nevertheless have remained inviolate. The question therefore arises, however successful the Schlieffen plan might have been, would it have led to a conclusion of the war? The historic answer is "No!" As in the days of Napoleon, England would have continued at war until she had built up another coalition, or until both she and Germany were faced with economic collapse, when a negotiated peace on traditional British lines would have ended it.

Time and again in the past, when England was involved in a continental war the historic lesson had been that as long as she commanded the seas, because her frontiers were un-attackable and her maritime communications secure, no continental nation, however powerful its land forces, could wrest the initiative from her. This was the governing factor, not only in the collapse of Germany in 1918, but also in her still more overwhelming collapse in 1945, and in both World Wars Germany failed to appreciate it.

Tactical stalemate and change of objectives

The operations which immediately followed the battle of the Marne led to a radical change in the orientation of the war. Each side first attempted to outflank the other's northern wing by reinforcing its own northern wing from its southern. But the race was so close that it ended in a dead-heat at Nieuport on the Channel. Then it was discovered that the magazine rifle had made the defensive so much stronger than the attack that when near the enemy, in order to exist, let alone fight, entrenching became imperative. Thus, as Bloch had predicted, the outcome was siege warfare.

But neither side was prepared to wage it, least of all the British, who were so ill-equipped for the task that they made hand grenades out of jam tins and converted field-gun cartridge cases into trench mortars. Catapults again came into use and wooden cannon were bored out of logs, from which oil drums filled with explosives were fired. Soon lines of entrenchments began to supplement each other, and though it was still possible at great cost to carry a front line entrenchment by assault, the ever-growing depth of trench systems, coupled with entanglements, soon prohibited complete penetration. Thus, until the advent of the tank, spade and barbed wire beat rifle and gun; mobility ceased on the western front and gave way to stalemate.

Meanwhile in the east, because of the disastrous retreat of the Austrians to the Dunajec, on September 15 Hindenburg was ordered to hold East Prussia with a minimum of his forces and transfer the bulk of his army to the Austrian left wing. This he did, and on November 1 was appointed commander-in-chief of the eastern front. But he was still too weak to force a decision, and when the Russians advanced again, their near approach to Silesia and their reoccupation of part of East Prussia so alarmed the Kaiser that pressure was brought on Falkenhayn to stop operations in the west and reinforce Hindenburg. This he was able to do in November, when the fighting in the Ypres area bogged down in the Flanders mud.

To save Austria, it was imperative to dislodge the Russians from the Carpathians, and on the suggestion of Field-Marshal Conrad von Hötzendorf, the chief of the Austrian General Staff, it was decided to break through the Russian front between Gorlice and Tarnow and wheel eastward behind the Russian left flank and sever its communications. In the east this was a feasible plan, because the Russian front was weakly entrenched, almost entirely unwired and held by little more than outposts.

At 6 a.m. on May 2, 1915, after four hours of bombardment, the German and Austrian infantry advanced, broke through the Russian front and captured 140,000 prisoners. But as the roads were rivers of mud, the pursuit was so slow that it was not until August 5 that the Russians were compelled to abandon Warsaw. Kovno and Grodno fell next, and by the end of September, after they had lost 325,000 men in prisoners alone and more than 3,000 guns, the Russians were forced back on the line Riga–Dvinsk–Pinsk–Tarnopol–Czernowitz. Although not driven out of the war, they were so weakened[1] that the armies of the Central Powers were free to select what objective they liked in 1916.

Meanwhile the Russian situation was made worse because Turkey had joined Germany, and to understand how this came about it is necessary to step back into pre-war history.

In 1883, in order to strengthen the Dual Alliance, General von der Goltz was lent by Germany to Turkey to reorganize her army, and two years later the defences of the Dardanelles were modernized. Twenty years later, when the Anglo-French entente was agreed, Admiral Sir John Fisher, then First Sea Lord, studied the Dardanelles problem and came to the conclusion that to force their passage, even with military support, would be "mighty hazardous". Next, in 1906 and again in 1911, the newly created British General Staff examined the question and decided "that owing to the impossibility of effecting a surprise, an attempt to disembark an army on the Gallipoli peninsula would be too hazardous to be recommended". In the meantime the British entente with Russia had drawn Turkey toward Germany, and to propitiate the Turks a British naval mission was sent to Constantinople. In order to counteract its activities, in 1913 a German military mission of 70 officers headed by General Liman von

---

[1] "Even before the end of the campaign in 1914," writes Mr. Lloyd George, "the Russian Army's resistance threatened to break down through lack of equipment" (*War Memoirs*, 1933, vol. 1, p. 441).

Sanders was sent to Turkey, and on August 2, 1914, a secret defensive and offensive alliance was signed by Germany and Turkey. It was followed immediately by the mobilization of the Turkish Army and the mining of the Dardanelles. No sooner was this treaty made than an unlooked-for event gave it life. Two warships, then being built in English yards for the Turkish Navy, were requisitioned by the British Government, and two German warships – the *Goeben* and *Breslau* – which were in the Mediterranean, after a series of adventures in which they successfully eluded the French and British fleets, entered the Dardanelles on August 10 and steamed for Constantinople. But they were not interned; instead they were nominally bought by the Turks to replace the two ships seized. This event more than any other determined the destiny of the war in the Mediterranean. Because of it, in September a British squadron was sent to watch the Dardanelles, and as this made the position of the British naval mission intolerable, the latter was withdrawn. This left the German military mission master of the field and it became obvious to the Allied Powers that war with Turkey was probable. It did not take long to come. On October 29 a Turkish squadron, under German command, entered the Black Sea and shelled Odessa, Sebastopol, and Theodosia. The following day the Russian Ambassador in Constantinople asked for his passports, and the British Government demanded the withdrawal of the German military mission within 12 hours. As this ultimatum was ignored, war with Turkey was declared by Russia on November 2, and by Britain and France on the 5th. This meant that all hope of the British and French to gain a southern approach to Russia was blocked.

The Turkish Army consisted of 36 divisions headed by Liman von Sanders, with General Bronsart von Schellendorf as his chief of staff. Its distribution was:

First Army, 13 divisions, based on Constantinople with one division on the Gallipoli peninsula. Second Army, six divisions on the coast of Asia Minor with one on the Asiatic side of the Dardanelles. Third Army, 11 divisions in Asia Minor, earmarked for the Caucasus. Two divisions in Yemen, two in Mesopotamia, and two in the Hejaz. Eventually, 70 new divisions were raised.

Although short of arms and ammunition, neither of which had been fully replenished since the Balkan wars, Enver Pasha decided on two campaigns – one against the Russians in the Caucasus and the other against Egypt. The aim of the first campaign was to

Before describing the Gallipoli operations, which he rightly calls "one of the greatest tragedies in British history", Fuller continues:

When the race between the British and Germans to the Channel ended at Nieuport, the mobile war both had set out to fight was so abruptly halted by the spade that Lord Kitchener exclaimed: "I don't know what is to be done—this isn't war." Unfortunately it was war, as every private soldier knew.[1] But ministers are not private soldiers, and the stalemate so shocked them that blame for it was heaped on the generals. Mr. Churchill, First Lord of the Admiralty, exclaimed: "Confronted with this deadlock, military art remained dumb; the Commanders and their General Staffs had no plan except the frontal attack which all their experience and training had led them to reject; they had no policy except the policy of exhaustion."[2] And on December 31, Mr. Lloyd George said: "I can see no signs anywhere that our military leaders and guides are considering any plans for extricating us from our present unsatisfactory position."[3]

' Thus it came about that the more silent the soldiers became, the more vociferous grew the politicians. But because there was no organ of strategical direction within or behind the Government at that time, no minister had any idea of what his colleagues were doing. "The men at the head of affairs," wrote Admiral Wemyss, "are ignorant of all technique; they think they have only to say 'Do it'—and it is done—wrong."[4] What was the result? General Sir William Robertson supplies the answer: "The Secretary of State for War, was aiming at decisive results on the Western front;

[1] "The enemy rose up and started to advance. They were stopped at once: with the parapet as a rest for our rifles it was impossible to miss. The attack was over before it had hardly commenced . . . ten men holding a trench could easily stop fifty who were trying to take it" (*Old Soldiers never Die*, Private Frank Richards, 1933, p. 36).
[2] *The World Crisis, 1915*, The Rt. Hon. Winston S. Churchill (1923), p. 20.
[3] *War Memoirs of David Lloyd George* (1933), vol. I, p. 356.
[4] *The Life and Letters of Lord Wester Wemyss*, Lady Wester Wemyss (1935), p. 194.

the First Lord of the Admiralty was advocating a military expedition to the Dardanelles; the Secretary of State for India was devoting his attention to a campaign in Mesopotamia . . . the Secretary for the Colonies was occupying himself with several small wars in Africa; and the Chancellor of the Exchequer, Mr. Lloyd George, was attempting to secure the removal of a large part of the British Army from France to some Eastern Mediterranean theatre."[1] This was at the time when the British Army in Flanders had lost half its men, and when there were no trained replacements at home to reinforce it.'

It was in 1915, depressed by the symptoms of deadlock on the Western Front, that the Allied statesmen first committed themselves to what Fuller, in a later book, has stigmatised as the "strategy of evasion."[1] There he has accurately defined its weakness:

> In what locality could Germany be most profitably struck? The answer depended on the most practical allied line of operations, which, in its turn, was governed by the location of the allied main bases. They were France and Great Britain, and in no other area than France could the ponderous mass armies of this period be fully deployed and supplied in the field. The main bases and the main theatre of war were fixed by geography and logistics, and no juggling with fronts could alter this. [2]

Nevertheless, the statesmen were determined to make the attempt, and it was naturally the most eloquent and forceful "juggler" who prevailed. So, assisted by the Russian appeal for aid, it was Winston Churchill's idea of forcing the Dardanelles Straits which carried the day. As an idea, it was undoubtedly attractive; no one has more clearly summed up the attraction than the most determined opponent of all "strategies of evasion", Field-Marshal Sir William Robertson, who became Chief of the Imperial General Staff in December 1915:

[1] Quoted in *Gallipoli, The Fading Vision,* John North (1936), p. 83.

[1] Fuller, *The Conduct Of War, 1789-1961,* Eyre & Spottiswoode, 1961.

[2] *Ibid.,* pp. 161-62.

The advantages to be derived from forcing the Straits were perfectly obvious. Such a success would, as the advocates of the project said, serve to secure Egypt, to induce Italy and the Balkan States to come in on our side, and, if followed by the forcing of the Bosphorus, would enable Russia to draw munitions from America and Western Europe, and to export her accumulated supplies of wheat. There is seldom any lack of attractive-looking schemes in war. The difficulty is to give effect to them, and one of the difficulties in the Dardanelles scheme was that nothing really useful could be achieved without the assistance, sooner or later, of troops, and, according to the War Minister, no troops were available.[3]

It was the sheer lack of necessary resources, from beginning to end, which chiefly bedevilled the Gallipoli Campaign – though other factors, such as the rawness of the troops and the ineptitudes of commanders, played their part. At first the whole affair was supposed to be a naval enterprise, pure and simple. Three indecisive bombardments of the Turkish forts guarding the Straits disposed of this idea, and after the failure of the third, on 18 March, it became clear that the Army would have to find troops somehow – in other words, "Gallipoli" would have to be a Combined Operation, for which neither Service possessed any training or equipment. The Commander-in-Chief appointed was General Sir Ian Hamilton, who failed to meet the measure of his difficult task. The first landings were made at Anzac[4] Cove and Cape Helles on 25 April. It is to be noted (though too often overlooked) that only three days earlier the Germans had launched the first Gas attack in the history of war at Ypres, plunging the British Expeditionary Force into a long-drawn-out battle which strained all its resources to the very limit and cost it sixty thousand casualties: *not* the best moment for embarking on a second major campaign.

The landings on 25 April had varying fortunes, and some of their episodes have passed into legend; their overall result was to establish footholds which the British only expanded by inches during the next three months. So far the whole effort had only succeeded in creating another deadlock as obstinate as that on the

---

[1] Robertson, *Soldiers And Statesmen*, Cassell, 1926.

[1] A.N.Z.A.C.—Australian & New Zealand Army Corps.

Western Front. As Fuller says: "It was the bullet, spade and wire which were the enemy on *every* front, and their geographical locations were purely incidental." [1] Meanwhile, the force at Gallipoli expanded, but never quickly enough to grasp its fleeting opportunities. It was clear that only some dramatic new stroke could save the campaign. This was attempted in August, in a new landing at Suvla Bay; the conjunction of elderly generals and raw, untrained soldiers, under a "permissive" C.-in-C. like Hamilton, proved fatal; the Turks found the "men of the hour" in their German Chief, Liman von Sanders and the brilliant and fiery Mustafa Kemal Bey. Once more the British gained footholds – and nothing more; "Gallipoli" became merely one more front in a war of attrition, but a front on which climate and disease added their own horrible contributions.

Hamilton was recalled in October, and replaced by General Sir Chalres Monro, who recommended evacuation. This was carried out in stages, Anzac and Suvla in December, Helles in January 1916, in all cases with complete success. Fuller remarks:
Thus were
concluded the sole successful operations of the campaign. In all, 410,000 British and 70,000 French soldiers had been landed, of whom 252,000 were killed, wounded, missing, prisoners, died of disease or evacuated sick. The Turkish casualties amounted to 218,000 men, of whom 66,000 were killed. The booty left behind was immense: "It took nearly two years to clean up the ground."

Thus ended one of the greatest disasters in British history, and one comparable with the siege of Syracuse in 415 B.C., because its root cause was the inability of a democracy to conduct a war. As Mr. Churchill has pointed out: "No man had the power to give clear, brutal orders which would command unquestioning respect. Power was widely disseminated among the many important personages who in this period formed the governing instrument." Therefore, as Mr. Lloyd George said: "There was no co-ordination of effort. There was no connected plan of action. There was no sense of the importance of time." But worst of all, there was no judgment; no clear strategical analysis of the initial problem; no proper calculation of its tactical requirements; and no true attempt to balance the means in hand with the end in view.

---

[1] *The Conduct Of War*, p. 161.

Progress of the War, 1915-1918

England was the strategical centre of gravity of the allied coalition; to win the war it was imperative for the Central Powers to drive her out of it. This demanded the defeat of France and Russia and the winning over of neutral support, so that, after the defeat of their allies, the British Government would be unable to raise another coalition. The British problem was to sustain the coalition. In the past this had been done by blockading the enemy, by subsidizing allies, and by employing the small British army in diversionary and distracting operations. Now, although Britain became the banker and arsenal of the coalition, she did not resort to full blockade from the outset and the army was not used as a diversionary force, but was transported to the western theatre of the war. Nevertheless, once stalemate was reached the British Government did not adhere to this new continental policy, but returned to the traditional policy of distraction.

Even before the Dardanelles diversionary venture had been decided on, two subsidiary campaigns were initiated, one in Egypt to protect the Suez Canal, and the other in the Persian Gulf to secure the Anglo-Persian oil installations at Abadan, and later, as we have seen, yet another expedition was sent to Salonika. These diversionary operations rapidly grew into major campaigns, and during 1917, when Russia was in death throes and the allied man-power problem reached its crisis, the first had grown into the Palestine campaign, in which the British ration strength was 340,000 men; the second into the Mesopotamia campaign, in which it was approximately 400,000; and the third into the Macedonian campaign in which, of 600,000 allied troops, 202,000 were British. These three campaigns cost the British Empire 174,500 men in killed, wounded, and dead of disease, to which must be added the 214,000 casualties sustained in Gallipoli.

This wastage of man-power was one of the main causes which prolonged the war; an even more important cause was the delay in establishing a full blockade of the Central Powers. This was because the British Government had in 1909 shackled themselves by the Declaration of London, which was based on the Declaration of Paris of 1856. This divided contrabands into two classes; one absolute, covering military stores, and the other conditional, which included foodstuffs and fodder destined for the enemy's armed forces. Because it was impossible to prove that the latter were not destined for Germany by way of neutral countries, the British blockade was hamstrung from the start, and on August 20, 1914, the first British Order in Council revising the Declaration of London was issued, and followed by the second on October 29. In reply to these revisions, which seriously curtailed supplies entering Germany and Austria, on February 4, 1915, the German Government declared that all waters surrounding Great Britain and Ireland would from the 18th be blockaded by submarine. It was a foolish decision politically, because the British Orders in Council had antagonized neutrals – particularly the United States – and the submarine blockade would inevitably modify neutral hostility toward Britain by embroiling Germany with every neutral Power trading with Britain. Events soon proved this to be so. On May 1 a United States merchantman was sunk and a week later the neutral world was shocked when the *Lusitania* was torpedoed.

In order to exploit the revulsion caused by the loss of this great vessel, on May 15 the British Government issued another Order in Council by which goods of any kind entering or leaving Germany were declared contraband. Thus full blockade was established. At the same time the Kaiser became so alarmed over American feelings that he ordered all attacks on passenger and neutral ships to cease. Had the United States then placed an embargo on munitions of war probably it would have brought the Allies to book, for their own factories were quite unable to supply the enormous demands of their armies.

When the German right wing was halted at Nieuport, the western front assumed the shape of a great salient that bulged westward between the Channel and the Vosges, with its apex near Compiègne. For 1915, Joffre's plan was to cut this salient off by a dual offensive; the British were to attack eastward from Artois, and the French northward from Champagne, the axes of their attacks to meet west of St. Quentin. Throughout the war this plan remained the norm of French strategy, and in accordance with it the following battles were fought in 1915: The First Battle of Champagne (December 20–March 17); the Battle of Soissons

(January 8–14); the Battle of Neuve-Chapelle (March 10–13); the Battle of Festubert (May 15–25); the Second Battle of Artois (May 9–June 18); the Battle of Loos (September 25–October 15), and the Second Battle of Champagne (September 25–November 6). None did more than dent the great salient.

Faced with winter on the Russian front, and aware that the abortive allied attempts to break through the western front had created in France a spirit of defeatism, toward the end of 1915 Falkenhayn decided once again to shift the main German effort to the west. His plan was to reopen the submarine campaign and simultaneously to strike at Verdun, which he selected as his objective because the French considered it impregnable. Could he wrest it from them, its loss might so lower their declining morale that it would lead to their collapse and the consequent isolation of England.

On February 21, 1916, the battle of Verdun was opened. Although, like all previous attacks against entrenched fronts, it failed to break through, it dragged on until July 11, by when the Germans had suffered 281,000 casualties and the French 315,000. A week after the battle began, the submarine campaign was launched, and with such startling success that at first it appeared that the Germans had at length discovered the weapon which would enable them to force their implacable enemy to terms. But on March 24, when the Folkestone–Dieppe packet, *Sussex*, was torpedoed without warning, the United States Government threatened to sever diplomatic relations with Germany unless she modified her submarine warfare. This so frightened the Kaiser that he agreed to restrict his submarines to purely military targets. Next, on July 7, the British Government rescinded the Declaration of London.

Though the battle of Verdun upset the allied spring offensive, a combined operation between Russia, France, and Britain was agreed, and on June 5 it was opened on the Russian front by General Brusilov. It came as welcome news to the English after their abortive naval battle off Jutland on May 31 and the loss of Lord Kitchener at sea five days later. Although by June 20 200,000 Austrians had surrendered to the Russians, between June 16 and 23 Brusilov was heavily counter-attacked by the Germans and pressed back. Nevertheless, this offensive continued until August 17, by when the Russians had lost over a million men and were bled white.

When the Brusilov offensive was at its height, on July 1, after enormous preparations and a seven-day preliminary bombardment, the French and British – the latter now under Sir Douglas Haig – opened their delayed offensive on the Somme, and again a battle of mutual attrition followed. It lasted until November 18 and each side lost more than 600,000 men in killed, wounded, and prisoners. Meanwhile, on August 27, the Rumanians declared war on the Central Powers, and two days later Falkenhayn was superseded by Hindenburg as Chief of the General Staff. On December 6 Bucharest capitulated to the Germans.

With the battle of the Somme the stalemate on all fronts became so complete that neither group of combatants appeared to have a chance of forcing a decision in the field, and the question of peace negotiations began to be considered in London, Berlin, and Vienna. On November 14, Lord Lansdowne, Minister without Portfolio in the Asquith coalition Government, laid a memorandum before the Cabinet in which he suggested that the possibilities of peace should be examined. The Asquith administration was tottering, and on December 7 it fell and Lloyd George, who was pledged to a more vigorous prosecution of the war, succeeded Asquith. Five days later Germany and her allies put forward four identical notes in which they stated their willingness to consider peace proposals. But whether Germany was sincere appears doubtful from what followed immediately. On December 18, President Woodrow Wilson indented a note to all belligerents asking them to state "the precise objects which would, if attained, satisfy them and their people that the war had been fought out," and, on January 22, 1917, in an address before the Senate, he declared for "peace without victory". Instead of courting the President, or offering to cede Alsace-Lorraine to France which, according to M. Viviani, French Minister of Justice, would have bought France out of the war, on January 31 the Kaiser commanded that the submarine campaign should from February 1 be placed on an unrestricted footing. To add to this folly, at the same time it became known in the United States that Germany had been urging Mexico to conclude an offensive alliance with her and Japan against the Americans should they enter the war. These things so exasperated the United States that, on February 3, diplomatic relations between Washington and Berlin were severed, and though peace conversations were continued, they were now bereft of all reality.

The reason why this stupidity was committed was that in Berlin it was considered that Russian morale had reached breaking point, and that if the havoc the submarine campaign had already caused were accentuated it would bring England to terms before the Americans could make their military influence felt. Clearly, what Germany should have done was to wait until Russia had collapsed, and then, when all was ready for an assault on the western front, to have opened the submarine campaign in full strength.

German prognostications about Russia were correct. In Petrograd 1916 had ended with a foreboding event. On December 29 the monk Rasputin, confidant of the Tsarina and the Svengali of the court, was assassinated, and from then on the situation in Russia slumped. On March 8, 1917, riots broke out in Petrograd and the bakers' shops were sacked. On the 11th, the troops were called out; they did not fire on the rioters but shot their officers and joined the mob. There were 190,000 soldiers in the capital and the mutiny, which started in the Imperial Guard, spread like wildfire. On the 12th revolution was in full swing, the Winter Palace was invaded, public buildings were burnt, and the prisons, including the fortress of St. Peter and St. Paul – the Russian Bastille – were opened and their inmates released. On March 15 Nicholas II abdicated and three days later a provisional Government, under Prince Lvov, was formed. Brusilov was appointed commander-in-chief and Kerensky Minister of Justice. In May, the latter became Minister of War, and in July Prime Minister. On March 22 the provisional Government was formally recognized by the allied Powers.

The March revolution was followed immediately by an extension of the conflict. On Good Friday, April 6, the United States declared war on the German Empire, and at about the same time the German Government sent Lenin (Vladimir Ilyich Ulyanov, 1870–1924) in a sealed train to Petrograd. These were the two most portentous events of the war, and they were destined to change the political axis of the world.

April 6, 1917, was the most fateful day in European history since Varus lost his legions, and in a mysterious way the American President sensed it to be so. On the night of April 1 – the day before he delivered his war message to Congress – in a conversation with Frank Cobb of the New York *World*, he is reported by the latter to have said:

". . . war would overturn the world we had known; that so long as we remained out there was a preponderance of neutrality, but that if we joined with the Allies the world would be off the peace basis and onto a war basis.

" 'It would mean that we should lose our heads along with the rest and stop weighing right and wrong. It would mean that a majority of the people in this hemisphere would go war-mad, quit thinking and devote their energies to destruction.' The President said a declaration of war would mean that Germany would be beaten, and so badly beaten that there would be a dictated peace, a victorious peace.

" 'It means,' he said, 'an attempt to reconstruct a peacetime civilization with war standards, and at the end of the war there will be no bystanders with sufficient peace standards left to work with. There will be only war standards' . . .

" 'Once lead this people into war,' he said, 'and they'll forget there ever was such a thing as tolerance. To fight you must be brutal and ruthless, and the spirit of ruthless brutality will enter into every fibre of our national life, infecting Congress, the courts, the policeman on his beat, the man in the street.' Conformity would be the only virtue, said the President, and every man who refused to conform would have to pay the penalty."

Had not public opinion, raised by propaganda to white heat, forced Wilson to take this fateful step, now that Russia was four-fifths out of the war and Germany thereby free to concentrate her forces against France, it is nearly certain that, without American support, France and Great Britain would have been forced on the defensive, that Germany would have failed to break their front decisively, and that because in May the British Admiralty by introducing convoying at sea,[1] began to master the submarine, a negotiated peace would have been agreed with the United States as referee before Lenin could have got into the saddle.

The wisdom of America's entry into the war was questioned by Mr. Ramsay Macdonald, leader of the British Labour Party. On August 17 he addressed a statement to Colonel House and the President, in which he wrote: "The majority of our people welcomed America's entry into the war, but a minority, much larger than newspapers or vociferous opinion indicates, regard it not

---

[1] After the convoy system was introduced, in which the United States Navy lent assistance, against the loss of 169 ships in April, between then and the end of the year, on the average losses were reduced by 75·5 ships a month, and not a single troopship was sunk.

with any hostile feelings but with regret. They come to that view because (a) they do not think that American military help was required in order to compel any of the Powers to make a reasonable peace; and (b) they think that America, out of the war, would have done more for peace and good feeling than in the war, and would also have had a better influence on the peace settlement." Further he wrote: ". . . whilst you can have peace without victory, history shows that as a rule nations have had victory without peace. . . . It would also compel them to welcome political activities parallel with military activities."

Years later – in August, 1936 – Mr. Churchill in a statement to William Griffen, editor of the New York *Enquirer*, is reported by the latter to have said that "America should have minded her own business and stayed out of the World War. If you hadn't entered the war the Allies would have made peace with Germany in the Spring of 1917. Had we made peace then there would have been no collapse in Russia followed by Communism, no breakdown in Italy followed by Fascism, and Germany would not have signed the Versailles Treaty, which has enthroned Nazism in Germany. If America had stayed out of the war, all these 'isms' wouldn't to-day be sweeping the continent of Europe and breaking down parliamentary government, and if England had made peace early in 1917, it would have saved over one million British, French, American, and other lives."

With Russia virtually out of the war and America as yet only nominally in it, the wisest course for the French and British to have adopted would have been to hold their front defensively, economize their man-power, and wait until America could develop her strength. Instead, they decided on a joint spring offensive eastward from Arras and northward from Rheims. When from the preparations the Germans gauged what was in hand, and in order better to hold their western front until reinforcements could arrive from Russia, they withdrew from the nose of the great western salient to what they called the *Siegfried Stellung*, and the allies called the Hindenberg Line. It was a vast system of entrenchments that stretched from near Arras to a few miles east of Soissons. This withdrawal threw the allied joint offensive out of gear and led to two separate battles – the battle of Arras (April 9–May 15) and the second battle of the Aisne (April 16–20). The former cost the British 158,000 casualties, and the latter, under the direction of General Nivelles, who had succeeded Joffre in December, 1916, ended in fiasco and cost the French 187,000 men. Worse, extensive mutinies followed, which meant that for the time being all further thought of a French offensive had to be abandoned. On May 15, Nivelles was replaced by General Pétain. Next, in the east, what was known as the Kerensky offensive was launched on June 29, and by July 18 was so crushed that no further Russian offensive was possible.

Before the battle of the Somme, Sir Douglas Haig had urged that the decisive battle should be sought in Flanders, and now, in order to draw the Germans away from the demoralized French, as well as to seize the German submarine bases at Ostend and Zeebrugge, he decided first to gain the Messines ridge, and next to break through the Ypres front and advance on Bruges and Ghent.

On May 21, under cover of 2,266 guns and nineteen mines, packed with a million pounds of explosives, the battle of Messines was launched, and by June 14 the ridge was successfully occupied. Next, on July 31, after a 13-day bombardment, a series of battles known as the "Third Battle of Ypres" was opened. The battle field was reclaimed swampland, and under the bombardment it reverted to a vast bog in which the attacking troops fought and wallowed until November 20, when the battle ended with a loss of 244,897 men.[1] To persist after the close of August in this tactically impossible battle was an inexcusable piece of pigheadedness on the part of Haig, because on the 20th of that month the French had recovered sufficiently to mount an attack at Verdun, which was continued until December 15 with the usual heavy losses.

Meanwhile in Italy, between October 24 and November 4, the Italians had suffered a catastrophic defeat in the battle of Caporetto, in which they lost 305,000 men, of whom 275,000 were captured. In order to prevent the Italians from being driven out of the war, British and French troops were rushed to Italy, and, on November 20, Haig attacked the Germans at Cambrai, a battle in which there was no preliminary bombardment and in which tanks for the first time were employed in mass. It opened with a startling success, and, on December 5, through lack of reserves, ended in failure and a loss of 45,000 men. By the close

[1] These are Sir James Edmonds' figures (*A Short History of World War I*, 1951, p. 252). According to the British *Official Strategical Abstract* (1920) between July 31 and December 31, the losses in the Third Battle of Ypres were 380,335, and in the Battle of Messines, 108,882.

of 1917, the British were bled white, the French were morally exhausted, the Italians nearly out of the war, and the Americans not yet sufficiently involved to make good a fraction of the enormous losses sustained.

Meanwhile on November 7 (old style October 25 – hence "the October Revolution") Lenin and Trotsky (Lev Davidovich Bronstein) seized power in Petrograd and overthrew the Kerensky Government. A month later, when hostilities between Russia and Germany were suspended, the Tsarist empire began to disintegrate. On January 22, 1918, the Ukraine declared its independence, which, on February 9, was recognized by Germany under the terms of the first Treaty of Brest-Litovsk. Next, between February 16 and May 30, Lithuania, Latvia, Estonia, Bielorussia, Georgia, Azerbaijan, Armenia, North Caucasia and Cossakia (Don and Kuban Cossacks) proclaimed their independence. Then, in order to bring the Bolshevik Government to heel and call a halt to Trotsky's interminable propaganda arguments, on February 18 the Germans recommenced hostilities, and immediately the Bolsheviks declared their readiness for peace. This led to the signing of the second Treaty of Brest-Litovsk on March 3, by the terms of which the Bolshevik Government recognized the independence of Finland and the Ukraine; surrendered Courland, Lithuania, Poland, Batum and Kars (the last two to the Turks); demobilized its army and fleet; and refrained from all propaganda in Germany. On May 7 followed the Treaty of Bucharest with Rumania.

While Russia was in anarchy, President Wilson considered peace, and on January 8 he outlined before Congress his settlement of the war in 14 points, and added four others later. Highly idealistic in character, they caught the imagination of a war-weary world and offered Germany an opportunity to end the war by a negotiated peace. This the Kaiser and his advisers refused to consider, in part at least because while Wilson waved his olive branch suggestions were voiced in America that the harshest possible terms should be imposed on the Germans and peace dictated in Berlin. Therefore, now that the war had been reduced to one front, the German Supreme Command decided to knock out the French and British before the Americans could get into their stride. Other than accepting the Fourteen Points, this was the only practical course open; for as Ludendorff has pointed out, the collapse of Russia had caused such an intensive relief within

Germany that everyone was eager for the offensive and dreaded a defensive campaign in face of the ever-mounting *matériel* of the enemy. Further, the stranglehold of the blockade was choking Germany to death, and only an offensive could break it rapidly.

The error committed by the Supreme Command was not that it decided on the offensive, but that it selected as its target the stubborn British instead of the war-weary French.

Once the western front had been reinforced by 70 divisions from Russia, the German plan was to break through the British Third and Fifth Armies north and south of Péronne, and directly penetration had been effected, to wheel the right attacking wing northward and drive the British away from the French.

On March 21 the *Kaiserschlacht* (Emperor Battle) was opened under cover of fog and gas shells, and it proved so successful that on the 26th, in order to meet the situation, General Foch was appointed co-ordinator of the allied armies. Nevertheless, by April 5 the momentum of the attack had exhausted itself and the Germans were left in an extensive salient with its apex nine miles east of Amiens. Frustrated in the Somme area, on April 9 a powerful attack was launched on the British First Army astride the Lys. On April 30 it petered out and left the Germans in yet another salient.

Only after these two abortive battles did the German Supreme Command decide to turn against the French on the Aisne. At one o'clock in the morning of May 27 the third great offensive opened; the ridge of the Chemin des Dames was stormed, and by the night of the 28th a large salient was pushed southward between Rheims and Soissons. On June 3 the Marne at Château Thierry was reached and a pause followed until the 9th, when the attack was renewed, but only to die out again on the 14th. On July 6 came the last German attack, this time east and west of Rheims, but the allies held fast and little progress was made.

In order to prevent a continuance of the offensive toward Paris, Foch decided to counter-attack the western flank of the salient, and on July 18 he struck eastward from Villers Cotterets, and by August 2 had forced the Germans back to the line Rheims–Soissons. By then, each side since March 21 had suffered about a million casualties. For the Germans these losses were absolute, because they could not be made good; but by now more than a million Americans had been landed in France, and they arrived at the rate of a quarter of a million each month. Thus the Americans, as Ludendorff said, "became the deciding factor in the war". Yet it was not the Americans who were to win the battle which decided it.

CHAPTER 7

The Battle of Amiens, 1918

The battle of Amiens, known to the French as the battle of Montdidier, was the most decisive battle of the First World War. It led not only to the collapse of the German armies on the western front, but also to the solution of the stalemate, and in solving this it established a tactical revolution. Nevertheless, had the German armies in 1914 been organized round the quick-firing field-gun and the machine-gun – the dominant weapons of the early twentieth century – instead of round the magazine rifle – the dominant weapon of the late nineteenth century – the probability is that there would have been no stalemate and that France would have been overrun almost as rapidly as she was in 1940 by two very different dominant weapons – the tank and the aeroplane. But they were not so organized, nor were their opponents, and, as we have seen, the result was that the rifle bullet was able to gain sufficient time for the spade to throw up bullet-proof entrenchments and neutralize the power of the gun. Only then did all armies set about to multiply their artillery and machine-guns, either in order to hold or to break an entrenched front, and because trenches and entanglements impeded the offensive and aided the defensive, as Bloch had foreseen, the latter became the stronger form of war.

To overcome this difference, the first solution was sought in the obliteration of trenches and entanglements by intense preliminary artillery bombardments,[1] and though, generally speaking, they guaranteed an initial success, they converted the battlefield into a cratered area and created as formidable an obstacle to forward movements of wheeled vehicles, without which the attackers could not be supplied, as the trenches and entanglements they demolished.[2] Besides, even when these artillery battles were successful they invariably left the attacker in a salient – that is, in a tactically

[1] The growth of the British preliminary bombardments was rapid: in the battle of Hooge (1915) 18,000 shells; in that of the Somme (1916) 2,000,000; at Arras (1917) 2,600,000; at Messines (1917) 3,500,000; and at Ypres III (1917) 4,300,000.
[2] During the third battle of Ypres the forward troops and guns had, as in mountain warfare, to be supplied by pack horses.

disadvantageous position. Thus, although the gun came into its own, because its destructiveness rendered it static it was unable to play a decisive part in a war of movement. Further, the cratered area favoured the machine-gun on the defensive. The outcome was that, instead of stalemate being liquidated by artillery fire, it became more and more consolidated.

Since the gun failed to solve the problem, on April 22, 1915, the Germans in the Ypres area resorted to discharges of chlorine gas.[1] But in spite of its initial success, because gas was easily neutralized by the box respirator, the problem remained unsolved.

Late in the war, in order to force a decision through demoralization, both sides resorted to aircraft attacks on civil populations. But they were no more than sideshows, for though they pointed to a deplorable future, throughout the war air power was not sufficiently developed to warrant decisive results.[2]

All these solutions were spurious, because the problem was not clearly understood. It was not to remove trenches and entanglements, but to neutralize the bullet; the question was how to disarm the mass of the enemy's riflemen and machine-gunners, not gradually but instantaneously. Obviously the answer was bullet-proof armour and not an increase in projectiles – whether bullets, shells, bombs, or even gas. Quite early in the war this was seen by Colonel E. D. Swinton[3] and others in England, and by General Estienne in France. Further, they saw that though the soldier could not carry bullet-proof armour, he could be carried, as the sailor was, in a bullet-proof armoured vehicle, and as this vehicle would have to travel across country it would have to move on caterpillar tracks instead of on wheels. Thus the tank, a self-propelled bullet-proof landship, was conceived. On September 15, 1916, it first went into action on the shell-blasted battlefield of the Somme.

Actually this solution was an exceedingly old one,[4] and in

[1] Toward the end of 1915 the Germans introduced phosgene gas shells, and in the summer of 1917 sneezing gas (diphenylchloroarsine, or Blue Cross), and mustard gas (dichloroethyl, or Yellow Cross). The last was a highly volatile vesicant liquid and a formidable weapon. The American gas casualties in the war were 74,779 (mostly due to mustard gas) or 27·3 per cent of the total; of these only 1·87 per cent were fatal.

[2] One hundred and eleven air attacks were made on England, in which 8,500 bombs weighing about 300 tons were dropped; 1,413 people were killed, 3,407 injured, and £3,000,000 worth of property was destroyed. In Germany 720 people were killed, 1,754 injured, and damage to property amounted to £1,175,000.

[3] See his book *Eyewitness* (1932).

[4] See *Tanks in the Great War*, J. F. C. Fuller (1920), chap. 1.

recent times had been examined with remarkable understanding by Colonel C. B. Brackenbury in an article entitled "Ironclad Field Artillery," which appeared in *The Nineteenth Century Review* of July, 1878. It is worth quoting at some length, for in it is clearly foreshadowed the "tank idea".

In condensed form, Brackenbury's argument ran: The leading lesson of the Plevna operations was "that troops of any kind under cover are practically invincible so long as the enemy is in front of them"; that the effect of artillery fire "increases as the range diminishes"; "that the destructive power of artillery at close quarters is practically annihilating"; but that, as the power of infantry "has immensely increased", it is not possible to advance the guns to annihilating range. Therefore the problem was how to protect the guns from bullets, and Brackenbury's suggestion was to carry forward "thin iron shields (in sections) capable of protecting the gunners against infantry fire" in "one or possibly two carriages to each battery". "Then the artillery might calmly await any attack whatever, certain to destroy an enemy long before he could reach the guns. All anxiety as to capture would be extinguished, and we might proceed to build up a system of tactics based upon the supposition that artillery will not need to run away from anything in front of it. . . . If two lines of artillery were contending against each other, surely the side which was safe from shrapnel bullets and the infantry fire of the other side ought to overwhelm its antagonist. . . . If we can prevent nine-tenths of the loss in killed and wounded, and nearly all the risk of capture, we can afford to disregard accidents. . . . As surely as ships of war can carry iron plates sufficient for defence against heavy guns, so surely can field artillery carry sufficient protection against the fire of infantry and shrapnel bullets. . . . The fire of infantry has become so formidable of late years that defensive measures must inevitably be adopted sooner or later by field artillery. . . . If we add the use of defensive armour which can be carried by artillery and cannot be carried by cavalry and infantry, a power will be created which must seriously modify the tactics of the battlefield. The development is as sure to come as the day to follow the night. We may hope that England will set the example instead of following other nations."[1]

[1] This was not to be. His idea was adopted by Colonel Schumann and tested in the 1899 and 1890 German autumn manœuvres. Also it was adopted by the Rumanian army (*Journal of the Royal United Service Institution*, vol. XXIV, pp. 867–889 and 1029–1035).

What is remarkable in Brackenbury's proposal is that he realized that "Moral effect is the object aimed at in a battle, for the killed and wounded have no influence on the final retirement" – this is the soul of the "tank idea". He saw as Frederick had seen, "that to advance is to conquer" because of the terrifying moral effect of a *continuous* advance. This was the underlying idea of the "bayonet school" of thought, an idea preeminently sound, but under the conditions that prevailed in 1914 – impossible. The "shell school" of 1914–1917 never grasped this idea; it could not, or did not, see that the problem was not to reduce the enemy's position to rubble, but *to advance the guns* under hostile rifle and machine-gun fire, and that could such an advance be sustained it would prove not *overwhelmingly destructive*, but *overwhelmingly demoralizing*. This is exactly what the tank – self-propelled armoured artillery – accomplished. It solved the two outstanding difficulties which had faced armies since the introduction of firearms – namely, how to harmonize movement and fire power and movement and protection. It increased mobility by substituting mechanical power for muscular; it increased security by neutralizing the bullet with armour plate; and it increased offensive power by relieving the soldier from the necessity of carrying his weapons and the horse from hauling them. Because the tank protected the soldier dynamically, it enabled him to fight statically; it superimposed naval tactics on land warfare.

The first occasion upon which tanks were used correctly was in the Cambrai attack on November 20, 1917. In this battle no preliminary artillery bombardment was employed. Instead, grouped in threes, tanks operated like a chain of mobile armoured batteries in advance of the infantry. With certain modifications these tactics were maintained until the end of the war and they vastly reduced casualties to ground gained. But although this battle showed that a true solution of the stalemate had been discovered, lack of reserves led to tactical failure, and it was not until the battle of Amiens that on a grand scale the same solution led to complete success.

Concurrent with the introduction of what was to become known as "armoured warfare", was the development of air warfare – the most mobile form of war – and this also was largely fostered by the stalemate. First, we see the aeroplane almost exclusively devoted to the direction of artillery fire; next, to air photography in order to produce special artillery trench-maps. These tasks stimulated fighting in the air, but it was not until the introduction of the German Fokker monoplane in the summer of 1915, which fired a fixed machine-gun between its propeller blades, that systematic air fighting began. Bombing of artillery positions and other targets was tentatively initiated during the battle of Loos; contact patrols were first introduced in the battle of the Somme; low flying attacks on trenches and artillery positions were developed in the battles of Messines and Cambrai; and, on April 1, 1918, the Royal Air Force was created as a separate arm to supersede the Royal Flying Corps. So enormous was the progress made that, whereas in 1914 the R.F.C. consisted of 165 officers and 1,264 other ranks, and took with it to France 63 aeroplanes, in the summer of 1918 the R.A.F. comprised 291,175 officers and men and 22,000 aircraft, of which 3,300 were in first line. It was the greatest air force in the world.

These preliminary tactical developments should be borne in mind when considering the great decisive battle fought east of Amiens between August 8 and 11.

Toward the end of June, when the British position on the Amiens front was much improved, General Sir Henry Rawlinson, in command of the Fifth Army, which since its defeat had been renumbered the Fourth, decided that the 4th Australian Division should occupy the village of Hamel and a neighbouring wood east of Corbie. On July 4, in cooperation with the 5th Tank Brigade, these objectives were taken so completely to plan and at so low a cost[1] that on the following day Rawlinson suggested to Haig a similar operation, but on a more extended scale. With this operation in mind, on July 12 Haig suggested to Foch – who two days before had been created a marshal of France – an offensive which would advance the allied front east and south-east of Amiens and disengage the town as well as the vital Amiens–Paris railway, both of which were under German gun-fire. Foch agreed, and on the following day Rawlinson was instructed to draft his plan. He submitted it on July 17, and on the 23rd it was approved by Foch and Haig.

The plan was that of Hamel enlarged, and its aim was a limited advance to the old Amiens outer defence line, lost in the previous

---

[1] It was the battle of Hamel more than the battle of Cambrai which made the reputation of the British Tank Corps (see *Tanks in the Great War*, Chap. XXVII, and *Memoirs of an Unconventional Soldier*, J. F. C. Fuller (1936), pp. 287–290.

April, and which on the Fourth Army front ran from le Quesnel on the Amiens–Roye road, through the village of Caix to a little east of Méricourt on the Somme.

While he waited for Haig's approval, Rawlinson had on July 21 assembled a conference at his headquarters in Flexicourt. It was attended by his three corps commanders, Lieutenant-General Sir Arthur Currie, Canadian Corps; Lieutenant-General Sir John Monash, Australian Corps, and Lieutenant-General Sir Richard Butler, IIIrd Corps, as well as by Lieutenant-General Sir Charles Kavanagh, commanding the cavalry, and representatives of the R.A.F. and Tank Corps. The original idea was somewhat enlarged at this conference and the number of tank battalions required raised from eight to twelve. Next, on July 26, Foch issued his formal orders for the operation, which began:

"1. The object of the operations is to disengage Amiens and the Paris–Amiens railway, also to defeat and drive back the enemy established between the Somme and the Avre.

"2. To do so, the offensive, covered in the north by the Somme, will be pushed as far as possible in the direction of Roye."[1]

Though the aim remained the same, the objective was pushed well beyond the Amiens outer defences, for Roye lies eight miles south-east of le Quesnel. At the same time zero day was fixed for August 8, and on July 28 the project was extended by Foch, who placed the French First Army, commanded by General Debeney, under Haig with instructions to employ it offensively on Rawlinson's right flank. Finally, on August 5, at a conference presided over by Haig, the aim of the operations was radically changed. Not only was the French Third Army, which stood on the right of the First, to be included in the attack, but Rawlinson was instructed to arrange for an advance eastward of the Amiens outer defence line, and, in order to facilitate the advance between Montdidier and Noyon of the French Third Army, he was further ordered to capture the line Roye-Chaulnes and thrust the enemy back on Ham – 15 miles south-east of Chaulnes. To assist him in this the Cavalry Corps was placed at his disposal.

To double the depth of penetration three days before the attack was due meant that corps commanders would not have time enough to change the intricate administrative detail which all offensive plans in this war demanded. It followed that the plans

[1] *Military Operations France and Belgium, 1918* (British Official History, edit. Sir James E. Edmonds, 1947), vol. IV, p. 3.

as they stood would have to be fitted to a situation for which they had never been contemplated. Further, it would seem that neither Foch nor Haig took into account the change in the character of the battlefield this extension carried with it.

North of the Somme the ground was cut up by gullies and spurs, which were serious obstacles for tanks, but the distance to be attacked over was short, because the Amiens outer defence lines were under 5,000 yards east of the starting line. South of the Somme and up to the Amiens outer defences lay perfect tank country, and the German works were indifferent. But beyond it lay the French part of the Somme battlefield of 1916; a jumble of decayed trenches, entanglements and shell holes. Not only was it difficult for tanks and infantry to fight over, but it constituted an ideal defensive area for enemy machine-gunners. Therefore, now that the depth of the attack had been extended to the line Roye–Chaulnes–Somme, the attackers were faced with two operations: as planned, how to advance up to the Amiens defence lines, and, as not planned, how to carry on the advance from there across the old Somme battlefield to the line Roye–Chaulnes. As the latter could not be rushed, strong infantry and tank reserves would be required to win it, and since they had not been budgeted for, as we shall see, like the battle of Cambrai, the battle of Amiens was virtually a one-day operation.

On August 8 General Rawlinson had under his command the following: on the left the IIIrd Corps, with the 12th, 18th and 58th Divisions in line, the 47th on the extreme left to secure the corps' left flank, and the American 33rd Division in reserve; in the centre the Australian Corps, with the 2nd, 3rd and 4th Divisions in line, and the 1st and 5th in reserve; and on the right the Canadian Corps, with the 2nd and 3rd Divisions in line, and the 1st and 4th in reserve. Also he had the Cavalry Corps, which consisted of the 1st, 2nd and 3rd Cavalry Divisions; the 5th Brigade R.A.F. – six corps squadrons, eight scout squadrons and three bomber squadrons – and the 3rd, 4th and 5th Brigades and the 10th Battalion of the Tank Corps. As a general reserve, the 17th, 32nd and 63rd Divisions were placed at his disposal.

The frontage of attack extended from Moreuil in the south to the river Ancre in the north. From Moreuil to the Amiens–Roye road it was held by the French XXXIst Corps; from the Amiens–Roye road to the Villers Bretonneux–Chaulnes railway (both inclusive) by the Canadian Corps; from this railway to the river

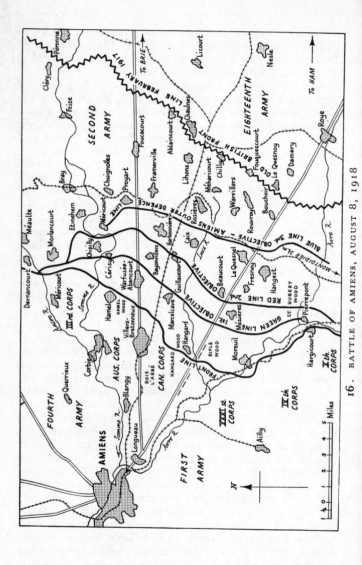

16. BATTLE OF AMIENS, AUGUST 8, 1918

Somme by the Australian Corps; and thence to the Ancre by the IIIrd Corps.

For the first day's battle the general idea was that the Canadian and Australian Corps were to carry out the main attack, while the French XXXIst Corps and the British IIIrd Corps formed defensive flanks on their right and left. The battlefield was divided into three objectives: Green Line, first objective, Red Line, second objective for all corps, and Blue and Blue Dotted Lines, third objective for the Australian and Canadian Corps respectively. A halt of two hours was to be made on the first objective, in order to provide time for the second wave of the attack to come up and leapfrog over the first.

Tank units were allotted as follows: the 4th Tank Brigade (1st, 4th, 5th and 14th Battalions) to the Canadian Corps; the 5th Tank Brigade (2nd, 8th, 13th and 15th Battalions) to the Australian Corps; the 10th Tank Battalion to the IIIrd Corps; and the 3rd Tank Brigade (3rd and 6th Battalions) to the Cavalry Corps.

The characteristics of the tanks these battalions were armed with are given in the table. The 3rd and 6th Battalions each had 48 Medium A (Whippet) tanks, and except for the 1st and 15th, which each had 36 Mark V Star tanks, the rest had 36 Mark V's apiece, and six in reserve to make good breakdowns. In all, 324 heavy tanks and 96 Whippets took the field, and besides them 42 were in reserve; also there were 96 supply tanks (converted Mark IV's) and 22 gun-carriers, also converted for supply; in all a grand total of 580 machines. In addition there was the 17th Tank (Armoured Car) Battalion, equipped with 12 armoured cars. It was placed under the 5th Tank Brigade, to operate with the Australians.

These distributions and allotments were more than sufficient to guarantee an advance to the Amiens outer defence lines; but for an advance beyond them to the Roye–Chaulnes line on August 9 they were insufficient, because all divisions and tanks were to be engaged on the 8th, and, therefore, all would require to be reorganized before a co-ordinated advance could be made on the 9th. The attacking forces on the 8th were over-strong and over-condensed. Divisional frontages averaged from 2,250 yards at the start to 3,000 at the finish. Had time permitted, these frontages could have been extended, and had this been done, probably two divisions and two tank battalions could have been

CHARACTERISTICS OF ARMOURED VEHICLES USED ON AUGUST 8, 1918

Characteristics	Mark IV		Mark V		Mark V Star		Medium Mark A	Gun-carrier
	Male	Female	Male	Female	Male	Female		
Length	26 ft. 5 in.	26 ft. 5 in.	26 ft. 5 in.	26 ft. 5 in.	32 ft. 5 in.	32 ft. 5 in.	20 ft. 0 in.	30 ft. 0 in.
Weight	28 tons	27 tons	29 tons	28 tons	33 tons	32 tons	14 tons	34 tons
Crew	1 Ofr. 7 O.R.	1 Ofr. 7 O.R.	1 Ofr. 7 O.R.	1 Ofr. 7 O.R.	1 Ofr. 7 O.R.	1 Ofr. 7 O.R.	1 Ofr. 2 O.R.	1 Ofr. 3 O.R.
Armament	2 6-pdrs. 4 Lewis guns	6 Lewis guns	2 6-pdrs. 4 Hotchkiss guns	6 Hotchkiss guns	2 6-pdrs. 4 Hotchkiss guns	6 Hotchkiss guns	4 Hotchkiss guns	1 Lewis gun
Engine	105 h.p.	105 h.p.	150 h.p.	150 h.p.	150 h.p.	150 h.p.	Two 45 h.p.	105 h.p.
Max. Speed	3·7 m.p.h.	3·7 m.p.h.	4·6 m.p.h.	4·6 m.p.h.	4·0 m.p.h.	4·0 m.p.h.	8·3 m.p.h.	3·0 m.p.h.
Average Speed	2·0 m.p.h.	2·0 m.p.h.	3·0 m.p.h.	3·0 m.p.h.	2·5 m.p.h.	2·5 m.p.h.	5·0 m.p.h.	1·75 m.p.h.
Radius of Action	15 miles	15 miles	25 miles	25 miles	18 miles	18 miles	40 miles	15 miles
Spanning Power	10 ft. 0 in.	10 ft. 0 in.	10 ft. 0 in.	10 ft. 0 in.	14 ft. 0 in.	14 ft. 0 in.	7 ft. 0 in.	11 ft. 6 in.

The Mark V Star tank could carry 20 men in addition to its crew.
Gun-carriers were originally designed to carry a 6-inch howitzer or a 60-pdr.
The Gun-carrier and Mark IV converted could transport 10 tons of stores.
Radii of Action approximate, depended on the nature of the ground.

added to the three divisions in reserve. Further, had the Cavalry Corps and its tank battalions been held back until August 9, five fresh infantry divisions, three fresh cavalry divisions, and four fresh tank battalions could have continued the battle on that day. This continuance of the forward movement was all important, because in order to maintain the momentum of the attack it was not only necessary to rout the enemy front line divisions, but to keep them routed before his reserve divisions could move up; for to throw back routed troops on unrouted ones is the surest way to disorganize and demoralize the latter.

Two German armies were involved, the Second and Eighteenth, the former commanded by General von der Marwitz and the latter by General Hutier. The front of the former extended from near Méaulte, on the left flank of the IIIrd Corps, to St. Hubert Wood, three and a half miles south of Moreuil, and the front of the latter from St. Hubert Wood to Noyon, which coincided with the right flank of the French Third Army. The Second Army had 10 divisions in line and four in reserve, and the Eighteenth Army 11 and four respectively.

On the Fourth Army front, the battle tactics were those of Cambrai. The tanks were to assemble 1,000 yards behind the infantry starting line, and before zero hour, which was fixed at 4.20 a.m., they were to move forward under an aircraft noise barrage to the starting line, from where at zero hour they were to lead the infantry forward under cover of a creeping barrage[1] fired by one-third of the guns of the army, while the remaining two-thirds bombarded the enemy's battery positions. Because the French First Army had few tanks, at zero hour a standing barrage was to be put down on the enemy trenches and batteries and maintained for 45 minutes, when the advance of the XXXIst Corps was to begin. The aircraft at the disposal of the Fourth Army numbered 800, and of the French First Army 1,104. As before the battle the opposing German armies had only 365 machines, the allies held the mastery in the air. Besides attempting to hold it during the battle, other tasks of the R.A.F. were to co-operate with the attacking troops, to bomb and machine-gun enemy ground targets; to supply ammunition to the forward attackers, and to bomb the rail centres at Chaulnes, Roye, Nesle and Péronne, as well as the crossings over the Somme.

The task given to the Cavalry Corps and the 3rd Tank Brigade

[1] The creeping barrage was introduced in 1916 during the battle of the Somme.

was to push through the leading infantry of the Canadian and Australian Corps at the first opportunity and to secure the Amiens outer defences and hold them until relieved. They were then to advance south-eastward on Roye–Chaulnes, cut the enemy communications and ease the advance of the French.

It was a fantastic task and strongly criticized by the Commander and General Staff of the Tank Corps, who held that tanks and horses could not work together successfully, because tanks were bullet-proof and horses were not. It was suggested that a better way to help the advance of the French would be to hold the two Whippet battalions back until the infantry and Mark V tanks had broken through, and then to move them forward from Villers-Bretonneux towards Rosières, swing right and sweep southward on a wide front through the rear of the German Second and Eighteenth Armies, and eventually emerge south-east of Montdidier. General Rawlinson considered this manœuvre too risky and it was decided to keep to the original task.[1]

Finally, secrecy and surprise were to be the soul of the attack. Troops were to remain unacquainted with the aim and attack orders until 24 to 36 hours before zero hour; all movements were to be made by night; forward reconnaissances and artillery registration were prohibited; normal work was to be carried on; the *pavé* roads were to be strewn with sand or straw; dumps were to be camouflaged; and a strong air barrage maintained to restrict enemy observation into rear areas. In spite of these precautions, early on July 29, the 5th Australian Division, then occupying the sector north of the Somme, carried out an asinine raid and captured 138 prisoners. On August 6 the all but inevitable retaliation followed. The German 27th (Württemberg) Division launched a violent attack on a 4,000-yard front against the inner flanks of the 18th and 58th Divisions of the IIIrd Corps – now in line – penetrated to a depth of 800 yards, and captured 236 prisoners. This attack completely upset IIIrd Corps preparations, and, as will be seen, led to serious consequences on August 8.

Between July 29 and early on August 8, without a hitch 14 infantry divisions, three cavalry divisions, three brigades of tanks and more than 2,000 guns were concentrated east of Amiens on a front of some 10 miles and within striking distance of an un-suspecting enemy. It was a triumph of organization and staff work.

[1] See *Memoirs of an Unconventional Soldier*, p. 299.

The night of August 7–8 was moonless and fine, but at 3 a.m. a ground mist began to rise, and when a little after four o'clock the tanks slowly moved forward from their assembly positions to the infantry starting line, it had grown so dense that visibility fell to nil. Exactly at 4.20 a.m., in one resounding crash, 2,000 guns opened fire. A hurricane of shells swept down on the Amiens outer defences and enemy batteries, while the creeping barrage fell 200 yards ahead of the leading tanks and infantry, to move forward at first at the rate of 100 yards every three minutes.

Although the mist compelled the attacking troops to break up into groups, and prevented air operations until 9 a.m., south of the Somme the surprise was complete. Led forward, because of the mist, by the first wave of skirmishers, the leading tanks advanced, and were followed by small columns of infantry in single file, behind which came the supports in company groups. No-man's-land, some 500 yards wide, was rapidly crossed, and the first line of the enemy swept back in rout.

On the right flank the French were late in starting, but when they did, the Germans were surprised by this extension of the battle front. Moreuil was occupied by 9.30 a.m. Then a fresh bombardment was opened for three hours and twenty minutes, and the French IXth Corps, on the right of the XXXIst, began to advance, but soon after was held on the Avre. Later, the XXXIst took Mézières, then halted for a further bombardment, and at 5.30 p.m. advanced again. At about nine o'clock this corps occupied Fresnoy, but failed to take le Quesnel. When we remember that the French had few tanks, they did not do so badly; for at a cost of 3,500 casualties they captured over 5,000 of the enemy and 161 guns.

Meanwhile, on the left, the advance of the IIIrd Corps was at once met by a barrage of gas shells, which compelled the attackers to move forward in their gas masks – a most exhausting task. Yet, in spite of heavy casualties, by 7.40 a.m. the first objective was reached in places; but from then on further attempts to advance were frustrated, and the result was that the left flank of the Australians, south of the Somme, suffered severely from the enfilade fire of the enemy batteries posted about Chipilly. This failure by the IIIrd Corps to fulfil its task was largely, if not entirely, due to the Australian raid on July 29.[1]

On the Canadian front, the leading brigades of the 3rd, 1st,

[1] See British Official History, 1918, vol. IV, p. 154.

and 2nd Canadian Divisions occupied the first objective at 7.45 a.m., and the second at about 11 a.m., when the 4th Canadian Division came up to move through them. Few German guns were then firing, and the rout of the enemy infantry was so complete that many officers present "thought that armoured vehicles could have gone anywhere."[1] This was true, for, as will be related, one was fortunate enough to break away from the cavalry and prove it to be so. From the second objective the Mark V Star tanks,[2] which carried machine-gun teams, were sent forward with the 4th Canadian Division to occupy the third objective. At the same time the 3rd Cavalry Division and the 3rd Tank Brigade were ordered to push ahead and seize Rosières. The final Canadian advance began at 12.40 p.m., and by 3.30 p.m. the third objective was reached along its whole front, except at le Quesnel. Undoubtedly this village would also have been taken if the French had not been held at le Fresnoy.

In the meantime, on the Australian front,[3] the 2nd Australian Division on the right and the 3rd Division on the left swept forward, and by 6.20 a.m. had captured the whole of the first objective. A halt was then made to allow the 4th and 5th Divisions to come up and push through to the second and third objectives. When these divisions moved forward at 8.20 a.m. they were accompanied by the 15th Tank Battalion, and the 1st Cavalry Brigade and 16 Whippet tanks were sent ahead, as well as the 17th Tank (Armoured Car) Battalion, whose cars had been towed over the broken roads by tanks. By 9.15 a.m. the second objective was reached by the 5th Division, but the 4th, on its left, was delayed by the German batteries on the Chipilly ridge, and did not occupy their part of the second objective until 10.30 a.m. The leading brigades of the 5th Division pressed on and reached the third objective between 10.30 a.m. and 11 a.m.; but again because of German enfilade fire the 4th Division was delayed, and only after it had suffered heavy casualties and had lost many of its tanks was it able to gain its final objective, except on the extreme left.

Throughout the Canadian and Australian advance the tanks

[1] *Ibid.*, p. 52.
[2] They were under-engined, slow, cumbersome and conspicuous. The teams carried suffered severely from exhaust gas and often were quite unfit for action when disembarked.
[3] The 1st Australian Division only arrived from the north on August 7, and was held in corps reserve.

proved of the utmost value in overcoming enemy machine-gun resistance. Nevertheless, as at Cambrai, their main effect was on morale. Faced by a weapon which they could not halt, the German infantry felt disarmed and instinctively took to their heels. They did so not because the fire of the tank six-pounders and machine-guns slaughtered them—it was too erratic to do so—but because the continuous forward movement of the tanks created a feeling of irresistible power. When tanks were faced with artillery, it was a different question, for during the day 109 tanks were knocked out by gunfire.[1] This was approximately 25 per cent. of the total engaged, a percentage which remained fairly constant for each day's tank action during the remainder of the war. But concerning the future rôle of tanks, the most instructive lesson on August 8 was the conspicuous failure of the attempt to combine them with cavalry.

As was foreseen by the Tank Corps General Staff, this combination proved impossible. They did not help each other; they impeded each other. Because the horsemen could move faster than the Whippets, the latter were left behind during the approach march, and because the cavalry could not face rifle and machine-gun fire, the Whippets forged ahead during the attack. The result was a continuous shuttle movement in which tanks advanced, cavalry retired, and tanks turned back to bring forward the cavalry. Also, because the Whippets were given no fixed objectives, they became little more than armoured guerrillas roaming from one enemy machine-gun to another. Although on the 8th glowing reports were received of cavalry charges[2] and actions around Rosières and Chaulnes, the bulk of the horsemen never crossed the Blue Line, although they did round up considerable numbers of the enemy left in rear by the impetuous attack. Long before dusk they were compelled to retire in order to water their horses, and with them went the Whippets!

It was apparent at the time that had the 3rd and 6th Tank Battalions been followed by infantry in lorries, which, like the armoured cars, could have been towed forward near to the Blue Line by the Whippets, and then had the infantry advanced on foot behind the tanks, it is probable that the high ground about Lihons and Chaulnes would have been occupied during the

[1] Nearly all, however, were repairable.
[2] There was one near Harbonnières, but the enemy turned out to be a German transport column. Forty-six of its men were killed and captured by the 1st Cavalry Brigade.

afternoon of the 8th. Had this ground been occupied, then, because the sole railway which fed the German Second and Eighteenth Armies ran from Chaulnes, *via* Roye, southward, the whole of the German forces facing the French First Army would almost certainly have fallen back.

Two incidents during the battle support this possibility. The first was the action of the 17th Tank (Armoured Car) Battalion, commanded by Lieutenant-Colonel E. J. Carter, and the second the action of a single Whippet which became detached from the cavalry and carried out a raid on its own.

The first incident occurred after the armoured cars had been towed to Warfusée-Abancourt – a little to the west of the Green Line – and unaccompanied by other troops had moved forward to Foucaucourt, some four miles east of the Blue Line, the third and final objective. There they surprised a German headquarters and threw it into panic. Under cover of this confusion the cars turned north and south of the Amiens–Brie road. Those which turned south met large columns of transport, and mounted officers and teams of horses, presumably belonging to the German corps headquarters at Framerville. These were fired on at short range – four officers were shot down by a single burst of fire. Soon after this the German headquarters was reached and the Australian Corps flag run up over the house which a few minutes before had been occupied by the German corps commander. About the same time one of the cars sighted a German train on the Amiens–Chaulnes railway and put it out of action. Later it was captured by the cavalry.

The cars which had turned northward entered Proyart and Chuignolles; two moved up to the Somme. At Proyart, German troops were found at dinner; the cars shot them down and scattered them in all directions. Next, they moved westward and saw in the distance masses of the enemy driven from their trenches by the Australians. To surprise them the cars hid in the outskirts of Proyart, and when they approached they rapidly moved forward and shot great numbers. The enemy scattered before the cars at Proyart, and made across country toward Chuignolles, but there the Germans were met by other cars and again fired on and dispersed. Near Chuignolles, one car obtained "running practice" with its machine-guns at a lorry full of troops until it ran into a ditch. Other cars followed German transport without being suspected until they opened fire at point-blank range.

Although more than half the armoured cars were out of action by the evening of the 8th, there were no casualties among their crews sufficiently serious to require evacuation.

The second incident was equally dramatic. "Musical Box" was a Whippet tank of B Company of the 6th Tank Battalion, and was commanded by Lieutenant C. B. Arnold. On the morning of the 8th it passed through the 2nd Australian Division, moved on parallel with the Amiens–Brie railway, and lost touch with its accompanying cavalry. Its first adventure was between Warfusée-Abancourt and Bayonvillers, where it attacked a German battery in the rear and put it out of action. It then moved on toward Guillaucourt; advanced eastward along the railway and helped two cavalry patrols; and then, as it approached Harbonnières it opened fire on a party of the enemy packing kits and killed and wounded some 60 of them. Next, at ranges of from 200 to 600 yards, it fired on lines of Germans as they retired, and after shooting up several columns of enemy transport, it caught fire and was put out of action.[1]

The confusion caused by these 12 armoured cars and one Whippet tank was phenomenal, and should it be multiplied by the number of Whippets which took the field on the 8th, it is probably no exaggeration to assume that, had they been concentrated around Chaulnes, they would have ruined the whole German command and administration from Albert to Montdidier and from Montdidier to Noyon, a front of some 50 miles.

In spite of this might-have-been, the battle of August 8 was the greatest allied triumph since the Marne. At a cost of some 12,000 men the two attacking armies had killed and wounded 13,000 of their enemy; captured 15,000; taken 400 guns; and had driven right through the German front. All that remained for the allies to do was to follow up their initial success with relentless exploitation.

This was the one thing for which they were not prepared. Also, the old Somme battlefield dictated that mobile warfare should give way to trench warfare. Although the tank had been designed as a trench warfare weapon, its true rôle lay in mobile warfare, and of the 300 tanks which still remained operative, the crews of those which had been engaged were exhausted, and all tanks which had been in action required repairs, munitions, and fuel. The result was that only 145 could be made ready for the

[1] For Arnold's full report, see *Tanks in the Great War*, pp. 230–235.

9th. Meanwhile, because Ludendorff was opposed to a withdrawal to the Hindenberg Line – which probably would have been the wisest course – six German reserve divisions had been rushed forward to reinforce the Second and Eighteenth Armies, and seven other reserve divisions were on their way.

For the 9th, General Rawlinson's orders were for the Fourth Army to advance to the line Roye–Chaulnes–Bray sur Somme–Dernancourt, while the French came up to Roye. But as his Chief of Staff writes: "Owing, however, to the difficulties of communication and other causes, the general movement did not begin till 11 a.m., and in the case of some brigades not until 1 p.m. As a result, the fighting was of a very disjointed nature throughout the day, the attacks of the various divisions and brigades starting at different times. Some of the attacks were covered by artillery or supported by tanks; others were carried out by infantry without support of the other arms."[1] Further, on the right flank the French attack showed little life.[2] Nevertheless, by nightfall, the battle front had been advanced to approximately the line Bouchoir–Rouvroy–Méharicourt–Framerville–Méricourt–Dernancourt.

On the night of the 9th–10th the Australian Corps was ordered to extend its left north of the Somme, and the 32nd Division was moved up to support the 3rd Canadian Division. On the 10th the objectives of the three British corps were to be the same as on the previous day.

On August 10 the battle front was extended by the French Third Army, on the right of the First, which joined in the offensive. As on the 9th, there was little co-ordination on the Fourth Army front and brigades moved forward piecemeal. German resistance had stiffened considerably, and more reserve divisions were thrown in. On the French First and Third Army fronts, because the German Eighteenth Army was now falling back, the advance was rapid; but on the Fourth Army front the Canadian Corps advanced no more than two miles, the Australians less, and the IIIrd Corps gained the whole of its first day's objective.

It was apparent to Haig and Rawlinson that along the whole of the Fourth Army front the offensive was petering out, and early on the 10th, in order to end it and reopen it further north, Haig sent a staff officer to General Sir Henry Horne, commanding the

[1] *The Story of the Fourth Army*, Major-General Sir Archibald Montgomery (n.d.), p. 52.
[2] *La Bataille de Montdidier*, Commandant M. Daille (1922), p. 197.

British First Army, to hasten the plan of an operation already in hand to capture La Bassée and the Aubers' ridge in conjunction with an advance of the Second Army against Kemmel and of the Third Army against Bapaume.

Soon after these instructions had been sent, Marshal Foch arrived at Haig's advanced headquarters at Wiry with a directive to push the offensive eastward in the direction of Ham. Because this would mean the continuance of a wholly frontal battle of attrition against ever-increasing odds, Haig proposed to slow the attack east of Amiens, and while his First and Second Armies made ready, to transfer the offensive to Sir Julian Byng's Third Army, which was in line on the left of the Fourth, with the right flank of the Germans opposing the Fourth Army and the French First Army as its target. But Foch was confident that the Germans were so demoralized that little resistance was to be expected from them. He had arrived at this conclusion because of the little resistance then offered to the French First and Third Armies. It would appear that he was unaware that the German Eighteenth Army and part of the Second were in retreat. Haig also would appear not to have known this, and half convinced by Foch, he ordered the directive to be carried out – much to Rawlinson's annoyance.

On the evening of August 10 the Fourth Army orders were for the IIIrd Corps to remain on the defensive on the 11th while the Canadian and Australian Corps pressed on to the Somme between Ham and Péronne and established bridgeheads on its right bank. At the same time the left of the French First Army was ordered to occupy Ham.

It became apparent on the 11th that both Haig and Rawlinson had been right and that Foch had misjudged the situation. "Owing to the increase of hostile artillery fire, the lack of tanks and sufficient artillery support," writes General Montgomery, "the Canadian attacks were cancelled by Sir Arthur Currie early on the 11th."[1] The Australians, after severe fighting, captured Lihons, and about noon, on the heels of a heavy bombardment, the Germans launched a series of determined counter-attacks against Chilly and between Damery and Fouquescourt on the old British front line of February, 1917. Although all were beaten back, they were a sure sign that it was time to end the battle.

At 3 p.m. Rawlinson held a conference of corps commanders

[1] *The Story of the Fourth Army*, p. 61.

at Villers-Bretonneux, at which it was decided to postpone offensive operations until August 15, and on the 12th the Cavalry Corps was withdrawn into reserve.

Thus, officially, the battle of Amiens was ended. Nevertheless, when Haig visited Foch at Sarcus on the 14th, again the latter pressed him to attack the enemy on the Chaulnes–Roye front. Haig writes in his diary: "I declined to do so because they could only be taken after heavy casualties in men and tanks. . . . I spoke to Foch quite straightly and let him understand that *I was responsible to my Government and fellow citizens for the handling of the British forces*. F's. attitude at once changed and he said all he wanted was early information of my intentions. . . . But notwithstanding what he now said, Foch and all his Staff had been most insistent for the last five days that I should press on along the south bank and capture the Somme bridges above Péronne, regardless of German opposition, and British losses."[1]

The casualties of this great battle were: French, 24,232; British, 22,202; and German estimated at 75,000. The French captured 11,373 men and 259 guns, and the British 18,500 and 240 guns. In killed and wounded, the losses of the Allies and the Germans were almost identical.[2]

Although neither Foch nor Haig realized then how decisive the battle had been, the events of the 8th alone were sufficient to convince not only the German generals, but also their soldiers, that it was a catastrophe. Whereas the former were already engaged upon preparations for a spring offensive, including the use of several thousand tanks, General Ludendorff acclaimed the 8th to be "the black day of the German Army in the history of this war."[3] Nor was he alone in this. The author of the German official monograph on this battle thus describes the situation on that fateful day: "As the sun set on 8th August on the battlefield the greatest defeat which the German Army suffered since the beginning of the war was an accomplished fact."[4] These expressions were not the mere afterthoughts of peacetime reflection; they were the heartfelt outbursts of the moment. As General von Cramon, German Military Plenipotentiary at the Austrian G.H.Q. records: "The turn of events on the Western Front had

[1] *The Private Papers of Douglas Haig, 1914–1919* (edit. Robert Blake, 1952), pp. 313–324.
[2] *British Official History, 1918*, vol. IV, pp. 154–155.
[3] *My War Memories*, vol. II, p. 679.
[4] Quoted in *British Official History, 1918*, vol. IV, p. 88.

a devastating effect upon Austria. The belief that German might could accomplish miracles was so deeply rooted in the mass of the Austrian people, that disillusionment struck them like a sledge-hammer. The Emperor himself was profoundly affected. He summoned me to his presence and informed me that the repulse on the Piave had not produced on his people an impression so overwhelming as the change in the situation on the Western Front."[1]

The nearly universal reason alleged for the German defeat was the employment of tanks in masses by the Allied Powers. But although the tank played a leading part in the German *débâcle*, had there not been deeper reasons, in all probability the results of the battle would have been not much greater than those after the battle of Cambrai.

Of the many causes of the German collapse, first and foremost stood the blockade. By the summer of 1918, if it had not been for the wheat of Rumania and the Ukraine the Central Powers would have been starved into capitulation. As it was, even with these extraneous supplies, their peoples were reduced to starvation level, and as their stomachs shrank their hearts sank. Further, although the German soldier was better fed than his civilian brother, his morale was shattered by the realization that the succession of offensives since March 21 had been in vain, and that their result was a defensive which could see no offensive dawn. Wedged as the German soldier was between his starving family and a hopeless future, it is little wonder that Ludendorff should record that during the battle the retiring troops shouted at the advancing reinforcements: "Blacklegs, you're prolonging the war!"[2]

Such was the gloomy background of Germany against which the power of the tank scintillated, and although Sir James Edmonds correctly points out that the material effect of the tank was small, because its moral effect was great – so he writes – "It has pleased the Germans to attribute their defeat in the field to the tank. The excuse will not bear examination."[3] What is missed here is what Colonel Brackenbury saw so clearly 40 years earlier: "moral effect is the object aimed at in battle." It was not the killing power of the tank which caused the author of the German

[1] *Quatre ans au G.Q.G. Austro-Hongrois*, p. 285.
[2] *My War Memories*, vol. II, p. 683.
[3] *British Official History, 1918*, vol. IV, p. iv.

monograph to entitle it "*Die Katastrophe des 8 August, 1918*," it was the terror it instilled; it precipitated not the final retirement, but the initial rout. Without the tank there would have been no surprise commensurate with the one achieved on the morning of the 8th, and it was the suddenness of the attack which detonated the panic. Added to this, the feeling of utter powerlessness of the soldier on foot when faced by an antagonist that no rifle or machine-gun bullet could halt instinctively led him to exaggerate the danger in order to mitigate the ignominy of immediate surrender or flight.

These exaggerations flooded the German Press. As an example, Baron von Ardenne wrote in the *Berliner Tageblatt*: "An attack by tanks has something appalling and demoniacal about it. It might terrify the superstitious . . . in the battle now raging the enemy made use of 500 armoured monsters. In addition to these there were numerous Whippet tanks which broke through our lines more quickly than an express train"(!) In a German Second Army order of August 25 we read: "People with anxious temperaments [usually every soldier under fire] saw everywhere squadrons of tanks, masses of cavalry and thick lines of infantry." A German prisoner said: "The officers and men in many cases come to consider the approach of tanks a sufficient explanation for not fighting. Their sense of duty is sufficient to make them fight against infantry, but if tanks appear, many feel they are justified in surrendering."[1] As will be seen, in the Second World War identical psychological incidents abound.

Ludendorff made no mistake over the situation the tank created. "Everything I had feared, and of which I had so often given warning," he writes, "had here, in one place, become a reality. Our war machine was no longer efficient. Our fighting power had suffered, even though the great majority of divisions still fought heroically.

"The 8th of August put the decline of that fighting power beyond all doubt and in such a situation as regards reserves, I had no hope of finding a strategic expedient whereby to turn the situation to our advantage. On the contrary, I became convinced that we were now without that safe foundation for the plans of G.H.Q., on which I had hitherto been able to build, at least so far as this is possible in war. Leadership now assumed, as I then stated, the character of an irresponsible game of chance, a thing

[1] *Weekly Tank Notes*, 10th August–2nd November, 1918, pp. 9, 14, 25, 26.

I have always considered fatal. The fate of the German people was for me too high a stake. The war must be ended."[1]

On August 11, the German Emperor summoned a conference of the senior army leaders. It assembled at Avesnes, Hindenburg's headquarters, and there he uttered the historic words: "I see that we must strike a balance. We have nearly reached the limit of our power of resistance. The war must be ended."[2] Two days later another conference assembled at Spa, at which Ludendorff reviewed the military situation and explained that "as it was no longer possible to force the enemy to sue for peace by an offensive," and "as the defensive alone could hardly achieve that object . . . the termination of the war would have to be brought about by diplomacy." The Emperor instructed the Secretary of State, von Hintze, "to open up peace negotiations, if possible, through the medium of the Queen of the Netherlands."[3]

Meanwhile the explosion of August 8–11 had detonated "the final battle of the world war," as Ludendorff calls it. It comprised a series of battles directed against the two sides of the great western salient; because of this a return was made to the strategy of Marshal Joffre.

On August 20 battle was opened simultaneously by the French Tenth and Third Armies between Soissons and Roye and by the British Third Army north of Albert. Immediately after this the front was extended south of the Somme by the British Fourth Army. In rapid succession battle followed battle, and on September 12 the American First Army joined in the fray and set out to reduce the St. Mihiel salient. The war in the west had entered its final phase; to use Foch's expression, it was until November 11 to be "*Tout le monde à la bataille.*"

On September 26, between the Meuse and Rheims, the American First Army and the French Fourth Army attacked. On the 27th, between Epéhy and Lens, the British Third and First Armies attacked. On the 28th, from Armentières to the Channel, the British Second Army, the Belgian Army, and the French Sixth Army attacked. And on the 29th, between La Fère and Epéhy, the French First Army and British Fourth Army attacked. Meanwhile, in Macedonia the Balkan front was broken by the allied armies under General Franchet d'Espérey, and

---

[1] *My War Memories*, vol. II, p. 684.
[2] Quoted in *British Official History*, vol. IV, p. 140.
[3] *My War Memories*, vol. II, pp. 684–687.

Bulgaria asked for a suspension of hostilities; on September 19 the battle of Megiddo was opened by General Sir Edmund Allenby, Damascus was entered on October 1, and on the 30th Turkey was out of the war.

Overwhelmed by defeat, at six o'clock on the afternoon of September 28, Ludendorff entered Field-Marshal Hindenburg's room and suggested that an armistice could no longer be delayed. "We did not consider any abandonment of territory in the East," he writes, "thinking that the Entente would be fully conscious of the dangers threatening them as well as ourselves from Bolshevism."[1] In this he was mistaken; nevertheless, on October 5, President Wilson's Fourteen Points were accepted as the basis for armistice negotiations.

[1] *Ibid.*, vol. II, p. 721.

EDITOR'S NOTE 6

The closing stages of the First World War deserve a somewhat closer inspection than Fuller gives them in the passage above. The significance of the Battle of Amiens is, of course, enormous. Ludendorff called it "the worst experience I had to go through". It undoubtedly marks the moment at which the German will to victory began to crack, and on this the comment of the British Official Historian, Brigadier-General Sir J. E. Edmonds, is worth quoting: "Thus the collapse of Germany began not in the Navy, not in the Homeland, not in any of the sideshows, but on the Western Front in consequence of defeat in the field."

It was a national – indeed, a world – misfortune that this conclusion was distasteful to the British Government of the day, dedicated as it was to "strategies of evasion". There was thus a persistent failure to appreciate the manner of the War's ending, and the large British contribution to that ending. In truth, Amiens was only the beginning of what must surely rank as the largest, most sustained, most successful British offensive campaign in history. Eight great victorious battles were fought by the British under Haig in continuous succession up to the Armistice.[1] Their effect was to give the Germans no respite; the climax of them all was the storming of the Hindenburg Line 27-29 September, which caused the German General Staff to demand an immediate armistice; and the final product may be judged from this table:
8 August – 11 November

Army	Prisoners	Guns taken
British	188,700	2,840
French	139,000	1,880
American	43,200	1,421
Belgian	14,500	474
	385,400	6,615

[1] See Terraine, *The Western Front*, pp. 180-81, Hutchinson, 1964.

National performances apart, the scale of German losses tells its own tale; 385,000 prisoners (over and above the very large number of killed and wounded) and the loss of over 6,600 guns (almost half their artillery) reveal a shattering defeat in the field which post-war propaganda should never have been allowed to disguise. But the national performances are also significant, because they show that Britain was entitled to a much stronger military voice in the armistice and Peace negotiations than she in fact enjoyed. The evidence is that this voice would have urged more realism and sanity than the political voices which dominated the council chambers. Fuller, however, has his own interesting and penetrating summary of the effects of the War, which requires to be quoted:

'The influences of the first of the world wars on vanquished and victors, and through them on history, were cataclysmic. Most of the Europe of a thousand years was shattered and the balance between its nations destroyed. Three empires were tumbled into the dust. Germany was reduced to economic ruin and slices of her frontier territories were amputated; Alace-Lorraine was returned to France, and parts of Silesia and Posen were given to a resuscitated Poland. Russia ceased to be a Christian country, and the autocracy of Marx was substituted for the autocracy of the Tsars. The Austro-Hungarian Empire was split into a congeries of squabbling states bereft of economic foundations, and Turkey was almost reduced to her original sultanate of Rum. Nor did the victors emerge much better. France, bled white, was left a demoralized, second-rate Power; Great Britain, who before the war had been the banker of the world, ended a debtor country, and for the *Pax Britannica* was substituted the League of Nations – a sham to replace a reality. The United States was left to pay for the war she had so blindly entered in order to disencumber herself of the consequences she had failed to foresee. Japan, who had played a minor part, alone emerged triumphant. Her empire was extended and the war raised her to a dominant position in the Far East and the western Pacific. Such were the sorry products of bankrupt statesmanship.

'Of these many disasters, the Russian Revolution and the replacement of the *Pax Britannica* by the League of Nations – the Wilsonian brand of a sovietized world – were, historically, the most momentous. Because the aim of the former was world revolution, and that of the latter world peace, and because no

arbiter was left to judicate between them, the world was split ideo-
logically in twain by a political Manicheism – it was not a struggle
between the powers of Light and Darkness, but between a world
to be made safe for American democracy and a world to be
secured by Russian autocracy. This meant the inversion of
Clausewitz's dictum that war is a continuation of peace policy.
In other words, because both policies were global, it led to the
establishment of a global state of "wardom."

Although the *Pax Britannica* had not prevented the outbreak of
continental wars, it prevented them from spreading to world-wide
dimensions and so had played the part of international arbiter.
And although the *Pax Britannica* was destroyed by the war, it was
because of the inept statemanship of Great Britain and America
that the war engulfed the entire world. This ineptness is worth
investigation, for the passing of the *Pax Britannica* was as catastrophic an historical event as had been the passing of the *Pax
Romana*.

When, in *King Richard the Second*, Shakespeare compares England
to a "fortress built by Nature for herself against infection and the
hand of war," and calls her "This precious stone set in the silver
sea, which serves it in the office of a wall," he summed up the
foundations of the *Pax Britannica*. And when, in his day, Napoleon
acclaimed that "England can never be a continental power and
in the attempt must be ruined," he did no more than accentuate
Shakespeare's dictum. In brief, the sea dictated England's foreign
policy, and of all her statesmen Chatham saw this the most clearly;
he realized that as a colonial empire, and not as a continental
power, England could go from strength to strength.

Later Canning saw it. "I do not say (God forbid I should!),"
he declared, "that it is no part of the duty of Great Britain to
protect what is termed the balance of power and to aid the weak
against the strong. I say, on the contrary, that it is her bounden
duty; but I affirm also, that we must take care to do our duty to
ourselves. The first condition of engaging in any war . . . is
that the war must be just; the second that, being just in itself,
we can also with justice engage in it; and the third . . . that we
can so interfere without detriment or prejudice to ourselves."[1]

Disraeli also understood. "The abstention," he said, "of England
from any unnecessary interference in the affairs of Europe is the

[1] Quoted from *The Foreign Policy of Canning, 1822–1827*, Harold Temperley (1925),
p. 463.

consequence, not of her decline of power but of her increased strength. England is no longer a mere European power; she is the metropolis of a great maritime Empire, extending to the boundaries of the farthest ocean. It is not because England has taken refuge in a state of apathy that she now almost systematically declines to interfere in the affairs of the Continent of Europe, England is as ready and as willing to interfere as in old days when the necessity of her position requires it."[1]

' Finally, Winston Churchill at the opening of his political career held the same idea in mind. When on May 13, 1901, the question of defence was being debated in the House of Commons he said: "Whereas any European Power has to support a vast army first of all, we in this fortunate, happy island, relieved by our insular position of a double burden, may turn our undivided efforts and attention to the Fleet. Why should we sacrifice a game in which we are sure to win to play a game in which we are bound to lose?"[2]

' In spite of this enormous initial blunder – the jettisoning of the *Pax Britannica* by Britain herself – if the United States had not entered the war on the side of the Entente, it is probable that in 1917 the war would have ended in a negotiated peace and most of the calamities which followed its American extension would not have befallen Europe. Therefore, and unquestionably, April 6, 1917, was the blackest of all days in modern European history. Although, as has been recorded in Chronicle 7, President Wilson foresaw the calamities that would follow American participation in the war, his propaganda-demented people could not see that the power of the United States was potentially so enormous that, as long as she refrained from participation in the war, it would make her the arbiter of the world. They also failed to see that although in all probability United States participation would decide the war, when it ended there would be no arbiter of peace left in the world.

'Had it not been for the octopus of propaganda, whose tentacles gripped him like a vice, there can be little doubt that Wilson would not have jettisoned the foreign policy which, in 1794, Washington outlined to Gouverneur Morris, and which since then had carried the United States from strength to strength.

' "Peace," he said, "has been the order of the day with me since

---

[1] Quoted from *The Cambridge History of British Foreign Policy*, vol. III, pp. 9–10.
[2] *Parliamentary Debates* ("Hansard"), vol. XCIII, Fourth Series, May 13, 1901, cols. 1574–1575.

the disturbance in Europe, first commenced. My policy has been, and will continue to be, while I have the honor to remain in the administration of the government, to be upon friendly terms with, but independent of, all the nations of the earth; to share in the broils of none; to fulfil our own engagements; to supply the wants and to be carrier for them all; being thoroughly convinced that it is our policy and interest so to do. Nothing short of self-respect, and that justice which is essential to a national character, ought to involve us in war."[1]

'The outstanding calamity of the war was that Wilson could not heed these words; it towered above all others, including the Russian revolution, because his war policy rendered Europe receptive to the Bolshevik contagion. What he did not, or could not, see, was that once involved in the war the only sane way to contain the contagion was to salve what remained of European stability; to prop up the tottering governments; to hold fast to the frontiers of 1913; to veto all territorial annexations; and to fight revolution by reinvigorating the existing European governments and in no way weaken them.

'Ever since the days of Charlemagne, who established the East Mark (Austria) as an outwork to secure Christendom against Slavonic and other barbarians of the east, the Germanic peoples began to form two great bastions – the northern eventually centred in Brandenburg–Prussia and the southern in Austria – which protected Europe against Asia. Wilson set out to weaken the northern bastion by refusing to treat with William II and his Government except on terms of total surrender, and the southern bastion he utterly destroyed in spite of the dictates of history.

'On October 17, 1805, a few weeks before the battle of Austerlitz, Talleyrand wrote to Napoleon: "The Austrian Monarchy is a combination of ill-assorted States. Such a power is necessarily weak, but it is an adequate bulwark against the barbarians [Russians] and a necessary one. In the future the Habsburg Empire will stand with its back towards Europe and its front to the East, thus protecting Western civilization from the aggression of Russia." And in 1848, the Czech historian, Frantisek Palanky, wrote: "If Austria did not exist she would have to be invented. The disintegration of the Austrian State into small republics would

---

[1] Quoted from *The Growth of the American Republic*, S. E. Morison and H. S. Commager (1942), vol. I, p. 358.

be an invitation to German and Russian Imperialism."[1]

What Wilson did not realize was that, as the Kremsier resolution put it, the old Austria was a valiant attempt "to unite all
lands and races of the monarchy into one great body politic,"
and that under Francis Joseph nine nationalities learned to live
and let live, and if they did not love one another, at least they
respected each other and fought as a united army. Instead, he
listened to the voices of the *émigrés*, and more particularly to that
of T. G. Masaryk – the future Czech President – and was brought
to believe that the Habsburg monarchy was a reactionary survival
from the Middle Ages and the gaoler of enslaved peoples.

'According to R. W. Seton-Watson, a close friend of Masaryk,
Wilson's exchange of notes during the battle of Vittorio-Veneto
"bore down the diplomatic defences of Vienna and Budapest,
killed the Emperor's project of Austrian federation at birth, and
wrested from him and his Government recognition of Czecho-
slovak and Jugoslav as an essential part of the foundation of the
new settlement. The Dual Monarchy crumbled before the impact
of Wilsonian diplomacy . . . no one factor contributed more to
this result than the Presidential thunderbolts."[2]

' Besides faulty statemanship, another cause, this time military,
underlay the many catastrophies the war begot. It was the tactical
stalemate which, as Bloch had foreseen, followed the initial onrush,
and, as he had predicted, led to a final decision through famine,
bankruptcy, and the break-up of the whole social order.

' Had there been no stalemate, the blockade would not have
been effective, and it was the allies' blockade – sea and not land
power – which finally broke the will of their enemies; it struck
every man, woman and child, every factory, and every farm in
the enemy countries. Only if the Central Powers at the outset had
been able to penetrate their enemies' fronts – that is, shorten the
range of the blockade – and thereby extend their food areas, would
the blockade have been broken. A parallel was the breaking of
the submarine counter-blockade by the convoy system which, so to
speak, penetrated it. As it was, it has been calculated that, during
the last two years of the blockade, "800,000 non-combatants died
in Germany from starvation or diseases directly attributed to
under-nourishment – about fifty times more than were drowned

---

[1] Both quoted from *Danubian Federation*, Lieut.-Col. F. O. Miksche (n.d.), p. 30.
[2] *Masaryk in England* (1943), pp. 113–114.

by submarine attack on British shipping."[1]

' The character of the war was as revolutionary as its results, and this was mainly because of the ever-increasing use of propaganda. Morality and common decency were cast to the winds, and in this respect the war differed markedly from both the Napoleonic and Franco-Prussian wars, in which, generally speaking, the contenders guarded against fostering revolution.[2] The use of alleged atrocities as a weapon became universal, and as the war lengthened people became more credulous and savage until all reason was lost in a primitive animalism; a frantic hysterical endeavour to injure the enemy by every means foul and damnable.

' When he wrote on the influence of British propaganda between 1914 and 1917 upon the American people, James Duane Squires said:

' "Fired by such notions [that German soldiers cut the hands off Belgian children] about the behaviour of the enemy and by others equally absurd,[3] the American people launched themselves into the war with an emotional hysteria that can only be understood by realizing the power of propaganda in generating common action by a nation under belligerent conditions. Those who did not accept the war ideology were usually few in number and always quite impotent. The almost primitive ecstasy that could sometimes grip the American people has been recently summarized in unforgettable fashion.

' " "We hated with a common hate that was exhilarating. The writer of this review remembers attending a great meeting in New England, held under the auspices of a Christian Church – God save the mark! A speaker demanded that the Kaiser, when captured, be boiled in oil, and the entire audience stood on chairs to scream its hysterical approval. This was the mood we were in. This was the kind of madness that had seized us.' "[4]'

---

[1] *Unfinished Victory*, Arthur Bryant (1940), p. 3. See also pp. 9 and 10.

[2] Napoleon could to his advantage have unleashed the "pent-up animality" of the Russian serfs and Ukrainians in 1812, and have stirred up a revolution in France during the Hundred Days, but he refrained (*Napoleon*, Eugene Tarle (1936), pp. 289, 381). The Duke of Wellington had a horror of fomenting revolution in any country, and, in 1871, Bismarck did not befriend the Paris Commune.

[3] For a vast number of other alleged atrocities see *Falsehood in War-Time*, Arthur Ponsonby (1936).

[4] *British Propaganda at Home and in the United States from 1914 to 1917*, James Duane Squires (1935), pp. 67–68. In the appendix is listed 277 publications and books of British propaganda sent to the U.S. between the above dates. Also see *Spreading Germs of Hate*, George Sylvester Viereck (1931).

' The means of fighting were also revolutionary, because for the first time in the history of war battles were as much tussles between factories as between armies. The production of weapons was more of a deciding factor in battles than the conscription of men. God had marched with the biggest industries in preference to the biggest battalions, and more often with tank and gun than with rifle and bayonet. As J. T. Shotwell says: "During the years 1914 to 1918 . . . war definitely passed into the industrial phase of economic history . . . the industry of war combines two techniques; the technique of peace which supplies war with its resources, and the technique of destruction."[1] The pecuniary profits of war shifted from plunder by the generals and troops to the gains made by financiers, war contractors, and manufacturers.

' Of the many changes which germinated in the war, probably the most ominous was that, contrary to common acceptance, the war *did* make the world safe for democracy in its several forms. From 1918 on, even more than in the Wars of Religion, the emotions of mass-man were to dominate human relations. Wresting reason from statecraft and strategy ". . . Demos rose a Demon, shriek'd and slaked the light with blood," and set a seal of madness and savagery on peace and war.[2] '

[1] *War as an Instrument of National Policy* (1929), pp. 34–35.
[2] For the bellicosity of democracies see Hoffman Nickerson's books: *Can We Limit War?* (1934) and *The Armed Horde* (1940).

The Russian revolution

When the nineteenth century opened, all the leading nations had changed from an agricultural to an industrial economy, and the progress made was so startling that it seemed to industrialized man that the new dispensation to which steam power had given birth made archaic all that had preceded it. Material progress was equated with happiness, and economic determinism accepted as the new religion. "The machine and the universe," writes Lewis Mumford in *Technics and Civilization*,[1] "were identified, linked together as they were by the formulae of the mathematical and physical sciences; and the service of the machine was the principal manifestation of faith and religion: the main motive of human action, and the source of most human goods." Man, who in the Age of Faith had been looked upon as only a little lower than the angels, was reduced to the status of an economic animal – the "beast of prey" of Oswald Spengler. For capitalist and socialist alike the worship of Mammon replaced the worship of God, and as it led to class-war, the socialists propounded the falsehood that classes could be extinguished, and thereby introduced a contradiction in the mammonic creed, because economic determinism leads to diversity and not uniformity of social status.

This contradiction was seized upon by Marx, who set out to do for the proletariat – the industrial workers – what Calvin had done for the elect, for his apocalypse gave them, as it has been well said, "the certainty of a triumph predestined by the majestic laws of the universe itself." The social world was not to be readjusted or reformed, but instead to be turned upside down, for according to his dialectics the new gospel was to be associated, not with amity but with enmity, not with charity but with violence. The whole Christian order was to be reversed; the principle of hate one another was to be substituted for that of love one another, and not until war on behalf of the proletariat had been made total – that is, world-wide – would the gates of his material paradise

[1] Published by George Routledge and Sons, Ltd., London, 1934.

open to the elect. Because, as Mumford has pointed out in *The Conditions of Man*, Marx believed "that material conditions and technical inventions were self-created entities, existing in and by themselves: prime movers, original sources of social power . . . he accepted the machine process as an absolute, imagined that the proletariat would simply take up capitalist production at the point that capitalism left off," and step straight into the social Eldorado. To Marx the proletariat was the new messiah and the organizer of an earthly kingdom in which the spiritual had no place.

Lenin accepted Marx's interpretation of the "dictatorship of the proletariat" and so became as much the victim of a theological obsession with doctrine as Luther and Calvin had been in their days. The process was simplicity itself. Through revolution the proletariat would become the governing class, and in the guise of a transitional state it would overthrow the bourgeoisie, wrest from it all means of production, exchange and distribution, and by centralizing them in its own hands would develop them for its own benefit until, after victory had been won and the entire people had been proletarianized, the State would die away into a self-sufficing and self-operating classless society.

This simplification was accepted by Lenin. Like Marx, he had never soiled his hands with a day's manual labour and knew nothing of the human side of the worker's life. Also like Marx, his views on national and industrial administration were naive. He declared that "we must break the old, absurd, savage, despicable and disgusting prejudice that only the rich [*i.e.*, the educated] can administer the State," since "every rank and file worker who is able to read and write can do organizational work." That "under Socialism all will administer in turn and will quickly become accustomed to nobody administering." Blindly he believed that "electrification plus socialism" was the highroad to the Communist New Atlantis, and was oblivious of the self-evident contradiction in Marx's gospel. Because everyone would own everything, nobody would own anything, and as this carried with it the elimination of individual incentive, who would keep the proletariat at work? This demanded the creation of a new class of taskmasters, which meant that the assumption that the proletariat could become the governing class was nonsense.

When, on November 7, 1917 (the October Revolution), Lenin, thanks to Trotsky's abilities as an organizer, began his struggle for power, he was almost unknown. But as everybody in Russia knew of the Social Revolutionary Party which had great influence with the peasants, he entered into coalition with its left wing, and between November 8 and December 31 issued 193 decrees. On November 9 he decreed that the property of the landlords was to be distributed among the peasants, and though this had nothing to do with Marxism, for Marx looked upon the peasants as "the barbarians of civilization," Lenin thereby gained the support of 80 per cent. of the Russian people. Little did the Social Revolutionaries and the peasants suspect at the time that Lenin's motive was to use the peasants to liquidate the bourgeoisie, and then in turn to liquidate them.

Later, on November 27, by another decree all industry was transferred to the workers, who became the governing class, and the Soviet of People's Commissars became their form of government, the task of which was to organize production and direct Communist affairs. The immediate result was that because the workers were incapable of organizing and directing anything, industry came to a standstill, factories were turned into debating clubs, and as the workers had nothing to exchange for food, the peasants ceased to cultivate the land, except for themselves. Thus the Marxian experiment was proved to be an illusion; it created nothing but confusion, and this because of its omission to take into account human nature. Yet it did prove something of inestimable future value – that the most certain way to wreck a potential enemy's economy is to plant Marxian communism in his realm.

Lenin was compelled to take his first decisive step away from Marx. On December 20 he formed a special police force, the Tcheka, on the lines of the old Tsarist Okrana. Ostensibly it was to fight counter-revolution; its real purpose was to compel the new governing class to cease misgoverning and to work. Since first of all food had to be provided for the workers, it was wrested from the peasants, and because of this the Social Revolutionaries broke away from Lenin. It was too late, a terror was at once unleashed by the Tcheka and the Marxian experiment drowned in blood. Lenin then formed a Political Bureau of five prominent members of the Bolshevik Party under his own leadership, which governed by means of the Tcheka and the Red Army Trotsky had created. The result was civil war. As this stimulated foreign intervention, it is opportune here to examine Lenin's foreign policy.

From the earliest days of the revolution there was one assumption upon which all the Bolshevik leaders were agreed; the revolution could not survive unless it became world-wide. It challenged the existing order of society, socially, politically, and economically. It not only offered to the world a new way of life, but its adherents held that it could not be established permanently until the old way was destroyed. As early as April 14, 1917, Lenin had proclaimed that "World Imperialism cannot live side by side with a victorious Soviet Revolution," and on March 12, 1919, in the name of the Central Committee he placed a report before the eighth congress of the Russian Communist Party in which he said:

"We are living not merely in a State, but in a system of States, and the existence of the Soviet Republic side-by-side with Imperialist States for a long time is unthinkable. One or the other must triumph in the end. And before that end supervenes a series of frightful collisions between the Soviet Republic and the Bourgeoise States will be inevitable."

Later, Stalin reiterated these words again and again, and summarized Soviet international policy as follows:

"The tasks of the Party in foreign policy are: (*1*) to utilize every contradiction and conflict among the surrounding capitalist groups and governments for the purpose of disintegrating imperialism; (*2*) to spare no pains or means to assist the proletarian revolutions in the west; (*3*) to take all necessary measures to strengthen the national liberation movement in the east; and (*4*) to strengthen the Red Army."

In order to make this subversive war world-wide, in March, 1919, Lenin founded the Third International, or Comintern; an instrument to unite all communist parties outside Russia in the struggle for world revolution, and its first task was to establish a communist régime in Germany. On the insistence of Poincaré, Clemenceau, Foch, and Klotz in France, and others in Great Britain, Germany was still under blockade, and out of desperation many Germans had turned to Bolshevism. So completely did the Paris peacemakers play into Lenin's hands that, in his own words, his plan was "To unite the proletariat of industrial Germany, Austria and Czechoslovakia with the proletariat of Russia, and thereby create a mighty agrarian and industrial combination from Vladivostok to the Rhine, from the Finnish Gulf to the blue waters of the Danube, capable of feeding itself and confronting the reactionary capitalism of Britain with a revolutionary giant, which with one hand would disturb the tranquillity of the East and with the other beat back the pirate capitalism of Anglo-Saxon countries. If there was anything that could compel the English whale to dance, it would be the union of revolutionary Russia with a revolutionary Central Europe."

One of the few men who realized this danger was Lloyd George who, on March 25, 1919, set forth his views:

"The greatest danger I perceive in the present situation is the possibility of Germany uniting her destiny with the Bolshevists, and placing her wealth, intellect and great organizing capacity at the disposal of the men who dream of conquering the world for Bolshevism by force of arms. This danger is no idle fancy. If Germany goes over to Spartacism [then being fostered by France] she will inevitably link her fate with that of the Bolshevists. If that takes place, all Eastern Europe will be drawn into the maelstrom of the Bolshevist Revolution, and a year hence we shall find ourselves opposed by nearly 3,000,000 men who will be welded by German generals and German instructors into a gigantic army equipped with German machine-guns and ready to undertake an offensive against Western Europe."

Because world revolution was Lenin's strategical goal, his tactics also had to be revolutionary. Their aim was not to persuade the enemy to change his mind by force of arms, but by force of ideas – in other words, to rot him internally and bring him to destroy himself. Before the Treaty of Brest-Litovsk he had said, "Let us give way in space, but gain time," because he saw that, once revolution was kindled in the west it would give back to Russia the space she had bartered, and without a fight.

He said: "We must be able to resort to all sorts of strategems, manœuvres, illegal methods, evasions and subterfuges only so as to get into the trade unions, to remain in them, and to carry Communist work within them at all costs. . . . The Communist Party enters such institutions not in order to do constructive work, but in order to direct the masses to destroy from within the whole Bourgeois State machine and Parliament itself."

Germany was the hub of the world revolution for Lenin and Trotsky because she was the strategical centre of gravity of Europe. Once she was won, the rest of Europe would become untenable and could be conquered. And when Europe was reduced to the position of a Soviet satrapy, the Mediterranean would also become untenable, and the Middle East could be

Bolshevized and Africa subverted. Finally, when the whole of the Old World was sovietized, the psychological conquest of the New World could be undertaken and the Soviet Republic of the World established.

The composition of the Russian empire prevented Lenin from launching out on this grandiose scheme. It was a mosaic of sub-jugated peoples held together by the centripetal autocracy of the Muscovite Tsar, which alone prevented the explosion of the centrifugal forces of discontent. Because of this, the overthrow of the Tsarist government in March, 1917, at once led to national uprisings among the non-Muscovites, with the result that at various dates – mostly following the October Revolution – 15 groups of subjugated peoples declared their autonomy. The first to do so was the Ukraine, the most populous of them, in which a Central Council of Liberation was formed on March 17, 1917. Next, on November 20, 1917, the Ukrainians formally proclaimed themselves to be a National Republic, and because Lenin could not prevent this, he acknowledged Ukrainian independence, and immediately began to establish a Communist shadow government at Kharkov. On December 17 it came into the open. It proclaimed the Ukraine a Soviet Republic and in accordance with Lenin's technique, appealed to the Soviet Government for aid. This was granted, and the Ukrainian War of Independence, which was to last until 1921, was started.

Meanwhile, immediately after the October Revolution, General Alexeyev in south Russia raised a volunteer army of White Russians (Imperialists) to fight the Bolsheviks, and was soon joined by General Kornilov and General Denekin. The former was killed in March, 1918, and when Alexeyev died the following September Denekin took over supreme command of the White Russian forces in the south. Two months later Admiral Kolchak raised his standard of counter-revolution at Omsk. At the moment when the Central Powers collapsed, civil war raged over most of Russia.

In the meantime foreign intervention had made confusion worse confounded. It was begun when the French supported the Czech prisoners captured by the Russians and formed by them into a corps to fight the Central Powers. After the Treaty of Brest-Litovsk the Czechs had elected to come under French command, and as they could not pass through Germany, they set out to reach France by way of Vladivostok.

By the close of 1918 the interventionist forces in Russia had reached a total of nearly 300,000 men – French, British, Americans, Italians, Japanese, German Balts, Poles, Greeks, Finns, Czechs, Slovaks, Estonians and Latvians – in Archangel, Murmansk, Finland, Estonia, Latvia, and Poland, as well as on the Black Sea, on the Trans-Siberian railway, and at Vladivostok. In April, 1919, Kolchak reached Kazan and Samara on the Volga, while Denekin advanced northward from the Black Sea. As Kolchak was considered the more dangerous, Trotsky sent General Tukhachevski against him. Tukhachevski won the battle of Busulug, set out from the Volga, crossed the Urals, and pursued his enemy to Vladivostok, 5,000 miles away. Next, in October, an offensive was opened against Denekin, who had advanced to Orel. He was pushed back, and once in retreat, because of the bandits and partisans who infested his rear communications, was unable to halt his demoralized men until they reached Novorossisk on the Black Sea. From there the remnants of his army were sent to General Wrangel in the Crimea. About the same time, General Yudenich, then advancing on Petrograd, was driven over the Estonian border, and intervention began to collapse. Two Powers were unwilling to give in; Japan, who had her eyes on territorial expansion in eastern Siberia, and France.

Because the French feared to lose the credits they had advanced Tsarist Russia and that, in revenge for the Treaty of Versailles, the Germans would link up with the Bolsheviks, their policy was contradictory. One aim was to restore the Tsarist régime, which would be grateful to France, and the other was to create an enlarged Poland which as a French ally would threaten Germany from the east.

On November 5, 1916, the independence of Poland had been sanctioned by the Central Powers, and when on November 11, 1918, they collapsed, the Regency Council established by them appointed Joseph Pilsudski (1867–1935) to the supreme command of all Polish troops. His first act was to declare himself head of the National Government, and his second to notify all belligerent and neutral Powers that Poland was an independent state.

Pilsudski, assured of French good will, credits, and munitions, needed little encouragement to make enormous territorial claims, for the key-note of his foreign policy was to restore the Polish frontiers of 1772 – roughly the line of the Dvina and Dnieper – and to make Poland the head of an anti-Bolshevik confederation.

In April, 1919, he invaded Lithuania, stormed Lida and occupied Vilna. In May he invaded east Galicia, which had been proclaimed a West Ukrainian Republic by General Petliura who, in November, 1918, had become head of the Ukrainian National Government, and so began the Polish-Ukrainian War.

Because the Supreme Council of the Allied Powers took little heed of these campaigns and failed to appreciate what manner of man Pilsudski was, on December 8, it fixed the eastern frontier of Poland along the line of the river Bug, and in the following year it became known as the "Curzon Line". It in no way satisfied Pilsudski, and soon after it was suggested the situation in the Ukraine grew so critical that, in the spring of 1920, Petliura came to terms with Pilsudski, and on April 22, peace between them was signed at Warsaw. Poland recognized the independence of the Ukraine and undertook to support the Ukrainians against Russia.

CHAPTER 8

The Battle of Warsaw, 1920

The civil war in Russia threw up one remarkable general—Mikail Tukhachevski. An able soldier, his outlook on civilization so closely reflected the Asiatic side of Bolshevism that to understand the future trend of the Russian Revolution it is worth while to examine it.

Born in 1892 of a noble family which traced its descent back to the Counts of Flanders, although his mother was an Italian, in character he was Tartar. From her he inherited his Latin looks, black hair, and the quick wit which enabled him to probe the Russian within him and the Tartar within the Russian. In 1914 he was gazetted a sub-lieutenant in the Imperial Guard, and in the following year was taken prisoner by the Germans.

By instinct he was a romantic barbarian who abhorred western civilization. He had the soul of Genghis Khan, of Ogdai and of Batu. Autocratic, superstitious, romantic and ruthless, he loved the open plain lands and the thud of a thousand hoofs, and he loathed and feared the unromantic orderliness of civilization. He hated Christianity and Christian culture because they had obliterated paganism and barbarism and had deprived his fellow countrymen of the ecstasy of the god of war and the glamour of "the carnival of death". Also he loathed the Jews because they had helped to inoculate the Russians with "the pest of civilization" and "the morale of capitalism." He said: "The Jew is a dog, son of a dog, who sows his fleas in every land."[1]

When he was incarcerated at Ingolstadt, he said to Fervacque, a fellow prisoner: "A demon or a god animates our race. We shall make ourselves drunk, because we cannot as yet make the world drunk. That will come."[2] Once Fervacque found him painting in discordant colours on a piece of cardboard the head of an atrocious idol. What is that? he asked him. "Do not laugh," replied Tukhachevski, "I have told you that the Slavs are in want of a new religion. They are being given Marxism; but aspects of that

[1] *Le chef de l'armée rouge, Mikaïl Tukhachevski*, Pierre Fervacque (1928), p. 24.
[2] *Ibid.*, p. 67.

theology are too modern and too civilized. It is possible to mitigate that disagreeable state by returning to our Slav gods, who were deprived of their prerogative and strength; nevertheless they can soon regain them. There is Daschbog, the god of the sun; Stribog, the god of the storm; Wolos, the god of human arts and of poetry; and also Pierounn, the god of war and of lightning. For long I have hesitated to choose my particular god; but, after reflection, I have accepted Pierounn, because once Marxism is thrust upon Russia, the most devastating wars will be let loose. . . . We shall enter chaos and we shall not leave it until civilization is reduced to total ruin."[1]

This was no sudden, imaginative whim caused by the boredom of imprisonment; when Tukhachevski was a small child he and his brothers scandalized their French governess by "baptising" three cats, amid dreadful howlings, in the name of "The Father, the Son and the Holy Ghost."[2] Every western virtue terrified him. "Honour, what is that," he cried? "Out-of-date word, which henceforth must be left to Occidentals."[3]

In his eyes, destruction justified everything because it unlocked the door which led to the road back to Seljuk, Tartar and Hun. "Seriously," he said, "it would be good for humanity were all books burnt, so that we could bathe in the fresh spring of ignorance. I even think that it is the sole means of preventing humankind becoming sterile." What he yearned for was a return to the days of Ivan the Terrible; "then Moscow will become the centre of the world of barbarians." "Had Nicholas II but followed in the footsteps of Peter the Great and Catherine II, how docile the Russians would have been, for they love a despot." "If Lenin is able to disencumber Russia from the old scrap iron of prejudices and de-westernize her, I will follow him. But he must raze all to the ground, and deliberately hurl us back into barbarism."[4]

In 1937 Stalin shot him, and in goodly company; for with Uborevitch, Primokov, Putna and others he returned to his god Annihilation.

This strange volcanic man, whose soul was in revolt with civilization, was destined to cross swords with Pilsudski, who was as violently anti-Russian as he was violently anti-European. Of the latter, Lord D'Abernon, who had exceptional opportunities to watch him, says: "An ardent patriot and a man of immense courage and force of character. A pronounced sceptic about

[1] *Ibid.*, pp. 73–75.   [2] *Ibid.*, p. 20.   [3] *Ibid.*, p. 111.   [4] *Ibid.*, p. 62.

orthodox methods, whether applied to military affairs or politics; he loves danger, his pulse only beating at a normal rate when he is in imminent personal peril. . . . Next to danger, he is said to love intrigue – a revolutionary by temperament and circumstances, his ingrained proclivity is to the secret and indirect."[1]

It was these characteristics – courage, unorthodoxy, and secrecy – coupled with success, which made Pilsudski a legendary figure. The day before his death, on May 12, 1935, he turned to General Smigly-Rydz and said to him: "To be vanquished and not surrender is victory, to vanquish and rest on laurels is defeat."[2] The first half of this saying sums up his generalship.

Before we describe the campaign which immediately followed the signing of the Treaty of Warsaw, it is as well to look at the opposing forces. Both were improvised, chaotically equipped and suffered from over-rapid growth. In November, 1918, when Pilsudski assumed command, the Polish army consisted of 24 battalions, three squadrons and five batteries; yet by January, 1919, these had respectively been raised to 100, 70, and 80, in all comprising some 110,000 men. A year later this figure had risen to 600,000 men, organized in 21 divisions and seven brigades of cavalry; but most were still in formation. Though manpower was sufficient, Poland possessed no arsenals and lacked munitions. A greater difficulty was an adequate supply of horses, because during six years of war the country had been searched repeatedly for remounts, and, as will shortly be seen, deficiency in the cavalry arm was Pilsudski's greatest weakness.

What of his opponent's army? Tukhachevski once said to Fervacque: "The Russian Army is not like yours – the French. It is a horde, and its strength is that of a horde."[3] Though these words were spoken during the World War, they are equally applicable to the campaign of 1920, because the army which faced Pilsudski was nothing more than a horde of peasants – whose sole idea was to get home[4] – leavened with a comparatively small number of fanatical revolutionaries. Though it was better equipped than the Poles – the rounding up of Denekin's and Kolchak's forces had supplied it with millions of pounds worth of French and British armaments – it was lamentably short of military

---

[1] *The Eighteenth Decisive Battle of the World*, Viscount D'Abernon (1920), pp. 38–39.
[2] Quoted from *Pilsudski Marshal of Poland*, Eric J. Patterson (1935), p. 127.
[3] *Le chef de l'armée rouge*, p. 36.
[4] See *The Eighteenth Decisive Battle of the World*, D'Abernon, p. 77.

transport and trained officers. The former consisted of thousands of peasants' carts, and the deficiency in the latter was made good by commissioning hundreds of officers of the old Imperial Army. But as their loyalty was suspect, Trotsky attached commissars to each formation. Most of these men were Jews, and, according to Lord D'Abernon, "they did everything in their divisions – commandeered food – gave orders—explained objectives."[1]

Both Poles and Russians desperately wanted peace, yet only on their own terms, which were: for the former, the old frontier of 1772; for the latter, the continuance of world revolution. So it came about that, when on December 22, 1920, the Soviet Government invited the Polish Government to negotiate a peace, though the proposal was accepted, nothing came of it.

At length, on April 25, diplomatic fencing was brought to an end by a sudden offensive launched by Pilsudski west of Zhitomir. His aim was to seize Kiev, and then to turn northward against Tukhachevski, who faced his left wing. Led by Pilsudski the Polish army, supported on its right by two divisions of Ukrainians under the Hetman Petliura, as well as by some Rumanians, swept towards the Dnieper, and, on May 7, occupied Kiev.

The forces faced each other as follows:

Russian: North of the Pripet, the Army of the West, under Tukhachevski, consisted of the Fourth, Fifteenth, Third and Sixteenth Armies, and the IIIrd Cavalry Corps (Gay Khan); and south of the Pripet the Army of the South-West, commanded by Yegorov, comprised the Twelfth and Fourteenth Armies, and five divisions of cavalry under Budienny. In all – possibly – 200,000 men.

Polish: North of the Pripet, the First and Fourth Armies, with a Reserve Army in rear near Vilna in process of formation; and south of the Pripet, the Third, Second and Sixth Armies. In all, some 120,000 men.[2]

Though the Russian numerical superiority was important, more especially as the bulk of it was opposed to the far weaker Polish left flank, what was more important was that the area between the Bug and the Dnieper was cut in half by the swamps of Polesia, a dead-level country practically impassable by large bodies of troops. This meant that a general action on the whole

---

[1] *Ibid.*, pp. 68, 76.
[2] Correct strengths for both sides are impossible to give. Throughout the campaign they changed constantly.

front of the two armies would at once develop into two separate actions which could not cooperate. When Comrade Sergei Kamenev, the commander-in-chief of all the Soviet armed forces,

17. POLISH-SOVIET CAMPAIGN, 1920

realized this, he ordered Tukhachevski to attack the Polish left wing. This he was eager to do, for frantic with revolution he dreamt of watering his horses on the Rhine[1] and of carrying the

[1] *Le chef de l'armée rouge*, Fervacque, p. 123.

war over the corpse of Poland into western Europe. At this time, Trotsky referred to Pilsudski as "a third rate Buonaparte", and, on May 2, he made the following forecast:

"There can be no doubt that the war of the Polish bourgeoisie against the Ukrainain and Russian workers and peasants will end with a workers' revolution in Poland. It would be a pitiful lack of spirit to be frightened at the first successes of Pilsudski. They are unavoidable. They were foreseen. They were a result of the earlier development of our relations with Poland. The deeper the right wing of the Polish troops penetrates into Ukrainia, turning against itself Ukrainian insurgents of all kinds, the more fatal for the Polish troops will be the concentrated blow which the Red troops will give them."[1]

Strategically this was correct, and when, on May 15, Tukhachevski selected as his objective the railway junction of Molodechno, and launched his Fifteenth Army against it, his aim was to drive it into the Pinsk swamps. Though the attack failed, it shook Pilsudski; but before he could reinforce his left wing, a formidable attack was launched against him in the south. There Budienny, who had served in the ranks during the Russo-Japanese War, at the head of 16,700 Cossacks, accompanied by 48 cannon, five armoured trains, eight armoured cars and 12 aeroplanes, struck at Pilsudski's right wing in the neighbourhood of Elizavetgrad on May 18. Next, he moved northward; attacked the Polish forces south and south-west of Kiev; broke through near Gaisin; raided west of Kiev; and swept into Berdichev and Zhitomir. On June 5 the Polish Third Army was nearly surrounded, but on the 13th it broke away and retired westward while Budienny's horsemen swept onward, crossed the Horyn on July 3, and two days later occupied Rovno. From there they pressed forward to Lutzk, Dubno, and the outskirts of Lvov (Lemberg).

As Pilsudski informs us, panic followed, and "the work of the State itself began to crack." He writes: "For our troops who were not prepared to meet this new offensive instrument, Budienny's cavalry became an invincible, legendary force. And it should be remembered that the farther in rear one goes, the more does such an obsession escape all reason – to become all-powerful and irresistible. Thus for me began to be created that most dangerous of all fronts – the inner one."[2] At the time, all he could do to meet

[1] *History of the Russian Revolution*, Trotsky (1932–35), vol. III, book 2, p. 102.
[2] *L'Année 1920*, Joseph Pilsudski (1929), p. 51.

this critical development was to save his left wing, the right flank of which had been turned by the defeat of his right wing; he therefore ordered its withdrawal.

When Pilsudski's left was in retreat, Tukhachevski set about to reorganize his chaotic army. During June he collected and incorporated nearly 100,000 deserters,[1] and though he complained bitterly of lack of equipment, the idea upon which he based his forthcoming attack was political rather than military. He considered that "the situation in Poland was favourable to revolution," and that a powerful rising of the city proletariat and peasants only awaited his arrival "on the ethnographical frontier of Poland." Further, he thought that Europe was ripe for revolution and that "a rapid and victorious offensive would hypnotize the peoples and draw them eastward." He arrived at these conclusions from exaggerated accounts of the conditions then prevalent: in Germany, where the people only awaited "the signal of revolt"; in England, where the situation resembled that in Russia in 1904; and in Italy, where the workers had occupied the factories and industrial establishments. He launched an advanced guard of propagandists to blaze a trail for his horde.[2] On this strategy, Lord D'Abernon writes:

"Moscow disposed of a host of spies, propagandists, secret emissaries and secret friends, who penetrated into Polish territory and undermined the resistance of certain elements of the Polish population . . . the services rendered by the unarmed were not less effective than those brought about by military pressure. The system adopted was to avoid frontal attack whenever possible, and to turn positions by flank marches, infiltration and propaganda."[3]

Though a cunning general, as an administrator Tukhachevski was, like most Russians, hopelessly inefficient. A Tartar at heart, he intended to live on the land and his system of supply closely resembled that of Attila or Genghis Khan. Fervacque probably exaggerates when he says that his 200,000 warriors were followed by a horde of 800,000 politicians, police, and pillagers, whose duty it was to bolshevize the conquered territories, by laying low the

[1] *Ibid.*, Annexe 1, "La marche au dela de la Vistula," M. Tukhachevski, p. 215.
[2] *Ibid.*, pp. 231–232.
[3] *The Eighteenth Decisive Battle of the World*, p. 28. This propaganda cut both ways. Chamberlin points out its discouraging effect on the Red soldiers, when on reaching the outskirts of Warsaw they "learned that there were some workers among the volunteers who were increasing the numbers of the Polish forces against them" (*The Russian Revolution* (1935), vol. II, p. 317).

wealthy and shooting the bourgeois and aristocrats.[1] Yet his exaggeration is not so great as it appears, because Tukhachevski tells us that his Fourth, Fifteenth, Third, and Sixteenth Armies were followed by 33,000 farm carts, and somewhat ironically adds: "It was a heavy burden for the local inhabitants."[2] This number of carts, at six men a cart approximately adds up to 200,000, and while these men devastated the Soviet rear, propaganda cleared the way on the Soviet front.

What the opposing strengths were at the end of June is problematical. The Polish armies would appear to have numbered approximately 120,000 men and the Soviet 200,000. Tukhachevski gives the figure of 150,188, made up of 80,942 rifles, 10,521 sabres, and 68,715 oddments;[3] and Pilsudski states that the total number placed under Tukhachevski's orders was 794,645 men and 150,572 horses, of which figure fighters numbered 200,000.[4] Whichever figures are correct, the Soviet forces constituted a magazine-rifle horde.

When the way had been cleared by propaganda, Tukhachevski launched his four armies into attack between the rivers Dvina and Pripet at dawn on July 4; the axis of their advance was the Smolensk–Brest-Litovsk railway. It was met by a stout resistance by the First and Fourth Polish armies, but confronted by a four to one superiority they were forced back. No attempt had been made to entrench,[5] because Pilsudski realized the uselessness of field works when fronts are long and forces are in comparison small. Besides, trenches could always be turned by the enemy's cavalry.

On July 7 the whole Polish front was in full retreat. On the 11th, a battle for Vilna opened. Vilna fell to the Soviet Fourth Army on the 14th, and the Polish situation became still more critical when the Lithuanian Army joined the Bolsheviks. By now, writes Pilsudski, Tukhachevski's continuous advance produced "the impression of something irresistible, a monstrous and heavy cloud which no obstacle could halt. . . . Under the threat of this cloud, munitioned with hail, the State settled down to sink; men trembled, and the hearts of our soldiers began to yield."[6] Everywhere around him he felt despair and impotence grow; the complete dissolution of Poland seemed imminent.

---

[1] *Le chef de l'armée rouge*, p. 124.
[2] *L'Année 1920*, Annexe 1, p. 218.   [3] *Ibid.*, p. 217.
[4] *Ibid.*, p. 16, quoting Froloff's *Approvisionnement de l'armée rouge sur le front occidental* (in Russian).
[5] *Ibid.*, p. 78, 84.   [6] *Ibid.*, pp. 113–114.

While Pilsudski clutched his retreating armies together, Tukhachevski moved on. On July 18 the latter ordered his Fourth Army to force the Niemen south of Grodno on the 21st; the Fifteenth to cross it on the 22nd; and the Third and Sixteenth to force the Shara river, north and south of Slonim. But the advance moved more rapidly than his orders; on the 19th Gay Khan and his horseman occupied Grodno and on the 21st Tukhachevski sent the following message to Moscow:

"Grodno was occupied on the 19th and Slonim yesterday. These two successes are witness to the fact that the line of the Niemen and Shara are forced and that the retreating enemy possesses no further positions upon which he can hope to hold us. We can now expect to complete our task in three weeks time."[1]

Kamenev was so thrilled by this that he imagined the Poles beaten beyond redemption and suggested the withdrawal of one of Tukhachevski's four armies in order to build up a reserve.

While north of the Pripet the Poles fell back, south of it the Polish Third Army, under General Smigly-Rydz, was so harassed by Budienny's Cossacks that it rapidly lost both energy and fighting spirit. Pilsudski says: "In the south the cavalry of Budienny were the motor of the war."[2]

When Grodno fell, Tukhachevski ordered Warsaw to be occupied on August 12. The reason he gives why he did not halt and reorganize his rear services and wait for 60,000 reinforcements to catch up with him is that, as his enemy was in rout, all that was necessary was to push on with the utmost energy.[3] This he did, while Pilsudski planned to hold the line of the Bug and counterattack Tukhachevski's left flank. But, on July 22 and 23, this line fell as well as that of the Niemen, and, on August 1, the Poles were driven out of Brest-Litovsk. Pilsudski's position was desperate, and because the Polesian swamps had been turned he expected that the two Soviet armies – Tukhachevski's and Yegorov's – would unite and crush his demoralized forces. Fortunately the situation was not so bad as it appeared, for Wrangel had emerged from his lair in the Crimea and so threatened Yegorov's rear that Tukhachevski agreed to detach part of the Twelfth Army[4] to help him. Although this did not relieve the immediate Polish situation, in the middle of August it had an important influence upon operations.

[1] *Ibid.*, Notes, p. 286.
[2] *Ibid.*, p. 120.
[3] *Ibid.*, Annexe I, p. 234.
[4] *Ibid.*, Notes, pp. 298–299.

On August 2 Pilsudski entered Warsaw to learn that the Narew was in his enemy's hands. On the following day Lomza was lost and the whole of the Polish First Army fell back on the capital. Annihilation seemed imminent; yet again the situation was not without hope, for the rapidity of the Bolshevik advance, nearly 300 miles in 30 days, had so disordered Tukhachevski's supply system that it was near dissolution. The situation was such that Tukhachevski could neither stand still nor retire; to halt and reorganize was out of the question for it would mean starvation. All he could do was to push on.

Further, the political situation favoured a continuation of the attack. In Austria, Czechoslovakia, and Germany the workers refused to allow munitions to pass through their countries to Poland. "On August 6 the British Labour Party published a pamphlet which stated that the workers of Great Britain would take no part in the war as allies of Poland." In Paris the French Socialists, through their organ L'Humanité, spoke of a "war against the Soviet Republic by the Polish Government on the orders of Anglo-French Imperialism, and cried 'Not a man, not a sou, not a shell for reactionary and capitalist Poland. Long live the Russian Revolution. Long live the Workman's International' ";[1] while in Danzig the dockers refused to unload munitions. Of all European peoples the Hungarians alone were friendly to the Poles, because under the hideous régime of Bela Kun they had tasted the fruits of the Bolshevik revolution.[2]

This dark political background to the Polish retreat of 375 miles convinced both Great Britain and France of the imminence of a Soviet victory—"Nothing could appear more certain than that the Soviet forces would capture Warsaw."[3] As early as July 12 this spirit of defeatism had already gripped the British Government. On that day, Lord Curzon, British Foreign Minister, who believed in the heresy that peace with Bolsheviks was possible, addressed a note to the Soviet Government, not only to propose a truce, but also that the frontier between Poland and Russia should be the line of the Bug. Five days later Chicherin suggested a conference, and, on August 10, Mr. Lloyd George in the House

[1] The Poland of Pilsudski, Robert Machray, pp. 112–113.
[2] On May 27, 1919, Lenin had written to the Hungarian Communists as follows: "Be firm. If there are waverings among the Socialists who came over to you yesterday, or among the petty bourgeoisie, in regard to the dictatorship of the proletariat, suppress the waverings mercilessly. Shooting is the proper fate of a coward in war" (Collected Works, Lenin, vol. XVI, p. 229).
[3] The Eighteenth Decisive Battle of the World, D'Abernon, p. 15.

of Commons advised Poland to accept the Bolshevik peace terms. These included among other things that the Polish army should be limited to 60,000 men supported by an armed militia of urban industrial workers "under the control of the labour organization of Russia, Poland, and Norway."[1]

As this meant the complete Bolshevization of Poland they were ‚ejected by Pilsudski who, as will be seen, four days before Mr. Lloyd George gave his fearful advice, when in the solitude of the Belvedere Palace an idea flashed into his mind which was to change the whole course of the war.

Meanwhile, the Bolshevik typhoon swept westward, and as something immediate had to be done by Great Britain and France, they decided to send a Mission to Warsaw. Lord D'Abernon, British Ambassador in Berlin, was instructed to proceed to Paris, where he was to be joined by General Weygand and others, and then hasten to Warsaw. When the Mission arrived there on July 25 it found that Pilsudski wanted shells, not advice.

To return to the war. On his arrival in Warsaw Pilsudski was confronted by the following situation. The bridgehead was well entrenched and wired, and was defended by 43 batteries of heavy guns. Further, it was flanked by the strong places of Deblin (Ivangorod) in the south and of Modlin (Novo-Georgievsk) to the north, as well as Plock, on the Vistula, further westward. Satisfied that the position was strong, he left it as it was, avoided the diplomatists, now busy considering the Soviet peace terms, and like Joffre before the battle of the Marne, he demoted many of his subordinates, placed General Haller in command of Warsaw, and raised a new Army, the Fifth, under General Sikorski.

The situation on the 200-mile battle front was: The Polish army was distributed in two groups – one around Warsaw and the other around Lvov – linked together by a weak centre. The northern group consisted of the Fifth Army (34,000), First Army (38,000), and Second Army (12,000), and the Fourth Army (23,500) – still falling back from the river Bug. The southern group consisted of the Sixth Army (22,000) about Lvov, with the Seventh Army, Ukrainians and Rumanians (24,000), to its south, and it was linked to the northern group by the Third Army (25,000). From

[1] *The Russian Revolution, 1917–1921*, William Henry Chamberlin (1935), vol. II, p. 208. See also *The Soviets in World Affairs*, Louis Fischer (1930), p. 267, and *The Eighteenth Decisive Battle of the World*, pp. 70–71.

north to south, in face of this long line stretched the Army of the West under Tukhachevski and the Army of the South-West under Yegorov. The former consisted of the Fourth Army (28,000), supported by Gay Khan's IIIrd Cavalry Corps (4,700), the Fifteenth Army (26,000), Third Army (20,000), Sixteenth Army (20,700), and the Mozyr Group (8,000); and the latter of the Twelfth Army (22,500), Fourteenth Army (18,000), and Budienny's First Cavalry Army (30,000). In all, 178,500 Poles and Ukrainians faced 177,900 Bolsheviks.

As the bulk of both armies was in the neighbourhood of Warsaw, Weygand's advice to Pilsudski was to defend the line of the Vistula – while a deliberate counter-offensive was prepared behind that river. In this he was supported by many of the Polish generals, who favoured a counter-attack based on Modlin with its right hinged on the Vistula. Their idea was to smash the Soviet right and drive it south of the river Bug and cut it off from the Warsaw–Bialystok railway.

While Weygand and the Polish generals talked, Pilsudski listened. He neither agreed nor disagreed, and seemingly their discussions left his mind blank. Then, on the night of August 5–6, he retired to his study in the Belvedere Palace, and his account of this inner struggle is so self-revealing that we will quote it in full.

"There is on record," he writes, "an admirable expression made by the greatest authority on the human soul in war time – Napoleon – who said of himself that, while about to take an important decision, he was like a girl on the point of giving birth to a child. Since that night I have often been reminded of the profound subtlety of this thought. He, who despised the weakness of the fair sex, compares himself, a giant in will and genius, to a frail young woman on her bed, a prey to the pains of labour. He used to say to himself that in those moments he was pusillanimous. I, myself, a prey to the same pusillanimity, could not overcome the absurdity of the problem of this battle, which condemned the bulk of the forces gathered at Warsaw to passive resistance. In my opinion, the counter-attack could not be launched from Warsaw nor from Modlin. This would mean a frontal attack against the main forces of the enemy, which, as I believed, were concentrated before Warsaw, and up to that time neither our forces nor our command had been able to hold the victorious enemy. Besides, the nightmare of defeat and the excuses of poltroons were sweeping over the whole town."

Pilsudski's meditations brought him to realize that to hold Warsaw was not enough, and if only to reinstate the morale of his army an offensive was imperative. But where was he to obtain the necessary troops for a counter-attack? – this was the question which perplexed him. Were he to withdraw them from either wing, the civil population of Warsaw or Lvov would almost certainly fall into a panic which might spread to his troops. He turned to his reports and his map, and was struck by the slow retreat of the Fourth Army. "The natural direction in which the enemy was pushing it," he writes, "was bringing it onto the Vistula between Warsaw and Deblin. Now, in that direction, there were neither bridges nor any other means of crossing. In the event of the enemy pushing vigorously in the centre, this army might be driven into a corner on the Vistula and find itself in an extremely critical position. It was, therefore, necessary to incline it either towards Warsaw or Deblin, or divide it into two sections, one diverted to the north and the other to the south."[1]

At length he made up his mind; he decided to order the bulk of the Fourth Army to fall back on Deblin, and as Budienny's cavalry had been driven back, at the same time to withdraw two divisions – the 1st and 3rd of the Legion – from the southern wing to Deblin. This he decided in spite of the risk that should Budienny learn of this he would again advance. Lastly, because the success of the counter-attack was so doubtful, he decided to command it in person.

When we look at the situation as it faced him, it will be seen that his basic idea was to take advantage of the separation of his enemy's forces: Tukhachevski's army was massed about Warsaw, and Yegorov's and Budienny's cavalry were in the vicinity of Lvov. The entire enemy front ran diagonally from north-west to south-east, the two armies were linked together by a weak centre about Lublin near the river Wieprz. Could the enemy about Warsaw and Lvov be held back, Pilsudski was convinced that, were he to interpose his counter-attack force south of the Wieprz between Deblin and Lublin – that is, at a right angle to the enemy's weak centre – he might well be able to attack Tukhachevski's Sixteenth Army in rear and simultaneously prevent that army penetrating his own weak centre between Warsaw and Deblin. Further, he knew that the Mozyr Group, which lay between the

[1] *L'Année 1920*, pp. 136–141.

Soviet Sixteenth and Twelfth Armies, was too weak and over-extended to offer much resistance; therefore, as he writes: "It was on that base [*i.e.*, the Wieprz] upon which the order of August 6, regulating the strategical distribution of the troops for the battle of Warsaw, was directed,"[1] and this in spite of the fact that on that day and the day following the three divisions (14th, 16th, and 21st) of the Fourth Army were still engaged. Also, not only did he realize that the withdrawal of the Fourth Army would entail a flank march in face of the enemy, but that the withdrawal of the 1st and 3rd Divisions of the Legion would open the door to Budienny.[2]

Could he carry out this counter-attack with extreme rapidity, and it must be remembered that he had little cavalry, then it was possible, once the Mozyr Group was dispersed, to fall on the rear of the Soviet Sixteenth Army, which he knew was already in a state of dislocation because of the ever-growing confusion in Tukhachevski's supply system.[3] To accentuate that confusion was the moral arrow he intended to fire from his strategic bow – the Wieprz. If it struck home, the rear of the Soviet Sixteenth Army would recoil on the rear of the Third, Fifteenth and Fourth Armies around Warsaw, and with their supply paralysed his own armies at Warsaw – the First and Fifth – would be able to advance to the counter-attack. In brief, his grand idea was to counter-attack with the bulk of his forces – a physical counter-attack detonated by the moral counter-attack of his Fourth Army. General Camon says that, taken as a whole, the manœuvre was Napoleonic, because it favoured a rear attack. It would be more apt to call it Alexandrian, because it more closely resembles the field strategy employed at the battle of Arbela. There, it will be remembered, the great Macedonian held his enemy's right, charged through the Persian weak left centre, and attacked the Persian right in rear, and this is what Pilsudski intended to do.

Once Pilsudski had formulated his plan, it was severely criticized by his generals and his general staff. His boldness winded them, for like mice they were hypnotized by the cat-like Tukhachevski, and instead of urging their chief to strengthen his counter-attacking forces, they could think of nothing better than

[1] *Ibid.*, p. 142.   [2] *Ibid.*, p. 146.
[3] For the state of Tukhachevski's army at this time, see Camon's *La Manoeuvre Liberatrice* (1929), p. 109.

to supplicate him to strengthen Warsaw.[1] Pilsudski held firm to his idea, and on August 6 the order for the assembly was issued.[2] He settled on August 17 as the day for his counter-attack, and on the 12th he left Warsaw for Deblin.

What was Tukhachevski's plan?

He was well aware that Lenin[3] attached the highest importance to the fall of Warsaw, and now that he stood before its gates, what course should he take? In reply he says that lack of troops prevented him from delivering a central attack or simultaneously attacking both his enemy's flanks, and that he was forced to choose between either a right or a left flank attack. To attack the Polish right would, so he says, have required a complicated regrouping of his army and the changing of its line of communications which ran through Kleshcheli (Kleszczele) and Brest-Litovsk. He decided to turn the Polish left and cut its communications with Danzig, and this in spite of the fact that he recognized that the outflanking army would have its back to East Prussia, which would place it at a disadvantage should the operation fail. He expected his left wing to be covered by Yegorov's army.

On August 8 he issued his instructions for an attack on the 14th. They were to be carried out as follows:

The Fourth Army to move north of Warsaw; to cover itself from the direction of Thorn, and force the Vistula at Plock. The Fifteenth Army to move on Plonsk; the Third on Wyszograd–Modlin; the Sixteenth on Nowo-Minsk–Garwolin and to force the Vistula south of Warsaw while the Mozyr Group forced the river in the neighbourhood of Deblin. He ended his project by saying: "Because of the high morale of our troops, we had the absolute right to count upon victory."[4] He said this although a copy of Pilsudski's order of August 6 had fallen into his hands; but fortunately for his enemy he believed it to be a bluff.

When we examine these instructions, it will at once be seen

[1] See Sikorski's *La campagne Polono-Russe de 1920*, pp. 70–77. Commenting on this, General Camon writes: "In the Polish G.H.Q., like the German in 1914, and also in other G.H.Qs. of the same period, the Operations Branch considered itself superior to the General-in-Chief – after all only an amateur – and G.H.Q. again and again returned to the idea of halting the Bolshevik advance by a counter-attack launched from the left flank of the front" (*La Manoeuvre Liberatrice*, p. 31), which was also General Weygand's idea.

[2] See *La Campagne Polono-Russe de 1920*, Sikorski (1929), pp. 53–56, and *La Manoeuvre Liberatrice*, Camon, pp. 34–41.

[3] In his *Collected Works*, vol. xvii, p. 308, we read: "All Germany boiled up when our troops approached Warsaw."

[4] *L'Année 1920*, Annexe I, pp. 244–245.

that they entail a general advance of the bulk of the Soviet forces directed north of Warsaw. The weakness of this attack did not lie in lack of numbers, but in lack of unity of command. Kamenev was in Moscow, Tukhachevski remained in Minsk, and Yegorov was in the neighbourhood of Lvov – over 200 miles distant from him. Worse still, he and Yegorov were at daggers drawn.

On August 10 Kamenev sent Yegorov an order to transfer Budienny and his cavalry to Tukhachevski's command, but as his message could not be deciphered, there was a three-day delay before it was re-transmitted. Then, on the 13th, when it became understandable, Yegorov started to argue. He was not interested in the Warsaw operations, and was intent upon taking Lvov, Przemysl and Sambor, and once he had forced the Dniester, to carry the war into Rumania. The result was that Kamenev's order was set aside and Budienny marched on Lvov as formerly had done the Tartar horde of Chmielnicki.

Meanwhile, what of Pilsudski? He tells us that August 6 to 12 were days of great anxiety while he watched his enemy creep round his left flank. On the 11th Tukhachevski launched an attack on Pultusk, garrisoned, as Sikorski informs us, by worn-out troops who looked like "living corpses" in rags and with naked feet.[1] This old fortress blocked the crossing of the Narew, and when, as they did, the Bolsheviks carried it, the sole remaining line of defence between it and the Vistula was the Wkra river, which joins the Bug near Modlin. The loss of Pultusk was in part compensated by General Smigly-Rydz's skilful withdrawal of the 1st and 3rd Divisions of the Legion from the Bug. Next, on the 13th, Tukhachevski's final orders for a general attack on the following day, sent out in clear by wireless, were intercepted, and the foreign diplomatists hastily retired from Warsaw to Lodz.

As we have seen, Tukhachevski's plan was to turn Warsaw from the north and, once its communications were cut, to fall upon its rear. On the 13th his Sixteenth Army advanced on the southern flank of the city, and his Third Army on its northern flank, while his Fifteenth Army moved on the Wkra, its centre on Nasielsk, and his Fourth swung round its right flank on to Plock. That day the Third Army launched an attack on the outer defences of Warsaw, which ran through Radzymin. These were held by the First Polish Army, while the Fifth, under Sikorski, occupied the line of the Wkra.

[1] *La Campagne Polono-Russe de 1920*, Sikorski, p. 79.

Pilsudski, accompanied by five staff officers, established his G.H.Q. at Pulawy, a little to the south of Deblin, and on this day – August 13 – he visited the units of his Fourth Army, to be in no way encouraged by what he saw. The troops were so ill-equipped that, as he says, "Throughout the entire campaign I had as yet never seen such ragamuffins."[1] He visited unit after unit, spoke to the men, and did all he could to raise their confidence and morale.

On August 14, Radzymin was lost by the Poles; this brought the Bolsheviks to within 15 miles of Warsaw. Simultaneously a fierce attack was launched against Sikorski on the Wkra and the situation became so critical that General Haller urged Pilsudski to start his counter-attack a day earlier than the date fixed. He agreed to do so, although another 24 hours would have been invaluable to him.

On August 15 the battle of the Wkra continued and a group of eight Polish armoured cars operated with signal effect in the area Raciaz–Drobin–Bielsk. Sikorski says: "With great skill they insinuated themselves in between the enemy units, attacked outposts and destroyed supply columns and communications, and rendered the highest service. They doubled their strength by their mobility; sowed confusion in the rear of the Russian divisions, and produced the impression that they were preparing the way for a formidable offensive."[2] The next day violent Bolshevik assaults were beaten back at Nasielsk; but under cover of these attacks Tukhachevski's Fourth Army wheeled round southward on to Plock, Wloclawek, Bobrowniki, and Nieszawa, all on the Vistula; the last-mentioned town was some 18 miles south-east of Thorn. The Polish situation grew worse and worse, for although the First Army held firm to Warsaw, Sikorski's left was turned, and in the vicinity of Plonsk a strong attack developed in his rear. Then from the Wieprz came salvation. That morning Pilsudski launched his counter-attack and during the next few days it was to advance to a depth of 150 miles.

On the Day of the Virgin, August 16, 1920, the Rubicon of Poland – the river Wieprz – was crossed, and the Polish Fourth Army was given as its objective the Warsaw–Brest-Litovsk road. Unlike Tukhachevski, who during his attack had remained at Minsk, Pilsudski passed the whole of this day in his motor-car and went from flank to flank to encourage his men and rapidly

[1] *L'Année 1920*, p. 147.   [2] *La Campagne Polono-Russe de 1920*, p. 181.

to estimate the situation. What astonished him most was the total absence of enemy forces. On the left Garwolin was occupied and passed without opposition; therefore for the 17th Pilsudski decided to swing forward the right wing of the counter-attack "and search for traces of the phantom enemy and for any signs of a trap." Again on the 17th he toured round his rapidly advancing front.

At the important railway station of Lukow, on the Brest-Litovsk line, he lunched with the headquarters staff of the 21st Division. Everyone affirmed "that there was no enemy in strength, and told him with enthusiasm that the whole of the civil population had risen in assistance, with the result that the few hostile groups met with were attacked by peasants armed with pitchforks accompanied by their wives carrying flails."[1] Of this day Pilsudski writes:

"Was I dreaming? But a few days back a veritable nightmare had obsessed me: a continuous movement of irresistible power, a movement in which I felt monstrous claws twining round my throat and suffocating me. Was it really true that my five divisions, freely and without any show of resistance, were boldly advancing over those self-same regions which but recently in the mortal agony of the retreat they had abandoned to the enemy? In spite of the joy of this dream, it seemed impossible that it could be real. A whole month of suggestions, suggestions of the superiority of the enemy refused to vanish. This happy dream could not be true. Thus I felt as I arrived that evening at Garwolin."[2]

A few hours later, as he sat by his bed drinking a cup of tea, away to the north he heard the distant thunder of cannon. "Then there was an enemy! It was not an illusion!" he exclaimed. "The shame which I had felt for the shock and my former terror, when engulfed in that monstrous nightmare which had all but conquered me by its savage illusive images, was not the dreamings of a madman and had been real. The enemy did exist, and the proof was the music of battle which rolled toward me from out the north."[3]

The next morning the cannonade had ceased, and although the countryside swarmed with Red Cossacks, again he set out in his car and drove to Kolbiel in order to catch up with the rear of his 14th Division, which had taken the town during the night and was then well on its way toward Nowo-Minsk. When he arrived there he found that the entire Soviet Sixteenth Army was in rout,

[1] *L'Année 1920*, p. 152.   [2] *Ibid.*, p. 152.   [3] *Ibid.*, pp. 152–153.

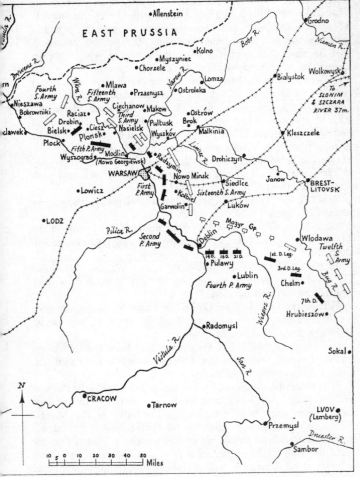

18 . BATTLE OF WARSAW, AUGUST 16-25, 1920

so he ordered his driver to head for Warsaw, to co-ordinate the advance of the First and Fifth Armies with the counter-attack. This was unfortunate, as he acknowledges, for once his powerful presence was not felt on the battlefield, the pursuit slackened, with the result that much of August 18 was wasted. Also he blames himself for not having assumed the direct command of the First and Fifth Armies, for had he done so he would have been better placed to impose his will on their commanders, who were still gripped by the terror which had so long obsessed them. He writes: "There everyone seized upon the most minute manifestation of activity on the part of the enemy in order still to believe in the possibility of disaster instead of believing in victory."[1]

On August 18 he issued the following orders:

Third Army: To hold fast to the area Lublin–Chelm and push back all fractions of the Twelfth Soviet Army met with.

Second Army: To occupy Brest-Litovsk and pursue the enemy toward Bialystok.

Fourth Army: To advance by forced marches northward to the Malkinia–Bialystok railway; to occupy Brok and Wyzskov, and to push the enemy toward the German frontier.

First Army: To advance north-east, axis on Warsaw–Wyzskov–Ostrow–Lomza, with its cavalry on the left front, and to work toward the German frontier.

Fifth Army: To annihilate Gay Khan's Cavalry Corps; advance on Mlawa-Przasnysz and cut off all fractions of the Soviet Fifteenth Army west of those towns.

Unfortunately the Polish First Army had been too split up to enable it to carry out its orders. This prevented the total annihilation of Tukhachevski's forces.

When Pilsudski launched his counter-attack, Tukhachevski was still at Minsk, 300 miles from Warsaw, and twice the distance Moltke had been from Paris during the battle of the Marne. There he would seem to have lost all contact, not only with his enemy, but with his own armies; and he tells us that it was not until the 18th that he received a telephone call from the Commander of his Sixteenth Army to inform him that an attack had been launched. He was then told that the attack by the "White Poles need not be taken seriously."[2] Tukhachevski was too good a general to view the situation in this light and at once issued the following orders:

[1] *Ibid.*, pp. 165–166.   [2] *Ibid.*, Annexe 1, pp. 250–251.

The Fourth Army was forthwith to fall back and concentrate in the area Ciechanow–Przasnysz–Makow, and *en route* help the withdrawal of the Fifteenth Army. The Fifteenth was to hold back the enemy and assist the concentration of the Fourth; while the Sixteenth withdrew behind the Liwiec river, protected by the Mozyr Group on its left flank. The Twelfth Army was ordered to halt the enemy who had crossed the Wieprz by attacking him in flank. Lastly, the Third and Sixteenth Armies were each instructed to send a division to Drohiczyn and Janow to form a reserve for the whole front.[2]

Tukhachevski informs us that he had foreseen the necessity for a general retirement to the line Grodno–Brest-Litovsk; but this may be discounted as an afterthought, for the truth is that, apparently unknown to him half his army was already in rout, while the remaining half – the Fourth Army and most of the Fifteenth – was so trapped that his orders to them were inoperative. As it happened, those dispatched to the Fourth Army were long delayed in transmission, and when they were received, because its commander had been told nothing of the general situation and considered it favourable, he set his instructions aside and continued to cross the Vistula in order to attack Warsaw in rear.

By August 21 the rout of Tukhachevski's right wing was complete. First, the Soviet Sixteenth Army, then the Third, and lastly the Fifteenth had been struck in flank more by terror than by fighting. As they broke eastward in panic, the whole countryside became the scene of pandemonium; units, fractions of units and innumerable stragglers, mixed pell-mell with thousands of supply carts, swept toward the Niemen; while Pilsudski's bare-footed and tattered men pressed the pursuit mile after mile without firing a shot.

To the north and north-west of Warsaw, the right of the Soviet Fifteenth Army put up a desperate fight at Ciechanow; but driven out of it on August 19, and out of Mlawa on the 20th, it carried away with it in its flight the supply train of the Fourth Army, which faced the crossings of the Vistula at Wloclawek and Plock.

The sole Soviet force which distinguished itself in the disaster was Gay Khan's Cavalry Corps. On the 20th he fell back on Mlawa, launched a night attack on Konopki and cut up a Polish battalion, and then was pursued eastward to Chorzele, where he

[2] *Ibid.*, Annexe I, pp. 251–252.

cut his way through two regiments at Myszyniec. Next, he headed for Kolno, where he came up against the Polish Fourth Army, which a few hours earlier had occupied it. Although greatly outnumbered and short of ammunition he again attacked and, on August 25 was driven pell-mell over the German frontier, as was the Soviet Fourth Army.

Eventually, on August 25, the remnants of the Soviet Army of the West reached the line Grodno–east of Brest-Litovsk–Wlodawa, where the pursuit ended. The booty taken was immense: 66,000 prisoners besides 30,000 to 40,000 disarmed in Germany; 231 guns, 1,023 machine-guns and 10,000 ammunition and supply wagons. During July and August the total Polish casualties numbered about 50,000 and the Soviet 150,000.

In spite of this great victory the campaign was not ended and two separate operations followed, one in the south and the other in the north. The first was carried out by Sikorski, who opened his offensive on September 12 and occupied Kovel, Lutzk, Rovno and Tarnapol on the 18th and Pinsk on the 20th. The second was led by Pilsudski who, after a masterful manœuvre, attacked Tukhachevski on September 20, destroyed the Soviet Third Army in the Battle of the Niemen, and occupied Grodno on the 26th. This victory was at once followed by the battle of the Shara (Szczara),[1] in which the remnants of the Soviet Armies were driven back to Minsk. In these two battles Pilsudski took 50,000 prisoners and 160 guns. On October 10 an armistice was agreed, and on March 18, 1921, by the Treaty of Riga the eastern frontier of Poland was fixed as it stood until 1939.

This marked the end of a remarkable campaign, fought between improvised armies of limited size in a vast theatre of war. It was a campaign of mobility and surprise, totally different from most of those fought during the World War. It was a contest between armies led mostly by young generals, and in which cavalry played an important part and field trenches no part at all, and above all, it was a war in which men were more important than *matériel*, and generals more important than their staffs.

The influence of this decisive battle on history was fully appreciated by Tukhachevski, who lost it, and by Lord D'Abernon, who watched it. Yet, strange to say, its importance was little

---

[1] For these two battles see articles by General Faury (French) in the *Revue militaire française* of February and March, 1922, and March, 1929. Faury was in 1920 attached to General Skierski, who commanded the Fourth Polish Army.

grasped by western Europe, and since has remained little noticed. Soon after his defeat Tukhachevski wrote:

"In all European countries Capitalism was staggering; the workers were lifting their head and rushing to arms. There is not the slightest doubt that, had we been victorious on the Vistula, the revolution would have set light to the entire continent of Europe. . . . Exported revolution is possible . . . and had it not been for our strategical mistakes and our defeat on the field of battle, perhaps the Polish war would have been the link which would have united the revolution of October to the revolution of Western Europe. . . . There cannot be the slightest doubt that had we succeeded in disrupting the Polish Army of bourgeois and lords, the revolution of the Polish class workers would have been a *fait accompli*, and the conflagration would not have halted on the Polish frontiers. Like an overwhelming torrent it would have swept into Western Europe. The Red Army will never forget this experiment in exported revolution, and if ever the bourgeoisie of Europe invites us to new struggles, the Red Army will succeed in destroying it and fomenting revolution in Europe."[1]

Later, in an article published in the *Gazeta Polska* of August 17, 1930, Lord D'Abernon set down his judgment as follows:

"The history of contemporary civilization knows no event of greater importance than the Battle of Warsaw, 1920, and none of which the significance is less appreciated. The danger menacing Europe at that moment was parried, and the whole episode forgotten. Had the battle been a Bolshevik victory, it would have been a turning point in European history, for there is no doubt at all that the whole of Central Europe would at that moment have been opened to the influence of Communist propaganda and a Soviet invasion, which it could with difficulty have resisted. . . . The events of 1920 also deserve attention for another reason: victory was attained, above all, thanks to the strategical genius of one man and thanks to the carrying through of a manœuvre so dangerous as to necessitate not only genius, but heroism. . . . It should be the task of political writers to explain to European opinion that Poland saved Europe in 1920, and that it is necessary to keep Poland powerful and in harmonious relations with Western European civilization, for Poland is the barrier to the everlasting peril of an Asiatic invasion."[2]

[1] *L'Année 1920*, p. 255.
[2] Quoted from *The Poland of Pilsudski*, Machary, p. 118.

Further, by shielding Central Europe from the full blast of Marxist contagion, the battle of Warsaw set back the Bolshevik clock. It deprived Russia of the plunder she badly needed to stem her desperate economic crisis and dammed the outward flow of discontent and almost drowned the Bolshevik experiment.

In 1920, life in the U.S.S.R. had reached bedrock. Transport was at a standstill. Compared with 1914, the number of locomotives in working order had been reduced from 17,000 to 4,000, and nearly 4,000 bridges had been destroyed during the civil war. The town dwellers starved; typhus daily claimed thousands; fodder for horses was unobtainable in the towns, wooden houses were pulled down for fuel, and in their thousands the workers abandoned the factories to seek food in the villages. In February, 1921, violent strikes broke out in the Petrograd factories, and again the Kronstadt sailors mutinied. The situation grew so critical that Lenin ceased to harbour the illusion that the proletariat was the governing class by right of birth. On March 8 he convoked the tenth congress of the Party and, in order to obtain bread, he revoked all Socialist decrees that affected agriculture, and allowed the peasants to return to private enterprise and to employ wage earners. Further, he authorized private internal trading, but kept in his hands finance, heavy industry, much of light industry, transport and foreign trade. Thus, according to his new economic policy, everyone became reasonably free except the proletariat. Yet it was not a return to capitalism, but a retreat in order to gain time – "one step back", as Lenin was wont to say, "to gain two steps forward". Nevertheless, the results were startling: the peasants began to sell, shops opened and private trading again appeared. Between October, 1921, and October, 1922, production increased by 46 per cent., and in the following year it was 44 per cent. higher than in the previous year.

On October 17, 1921, Lenin openly admitted his failure. To a congress of the political storm troops of the Party he said: "We supposed that it would be possible to change the old Russian economy into a State economy on a communist base. Unfortunately we made a great mistake in trying to do this. . . . Being so uncultured as we are, we cannot destroy capitalism by one attack. . . . In the civil war we were able to win because we established in the army the severest discipline. We have yet to establish the most brutal discipline in our working army in order to secure our country, our republic. . . ."[1] Necessity and not Marx turned Russia back to Peter the Great and Ivan the Terrible.

On January 21, 1924, Lenin died at Gorky, near Moscow, and power passed to Stalin (Joseph Dzhugashvili, 1879–1953), who, because of his unbridled brutality, had been made secretary-general of the Party by Lenin. What remained of Marxism was grafted by him to the Russian Asiatic-Byzantine tradition, totalitarian State Capitalism was rapidly developed and everyone reduced to a proletarian level. The Political Bureau became dictator, with the secret police as its instrument of rule, and the ever-growing bureaucracy emerged as the new middle class. Oswald Spengler wrote in 1931: "What the Soviet régime has been attempting for the last fifteen years has been nothing but the restoration, under new names, of the political, military, and economic organization that it destroyed."[2] An observation proved correct to the letter, when the Russia of Stalin is compared with what the Marquis de Custine has to say of the Russia of Nicholas I in 1839.[3]

The State, instead of withering away, was established as an object of worship with Stalin as its omniscient prophet. Marxist terminology was retained as a liturgical language. "In this language," writes Borin, "totalitarian state capitalism would be called Communism. The dictatorship of the Political Bureau of the Communist Party would be named the dictatorship of the proletariat. The prosperity of the new governing class would be known as the prosperity of the working people. While preserving Marxist terminology the State Communistic bureaucracy pronounced the spirit of Marxism as reactionary, counter-revolutionary and Fascist. Marxism in Russia meant Political Bureau and State Police. Anybody who thought otherwise must die."[4]

As Tukhachevski had foreseen, Marxism was found to be a theology too modern and too civilized for the Russians and a return was made to their old Slav gods. The U.S.S.R. reverted to the historic Russia of the "Third Rome," and Tukhachevski's defeat by Pilsudski at Warsaw was not the least of the factors which brought her back on to the old, traditional Tsarist path.

[1] Quoted from *Civilization at Bay*, V. L. Borin (1951), p. 91.
[2] *Man and Technics* (English edit., 1932), p. 99.
[3] See *Journey for our Time*, trans. Phyllis Perm Kohler (English edit., 1953).
[4] *Civilization at Bay*, p. 103.

The rise of the Third Reich and the origins of the Second World War

War alliances against a common enemy are proverbially ephemeral, for once the enemy has been defeated the alliance's centre of gravity is destroyed. There was little reason to suppose that the entente between America, France, and Great Britain, which won the First World War, would be more durable than the Holy League after Lepanto, or the congress of victorious powers after Waterloo. But when compared with the latter there was a profound difference: whereas after the final defeat of Napoleon, for 100 years the *Pax Britannica* maintained a balance of power between the squabbling nations of Europe, during the First World War it was destroyed and after it, thanks to American participation in the war, it was replaced by the League of Nations, an instrument designed neither to remove the causes which had precipitated the war, nor to re-establish the balance of power which had perished in it. Instead it rigidly imposed a peace on the world on lines which conformed neither to history, nor to geography, nor to economics. Instead of being designed as a permanent conference of sovereign Powers for the settlement by discussion of disputes between its members, it was fashioned as an autocratic instrument which legalized war against any Power which threatened its members' territorial integrity and political independence, and outlawed all other forms of war. It was a covenant of words without the sword, which caused ever-increasing discontent and friction and, as a reaction to its futile and disingenuous efforts, led to an outcrop of tyrants who challenged its authority and exploited its impotence.

Among these artists of power were two men possessed of a new philosophy – Benito Mussolini and Adolf Hitler. They challenged the myth of Economic Man, the fundamental factor in Capitalism, Socialism, and Communism, and exalted in its stead the myth of Heroic Man. This myth has been clearly defined by that remarkable French soldier René Quinton, in his *Maximes sur la guerre*:[1]

---

[1] Translated into English by Douglas Jerrold under the title *Soldier's Testament* (1930), from which the quotations are taken.

"The hero is the man who forgets himself for others. . . . Nature created the hero not to live but to serve . . . The hero is unique among men because his life is the apotheosis of devotion and not of effort. . . . Wars give back religion to men who have lost it. . . . It is security of life that has killed the gods. . . . By death man saves the life of the world. . . . Ideas, not men, are the founders of races."

In Hitler's eyes the aims of international Capitalism and Marxism were one and the same. Both, he said, repudiated "the aristocratic principle of Nature"; both were destroyers of quality, not of things but of life. He held that both lacked the self-justification of sacrifice, fought against Nature, and were destroyers of the race. Hence his creed of the blood, cryptically embalmed in his dogma *"ein Volk, ein Reich, ein Führer"*, which perversely he adulterated with confused ideas on Aryanism and Teutonic superiority, mixed with vitriolic hatred for the Jews. Like Cromwell, he created an Association, not of tapsters and decayed serving men, but of men of spirit who "made some conscience of what they did." And when we turn to his autobiographical bible – *Mein Kampf* – we find remarkable parallels to the maxims of René Quinton:

"Men do not die for business but for ideals. . . . He who would live must fight. He who does not wish to fight in this world, where permanent struggle is the law of life, has not the right to exist. . . . To recover Germany's power you must not ask 'How are we to manufacture arms?' but 'How are we to breed the spirit that makes a people capable of bearing arms?' . . . The greatness of the Aryan is not based on his intellectual powers; but rather on his willingness to devote all his faculties to the service of the community. . . . This mental attitude, which forces self-interest to recede into the background in favour of the common weal, is the first pre-requisite of any kind of really human civilization. . . . The renunciation of one's own life for the sake of the community is the crowning significance of the idea of all sacrifice. . . . Posterity will not remember those who pursued only their own individual interests, but it will praise those heroes who renounced their own happiness."

The comments of Peter F. Druker on this creed are illuminating. "It is a common and stupid mistake," he writes in *The End of Economic Man*, "to look at this exaltation of sacrifice in totalitarianism as mere hypocrisy, self-deception, or a propaganda stunt. It grew out of deepest despair. Just as nihilism in the Russia of 1880 attracted the noblest and bravest of the young people, so in Germany and Italy it was the best, not the worst representatives of the post-war generation who refused to compromise with a world that had no genuine values worth dying for and no valid creed worth living for."

Unless the struggle between these two myths – Economic Man and Heroic Man – is accepted and understood, the cataclysm which in 1939 submerged the world is almost incomprehensible and the age to which it gave birth little more than the plaything of chance.

Hitler, an Austrian by parentage, was born at Braunau-am-Inn on April 20, 1889, and when on the outbreak of war in 1914 he enlisted into the 16th Bavarian Infantry Regiment, no other recruit had a better claim to be called "the complete proletarian." Through sheer merit, he won the Military Service Cross with Swords, the Regimental Diploma for Gallantry, and the first-class order of the Iron Cross. Yet, strange to say, he never rose above the rank of corporal.

While the victors of the war inscribed their triumph on the memorial they erected at Rethondes in the forest of Compiègne, which read: "*Ici le 11 Novembre 1918 succombra le criminel orgeuil de l'empire Allemand, vaincu par les peuples libres qu'il prétendait asservir*", Corporal Hitler lay in hospital at Pasewalk in Pomerania half-blinded by poison gas. Little did they suspect that a day would dawn when this obscure soldier would at the foot of that same monument receive the surrender of the eagles of France and carry his swastika flag from the Atlantic to the Volga.

What was the power which enabled him to achieve this? In part his political genius, also in part his remarkable gift of leadership, but above all that he believed himself to be the divinely appointed regenerator of the Germanic peoples. He was a god-intoxicated man, the spiritual precipitate of the law of retribution, that he who soweth iniquity shall reap calamity.

The demons that exalted him were the Treaty of Versailles, which bore no resemblance to Wilson's Fourteen Points – "*Quatorze commandements! C'est un peu raide!*" had cried Clemenceau, "*Le bon Dieu n'en avait que dix!*" – the invasion of the Ruhr by Poincaré in 1923, which debauched the German currency and wiped out the German middle classes; the influx of £750 m. in foreign loans between 1924 and 1930, which debauched the German people, and lastly the crash on the American stock exchange, which begat the world-wide monetary depression of 1929–1931.

In 1930, 17,500,000 Germans were supported by the State, and in 1931 the Communist electorate in Germany rose to over five million. In that year the American journalist H. R. Knickerbocker in his book *Germany – Fascist or Soviet?* estimated that at least 15 million Germans were partially starving; that two-thirds of the voters were hostile to Capitalism, and more than half were hostile to the existing political system called democracy. In the following year these calamities led to Hitler's triumph. In 1919 – a "human-nothing", as he called himself – he had become the seventh member of an obscure political group the six members of which called themselves "the German Workers' Party". In 1932, this party, renamed the "National Socialist German Workers' Party", gained 13,779,017 votes out of 36 million votes in the July Reichstag elections, and on January 30, 1933, President Hindenburg called upon Hitler, leader of the largest political party in Germany, to fill the appointment of Chancellor and form a government. A year later, on June 30, Hitler purged his party in a series of hideous assassinations in which Ernst Röhm, General von Schleicher and General von Bredow, Gregor Strasser, and many hundreds of others were murdered. Lastly, when on August 2, Field-Marshal Hindenburg died, the office of President was abolished, and Hitler became Führer of the German people.

Save by those who witnessed it, the exultation of the masses on Hitler's advent to power is unbelievable, and when early in 1934 Rudolf Hess swore in the entire party to Hitler in a mass spectacle which brought millions of people to the microphone the words he spoke were those which echoed in every German heart. He said: "By this oath we again bind our lives to a man, through whom – this is our belief – superior forces act in fulfilment of Destiny. Do not seek Adolf Hitler with your brains; all of you will find him with the strength of your hearts. Adolf Hitler is Germany and Germany is Adolf Hitler. Germany is our God on earth."

Whether this extraordinary man was devil or madman, as his enemies proclaimed him to be, in no way belittles the fact that he stamped out Bolshevism in Germany and accomplished astonishing things. The truth would appear to be that he was a Jekyll and Hyde,[1] at one moment a normal being and at another an

[1] The writer, who met Hitler on a number of occasions, is of opinion that he possessed a dual-personality. At one moment he was Adolf, like any normal man, and at another *Herr Gott*, when to argue with him was, of course, absurd.

inspired paranoic. If that is not the truth it is difficult to explain how so intelligent a man as Lloyd George, on his return to England after a visit to Hitler in 1936, could say: "I have never seen a happier people than the Germans. Hitler is one of the greatest of the many great men I have ever met"; and that Winston Churchill in *Step by Step* could write of him: "If our country were defeated, I hope we should find a champion as indomitable to restore our courage and lead us back to our place among the nations."

Hitler's goal was Napoleonic: to establish a German Continental System under the aegis of Germany. Also, his means were not far removed from those of the great emperor: to liberate Germany from the shackles of international loan-capitalism, to unite all Germanic peoples into the Third Reich, and to establish in eastern Europe what he called the German *Lebensraum* (living space) which he considered as essential to the economic security of Germany as Napoleon had considered the Confederation of the Rhine essential to the strategic security of France.

Hitler held that, as long as the international monetary system was based on gold, a nation which cornered gold could impose its will on those who lacked it. This could be done by drying up their sources of exchange, and thereby compelling them to accept loans on interest in order to distribute their wealth – their production. He said: "The community of the nation does not live by the fictitious value of money, but by real production which in its turn gives value to money. This production is the real cover of the currency, and not a bank or a safe full of gold."[1] He decided: (1) To refuse foreign interest-bearing loans, and base German currency on production instead of on gold. (2) To obtain imports by direct exchange of goods – barter – and subsidize exports when necessary. (3) To put a stop to what was called "freedom of the exchanges" – that is, licence to gamble in currencies and shift private fortunes from one country to another according to the political situation. And (4) to create money when men and

---

[1] Mr. Churchill, who, as Chancellor of the Exchequer, reintroduced the gold standard in Britain in 1925, in 1931 held identical views. He said: "Is the progress of the human race in this age of almost terrifying expansion to be arbitrarily barred and regulated by fortuitous discoveries of gold mines? . . . Are we to be told that human civilization and society would have been impossible if gold had not happened to be an element in the composition of the globe? . . . These are absurdities; but they are becoming dangers and deadly absurdities. . . . I therefore point to this evil and to the search for the methods of remedying it as the first, second and the third of all the problems which should command and rivet our thoughts."

material were available for work instead of running into debt by borrowing it.

Because the life of international finance depended upon the issue of interest-bearing loans to nations in economic distress, Hitler's economics spelt its ruination. If he were allowed to succeed, other nations would certainly follow his example, and should a time come when all non-gold-holding governments exchanged goods for goods, not only would borrowing cease and gold lose its power, but the money-lenders would have to close shop.

This financial pistol was pointed more particularly at the United States, because they held the bulk of the world's supply of gold, and because their mass-production system necessitated the export of about 10 per cent. of their products in order to avoid unemployment. Further, because the brutalities meted out to German Jews by Hitler understandably had antagonized American Jewish financiers, six months after Hitler became Chancellor, Samuel Untermyer, a wealthy New York attorney, threw down the challenge. He proclaimed a "holy war" against National Socialism and called for an economic boycott of German goods, shipping, and services. Cordell Hull, American Secretary of State, under the terms of the Trade Agreement Act of 1934, insisted that American foreign trade should not be undercut by exchange controls, government monopolies, and the barter system.

Between 1933 and 1936, Hitler had reduced German unemployment from six millions to one, and prosperity had so far returned that, like Arthur Balfour in 1907, in 1936 Winston Churchill is reported to have said to General Robert E. Wood of America: "Germany is getting too strong and we must smash her." Then in September, 1937, a new American depression set in and developed with such startling rapidity that, on October 19, the stock market collapsed, and in the following month the census of unemployment showed about 11 million totally unemployed and 5,500,000 partially so. Something had to be done to divert public attention from this desperate internal situation – especially as the presidential elections were impending – and on October 5, at Chicago, President Roosevelt delivered his notorious "Quarantine Speech". He spoke of "a haunting fear of calamity . . . the present reign of terror . . . the very foundations of civilization are seriously threatened . . . let no one imagine that America

will escape, that the Western Hemisphere will not be attacked",
and that the easiest measure to enforce moral standards was an
international quarantine against aggressors. Soon after this the
main aggressor was named. Mr. Bernard Baruch told General
George C. Marshall that "We are going to lick that fellow Hitler.
He isn't going to get away with it". With what? Presumably his
barter system, for in September, 1939, Baruch released a report
of an interview he had with the President in which he said:
"If we keep our prices down, there is no reason why we shouldn't
get the customers from the belligerent nations that they have had
to drop because of the war. In that event Germany's barter system
will be destroyed."

In Great Britain a similar challenge to the barter system was in
full blast, and on March 9, 1939, the Polish Ambassador in
London reported to his Government that Mr. R. S. Hudson, the
Parliamentary Secretary for Overseas Trade, had said to him:
"The British Government were . . . determined not to abandon
a single European market and not to renounce their economic
advantages in favour of the German Reich. . . . Today we are
making negotiations in the economic sphere and shattering the
German barter system." So fiercely was the economic war waged
that Robert E. Sherwood records in *The White House Papers of
Harry L. Hopkins* that, in April, 1939, the acting military attaché
in the American embassy at Berlin reported: "The present situation when viewed in the light of an active war which Germany
is now in the process of waging becomes clear. It is an economic
war in which Germany is fighting for her very existence. Germany
must have markets for her goods or die and Germany will not
die."

When we consider these economic causes of the Second World
War it must be borne in mind, like with those of the first, that the
struggle between the two economic systems is not a question of
right and wrong, but of survival values. It was no more right or
wrong for loan-capitalism to fight for its supremacy than it was
for Hitler to fight for his barter system. Each was vital to the party
concerned; both were the product of trade competition – the curse
born of the Industrial Revolution.

Besides this cause of war, between 1933 and 1939 others helped
to inflame the international situation, and of these the most important was the violence with which Hitler set out to carry out
his programme of German regeneration. Firstly, on October 19,

1933, in order to clear his political decks, he withdrew from the League, and secondly, to secure Germany's eastern flank, on January 26, 1934, he entered on a 10 year peace pact with Poland, which in September was in part neutralized when the Soviet Union joined the League. Next, once the Saar plebiscite had gone in favour of Germany, on March 16, 1935, Hitler repudiated the arms provisions of the Treaty of Versailles and reintroduced conscription, which he justified by pointing at the enormous Soviet army. On May 2 this was countered by the Franco-Soviet Pact of Mutual Assistance, which made nonsense of the League, as also did the Anglo-German Naval Agreement of June 18, by which the strength of the German fleet was fixed at 35 per cent. of the British fleet.

The next crisis was further to increase Hitler's power and to bankrupt the League. In accordance with the secret treaties of the World War, Italy had been promised economic control in Abyssinia and, in order to purchase peace in Tunisia, in January, 1935, France had made a deal with Mussolini over Abyssinia – a member of the League. When Mussolini failed to obtain satisfaction at Geneva, on October 3 he invaded Abyssinia, and on November 18 the League, headed by Great Britain, enforced economic sanctions against Italy. Although they in no way impeded her, they threw Mussolini into Hitler's arms. In the end the 50-odd nations of the League were irretrievably discredited, and on March 7, 1936, Hitler declared the Franco-Soviet pact, which was then about to be ratified, a violation of the Treaty of Locarno, and reoccupied the demilitarized Rhineland.

The next crisis followed immediately. Since February, 1936, the misrule of the Popular Front Government in Spain had led to such chaos that, in order to quell anarchy, on July 18 General Francisco Franco raised his standard of revolt; he was supported by Italian troops, and the Republicans by Russian. Here again was an opportunity not to be missed by Hitler. On November 25 he entered into an Anti-Comintern Pact with Japan, and directly it became apparent that Franco was winning, on March 13, 1938, he annexed Austria.

A fortnight later the Sudeten Germans in Czechoslovakia demanded a restricted form of self-government, and were at once supported by Hitler, not only because of his racial principle, but because Czechoslovakia was a Franco-Soviet air pistol pointed at

Germany. He had not forgotten that, in 1919, the Allies had agreed that should Germany refuse to sign the peace treaty, she would be bombed from the Bohemian airfields. This crisis simmered until September 1, when Henlein, leader of the Sudeten Germans, visited Hitler at Berchtesgaden. The European atmosphere then grew so explosive that, on September 15 and again on the 22nd, the British Prime Minister, Mr. Neville Chamberlain, visited Hitler. On the 24th, Sir Eric Phipps, British Ambassador in Paris, informed Lord Halifax, British Foreign Minister, that "All the best in France is against war, almost at any price," and that the sole group in favour of war was that of the Communists, who were "paid by Moscow." Finally, on September 29, with M. Daladier and Signor Mussolini, for the third time Chamberlain flew to Germany and met Hitler at Munich, and, in order to avert war, he agreed to the secession of the Sudetenland to Germany. Mutinies had broken out in the French army and, according to Sir Neville Henderson, the British Ambassador in Berlin, England "did not possess any Spitfires . . . had only one or two experimental Hurricanes, and only seven modern A.A. guns for the defence of London."

These never-ending crises generated a violent propaganda against Hitler. Foreign affairs lost all objectivity and became wrapped in an explosive animosity which so perturbed Dr. Goebbels, the German Minister of Propaganda, that he appealed to the American Ambassador in Berlin, who replied that the "most crucial thing that stood between any betterment of American Press relationships was the Jewish question."

It was in no way improved when, on November 7, 1938, a young Polish Jew assassinated the third secretary at the German Embassy in Paris, because the murder at once precipitated a pogrom against the Jews in Berlin which added fuel to anti-German sentiment in America. The situation as it was at the end of the year is so illuminatingly described by the Polish Ambassador at Washington, Count Jerzy Potocki, in a report to the Polish Foreign Office, dated January 12, 1939, that we will quote from it fully:

"Public opinion in America nowadays," he wrote, "expresses itself in an increasing hatred of everything . . . connected with National Socialism. Above all, propaganda here is entirely in Jewish hands . . ." and "when bearing public ignorance in mind, their propaganda is so effective that people here have no real

knowledge of the true state of affairs in Europe. . . . It is interesting to observe that in this carefully thought-out campaign –
which is primarily conducted against National Socialism – no
reference at all is made to Soviet Russia. If that country is mentioned, it is referred to in a friendly manner and people are given
the impression that Soviet Russia is part of the democratic group
of countries. Thanks to astute propaganda, public sympathy in
the U.S.A. is entirely on the side of Red Spain. Side by side with
this propaganda an artificial war-panic is created. . . . No effort
is spared to impress upon the American mind that in the event
of a world war the U.S.A. must take an active part in a struggle
for freedom and democracy. President Roosevelt was first in the
field to give expression to this hatred of Fascism. He had a two-fold
purpose in mind: firstly, he wanted to divert American public
opinion from difficult and complicated domestic problems. . . .
Secondly, by creating a war-panic . . . he wanted to induce
Americans to endorse his huge program of armaments. . . .

"Furthermore, the brutal treatment meted out to the Jews in
Germany as well as the problem of the refugees are both factors
which intensify the existing hatred of everything connected with
German National Socialism. In this campaign of hatred, individual Jewish intellectuals such as Bernard Baruch, Lehman,
Governor of New York State, Felix Frankfurter, the newly
appointed Supreme Court Judge, Morgenthau, the Financial
Secretary, and other well-known personal friends of Roosevelt
have taken a prominent part in this campaign of hatred. All of
them want the President to become the protagonist of human
liberty, religious freedom and the right of free speech. . . . This
particular group of people, who are all in highly placed American
official positions and who are desirous of being representatives of
'true Americanism', and as 'Champions of Democracy', are, in
point of fact, linked with international Jewry by ties incapable of
being torn asunder. For international Jewry – so intimately concerned with the interests of its own race – President Roosevelt's
'ideal' role as a champion of human rights was indeed a godsend.
In this way Jewry was able not only to establish a dangerous centre
in the New World for the dissemination of hatred and enmity, but
it also succeeded in dividing the world into two warlike camps.
The whole problem is being tackled in a most mysterious manner.
Roosevelt has been given the power to enable him to enliven
American foreign policy and at the same time to create huge

reserves in armaments for a future war which the Jews are deliberately heading for."[1]

Two days after Count Potocki penned this dispatch, he was assured by William C. Bullitt, American Ambassador to France, that, in the event of war, the United States would be prepared "to intervene actively on the side of Britain and France." Then came the next crisis, for soon after this assurance was given Hitler decided to complete the subjugation of Czechoslovakia. He fomented a *coup d'état* which liberated Slovakia, and on March 15, 1939, he occupied Prague and proclaimed the Protectorate of Bohemia and Moravia. Not content with these aggressions, he had moved toward his final one. On October 24, 1938, Joachim von Ribbentrop, his Foreign Minister, suggested to the Polish Ambassador in Berlin that the Polish Government should agree to a "reunion of Danzig with the Reich" and should consent to the building of "an extraterritorial motor road and railway line across Pomorze" – that is, across the Polish Corridor – which 20 years earlier Mr. Lloyd George had declared, "must sooner or later lead to a new war in the east of Europe." Arguments followed, during which Mr. Chamberlain produced a formula whereby Britain, France, Poland, and Russia would sign a declaration that they "would act together in the event of further signs of German aggressive ambitions". Strangely enough, Josef Beck, the Polish Foreign Minister, rejected the proposal and, equally inexplicable, when in its stead Beck suggested a bilateral agreement between Britain and Poland, Chamberlain agreed to it, and on March 27 the British Foreign Office informed Beck that if the Poles would undertake to defend themselves in event of a German attack, Britain would pledge "all her forces and resources to their assistance." This agreement was made public on March 31.

The effect Chamberlain's Polish guarantee had on Hitler was immediate; for though the latter was aware that an attack on Poland was likely to involve him in a war on two fronts, on April 3 he issued a directive to prepare an invasion of Poland after

---

[1] *German White Paper of Polish Documents*, New York (1940), pp. 29–31. Addressing the Reichstag on January 30, 1939, Hitler said: "I want to-day once again to make a prophecy: if the international Jewish financiers within and without Europe succeed once more in hurling the people into a world war, the result will be, not the Bolshevization of the World and with it a victory of Jewry, but the annihilation of the Jewish race in Europe." This was to be only too true, for according to Goebbels: "About 60 per cent. of them will have to be liquidated; only 40 per cent. can be used for forced labour" (*Diaries*, p. 103).

September 1, and on April 17, in order to avoid a two-front war, he opened negotiations with the Kremlin.

That by now war had been decided on by others besides Hitler is clear; for Karl von Weigand, the doyen of American journalists in Europe, informs us that, on April 25, he was called to the American Embassy in Paris and told by Bullitt, " 'War in Europe has been decided upon. Poland', he said, 'had an assurance of the support of Britain and France, and would yield to no demands from Germany. America,' he predicted, 'would be in the war after Britain and France entered it.' "[1] This statement is corroborated by *The White House Papers of Harry Hopkins*, in which their editor says that, about this time, Winston Churchill told Bernard Baruch: "War is coming very soon. We will be in it and you (the United States) will be in it. You (Baruch) will be running the show over there, but I will be on the sidelines over here."

Throughout the summer the crisis fluctuated, and both Chamberlain and Hitler bid for Russian support; the one to enable him to honour his Polish pledge, and the other to avert a two-front war. At length on August 23 the latter won; that day a treaty of non-aggression was signed in Moscow between Germany and the U.S.S.R., and in accordance with a secret protocol, Poland was to be divided between Germany and Russia. On the 24th the treaty was published, and on the following day the Anglo-Polish Agreement of March 27 was formally signed.

On September 1 – the anniversary of Sedan – without a declaration of war, German troops crossed into Poland, and President Roosevelt issued an appeal to Britain, France, Germany, and Poland to refrain from bombing unfortified cities and civil populations. Hitler immediately endorsed the President's plea, and on the 2nd the British and French governments issued a declaration in which they stated that they were in sympathy with the humanitarian sentiments expressed by the President.

At 9 a.m. on September 3 the British Ambassador in Berlin delivered an ultimatum to the German Foreign Office that unless before 11 a.m. assurances were given of a suspension of hostilities, Britain would declare war on Germany. At noon the French

---

[1] The writer met von Weigand in Berlin on April 19, and was told by him that he had learnt from a high authority that Germany expected to overrun Poland in a minimum of three weeks or a maximum of six: that there would be no attack on the Western Front, and that Italy would probably remain neutral. Of the British guarantee to Poland he said: "Well, I guess your Mr. Prime Minister has made the biggest blunder in your history since you passed the Stamp Act."

Ambassador handed in a similar ultimatum to expire at 5 p.m. Both were unanswered.

When Hitler received the British challenge he sat in silence unmoved, and when Paul Schmidt, his interpreter, left the room, Göring turned to him and said: "If we lose this war, then God have mercy on us."

For a long time the possibility of Germany losing the war did not seem substantial. There is no doubt that, during the inter-war years, the Germans made a better application of the lessons of the First World War than the French or British. But this is not saying much; there remained grave defects in German forward thinking which would ultimately have disastrous effects upon her performance. In 1939, however, these had yet to be revealed, and the strength of the German military machine appeared most formidable. Fuller writes:

'As is usual in war, it was the losing side which learnt most. Whereas the victors looked upon the war as an incident which had been liquidated, the vanquished saw in it the consequence of faulty action. To Russia and Germany the supreme lessons of the war were: the increasing necessity for (*1*) political authority in war; (*2*) national discipline in war; (*3*) economic self-sufficiency in war; and (*4*) technology in war. And the same factors affected peace also, in order to be prepared for war.

'Of the last requirement, three radically new weapons had been experimented with – the aeroplane, tank, and lethal gas – and in each case the experiments had pointed to an extension of gun power – the gun was the dominant weapon. The tank had been used as a self-propelled armoured gun; the aeroplane as a long range gun or machine-gun; and lethal gas as molecular shrapnel. Had the war lasted another year, it would have become apparent that in themselves tanks and aircraft were not weapons, but instead vehicles in which anything could be carried up to their maximum loads. Further, it would have been seen that as their dominant characteristic was a new means of movement, made practical by the common prime-mover, petroleum, entirely new fighting organizations could be built around them – namely, self-propelled armoured armies and airborne armies, and not merely self-propelled armoured guns and airborne artillery.'

On 1 September 1939 the world made its first acquaintance

with the Blitzkrieg, a form of war evolved by the Germans from studies at least partly based on Fuller's own writings, stemming from his experience as a Tank officer in World War I. Here is Fuller's description of the German system as revealed in 1939 in Poland, and later in Belgium and France:

'The tactical policy of Germany was based on the offensive and designed to overcome the linear defensive of her opponents by means of the attack by paralysation, which was adopted as the basis of her *Blitzkrieg*. Her army was fashioned into an armour-headed battering ram which, under cover of fighter aircraft and dive-bombers – operating as flying field artillery – could break through its enemy's continuous front at selected points. The soul of German policy was mobility – a sharp, rapid and short war on one front only. This was to be the outstanding difference between the Second World War and its predecessor. Nevertheless, this policy was founded on a strategical oversight; it took no account of the possibility that, were England to support France, the next continental war would be a two-front war – a front on the land and a front on the sea. To break the second of these fronts was Germany's key problem, for should England throw in her lot with France, she would, as in the past, become the strategical centre of gravity of the alliance. Yet so ill-prepared was Hitler to break the sea front that, on the outbreak of the war, he had no more than an insignificant surface fleet; only 57 submarines, of which 26 were suitable for Atlantic operations; not a single landing-craft; an air force neither designed nor trained for an oversea invasion of the first magnitude; and above all – he had no plan.'

The collapse of Poland in eighteen days, the depressing Anglo-French campaign in Norway, and the Fall of France in six weeks in 1940 are all by now well-covered ground. No less than three books on the French débâcle appeared by English authors in 1968–69: *The Ides Of May* by John Williams (Constable, 1968), a sound and very readable account; *Why France Collapsed* (Cassell, 1968) by Guy Chapman, also sound but somewhat dense in style; *To Lose A Battle* by Alistair Horne (Macmillan, 1969), the all-round best of the three. There is no major conflict between what Fuller wrote in 1956, and what these writers have added since, although they have had the advantage of fresh information which has come to light. But in view of this considerable literature (to say nothing of what has appeared in other languages) Fuller's narrative of the Battle of Sedan and the French campaign of 1940 does not need to be presented here. Some of his comments are, however, worth noting. On the evacuation of the British Expeditionary Force (and nearly 150,000 Frenchmen) from Dunkirk:

That, in face of the most powerful army and air force in the world, a third of a million men were safely brought back to Britain in nine days, thrilled the peoples of the British Empire. It was a unique achievement, and its completion on 3 June marks the day when spiritually the British people full-heartedly entered the war. To France it was a catastrophe.

Next, on the frames of mind which possessed the Allies in the final stage, marked by the German attack on the Aisne which began on 9 June:

'From the launching of the battle of the Aisne to June 25 we enter a dreamland of political fantasy, in which the tilting at windmills passed from fiction into history. On June 10 the French Government abandoned Paris, and followed by several millions of refugees[3] first sought refuge in Tours, and then in Bordeaux. On the 14th Paris was occupied by the Germans and the heart of France ceased to throb; nevertheless, utopian panaceas were proposed. For the most part they emanated from the fertile brain of Mr. Churchill: Brittany should be held as a redoubt; the French Government and 500,000 French soldiers should seek refuge in Algeria;[4] *a levée en masse* should be proclaimed; and more imaginative still, the French should take to guerrilla war and wear down the Germans until they succumbed to famine. Of these fantastic schemes, it was fortunate for Mr. Churchill that the only feasible one, the transference of the French Government to Algeria was not adopted, for had it been, as Weygand points out, the almost inevitable outcome would have been a German invasion of North Africa, which was the one thing Mr. Churchill should most have dreaded.

'On June 16, when the British Prime Minister's imagination hit the bottom of 1,000 years of cantankerous Franco-British history by a proposal of an "indissoluble union" of Britain and France, it so startled Monsieur Reynaud that at 8 p.m. he resigned the premiership and President Lebrun empowered Marshal Pétain to form a new Ministry. Pétain was 84 years old. In the First World War he had been proclaimed "the saviour of France", now he was called upon to become her undertaker. Although a slow and cautious soldier, he acted with a promptness which belied his years. At 12.30 a.m. on June 17 he asked the Spanish Ambassador to transmit to Hitler a request for an armistice. On the 22nd it was signed at Rethondes in the same railway coach in which the armistice of November 11, 1918, had been concluded.[1] Three days later hostilities in France ended, and Britain stood alone. '

Finally, on the campaign as a whole:

' The entire campaign was a dramatic vindication of the attack by paralysation. "The French High Command," writes Major Ellis, "was beaten not only by superiority of numbers and equipment, but by the pace of enemy operations, by inability to think ahead. . . ." Lord Gort, who should know better than any man, wrote in his "Despatches": "The speed with which the enemy exploited his penetration of the French front, his willingness to accept risks to further his aim, and his exploitation of every success to the uttermost limits emphasized, even more fully than in the campaigns of the past, the advantage which accrues to the commander who knows how best to use time and to make time his servant and not his master." '

When Britain, under Winston Churchill's leadership, showed no disposition to capitulate after the Fall of France, the logical next step for Germany was clearly an invasion of the British Isles. Yet, as Fuller points out, in all German preparations for such a deed, there was an element of unreality, despite the apparent overwhelming strength of the German Army and the Luftwaffe. The first directive for invasion of England was issued in mid-July, under the code-name OPERATION SEA-LION; Fuller comments:

The landing was to come as a surprise on a broad front from Ramsgate to the Isle of Wight, and all preparations were to be completed by the middle of August, a palpable absurdity,

[1] The armistice terms were lenient: The constitution of the Third Republic remained in full force; 40 departments were not occupied; an army of 100,000 men in France and 180,000 in Africa was allowed; the fleet was left intact, and so was the French Empire.

as thirty-nine divisions were involved – thirteen in first flight and twenty-six in support, and 1,722 barges, 471 tugs, 1,161 motor-boats and 155 transports had to be fitted and assembled in the Channel Ports.

By comparison, Fuller notes in passing, the Anglo-American invasion of North Africa in 1942 took well over nine months to prepare – a proof, if any more were needed, that Hitler's project was ridiculous. Equally ridiculous was his deferment of the decision to invade until "after the Air Force has made concentrated attacks on Southern England for one week." "The truth is," says Fuller, "with the possible exception of Göring, the Luftwaffe commander, nobody believed in Operation Sea Lion. Certainly the German admirals did not, nor the generals, nor Hitler himself who, according to General Blumentritt, in July told Runstedt privately that 'he did not intend to carry out Sea Lion'."

Instead, the Germans launched the air offensive which has gone down in history as the Battle of Britain. Had this battle ended otherwise, if the Royal Air Force and the industries behind it had been knocked out, then, possibly, an attempt at invasion might have been made. But what happened was the first complete check to the apparently invincible Luftwaffe, and the revelation of its utter inadequacy as a strategic weapon. This was the price of Blitzkrieg victories; the German Air Force excelled as an Army support weapon, but the very aircraft which enabled it to do so now proved useless for the larger task. On 18 August the Ju 87 dive-bomber (Stuka) which had paved the way for victory after victory on the Continent had to be withdrawn from the battle because it was "a sitting duck for Hurricanes and Spitfires".[1] On 30 September the German twin-engined bombers (i.e. their whole bomber force) were relegated to night operations. These defects, in conjunction with brilliant handling of the R.A.F. Fighter Command by Air Marshal Dowding, with the aid of radar, spelt the first German defeat of the war. Fuller comments:

'Rightly in England and throughout her Empire the Battle of Britain was turned into a great propaganda victory: yet never once were the British Isles in any real danger, nor was Fighter Command ever reduced to its last cartridge, as was put about in order to magnify the German peril. Because it came so soon on

[1] Wood and Dempster, *The Narrow Margin*, Hutchinson, 1961.

the heels of the fall of France, it not only showed that the Germans were not invincible, but it made Hitler look ridiculous, and in doing so it added vastly to British prestige. In consequence, the Battle of Britain was not the least of the factors which stimulated American support of England. Further, it persuaded Hitler to turn on Russia before Britain had been driven out of the war and this, as will be seen, was the road to his ruin. '

Operation Barbarossa and the Lend-Lease Act

As soon as the direct attack on England had been abandoned, Hitler turned to the indirect approach. Already on June 30, in a memorandum on the "Continuation of the war against England," General Jodl had suggested as an alternative to operation "Sea Lion" that the Mediterranean should be sealed off by the occupation of Gibraltar and Egypt; the former aim to be effected in cooperation with Spain, and the latter with Italy. Two months later – on August 21 – Ciano mentions in his diary that Mussolini was "entirely occupied" with his plan to attack Egypt on September 6, and that General Keitel had told the Duce that to take Cairo was more important than to take London. Significantly, on September 6 Admiral Raeder presented a report to Hitler to revive Jodl's suggestion. "Preparations for this operation," he wrote, "must be begun at once so that they are completed before the U.S.A. steps in. It should not be of secondary importance, but as one of the main blows against Britain." This was strategically sound, because Egypt was both the centre of Britain's imperial communications and her sole remaining oversea base within striking distance of Europe. Should Egypt and Gibraltar be wrested from her, the Mediterranean would become an Italian lake, Turkey could be pinched out, and the road to Russia by way of Armenia and Georgia opened; and finally Britain would be placed in so desperate a position that American ardour in her support might fall to zero. Could such a situation be brought about, England would be compelled to accept a negotiated peace, for without American economic support she could not continue the struggle.

Hitler did not set aside Raeder's suggestion, but seized on it and opened negotiations with Spain. First he decided that the submarine campaign should be intensified and the bombing of London continued, and then, on October 23, he met Franco at Hendaye in order to gain his consent to the free passage of German troops through Spain. He pressed for an immediate agreement which, to his annoyance, Franco refused to give. Five days later the whole situation was suddenly changed; without reference to Hitler, Mussolini invaded Greece. It was an act of strategic madness, because it involved Italy in a war on two fronts when she was having the utmost difficulty in supplying General Graziani's front in North Africa.

The immediate result of this piece of foolishness was the British occupation of Crete and Lemnos on November 3, and as this advance halved the bombing distance between Egypt and the Rumanian oilfields, Hitler decided, while preparations to seize Gibraltar continued, to impose his will on Bulgaria and Rumania and to invade Yugoslavia and Greece. On November 17 King Boris of Bulgaria was summoned to Germany and his good will won. Ten days later General Antonescu carried out a *coup d'état* in Rumania and joined the Axis.

Barely were these arrangements made than another unlooked for event upset Hitler's calculations. On December 9, Sir Archibald Wavell, British commander in the Middle East, routed Graziani in the Battle of Sidi Barrani, and the defeat was so complete that it became imperative for Hitler to succour the Italians. Without the loss of a minute, on December 10 he ordered formations of the *Luftwaffe* to the south of Italy in order to attack British sea communications, and ordered the despatch to North Africa of at least one armoured division under General Rommel. Further, and more important, the Italian defeat so alarmed Franco that the projected seizure of Gibraltar had to be dropped, and this, coupled with the British advance in the Aegean, led to Hitler's fateful decision – to strike at Russia before he had settled his accounts with England.

On December 16 he issued Directive No. 21, designated "Operation Barbarossa". In it we read:

"The German Armed Forces must be prepared to crush Soviet Russia in a quick campaign even before the end of the war against England. For this purpose the Army will have to employ all available units with the reservation that the occupied territories must be safeguarded against surprise attack. . . . Preparations are to be completed by May 15, 1941. . . . The ultimate objective of the operation is to establish a defensive line against Asiatic Russia from a line running approximately from the Volga river to Archangel."

Further, Hitler directed that the concentration of forces for "Barbarossa" was to be camouflaged as a feint for "Sea Lion" and his projected attack on Greece. It was to be made "the greatest deception in history."

This was not altogether a gesture of frustration; there was logic behind this decision: If England would not come to terms – so he argued – then her one and only hope must lie in the intervention of Russia and the United States. Were Russia, as a prospective British ally, to be eliminated, England would be left with the United States, and because neither would be able to recruit a continental partner, was it likely that America would continue to support Britain? If not, then Britain would be compelled to negotiate, and even were the United States to continue her support, the two allies would be faced with the whole might of Germany on one front, and probably by that of Japan on another.

In Martienssen's[1] opinion, Hitler's directive of December 18 was "perhaps the biggest military blunder of all time." Events proved that it was certainly the biggest blunder he made, although at the beginning there was one factor which had Hitler grasped it would in all probability have led to the complete overthrow of the Soviet colossus within a few months – that was, the composition of the Russian empire.

As discussed in Chronicle 9, Russia is a mosaic of subjugated peoples who in 1940 were as violently opposed to the autocracy of their Bolshevik masters as previously they had been opposed to the autocracy of their Tsars. Had Hitler only appreciated what this meant, he would have offered the Ukrainians, Bielorussians (White Russians), Turkomans, and the other subjected peoples liberation from Soviet rule and unfettered autonomy. He would have decided to have advanced into Russia as a liberator, not a conqueror, and had he done so he would have caused such an explosion that the U.S.S.R. would have disintegrated. It is true that this alone would not have given him the *Lebensraum* he sought; yet it is equally true that once the Soviet Imperium had been destroyed, he could have enforced his will on its shattered parts. As will be seen – setting morality aside – his barbarities toward the subjugated peoples as well as the Muscovites were not so much misplaced as mistimed; for they could only be profitable to him were they to follow the fall of the Soviet régime. Because of this they should have been rigorously excluded before the collapse. Although Hitler was as brutal as Lenin, he was less astute; while

[1] Editor of the *Fuehrer Conferences on Naval Affairs* and author of *Hitler and his Admirals* (1948).

Lenin understood how to make brutality his servant, Hitler through sheer grossness of mind became its victim, and ultimately it strangled him.

His most implacable enemy, President Roosevelt, had not been idle, and in spite of his manifold enunciations to keep the United States out of the war, he was bent on provoking some incident which would bring them into it. His aim, like Mr. Churchill's, was to destroy Hitlerism, root, trunk, and branch. He said, "There is absolutely nothing important in the world to-day but to beat Hitler," and as this would become impossible were Great Britain to accept a negotiated peace, in spite of international law, the laws of America and the neutral status of the United States, Roosevelt set out to do everything in his power to help her. His one great difficulty was to overcome isolationism at home, which meant that most Americans wanted to mind their own business. His policy to overcome this difficulty was double-faced. Like Mahomet II, "peace was on his lips, while war was in his heart." "We will not participate in foreign wars," he said, "and we will not send our Army, naval and air forces to fight in foreign lands. . . . I have said this before, but I shall say it again and again and again: Your boys are not going to be sent into any foreign wars. . . . Your President says this country is not going to war." But he left no stone unturned to provoke Hitler to declare war on the very people to whom he so ardently promised peace. He provided Great Britain with American destroyers, he landed American troops in Iceland, and he set out to patrol the Atlantic seaways in order to safeguard British convoys; all of which were acts of war.

The crucial danger which faced Great Britain was neither the German direct attack nor the German indirect approach. The battle of Britain had been won, and the battle of the Mediterranean was successfully waged; but the one battle in which Britain fought a desperate rear guard action remained – it was the battle of the dollar. Without dollars to pay for her food, munitions, and shipping, she was faced with strategical bankruptcy. Thus far she had paid for them on a "cash-and-carry" basis – that is, by selling her foreign assets; but by the end of 1940 she was scraping the bottom of her dollar barrel, and unless it could be replenished the ultimate issue before her was a negotiated peace. So desperate was her situation that, on December 8, Mr. Churchill, in a long letter to Roosevelt, informed him that the moment approached when further payment could not be made.[1] Rightly he says that this was one of the most important letters he ever wrote. It changed the axis of the entire war.

Roosevelt received this letter while on a cruise in the Caribbean, and for several days he pondered. On December 17, at a Press conference, he talked of how to "get rid of the silly, foolish old dollar sign", and on the 29th he delivered over the radio one of his educational fireside chats. It opened with the usual pronouncement that it was his purpose to keep the people, their children and their grand-children "out of a last-ditch war." In order to terrify them into one, he added, "Never before since Jamestown and Plymouth Rock has our American civilization been in such danger as now. . . . If Great Britain goes down, the Axis Powers will control the continents of Europe, Asia, Africa, Australasia (*sic*) and the high seas." Then "all of us would be living at the point of a gun loaded with explosive bullets." Then came the catch-line of his speech: "We must be the great arsenal of democracy. We have furnished the British great material support and we will furnish far more in the future." Typically, this chat ended with another wave of the olive branch – "We have every good reason for hope – hope of peace."

The great arsenal of democracy referred to the Lend-Lease Bill – "an Act to promote the defense of the United States" – introduced into Congress on January 10, 1941. On March 8 it passed the upper house by 60 votes to 31, and on the 11th was signed by the President, who on the same day proclaimed that the defence of Britain and Greece was "vital to the defense of the United States," and four days later China was included.

The powers granted to the President by this Act were unprecedented. It enabled him to designate as a beneficiary any country in the world; to manufacture and procure whatever munitions he wanted; to sell, transfer, exchange, lease and lend any articles of defence he liked; to repair and recondition the articles of defence of the designated governments; to communicate to these governments any defence information he considered necessary; and to determine the terms and conditions of receipt and payment. All

[1] "We had paid out over 4,500 million dollars in cash. We had only 1,000 millions left, the greater part in investments, many of which were not readily marketable. It was plain that we could not go on any longer in this way. Even if we divested ourselves of all our gold and oreign assets, we could not pay for half we had ordered, and the extension of the war made it necessary for us to have ten times as much" (Churchill, in *The Second World War*, 1949, vol. II, p. 493).

these things he could do at his pleasure "notwithstanding the provision of any other law."

The signing of the Lend-Lease Act on March 11, 1941, was as fateful an event in world history as the American declaration of war on April 6, 1917. By allying the United States with all countries fighting the Axis it enabled their President to make war, declared or undeclared, in any quarter of the globe. It meant that when America entered the war, again there would be no neutral arbiter left. In 1917, Woodrow Wilson had foreseen where he was going, but in 1941 Franklin D. Roosevelt stepped blindly on to the road of global war. In order to bracket the Lend-Lease Act with the Declaration of American Independence, he had numbered the Bill "1776". Yet instead of liberating Europe, under his leadership it was to become above all other instruments the one which was to bring half the world under the servitude of Moscow. Hitler's barbarities redounded to Stalin's profit and the blindness of the American President led to the triumph of the Muscovite dictator.

The first step in Hitler's projected invasion of Russia was to consolidate his position in the Balkans so that he might protect his right flank and rear and safeguard the vital Rumanian oilfields. By February 28 all was ready, and on that day, with the connivance of King Boris, Bulgaria was occupied and became party to the Three Power Pact, which had been signed by Germany, Italy, and Japan on September 27. Pressure was then brought on Yugoslavia and Greece and the latter called for British aid. On March 24, the Yugoslav Government capitulated, but three days later, when German troops were about to cross the Yugoslav frontier, General Simovitch carried out a *coup d'état* and repudiated the capitulation. With his accustomed celerity, on April 6 Hitler ordered his troops to cross the Yugoslav frontier, and 11 days later the Yugoslav army capitulated. Meanwhile, on March 7, British troops had begun to land at the Piraeus, but no sooner were they in line with the Greeks than, on April 8, they were attacked, and on the 21st Greece was out of the war. A month later a German airborne attack was launched on Crete, and on May 27 the island was in German hands.

Once Greece had been overrun, on April 30, at a conference of his generals, Hitler chose June 22 as the date to launch "Barbarossa". Actually, it must have been decided some days earlier, because on April 24 the German naval attaché in Moscow telegraphed O.K.M.: "Rumors current here of alleged danger of war between Germany and the Soviet Union. . . . According to the Counselor of the Italian Embassy, the British Ambassador predicts June 22 as the day of the outbreak of war."

While these campaigns were under way, Rommel opened his first offensive in Libya. By the middle of April he had won back nearly all that Graziani had lost. His success was so startling that on May 30 Admiral Raeder and the Naval Staff, in a memorandum they regarded as "one of the most important documents in all the war records," put forward the proposal of "a decisive Egypt–Suez offensive for the autumn of 1941"; a step which they considered would be "more deadly to the British Empire than the capture of London." Strategically they were right, for if Rommel had been reinforced with one or two armoured divisions, the probabilities are that he would have occupied Egypt long before the end of 1941. But Hitler would not listen to this until operation "Barbarossa" had been finished. What he failed to appreciate was that the conquest of Yugoslavia and Greece had added vastly to his negative front, and would increasingly do so as long as the British were left in occupation of Egypt and the Middle East. He had failed to occupy north-west Africa after the fall of France, now he set aside the opportunity to seize Egypt after the fall of Greece. Both were strategic blunders of the first order, and why he committed them would appear to be that he was incapable of appreciating the potentials of sea power, which became more and more formidable as his negative front was extended.

CHAPTER 9

The Battles for Moscow

With the occupation of Crete, Hitler had to his credit a series of conquests which no general in history had gathered in so brief a space of time. He had conquered Poland in 27 days, Denmark in one, Norway in 23, Holland in five, Belgium in 18, France in 39, Yugoslavia in 12, Greece in 21, and Crete in 11. Russia, in spite of her overwhelming might, had taken over 100 days to bring the Finns to heel. With this record behind him and with Russian inefficiency to mislead him, his assumption that he could overthrow Russia before winter set in was not only to his uncritical mind in no way astonishing, but it was accepted by the world in general as a high probability. He expected to destroy Russia's fighting power and to gain the line of the Volga–Archangel within three or four months; after which he could leave some 50 to 60 divisions to hold the conquered area and employ the remainder of his forces against England. This is why, before the campaign started, winter clothing for no more than a fifth of the invading armies was budgeted for.[1]

An essential of so rapid a campaign was the best of ground conditions at its start, and because the spring of 1941 had been exceptionally wet, and well into May the Bug and its tributaries were still at flood level,[2] it is improbable, as has so often been asserted, that the Yugoslav and Greek campaigns delayed the invasion by as much as six weeks, if at all, and in consequence that they were one of the main factors which led to its ultimate failure. The choice of objectives was more to blame. To destroy Russian fighting power demanded the selection of a goal which could not be abandoned by the Russian armies and which would compel them to accept battle within striking range of the Germans. The sole target which filled this bill was Moscow. It was the hub of Russian rail communications, and therefore strategically indispensable, and it was also the Mecca of world communism, the headquarters of a highly centralized government, and a great

---

[1] See *The German General Staff*, Walter Görlitz (1953), p. 389.
[2] See *Panzer Leader*, General Heinz Guderian (1952), p. 145.

industrial centre which employed over a million workers. This was the objective Field-Marshal Brauchitsch and General Halder wished to strike at, but Hitler would have none of it. " 'Only completely ossified brains, absorbed in the ideas of past centuries,' he said angrily, 'could see any worthwhile objective in taking the capital.' *His* interest lay in Leningrad and Stalingrad, the breeding grounds of Bolshevism. Destroy these two cities . . . and Bolshevism would be dead."[1]

This outlook is not as absurd as it may at first seem, because Hitler saw that his problem was very different from the one which had faced Napoleon. It was not wholly a strategical question – the defeat of the Russian armies; it was profoundly political – the defeat of the Bolshevik régime – not by the occupation of cities, but by the fomentation of revolution within Russia.[2] If he had from the start of the campaign assumed the role of liberator, he would have been right to consider his generals addle-pated. But to imagine that because of their names the occupation of Leningrad and Stalingrad would shatter the Soviet system was a piece of mystical bunkum, which he further confused when he coupled it with two primary economic objectives – the conquest of the Ukraine and of the Caucasus. The objective of the one was to deprive Russia of her main resources of food stuffs and 60 per cent. of her industries, and of the other to deprive her of the bulk of her oil. The result was a confused multiplicity of objectives which over-extended the German armies and meant the inevitable adoption of half-measures.

In spite of the "ossified brains" of the German generals, Directive 21 was a compromise between Hitler's views and theirs. Moscow was not to be abandoned, but given second place to Leningrad and the Ukraine, with the risk that unless the autumn were exceptionally dry it would not be occupied when winter set in.

The General Intention was:

"The mass of the army stationed in Western Russia is to be destroyed in bold operations involving deep penetrations by armoured spearheads, and the withdrawal of elements capable of combat into the extensive Russian land spaces is to be prevented.

"By means of a rapid pursuit a line is then to be reached, from beyond which the Russian air force will no longer be capable of

---

[1] *Hitler as War Lord*, Franz Halder (1950), p. 41.
[2] See Kleist's views in *The Other Side of the Hill*, B. H. Liddell Hart (1951), p. 259.

attacking the German home territories" – namely the line Volga–Archangel, as already mentioned.

Next, after a paragraph on the tasks of the Finns and Rumanians, followed *The Conduct of Operations*, in which the more important items were:

"The area of operations is divided into southern and northern halves by the Pripet Marshes. The point of main effort will be made in the *northern* half. Here two army groups are to be committed.

"The southern of these two army groups – in the centre of the whole front – will have the task of breaking out of the area around and to the north of Warsaw with exceptionally strong armoured and motorized formations and of destroying the enemy forces in White Russia. This will create a situation which will enable strong formations of mobile troops to swing north; such formations will then co-operate with the northern army group – advancing from East Prussia in the general direction of Leningrad – in destroying the enemy forces in the area of the Baltic states. Only after the accomplishment of these offensive operations, which must be followed by the capture of Leningrad and Kronstadt, are further offensive operations to be initiated with the objective of occupying the important centre of communications and armaments manufacture, Moscow.

.   .   .   .   .

"The army group *south of the Pripet Marshes* will make its point of main effort from the Lublin area in the general direction of Kiev, with the object of driving into the deep flank and rear of the Russian forces with strong armoured formations and of then rolling up the enemy along the Dnieper.

.   .   .   .   .

"Once the battle south or north of the Pripet Marshes has been fought, the pursuit is to be undertaken with the following objectives:

"*In the south* the rapid occupation of the economically important Donetz Basin,

"*In the north* the speedy capture of Moscow.

"The capture of this city would be a decisive victory both from the political and from the economic point of view; it would

19. THE MOSCOW CAMPAIGN, 1941–1942

involve, moreover, the neutralisation of the most vital Russian rail centre."[1]

The composition of the three army groups laid down in the directive was:

Army Group North, Field-Marshal von Leeb: Eighteenth Army, General von Küchler; Sixteenth Army, General Busch; and Fourth Armoured Group, General Hoeppner – a total of 20 infantry divisions, three armoured and three motorized, supported by the First Air Fleet, General Keller.

On its northern flank was the Finnish Army (Marshal Mannerheim), which comprised 16 Finnish divisions (150,000 men) and four German divisions – two infantry and two motorized.

Army Group Centre, Field-Marshal von Bock: Ninth Army, General Strauss, with the Third Armoured Group, General Hoth, and the Fourth Army, Field-Marshal von Kluge, with the Second Armoured Group, General Guderian – a total of 31 infantry divisions, nine armoured, seven motorized, and one cavalry, supported by the Second Air Fleet, Field-Marshal Kesselring.[2]

Army Group South, Field-Marshal von Rundstedt: Sixth Army, Field-Marshal von Reichenau; Seventeenth Army, General von Stuelpnagel, and the First Armoured Group, General von Kleist – a total of 30 infantry divisions, five armoured and four motorized. It also included the IIIrd Italian Corps (four divisions), General Messe; a Hungarian Corps, a Slovak division, and a Croatian regiment. The whole was supported by the Fourth Air Fleet, General Loehr.

To the south of this Army Group and attached to it were the Eleventh German-Rumanian and the Third and Fourth Rumanian Armies, nominally commanded by Field-Marshal Antonescu. Their task was to protect the right flank of Army Group South.

General Reserve: 24 infantry divisions, two armoured and two motorized.[3]

Two points should be noted about these forces; one refers to tanks, the other to transport.

When the campaign in the west was over, in order to multiply the Panzer divisions the number of their tanks was reduced by a

---

[1] Quoted from Guderian's *Panzer Leader*, Appendix XXII, in which Directive 21 appears in full.

[2] On July 3, 1941, both armoured groups were temporarily subordinated to the Fourth Army, and the infantry corps of the Fourth Army were formed into the Second Army under General von Weichs.

[3] The bulk of these figures are those given by General Wladyslaw Anders in his *Hitler's Defeat in Russia* (1953), pp. 32–34. Other authorities vary slightly.

half. The yearly output of tanks was then no more than 1,000, and when the invasion opened the total German tank strength was barely 3,200 machines. Later, the monthly output would appear to have risen from 80 to 210 machines, still a fantastically low figure to make good wastage, let alone to increase the number of Panzer divisions.

Even more important was the second point, which was governed by Germany's limited supply of motor fuel. There was only sufficient for a fraction of the transport to be motorized, and the lack limited the number of motorized divisions. Much of the divisional transport was horsed, and as enough lorries could not be produced in Germany, the new divisions were allotted lorries of French design, which were found not strong enough for the Russian roads. Without question it may be said that the lack of tracked supply vehicles was as vital a factor in the ultimate failure of the campaign as was Napoleon's lack of horse and ox shoes in 1812.

When we turn to the Russian plan, in fact to any Russian operation, the first and enduring difficulty is lack of documentation. It does not exist, because Soviet history is subordinated to Soviet politics, and as the latter is always changing, no general dare write his memoirs, nor can the Soviet Government produce an official history for fear that after publication it may contravene some future political change.[1] We are left with foreign sources, more particularly German, which are apt to be prejudiced.

What we do know is that instead of making use of the vast depths of Russia in order to wear down the German initial advance, and when its momentum was exhausted to counter-attack in strength, the Russian High Command deployed its forces close to the German frontier of 1941. According to General Alexei Markoff, a former major-general in the Soviet army and air force, when the invasion began "There were no reserve echelons backing up the front-line troops, because defense in depth was waved aside as sheer nonsense. No defensive war plans were made or even contemplated. Giant supply depots were filled to bursting with arms, ammunition and fuel not in the safe rear, but so close to the frontier as to be within range of Nazi heavy artillery."[2]

---

[1] Colonel G. A. Tokaev, a Caucasian officer in the Russian army, who in 1948 sought refuge in the west, writes: ". . . it must be remembered that in the Soviet Union any attempt to reconstitute the true history of even the recent past is considered a capital offence" (*Betrayal of an Ideal*, 1954, p. 6).

[2] See his article in *The Saturday Evening Post* of 1950, vol. 222, No. 46; quoted by Raymond L. Gartoff in his *How Russia Makes War* (English edit., 1954), p. 437.

Further, we know that in June, 1941, the Red Army had not recovered from the purges of 1937–1938, in which three marshals, 13 army commanders, 57 corps commanders, 110 divisional and 220 brigade commanders were liquidated – that is, half its senior officers – and that it was still in a state of reorganization. Judged by western standards it was a primitive fighting force, and although it possessed, according to German estimates, about 15,000 tanks and 10,000 aircraft, most of these were of obsolete types. Its transport and supply systems were archaic,[1] and its attack tactics were heavy and clumsy; but, as in past campaigns, its soldiers were tough fighting peasants who, although they lacked initiative, were endowed with astonishing powers of endurance.

When the campaign opened, according to not very reliable German sources, the distribution of the Russian forces was:[2]

Finnish Group, Generals Meretzkov and Govorov; 20 infantry divisions, two cavalry divisions and five armoured brigades, east and west of Lake Ladoga, to operate against the Finns.

Baltic Group, Marshal Voroshilov: 19 infantry divisions, seven cavalry divisions and five armoured brigades, in Lithuania and Latvia, to cover Leningrad.

Bielorussian Group, Marshal Timoshenko: 50 infantry divisions and two armoured brigades, in east Poland and Bielorussia west of Minsk, to cover Moscow.

Ukrainian Group, Marshal Budienny: 69 infantry divisions, 11 cavalry divisions and 28 armoured brigades, in south-east Poland and Bessarabia, to cover the Ukraine.

According to General Halder, on June 21, 1941, the estimated strength of the Russian army in western Russia was: 154 infantry divisions, $25\frac{1}{2}$ cavalry divisions, and 37 armoured brigades, and that it was faced by 102 German infantry divisions, 19 armoured divisions, 14 motorized, five special, and one cavalry.[3]

The strength of Russia did not lie so much in her armed might, but as in the days of Charles XII and Napoleon, it lay in her immense spaces, her primitive roads, her vast forests, broad rivers and swamps, coupled with her short summer, long winter and spring thaws. Added to these were the scarcity and broad gauge of her railways, and she was a difficult country for tanks and

[1] See *An Outspoken Soldier*, Lieut.-General Sir Giffard Martel (1949), p. 226.
[2] Mainly quoted from *La défaite Allemande à l'est*, Colonel Léderrey (1951), p. 31.
[3] *The Halder Diaries* (copyright 1950, *Infantry Journal, Inc.*), June 21, 1941, vol. VI, p. 160.

motor vehicles. When it rained the roads became rivers of mud, and when it did not, either they were snow-bound, or the dust raised by traffic clogged the tank engines, and in winter the frost was frequently so intense that they could not be started until fires had been lit under them. It was imperative for the Germans to subdue Russia up to the Volga in the shortest possible time, and before her vast manpower could be called to arms, if not the campaign would tactically become an interminable struggle.

Hitler put his trust in the superiority of the German tactics to gain a rapid victory. His idea was to pinch out one Russian army after the other by a series of vast tank encircling manœuvres. The procedure was that two armoured groups were rapidly to advance against the flanks of the forces selected for destruction, to penetrate them, and then to wheel inwards well to their rear and cut them off from their communications and paralyse their command. Simultaneously the German infantry were to engage the Russian front, pushing in on the flanks of their enemy and so effect an inner encirclement, and then mop him up.

These tactics were set in motion on Sunday, June 22, 1941, when at 3.15 a.m. on the front of Army Group Centre – the one which most concerns us in this chapter – the artillery barrage opened, and 25 minutes later the first dive-bomber attack went in. At 4.15 a.m. from about Suvalki and Brest-Litovsk, the Third (Hoth's) and Second (Guderian's) Armoured Groups set out to encircle Timoshenko's group of armies west of Minsk. In this initial advance some of Guderian's tanks were waterproofed and equipped with the Schnorkel device – later adopted by the German submarines – which enabled them to cross the bed of the river Bug.[1]

In spite of the many warnings the Kremlin had received,[2] the attack surprised it. Halder says: "Tactical surprise of the enemy has apparently been achieved along the entire line. All bridges across the Bug river, as on the entire river frontier, were undefended. . . . That the enemy was taken by surprise is evident from the fact troops were caught in their quarters, that planes on the airfields were covered up, and that enemy groups faced with the unexpected development at the front inquired at their Hqs. in the rear what they should do. . . . A Gp. Center reports

---

[1] See *The Other Side of the Hill*, B. H. Liddell Hart, p. 268, and Guderian, p. 153. In 1918 a type of Schnorkel was suggested by the British Tank Corps in order to cross the Rhine in 1919.

[2] See *How Russia Makes War*, pp. 434–435.

wild flight on the Brest-Litovsk–Minsk road. Russian command organization in complete confusion."[1]

By June 24 over 2,000 Russian aircraft had been destroyed, either in the air or on the ground. "From the second day onwards," writes Kesselring, "I watched the battle with the Russian heavy bombers coming from the depth of Russia. It seemed to me almost a crime to allow these floundering aircraft to be attacked in tactically impossible formation. One flight after another came in innocently at regular intervals, an easy prey for our fighters. It was sheer 'infanticide'."[2]

On June 26 Hoth's Panzer divisions reached their objective, Minsk, and on the following day were joined by those of Guderian. While the German infantry were still far behind, the pincers closed on Timoshenko. On July 3, the first great battle of the campaign, that of Bialystok–Minsk, ended in pouring rain that turned the roads into bogs.[3] According to Admiral Assmann, it cost the Russians 290,000 men in prisoners alone, 2,585 tanks, and 1,449 guns.[4] In the meantime Army Group North captured Dvinsk and forced a crossing of the Dvina, while Army Group South crossed the Bug near Chelm, and advanced on Lutsk and Rovno.

Halder was so elated by the initial successes that, on July 3, he entered in his diary: "It is thus probably no overstatement to say that the Russian Campaign has been won in the space of two weeks."[5] By this he did not mean that the invasion was as good as over, but that its first phase had been won, and he was right. What of the second phase?

It opened with a tactical argument, which shows what little unanimity the German high command possessed. The original instructions were for the two armoured groups of Army Group Centre to drive straight to Smolensk–Roslavl, and O.K.H. still adhered to this idea. But because the infantry were now some 14 days in rear, Hitler, who wanted to gather prisoners, did not push on and disintegrate his enemy's command, but desired most of the armoured groups to fall back and help the infantry in their task of mopping up. In this he was supported by Kluge, though

---

[1] *Halder Diaries*, June 22, 1941, vol. VI, pp. 161–162.

[2] *The Memoirs of Field-Marshal Kesselring* (English edit., 1953), p. 90.

[3] *Halder Diaries*, July 3, 1941, vol. VI, p. 194.

[4] "The Battle for Moscow, Turning Point of the War," Vice-Admiral Kurt Assmann, *Foreign Affairs*, vol. 28, No. 2, p. 314. Throughout this campaign the enormous captures of tanks must have been because they ran out of petrol.

[5] *Halder Diaries*, July 3, 1941, vol. VI, p. 196.

Hoth and Guderian wanted to press on and Bock wanted both groups to be placed under Kluge so that he himself might be relieved of responsibility in their use. Hitler agreed to this on July 3.

A series of contradictory orders then followed, and Guderian – one of the few German generals who refused to be petrified by Hitler – cut the Gordian knot. He prepared to continue the advance, and by the time Kluge was able to intervene the preparations had gone so far that he was unable to stop them. The result was that, on July 7, the two groups pushed on, that of Hoth by way of Vitebsk and that of Guderian by Mogilev and Orsha. The semi-mythical Stalin Line, which ran from Narva to Polotsk, Vitebsk, Orsha, Mogilev, and thence by way of Vinnitza to the Black Sea, was broken through, and in spite of Kluge's intervention Guderian's leading tanks crossed the Dnieper on July 10, and undeterred by heavy Russian counter-attacks reached Smolensk on July 16. Four days later, Elnya – 50 miles south-east of Smolensk on the Dnieper – was captured, but here Guderian's forces were heavily counter-attacked. Hoth's group came in on the north of Smolensk.

Thus, by July 16, as the crow flies, two-thirds of the way to Moscow had been traversed – 440 miles had been covered at an average of 20 miles a day. The battle of Smolensk lasted until August 8 and ended in another encirclement, during which, between July 3 and July 25, Army Group Centre claimed as its booty 185,487 prisoners captured as well as 2,030 tanks and 1,918 guns.[1]

This bold and skilfully executed advance was one of the most remarkable tank operations of the war. According to General Blumentritt, the country was appallingly difficult for tank movements – "great virgin forests, widespread swamps, terrible roads, and bridges not strong enough to bear the weight of tanks." The great unfinished motor road leading from the frontier to Moscow, he tells us, was the only road a westerner would call a "road", all others were only sandy tracks. "Such country," he says, "was bad enough for the tanks, but worse still for the transport accompanying them. . . . Nearly all this transport consisted of wheeled vehicles, which could not move off the roads, nor move on them if the sand turned into mud. An hour or two of rain reduced the Panzer forces to stagnation. It was an extraordinary sight, with

[1] *Halder Diaries*, July 25, 1941, vol. VI, p. 270.

groups of them strung out over a hundred miles stretch, all stuck
– until the sun came out and the ground dried."[1] An additional
obstruction was that every time a difficulty arose in rear, Kluge
stopped the advance until it had been overcome. Here it may be
observed that, like a jockey, a bold tank general should have his
eyes fixed on the winning post, and not, like a cautious transport
leader, on the tail of his convoy.

When this remarkable operation was under way, on July 5
Army Group North burst through the Stalin Line in the region
of Lake Peipus; captured Ostrov, Pskov, and Porkhov, and then
advanced on Novgorod to cut off Leningrad from the east; and
at the same time Army Group South broke through the Stalin
Line between Zhitomir and Berdichev and thrust toward Kiev.

Hitler was a man who usually could no more break away from
a preconceived idea than Joan of Arc could abandon her angelic
voices. Once he had made up his mind, he stuck to his plan as if
it were holy writ. This is why he would not abandon or modify
Directive 21, and the deeper his armies penetrated into Russia
the more pertinaciously he held to it.

When, on July 19, the battle of Smolensk was at its height, he
did not wait for its outcome, but issued Directive 33. It comprised
two operations to be carried out by the two armoured groups of
Army Group Centre. The Second (Guderian) in cooperation with
Army Group South, was to help to encircle the Russian forces
about Kiev by moving on them in a southerly direction, while the
Third (Hoth) was to advance northward, cut the Leningrad–
Moscow line of communications, and help Army Group North
in its assault on Leningrad. "Thus," writes Assmann, "began a
turning point in the war, incomprehensible to the Russians –
'Marne miracle' as a Russian general called it – which was to save
Moscow just as Paris was relieved in 1914."[2] Actually, there was
no turning point, because the "Marne miracle" was implicit in
Directive 21.

Timoshenko had succeeded in extricating nearly half a million
men during the battle of Smolensk and he now withdrew them to a
defensive line closer to Moscow. They had put up some very tough
fighting, and to Halder's consternation he discovered that the
Russians possessed more than the maximum of 200 divisions
originally estimated by O.K.H.; 360 divisions had already been
identified. In spite of this, O.K.H. wanted to press on to Moscow,

[1] *The Other Side of the Hill*, p. 271.   [2] *The Battle for Moscow*, p. 315.

but Hitler would not listen to Brauchitsch and Halder and, on July 26, in order to start off the southern operation, he instructed Guderian's armoured group, in collaboration with the German Second Army, to round up a strong enemy force at Gomel. Halder's comment on this is illuminating. "Such a plan," he writes, "implies a shift of our strategy from the operational to the tactical level. If striking at small local enemy concentrations becomes our sole objective, the campaign will resolve itself into a series of minor successes which will advance our front only by inches. Pursuing such a policy eliminates all tactical risks and enables us gradually to close the gaps between the fronts of the Army Groups, but the result will be that we feed all our strength into a front expanding in width at the sacrifice of depth and end up in position warfare!"[1] – this is almost exactly what happened.

While the Gomel operation was still under discussion, on August 4 a conference was held at headquarters Army Group Centre. Field-Marshal Bock, supported by Hoth and Guderian, pressed for a continuation of the offensive against Moscow. But Hitler brushed this suggestion aside and said that the industrial area about Leningrad was his primary objective, and after that the Ukraine, because its produce was vital to Germany for the further prosecution of the war. Further, to safeguard the Rumanian oilfields from Russian air attack, he considered it essential to occupy the Crimea. Six days later Army Group North's offensive on Leningrad was repulsed.

Between August 4 and 21, priceless time was wasted in arguments about objectives; but Hitler remained obdurate, and on the 21st issued Directive 34. Its opening paragraph reads: "The principal objects that must be achieved . . . before the onset of winter, is not the capture of Moscow but rather, in the South, the occupation of the Crimea and the industrial and coal region of the Donetz, together with isolation of the Russian oil region in the Causasus and, in the North, the encirclement of Leningrad and junction with the Finns."[2]

In accordance with Directive 33, the main operation was to ease the advance of Army Group South toward Rostov–Kharkov by means of a double envelopment carried out by the inner wings of Army Groups Centre and South to annihilate the Russian Fifth Army east of Kiev. "Not until we have tightly encircled Leningrad,

[1] *Halder Diaries*, July 26, 1941, vol. VI, p. 271. See also Guderian, pp. 182–183.
[2] *Halder Diaries*, August 22, 1941, vol. VII, p. 59.

linked up with the Finns and destroyed the Russian Fifth Army," we read, "shall we have set the stage and can we free the forces for attacking and beating the enemy Army Group Timoshenko with any prospect of success." Moscow, it was stated, "is of secondary importance."[1]

Brauchitsch sent Guderian to persuade Hitler to abandon this madness, which must lead to a winter campaign, but when Guderian met Hitler on August 23, all the latter told him was that the German generals knew nothing about the economic aspects of the war.[2] Guderian was ordered on August 25 to set out for east of Kiev.

Kesselring's opinion on this is worth quoting, because it shows the magnitude of Hitler's error. "If on the conclusion of the encirclement battle of Smolensk . . ." he writes, "the offensive had been continued against Moscow after a reasonable breather, it is my opinion that Moscow would have fallen into our hands before the winter and before the arrival of the Siberian divisions. The capture of Moscow would have been decisive in that the whole of Russia in Europe would have been cut off from its Asiatic potential and the seizure of the vital economic centres of Leningrad, the Donetz basin and the Maikop oilfields in 1942 would have been no insoluble task."[3]

On August 17, although Army Group North captured Narva, its second assault on Leningrad failed, and at the beginning of September Timoshenko, no longer confronted by German armour, launched a powerful counter-attack on the German Fourth Army and claimed the destruction of eight German divisions.

The battle of Kiev, which opened on August 25 and ended on September 26, was the greatest battle of encirclement of the war. Its aim was to annihilate the bulk of Marshal Budienny's Army Group in the vast salient which extended from Trubechevsk in the north to Kremenchug in the south, with Kiev as its apex. The German plan was to pinch it out by an inner and an outer encirclement. The former was to be carried out by the Second Army (von Weichs) moving southward from Gomel–Novosybkov, and by the Seventeenth (von Stuelpnagel) advancing northward from Kremenchug–Cherkasy, while the Sixth (von Reichenau) pinned the main Russian forces down on the Kiev front. The outer encirclement was the task of the Second and First Armoured Groups, commanded respectively by Guderian and von Kleist.

[1] *Ibid.*, vol. VII, pp. 60, 61.   [2] Guderian, pp. 199–200.   [3] *Memoirs*, p. 98.

The one was to advance southward from west of Trubechevsk on Lokhvitsa, and the other northward from Kremenchug on Lubny, both destinations were about 125 miles east of Kiev.

On September 9 Guderian captured Romny and on the 16th he established his headquarters there and made contact with

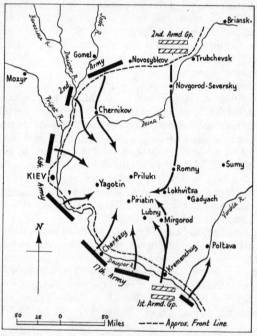

20. BATTLE OF KIEV, AUGUST–SEPTEMBER, 1941

von Kleist's group. The Second Army had crossed the Desna at, and on, the flanks of Chernikov, and the Seventeenth moved northward on a wide front between Kremenchug and Cherkasy, its right flank protected by a detachment directed on Poltava. On the 17th, the inner ring began to close in on Yagotin and Piriatin, 50 to 90 miles east of Kiev, and on the 19th, amid "wild chaos,"[1] Kiev was occupied by the German Sixth Army. On September 26, the day the battle ended, the Eleventh Army,

[1] *Halder Diaries* September 19, 1941, vol. VII, p. 111.

under von Manstein, broke through the isthmus of Perekop and overran the Crimea.

The booty captured in the battle of Kiev was immense: besides 665,000 prisoners, it included 884 tanks, 3,718 guns and 3,500 motor vehicles. It is understandable that Hitler was elated. He called it "the greatest battle in the history of the world", but Halder termed it "the greatest strategic blunder of the eastern campaign."[1] Strategically the latter was right; yet had Hitler appreciated the political significance of the Ukraine, he could have turned the battle of Kiev into the most decisive operation of the war and could have exterminated Bolshevism.

Since the campaign began his armies had captured nearly 1,500,000 Russians, over 7,000 tanks, and approximately 9,000 guns. The first figure is significant, because the capture of such hordes of prisoners in the first phase of a war which was to last for nearly four years is unique in history. The reason is given by General Anders: "Even the first battles of 1941," he writes, "disclosed the widespread disinclination of the Soviet soldier to fight in the defense of the 'Fatherland of the proletariate', and his hatred of the régime, which was shared by the great majority of the population of the U.S.S.R. Many soldiers, seeing the war as an opportunity for a change of order in Russia, wished for German victory and therefore surrendered in great masses. . . . The surrender was not limited to enlisted men and lower ranks; many high Soviet officers went over to the enemy offering to fight against the Soviets."[2] One of them was Marshal Timoshenko's chief of staff.

What is astonishing is that Hitler, a man of exceptional political perspicacity, who had reckoned on the collapse of the Soviet régime as the first fruits of the invasion, made no effort to win over the subjugated peoples of western Russia, but deliberately set out to antagonize them. This colossal political blunder lost him his 1941 campaign and added insuperable difficulties to those that followed. With him it was *aut Caesar aut nullus,* and it would seem that the profusion of prisoners captured did not reveal to him the horror of the Russian masses for Soviet rule, but led him to assume that the surrenders were solely due to the brute force of his armies.

He would seem to have been oblivious of events: that when the invasion was in its initial stage, the Germans were everywhere

[1] *The Battle for Moscow,* p. 119.
[2] *Hitler's Defeat in Russia,* General Wladyslaw Anders, p. 168.

welcomed by the common people as liberators; that the Ukrainians looked upon him as the saviour of Europe;[1] that the Bielorussians (White Russians) were eager to fight on the German side; that whole regiments of Cossacks deserted to their enemy; and that Georgians, Armenians, Turkomans, Tartars, and Usbeks, as well as Ukrainians, Bielorussians and Cossacks surrendered in droves. Often the German soldiers were greeted with flowers and gifts by the peasantry, and Guderian tells us that "women came out of their villages on to the very battlefield bringing wooden platters of bread and butter and eggs and, in my case at least, refused to let me move on before I had eaten."[2] Even as late as December, 1941, Rundstedt, when he left Uman, was presented with flowers and an embroidered Ukrainian table cloth. At Rostov, writes Erich Kern, "all over the city there were people waiting on the streets ready to cheer and welcome us in," and on one occasion an old Russian woman thanked him for being kind to her and before he left, said, "I shall tell you a great truth; the Russian people will not be saved by the man with the bigger gun but by the man with the greater soul." "Never before," writes Kern, "had I seen such a sudden transformation. Of Bolshevism, there was no more. The enemy had gone. . . . Wherever we went now we met laughing and waving people. ... . The Soviet Empire was creaking at the joints."[3]

If Hitler had possessed the wisdom of the old Russian woman who told Erich Kern "the great truth", in spite of his strategic bunglings he might with ease have exploded the Soviet Imperium and have marched into Moscow garlanded with flowers. Many had foreseen this,[4] notably Alfred Rosenberg, a Balt who understood the conditions that prevailed within the U.S.S.R. Shortly after the invasion started he was made Minister of the Eastern Territories, and, on July 7, 1941, in an address he set forth his suggested policy:

"Russia," he said, "has never been a national State, but a State of nationalities", as Mommsen had appreciated when he wrote: "The Russian Empire is a dust-bin that is held together by the rusty hoop of Tsardom." The German task was not to reconstruct it, but to dissolve it; not to impose a new political

---

[1] *The Goebbels Diaries* (1948), p. 135.   [2] Guderian, p. 193.
[3] *Dance of Death* (English trans., 1948), pp. 102, 69, 94, 86. Kern was a n.c.o. in the *Leibstandarte Adolf Hitler*.
[4] Among them Halder, Count von der Schulenburg, former German ambassador at Moscow, Goebbels, and most of the generals.

15

system upon its subjugated peoples, but to recognize each nationality and foster each nation's independence. He proposed to do this by cutting out of western Russia three great blocks of peoples and forming them into buffer states between the rest of Russia and Europe. Besides Finland, which was already independent, Bielorussia and the Baltic States should form one block, the Ukraine a second, and Caucasia a third. Any attempt to hold down the Ukrainians, he said, "would mean to put a soldier behind every farmer." Of Russia proper – the area between Leningrad, Moscow, and the Urals – "We should declare," he proposed, "that we are not fighting the Russian people but the Bolshevik system," and that "our fight for re-organization will take place in the name of national self-determination of nations." He ended by stating that the two main German tasks in Russia were: "To safeguard the German food and war economies, and to free Germany for ever from the political pressure of the East: it is the political aim of our fight. . . ."[1]

Hitler would have none of this and on August 16, 1941, at a conference of his myrmidons he set forth his policy:

"Fundamentally," he said, "our policy is to cut the gigantic cake with skill, so that it can be first mastered, secondly administered, thirdly exploited. . . . The Russians have now given an order for guerrilla war behind our lines. This has its own advantage: it provides us with the opportunity to destroy whatever is against us . . . under no circumstances can anyone but Germans carry weapons. This is particularly important, for it is wrong to induce any subjected people into rendering us military assistance, even though it may appear more convenient at first sight . . . the whole Baltic area has to become Reich's territory. The Crimea, too, has to be incorporated in the Reich, with possibly a large area to the north . . . the German Volga colony has to become a territory of the Reich, and similarly the area around Baku. . . . The affiliation of Finland as a federal State has to be prepared," and Leningrad is to be razed to the ground and handed over to the Finns. . . . "Naturally, the vast territories have to be pacified as soon as possible; this can best be achieved by shooting everybody who shows a wry face."[2]

[1] Abstracted from *Russian World Ambitions and World Peace*, R. Ilnytzky (1953), pp. 4–12.
[2] *Ibid.*, pp. 12–15, citing Nuremberg Documents in evidence at the trial before the International Military Tribunal, Nuremberg, 1945–1946. See also *Hitler, a Study in Tyranny*, Alan Bullock (1952), pp. 633–644.

This policy was put into force, and although Rosenberg remained Minister of the Eastern Territories, their pacification – as it was called – was handed over to Himmler and his Security Service (*Sichereitsdienst*), a sister organization of the Gestapo and divorced from O.K.H., which was strongly opposed to it. It was this infamous Security Service, and not the army, which carried out the mass killings. Early in 1942 Dr. Berthold, a leading official of the German Administration in Poland, told von Hassell that the brutal treatment of the Russians and Ukrainians "exceed anything yet known."[1] For example, because a transmitter was found to be damaged 400 men were shot in Kiev.

Erich Kern points out that at the time when Bolshevism was politically bankrupt, it was saved by Himmler and his assassins. "By rousing the Russian people to a Napoleonic fervour," he writes, "we enabled the Bolsheviks to achieve a political consolidation beyond their wildest dreams and provided their cause with the halo of a 'patriotic war'."[2] And Görlitz writes: "The fact that the destruction of Bolshevism began soon to mean simply an effort to decimate and enslave the Slav people was the most fatal of all the flaws in the whole campaign."[3]

This madness went far to stimulate the guerrilla war proclaimed by Stalin within a fortnight of the invasion and first mentioned by the Germans on July 25, 1941. But it was not until December that the partisan menace grew formidable. This was firstly because of the atrocities perpetrated by the German Security Service, and secondly because of the scientific devilry of the N.K.V.D. (Russian Security Police) which controlled the partisan movement.

The first task of the N.K.V.D. was to end collaboration with the Germans, and only after this had been achieved did they turn to the allotment of military tasks to the partisans. As the simplest way to accomplish the former end was to terrorize the population, the N.K.V.D. at first left the Germans in peace and waged a war of terror against the population behind the German front. Men and women were trained for this purpose; they either passed through the German lines or were dropped from aircraft behind them, and then they organized bands of wandering soldiers and would-be partisans into terror squads. The Germans

[1] *The von Hassell Diaries, 1938–1944* (1948), p. 219. Even Goebbels wrote in his diary on April 25, 1942: "In the long run we cannot solicit additional workers from the East if we treat them like animals within the Reich" (p. 136).
[2] *Dance of Death*, p. 108.   [3] *The German General Staff*, p. 397.

were little molested in this opening phase of the partisan campaign and they took no steps to protect the population; but as fear of the partisans grew the prestige of the Germans declined. When the population had been so terrorized that they would not collaborate, the partisans were instructed to kidnap German soldiers, torture them to death, and expose their mutilated bodies in places which would incriminate the local inhabitants. German reprisals followed; villages were burnt, hostages shot, cattle removed, and sometimes entire districts in which partisans operated were devastated. The results of reprisals were negligible, because all that the partisans had to do was to move into another district and repeat their devilry. But for the Germans they were disastrous. The peasants, deprived of means of living and filled with intense hatred for those whom they had welcomed as liberators, joined the partisans in tens of thousands. On March 6, 1942, Goebbels' entered in his diary: "The partisans are in command of large areas in occupied Russia, and are conducting a régime of terror there." Later in the war their numbers ran into hundreds of thousands, and they became so formidable a menace that Hitler was compelled to rescind his "wry face" policy; but it was too late.[1]

As soon as the battle of Kiev opened Hitler suddenly changed his strategy. Rebuffed before Leningrad, he decided to invest it, not to carry it by assault, and as soon as the battle of Kiev had been won – which he took for granted it would be in some 10 days – to annihilate Timoshenko's forces west of Orel-Rzhev, and then triumphantly to march into Moscow. This decision was embodied in Directive 35, issued on September 6. Army Groups North and South were to reinforce Army Group Centre with armoured troops, after which Army Group Centre was to carry out the offensive as follows:

The Fourth Army (Field-Marshal von Kluge) and Hoeppner's Fourth Armoured Group in the centre, between Smolensk and Roslavl, were to envelop Viazma from the south; the Ninth Army (General Strauss) and Hoth's Third Armoured Group on its left, between Smolensk and Olenino, were to envelop Viazma from

---

[1] Largely extracted from General Anders's *Hitler's Defeat in Russia*, chap. VII. What made the partisan war so formidable was that it could be controlled by radio and supplied by aircraft. The ruthlessness of the N.K.V.D., even toward their own partisans, is illustrated by the following order of May 11, 1943: "The repeated intercourse with women (partisans) resulted in several cases of pregnancy. These women are a nuisance to the regiment. Shoot them!" (Anders, p. 211).

the north; and the Second Army (General von Weichs) between Roslavl and Novogorod-Seversky, was to envelop Briansk. Unlike the previous battles, in which after two flanks had been created,

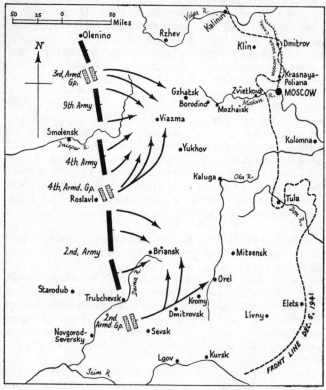

21. BATTLE OF VIASMA-BRIANSK, OCTOBER 1941

the enemy's centre was rolled up, two great mouthfuls were to be bitten out of his front on a frontage of over 300 miles – about the distance of London from Berwick-on-Tweed. Further, besides investing Leningrad, Army Group North was to cover the left flank of Army Group Centre, and Army Group South was to aid its attack by a simultaneous advance on Poltava–Kharkov–Izyum.

On September 30 the great battle of Viazma-Briansk was opened by Guderian, who set out from Novgorod-Seversky and completely surprised the Russians; by October 1 he had penetrated to a distance of 85 miles.[1] On October 2, the main attack was launched from north and south of Smolensk. Its impetus was so great that by the evening of the 3rd the infantry had penetrated to a depth of 25 miles and the armoured forces more than 30 miles. On this day Guderian captured Orel. On the 4th Hoth's Armoured Group began to wheel in on the north of Viazma; Hoeppner's group advanced to the north-east of Roslavl and swung in from the south, while Guderian directed part of his group northward on Briansk, and part on Mitsensk, which was captured. On the 7th Viazma was encircled by Hoth and Hoeppner, and on the following day Briansk was encircled by Guderian and the Second Army, which made some tremendous marches. Mopping up lasted until October 20, during which Gzhatsk was occupied on the 9th; Kaluga on the 16th; and Mozhaisk – only 65 miles from Moscow – on the 18th. Again the number of prisoners was astronomical: this time 663,000, as well as 1,242 tanks and 5,412 guns.

So great was the threat to Moscow that, with the exception of Stalin, the Soviet Government abandoned the capital and withdrew to Kuibishev (Samara) on the Volga; Budienny was replaced by Timoshenko, and Marshal Zhukov took over the latter's command to prepare to defend Moscow, not by resistance, but by counter-attack. It appeared to the Russians and to the world in general that the fate of Moscow was sealed. Hitler, in an outburst of excusable elation, announced that the Soviet armed forces had been annihilated, and even the pessimistic Halder jotted in his diary: "With reasonably good direction of battle and moderately good weather, we cannot but succeed in encircling Moscow."[2]

This was true enough, and had the battle of Viazma-Briansk been fought a month earlier it would have been more certain. But in October any large offensive could not be other than a gamble with weather, and when Mozhaisk was reached it rained. The roads became rivers of mud, and that of Orel-Tula so impassable that Guderian's Second Armoured Army – for so it became known on October 6 – was bogged down for days on end, and had to be supplied by air. On October 29 it splashed forward

---

[1] Guderian, p. 230.
[2] *Halder Diaries*, October 8, 1941, vol. VII, p. 147.

within two miles of Tula, but failed to take it; there it was compelled to halt until frost solidified the roads.

In the meantime Army Group North closed in on Tikhvin and Lake Ladoga, and gained contact with Army Group Centre at Ostashkov, south of the Valdai Hills. Army Group South approached Bielgorod and Kharkov, and in the battle of the Azov Sea 100,000 prisoners, 672 guns and 212 tanks were captured, and the First Armoured Army (von Kleist) in the south occupied Stalino, while in the Crimea the Eleventh Army advanced on Sebastopol and Kerch.

During the night of November 3–4 the first frost set in, and although it eased road movements, the German troops suffered severely because they had no winter clothing. On the 7th there were many cases of frostbite and on the 12th the temperature dropped to 5 degrees Fahrenheit. The question whether the offensive should be suspended or continued was brought to the fore. Rundstedt wanted to suspend it, but as Moscow was only 40 miles distant Hitler would not consider it, and for once he was supported by Brauchitsch, Halder, and Bock. On November 13 a conference of chiefs of staff was held, after which orders for what was called "the autumn offensive" were issued: Moscow was to be taken, and the Kremlin blown up, "to signalize the overthrow of Bolshevism."[1]

The plan of attack was that von Kluge's Fourth Army – 36 divisions in all – was to make a frontal advance on Moscow, while on its left Hoth's and Hoeppner's armoured groups were to encircle the capital from the north and west, and on its right Guderian's armoured army was to do the same from the south. The northern flank of this triple attack was to be protected by the Ninth Army and its southern by the Second.

The battle of Moscow was opened on November 16. Slowly Hoth advanced in a south-easterly direction; on the 23rd he captured Klin, and on the 28th reached the Moscow–Volga canal at Krasnaya-Poliana – 14 miles from the capital – and in the distance glimpsed the towers of the Kremlin. South of him Hoeppner advanced on Zvietkova, west of Moscow, and in the meantime Guderian by-passed Tula and advanced on Kolomna. For the first time during the campaign Siberian troops were captured.

The two armoured wings depended for their success on the

[1] *The Other Side of the Hill*, p. 285.

advance of the Fourth Army in the centre, for if it were held up they would be isolated north and south of Moscow. This is what happened, for no sooner had the battle opened than the right flank of the Fourth Army was so heavily attacked that Kluge had to commit his reserves in its support, and because of this he held back his left and centre until November 19, when his right again advanced. Although it made some progress, Field-Marshal von Bock was "so profoundly affected by the severity of the fighting" that, on the 22nd, he took over personal command of the battle and, as Halder writes, with "enormous energy" drove forward everything that could be brought to bear, because, as he said, the situation was similar to that on the Marne in 1914, "when the last battalion that could be thrown in turned the balance." But in spite of his energy the right wing of the Fourth Army was so exhausted that it could not move.

The Russians threw in more and more troops, but although von Bock feared that "the operation would become a second Verdun, *i.e.*, a brutish chest-to-chest struggle of attrition,"[1] the left wing of the Fourth Army pressed on, and on November 30 the centre was ordered to renew the offensive on December 1. At first it made good headway, but on the 2nd its advance was held up by strong defences in the forests round Moscow. Then, says General Blumentritt, von Kluge's chief of staff:

"A few parties of our troops, from the 258th Infantry Division, actually got into the suburbs of Moscow. But the Russian workers poured out of the factories and fought them with their hammers and other tools in defence of their city.

"During the night the Russians strongly counter-attacked the isolated elements that had penetrated their defences. Next day our corps commanders reported that they thought it was no longer possible to break through. Von Kluge and I had a long discussion that evening, and at the end he decided to withdraw these advanced troops. Fortunately the Russians did not discover that they were moving back, so that we succeeded in extricating them and bringing them back to their original position in fairly good order. But there had been very heavy casualties in those two days' fighting."[2]

Two days later, when the temperature fell to minus 32 degrees,

---

[1] The above is based on the *Halder Diaries* of November 16–29, 1941, vol. VII, pp. 164–192.
[2] *On the Other Side of the Hill*, p. 207.

because "the troops were no longer strong enough to capture Moscow", with a heavy heart Guderian decided to fall back.[1]

The final offensive on Moscow had petered out, not so much because of Russian resistance, but because of the frost. Snow had fallen for days on end, blizzards had covered the villages, and drifts had blocked the railways and roads. Lorries ceased to run, locomotives could no longer be fired, the troops could not be supplied, tanks would only start after hours of warming-up, aircraft dropped out of action because their lubricants froze, telescopic sights frosted over and became useless, machine-guns ceased to fire, and worst of all, thousands of men who lacked winter clothing were crippled by frostbite, and hundreds were frozen to death. That the German soldier, utterly unprepared for winter warfare, accomplished what he did is one of the greatest feats of endurance which the history of war records.

While this battle was fought, on November 21 von Kleist's First Armoured Army took Rostov, but on the 28th it was violently attacked by Timoshenko, driven out of the town and forced to fall back westward. This was the first successful big Russian counter-attack of the campaign, and when Field-Marshal von Rundstedt asked for authority for Kleist to withdraw to a defensive position on the Mius River, he was ordered by Hitler on no account to do so. Rundstedt felt unable to obey this order and asked to be relieved of his command. His resignation was accepted, and Field-Marshal von Reichenau, commander of the Sixth Army, was given command of Army Group South. Meanwhile von Kleist was forced back, and soon after this Hitler sanctioned his occupation of the Mius line.

The withdrawal of the Fourth Army on the night of December 3 was only just in time to avert a major disaster, because soon after it had fallen back Marshal Zhukov launched his long prepared counter-offensive, in which many fresh Siberian divisions took part. On December 6 he broke through the German positions east of Kalinin, and on the following day forced his enemy out of Klin. The blow was so formidable and the Germans so ill-prepared to meet it that Halder urged the withdrawal of the Fourth Army to the line Mozhaisk–Rzhev–Ostashkov. Hitler refused to countenance a retreat. On the 9th the Second Army front was breached at Livny, and on the following day Guderian's army was broken through west of Tula. Soon the counter-offensive

[1] Guderian, p. 260.

was taken up along the entire German front from the Gulf of Finland to the Black Sea. On December 18 Field-Marshal von Bock fell ill and was replaced by von Kluge, and on the following day Field-Marshal von Brauchitsch was relieved of his appointment and Hitler took over supreme command of the German army. On the next day his first order was issued: "Every man must fight back where he stands. No falling back where there are no prepared positions in rear."[1]

When reports of the Russian counter-offensive were received in Berlin, and with them the momentous news that the United States had become a belligerent, the capital was rocked to its foundations. "Unrest grew among the people," writes Arvid Fredborg. "The pessimists remembered Napoleon's war with Russia, and all the literature about La Grande Armée suddenly had a marked revival. The fortune-tellers busied themselves with Napoleon's fate and there was a boom in astrology. . . . Even the most devoted Nazi did not want a war with America. All Germans had a high respect for her strength. Nobody could help remembering how America's intervention had decided the first world war. The 1917 perspective was uncomfortable."[2]

Although the German generals repeatedly counselled retreat, both Guderian and Hoeppner were relieved of their commands because they fell back without authority; Hitler, the visionary, saw that a retreat could only end as did that of Napoleon. Although it was his obstinacy which had brought the campaign to the brink of disaster, it was his obstinacy which was to save it from plunging into the abyss. His refusal to draw out of Russia or to west of Smolensk undoubtedly saved his army from an even greater catastrophe than that of 1812.

Hitler's problem was to get his troops under shelter before they were frozen to death, and to hold on to communications so that the armies could be re-equipped and supplied.

The vital communications in the Moscow sector were the railways, Moscow–Rzhev–Velikye Luki, Moscow–Viazma–Smolensk, Moscow–Kaluga–Briansk, and Moscow–Tula–Orel, all of which were linked by the lateral line Velikye Luki–Vitebsk–Smolensk–Briansk–Orel. Also, from Orel a railway ran south to

[1] *Halder Diaries*, December 20, 1941, vol. VII, p. 235.
[2] *Behind the Steel Wall* (1944), pp. 60–61. Fredborg was a Swedish journalist in Berlin. It is interesting to be told that Caulaincourt's *Memoirs* were in great demand; they were diligently studied by von Kluge (*The Other Side of the Hill*, p. 284) and ultimately their circulation was prohibited (*How Russia Makes War*, p. 433).

Taganrog on the Sea of Azov. On all these railways there were one or more advanced depôts from which the front was fed. The more important were: Staraya Russa, Rzhev, Viazma, Kaluga, Briansk, Orel, Kursk and Kharkov. Between them there were minor depôts, and all were fully stocked and afforded shelter. It was essential to hold them and to get the troops back to them.

Hitler decided to turn these advanced depôts into entrenched camps, and to fall back on them. This would gain shelter for his troops, who could live on their dumps while the lines of supply were put into working order.[1] His plan was not a retreat, as had been that of Napoleon, but a manœuvre to the rear.

Each of the main fortified regions covered many square miles, and in some cases could shelter an entire army. The Germans called them *Igels* ("hedgehogs") after the squares of medieval Swiss pikemen formed to resist cavalry, because their defences bristled in all directions. Sometimes they were supplied by aircraft.

Generally speaking, the Russian advance was not so much a counter-offensive as a steady forward percolation which lapped round the points of German resistance and flowed between them. Because movements had to be made across country rather than by road, the Russians relied extensively on Cossack divisions reinforced with sledge-mounted artillery, sledge-borne infantry, and ski-troops; the landing-wheels of fighter aircraft were replaced by skis. Fighting became brutal in the extreme because of the guerrilla bands in rear of the German front.

The German withdrawal embraced the entire front and was deepest in the Moscow sector between Kalinin and Tula. Once these towns had been captured, extensive pincer operations were developed against Rzhev, Gzhatsk, and Viazma. At the close of December Kaluga was captured by the Russians. It was the most important single Russian success of the whole winter campaign, because Kaluga was a major "hedgehog."

From Kaluga the Russians advanced north-west on Yukhnov, a "hedgehog" south-east of Viazma, and pushed a deep salient into the German front. At the same time in the north they lapped round the west of Rzhev toward Vitebsk and to the north of the latter reached Velikye Luki. These two advances round Viazma brought the Russians within 50 miles of Smolensk. In the meantime, on January 20–22, Mozhaisk was occupied.

[1] Thousands of German lorries and hundreds of locomotives were frozen up. The damage took weeks to repair.

On the Leningrad front, Tikhvin was abandoned by the Germans on December 9, and when the Russians pressed on and crossed the Volkhov river the Germans linked up Schüsselburg with Novgorod, and position warfare set in. In the extreme south the Russians opened a counter-offensive in the Crimea, and north of the Sea of Azov the "hedgehogs" of Taganrog, Stalino and Artemovsk were by-passed in order to concentrate all available forces against the "super-hedgehog" of Kharkov. It stood firm, though Losovaya to the south of it was captured and the advance pushed to within 30 miles of Poltava.

With mid-winter and the increased depth of the snow, the Germans expected a respite. But the Russians continued their percolation although no decisive gains were won except on the Leningrad front, where they built a motor road over the ice of Lake Ladoga, regained contact with Leningrad, and on February 22 cut off a considerable portion of the German Sixteenth Army in the Staraya-Russa area.

On the central front, in February and March, the Russian gains were consolidated and the small "hedgehogs" of Sukhinichi and Yukhnov were captured. In April the thaw brought operations to a standstill except in the Crimea, where the Germans made some progress against Kerch, which earlier in the winter had been recaptured by the Russians, as also had Theodosia.

The German casualties in this campaign are given by Halder. Between June 22 and December 31, 1941, they were 830,403, including 173,722 dead,[1] and between June 22, 1941, and February 28, 1942, 1,005,636, of which the dead numbered 210,572.[2] Whether these figures include casualties from frost is not mentioned, but, according to Goebbels, up to February 20, 1942, they numbered 112,627, of which 14,357 required major amputations.[3] The Russian casualties cannot be ascertained and are probably unknown; but, according to Raymond Cartier, by January 1, 1942, the Red Army was reduced to 2,300,000 men which, he states, was the lowest strength up to the present day (1946).[4] Since in June, 1941, the total strength of the Red Army was over 5,000,000 men, the German claim to have captured well over 2,000,000 does not appear to be exaggerated.

---

[1] *Halder Diaries*, January 5, 1942, vol. VII, p. 248.
[2] *Ibid.*, March 5, 1942, vol. VII, p. 279.
[3] *The Goebbels Diaries*, p. 72.
[4] Quoted by Genl. Anders (p. 80) from *Les secrets de la guerre devoilés par Nuremberg* (1946), p. 297.

Although these enormous losses in Soviet manpower could in time be made good, the loss of war resources necessitated American and British aid, and then it could be made good only in part. According to Professor Prokopowicz, by December, 1941, the Germans had occupied 26·6 per cent. of Russia in Europe, which contained 40 per cent. of its population, and furnished 39·3 per cent. of its agricultural produce, 49 per cent. of its horses, 45 per cent. of its cattle, 66·6 per cent. of its iron, and 60 per cent. of its coal.[1] Set off against these staggering losses, the moral loss of the Germans was irreparable. In the "hedgehogs" of the winter months the cutting edge of the Grand Army of 1941 was blunted, and its temper could not be restored by the addition of the base metal of Italian, Rumanian and other satellite levies. Further, the economic gains in Russia were more than cancelled by the growing stranglehold of the British and American blockade.

Finally, what was the significance of Hitler's failure to take Moscow? Admiral Assmann's answer is that it was "the turning point of the war." But if this were so, would the turning point have been avoided had Hitler occupied Moscow? Beyond it extended 4,500 miles of unconquered territory, and since December 11 the United States had become involved in the war against Germany. Is it likely that, at this critical moment for Hitler, Stalin would have accepted a negotiated German peace, and even had he done so, would Hitler have trusted him to abide by its terms?

The turning point of the war was not Hitler's failure to occupy Moscow, but Roosevelt's astuteness in bringing the United States into the war, and this could only have been avoided, or its results mitigated, had Hitler grasped that, as Roosevelt's problem was how to unite the Americans in a war against Germany, his problem was how to detach the subjugated peoples of the U.S.S.R. from their masters in the Kremlin. Although this is a hypothetical question, it would seem probable that, had he come to them as a liberator, he would have dissolved most of the Soviet Army and have overthrown the Bolshevik régime months before Roosevelt had accomplished his self-appointed task, and had he succeeded in doing so, the one thing he dreaded most would have been avoided – namely, a war on two fronts. His error was political more than strategic; he struck at the iron head of his monstrous antagonist instead of at his feet of clay. Had he struck at the

[1] Quoted by Léderrey in *La défaite Allemande à l'est*, p. 58.

486

latter – that is, had he relied on counter-revolution and not on conquest – possibly there would have been no turning point at all. In any case, the whole outcome of the war would have been different; either Germany would have been defeated without Russian aid, or the war would have ended in a negotiated peace in which the Kremlin would have played no part.

Not for nothing, when he embarked on autobiography, did General Fuller call his book *Memoirs Of An Unconventional Soldier*. His analysis of the motivations and transactions of Allied leaders during the Second World War conforms entirely to this view of himself, and should convince anyone of its truth. Thus:

'At nine o'clock on the evening of the day Hitler invaded Russia, Mr. Churchill said in a broadcast to the British people: "I have to declare the decision of His Majesty's Government. . . . We have but one aim and one single irrevocable purpose. We are resolved to destroy Hitler and every vestige of the Nazi régime. . . . We will never parley, we will never negotiate with Hitler or any of his gang. . . . Any man or state who fights on against Nazidom will have our aid. Any man or state who marches with Hitler is our foe. . . . That is our policy and that is our declaration. It follows therefore that we shall give whatever help we can to Russia and the Russian people."

'From this and similar utterances it is clear that Mr. Churchill had no conception of the task demanded of him in his capacity of Prime Minister and Minister of Defence. Firstly, it should have been to win a peace which would be profitable to his country, and there could be neither moral nor political advantage in substituting Stalin for Hitler. Secondly, because he had postulated the extirpation of Hitler and Hitlerism as his aim, he should have differentiated between the Nazi régime and the mass of the German people. Had he done so, he would have seen that his most profitable ally was the extensive anti-Hitler faction in Germany, and in accordance with his declaration he would have given it his aid. But, overmastered by his emotions, he committed the selfsame blunder that Hitler had made when he failed to distinguish between the pro- and anti-Stalinist peoples of the U.S.S.R. This blunder prolonged the war by years, and in spite of ultimate victory, it lost the peace and made the war an absurdity.

'Thirdly, bound to Poland as the British Government was by the Anglo-Polish treaty, and faced with her partition – in which Stalin was as guilty as Hitler – Mr. Churchill should not have impulsively thrown his country into the arms of the Soviets, but should have paused until Stalin had sought his aid, and only then have proffered it on the understanding that the Ribbentrop-Molotov Pact of August 23, 1939, was first annulled, and that all Polish prisoners and deported Poles in Russian hands were released.

' His partner in this negation of statesmanship was the American President who, obsessed by the collection of votes, sedulously cultivated the Communists and their fellow travellers, who held the balance of power in New York State. The outcome was, an American writer says: when Hitler invaded Russia the New Deal bureaux became the "roosting places for droves of Communist termites." Almost unbelievably, this infiltration was so successful that American Communists – agents of the Kremlin – obtained controlling positions in many of the government departments.[1] It was the work of these agents which deluded the President and thereby helped to shape his war policy toward Russia.'

Fuller's thesis is that President Roosevelt was determined to bring the United States into the war; that his only problem was how to do it; and that his answer was to provoke Japan deliberately into an act of war which would rally the American people. This is an interesting proposition, which, clearly there is not space enough to argue out here. It leads Fuller to the conclusion that the famous meeting between Churchill and Roosevelt, in August 1941, at Placentia Bay, was about the method and timing of this provocation of Japan more than anything else – "he (Roosevelt) promised Churchill that the United States 'even if not herself attacked, would come into the war in the Far East.' " Fuller continues:

' As these commitments could not be made public, the notorious Atlantic Declaration, or Charter, was concocted. It was nothing more than a publicity hand-out, and was never intended to be a

---

[1] For a score or more of these agents see *The Twenty-Year Revolution from Roosevelt to Eisenhower*, Chesly Manly (1954), pp. 99–103. Manly quotes the following evidence before the Senate sub-committee on August 14, 1951: "I would say that our best ones [Communist agents] were Henry Dexter White and Lauchlin Currie. . . ." The former became assistant secretary to the Treasury and the latter administrative assistant on eastern affairs to the President.

formal state paper, nor was it inscribed, signed and sealed; it was merely mimeographed and released. It was a highly idealistic document in which it was laid down that no territorial changes would be made which did not accord with the freely expressed wishes of the people concerned; that all peoples were to be given the right to choose the form of government under which they wished to live; that all States, victor or vanquished, were to have access on equal terms to the trade and raw materials of the world; and that after the final destruction of Nazi tyranny a peace was to be established which would permit all nations to dwell safely within their own boundaries, so that all men in all lands might live out their lives in freedom from fear and want.

'Had it been adhered to, it would have been impossible to implement; as it happened, all it did was to delude the world. Nevertheless, until it was scrapped at the Teheran Conference, it was first-class propaganda, and probably the biggest hoax in history.'

What cannot be expunged from history is the fact that, whether or not Roosevelt himself, or his left-wing advisers, were being as Machiavellian as Fuller suggests, the event as it transpired was neither to their taste nor to their advantage. (In passing, it may be said that the weakness of his argument is that it ignores Japanese attitudes and policies.) Anyway, the dénouement was the virtual destruction of the American Pacific Fleet at Pearl Harbour by surprise air attack on 7 December 1941. This put the United States fairly and squarely into the war, and, as Fuller says, because she was "the greatest industrial power in the world, from the moment she entered the war she became potentially the dominant belligerent."

Unfortunately for the world, because her leaders lacked historic sense and looked upon war as a lethal game rather than an instrument of policy, battles began to lose their political value as soon as the United States entered the war. So much was this so that, during the latter half of the war, their results were as often as not neutralized by political events. Thus, it came about that conferences, such as those held at Casablanca, Teheran, and Yalta, were not only far more decisive than any battle fought, but they annulled the decisions the latter achieved. Further, whereas in the military sphere, because of the enormous strides made in technology, the generals-in-chief increasingly became the rubber-stamps of a host of technicians and industrialists, on the political plane power increasingly passed from cabinets and parliaments into the hands of single statesmen – heads of state – who at times, advised as they were by military simpletons and political crackpots and deluded by their own propaganda, committed the most egregious strategical and political blunders.'

The first of the Anglo-American Conferences ("ARCADIA", December 1941 – January 1942) displayed both the strength and the weakness of the new method of running a coalition war. On the military side, straight away, a tremendous step forward was taken which ensured that the endless, sterile disputations about "Unity of Direction" which had haunted Allied strategy during the First World War would not be repeated: the setting up of the "Combined Chiefs of Staff Committee", consisting of the British and American Chiefs of Staff, or their representatives, to exercise continuous strategical control of the war. The value of this can hardly be over-stated. On the political side, however, it was a different story. Here, says Fuller, one sees "the fateful beginning of the end – the initiation of a policy which was to cost the two western allies the peace."

'It was the pet idea of President Roosevelt and was called by him the "Great Design." It was a reversion to the Wilsonian policy of 1917–1918 without the 14 points, and may be compared with a pot of political ale – all froth. His proposal was that, once the war was at an end, the nations of the world should be united into a great organization for peace. This association of sovereign Powers was to be modelled on the American inter-state system and be based on the principles of the Atlantic Charter. Since it was essential that this band of brothers should include Russia, nothing must be left undone to win Stalin's collaboration. In the President's opinion this presented no insuperable difficulty, because Harry Hopkins, his *eminence grise*,[1] who had visited Stalin soon after the German invasion, had told him that it was ridiculous to think of Stalin as a communist; he was nothing of the sort, he was a great Russian nationalist and patriot. Whatever his views might be about the future of Europe, he must be won over. Although the President did not then realize it, appeasement of Russia was to become the linch-pin in allied policy.

' This sublime nonsense, christened by the President the "United Nations", was accepted by the conference as the peace programme

[1] Sherwood calls him "the *de facto* Deputy President" (*The White House Papers of Harry L. Hopkins*, 1946, vol. 1, p. 267); Churchill – "high among the Paladins," and Representative Dewey Short of Missouri – "The White House Rasputin."

of the allied Powers, and on January 1, 1942, a joint declaration was signed by the United States and United Kingdom, as well as 24 other nations, including the U.S.S.R. It endorsed the Atlantic Charter and proclaimed that the signatories were "convinced that complete victory over their enemies is essential to defend life, liberty, independence, and religious freedom, and to preserve human rights and justice in their own lands as well as in other lands, and that they are now engaged in a common struggle against savage and brutal forces seeking to subjugate the world."

' Thus was created the policy which was to render abortive every victory won by the two great western allies; bring the Slav back to the Elbe; and replace Hitler by Stalin.'

Meanwhile, whatever may have been the causes of her entering the war, Japan was signalising her presence with a series of conquests which caused the utmost embarrassment to the Allies. Hong Kong was bombarded on the same day as Pearl Harbour; almost simultaneously, the Japanese landed in Malaya. On 10 December they sank the two British capital ships, PRINCE OF WALES and REPULSE, and on the same day invaded the Philippines. A week later they attacked Sarawak, and a week after that Hong Kong surrendered. Manila fell on 2 January, and on the 3rd the Japanese arrived in Borneo. On the 23rd they were in New Guinea, and on the 29th in Java. Everywhere their enemies crumbled before them; neither British, nor Dutch, nor American forces seemed able to withstand the ferocious tide unleashed in so many directions at once. The great British Far Eastern fortress of Singapore fell on 15 February, and eighty-five thousand men laid down their arms – the greatest single military disaster in British history. Already the invasion of Burma had begun. On 9 March the Japanese captured Rangoon, and on the same day Java surrendered, marking the effective end of Dutch resistance in the East Indies. On 9 April the American forces in Bataan (Philippines) surrendered. On 1 May the Japanese were in Mandalay. On 6 May the last Americans in the Philippines surrendered at Corregidor. On 15 May the British were out of Burma. In five and a half months the British and Dutch Empires in South East Asia had been snuffed out; American power and prestige had taken a fearful knock; the Japanese stood at the gates of India, and Australia feared imminent invasion. Yet all this glittering success proved illusory; Fuller writes:

' In spite of these initial successes, the Japanese plan was based on two miscalculations. It not only challenged the two greatest naval powers, but also the two greatest industrial powers in the world, and the United States could not be crippled permanently even were Germany to win the war in Europe. What the Japanese overlooked was that the industrial potential of the United States was so vast that in time she could overcome all strategical obstacles of space and distance, and that the United States was a Power which, as they should have known, would choose to overcome them at whatever cost rather than negotiate a limited peace. Of all Japan's blunders this was the greatest: she believed that America would be willing to barter "losing face" for a short war, when she herself was willing to risk her existence in a long war rather than "lose face" by a withdrawal from China.'

The war in the Far East now entered a new phase, dominated by American power (although the decision of the Combined Chiefs of Staff that the defeat of Germany should be the main objective of the Allies still stood). The American effort expressed itself, strategically, in two ways: first, the bold decision to make Australia the base for Army operations against the Japanese, under General Douglas MacArthur, despite the immense distances involved (San Francisco to Sydney, direct—6,590 miles) across an ocean where the Japanese Navy was, for the time being, supreme. Secondly, there was the dramatic, almost unbelievable revival of American naval strength, which found its first expression as early as 4 June 1942, at the Battle of Midway.

Midway, like its "curtain-raiser", the Battle of the Coral Sea a month earlier, confirmed that a new era of naval warfare had arrived. In both actions, apart from anti-aircraft fire and the operations of submarines, the fight was entirely waged by carrier-borne aircraft – "not a shot was fired between surface craft." At the Coral Sea the Americans emerged from "a fantastic chapter of accidents and blunders"[1] with a narrow margin of strategic advantage; by contrast "the battle of Midway was one of the most brilliant ever fought, and a decisive turning point in the Pacific War."[1] The advantage of numbers still lay with the Japanese, but the Americans, under the firm handling of Admiral Nimitz, having broken the Japanese naval cipher, made the most of their opportunity. Four Japanese carriers were sunk, at a cost of one American carrier and one hundred and forty seven aircraft. Fuller writes:

[1] Peter Young, *World War 1939-45*, Arthur Barker, 1966.

' "The Battle of Midway," writes Admiral King, "was the first decisive defeat suffered by the Japanese Navy in 350 years."[1] It was one of those rare battles in which a numerically inferior fleet suddenly snatched victory from a superior force, and thereby changed the course of war. The destruction of two-thirds of Japan's fleet carriers knocked the bottom out of her grand tactical scheme to hold the Pacific by means of "hedgehogs" and mobile forces, and it threw her on the passive defensive. For the remainder of the war it secured the central Pacific for the United States; put into pawn the Japanese occupation of Attu and Kiska in the Aleutians, and restricted Japan's ambitious plan to conquer Fiji, Samoa and New Caledonia in order to sever Australia from North America. Finally, it struck a mortal blow at Japanese prestige.'

In *The Conduct Of War* Fuller has stated with perfect clarity a thought which has always been central in his military studies: "the true aim of war is peace and not victory; therefore that peace should be the ruling idea of policy, and victory only the means towards its achievement." It is this thought which guides his analysis of the Anglo-American campaigns in North Africa and Europe, and which supplies, for him, a special significance of the war against Italy. He says:

' Because the aim of the two western allies – the United States and the United Kingdom – was to exterminate Hitlerism, there could be no political advantage were Hitlerism to be replaced by Stalinism, and because Hitler's failure to occupy Moscow had shown that his expectations of driving Russia out of the war before the United States entered it, had been frustrated, the aim of the western allies clearly had become not only to extirpate Hitlerism, but simultaneously to prevent its replacement by Stalinism. Should they fail to do so, then, the more Germany was crushed, the more would the war politically be lost by the West.

' This dual aim could only be attained if Germany were driven out of the war before Russia developed her full strength, and because the western allies could not hope to defeat the German armies and occupy Germany before this became probable, their sole rational course was to help Russia to withstand defeat while they entered into close cooperation with the extensive anti-Nazi faction in Germany to foment revolution within the Reich and at the same time to knock Italy out of the war. Could this latter aim be attained while they stimulated revolt in Germany, then except for the improbable event of a renewal of the Nazi-Soviet

Pact of 1939–1941, whatever happened in Russia the western allies would strategically be well placed, not only to penetrate the centre of the German southern front, which extended from the Bay of Biscay to the Black Sea, but also to flank from the south a Russian advance into eastern and central Europe, and thereby bring Russia to heel. Vienna, and not Paris, was the goal of their military strategy. Could they but turn these two keys in their respective locks; could they foment revolution within the Reich and simultaneously occupy, or even only threaten, Vienna, there would be every chance that they would be able to exterminate Hitlerism while Hitler was still engaged in Russia, and thereby become the arbiters of the peace which would follow the war. It was for this reason, and it should have been as obvious at the time as it was when the war ended, that Stalin so insistently pressed for the opening of a second front in northern France – that is, to get his allies as far away from Vienna as possible.'

Until the end of 1942 there was no difficulty about keeping the western powers away from Vienna. The Americans were not engaged against the German and Italian land forces at all; the British were only engaged in Libya – and there the pendulum swings of desert warfare had, by July of that year, brought them right back to their start-line inside Egypt. Fuller writes:

'Since it is not the intention here to consider in any detail the campaigns which immediately followed, it is as well to appreciate why Libya was for so long the racecourse of the war: each army in turn galloped forward until its momentum was exhausted, and then was compelled to gallop back to avoid annihilation. The reason centred almost entirely in supply and, like a piece of elastic, the line of supply of both armies could be stretched with comparative safety to between 300 and 400 miles from its base – Tripoli on the one hand and Alexandria on the other. But as these two main bases were over 1,400 miles apart, to try to stretch them farther before intermediate bases were established was to risk snapping the elastic. The supply problem of both sides was how to increase the elasticity of their respective supply systems. This could only be done by building up stockpiles at their respective main bases, and step by step pushing forward the advanced bases. As both sides were separated from their homelands by the sea, the tussle was governed by sea communications.'

Throughout the Desert campaigns the island of Malta remained a thorn in the side of the Axis forces; shipping losses created a steady drain on their resources; not even the tactical genius of General Rommel, nor the battle-skill of his Afrika Korps, could rise above 75 per cent sinkings, which was what the monthly rate on one occasion mounted to. On 1 July 1942 the Axis forces, though victorious, were already seriously weakened by this interruption of supply and reinforcement. Nevertheless, Rommel elected to make another try for Egypt, and it was on that day that the decisive First Battle of El Alamein began. It swayed back and forth on a narrow front for seventeen days, and at the end of it Rommel was a beaten man. The victor was General Auchinleck, who had replaced Wavell as Commander-in-Chief, Middle East, a year before; he was the victor in the full and true sense of the word, because when his army had faced severe defeat in June he had taken personal command in the field. This was his vindication.

> On 17 July 1942, Auchinleck had won a historic battle. It had been as desperate, difficult and gallant as Wellington's repulse of Napoleon at Waterloo, but for Auchinleck there was no Blücher with forty thousand fresh men to come up on the flank and turn defeat into rout. Nevertheless Auchinleck had saved the Middle East, with all that this implied for the general course of the war. It was the turning point.[1]

It is an irony that, only a fortnight later, the victorious general was replaced in his command – the penalty of forfeiting political goodwill. Churchill at this time was like Lincoln, restlessly seeking the right general until he found Grant in 1864. Churchill found two "right generals" – Alexander, who took over from Auchinleck as overall theatre commander, and Montgomery, who took command of the field (8th) army. "Montgomery," says Fuller, "was a man of dynamic personality and of supreme self-confidence. Known to his officers and men as 'Monty', he was a past-master in showmanship and publicity; audacious in his utterances and cautious in his actions. . . . He was the right man in the right place at the right moment; for after its severe defeat[2] the Eighth Army needed a new dynamo and Montgomery supplied it." But the first battle of the new command was a defensive one; Rommel, despite ever-mounting supply problems,

[1] Correlli Barnett, *The Desert Generals*, Kimber, 1960, p. 207.

[2] Fuller is clearly alluding to the defeats *before* the First Battle of El Alamein.

determined on one more throw for the Nile Delta. The three-day Battle of Alam Halfa, which began on 31 August, marked the doom of a hope which had never been more than forlorn. Montgomery had proved himself a master of the defensive; he now showed himself to be a patient, meticulous preparer of the offensive.

The Second Battle of El Alamein (23 October – 5 November) has rightly gone down as a large event in British military history. So it was; it marked the transition to continuous offensive warfare against the Axis – for Montgomery, a long, satisfying march from Egypt to Lüneburg Heath. Yet its significance has – especially by British writers – been exaggerated, and some of its lessons distorted. The 13,500 British casualties in thirteen days have been contrasted with the 415,000 (in four and a half months) of the Battle of the Somme in 1916, which was the watershed of the First World War. This misses the point that, while Montgomery engaged and defeated four German divisions at El Alamein (the bulk of Rommel's troops being the now largely demoralised Italians), Haig's armies on the Somme engaged and defeated eighty-three German divisions – a proceeding liable to cause heavy loss. Further, while El Alamein certainly revealed a satisfying British military revival, nevertheless the changing texture of the war very soon relegated the British to a junior rôle in the great drama. To that extent, the bells which rang in Britain for the victory of Alamein were like those which rang for Cambrai in November 1917: they celebrated illusion.

The fighting at El Alamein ended on 5 November, with Rommel in full retreat and Montgomery in cautious pursuit. Three days later the Anglo-American landings in French North Africa began – significantly, under an American Supreme Commander, General Dwight D. Eisenhower, of whom more would be heard. When Montgomery's Eighth Army joined up with the force in North Africa, at the end of the two-thousand-mile march of victory from Alamein to Tunis, the British were once more the preponderant part of the Allied array. Under the skilful handling of Alexander the Allies (among whom French units were now included) remorselessly closed in on the Axis forces. On 12–13 May says Fuller:

250,000 Germans and Italians laid down their arms and only 663 escaped by sea. . . . After two and a half years of tilting up and down North Africa, the decisive battles of El Alamein and Tunis ended the first victorious allied campaign of the war. A base had been established from which Italy could directly be attacked and a road to central Europe opened. All that remained for America and Britain to do was with the utmost speed to exploit their success and drive Italy out of the war.

Already, however, political infirmities had gravely affected both the Allied capacity to profit from success and the opportunity to undermine the Axis from within. At the Casablanca Conference in January 1942, President Roosevelt coined the unfortunate definition of Allied war aims: "unconditional surrender". Fuller writes:

'The implication of this slipshod slogan were even more fatal to the future of the western world than Woodrow Wilson's "self-determination". Here it may be remarked that a statesman should never publicly bind himself to an irreversible decision, and that of all men Mr. Churchill should, from constant practice, have been aware that the essence of successful politics is ability to turn somersaults without loss of face.

'Firstly, what unconditional surrender implied was that war was no longer to be accepted as an instrument of creative policy –the establishment of a profitable and stable peace–but that it was to be an instrument of pure destruction. From Casablanca a vulture was unleashed to batten on the entrails of Europe.

' Like the Bourbons, Roosevelt and Churchill had learnt nothing and forgotten nothing. Both had before them the example of the abortive peace-making of 1919, from which Hitler had sprung, and although both the American and British psychological warfare experts pressed for a definition of what "unconditional surrender" meant, all their efforts foundered on the rock of Roosevelt's opposition. When, on March 16, 1944, a committee set up by the United States Joint Chiefs of Staff to study the implications of the slogan recommended that the allies should declare that, although war criminals would be punished, there would be no indiscriminate penalization of the German people because Germany's cooperation would be needed in the future peace, Roosevelt's reply on April 1 was an "uncompromising negative."

' Of all the judgments which have since been passed on this

monstrous and momentous slogan, the most powerful is the one made by a statesman the best qualified to make it. In his book *Politics Trials and Errors*, Lord Hankey writes: "It embittered the war, rendered inevitable a fight to a finish, banged the door on any possibility of either side offering terms or opening up negotiations, gave the Germans and Japanese the courage of despair, strengthened Hitler's position as Germany's 'only hope', aided Goebbel's propaganda, and made inevitable the Normandy landing and the subsequent terribly exhausting and destructive advance through North France, Belgium, Luxemburg, Holland, and Germany. The lengthening of the war enabled Stalin to occupy the whole of eastern Europe, to ring down the iron curtain and so to realize at one swoop a large instalment of his avowed aims against so-called capitalism, in which he includes social democracy. By disposing of all the more competent administrators in Germany and Japan this policy rendered treaty-making impossible after the war and retarded recovery and reconstruction, not only in Germany and Japan, but everywhere else. It may also prove to have poisoned our future relations with ex-enemy countries. Not only the enemy countries, but nearly all countries were bled white by this policy, which has left us all, except the United States of America, impoverished and in dire straits. Unfortunately also, these policies, so contrary to the spirit of the Sermon on the Mount, did nothing to strengthen the moral position of the Allies."'

The ill results were soon seen. On 10 July the Anglo-American forces invaded Sicily, and on 24 July Mussolini was overthrown. Ten days later Italian envoys arrived in Lisbon to discuss terms of surrender with the Allies. But Roosevelt was still publicly proclaiming "unconditional surrender" or nothing (though privately both he and Churchill were in some doubt as to what it meant in such a situation). It took a month to work out a compromise solution which could bring Italy out of the Axis camp into that of the Allies – a lamentable loss of time and opportunity. As Fuller says:

Unfortunately for the western allies the wrangling gave Hitler over four weeks to pour reinforcements into Italy. The first fruits of unconditional surrender were that the gilt was rubbed off the El Alamein and Tunis gingerbread, and that the offspring of these decisive battles was the most unprofitable allied campaign of the war.

'But their immediate results were highly profitable to the two western allies because the conquest of North Africa had reopened the Mediterranean and so released millions of tons of allied shipping; it had doubled the area of occupied Europe which could be threatened and thereby had added vastly to the liabilities of Hitler's negative front; it tested the requirements of big amphibious operations; and it smoothed the rough edges off American and British cooperation and welded together their respective fighting forces. '

The foundations of the Stalingrad campaign

The situation which faced Hitler in the spring of 1942 was very different from that of nine months before. Then his prestige was at its height; his armies swept victoriously into Russia, England was isolated, and America, although truculent, was still nominally neutral. Now he was faced by a war on two fronts, the one thing he had dreaded most, and to disentangle himself from this disastrous situation it should have been apparent to him that, since his fatal policy had antagonized the subjugated peoples under Muscovite rule and had bereft him of all hope of the subjugation of Russia by internal revolution, he was left with two alternatives: either to destroy Russia's military power or to render it impotent before the Americans and British could develop their full fighting strength. The first he had already attempted and had failed, and as the Russians had unlimited space in which to fall back, which carried with it a progressive weakening of the German armies by lengthening their communications through hostile country, there was no reason to suppose that in 1942 it would prove more successful than it had in 1941. Hitler was left with the second alternative. What did it demand?

Firstly, the occupation of Moscow to cripple Russian communications; secondly, the occupation of Vologda to block the ingress of lend-lease supplies from Archangel; and thirdly, the occupation of Kirov, Kazan, Ulanovsk, Kuibishev, and Saratov to sever the Russian armies west of the Urals from the resources and man-power of Asiatic Russia. In brief, he had to establish a defensive line along the upper and middle Volga, approximately as laid down in Directive No. 21 of December 18, 1940. Could this be done in 1942, then a situation would be created in the east in which Russia's fighting power would progressively so weaken that, by the time America and Britain could take the field in strength, it would be possible to leave a minimum of forces in Russia and concentrate a maximum in the west. But Hitler did not implement this policy. The primary idea of the plan he adopted was to strengthen his military potential by the seizure of Russian oil, and the secondary consideration was that the enemy would be weakened because of its loss.

The plan decided on was his own, for since his failure to take Moscow Hitler seldom consulted his General Staff. He exaggerated the capacity of his own armies as grossly as he underrated that of his enemy, and when a statement was read to him in which it was pointed out that Stalin was still able to muster 1,500,000 men in the region north of Stalingrad, besides 500,000 in the Caucasus, according to Halder, "he flew at the man who was reading with clenched fists and foam in the corners of his mouth, and forbade him to read such idiotic twaddle." Halder remarks: ". . . his decisions had ceased to have anything in common with the principles of strategy . . . as they had been recognized for generations past. They were the product of a violent nature following its momentary impulses, a nature which acknowledged no bounds to possibility, and which made the wish the father of the deed."

He was profoundly influenced in this by his leading industrialists and economic advisers, who constantly impressed upon him that, unless the Caucasian oilfields were won, the Reich would collapse. Without further ado he accepted this at face value and decided that the occupation of these oilfields should be the goal of his 1942 campaign.

He was easily persuaded, for since the war began oil had been his nightmare. In 1941 his total supply had amounted to 8,929,000 tons, and he had only been able to carry on the war by withdrawing 1,140,000 tons from his reserves, which, excluding the needs of the navy, had by the end of 1941 fallen to 797,000 tons – barely one month's supply. In 1941 the yield of the Rumanian oilfields provided him with some 5,500,000 tons, half of which was earmarked for Rumania and her army, and synthetic production was about the same. Together they were insufficient to wage an extensive campaign on two fronts; sufficiency of oil was indeed a vital problem. Nevertheless the fact remained that wars are based on strategy, and although the foundations of strategy are in part economic – food, coal, oil, iron – economic security cannot compensate for the lack of military sanity. Hitler should have thought of this before he went to war, but once he had crossed the Rubicon, there was little chance of winning it were strategy subordinated to economics.

According to Goebbels who, on March 20, 1942, discussed the situation with Hitler, the latter had "a perfectly clear plan for the coming spring and summer. He does not want," he writes, "to overextend the war. His aims are the Caucasus, Leningrad, and Moscow. If these aims are attained, he is determined, whatever the circumstances, to end the campaign at the beginning of next October and to go into winter quarters early. He intends possibly to construct a gigantic line of defence and to let the eastern campaign rest there." On this Goebbels comments: "Possibly this may mean a hundred years' war in the East, but that need not worry us."

Save for local pressure on Leningrad, Hitler decided to assume the defensive on the whole front, except in the south, and whatever he may have said to Dr. Goebbels he had no intention to take Moscow. His aim was to occupy the Caucasus up to the line Batum–Baku and, in order to cover this operation, to establish a defensive front along the Don from Voronezh to Stalingrad. To accomplish this, he decided to break through the Russian front between Taganrog and Kursk.

This plan was radically unsound. Not only were the troops at his disposal – more especially German – insufficient simultaneously to carry out both operations, but to stretch the covering forces over a distance of 360 miles was to offer an enormous flank to Russian attack. If the Russians broke through this vulnerable flank and occupied Rostov the whole of the German forces in Caucasia would be cut off from their base.

It would appear that, when he came to these decisions, Hitler took no notice whatsoever of the Russian railway communications leading to the Voronezh–Stalingrad front, of which Saratov was their strategic centre. Saratov was linked to Moscow by rail; to the Ural industrial region by rail and river; to Astrakhan by rail east of the Volga; and to Chkalov on the river Ural by rail, near which a pipe-line ran to the north Caspian oilfields. Troops, munitions, fuel, and supplies could therefore be poured into the Saratov area from Moscow, Archangel, Siberia, Kazakh, Caucasia and Persia. Further, the lateral railways Tula–Penza–Syzran, Michurinsk–Tambov–Saratov, Tambov–Balashov–Kamishin, Voronezh–Rojestvenskoe–Stalingrad, when coupled with the longitudinal railways Moscow–Voronezh and Gorki–Penza–Balashov, made the area north of the Don well suited for the concentration of troops and supplies.

South of Stalingrad, Astrakhan played a similar though subordinate part. By way of Saratov it was linked by rail to the whole of unoccupied Russia, and by way of the Caspian to Persia and thence to the outer world; for in the south the Caspian Sea played the same strategic role as that of the White Sea in the north. Stalingrad was of little strategic importance; it was too distant to cover the forces operating in Caucasia, and it did not block the Volga any more efficiently than did Saratov. In any case, the Volga was ice-bound for five to six months in the year.

By the spring of 1942 Hitler had under his command 232 divisions, of which 171 were German and 61 satellite. The former consisted of 134 infantry, 24 armoured, and 13 motorized divisions, and the latter of 22 Rumanian, 10 Italian, 10 Hungarian, 17 Finnish, one Spanish and one Slovak, of which four were armoured. Though numerically a much larger army than that of 1941, it was weaker. The satellite divisions were indifferently armed and equipped – according to Antonescu, the Rumanians were next to worthless – and the strength of the German infantry divisions had been reduced from nine to six battalions, and only 10 of the original 20 armoured divisions had been brought up to full strength, because priority had been given to submarine construction.

Because of the enormous losses suffered in 1941, the Soviet Army of 1942 was largely composed of Asiatics, the tough Hunnish peoples of central Asia who centuries before had followed Attila and Genghis Khan. Although of low intelligence and almost wholly illiterate, they possessed immense natural tenacity and endurance. They not only replenished their supplies from the regions through which they advanced, but also their numbers; all able-bodied men found *en route* were conscripted straight into the front line units. Field-Marshal von Manstein says that "the dynamic of the Red Army was the same as that of the revolutionary armies of France, a combination of fanaticism and terror," and General Dittmar considered that the Russians' chief asset was "the soulless indifference of the troops" which was "something more than fatalism."

According to Field-Marshal von Rundstedt, none of the Russian generals of 1941 was any good; but by the spring of 1942, the war had winnowed away much of the chaff and not a few of the higher commanders were as efficient as the German, particularly Marshal Zhukov, who in 1921–1923 had studied strategy under General von Seeckt in Germany. Nevertheless, in order to fit the low intelligence of the bulk of the troops, tactical plans and operations had to be kept simple and rigid, and in consequence were easy to dislocate. According to Manstein, the Soviet Army was more effective in advance than in retreat. The vast numbers it could bring into the field enabled it simultaneously to attack at a large number of places; wave after wave of infantry advanced until a weak spot was found, when the armoured units would break through and the infantry follow.

In 1942 the Russian armoured formations were manned by picked troops, and the Russian T.34 tank, in design simple to the point of crudity, was superior to any German tank before the introduction of the Panther and Tiger in 1943. Cavalry were still employed in large numbers and were particularly useful during the spring thaws. The transport and supply services remained indifferent, and in General Geyr von Schweppenburg's opinion, had it not been for the thousands of lend-lease trucks which, in 1942, began to pour in from America, the Russian armies would never have survived the 1942 campaign. Against this must be set the statements of a considerable number of German generals made to Captain Liddell Hart after the war. They held that "the Russians' greatest asset was the way they could do without normal supplies," and General von Manteuffel told Liddell Hart that "The advance of a Russian Army is something that Westerners can't imagine. Behind the tank spearheads rolls on a vast horde, largely mounted on horses. The soldier carries a sack on his back, with dry crusts of bread and raw vegetables collected on the march from the fields and villages. The horses eat the straw from the house roofs – they get very little else. The Russians are accustomed to carry on for as long as three weeks in this primitive way, when advancing. You can't stop them, like an ordinary army, by cutting their communications, for you rarely find any supply columns to strike."[1]

Although Halder was still Chief of Staff, the 1942 plan of campaign was entirely Hitler's, and in April he reshuffled his forces. Army Group South was disbanded and replaced by Army Groups A and B. The former was commanded by Field-Marshal List; it consisted of the First Panzer Army (General von Kleist), the Seventeenth Army (General Ruoff), supported by the Fourth Air Fleet, and its task was to conquer the Caucasus. The latter, whose task was to cover the northern flank of Army Group A by

[1] This cannot have applied to the Russian armoured and motorized forces.

the occupation of the Stalingrad area, was commanded by Field-Marshal von Bock, and it comprised the Second Army (General von Weichs), the Fourth Panzer Army (General Hoth), and the Sixth Army (General von Paulus), supported by Luftwaffe Don Command. Behind these two groups in second *échelon* were the Second Hungarian, Eighth Italian, and Third Rumanian Armies, and apart from them in the Crimea General von Manstein's Eleventh Army, which included the Fourth Rumanian Army. In all, 60 German divisions, of which 10 were armoured and six motorized, and 43 satellite divisions were allotted to the southern front.

The combined operation of the two army groups was code-named *"Blau"* (Blue), and the campaign was to be carried out on the following lines:

From the south of Kursk, the Fourth Panzer Army of Army Group B was to advance on Voronezh, but not to occupy it. Followed by the Sixth Army, it was then to wheel south-eastward and move down the right bank of the Don toward Stalingrad, and as these two armies did so, the Second German, Second Hungarian, Eighth Italian, and Third Rumanian Armies were to take over the defence of the river to its bend west of Stalingrad; later the Fourth Rumanian Army was to hold the front south of Stalingrad. Under cover of this manœuvre, Army Group A was to advance from between Taganrog and Iyzum toward the lower Don about Rostov. The First Panzer Army was to pave the way for the Seventeenth Army, which was to join in the offensive once the former had crossed the Don, and by the Eleventh Army after it had reconquered the Crimea.

It is opportune here briefly to describe Hitler's system of issuing orders, because it led to endless confusion. Each evening the approximate positions of the forward troops were sent by wireless to Army Headquarters, and thence transmitted to Supreme Headquarters and placed before Hitler during the following morning, when orders for the day were issued. As they seldom reached the front line troops until late in the afternoon, by when their positions had frequently completely changed, as often as not they were inapplicable, and when they were not obeyed violent altercations followed. Compared with Napoleon's system that of Hitler was amateurish in the extreme.[1]

On May 8, 1942, the campaign in the Crimea was reopened by

[1] See pp. 105-6

Manstein's Eleventh Army, which consisted of seven German and six Rumanian divisions; the defences around Kerch were broken through, and on May 15 the town of Kerch was occupied. In spite of the numerical superiority of the Russians, again their losses were phenomenal, for Manstein captured 150,000 prisoners, 1,133 guns, and 255 tanks. On June 2, he laid siege to Sebastopol, and after a month's severe fighting the fortress and 100,000 Russians surrendered to him.

In the meantime, Marshal Timoshenko opened a violent offensive north-east and south-east of Kharkov on May 12. He broke through the German defences and next struck at Krasnograd; then his momentum petered out. On May 17 he was counterattacked by Kleist's First Panzer Army, supported by the Seventeenth and Sixth Armies, and was forced back. He was unable to withdraw his troops around Izyum and on May 26 they were surrounded. On the following day they were forced to capitulate. This abortive spoiling attack, which had little influence on the German preparations, cost Timoshenko 240,000 men captured, 2,026 guns, and 1,249 tanks. In subsequent operations in June around Volchansk, Izyum, and Kupyansk the Germans captured another 38,000 Russians.[1]

Understandably Hitler was elated by these captures, but unfortunately for him they would seem to have convinced him that he was right and his generals were wrong; that he had nothing further to fear from the Russians, and that by October Operation *"Blau"* would bring the war in the east to a victorious end.

---

[1] All these figures are from German sources, and therefore may be exaggerated.

CHAPTER 10

The Battle of Stalingrad, 1942-1943

On June 28, 1942, the Stalingrad campaign was opened by a sudden advance of the Second Army and the Fourth Panzer Army of Army Group B from about Kursk eastward on Voronezh. It came as a complete surprise to the Russians who, because of the lack of roads eastward of the line Kurzk–Izyum, did not expect a major German advance in that area, and in consequence the line of the Oskol river was held by little more than outposts. On June 30, the Sixth Army struck eastward from between Bielgorod and Volchansk and the advance of all three armies was so rapid that it appeared to Hitler that Russian resistance was at an end. On July 3 the advanced guards of the Second Army and Fourth Panzer Army neared Voronezh, and those of the Sixth, which by then had crossed the Oskol, pressed toward Korotoyak on the Don. Voronezh was reached on July 5, where the first severe fighting was experienced; but as Hitler did not intend to occupy the town, he ordered the Fourth Panzer Army, when relieved by the Second Army, to wheel southward down the Don, while the Sixth Army wheeled to the south-east on Rossosh.

No sooner were these movements under way than, on July 9, from between Izyum and Kupyansk the First Panzer Army set out down the northern bank of the Donetz, took Lisiachiansk, and on the 10th, when it approached Millerovo, the Fourth Panzer Army occupied Kantemirovka. The aim of these movements was to come down in rear[1] on the Russian communications in the Rostov area, and simultaneously to cover the advance of the First Panzer Army from the north and east. Because an attempt to enter Voronezh caused a delay which annoyed Hitler, on July 13 Field-Marshal von Bock was relieved of his command and replaced by General von Weichs, and the command of the Second Army was given to General von Salmuth.

General Halder describes the situation on July 16: "North of Kamiensk all the way to the Millerovo area a zone of confused

[1] *The Halder Diaries,* July 11, 1942, vol. VII, p. 347.

22 · THE STALINGRAD CAMPAIGN, 1942–1943

battles, in which the enemy elements, squeezed between First Panzer Army from the west and Fourth Panzer Army from the north, are trying to break out in several groups in all directions. Meanwhile, east of this seething mass, the Grossdeutschland and 24th Armoured Divisions are racing to the Don without serious check by the enemy."[1]

The Russians abandoned Voroshilovgrad on July 17 and fell back to the south-east hotly pursued by the Seventeenth Army, which had advanced from north of Taganrog. On the same day the First Panzer Army crossed the Donetz at Kamiensk, and west of the Donetz in the north the Fourth Panzer Army moved down the Don with the Sixth Army on its western flank; neither met opposition. It was also on the 17th that Hitler took a step which went far to ruin the campaign. Fearful that von Kleist's First Panzer Army would not prove sufficiently powerful to force crossings over the lower Don he ordered Hoth to move the bulk of his Fourth Panzer Army to his support and thereby left the Sixth Army single-handed to continue its advance on Stalingrad. Halder strongly opposed this change.[2] But Hitler would not listen, although it should have been apparent to him that if the pace of the advance could be maintained Stalingrad was likely to fall before it could be put into a state of defence; and that the momentum of the Sixth Army depended on the Fourth Panzer Army's cooperation. Thus, again by a major diversion of his forces, Hitler ruined his campaign. As has been seen, in 1941 he failed to take Moscow because he diverted Guderian's armour toward Kiev, and his failure to take Stalingrad was primarily because of the diversion of Hoth's Panzer Army from the middle to the lower Don.

The battle for the crossings of the Don was vigorously pushed and on July 19 the advanced guard of Hoth's Fourth Panzer Army won a bridgehead over the river at Tsymlanskaya. Two days later Kleist's First Panzer Army came down on Rostov from the north and, according to Halder, broke through "a totally demoralized enemy."[3] On July 22, the Russian inner defences of Rostov collapsed and the Seventeenth Army crossed the Don in four places. The Sixth Army had continued its advance on Stalingrad and on July 24 approached the bank of the Don to the west of the city.

[1] *Ibid.*, July 16, 1942, vol. VII, p. 352.   [2] *Ibid.*, July 23, 1942, vol. VII, p. 358.
[3] *Ibid.*, July 21, 1942, vol. VII, p. 356.

By July 23 the confusion caused by the concentration of the two Panzer armies in and to the east of the Rostov area caused Hitler to assemble a conference at which in a violent scene he threw the entire blame for the muddle on his General Staff. Halder wrote in his diary: "The situation is getting more and more intolerable. There is no room for any serious work. This 'leadership', so-called, is characterized by a pathological reacting to the impressions of the moment and a total lack of any understanding of the command machinery and its possibilities (*i.e.*, Hitler is incapable of grasping that his constant interference is throwing everything in disorder)."[1] In spite of Hitler's interference the Russians had shown such incapacity to stay the German advance that the campaign had been an unqualified success. Their situation was so critical that the Kremlin, through its agents in America and Britain, launched a frenzied propaganda campaign in which the immediate opening of a second front in the west was demanded.[2] In August this led to the abortive British landing at Dieppe, which nevertheless so startled Hitler that he ordered two of his best divisions to be transferred to the west.[3]

When driven back from the lower Don the Russians withdrew to the river Manich, but were rapidly ejected by Kleist's First Panzer Army, which on July 27 began to fan out on a wide front in three columns toward the Black Sea; one on Voroshilovsk, one on Maikop, and, in between, one on Armavir.

By the end of July the situation was as follows: In the north the Sixth Army, because of lack of fuel and ammunition,[4] and shortage of armour due to the diversion of the Fourth Panzer Army, was, after violent fighting, halted on the Don immediately west of Kalach; the Fourth Panzer Army had reached Proletarskaya on the Novorossisk–Stalingrad railway; and in the south the First Panzer Army advanced on the line Maikop–Voroshilovsk, while the Seventeenth Army, and the Fourth Rumanian Army from the Crimea, after they had thrown the enemy into "wild rout,"[5] moved on Novorossisk and Tuapse.

On July 30, Hitler again made a fateful decision, through Jodl

---

[1] *Ibid.*, July 23, 1942, vol. VII, p. 358.

[2] See *Hitler's Defeat in Russia*, General W. Anders (1953), p. 105.

[3] See *The Other Side of the Hill*, edit. by B. H. Liddell Hart (1951), p. 313.

[4] Halder records, on July 25 (vol. VII, p. 360) "Lack of fuel and ammunition"; and on July 29 (vol. VII, p. 362) ". . . fuel supply to Sixth Army is not functioning. Insufferable tirades about other people's mistakes, which are nothing but duly executed orders of his [Hitler's] own congestion of armoured forces in Rostov area."

[5] *Ibid.*, July 30, 1942, vol. VII, p. 363.

he announced at a conference of his generals: ". . . that the fate of the Caucasus will be decided at Stalingrad, and that in view of the importance of the battle it would be necessary to divert forces from Army Group A to Army Group B . . . that the first Panzer Army must at once wheel south and southwest to cut off the enemy now being pushed back step by step from the Don by Seventeenth Army, before he reaches the Caucasus." Halder writes: "This is rankest nonsense. This enemy is running for dear life and will be in the northern foot hills of the Caucasus a good piece ahead of our armour and then we are going to have another unhealthy congestion of forces before the enemy front."[1]

To comply with the first item of these instructions, on August 1 Hoth's Panzer Army was returned to Army Group B[2] and ordered to move north-eastward along the Novorossisk–Stalingrad railway. It was little opposed at first and its advance was rapid. On August 3 it occupied Kotelnikovo, but from then on it was so fiercely opposed that on August 9 it was forced on the defensive and in consequence had to abandon all idea that it could seize Stalingrad single-handed.

While Hoth was thus engaged the Sixth Army resumed its offensive and, in spite of strong opposition, it gained a crossing over the Don; drove the Russians out of Kalach; and set out on its final lap towards Stalingrad. On August 23 it reached the Volga north of Stalingrad and occupied the northern outskirts of the city. Immediately afterward it closed the gap between the Don and the Volga – that is, from Kachalinskaya to Dubovka – and on September 2 established contact with Hoth at Kotelnikovo. On September 12 its commander, General von Paulus, received an order from Hitler to carry Stalingrad by storm on the 15th.

In the south, Army Group A advanced against little resistance at high speed; the Seventeenth Army on Krasnodar and Novorossisk; and the First Panzer Army on Voroshilovsk and Maikop. On August 3 Armavir and Voroshilovsk were captured, and on the 9th, when the Seventeenth Army seized Krasnodar, the First Panzer Army reached the Maikop oilfields, and on the following day its eastern column captured Piatigorsk. According to Colonel Léderrey – quoting Krylov's *Journal* – Kleist's rapid advance was partly because of the mutiny of the Kuban Cossack divisions under

[1] *Ibid.*, July 30, 1942, vol. VII, p. 363.
[2] *Ibid.*, August 1, 1942, vol. VII, p. 365.

General Lvov. Later, 15,000 of their officers and men were sent to Astrakhan and of every three, one was shot.[1] On August 22 men of von Kleist's army hoisted the swastika flag on the summit of Mount Elbrus (18,526 ft.),[2] and on the 25th Mosdok on the Terek river was captured. On September 6, Novorossisk, the last Soviet naval base on the Black Sea, fell to the Seventeenth Army.

In spite of these achievements, since the middle of August the momentum of Army Group A had rapidly declined, and on September 9 Keitel informed Halder that Hitler had decided to remove Field-Marshal List from his command.[3] He was succeeded by General von Kleist, and the command of the First Panzer Army was given to General Eberhard von Mackensen.

This change in command in no way solved the problem, because the primary cause of the loss of momentum was lack of petrol. "The bulk of our supplies," says von Kleist, "had to come by rail from the Rostov bottleneck, as the Black Sea route was considered unsafe. A certain amount of oil was delivered by air, but the total which came through was insufficient to maintain the momentum of the advance, which came to a halt just when our chances looked best." He adds: "But that was not the ultimate cause of the failure. We could still have reached our goal if my forces had not been drawn away bit by bit to help the attack on Stalingrad. Besides part of my motorized troops, I had to give up the whole of my flak [anti-aircraft] corps and all my air force except the reconnaissance squadrons."[4] Other generals, writes Captain Liddell Hart, "confirmed Kleist's evidence on the causes of the failure, especially the shortage of petrol – the armoured divisions were sometimes at a standstill for weeks on end, waiting for fresh supplies. Owing to this shortage the petrol lorries themselves were immobilized and petrol was brought forward on camels. . . ."[5]

By September 12, when Stalingrad was about to be stormed, the advance in the Caucasus had stopped on the line Tuapse–Elbrus–Ordzhonikidze–Mosdok–Elista;[6] the German front in the south, which ran from Kursk and Voronezh through Stalingrad, Elista, Elbrus to Tuapse, was stretched over more than 1,250 miles. When these miles are added to the 800 miles between Kursk and Leningrad, the total German frontage in Russia was

[1] *La défaite Allemand à l'est* (1951), p. 94.
[2] *The Halder Diaries*, August 22, 1942, vol. VII, p. 380.
[3] *Ibid.*, September 9, 1942, vol. VII, p. 391.
[4] *The Other Side of the Hill*, p. 303.   [5] *Ibid.*, p. 305.
[6] Elista, halfway between Mozdok and Stalingrad, was occupied on August 16.

well over 2,000 miles in length. This, when set against the forces and resources at Hitler's disposal, the vastness of the communications required to maintain this front, and the formidable proportions of guerrilla warfare in rear, shows the ineptitude of Hitler as a strategist more than anything else.

In 1942 Stalingrad was a long, narrow industrial city of about 500,000 inhabitants. It straggled for some 18 miles along the right bank of the Volga immediately north of its elbow, from where the river flows south-eastward into the Caspian Sea at Astrakhan. It was also an extensive inland port, ice-free for half the year, and in its northern sector were three large groups of factories which produced over a quarter of the tractors and mechanical vehicles of the U.S.S.R., as well as tanks, guns, and other armaments. West of the two southern groups rose the Mamaiev hill, also called the "Iron Heights", from which an extensive view could be obtained over the Volga. By September, thanks largely to Hitler's interference and the consequent slowing of the Sixth Army's advance, time had been gained by the Russians strongly to garrison the city. Its commander was General Chuykov.

East of the northern and southern quarters of Stalingrad the Volga, like the Piave, flows through several channels created by a number of islands and its main channel varies from two to two and a half miles in breadth. The river presented the Germans with a formidable bridging problem, and until it was solved it was not possible to invest the city on its eastern side. Could the Germans establish themselves on the left bank of the Volga, then a comparatively small, well-entrenched force would stop all river traffic, complete the investment, and reduce the city through starvation.

It is of some interest to examine this problem, because in nearly all opposed river crossings the determining factor is not width of river – though this is important – but the length of river frontage held by the attacker. Should the frontage be extensive, by feinting here and there the would-be crosser can so distract his opponent that, sooner or later, he will be able to throw a bridge over the river at some unprotected or lightly held point and establish a bridgehead on its far side. Because it takes longer to bridge a wide river like the Volga, the longer should be the operative stretch on which to feint. The initial German problem was to establish this operative front. But instead they resorted to direct attack – that is, an attempt was made to carry the city by batter and storm.

Once General von Paulus had sealed off the gap between the Volga and Don he established his airfields and supply dumps in the area between the two rivers. This was no easy task because he was dependent upon two indifferent railways – the Novorossisk–Stalingrad and the Rostov–Stalingrad. The latter ran by way of Tchirskaya, with a short branch line to Kalach; it was in a shocking state of repair and was constantly cut by partisans.

Hitler was not unaware that the troops which held the Don north-west of Stalingrad were inadequate for the task set them, but he trusted that a quick capture of Stalingrad would set free sufficient forces to reinforce them. Halder disagreed with this, and once it became obvious that Stalingrad could not be rushed, he urged the abandonment of the operation and a withdrawal westward. Instead Hitler took more and more German troops from the defensive wing and sent them to von Paulus.[1]

This piece of folly, coupled with a strong Russian counteroffensive in the Rzhev area, led to the final clash between Hitler and Halder, and the outcome was that the latter was relieved of his appointment and General Kurt Zeitzler, then in France, was ordered to replace him as Chief of Staff, O.K.H.[2]

The battle proper for Stalingrad opened on September 15, and after a week's desperate fighting the Germans penetrated to the centre of the city. On the 26th and 27th they broke into the factory district and seized the "Iron Heights", but on the 29th they were ejected. Reinforcements were then brought up and on October 4, supported by large numbers of tanks and bomber aircraft, the attack was renewed. For 10 days the attack was pressed with the utmost ferocity, street by street, house by house, both day and night, until the attackers were physically and morally exhausted. Stalingrad had become a second Verdun.

Hitler ordered a change of tactics; storming was to cease and the city systematically to be devastated by artillery fire and bombing. This was a senseless operation because it substituted rubble heaps for houses, and the former are the more easily defensible. The battle became one of prestige; Stalin was determined to hold the city which bore his name, and because of its name Hitler was equally determined to wrest it from his adversary. Yard by yard, over ground and under ground, the attackers

[1] See Warlimont's account in *The Other Side of the Hill*, p. 315.
[2] *The Halder Diaries*, September 24, 1942, vol. VII, p. 397. This entry concludes the *Diaries*, and the invaluable Halder deserts us.

18

fought their way through the ruins in what became known as the *Rattenkrieg* ("rat war"). On November 9 Hitler announced that "not one square yard of ground will be given up."[1] The battle continued until November 12, when in the last German general assault the Volga was reached in the south of the city.

By mid-November the German situation was as follows:

The Fourth Panzer Army, considerably reduced in strength and which on November 10 had been withdrawn to refit, was in the Kotelnikovo area.

The Sixth Army was in and around Stalingrad, and also held the gap between the Volga and Don as well as the Don between Kachalinskaya and Kletskaya, with the exception of a small bridgehead the Russians had established at Kremenskaya.

West of Kletskaya to Veshenskaya stood the Third Rumanian Army, and since November 2 the Fourth Rumanian Army – part of Manstein's Eleventh Army – had been brought up to hold the Ergeni Hills south of the Volga elbow in order to cover the right flank and the Novorossisk–Stalingrad railway. The rest of Manstein's army was ordered to the Leningrad front.

In the Caucasus the head of Army Group A was still about Mozdok, and a weak Rumanian force held Elista.

North of the Third Rumanian Army lay the Eighth Italian Army on the Don between Veshenskaya to west of Pavlovsk, and to its north stood the Second Hungarian Army as far as Korotoyak, where it contacted the right of the Second German Army in the Voronezh area.

It was early November and Hitler's attention was suddenly attracted to events in North Africa. The battle of El Alamein had been fought and won by Montgomery on November 5, and Morocco and Algeria invaded by Eisenhower on November 8. To counter this extension of the war in the south, German reinforcements were not sent east, but were sent west into France and to Tunisia. The moment was propitious for a Russian counteroffensive.

It was no sudden inspiration on the part of the Russians, for since early July they had prepared a counter-offensive, and by November, when winter would favour them, they had concentrated powerful forces in the forests north of the Don. Further, in preparation of their counterstroke, while their enemy pressed into the Caucasus and closed in on Stalingrad, they had carried out

[1] *Hitler's Defeat in Russia*, p. 119.

a series of violent attacks in the Voronezh area in order to pin down the German Second Army, and had also made many local attacks along the Don. They had seized a number of fords along the Don and had established several bridgeheads, including one at Serafimovitch. On October 25 a report was received at head-quarters O.K.W. that the Russians had started bridging, and on November 2 this was confirmed by air reconnaissance. Two days later German agents reported that in the near future the Kremlin had decided to launch a powerful offensive, either over the Don or against Army Group Centre. They intended to do both.

These counter-offensives were planned and organized by Marshal Zhukov and his Chief of Staff, General Vassilevski. The attack over the Don was to be carried out in three phases by three armies north of the river in cooperation with an attack south of Stalingrad. The three northern armies were commanded by General Rokossovski, General Vatutin, and General Gorlikov, and respectively were deployed on the fronts Volga–Serafimovitch, Serafimovitch–Veshenskaya, and Veshenskaya to south of Voronezh. Approximately they faced the left wing of the German Sixth Army and the Third Rumanian Army, the Italian Eighth Army, and the Second Hungarian Army. The southern attack was to be made by General Yeremenko's army against the Fourth Rumanian Army on the Ergeni Hills. The second counter-offensive was to be launched against the German central sector between Vielikye-Luki and Rzhev, so as to impede reinforcements to the Don front; the attack began on November 25, and does not concern us.

The aim of the Don counter-offensive was to pinch out the German Sixth Army by a concentric attack on Kalach by the armies of Rokossovski and Yeremenko, and in which Vatutin's left wing was to protect Rokossovski's right flank. Once it was under way Vatutin was to break through the Eighth Italian Army and advance on Likhaya on the Stalino–Stalingrad railway, and thence on Rostov, the bottleneck of German communications. Gorlikov was to follow Vatutin and break through the Second Hungarian Army, force the German Second Army westward of Voronezh, and then advance south-westward on Bielgorod and Kharkov.

On November 19 the offensive was opened by Rokossovski. With three armoured corps and four cavalry corps in first line and 21 infantry divisions in second line, he debouched from bridgeheads between Serafimovitch and Kletskaya; broke through the right of the Third Rumanian Army, and while his right wing, in cooperation with Vatutin's left, pressed the enemy in rout toward the Chir river, with his centre he advanced on Kalach. Immediately after this attack his left wing moved against the Don–Volga gap, but was repulsed by the Sixth Army.

On the following day, Yeremenko, with two armoured corps and nine infantry divisions, broke through the Fourth Rumanian Army on the Ergeni Hills; then, while his left wing advanced on Kotelnikovo, his right wing swung northward toward Kalach where he linked up with Rokossovski on November 22. This meant that the Sixth Army, of about 200,000 combatants and 70,000 non-combatants, was surrounded; but the Russians were not sufficiently organized to prevent von Paulus from breaking out, which in all probability he could have done at any time during the following week.

When the news of the Russian offensive was received at Hitler's headquarters, General Zeitzler urged Hitler to order Paulus to cut his way out, and he nearly persuaded him to do so, but Göring – an incorrigible boaster – guaranteed that he would supply him by air with 500 tons a day of munitions, fuel, and rations. On November 24, because of this vain boast, Hitler ordered Paulus to "hedgehog" himself in, and commanded that his army should become known as "Fortress Stalingrad." The next problem was how to relieve it.

For once Hitler did the right thing. He called to his aid the ablest of his subordinates, Field-Marshal von Manstein, then at Vitebsk; renamed his Eleventh Army—largely dispersed—"Army Group Don", and subordinated to it the Sixth Army, Fourth Panzer Army, and the Third and Fourth Rumanian Armies. Manstein's task was not to open a way for the Sixth Army's retreat, because Hitler had no intention to withdraw it, but instead it was to defeat the Russians who encircled it and to re-establish the Stalingrad front.

Because of his indifferent railroad communications, Paulus's supply situation had throughout been precarious; now it grew critical. His army needed 700 tons of supplies daily and, according to General Anders,[1] O.K.W. were aware that once his reserves were exhausted he would require over double this amount.

---

[1] *Hitler's Defeat in Russia*, pp. 126–127, citing *Die Oberste Wehrmachtfürung*, Helmuth Greiner (1951), p. 425.

Göring had guaranteed to deliver 500 tons although there was only sufficient transport aircraft to lift 300 tons, and this amount did not allow for losses or the weather. The tonnage delivered between November 26 – when the operation was initiated – and January 3 is not specified by Greiner, but he records that on January 4 250 tons were delivered, on the 5th 150 tons, on the 6th 45, and from then to January 21, when it would appear that air supply ceased, the average was well under 100 tons daily.[1] During December alone this futile operation cost the *Luftwaffe* 246 transport aircraft.

When, on November 27, Manstein took over command of Army Group Don the situation with which he was faced was as follows: The remnants of the Third Rumanian Army, reinforced by improvised bodies of Germans, under command of General Karl Hollidt, precariously held the northern front from Veshenskaya on the Don southward along the river Chir. On the southern front about Kotelnikovo stood Hoth's Fourth Panzer Army and remnants of the Fourth Rumanian Army, and to this group reinforcements were rushed from the north and the Caucasus. The Sixth Army was sandwiched between these two fronts in and around Stalingrad. Disturbing reports came in that the Russians north of the Don were concentrating large forces opposite the Eighth Italian and Second Hungarian Armies.

Manstein's plan, largely dictated by Hitler, was to advance Hoth's Fourth Panzer Army up the Kotelnikovo–Stalingrad railway against Yeremenko; to throw him back, and then to wheel against Rokossovski's right flank while Paulus struck at it from Stalingrad. Then he intended to launch the Hollidt group eastward over the Chir against Rokossovski's right – in brief, to defeat Yeremenko and then to encircle Rokossovski. The latter operation was an impossible task, and it would seem that Hitler had little information about the strength of Vatutin's army.

On December 12 Manstein's counter-offensive opened, and it made good progress for two days before it slowed. Nevertheless, by December 21 it was pushed forward to within 30 miles of the Stalingrad "hedgehog". Manstein's situation then became so critical that he decided to defy Hitler, and sent to von Paulus an order to be prepared to break out and join him within 24 hours. Paulus replied that he was unable to do so because his tanks had fuel only for 20 miles, and although he was urged by his generals to

[1] *Ibid.*, pp. 127-128 and pp. 425-435.

abandon his impedimenta and cut his way out with his infantry, he refused to do so. The truth would appear to be that he had no intention to withdraw from Stalingrad without a direct order from Hitler.

Why Manstein's request was so urgent was that on December 14 Hollidt had been violently attacked by Vatutin. On the 17th his front on the Chir collapsed, and on the following day Vatutin's right and centre crossed the frozen Don and struck at the Italian Eighth Army; on the 19th it was thrown back in rout toward the Donetz. Threatened as he was by encirclement, on December 24 Manstein ordered Hoth to send reinforcements to Hollidt, and then rapidly withdrew westward. On Christmas Day Hoth was in full retreat.

On December 29 von Paulus sent General Hube, commander of his XIVth Corps, by air to place the situation of the Sixth Army before Hitler. It was a futile journey, for the order Hitler sent back was to hold fast to Stalingrad until the spring. Nevertheless, on the same day, after he had repeatedly been pressed by Zeitzler to withdraw Army Group A from the Caucasus, he consented.

The next weeks were spent by Manstein in a desperate struggle to keep a corridor open for the retreat of Army Group A. He succeeded, and on January 18 Kleist reached the Don, and crossed it by the 22nd. While this retreat was in progress Gorlikov struck at the Second Hungarian Army and sent it back in rout. By the end of January, 1943, the whole of the German Don front had collapsed and a gap over 200 miles wide separated Manstein's left flank at Voroshilovgrad from Voronezh in the north.

The situation within Fortress Stalingrad rapidly deteriorated during Manstein's desperate struggle and Kleist's brilliant retreat. Soon rations had to be reduced to below subsistence level; artillery ammunition began to fail; medical stores and fuel, even for cooking, became exhausted; typhus and dysentery claimed thousands of victims, and frost as many more – the thermometer fell to 28 degrees below zero.

On January 8 Rokossovski called upon von Paulus to capitulate, and when he refused to do so, on the 10th Rokossovski ordered a general assault to be made on the doomed army. On the 14th the Pitomnik airfield, 14 miles west of the centre of the city, was captured by the Russians, and by then Paulus's situation had become so bad that he reported to Hitler that his troops could no longer bear their sufferings. The answer he received was:

"Capitulation is impossible. The Sixth Army will do its historic duty at Stalingrad until the last man, in order to make possible the reconstruction of the Eastern Front."[1]

On January 25 the Russians captured the last remaining German airfield, the loss of which deprived Paulus of all further physical contact with the outer world. On January 31 Hitler promoted him a field-marshal, and on the same day the radio of Sixth Army headquarters sent its final message: "The Russians are before our bunker. We are destroying the station."[2] Immediately after this, except for the XIth Corps, commanded by General Strecker, the Sixth Army laid down its arms, and on February 2 the XIth Corps surrendered.

When Hitler received the news of the surrender, first he compared the Sixth Army with the Three Hundred at Thermopylae, and declared that it had shown the world "the true spirit of National Socialist Germany and its loyalty to its Fuehrer," then he raved against Paulus and shouted that, like Varus, he should have thrown himself upon his sword rather than accept captivity.[3]

With Paulus, 23 generals, 2,000 field and junior officers, 90,000 other ranks, and about 40,000 non-combatant soldiers and civilians surrendered. About 34,000 wounded and sick had been evacuated by air during the siege, and over 100,000 were killed, died of sickness, hunger and frost, and left sick and wounded in Stalingrad. If Erich Kern is to be believed, these last-mentioned unfortunates were massacred by the Russians, who threw explosive charges into the hospital shelters, and on February 3 thousands were buried alive in the enormous Timoshenko bunker when its entrances were dynamited. Kern also informs us that "of the 90,000 prisoners, between 40,000 and 50,000 died of starvation within the first six weeks [of captivity] in the prison camp Bektoffka on the Volga, some forty miles south of Stalingrad."[4] As regards losses of material, Chester Wilmot states that "the records of the Army High Command show that at Stalingrad the Wehrmacht lost the equivalent of six months production of armour and vehicles, three to four months production of artillery, and two months production of small arms and mortars."[5] To these losses,

---

[1] *Hitler, a Study in Tyranny*, Alan Bullock (1952), p. 631, citing von Paulus's evidence at the Nuremberg Trials.
[2] Quoted by Anders, *Hitler's Defeat in Russia*, p. 142.
[3] *Hitler, a Study in Tyranny*, pp. 631–632.
[4] *Dance of Death* (1948), p. 246.
[5] *The Struggle for Europe*, p. 149.

according to General Pickert, who was in charge of the air supply of the Sixth Army, must be added over 500 transport aircraft.[1]

Stalingrad was a second Poltava in which Hitler was as much the architect of his own ruin as was Charles XII in 1709. Into the minds of a hundred million Muscovites flashed the myth of Soviet invincibility, and it forged them into the Turks of the North. If they could overcome the legions of Hitler, what had they to fear from the nations he had trampled in the dust? The German victories had thrown Europe into chaos and so had blazed a trail for the Third Rome. This decisive victory, which came on the heels of El Alamein, and at the moment when in Tunisia the Fascist cause had reached its nadir, inspired propaganda intoxicated peoples of the west. Stalingrad exalted Stalin into the champion of all for which they so ardently yearned. Tragically they were to be disillusioned.

In spite of the vastness of the German defeat, Stalingrad was only the signal of Hitler's ruin – it was not its cause. This, as described in Chapter 11, was because in his blind arrogance he had failed to differentiate between potential friends among the subjugated peoples of the U.S.S.R. and his active enemies. Also, Great Britain and the United States committed the same blunder when they did not distinguish between the Nazi and anti-Nazi factions in Germany, and did not establish the second front they were seeking within instead of outside the frontiers of the Third Reich. Had they done so, while still supporting Russia, the German *débâcle* at Stalingrad would have opened to them the road which almost certainly would have led to the end of the war in the spring or summer of 1943.

Because of the pointless sacrifice of the Sixth Army, never at any time during the war was revolt against Hitler nearer to success than in January, 1943. Generals Beck and Zeitzler and most of the field-marshals were involved, but without some assurance of British and American support they had nothing to offer the large middle group of officers who wavered. After the war one of the conspirators said to Mr. Francis Russell: "Our conspiracy was a great tragedy. We might have ended the war a year and a half earlier if your government had given us some encouragement. . . . We had our intermediaries in Sweden; we wanted to know what the Anglo-American conditions would be, what terms they would give a new government if we succeeded in doing away with Hitler.

[1] *Defeat in the West*, Milton Shulman (1947), p. 72.

They took our memorandum, it was given to Eden – but there was never any reply."[1]

On January 22 the two main rebel factions – those who wanted forcibly to remove Hitler, which could only mean assassination, and those who wanted to subject him to the General Staff – met in the house of Count Peter von Wartenburg in Berlin-Lichter-felde to square their differences. Then, on the following day, before they had arrived at a decision, Roosevelt's and Churchill's proclamation of unconditional surrender came from Casablanca; "a formula which," Görlitz declares, "gave the death blow to any hope that may have been entertained either by the 'shadow government' or by the oppositional elements in the General Staff, that their enemies would negotiate with a 'respectable' government."[2]

In spite of this setback, on March 13 the first definite plan to assassinate Hitler was put into force by a group of officers at von Kluge's headquarters. Unfortunately for them the bomb smuggled into Hitler's aeroplane failed to explode;[3] nevertheless, six other attempts on Hitler's life were planned in 1943. "Death," Görlitz says, "was already stalking Hitler unseen – which only shows how weak was the real basis of his authority."[4]

At this climax in the war, what staggers one is the political blindness of British and American statesmen. They completely failed to realize the politico-strategical situation with which they were faced, and this is so clearly unfolded in an exchange of notes between Sir Samuel Hoare (later Viscount Templewood), British Ambassador in Spain, and Count Jordana, the Spanish Foreign Minister, immediately after the German defeat at Stalingrad, that it is worth while to quote them at some length.

General Franco's views were "that there were two separate wars in progress, the war in the east against communism in which Spain was directly involved, and the war in the west between the Anglo-Saxon powers and Germany, in which Spain took no part."[5] To convince him that there was only one war, Sir Samuel

---

[1] "Pictures from Germany," *The New English Review*, June, 1948, p. 551.
[2] *The German General Staff* (1953), p. 430. Chester Wilmot writes that ". . . when the Allies proclaimed their demand for 'Unconditional Surrender' even commanders like von Kluge and von Manstein, who foresaw where Hitler's policy was leading Germany, refused to act against him. Since it seemed that the Allies were determined to destroy the German military caste. . . ." (*The Struggle for Europe*, p. 166).
[3] See *Revolt Against Hitler*, Fabian von Schlabrendorff (1948), chap. VI.
[4] *The German General Staff*, p. 434.
[5] *Ambassador on Special Mission*, Rt. Hon. Sir Samuel Hoare (1946), pp. 184–185.

Hoare entered into correspondence with Count Jordana, and on February 19, 1943, he stated in a memorandum to the latter: "The victory at the end of this war will be an Allied, not a Russian victory, namely a victory in which the British Empire and the United States of America will exercise the greatest possible influence. Moreover, M. Stalin declared on November 6th, 1942, that it was not the future policy of Russia to interfere in the international affairs of other countries."

On February 21 Jordana replied to this note, and among other things wrote:

"If events develop in the future as they have done up to now, it would be Russia which will penetrate deeply into German territory. And we ask the question: if this should occur, which is the greater danger not only for the continent but for England herself, a Germany not totally defeated and with sufficient strength to serve as a rampart against Communism, a Germany hated by all her neighbours, which would deprive her of authority though she remained intact, or a Sovietized Germany which would certainly furnish Russia with the added strength of her war preparations, her engineers, her specialized workmen and technicians, which would enable Russia to extend herself with an empire without precedent from the Atlantic to the Pacific? . . .

"And we ask a second question: is there anybody in the centre of Europe, in that mosaic of countries without consistency or unity, bled moreover by war and foreign domination, who could contain the ambitions of Stalin? There is certainly no one. . . . We may be sure that after the German domination, the only domination which could live in these countries is Communism. For this reason we consider the situation as extremely grave and think that people in England should reflect calmly on the matter, since should Russia succeed in conquering Germany, there will be no one who can contain her. . . . If Germany did not exist, Europeans would have to invent her and it would be ridiculous to think that her place could be taken by a confederation of Lithuanians, Poles, Czechs, and Roumanians which would rapidly be converted into so many more states of the Soviet confederation. . . ."

On February 25, Sir Samuel Hoare replied:

"The Minister says that the great danger to Europe is Communism and that a Russian victory will make all Europe Communist. . . . The British view is very different. . . . Will any single country be able to dominate Europe at the end of this war? Russia, at least, will need a long period of reconstruction and recovery in which she will depend greatly upon the British Empire and the United States of America for economic help. . . . Whilst, however, giving full credit and admiration to the Russian army, we are convinced that the final victory will not be the victory of any single Ally but of all the Allies. . . . There will then undoubtedly be great British and American armies on the Continent. . . . They will be composed of fresh, first line troops, whose ranks have not been previously devastated by years of exhausting war on the Russian front.

"As for ourselves, I make the confident prophecy that at that moment Great Britain will be the strongest European military Power. . . . British influence, it seems to me, will be then stronger in Europe than at any time since the fall of Napoleon. . . . We shall not, however, shirk our responsibilities to European civilisation or throw away our great strength by premature or unilaterial disarmament. . . . There is no reason to think that the alliance formed under the stress of war will not continue in the peace and provide a peaceful and stabilising force in European politics."[1]

This correspondence reveals, against the sombre background of Spanish realism, the idealistic war policy which the American and British governments followed, and how misjudged this policy was became fully apparent to Mr. Churchill four days after his war aim of June 22, 1941 – "to destroy Hitler and every vestige of the Nazi régime" – had been attained. On May 12, 1945, in a telegram addressed to President Truman – which he calls "the 'Iron Curtain' telegram" – he said:

"I am profoundly concerned about the European situation. . . Anyone can see that in a very short space of time our armed power on the Continent will have vanished, except for moderate forces to hold down Germany. . . . What will be the position in a year or two, when the British and American Armies have melted and the French has not yet been formed on any major scale, when we may have a handful of Divisions, mostly French, and when Russia may choose to keep two or three hundred on active service? An iron curtain is drawn down upon their front. We do not know what is going on behind. There seems little doubt that the whole of the regions east of a line Lübeck–Trieste–Corfu will soon be completely in their hands. . . . Thus a broad band of many

[1] *Ibid.*, pp. 190–195.

hundreds of miles of Russian-occupied territory will isolate us from Poland. . . . Meanwhile the attention of our peoples will be occupied in inflicting severities upon Germany, which is ruined and prostrate, and it would be open to the Russians in a very short time to advance if they chose to the waters of the North Sea and the Atlantic."[1]

In this apocalyptic appeal to the new President is revealed the political importance of the battle of Stalingrad. Because of the allied policy of unconditional surrender, which crystallized all that President Roosevelt and Mr. Churchill stood for, it was, with the exception of the battle of Normandy – its copestone – the most decisive of all the battles of the war. It was, Lieutenant-Colonel F. O. Miksche declares, "a defeat for Europe as a whole."[2]

[1] *The Second World War*, vol. VI, pp. 498–499.
[2] *Unconditional Surrender* (1952), p. 254.

The political and second fronts

The year 1943 was one of decisive political changes that shaped the outcome of the war and radically influenced the course of history. It opened with the proclamation of unconditional surrender at Casablanca and by its emphasis on a war of annihilation bereft the western allies' cause of a sane aim, a decision which Stalin was not slow to capitalize.

Stalin sought to exploit the West's enthusiasm over the Soviet victory at Stalingrad, and resorted to Lenin's maxim: "one step back to gain two steps forward." On May 22 he announced the dissolution of the Comintern and so deluded the British and American peoples and governments into a belief that the Kremlin had abandoned for ever its policy of interference in the internal affairs of other countries; Russia could be accepted by them as a friendly, near-democratic partner. Because of this chameleon-like change and their own policy of unconditional surrender, the western allies left the political initiative to Russia at the very moment when Italy was on the point of collapse and the road was about to open to them to seize their opportunity in southern Europe and establish a profitable second front.

In the meantime Hitler inverted everything he had so far held to be essential. He abandoned his plan to impose his will on Europe and establish a German *Lebensraum* in western Russia and instead set out to champion European freedom in order to prevent the establishment of a Soviet *Lebensraum* in eastern and central Europe. He knew that all continental nations were terrified at the prospect of a Russian victory, and that the age-old policy of England was antagonistic to the dominance of Europe by any one Power. He substituted *Festung Europa* for *Lebensraum*, made propaganda capital of the unconditional surrender policy and so turned it into a blood transfusion for the Germans, and proclaimed a crusade of Europe against Asia. Such were the main political transformations of 1943.

Although their policy was dismal, the strategic prospects of America and Britain were bright. By the summer of 1943 the submarine had been mastered and the so-called Battle of the

Atlantic won;[1] supremacy in the air had been gained; the output of American industry reached its peak; an enormous American army was in training; and Great Britain had recovered from her disaster at Dunkirk, and was in the process of raising a powerful army at home. The allied problem was how best to employ these enormous and ever-increasing assets; in other words, how to establish the long awaited Second Front which had been accepted as their strategic goal as early as the Arcadia Conference, and at which three possible directions were foreshadowed – across the Mediterranean, from Turkey into the Balkans, and in western Europe.

Because the Second Front could not be opened in 1942, when Stalin vociferously demanded it, and because something had to be done to satisfy him, the invasion of North Africa had been undertaken as a stopgap, but only on the understanding that the preparations for the invasion of France ("Bolero") would in no way be impeded. It was decided at the Casablanca Conference to set up an inter-service staff, under Lieutenant-General F. E. Morgan as Chief of Staff to the Supreme Allied Commander designate (COSSAC), to prepare a definite plan for the invasion of France in the spring of 1944. It superseded "Bolero" and was code-named "Overlord". Lastly, the successes which sprang from "Torch", especially the invasion of Italy, introduced a strategical complication that was to become a bone of contention between Mr. Churchill and the Joint Chiefs of Staff – more particularly General Marshall – and bedevil allied strategy up to and beyond the establishment of the Second Front in Normandy.

The crux of this question would appear to have been that Mr. Churchill's ideas on where he wanted the second front to be opened were mixed. Although he agreed with "Overlord", once a front had been established in Italy he did not want "Overlord" to cripple it. Nor – and he is most emphatic about this – did he want to open a second front in the Balkans. Nevertheless, from the earliest days of the war his thoughts were directed on the possibilities of a south-eastern front, and in September, 1941, he had considered that the only means to help Russia was to establish with Turkish aid "a second front somewhere in the Balkans".

[1] In the opinion of the author, the struggle for the mastery of the Atlantic is erroneously called a "battle". It was a series of co-ordinated and *ad hoc* operations in which their sum, and no single engagement, was decisive. It may be compared with the struggle for air or industrial supremacy. It was a continuous operation which only ended with the termination of the war.

When Sicily was invaded he expressed the opinion that "the Balkans represented a greater danger to Germany than the loss of Italy," and he hoped to bring in Turkey when allied troops "had reached the Balkan area" – presumably Venezia Giulia. In spite of this, on October 20, in a note to Mr. Eden – then in Moscow – he wrote: "I would not debouch from the narrow leg of Italy into the valley of the Po. . . . Would they [the Russians] be attracted by the idea of our acting through the Aegean, involving Turkey in the war, and opening the Dardanelles . . . so that we could ultimately give them our right hand along the Danube?"

Because of this persistent reference to the Balkans the Joint Chiefs of Staff assumed that Mr. Churchill's heart was in the south-eastern front and not in "Overlord" – the north-western front. Although we do not wish to ascribe to Mr. Churchill an opinion he never held, it would seem that his outlook at this time, when compared with that of the Joint Chiefs of Staff, was not far removed from that of Constantin Fotitch, the Yugoslav Minister in Washington. On October 16, Fotitch broached to President Roosevelt the question of an invasion of Europe by way of the Balkans, and pointed out that this strategy, "already suggested by Churchill, would prevent the installation of Soviet puppet régimes in the Balkans and in Central Europe." The President replied that the problem would be decided "purely upon its military aspects." Fotitch observed, ". . . that it was a costly absurdity to fight a war for purely military reasons, with no moral and political objectives." The bone of contention would appear to be that while the President and his Chiefs of Staff aimed at a purely military victory, Churchill had his eye on the political outcome of the war, and this involved Russia as fully as it did Germany. Should this be correct, then undoubtedly he was right, for a war without a political aim is military nonsense. But was it correct? It is difficult to determine, because on July 25, the day Mussolini resigned, Churchill decided to send Mr. Fitzroy Maclean, M.P., on a mission to Marshal Tito, and when Maclean pointed out to him that if the Yugoslav partisans were victorious Tito would in all probability establish a Communist régime in Yugoslavia closely linked to Moscow, and asked for His Majesty's Government's views on such an eventuality, Churchill replied: "So long as the whole of western civilization was threatened by the Nazi menace, *we could not afford to let our attention be diverted from the immediate issue by considerations of long-term policy. . . ."* "My task," writes Maclean, "was simply to find out who was killing the most Germans and suggest means by which we could help them to kill more. *Politics must be a secondary consideration.*"[1] Even as late as February 27, 1945, 10 weeks before the war ended, Churchill told Parliament that the two principles which guided his approach to continental problems were: "While the war is on, we give help to anyone who can kill a Hun; when the war is over we look to the solution of a free, unfettered democratic election." Apparently it never occurred to him that as Russia would by then have done most of the killing, she would seek a solution of her own.

On August 17, when the Germans had just suffered in the great battle of Orel–Kursk as catastrophic a defeat as that at Stalingrad, Churchill and Roosevelt, attended by the Combined Chiefs of Staff, met in Quebec to discuss "Overlord". Their main decisions were that as a prerequisite of "Overlord" highest priority was to be given to the strategic bombing of Germany; that resources for the prosecution of "Overlord" were to have priority over operations in the Mediterranean; that a landing in the south of France, code-named "Anvil" (later changed to "Dragoon"), was to supplement "Overlord"; and that the "target date" for "Overlord" was to be May 1, 1944.

These important decisions were overshadowed by a forecast made in a document which Harry Hopkins brought with him to the conference. It was entitled *Russia's Position*, and was attributed to "a very high level United States military strategic estimate." It stated that: "Russia's post-war position in Europe will be a dominant one. With Germany crushed, there is no power in Europe to oppose her tremendous military forces. It is true that Great Britain is building up a position in the Mediterranean *vis-à-vis* Russia that she may find useful in balancing power in Europe. However, even here she may not be able to oppose Russia unless she is otherwise supported.

"The conclusions from the foregoing are obvious. Since Russia is the decisive factor in the war, she must be given every assistance and every effort must be made to obtain her friendship. Likewise, since without question she will dominate Europe on the defeat of the Axis, it is even more essential to develop and maintain the most friendly relations with Russia.

[1] *Eastern Approaches* (1949), p. 281, italics added.

"Finally, the most important factor the United States has to consider in relation to Russia is the prosecution of the war in the Pacific. With Russia as an ally in the war against Japan, the war can be terminated in less time and at less expense in life and resources than if the reverse were the case. Should the war in the Pacific have to be carried on with an unfriendly or a negative attitude on the part of Russia, the difficulties will be immeasurably increased and operations might become abortive."

This estimate is reflected in a telegram sent by Mr. Churchill to Field-Marshal Smuts a few days after the conference ended. "I think," he said, "that Russia will be the greatest land Power in the world after this war, which will have rid her of the two military Powers, Japan and Germany."

These predictions meant that once Germany was crushed, the totalitarian rule of Stalin over Europe would replace that of Hitler; as far as the western allies were concerned, the war would lose its political aim, and in consequence it would be absurd to continue it.

It would appear that this vitally important inference was not discussed for a moment. Had it been discussed it would have become apparent that in order to attain their political aim, it was essential for the western allies not only to destroy Hitlerism, but simultaneously to prevent its replacement by Stalinism. And if psychological attack is omitted, this could only be accomplished if they adapted their military operations to this political end.

In the time at their disposal there was only one course they could have taken, and that was to accept the front, then about to be established by General Eisenhower and General Alexander in Italy, as the Second Front, and to have put "Overlord" into cold storage. Had they done so, then, when Alexander had been reinforced with the resources earmarked for "Overlord" – more particularly landing craft – by a series of amphibious operations up the leg of Italy he rapidly could have compelled Field-Marshal Kesselring to withdraw beyond the river Po, and by a landing in the Trieste area he could have forced him either to abandon Italy or risk the loss of his communications. Such an eventuality, which was by no means impracticable, would win for the western allies the road to Vienna, Budapest, and Prague. In any case the Chiefs of the Combined Staff should have seen that, instead of striking at the apex of the German salient Leningrad–Brest–Athens, strategy dictated that, were the means available, its reduction should be sought by striking at its waist – Lübeck–Trieste. Because it was more difficult to strike at the former target than the latter, a second front in the Trieste area was the only practical operation in the time available to eliminate the rival totalitarian systems.

The next conference, that of the allied Foreign Ministers, which had been agreed at Quebec, assembled at Moscow on October 18. Mr. Eden there broached two main subjects. The first was a meeting of the three heads of the allied governments, which Roosevelt had long requested. Stalin agreed, but insisted that the conference should be held at Teheran. The second subject was the problem of the Second Front, and Mr. Eden reported to Mr. Churchill "that the Russians were completely and blindly set on our invasion of Northern France." The latter replied that Eden should tell Stalin: "I will not allow . . . the great and fruitful campaign in Italy . . . to be cast away and end in a frightful disaster, for the sake of crossing the Channel in May. The battle must be nourished and fought out until it is won. We will do our very best for 'Overlord', but it is no use planning for defeat in the field in order to give temporary political satisfaction. . . . Eisenhower and Alexander must have what they need to win the battle, no matter what effect is produced on subsequent operations." This was a brief glimpse of strategical daylight.

That the daylight lasted so short a time was largely because of Roosevelt's obsession that he was Beauty and Stalin a Beast who could be charmed into a fairy prince with whom Europe could live happily ever after. When William C. Bullitt, former United States Ambassador in Moscow, protested that his Russian policy would fail because Stalin could not be trusted, the President replied: "Bill . . . I don't dispute the logic of your reasoning. I just have a hunch that Stalin is not that kind of man. Harry says he's not, and that he doesn't want anything but security for his country. And I think that if I give him anything I can and ask nothing from him in return, noblesse oblige, he won't try to annex anything and will work with me for a world of peace and democracy." In this frame of mind the President set out on November 13 for Cairo, where he conferred with Churchill and Chiang Kai-shek, and on November 27 he flew with Churchill to Teheran to meet Stalin.

Before they left Cairo he and Churchill had agreed to suspend a final decision on Anglo-American strategy for 1944 until after the conference. Nevertheless, the American Chiefs of Staff had long made up their minds, and, according to Sherwood, were prepared "for battles at Teheran in which the Americans and Russians would form a united front." This was facilitated by the arrangements made to house the President and Prime Minister. Churchill was lodged in the British Legation, and to make sure that he had the President in his pocket, on a pretext of security Stalin invited him to take up residence in the Soviet Embassy and not in the American Legation.

The first plenary meeting was held on November 29, and as there was no agenda discussions were *ad hoc* and confused. It would appear that, as usual, Churchill did most of the talking, and this suited Stalin admirably, because he alone of the "Big Three" knew exactly what he wanted. Above all his wish was for a Second Front in France in May, and bluntly he asked Churchill whether he really believed in "Overlord", or was "only thinking about it to please the Soviet Union?" Churchill replied that there was no question of shelving "Overlord", and that it would be launched in May, June, or July; but that the immediate problem was what to do in the Mediterranean during the next five months. He emphasized the importance of the Balkans and suggested that support should be given to Tito's partisans in Yugoslavia and withdrawn from those of Milhailovich. After the capture of Rome, he said, there would be "no advance in Italy beyond the Pisa–Rimini line." Nevertheless, when the subject of an invasion of southern France cropped up – which Stalin favoured – he said that although he was not opposed to it, he "preferred a right-handed movement from the north of Italy, using the Istrian peninsula and the Ljubjana Gap towards Vienna." Stalin was adamant against this and any Balkan or Turkish venture.

The subject of Poland was raised by Churchill. "Nothing was more important," he said, "than the security of the Russian western frontier." Poland should relinquish all her territory east of the Curzon Line (approximately the Ribbentrop–Molotov line) to Russia, and move westward into Germany. "If Poland trod on some German toes," he remarked, "that could not be helped, but there must be a strong Poland." He added that he "would always support the movement of Poland's frontier westward."

Stalin suggested that the Poles should be allowed to move west as far as the Oder. He said that he did not want anything belonging to other people, but would like Königsberg – which did so belong. Churchill replied that the Poles would be foolish if they did not accept the Curzon and Oder frontiers, and that he would remind them "that but for the Red Army they would have been utterly destroyed." Anyhow, he was not going to break his heart about the cession of part of Germany, although it meant shifting 9,000,000 people. This was the end of the Atlantic Charter and the Anglo-Polish Guarantee of 1939. Apparently Mr. Churchill had forgotten that, on December 27, 1941, he had said to Mr. Jan Ciechanowski, Polish Ambassador to the United States: "We shall never forget what glorious Poland has done and is doing. . . . Great Britain has set for herself the aim of restoring full freedom and independence to your nation overrun by Hitler. That is, and will remain our foremost concern. I can assure you that Great Britain will never tarry in the fight until that aim is achieved."

After Poland came Finland. Churchill urged that "Russia must have security for Leningrad and its approaches," and that the Soviet Union must be assured "as a permanent naval and air Power in the Baltic." As with Poland, no mention would appear to have been made of Russia's unprovoked attack on Finland in 1939, but because the Finns had retaliated in 1941 Stalin demanded the restoration of the 1940 treaty, the cession of Hangö or Petsamo, and compensation in kind for 50 per cent. of the war damage suffered.

The problem of Germany was examined at considerable length. Stalin said he wanted Germany to be split; the President warmly agreed and suggested that it should be divided into five parts: (1) Prussia; (2) Hanover and north-west Germany; (3) Saxony; (4) Hesse-Darmstadt and Hesse Cassel; and (5) Bavaria, Baden, and Württemberg. Each part should be self-governing; but Kiel, the Kiel Canal, Hamburg, the Ruhr, and the Saar should be governed by the United Nations.

Churchill put forward another scheme. He considered that the root evil lay in Prussia, the Prussian Army, and the General Staff[1] and proposed that Prussia should be isolated; Bavaria, Württemberg, the Palatinate, Saxony, and Baden detached, and that Bavaria with Austria and Hungary should be formed into a non-aggressive confederation. "We all deeply feared," he comments, "the might of a united Germany. . . . It would be possible, I thought, to make a stern but honourable peace with her,

---

[1] An astonishing statement, which shows how ignorant Mr. Churchill was of the antagonism of the General Staff to the Nazi régime.

and at the same time to create in modern forms what had been in general outline the Austro-Hungarian Empire. . . ." Stalin thought not. He saw no fundamental difference between north and south Germany—"all Germans fought like beasts," he said—Austria and Hungary should exist independently, and after the break up of Germany it would be most unwise to create a new Danubian combination. The President fully agreed.

Stalin assured the President that the United States need have no fear about the Pacific, since the Soviet Union would declare war on Japan once Hitler had been defeated. "Then," he said, "by our common effort we shall win." This Delphic utterance vastly pleased the President and his Chiefs of Staff, and, so it would appear, out of gratitude and behind Churchill's back, Roosevelt, in one of his several private conversations with Stalin, discussed the question of a common front against the British and proposed that he and Stalin would back Chiang Kai-Shek against Churchill on the question of Hongkong and Shanghai. Elliott Roosevelt's explanation of this is that "the biggest thing was" to make "clear to Stalin that the United States and Great Britain were not in one common block against the Soviet Union." Further, Roosevelt mentioned to Stalin "the possibility that Russia might have access to the port of Darien in Manchuria" (incidentally, this was Chinese territory).

In the end little was formally agreed: the partisans in Yugoslavia were to be supported; Turkey was to be encouraged to enter the war; "Overlord" was to be launched in May, 1944; and the Staffs of the three Powers were to keep in close touch with each other. Actually, Stalin scooped the pool; Churchill got nothing, except the arch-Communist Tito as a collaborator; and the President received Stalin's grateful thanks. "Pushed by the Russians and pulled by the Americans," writes Wilmot, "the overall strategy of the Western Powers had been diverted away from the area of Soviet aspirations. Even before Teheran it was inevitable that the enforcement of 'Unconditional Surrender' upon Germany would leave the U.S.S.R. the dominant power in Eastern Europe, but it was by no means inevitable that Russian influence would extend deep into Central Europe and the Balkans. After Teheran it became almost a certainty that this would happen. Thus the Teheran Conference not only determined the military strategy for 1944, but adjusted the political balance of post-war Europe in favour of the Soviet Union."

On December 1 the conference ended and on the following day Roosevelt and Churchill were back in Cairo. Eisenhower was selected as Supreme Commander for "Overlord" on December 6, and the Combined Chiefs of Staff decided that "Overlord" and "Anvil" would be "the supreme operations for 1944. . . . They must be carried out during May. Nothing must be undertaken in any part of the world which hazards the success of these two operations."

The Battle of Normandy, 1944

The invasion of Normandy was the supreme effort of the western allies in Europe, but although it was tactically decisive, it utterly failed to win the peace of President Roosevelt's dreams. The reason was, as the American official historian points out, that the Joint Chiefs of Staff developed "a purely military perspective that considered political implications chiefly with an eye to avoiding them."[1] This is fully corroborated by the President who, in a conversation with his son at Teheran, said:

"Elliott: our chiefs of staff are convinced of one thing. The way to kill the most Germans with the least loss of American soldiers, is to mount one great big invasion and then slam 'em with everything we've got. It makes sense to me. It makes sense to Uncle Joe. It makes sense to all our generals, and always has, ever since the beginning of the war. . . . It makes sense to the Red Army people. That's that. It's the quickest way to win the war. That's all.

"Trouble is, the P.M. is thinking too much of the *post*-war, and where England will be. . . . He's scared of letting the Russians get too strong.

"Maybe the Russians will get strong in Europe. Whether that's bad depends on a whole lot of factors.

"The one thing I'm sure of is this: if the way to save American lives, the way to win as short a war as possible is from the west and from the west alone, without wasting landing craft and men and materials in the Balkan mountains, and our chiefs are convinced it is, then that's that!"[2]

Throughout this chapter the reader should bear these words in mind, because they explain why and how the invasion of Normandy and the events which followed it led to the establishment over half of Europe of a Soviet dictatorship equally vile to the one Russia had helped to destroy.

[1] *United States Army in World War II* (American Official History), "Cross-Channel Attack", Gordon A. Harrison (1951), p. 92.
[2] *As He Saw It*, Elliott Roosevelt (1946), p. 185.

Soon after General Eisenhower's nomination to command "Overlord" the following appointments were made: General Sir Henry Maitland Wilson to become British Supreme Commander in the Mediterranean; Air Chief Marshal Sir Arthur Tedder to be Eisenhower's deputy Commander; and General Sir Bernard Montgomery to command the cross-Channel invasion forces, known as the Twenty-First Army Group, until such time as Eisenhower could transfer his headquarters to France. Besides these appointments, Admiral Sir Bertram Ramsay was given command of the Allied Naval Expeditionary Force, and Air Chief Marshal Sir Trafford Leigh-Mallory was given command of the Allied Expeditionary Air Force.

On January 1, 1944, Montgomery left Italy for England; broke his journey at Marrakesh, where Mr. Churchill was convalescing, and was shown by him the draft COSSAC plan prepared by General Morgan. It was proposed to launch the invasion in the Bay of the Seine between Grandcamp and Caen with one corps of three divisions, with a build-up to nine divisions by the fifth day. After his arrival in England on January 2, Montgomery considered this plan in detail and came to the conclusion that the frontage was too narrow and the assault force too weak. At a conference with Ramsay and Leigh-Mallory it was decided that the assault should be made on a frontage of two armies, the First United States Army on the right with two divisions in first wave, and the Second British Army on the left with three divisions. To meet this increase of force, the front of assault was extended westward to les Dunes de Varreville, on the eastern coast of the Cotentin peninsula, and eastward to Cabourg, east of the river Orne. The dividing line between the two armies was to be Port en Bessin–Bayeux, both inclusively allotted to the Second British Army. Because this increase of force demanded additional landing craft it was proposed to postpone the date of the invasion (D-day) from May 1 to May 31, in order to obtain an additional month's production of craft, and to take over the landing craft earmarked for "Anvil" – the invasion of southern France.

The shortage of landing craft was not the fault of production, but of allocation, for by May 1 Fleet-Admiral King, C.-in-C. U.S. Fleet, had at his disposal the bulk of the landing craft, but as his heart was in the Pacific and not in Europe he allotted only a small fraction of the number as the American quota to "Overlord". The crux of the difficulty, as Mr. Henry L. Stimson, United

States Secretary for War, points out, was that the Joint Chiefs of Staff were "incapable of forcing a decision against the will of any one of its members. . . . Only the President was in a position to settle disagreements" between them, which he was reluctant to do.[1] The results of King's close-fistedness were that the date of "Anvil", which was to coincide with "Overlord", had to be postponed, and that General Alexander was deprived of the means to carry out amphibious operations up the leg of Italy, in consequence of which his campaign was ruined.

On January 21 Eisenhower accepted the revised plan, the general idea of which was: (1) to secure a footing on the Normandy coast from north of the Carentan estuary to the river Orne; (2) to occupy Cherbourg and the Brittany ports; (3) when once firmly established, to threaten to break out with the Second British Army in the Caen area, in order to draw the enemy reserves toward that sector; (4) once this had been done, to break out with the First and Third U.S. Armies[2] on the western flank and advance southward to the Loire; and (5) to pivot the whole front on Caen and swing the right wing eastward to the Seine.[3]

Across the Channel Eisenhower was faced by Field-Marshal von Rundstedt who, in March, 1942, had been appointed C.-in-C. West, a command which included France, Belgium, and Holland. In the spring of 1944 he had at his disposal two Army Groups and the Panzer Group West. They included these formations:

Army Group B (Field-Marshal Rommel) consisted of the LXXXVIIIth Corps (General Christiansen) of three divisions in Holland; the Fifteenth Army (General von Salmuth) of four corps of 17 divisions, between Antwerp and the river Orne; and the Seventh Army (General Dollmann) of three corps of 15 divisions (one in the Channel Islands) between the Orne and the Loire.

Army Group G (General Blaskowitz) comprised the First and Nineteenth Armies, the one of five and the other of eight divisions. The former garrisoned the area between the Loire and the central Pyrenees, and the latter the Mediterranean coast from Perpignan to Mentone.

In all there were 48 divisions, of which 38 were located along, and 10 behind the coast. Of the latter, five were between the

---

[1] *On Active Service in Peace and War* (English edit., n.d.), p. 287.
[2] The Third Army was to follow the First Army at a date subsequent to D-day.
[3] *Normandy to the Baltic*, Field-Marshal Montgomery (n.d.), pp. 15–16.

Scheldt and the Somme, two between the Somme and the Seine, and three in Normandy.

Panzer Group West (General Baron Geyr von Schweppenburg) was responsible for the administration and training of 10 Panzer and Panzer grenadier divisions, located as follows: North of the Loire, 1st S.S. Panzer Division (*Leibstandarte Adolf Hitler*) at Beverloo (Belgium); 2nd Panzer Division in the Amiens area; 116th Panzer Division east of Rouen; 12th S.S. Panzer Division (*Hitler Jugend*) in the Lisieux area; 21st Panzer Division in the Caen area; and the Panzer-Lehr Division in the Orléans area south of the Loire; the 17th S.S. Panzer Grenadier Division was in the Poitiers area; 11th Panzer Division in the Bordeaux area; 2nd S.S. Panzer Division (*Das Reich*) in the Toulouse area; and 9th Panzer Division in the Avignon area. Of these divisions the 2nd, 116th, 21st and 12th S.S. were under Rommel's command, and the rest in O.K.W. reserve.[1]

The Third Air Fleet (Field-Marshal Sperrle), which was reduced to 90 bombers and 70 fighters fit for action, came under Göring's orders, although it was centred in France.

Taken as a whole the troops were of poor quality, reinforced with invalids and foreigners, and most of their divisional transport was horse drawn.

The so-called Atlantic Wall, which skirted the coasts of Holland, Belgium, and France, had been laid out by the Todt Organization, and in 1943, with the exception of port defences and the Pas de Calais section, consisted of little more than coastal earthworks. In November, 1943, when Rommel was appointed to command Army Group B, he was instructed to inspect the coastal defences, independently of Rundstedt, and in his report to Hitler, dated December 31, he expressed the opinion that "the focus of the enemy landing operation" would "probably be directed against the Fifteenth Army's sector . . . between Boulogne and the Somme estuary. . . ."[2] Nevertheless, he turned his attention to the Normandy stretch, possibly because Hitler was one of the few who believed that the landing would be attempted there.[3] The result was that the coastal defences in the Seine Bay were extensively added to: concrete works were built, minefields and entanglements extended, anti-tank obstacles constructed on the

[1] *Panzer Leader*, General Heinz Guderian (1952), pp. 331–332.
[2] *The Rommel Papers*, edit. B. H. Liddell Hart (1953), p. 453.
[3] See *Von Rundstedt*, Guenther Blumentritt (1952), p. 218, and *The Struggle for Europe*, Chester Wilmot (1952), p. 205.

beaches, and under-water obstacles added. Extensive areas were flooded in the marshy ground bordering the Carentan estuary.

The question of the location of the strategic reserve led to a somewhat academic argument between Rundstedt and Rommel, because ever since 1941 Hitler had decided that were a landing attempted it was to be fought *à outrance* on the beaches. Rommel was of the same opinion, and because of the enemy's air superiority, which he rightly maintained would prohibit daylight movements, besides holding the beaches in strength he wanted the reserves, particularly the armoured divisions, to be located near the coast.[1] Rundstedt, supported by Geyer and General Guderian, Inspector-General of the Panzer Troops,[2] with equal right maintained that until it was known where the enemy intended to land such a course might mean that the reserves would be wrongly positioned when the enemy did land. The outcome was a compromise: the 21st Panzer Division was left at Rommel's disposal, but the 116th, 12th S.S., and Panzer-Lehr Divisions were on no account to be used without Hitler's authority. The greatest defect in the whole defence scheme was that Hitler arrogated to himself the right to issue orders direct to those who should have been Rundstedt's subordinates – Rommel, Sperrle, and others – but who actually were no more than his collaborators. There was no unity of command during the campaign.

The forces in England ready for use at the time of the invasion were: 17 British divisions, including three Canadian; 20 American divisions, one French and one Polish; 5,049 fighter aircraft, 3,467 heavy bombers, 2,343 other combat aircraft, 2,316 transport aircraft, and 2,591 gliders. The total landing craft, merchant vessels and warships exceeded 6,000 vessels.[3] There were also assault engineer tanks; tank-carried bridges for crossing anti-tank ditches; mat-laying tanks for crossing soft patches on the beaches; ramp-tanks over which vehicles could scale sea walls; flail tanks for exploding land mines; amphibious tanks, known as D.D. tanks because of their duplex drive – twin propellers as well as tracks[4] – and C.D.L. tanks, which were fitted with projectors for night operations.[5] Seventy old merchant vessels and four old warships were prepared for the planting of breakwaters (code-named "Gooseberries") in each divisional sector; two artificial harbours

---

[1] *The Rommel Papers*, pp. 468–469.   [2] *Von Rundstedt*, p. 213.
[3] *Crusade in Europe*, Dwight D. Eisenhower (U.S. edit., 1948), p. 53.
[4] *Normandy to the Baltic*, p. 24.
[5] *The Second World War*, J. F. C. Fuller (1948), Appendix, pp. 413–415.

(code-named "Mulberries") built of concrete caissons, which could be towed over the Channel, were in readiness, and a cross-Channel pipe line (code-named "Pluto") was available through which sea-going tankers could discharge petrol direct on the Normandy shore.

The order of battle of the initial assault forces was:

Airborne: the 6th British and the 82nd and 101st American Airborne Divisions.

First U.S. Army (Lieutenant-General Omar N. Bradley): VIIth Corps (Major-General J. L. Collins) four divisions – the 4th, followed by 90th, 9th, and 79th. Vth Corps (Major-General L. T. Gerow) three divisions – 1st and 29th, followed by the 2nd.

Second British Army (Lieutenant-General M. C. Dempsey): XXXth Corps (Lieutenant-General G. C. Bucknall) three divisions – 50th Division and 8th Armoured Brigade, followed by the 7th Armoured Division and 49th Division. 1st Corps (Lieutenant-General J. T. Croker) three divisions – 3rd Canadian Division and 2nd Canadian Armoured Brigade, followed by Commandos and 4th Special Service Brigade; and the 3rd British Division and 27th Armoured Brigade, followed by the 1st Special Service Brigade, 51st Highland Division and 4th Armoured Brigade.

On land, sea, and in the air there were in all 2,876,439 allied officers and men.

The objectives of the forces are shown on the assault plan. It will be seen that the two airborne groups were to form flank guards, the U.S. 82nd and 101st Airborne Divisions around Ste. Mère-Eglise on the right of the assault area, and the British 6th Airborne Division between Cabourg and the river Orne on its left. Five landing areas were allotted to the four assault corps: "Utah" for the U.S. VIIth Corps; "Omaha" for the U.S. Vth Corps, and "Gold", "Juno" and "Sword" for the British XXXth and 1st Corps. The final objectives for D-day are shown on the plan.

Probably the most important step in readiness for invasion was the adoption of a rational strategic bombing policy. Since May 11, 1940, when Mr. Churchill inaugurated the bombing of German cities,[1] the policy of obliterating the enemy's industrial and residential areas had proved a failure; it had not reduced production, which had advanced by leaps and bounds, and it had fortified, not lowered, German civil morale.[2] It was too scattered

---

[1] See *Bombing Vindicated*, J. M. Spaight (1944), pp. 68 and 74.
[2] See *United States Strategic Bombing Survey, Over-all Report (European War)*, 1945.

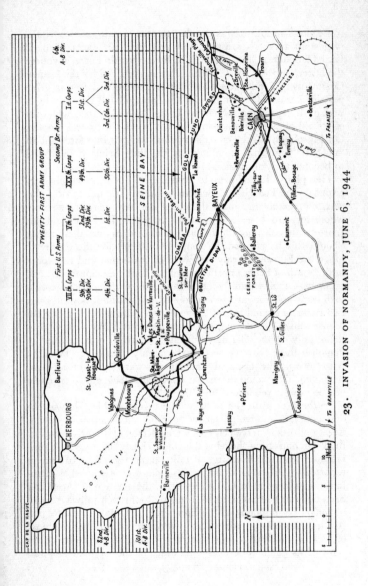

23 · INVASION OF NORMANDY, JUNE 6, 1944

to be decisive and it was decided to concentrate on two vitally important targets – transport and synthetic oil plants. General Carl C. Spaatz, Chief of the U.S. Strategic Air Force, favoured the latter, and Air Chief Marshal Sir Arthur Tedder the former. Of the two, Tedder's was the better choice, and it was given priority because the bombing of transport offered the only prospect of disorganizing the enemy in the time available, while the effect of bombing oil plants might not be felt for several months. On March 30, 1944, Tedder's proposal was put into force and at long last "strategic" bombing, for the time being at least, was to become truly strategic.

The plan adopted was to restrict the enemy's mobility by crippling the French and Belgian railways. The underlying idea was, not merely to isolate the allied landing area, but also the whole forward zone of operations between the Seine and the Loire by demolishing the rail and road bridges over these rivers. Should this be effected, it would be difficult for the enemy to move the Fifteenth Army westward of the Seine, and his troops in the south of France northward of the Loire. Except for the gap between Orléans and Fontainebleau, these demolitions would turn the whole forward zone into a strategic island. Beyond these two rivers, a second line of "interdiction" was selected along the Meuse and Albert Canal, the crossings over which were vital to the supply of the German Fifteenth Army. It was decided to demolish these crossings so that the supply lines of the Fifteenth Army would be crippled and its westward lines of advance restricted. This would mean that the German Seventh Army could not be rapidly reinforced from the east.

In the attack on the railways the primary objective was the destruction of motive power by bombing the locomotive depôts. Eighty of these "nerve centres" were selected and by D-day more than 50 had been heavily damaged. Early in May, Colonel Höffner, who was in charge of rail transport for von Rundstedt, reported to O.K.W. that 100 trains a day were required to maintain the *Wehrmacht* in France, and that the average for April had been 60, and had fallen to 32, because the French railways could no longer be supplied with Belgian coal.[1] By D-day, in the Région Nord, of 2,000 locomotives 1,500 were immobilized by air action, or lack of maintenance and fuel, and traffic had fallen to 13 per cent. of its January level. By June 5, "of the 24 road and rail

[1] Cited by Wilmot in *The Struggle for Europe*, p. 211.

bridges over the Seine between Paris and the sea, 18 had been destroyed, three were closed for repair, and the remaining three were under such threat of air attack that they could not be used for any large-scale movement in daylight."[1]

During the three months before D-day 66,000 tons of bombs were dropped, "thus creating," Mr. Churchill writes, "a 'railway desert' around the German troops in Normandy."[2] Besides these operations, preparatory attacks were made by the allied air forces on the enemy coastal defences, radar stations and airfields, which for several weeks before D-day were systematically bombed, and on the eve of D-day 10 super-heavy radar-sighted batteries on the Normandy coast were obliterated. In all, more than 14,000 tons of bombs were dropped on these targets. On the same night the remaining enemy radar stations were jammed, so that when the airborne attacks were launched they were not intercepted, nor were the invasion forces discovered until they neared their objectives.

The more important naval tasks were to escort the invasion fleet, to sweep channels through the enemy's mine barrier, and to cover the landings by bombardment. Admiral Ramsay had two task forces at his disposal; the eastern force, under Rear-Admiral Vian, R.N., to assist the landings on the British sector, and the western force, under Admiral Kirk, U.S.N., to help the American landings. In all, 29 flotillas of minesweepers were allotted to these forces.

An elaborate deception plan was put into force to cover the tactical operations. Its aim was to mislead the enemy about the date of the attack by persuading him that the attempt to cross the Channel would not be made until about six weeks after the actual day selected, and to indicate that it would be delivered in the Pas de Calais area. For every air mission flown over Normandy, two were flown over the Pas de Calais, and for every ton of bombs dropped west of le Havre, two tons were dropped north of it. In addition, many dummy landing craft were assembled in the ports of south-east England; an elaborate dummy headquarters was erected at Dover; and dummy roads, railways and sidings were laid in Sussex and Kent.

Of the many perplexing problems Eisenhower was called upon to solve, one of the most intricate was the choice of D-day. "It was decided," Montgomery states, "that the best conditions would

[1] *Ibid.*, p. 212.   [2] *The Second World War*, vol. v, p. 465.

obtain if H-hour [the old zero-hour] were fixed at forty minutes after nautical twilight on a day when at this time the tide was three hours before high water mark,"[1] but because the flow of the tide up the Channel did not permit these conditions to be obtained on all beaches simultaneously, a separate H-hour had to be fixed for each beach; they varied from 6.30 a.m. to 7.45 a.m. Also, as it was desirable that the invasion should be made under a full moon, D-day was restricted to one of three days in each lunar month, and the first three after May 31 were June 5, 6, and 7. The first date was selected; full moon was on the 6th.

June opened with high winds and rough seas, and on June 3 and 4 meteorological predictions were so unfavourable that Eisenhower decided to postpone the invasion for 24 hours. Although conditions had only slightly improved on the 5th, at 4 a.m. that day he took the bold decision to launch the cross-Channel assault on the 6th.

The timetable was that airborne troops, carried in 2,395 aircraft and 867 gliders, were to land at 2 a.m.; the air bombardment, in which 2,219 aircraft were to participate, was to open at 3.14 a.m., to be augmented by a naval bombardment at 5.50 a.m.; and the first wave of the invading forces, carried in 4,266 landing ships and landing craft, were to land between 6.30 a.m. and 7.45 a.m.

At the appointed hour the bombardment was opened by an intense bombing of the enemy's coastal defences and beach obstacles; 7,616 tons of bombs were dropped on them. Then, while the 2nd British and 9th U.S. Tactical Air Forces covered the invasion flotillas, the heavy guns of the combined fleets bombarded the enemy's fixed batteries and concrete defences.[2] At closer range, the lighter defences were bombarded by the lighter ordnance. Finally, as the first wave of the assault neared the shore, a standing barrage was placed on the beaches, which was timed to lift immediately the troops landed. For this, Commander Edwards states, destroyers and L.C.G.'s (landing craft gun) – the modern equivalent of the old floating batteries – literally "drenched" every yard of the beaches with high explosives. Further to increase the density of the fire, rockets were fired from landing craft – L.C.R.'s. "For purposes of short-range 'drenching fire'," Commander Edwards writes, "one such craft

---

[1] *Normandy to the Baltic*, p. 26.
[2] Both bombardments did little damage to the concrete casemates (see *Supreme Commander's Report*, p. 27).

has a fire-power equivalent to over 80 light cruisers or nearly 200 destroyers.'[1] These operations were covered by a standing patrol of 10 fighter squadrons, and as far as the high seas permitted the troops were led to the beaches by D.D. (amphibious) tanks. Eisenhower writes: "The use of large numbers of amphibious tanks to afford fire support . . . had been an essential feature of our plans, and, despite the losses they suffered on account of the heavy seas . . . it is doubtful if the assault forces could have firmly established themselves without the assistance of these weapons."[2]

The airborne invasions were eminently successful in spite of the stormy weather. The 6th British Airborne Division was dropped around Breville; the 101st American Division south of Ste. Mère-Eglise, and the 82nd to its west. The first division captured the bridges over the Orne and blew those over the Dives; the second occupied the villages of Pouppeville and St. Martin-de-Varreville, west of "Utah" beach; and the third, in spite of wide dispersion, seized Ste. Mère-Eglise and thereby blocked the Caen–Carentan–Cherbourg road.

These operations came as a rude shock to the enemy who, because of the bad weather, had been taken off-guard. But he was not completely surprised, because between 9.15 and 9.30 p.m. on June 5, a wireless signal had been intercepted and decoded which called all the French Resistance Movement to battle at midnight June 5–6. By 10.30 p.m. both Army Groups B and G and the Third Air Fleet were put on the alert, but unfortunately for the Germans Rommel was on a visit to his wife at Heerlingen, near Ulm; Sepp Dietrich, commander of the 1st S.S. Panzer Corps, was in Brussels; and Dollmann, C.-in-C. Seventh Army, was at Rennes directing a war game.[3] About 1 a.m. on June 6 O.K.W. was informed of the intercepted message, and between 2 a.m. and 3 a.m. it was informed of the airborne landings. When the seaborne landing was announced Rundstedt asked O.K.W. to release the Panzer divisions in reserve. But permission to use them was not given until between 3 and 4 p.m., when it was too late to bring them into action that day. This, according to Blumentritt, was because it was Hitler's habit to work into the

[1] *Operation Neptune* (1946), p. 89.
[2] *Supreme Commander's Report*, p. 30. The author first proposed the use of amphibious tanks in a lecture given at the Royal United Service Institution on February 11, 1920, entitled "The Development of Sea Warfare on Land and its Influence on Future Naval Operations."
[3] See *Von Rundstedt*, p. 221.

early hours of the morning and then to sleep until a little before noon, and as no one at O.K.W. had the courage to wake him, "he received detailed information only when the invasion had been in full swing for several hours."[1]

None of the seaborne landings was repulsed; all were successful, though in varying degrees. On Utah beach the 4th U.S. Division, preceded by amphibian tanks that had been launched 5,000 yards off shore, penetrated to a depth of over six miles and made contact with the 101st Airborne Division. On Omaha beach, the two regimental combat teams of the 29th and 1st U.S. Divisions, deprived by the rough sea of full amphibious tank support, were vigorously opposed by the 352nd German Division and were pinned down on the shore line until late in the day, when they fought their way forward to the coastal road. The Second British Army, which also used amphibious tanks, was more fortunate, for although the right of the 50th Division on Gold beach was strongly opposed at le Hamel (two miles east of Arromanches), its left rapidly advanced inland almost to the Bayeux–Caen road. The 3rd Canadian Division on Juno beach met with stiff resistance on the beach, but it pushed forward steadily to a depth of nearly seven miles. On the left of the Second Army the 3rd British Division's assault on Sword beach went according to plan, and by the late afternoon Bieville and most of Ouistreham had been secured, and a counter-attack by German infantry supported by some 20 tanks of the 21st Panzer Division had been repulsed by the 3rd British and 3rd Canadian Divisions.

This counter-offensive was a muddled affair. In the absence of Rommel, General Speidel ordered forward the 21st Panzer Division. But, meanwhile, its commander, General Edgar Feuchtinger, had advanced part of it against the enemy airborne troops east of the Orne, and before it could accomplish its task he was ordered to withdraw it to deal with a critical situation west of the Orne. He was unable to intervene until 3 p.m., and for lack of sufficient infantry support his counter-attack, after it had penetrated to the coast, was beaten back by self-propelled anti-tank artillery.

[1] *Ibid.*, p. 225. According to Fabian von Schlabrendorff, when General Hans Speidel, Rommel's chief of staff, telephoned General Jodl at O.K.W., the officer on duty did not dare wake him until 9 a.m., and in his turn Jodl waited for another hour before he informed Keitel. "Both men then considered themselves bound by the strict order never to disturb Hitler's sleep. So it was not until his usual midday meeting that Hitler heard the news" (*Revolt against Hitler*, pp. 129–130).

Throughout the day the allied command of the air was absolute. The *Luftwaffe* did not shoot down a single aircraft of the 14,600 sorties that were flown. By nightfall, between the Vire and Orne the allies had broken through the Atlantic Wall on a front of some 30 miles; but gaps between the landing stages still remained to be filled in, and not one of the final objectives had been gained.

Hitler, Rundstedt, and Rommel – who had returned on the afternoon of the 6th – for once agreed in the belief that the assault west of the Seine was a feint intended to cover the main invasion in the Pas-de-Calais. They decided not to call in the Fifteenth Army, and to deal with the immediate situation. Rommel's plan was to seal off the American penetrations with infantry, and to counter-attack the British in the Caen sector with the 1st Panzer Corps. So that this might be done without delay, Dietrich was instructed not to wait for the Panzer Lehr Division, but to attack all out with the 21st and 12th S.S. Panzer Division as early as he could on June 7.

Soon after midnight on June 6–7, General Kurt Meyer, Commander of the 12th S.S. Panzer Division, arrived at Feuchtinger's headquarters in Caen. Between them they had some 160 tanks, a formidable force, but because of delay in refuelling, aggravated by a fighter-bomber attack at dawn and the involvement of the 21st Panzer Division in a British attack north of Caen, Meyer went forward with only part of his division. He struck at the Canadians who then threatened Caen from the west, and early on June 8 Rommel ordered Dietrich to strike again, this time with all three of his divisions, between Caen and Bayeux. But this was not possible, because the Panzer Lehr Division had not yet come up and the 21st was unable to disengage. All Dietrich could do was to reinforce Meyer, and again Meyer struck at the Canadians, who had advanced to the Caen–Bayeux road at Bretteville. But his infantry was cut off from his tanks and before dawn on the 9th a Canadian counter-attack took back the ground he had gained. After this abortive operation Rommel decided to postpone further counter-attack until he could concentrate his armour.

"From 9th June onwards," writes Speidel, "the initiative lay with the Allies, who fought the battle entirely as it suited them."[1] This is corroborated by Rommel who, on the 10th, in a long report to Hitler, wrote: "During the day, practically our entire

[1] *We Defended Normandy*, p. 99.

traffic – on roads, tracks, and open country – is pinned down by powerful fighter-bomber and bomber formations, with the result that the movements of our troops on the battlefield is almost entirely paralysed, while the enemy can manœuvre freely. Every traffic defile in the rear areas is under continual attack and it is very difficult to get essential supplies and ammunition and petrol to the troops."[1]

Montgomery had firmly established his bridgehead by June 12, and 326,000 men, 54,000 vehicles, and 104,000 tons of stores had been landed.[2] By then the VIIth U.S. Corps had pushed out to Montebourg, north-east of Ste. Mère-Eglise, and also had occupied Carentan, east of which it had linked up with the Vth U.S. Corps. The latter had advanced its front to the Vire, eight miles north of St. Lô; had occupied the Forest of Cerisy, and had pushed its left well beyond Balleroy. On the British front the XXXth Corps had captured Bayeux and had fought forward to the Balleroy–Caen road. On its left the Ist Corps had established itself on a front that ran from Bretteville round Caen and thence to Ste. Honorine, from where its left was swung northward to Franceville-Plage on the Channel, west of Cabourg.

In spite of Rommel's failure to drive his enemy into the sea, on the night of June 12–13 renewed hope was awakened in Germany. The first flying-bomb had fallen on London. It was a pilotless jet-propelled aircraft with a warhead of 1,000 kg., but although it did considerable damage the expectations placed in it were soon found to have been grossly exaggerated.[3]

Once the German counter-attack had been repulsed, Montgomery set out to take Cherbourg and Caen; the former in order to gain a port which would supplement his precarious prefabricated harbours and beach supply, and the latter to establish a fulcrum for his strategic lever – the break-through on his western flank. Rommel, after his failure at Caen, set out to frustrate an advance on Cherbourg, and on June 13–15 he made a violent attempt, in which the 17th S.S. Panzer Division was committed, to break through the junction of the VIIth and Vth U.S. Corps in the Carentan area; but again he was repulsed. Simultaneously

---

[1] *The Rommel Papers*, pp. 476–477.   [2] *Normandy to the Baltic*, p. 57.
[3] In all some 8,000 flying-bombs were launched against London, of which 2,400 got through; 23,000 houses were destroyed, over 700,000 damaged, 6,000 people killed and 18,000 injured. On September 8 the first long-range rocket-bomb (V2) fell in London. It was a novel and revolutionary weapon, its maximum range was 200 miles and its speed remarkable, but it was too inaccurate to be anything more than a terror weapon.

the Americans captured Montebourg, and on the 14th the 9th U.S. Division and the 82nd Airborne Division advanced westward on St. Sauveur-le-Vicomte. They captured it on the 16th and two days later reached the west coast of the Cotentin Peninsula at Barneville. The VIIIth U.S. Corps then became operative and took over command of the two airborne and 90th divisions and faced south so as to cover the advance of the VIIth Corps on Cherbourg.

On June 19 the allied calculations were upset by a furious and unforecasted gale. It blew hard for three days, wrecked the American "Mulberry" at St. Laurent-sur-Mer, and damaged the British "Mulberry" at Arromanches. When the storm subsided it was found that 800 craft were stranded on the beaches and that allied shipping had sustained five times the damage caused by the enemy on D-day.

On June 21, the 4th, 79th, and 9th Divisions of the VIIth U.S. Corps closed on Cherbourg, and on the following day, supported by naval gunfire, they opened an assault on the fortress, which was commanded by General Karl von Schlieben. On the 25th they broke through its defences, captured von Schlieben on the 26th, and on the 27th Cherbourg surrendered with 39,000 men. The port was found so thoroughly wrecked that it did not become operative until late in August.

While Cherbourg was stormed, on June 25 the XXXth, VIIIth, and Ist Corps of the Second British Army made a determined attack on Caen. The country was exceedingly difficult and strewn with land mines, and although in the centre the VIIIth Corps reached the river Odon west of Caen, the other two corps made little progress. On the 29th the 1st and 2nd S.S. Panzer Divisions were encountered, and were soon followed by the 9th S.S. Panzer Division with elements of the 10th S.S. Panzer Division, both from the eastern front. This stiffening of the enemy armour decided Montgomery to hold the ground he had won and to re-group.

When the Second Front, so long called for by Stalin, was opened in Normandy, the Russians made ready their summer offensive. On June 23 it was opened between Vitebsk and Gomel, and by the end of July the Niemen was reached. South of the Pripet a second great offensive followed on July 13, and 17 days later the Vistula was crossed south of Sandomir. By mid-August the German situation was catastrophic – the Russians were at the

Carpathians and the borders of east Prussia. On August 22 after a *coup d'état* in Bucharest the Rumanian Government capitulated, and three days later the Finns sued for an armistice. From July 1 the doom of the Third Reich was no longer in doubt; the hour for the break-through in Normandy was about to strike and at long last the end of the war was in sight.

On the day after the fall of Cherbourg, Rundstedt and Rommel were summoned to Berchtesgaden and, on June 29, in conference with Hitler, Rundstedt demanded a free hand, and Rommel urged that the Seventh Army should be withdrawn to the Seine. Hitler would not listen to these proposals and the outcome was that on July 3 Rundstedt tendered his resignation and was succeeded by Field-Marshal von Kluge.

Meanwhile Montgomery decided to take Caen, and at the same time to advance the First U.S. Army toward the line Coutances–St. Lô, preparatory to a break-out on the western flank. This dual offensive was opened by Bradley on July 3, but because of the difficult *bocage* country and the stubborn resistance of the enemy it made slow progress. On July 7–8 came the attack on Caen, a typical Montgomery battle of *matériel*. Bomber Command R.A.F. was called in to support Dempsey's advance, and although Montgomery asserts that "it played an important part in the success of the operation,"[1] eyewitness reports do not corroborate this.[2] Two thousand five hundred tons of bombs were dropped on Caen, the streets of which were so blocked by rubble that it was impossible for tanks to move along them until passages had been cleared by bulldozers.[3] The delay caused by the bombing enabled the Germans to withdraw from Caen, on the northern side of the Orne, to the Faubourg de Vaucelles, on the river's southern side, and so to frustrate a complete break-through.

By July 10, a crisis was reached: the American offensive was bogged down; the Germans in Vaucelles still blocked the way to the Falaise plain; and four German divisions from southern France had been brought up to reinforce the right of the Seventh Army. Because these reinforcements enabled Rommel to relieve his Panzer divisions, which he began to move toward the American

---

[1] *Normandy to the Baltic*, p. 74.

[2] See *Eclipse*, Alan Moorehead (1945), p. 112, and *European Victory*, John D'Arcy-Dawson (n.d.), pp. 87–88.

[3] General de Guingand, Montgomery's Chief of Staff, records: "The trouble then was that *too much disruption* was caused, and our advance was impeded by the effects of the bombing" (*Operation Victory*, 1947, p. 396).

front, it became imperative for Montgomery to attack again in order to put a stop to this.

His plan was that while Bradley restocked his ammunition dumps and made ready to capture St. Lô and drive the enemy back to the Périers–St. Lô road, in preparation for a break-out (Operation "Cobra") on July 20, on the night of July 15–16 Dempsey was to make a feint attack to the west of Caen, which on the 18th was to be followed by a decisive attack (Operation "Goodwood") by his VIIIth Corps and three armoured divisions from the Orne bridgehead southward and to the east of Caen. In a note to Lieutenant-General Sir Richard O'Connor, G.O.C. VIIIth Corps, Montgomery explained his project as follows: "A victory on the eastern flank will help us gain what we want on the western flank. But the eastern flank is a bastion on which the whole future of the campaign in North-West Europe depends."[1] In brief, his plan was to draw in the maximum German forces on Caen so that the minimum would be left to operate against Bradley's First Army in the St. Lô area.

The feint attack at first succeeded in deceiving the Germans, and was notable for its use of an expedient called "artificial moonlight." Beams of massed searchlights were focussed on the clouds, from which their light was reflected back to the ground.[2] But on the following night a *Luftwaffe* reconnaissance, using flare-lights, reported traffic across the Orne bridges. As this pointed to a break-through, early on July 17 Rommel went forward to make sure of the defensive dispositions. On his return in the afternoon, when on the road from Livarot to Vimoutiers, near the village of Ste. Foy-Montgomery, his car was attacked by a British fighter aircraft and he was so severely wounded that at first it was thought he was dead. When von Kluge heard of this, he did not appoint a successor to Rommel, but took over command of Army Group B.

The attack on July 18 (operation "Goodwood") was a super-Montgomery operation. The plan was to bridge the Orne canal; to send over three armoured divisions (the Guards, 7th, and 11th) with supporting tanks and infantry, and then, under cover of a "super-colossal crack", to swing southward toward Falaise and cut off and destroy three German divisions. To clear a way for the tanks, heavy bombers were to bomb on each side of an area

[1] Cited by Wilmot in *The Struggle for Europe*, p. 354.
[2] Montgomery's assumption that this expedient "was used for the first time in battle" (*Normandy to the Baltic*, p. 78) is incorrect. As we have seen (Chapter 8, p. 314) it was first employed in Italy by the British 7th Division in August, 1918.

4,000 yards in width and silence the enemy anti-tank guns on the flanks of the attacking armour. Between these two walls of bursting bombs lighter aircraft were to drop fragmentation (non-cratering) anti-personnel bombs, so as not to make the ground impassable. The tanks were then to advance through the bomb-swept lane under cover of a creeping artillery barrage. Eisenhower informs us that the attack was preceded "by what was the heaviest and most concentrated air assault hitherto employed in support of ground operations." Twelve thousand tons of bombs were dropped, 5,000 "in less than forty-five minutes. . . . At the same time, a strong naval bombardment was made to supplement the air effort."[1]

Unfortunately for Montgomery, the Germans withdrew their troops and prepared a zone of anti-tank defences on a line a few miles behind the prospective lane. Their gunners remained under cover until the bombing was over and then they emerged and opened fire on the hundreds of vehicles deployed across the plain. They knocked out between 150 and 200 of the attacking tanks – the 11th Armoured Division lost over 100 – after which some 50 German aircraft heavily bombed the British position during the night. On the following day the weather broke and the plains of Caen became a sea of mud; the battle ended.[2]

The break in the weather persuaded General Eisenhower to postpone Bradley's attack (Operation "Cobra") until July 25, when the plan was to advance on a three-divisional front west of St. Lô, with the line Marigny–St. Gilles as the primary objective. Then it was planned that three fresh divisions would leap-frog through the leading three divisions, and lastly a turn westward was to be made in order to strike at Coutances and Granville.

The air tactics were that fighter-bomber attacks were made on all enemy bridges over the river Vire south of St. Lô, so as to isolate the area of advance. Then, "at 1.40 hours," writes General H. H. Arnold, Commanding General U.S. Army Air Forces, "P.47 Thunderbolts with bombs and incendiaries crossed east to west in seven waves, 2 or 3 minutes apart. Then for an hour more than 1,500 Fortresses and Liberators dropped 3,431 tons of explosives. P.38 Lightnings followed in eight waves lasting 20

---

[1] *Supreme Commander's Report*, pp. 45–46.
[2] According to General Wisch, commander of the 1st Panzer Division, on the evening of July 18 his Panther tanks surprised approximately 100 British tanks in leaguer and knocked out 40 during the night and another 40 next morning (*Defeat in the West*, Milton Schulman, 1947, p. 141).

minutes, laying more incendiaries. Then 400 medium bombers attacked the southern end of the area with 500-pound bombs, concentrating on crossroads and German concentrations of tanks and troops in the village of St. Gilles. Incendiaries started flames that swept unchecked over German bivouac areas and dugouts."[1]

As in the Caen attacks, this mighty air blow "did not cause a large numbers of casualties to the enemy, but it produced great confusion." And "Again, as at Caen, this stunning effect was only temporary. . . . The advance was met with intense artillery fire, from positions not neutralized by the air bombing."[2]

The infantry attack was made on a four-mile front, with tanks in support, and the most interesting thing about it was the air cooperation. "As our troops went forward," writes General Arnold, "fighters and fighter-bombers in closest communication and under common direction ranged ahead of them destroying military targets. . . . Fighters in direct communication with tanks by radio flew constant alert over our armored columns. Ground officers called on the fighters to bomb or strafe artillery or armor in their path. Pilots warned tank commanders of traps at crossroads or woods. German armored units, without aerial eyes, fought at a disadvantage."[3] This was *blitzkrieg* on the grand scale.

During July 27 the towns of Périers and Lessay were occupied, and on the 28th the escape route through Coutances was closed and 4,500 Germans captured. In the meantime, to the east, the Canadian IInd Corps' advance toward Falaise had been halted by a strong defensive belt of anti-tank guns, dug-in tanks, and mortars.

Five days later, the Third U.S. Army, which consisted of the VIIIth, XIIth, XVth, and XXth Corps, under General Patton, officially came into being; Lieutenant-General C. H. Hodges was given the command of the First U.S. Army (Vth, VIIth, and XIXth Corps), and the two armies were formed into the Twelfth Army Group under General Bradley. This left Montgomery in command of the Twenty-First Army Group, namely the Second British Army and the First Canadian Army, under Lieutenant-General H. D. G. Crearer, which had become operational on July 23. Nevertheless, until September, Montgomery continued in control of all of Eisenhower's land forces.

---

[1] *Second Report*, 27th February, 1945, pp. 11 and 14.
[2] *Supreme Commander's Report*, pp. 47–48.
[3] *Second Report*, 27th February, 1945, p. 14.

When Coutances was taken, the plan for the Third U.S. Army was to drive south, break through Avranches into Brittany, and seize the area Rennes–Fougères. Then it was to turn westward and secure the ports of St. Malo and Brest while the First U.S. Army advanced south to seize the Mortain–Vire area. At the same time the Second British Army was to thrust forward in the Caumont area. This time, whatever the weather, Eisenhower decided "to indulge in an all-out offensive and, if necessary, throw caution to the winds."[1] It was high time to do so, because he had absolute command in the air, at least two men to his enemy's one, and a tank and gun superiority of about three to one in his favour.

On July 29 Patton's leading tanks crossed the river Sienne (south of Coutances), and two days later Avranches was captured. "No effective barrier," writes Eisenhower, "now lay between us and Brittany, and my expectations of creating an open flank had been realized. The enemy was in a state of complete disorganization. . . ."[2] At the same time Montgomery launched his thrust south of Caumont, preceded by a smashing air bombardment delivered by 1,200 aircraft. Évrecy and Esquay, south-west of Caen, were stormed on August 4, and Villers-Bocage occupied on the 5th.

After the capture of Granville and Avranches, Patton met negligible resistance. On August 2 Rennes was entered and St. Malo by-passed. By August 6, the line of the Vilaine river was held from Rennes to the sea and the Brittany peninsula cut off. On August 7 the 6th U.S. Armoured Division stood before Brest, and on the 10th Nantes was in American hands.

The day after the occupation of Rennes, Bradley ordered Patton to leave a minimum of force in Brittany, and with the bulk of his army to drive all out for Paris. Patton set out to do this on August 4.

It was clear to von Kluge, threatened as he was by Patton's break-out from Avranches, that the only sane thing to do was to withdraw to the Seine. But Hitler would not listen to this, and on the day Patton set out for Paris Hitler ordered Kluge to assemble eight of his nine Panzer divisions and, on the night of August 6–7, to launch them from Mortain against the bottleneck of Patton's communications at Avranches. This would have been a sound enough proposition had Kluge held command of the air,

[1] *Supreme Commander's Report*, p. 50.
[2] *Ibid.*, p. 50.

but as he did not, it was suicidal.[1] Kluge was fully aware of this, but as he had been involved in the plot of July 20 to assassinate Hitler[2] he feared that were he to press his disagreement Hitler might suspect him of treason. In spite of this fear he found it impossible to disengage from the battle more than four Panzer divisions – 250 tanks in all – and two infantry divisions.

Unfortunately for Kluge, his preparations could not be hidden from his enemy's air reconnaissances, and directly Bradley learnt of them he deployed five divisions between Vire and Mortain to meet the threatened thrust. He also ordered Patton to hold back three divisions at St. Hilaire on the southern flank of the German advance. On August 6 Bradley struck against Vire, which compelled General Paul Hausser, in command of the Seventh German Army, to throw in part of the counter-attacking force in order to secure its right flank. Lastly, on the night of August 6–7, Hausser struck westward, advanced seven miles toward Avranches, and then was halted by American armour.

On August 7 the German columns that crowded the roads around Mortain were mercilessly bombed by American Thunderbolt and R.A.F. Typhoon aircraft and Montgomery ordered the First Canadian Army to thrust southward down the Caen–Falaise road against the rear of Hausser's right flank. "The plan," writes Montgomery, "was to attack under cover of darkness after a preliminary action by heavy bombers; the infantry was to be transported through the enemy's zone of defensive fire and forward defended localities in heavy armoured carriers. These vehicles, which became known as 'Kangaroos', were self-propelled gun carriages converted for transporting infantry."[3] On August 8 Montgomery asked Bradley to order Patton to swing his XVth Corps, which the day before had occupied Le Mans, northward on Alençon, so as to meet the Canadian thrust on Falaise and thereby close in from south and north on the enemy's communications.

[1] According to General Bayerlein: "Without the U.S.A.A.F. and the R.A.F. this attack . . . would almost certainly have resulted in a resounding victory. Hence, like the invasion battle itself – and this was the opinion of Rommel and most of the leading commanders – the battle was lost only because of the total supremacy which the Allies enjoyed in the air" (*The Rommel Papers*, pp. 490–491).

[2] For this plot see *Revolt Against Hitler*, Fabian von Schlabrendorff, chap. x. So little did the Allies appreciate the value to themselves of the anti-Nazi revolt that after July 20 they indicated "that Hitler's removal from power would not mean any modification in the demand for 'Unconditional Surrender'" (*The Struggle for Europe*, p. 318). Actually the attempted assassination strengthened more than weakened Hitler's position.

[3] *Normandy to the Baltic*, p. 97. It is strange that these vehicles were not used earlier because armoured infantry transporters were built in 1918.

This thrust became apparent to Kluge on the morning of the 10th, and as he could not meet it, a withdrawal from the Mortain area was imperative. Nevertheless he hesitated to suggest it to O.K.W. until midday on the 11th, and then only in a vague way. The reply he received was that, once he had driven back the XVth American Corps, he was to adhere to the counter-attack. But before he could act on this order the XVth Corps captured Alençon on August 12, and by the evening of the following day had advanced to Argentan. This placed most of the Seventh German Army in an impossible position. It occupied a sausage-shaped salient, 40 miles in length and 15 miles in breadth at its base – Falaise–Argentan – and whatever Hitler might dictate its withdrawal had become compulsory.

So that Patton might resume his advance on Paris, on August 12 Bradley relieved his XVth Corps at Argentan by the Vth Corps of the First U.S. Army, and on the 14th the Canadians resumed their advance on Falaise, but failed to occupy it until the 16th. On that day Patton's XIIth Corps captured Orléans and his XXth entered Chartres, and 24 hours later his XVth was in Dreux, from where it was ordered to advance to the Seine at Mantes – north-west of Paris. There it established a bridgehead over the Seine on the 19th. In the meantime Hitler, who suspected that Kluge had betrayed him, replaced him by Field-Marshal Walter Model.[1]

On August 17 the Vth American Corps from Argentan, and the 4th Canadian and 1st Polish Armoured Divisions from Falaise set out to close the exit of the shrinking pocket in which the remnants of 15 German divisions and elements of others were now squeezed into a space 20 miles long and 10 wide at its eastern end. Their only escape routes were through Chambois and St. Lambert, which were under fire from both flanks and unceasingly bombed. "P.47 Thunderbolts," writes General Arnold, "caught German tanks and trucks in column moving three abreast, bumper to bumper, on three highways of Argentan. The planes bombed the leaders of the columns, blocking the roads, and then roamed over them strafing and bombing. . . . A.A.F. Fighters kept up the attack all day despite intense flak and foul weather. The smoke was so thick along some roads that pilots could not tally the destruction exactly, but they estimated 1,000

---

[1] Kluge handed his command over to Model on August 16, and a few days later committed suicide. Rommel was compelled to do the same on October 14.

vehicles destroyed. Next day in the Royal Air Force area, Spitfires, Mustangs, and Typhoons destroyed another thousand."[1]

In spite of this terrific pounding, on August 20 the 2nd Panzer Division broke through the Canadians at St. Lambert and for six hours kept open an escape road for the fleeing remnants of the Seventh Army. That any of its men escaped, and over a third did, would appear to be because the thrust from Falaise had been made in insufficient strength and because of the relief of the American XVth Corps by the Vth, which must have delayed the advance northward of Argentan. The destruction of the Seventh German Army and not the occupation of Paris should have been the strategical objective at that time But later, in April, 1945, as we shall see, when Berlin was within Eisenhower's grasp, it was the reverse.

On August 15, when the battle of Falaise was at its height, Operation "Dragoon" – previously code-named "Anvil", was put into force. Had this happened immediately before or simultaneously with "Overlord", strategically there might have been some slight profit, but after D-day "Anvil" had lost its *raison d'être*. This diversion of forces from Italy wrecked Alexander's campaign, which after the fall of Rome, on June 4, had progressed rapidly northward, and prevented Alexander from advancing into central Europe and so went far to deprive the victory in Normandy of its political significance. After the successful landing on June 6, in any set of circumstances the defeat of Germany was assured in the immediate future; the time had come to suit strategy to policy. Although in the circumstances that prevailed, Normandy and Poland were strategically the decisive theatres of the war, the backbone of the decisive political theatre remained the line Vienna–Prague–Berlin. Were the western allies the first to gain that line, in spite of their purblind commitments at Teheran they would still be able largely to shape the eventual peace; but were the Russians to do so, then, faced by Russia's military might, they would be compelled to toe the line.

This was foreseen by Mr. Churchill, by the British Chiefs of Staff, and by General Wilson, General Alexander, and General Montgomery. On June 19 Wilson had pointed out to Eisenhower that should the strategical aim be to defeat Germany in 1944, "the strategy best calculated to aid the assault on Northern France," was "to strike a blow which would force the enemy to

[1] General Arnold's *Second Report*, pp. 14 and 28.

divert divisions from France and, at the same time, confront him with the prospect of defeat in 1944." Instead of "Anvil" he urged "a continuation of General Alexander's campaign into the Po Valley and to the Ljubljana gap – thereby threatening an area vital to the enemy,"[1] and, incidentally, vital to the Russians also.

But Eisenhower would have none of this and he was strongly supported by the American Chiefs of Staff, more particularly by General Marshall. Mr. Churchill points out that they held "rigidly to the maxim of concentrating at the decisive point, which in their eyes meant only North-West Europe."[2] What they failed to understand was that a decisive point of the first importance must be politically profitable as well as strategically attainable, and that to land an army in southern France in order eventually to storm the winter sports resorts of the Black Forest was about the most indecisive thing they could do. On the contrary, Wilson's suggestion, which led toward Vienna, would endow a victory in France with the utmost political profit, because it would bring the Americans and British into central Europe, and only in central Europe could the war be won politically. Eisenhower's contention that "there was no development of that period which added more decisively to . . . the final and complete defeat of the German forces than did this secondary attack coming up the Rhone Valley,"[3] shows that, even as late as 1948, he still failed to realize that war is a political instrument.

Eisenhower was supported by the President, who had political reasons for doing so. In a long cable dispatched to Churchill on June 29, Roosevelt said: "Since the agreement was made at Teheran to mount an 'Anvil', I cannot accept, without consultation with Stalin, any course of action which abandons this operation. . . . Finally, for purely political considerations over here, I should never survive even a slight set back in 'Overlord' if it were known that fairly large forces had been diverted to the Balkans."[4] For the President, the decisive point was neither in north-west France nor central Europe, it was the November presidential elections, and in part, at least, "Anvil" was launched to secure for him his fourth term in office.

That was why early in July Alexander was ordered to withdraw the VIth U.S. Corps (three divisions); the French Expeditionary

[1] *Report by the Supreme Allied Commander Mediterranean, etc.* (1948), part II, p. 35.
[2] *The Second World War*, vol. VI, p. 52.   [3] *Crusade in Europe*, p. 294.
[4] *The Second World War*, Winston S. Churchill, vol. VI, p. 664.

Force (three divisions in Italy and four in North Africa); and a considerable part of his air force in order to build up the Seventh U.S. Army, under Lieutenant-General Alexander M. Patch, for the invasion of southern France on August 15. Mr. Churchill points out that thereby General Mark C. Clark's Fifth U.S. Army in Italy alone was reduced from some 250,000 to 153,000 men,[1] and Alexander's campaign wrecked.

Ten days after the Seventh U.S. Army had landed – virtually unopposed – between Cavalaire and Agny on the French Riviera,[2] Paris was liberated by the 2nd French Armoured Division, under General P. E. Leclerc. The battle of Normandy was at an end; the Seventh German Army was in rout. "From the point of view of equipment abandoned," says General Dietrich, who conducted the withdrawal, "the Seine crossing was almost as great a disaster as the Falaise Pocket."[3] The battle had cost the Germans little short of half a million men, of whom 210,000 were captured; 3,000 guns; 1,500 tanks; 2,000 aircraft; 20,000 vehicles; and masses of equipment and supplies.

On September 1, Eisenhower took over personal command of all his land forces, and Montgomery, promoted field-marshal, was left with the Twenty-First Army Group. A second Jena had been won and the western road to Berlin opened; all that remained was to exploit the victory, as Napoleon had done in 1806. But unfortunately for the allies, through force of circumstances, and even more because of difference of character, Eisenhower was neither a Montgomery nor a Napoleon.

When the war began Eisenhower was a junior lieutenant-colonel in the Philippines on General Douglas MacArthur's staff. Since then, and until July, 1942, when he was selected over the heads of 366 senior officers to command "Torch", he had held no command other than that of an infantry battalion. His outlook on the war was typical of most Americans. He says that the war was a crusade in which "the utter destruction of the Axis" was demanded, in order to create "a decent world."[4] "Throughout my life," he said during his 1952 electoral campaign for the presidency, "the major events have always had that extra spiritual factor to make them a crusade. . . . How else can you explain

[1] *Ibid.*, vol. VI, p. 76.
[2] On September 15 the French divisions were grouped into the First French Army (General de Lattre de Tassigny) and with the Seventh U.S. Army were formed into the Sixth Army Group, under General J. L. Devers.
[3] Cited in *The Struggle for Europe*, p. 434.   [4] *Crusade in Europe*, p. 157.

the successful landings in North Africa and the campaigns that followed through Sicily and Italy except in terms of a crusade? . . . How could Hitler's Fortress Europe have been breached, and how could the Nazi armies have been rolled back to ultimate destruction unless the spirit of every man involved was a spirit of crusade?"[1] In 1944, Henry Morgenthau quotes him as characterizing "the whole German population" as "synthetic paranoid;"[2] he held that "membership in the Gestapo and the S.S. should be taken as *prima facie* evidence of guilt," and that the war-making power of Germany should be eliminated.[3] Whether this was to be the task of the western allies or Russia does not seem to have concerned him, because in his opinion, "The ordinary Russian seemed to" him "to bear a marked similarity to what we call an 'average American',"[4] and that, "In the past relations of America and Russia there was no cause to regard the future with pessimism. . . . Both were free from the stigma of colonial empire building by force."[5]

When his generalship is criticized, it should be borne in mind that his upbringing placed him in an exceptionally difficult position as an allied commander. It would appear that he was not a highly educated or deeply read soldier, and he had little comprehension of the relationship between strategy and policy. "Political estimates," he writes, "are functions of governments, not of soldiers,"[6] which though true in the abstract, is often fatal in the concrete, more especially when the soldier is a general-in-chief. Because in service he was a comparatively junior officer, and a man of amiable rather than forceful character, he was dominated by General Marshall and over apt to yield to his subordinates. It was made more difficult for him not to give way to the latter because he commanded an allied army, and in such a body envy and jealousy, if not active, are always latent. It was imperative for him to establish harmony between his leading generals, and this he did admirably. But it was equally imperative in order to win the war in the shortest time and at the least cost, that strategy should not be subordinated to concord. Because he failed to understand this, as a general-in-chief he was more of a coordinator than a commander. In order to keep his turbulent

---

[1] *The Times*, London, October 22, 1952.
[2] *America's 2nd Crusade*, William Henry Chamberlin (1950), p. 303.
[3] *Crusade in Europe*, p. 287.   [4] *Ibid.*, p. 474.
[5] *Ibid.*, p. 457. This would be an extraordinary statement even for a schoolboy.
[6] *Ibid.*, p. 80.

barons occupied and tranquil he cut the strategic cake into slices and gave each a slice to eat; in so doing he violated the principle of concentration and prolonged the war.

On August 31 the rosters of Allied Supreme Headquarters showed that by then a total of 2,052,297 men and 436,471 vehicles had been landed, and that in northern France Eisenhower had at his disposal 23 infantry divisions and the equivalent of 15 armoured divisions. "The ratio of combat effectives," states Mr. Cole, "was approximately 2 to 1 in favor of the Allies. . . . Allied superiority in guns was at least 2½ to 1, that in tanks approximately 20 to 1;" and allied air strength numbered 13,891 combat aircraft, as well as hundreds of reconnaissance, liaison, and transport aircraft, against 573 serviceable aircraft of all types in the German Third Air Fleet.[1]

Although Eisenhower was unaware of these ratios, at least he knew as much as Bradley, which was that "By the first of September the enemy's June strength on the Western front had been cut down to a disorganized corporal's guard. The total of all German remnants north of the Ardennes equaled only 11 divisions, of which but two were panzers."[2] The problem Eisenhower had to solve was clearly one of pursuit. His four armies in northern France were in line: the First Canadian on the left, the Second British and First American in the centre, and the Third American on the right; and together they had pushed out a great salient from Abbeville in the north and Orléans in the south, with its apex at Verdun. To launch a pursuit with all four armies was out of the question because, Eisenhower points out, truck supply of petrol had become "utterly inadequate" and, in order to maintain the momentum of the Third Army, he had already been compelled to supply it by air-lift.[3] His problem was to decide which of his armies to halt so as to accumulate sufficient petrol to sustain those which were to pursue.

Montgomery had considered this problem; already on August 17 he had suggested to Bradley that, once the Seine was crossed, a powerful thrust should be made, not along the whole front, but north of the Ardennes. On August 23, he proposed to Eisenhower, "one powerful full-blooded thrust across the Rhine into the heart

[1] *The United States Army in World War II*, "The Lorraine Campaign," H. M. Cole (1950), pp. 2–4.
[2] *A Soldier's Story*, p. 411.
[3] *Supreme Commander's Report*, p. 60. See also General Arnold's *Second Report*, p. 30, and Sir Trafford Leigh-Mallory's "Despatch", *London Gazette*, December 31, 1946.

of Germany" by way of Belgium so as to gain the plains of northern Germany, where superiority of armour could be exploited. "If we could maintain," he writes, "the strength and impetus of our operations beyond the Seine sufficiently to keep the enemy on the run straight through to the Rhine, and 'bounce' our way across that river before the enemy succeeded in reforming a front to oppose us, then we should achieve a prodigious advantage."[1] But to supply this thrust demanded that Patton's Third Army should be halted temporarily. Eisenhower would not agree to this: he considered it politically impossible, because "the American public would never stand for it."[2] And from a military point of view he held that the proposal was "completely fantastic"; he called it a "pencillike thrust."[3]

Eisenhower's plan was to "push forward on a broad front, with priority on the left," and at the same time to advance the Third Army eastward toward the Saar Basin, to make contact with the Sixth Army Group, then advancing up the Rhône Valley. "This linking up of the whole front," he writes, "was mandatory," it "would allow us to use all our troops in facing and fighting the enemy and would prevent the costliness of establishing long defensive flanks along which our troops could have nothing but negative, static missions. . . . We wanted to bring all our strength against him, all of it mobile and all of it contributing directly to the complete annihilation of his field forces."[4]

It would appear that it was because of Bradley's and Patton's protests that Eisenhower did not allot the leading rôle to Montgomery, and also that he entirely misread the situation. He did not exploit his victory, but began preparations for another major battle and so missed the opportunity to make his victory strategically decisive.

Whether Montgomery's "full-blooded thrust" would have succeeded, we cannot say, but what we do know is that it was what the Germans expected. "Since the war," writes Wilmot, "Rundstedt and other German generals . . . have declared that a concentrated thrust from Belgium in September must have succeeded. . . . Blumentritt says: 'Such a break-through *en masse* with air domination, would have torn the weak German front to pieces and ended the war in the winter of 1944'."[5]

[1] *Normandy to the Baltic*, p. 119.
[2] Cited by Wilmot, *The Struggle for Europe*, p. 468.
[3] *Crusade in Europe*, pp. 252 and 306.
[4] *Ibid.*, p. 226.   [5] *The Struggle for Europe*, p. 539.

Liddell Hart corroborates this: "All the German generals to whom I talked," he records, "were of the opinion that the Allied Supreme Command had missed a great opportunity of ending the war in the autumn of 1944. They agreed with Montgomery's view, that this could best have been achieved by concentrating all possible resources on a threat in the north, towards Berlin."[1] Finally, General Speidel says: "The events of the last weeks of August were like a foaming torrent that nothing could stem. . . . Then something unexpected occurred, a German variation of the 'miracle of the Marne' for the French in 1914: the furious advance of the Allies suddenly faded away. . . . The method of Allied Supreme Command was the main reason. . . . Had the Allies held on grimly to the retreating Germans they could have harried the breath out of every man and beast and ended the war half a year earlier. There were no German ground forces of any importance that could be thrown in, and next to nothing in the air."[2]

Still further to cripple allied strategy, during the Second Quebec Conference, which assembled on September 10, Mr. Henry Morgenthau, Secretary of the United States Treasury, who in 1944 began to play a decisive part in shaping American foreign policy,[3] brought forward a plan on how to deal with Germany. It was largely the work of Harry Dexter White, Morgenthau's assistant secretary, who, in August 14, 1951, was cited before the Senate security sub-committee, and was found to be a Soviet agent.[4] The main features of the plan[5] were that Germany was to be deprived of east Prussia, most of Silesia, the Saar, and an extensive area on the left bank of the Rhine. The rest of Germany was to be partitioned into North and South and an International Zone, the latter to extend from Frankfort to the Baltic and Bremen, and to include the Ruhr. In this zone it was laid down that "all industrial plants and equipment not destroyed by military action shall be completely dismantled or removed from the area, or completely destroyed, all equipment shall be removed from the mines and the mines shall be thoroughly wrecked." Forms of restitution were to include, besides transfer of plant and equipment, "forced German labor outside Germany." The last proviso is of particular interest, for had it been put into effect it would have led to the

[1] *The Other Side of the Hill*, p. 429.   [2] *We Defended Normandy*, pp. 151–153.
[3] See *Memoirs of Cordell Hull* (English edit., 1948), vol. I, p. 207.
[4] See *The Twenty-Year Revolution from Roosevelt to Eisenhower*, Chesly Manly (1954), pp. 102, 103.
[5] See *Germany Is Our Problem*, Henry Morgenthau, Jr. (1945), pp. 1–4.

domination of Germany by Russia. It reads: "The primary responsibility for the policing of Germany and for civil administration in Germany should be assumed by the military forces of Germany's continental neighbors. Specifically these should include Russian, French, Czech, Polish, Greek, Dutch, and Belgian soldiers. Under this program United States troops could be withdrawn within a relatively short time."

The Morgenthau plan was accepted by the President and Mr. Churchill, and on September 15 they initialled an agreement providing that the industries in the Ruhr and the Saar would be "put out of action and closed down." The two areas were to be placed under some international organization, "which would supervise the dismantling of these industries, and make sure that they are not started up again by some subterfuge. This programme for eliminating the war making industries in the Ruhr and the Saar is looking forward to converting Germany into a country primarily agricultural and pastoral in its character. The Prime Minister and the President were in agreement upon this programme."[1]

On September 24 the plan was made public,[2] and as it appeared to define in detail what unconditional surrender meant, it convinced the millions of Germans who were opposed to the Nazi régime that it was better to go down fighting under Hitler than to accept a Carthaginian peace. It awakened in them the spirit of 1813. In the words of Macbeth, the cry of every German was:

> "Ring the alarum-bell! Blow wind! come wrack!
> At least we'll die with harness on our back."

After this insane spiritual blood transfusion, coupled with Eisenhower's broad-front strategy, throughout the autumn there was a series of desperate offensives, desperately resisted, along the 350 miles from Nijmegen to Colmar, until in mid-December Hitler's counter-offensive in the Ardennes clearly demonstrated the folly of Eisenhower's linear strategy. Though it failed, it cost the allies 77,000 men, and it was almost as great a blow to American prestige as the Japanese surprise attack on Pearl

---

[1] In full see *On Active Service in Peace and War* (English edit., n.d.), Henry L. Stimson and McGeorge Bundy, p. 33.

[2] It was heavily criticized, and when Stimson, U.S. Secretary of War, read to the President the words about converting Germany into a pastoral country, Stimson records that: "He was frankly staggered by this and said he had no idea he could have initialled this; that he had evidently done it without much thought" (*ibid.*, p. 336).

Harbour. It so impressed Stalin that he seized the opportunity, while his western allies were embarrassed, to agree to another Big Three meeting toward the end of January, for which the President had pressed since his re-election. Also, since Hitler had committed his entire strategic reserve in the Ardennes offensive, Stalin decided to open the Russian winter campaign in mid-January; he hoped that by the time the "Big Three" met his armies would have overrun the whole of Poland and be in a position to present his allies with a *fait accompli*.

The Russian offensive, led by Zhukov and Koniev, opened on January 12. It burst like an avalanche through the German front and swept forward at such speed that by February 4 the two marshals had carried their armies to the Oder at Küstrin and Breslau. That same day the Big Three met at Yalta in the Crimea. On Mr. Churchill's suggestion, it was prophetically code-named "Argonaut", for Stalin played the part of Jason and in triumph carried back with him to the Kremlin the fleeces of Poland and several other countries.

Roosevelt left America for the Crimea with high hopes and little preparation;[1] the war in Europe neared its end and peace glimmered on the horizon. The moment had come to assure himself of Stalin's full-hearted collaboration. This appeared an easy task, for he could see no fundamental clash of interests between the Soviet Union and the United States. Also, although Churchill was a full-blooded imperialist, Stalin, so he fondly held, was nothing of the kind, and, in order to liquidate the British, French, and Dutch Asiatic empires, he needed his support. He also needed Stalin's aid to finish off the Japanese, because his Chiefs of Staff had warned him that without Russia it might cost the United States "a million casualties" to conquer Japan.[2] Before the conference assembled, he had made up his mind to give Stalin a free hand in Europe as a *quid pro quo*.

Because of Stalin's realism and the President's idealism – he was advised by Harry Hopkins, and among others by Algar Hiss of the State Department – the results of the Yalta Conference were a super-Munich.

It was unanimously agreed that Germany was to be partitioned into zones and each zone occupied by an allied army; that unconditional surrender was to be enforced; that forced labour was to

[1] See *Speaking Frankly*, James F. Byrnes (English edit., n.d.), p. 23.
[2] *On Active Service in Peace and War*, Henry L. Stimson, p. 365.

be imposed; and that 20 billion dollars in reparations, of which Russia was to receive half, should be considered.

Once Stalin had agreed to take part in the United Nations Conference in April, Poland, for whose integrity Great Britain had entered the war, was thrown to the Russian wolves. Her eastern frontier was approximately fixed on the Curzon Line; her western frontier provisionally pushed out to the Oder and western Neisse; and the Lublin Committee of Soviet stooges, which at the instigation of the Kremlin had, on December 31, 1944, proclaimed itself the "Provisional Government of Liberated Democratic Poland", was, when diluted with a few members of the *émigré* government, to be accepted, on condition that free elections were held, but these were not to be supervised by neutral observers, as this would insult the Poles!

Lastly, once Poland had been pledged to the Soviets, at a secret meeting, from which Churchill was excluded, Roosevelt secured Stalin's aid against Japan. In exchange he agreed to acknowledge the *status quo* in Outer Mongolia; the restoration to Russia of all territories lost in 1904–1905, southern Sakhalin and the Kurile Islands; and also he agreed to Russian joint control with China of the eastern and southern Manchurian railways. As much of these territories was Chinese, it would appear that the President had either forgotten about imperialism and the Atlantic Charter, or was *non compos mentis*.

The conference ended on February 10, and at the dinner which followed, when he proposed Stalin's health, Mr. Churchill, with true prophetic vision, said: ". . . he knew that in peace no less than in war Marshal Stalin would continue to lead his people from success to success."[1] The following day a statement was signed and issued by the Big Three. It contained, among other things, many of the economic proposals of the Morgenthau Plan, and ended with a declaration that "in the words of the Atlantic Charter" the agreements offered assurances which would permit all men in all lands to "live out their lives in freedom from fear and want."[2]

Three days before these hopeful words were published, the final stage of Eisenhower's phalangial advance on the Rhine opened in appalling weather. On the left the Rhine was reached by the

---

[1] *The White House Papers, etc.*, vol. II, p. 857. "Stalin replied in the best of tempers" (Churchill, vol. VI, p. 343).
[2] In full see *Roosevelt and the Russians, etc.*, Edward R. Stettinius, pp. 295–302.

First Canadian Army opposite Emmerich on February 14, but not until March 3 was the Ninth U.S. Army, on the right of the Canadians, able to make contact with it at Geldern, for besides the evil weather the enemy put up fanatical opposition. Next, on March 5, advanced elements of the IIIrd Corps of the First U.S. Army captured the bridge over the Rhine at Remagen. Lastly, on March 22, Patton crossed the Rhine near Oppenheim, south of Mainz, and on the following day the Twenty-First Army Group and the Ninth U.S. Army, both under Montgomery, crossed at Wesel.

From the Rhine the Germans fell back on the Ruhr. There they put up a desperate resistance, but were surrounded, and on April 13 Field-Marshal Model with 325,000 officers and men capitulated. The road to Berlin was now unbarred and the Russians, under Zhukov and Koniev, were still on the Oder and Neisse. On this same day in the south Marshal Malinovsky occupied Vienna, the southernmost of the three great political and strategical centres in central Europe.

There still remained Berlin and Prague. There was little between Eisenhower and the former, neither prepared defences nor field army, and although Berlin was in the centre of the agreed Russian zone of occupation it had never been suggested that it was the perquisite of any one allied army. It was imperative that Eisenhower should advance on it because the Russians had broken or disregarded every important item of the Yalta Agreement which by then had been put to the test, and Berlin in Anglo-American hands would place Great Britain and the United States in a strong position from which they could insist that the Russians honoured their agreements. "If we did not get things right," says Mr. Churchill, "the world would soon see that Mr. Roosevelt and I had underwritten a fraudulent prospectus when we put our signatures to the Crimea settlements."[1]

Although this should have been obvious, political values were of secondary importance to Eisenhower, and coupled with this outlook was his belief that Hitler intended to abandon Berlin and fall back on what was called the "National Redoubt" – western Austria and southern Bavaria.[2] "Military factors, when the enemy

---

[1] *The Second World War*, vol. VI, p. 370.
[2] Bradley writes: "Months before, G.-2 had tipped us off to a fantastic enemy plot, for the withdrawal of troops into the Austrian Alps . . . for a last-ditch holdout. . . . I am astonished we could have believed it as innocently as we did" (*A Soldier's Story*, p. 536).

was on the brink of final defeat," he writes, "were more important in my eyes than the political considerations involved in an Allied capture of the capital. The function of our forces must be to crush the German armies rather than dissipate our strength in the occupation of empty ruined cities."[1] That was why his plan was to leave Berlin to the Russians, and, under Bradley, to move the axis of his advance through central Germany toward Marshal Koniev in the Leipzig–Dresden area and so cut off Hitler from the National Redoubt, while his right wing, under Patton, occupied that mythical lair, and his left wing, under Montgomery, moved on Hamburg and the Baltic. Already, on March 28, he had cabled the gist of his plan to Washington, London, and Moscow; Stalin was delighted and Churchill furious, but the latter was hamstrung because the American Chiefs of Staff supported Eisenhower. On March 31 Marshall cabled the British Chiefs of Staff: "The battle of Germany is now at a point where it is up to the Field Commander to judge the measures which should be taken. To deliberately turn away from the exploitation of the enemy's weakness does not appear sound. The single objective should be quick and complete victory."[2] On April 6 he stated: "Such psychological and political advantages as would result from the possible capture of Berlin ahead of the Russians should not override the imperative military consideration which, in our opinion, is the destruction and dismemberment of the German armed forces."[3]

The van of the Ninth U.S. Army entered Magdeburg on April 11, and on the following day it crossed the Elbe. "At that time," writes Bradley, "we could probably have pushed on to Berlin had we been willing to take the casualties Berlin would have cost us. Zhukov had not yet crossed the Oder and Berlin now lay midway between our forces."[4] On the 14th, two days after President Roosevelt died and Mr. Harry S. Truman had succeeded him, Eisenhower halted his troops on the Elbe, and on the 21st he informed the Soviet High Command that, except for an advance on Lübeck, he did not intend to advance east of the Elbe, nor beyond the western frontier of Czechoslovakia; instead his Third and Seventh Armies would occupy the National Redoubt! Prague also was abandoned to the Russians.

The doom which, since the allied landings in Normandy, had

[1] *Supreme Commander's Report*, p. 131.   [2] *Crusade in Europe*, p. 402.
[3] Cited by Wilmot in *The Struggle for Europe*, p. 693.   [4] *A Soldier's Story*, p. 537.

threatened Hitler like the open jaws of some monster, closed with a snap. On April 29 General Heinrich von Veitinghoff, in command of the German forces in Italy, with nearly one million men,

25. ALLIED ZONES OF OCCUPATION AND RUSSIA'S
WESTERN FRONTIER IN 1945 COMPARED WITH
CHARLEMAGNE'S EASTERN FRONTIER IN 814

surrendered unconditionally to Field-Marshal Alexander. At 3.30 p.m. on the following day Hitler shot himself, and on May 2 the Russians established themselves in Berlin. Two days later,

Admiral Friedeburg and other representatives of the German High Command, at Montgomery's tactical headquarters on the Lüneburger Heide, where in 1935 Hitler had held his first manœuvres, signed an armistice providing for the surrender of all German forces in north-west Germany, Denmark, and Holland. Three days later the instrument of the *Wehrmacht's* unconditional surrender was signed by Jodl and Friedeburg at Eisenhower's headquarters in Rheims; at midnight May 8–9 hostilities ceased, and on May 9 the Russians marched into Prague.

For the United States and Great Britain, the fruits of the battle of Normandy were apples of Sodom, which turned to ashes as soon as they were plucked. Hitler and his legions were destroyed, and in their stead stood Stalin and his Asiatic hordes. Because "Victory – victory at all costs"[1] had been the western allies' aim, and because of their insistence that "it was to be the defeat, ruin, and slaughter of Hitler, to the exclusion of all other purposes, loyalties and aims,"[2] Stalin, the supreme realist, whose strategy had throughout kept in step with his policy, had been able to impose his messianic cult upon Estonia, Latvia, Lithuania, part of Finland, Poland, eastern and central Germany, a third of Austria, Czechoslovakia, Yugoslavia, Hungary, Rumania, and Bulgaria. Vienna, Prague, and Berlin, the vertebrae of Europe, were his, and except for Athens, so was every capital city in eastern Europe. The western frontier of Russia had been advanced from the Pripet Marshes to the Thuringerwald, a distance of 750 miles, and as in the days of Charlemagne, the Slavs stood on the Elbe and the Böhmerwald. A thousand years of European history had been rolled back. Such were the fruits of the battle of Normandy, fructified by inept strategy and a policy of pure destruction.

[1] *The Second World War*, Winston S. Churchill, vol. II, p. 24.
[2] *Ibid.*, vol. III, p. 21.

There remained Japan. Thrown on to the defensive after Midway, her too-distant European allies crumbling, facing the most formidable swift build-up of military and naval power ever seen in history, her fate was sealed. Yet, such was the difficulty of the vast Pacific theatre of war, such was the ruthless tenacity of the Japanese commanders, and the sacrificial heroism of the soldiers – and such was Allied political ineptitude – that it took over three years to reach the inevitable end.

It has always to be remembered that Japan's war was conducted, until 1945, on four fronts: in the South-west Pacific they faced General MacArthur's mounting offensive through New Guinea to the Philippines; in the central Pacific they faced Admiral Nimitz, also driving in on the Philippines, which would become the base for combined action against the Japanese home islands; in Burma they faced Admiral Mountbatten's South East Asia Command, advancing on Singapore and the Dutch East Indies; and there was always China, where their war had begun, a great sponge which, as late as April 1945, absorbed over fifty of their divisions.

The British campaign in Burma displayed another satisfying military revival. When Mountbatten set up his new Command at the end of 1943, he took over a theatre in which nothing had gone right, where morale was at a decidedly low ebb, and which was bound to remain low in the Allied priority list for supply and equipment. By May 1945, when the British re-entered Rangoon, this picture had been totally transformed by a year of continuous victory – victory not merely over the Japanese, but over the jungle, the monsoon and the tropical diseases which had wasted every previous force in that area. Under General Slim, probably the best British general of the war, the Fourteenth Army won one of the most ably planned and executed victories in British military history: the double battle of Meiktila-Mandalay, from which the Japanese in Burma never recovered. All this was gratifying, and played its part in Japan's downfall: but a minor part. It was the huge American effort in the Pacific which really defeated Japan.

MacArthur's first objective was the Japanese forward base at Rabaul. This he attacked by a two-pronged drive, through the Solomons, where the Japanese suffered severe defeat at Guadalcanal, and through and round New Guinea, where Australians and Americans side by side met and overcame fierce resistance. American air power, and the skilful use of amphibious operations were the chief ingredients of MacArthur's success, which, by November 1943 had neutralized Rabaul and cut off over 135,000 Japanese, as Fuller says, "beyond hope of rescue." He continues:

' Nimitz's problem differed from MacArthur's. The latter was land-based, but Nimitz had to move his base along with him, which meant that his fleet had to be both his base of operations and his striking force. It was, therefore, a four-fold organization – a floating base, a fleet, an air force, and an army, combined in one. That it was designed, built and assembled within 18 months of the battle of Midway Island is without question the greatest organizational feat of naval history.

' This great instrument of destruction enabled Nimitz and his subordinate admirals to operate on so broad a front that the Japanese were compelled to deploy their inferior strength – particularly their air force – over such wide spaces that they could seldom, if ever, concentrate it at any critical point. The consequence was that because most of the Pacific islands are too small to be converted into really formidable positions and are incapable of housing garrisons of sufficient strength to put up a prolonged resistance, they could be knocked out before aid could be brought to them. Further, once one or more air bases in a group of islands had been seized and put into use the remaining islands could be so completely cut off from succour that they could safely be by-passed and left to starvation. Because the instrument was not only most powerful, but also because it was self-sufficient and carried out all operations, including its own supply, maintenance and repair, and therefore possessed indefinite range of action, it rapidly knocked the bottom out of the Japanese defensive strategy and transformed the vastness of the Pacific from an ally into a deadly enemy of the Japanese. '

By August 1944 the two American campaigns had fused into one, and poised themselves for re-entry into the Philippines. It became the task of the Imperial Japanese Navy, which had been the prime instrument of all Japan's conquests, to prevent or mar this American advance. But this was not the Navy of 1941: the Japanese carrier-borne air-power had been shattered in the Battle of the Philippine Sea in June. Only six carriers remained, but even these were now gravely short of aircraft and trained air crews. Fuel shortage, due to American submarine and air attacks on tankers, affected the whole fleet. Japanese strategy now became a strategy of suicide: the naval Commander-in-Chief, Admiral Toyoda, explained after the war that "were the Philippines lost, even though the fleet should be left, the shipping lane to the south would be so completely cut off that even if the fleet should come back to Japanese waters it would not be able to obtain its fuel supply. If it should remain in southern waters it could not receive supplies of ammunition and arms. 'There would be,' he added, 'no sense in saving the fleet at the expense of the loss of the Philippines.'" In other words, the fleet had become expendable, and the Japanese plan became quite simply to extract the last ounce of its damage-potential by a concentrated attack on the Americans, aiming at coming to close quarters where gunfire would tell, and not concerned with survival. The result was the greatest naval battle in history, at Leyte Gulf, fought between 23 – 26 October 1944. Fuller sums up:

'For the Americans, the battle for Leyte Gulf was a cheap victory; for the Japanese it was a catastrophic defeat. In the four days' fighting the former lost a light carrier, two escort carriers, two destroyers, a destroyer escort and a motor-torpedo-boat, and the latter lost three battleships, one large and three light carriers, 6 heavy cruisers, four light cruisers, and nine destroyers. The Japanese Navy had ceased to exist, and, except by land-based aircraft, their opponent had won undisputed command of the sea. When Admiral Ozawa was questioned on the battle after the war he replied: "After this battle the surface forces became strictly auxiliary, so that we relied on land forces, special [*Kamikaze*] attack, and air power. . . . There was no further use assigned to surface vessels, with exception of some special ships." And "Admiral Mitsumasa Yoni, Navy Minister of the Koiso Cabinet, said he realized that the defeat at Leyte 'was tantamount to loss of the Philippines.' As for the larger significance of the battle, he said, 'I felt that that was the end.'"

'This "larger significance" was missed by President Roosevelt and his advisers, who failed to appreciate the political implications of their overwhelming victory. They looked upon the war as a contest between Christian and Appollyon, instead of regarding it as a surgical operation. They failed to understand that, what the scalpel is to the surgeon, war should be to the statesman, and whatever the causes of war may be, should the aim of the statesman be purely destructive, then the activities of the soldier will become those of the slaughterhouse. But if, instead, the aim is constructive and curative, then these activities become those of the surgery. Because of mischance or misunderstanding, or lack of knowledge or skill, a surgical operation may fail; but when the aim of the slaughterer becomes the aim of the surgeon, it must fail, there can be no póssible alternative. To be a sane political instrument, war demands a sane political end, and to be attainable that end must be strategically possible.

'After the battle for Leyte Gulf, this strategical possibility had been fully established: there could be no question that Japan could win the war. As she was doomed to lose it, the American problem was predominantly political – how could her defeat be brought about at the highest profit to the United States?

'It was a far simpler problem than the one that faced the President in Europe. There he had to consider his allies, but the war with Japan was 95 per cent. an American war, and to win it at the highest profit it was essential, in order to avert complications, that the United States should win it single-handed. Had this been understood, it would have been appreciated that as Russia was the only Power who could complicate the issue it was highly desirable for the United States to bring the war with Japan to an end before or immediately after Germany collapsed – that is, while Russia was still at grips with her. Was this possible? The answer is an unqualified "yes", provided that the strategical and political centres of gravity of the problem were firmly kept in mind.'

Japan, says Fuller, was by now facing complete economic collapse. He cites impressive figures to support his case. As an island power, Japan, like Britain, depended for life on sea-borne supply. "At the opening of the war," says Fuller, "Japan had 6,000,000 tons of merchant shipping of over five hundred tons gross weight, and during the war an additional 4,100,000 tons were built or captured. Of the total, 8,900,000 tons were sunk, and of this loss 54·7 per cent of the total was attributed to submarines." Air attack on Japanese cities and industry increased the ruin, but many of the factories and production plants attacked, says Fuller, were already almost closed down through lack of raw materials. The Americans did not, apparently, grasp the extent of the economic damage they had done; they also committed a serious political blunder:

' Unfortunately for the aftermath of the war, Japan's political centre of gravity eluded the vision of the President and his advisers. It lay in the person of the Emperor, or Tenno ("Heavenly King"), and because he was the godhead of the armed forces, and in the eyes of his people a divinity, he was the supreme symbol of Japanese life and thought. Yet there was one thing he could not do, and that was to order his people to surrender unconditionally and thereby acquiesce in his becoming a war criminal, to be placed on trial or shot at sight. '

Once more, "unconditional surrender" was having its miserable effect in prolonging the war – but this time against the background of a deeper tragedy for the whole human race. Denied an opportunity to negotiate peace, the Japanese fought on with savage determination: in the defence of Iwojima in February 1945, out of a garrison of twenty thousand only two hundred and sixteen were taken prisoner. In the three-month campaign on Okinawa, some eighty thousand Japanese were killed, only ten thousand taken prisoner. As the American Official History says: "There was only one kind of Japanese casualty – the dead." The question what it would be like to fight men like these in their homeland was very real and very daunting. But the answer supplied was all that and more.

On 17 July 1945 the Allied leaders assembled for their last war-conference at Potsdam. Roosevelt was dead; his successor, Mr. Truman, and Churchill were informed of the successful explosion of an atomic bomb in New Mexico. The opportunity was thus presented of bringing the war to a quick end if the Japanese still refused to accept the Allied terms. These were once again presented on 26 July: once again the demand was for "unconditional surrender". "Not a word was said about the Emperor, because it would be unacceptable to the propaganda-fed American masses." The Japanese again rejected the ultimatum, and events followed their prescribed and mournful course. On 6 August an atomic bomb was dropped on Hiroshima. On 8 August Russia declared war on Japan, so that even the important political advantage of excluding the Soviet from the Far Eastern settlement was lost. On 9 August the Russians invaded Manchuria, and on the same day a second atomic bomb was dropped on Nagasaki. On 14 August Japan accepted the Allied terms. The Emperor told his people: "It is Our desire to initiate an era of peace for future generations by tolerating the intolerable and enduring the unendurable." The instrument of surrender was signed in Tokyo Bay aboard the U.S.S. MISSOURI on 2 September. The Second World War was over; it had lasted exactly six years. And the Emperor remained, after all; at the moment of writing, he is still on his throne, twenty-five years after the great tragedy. The greater tragedy is that had it been possible to foresee this, had the Allies not been so obdurate in proclaiming a policy which proved impossible to implement, the war might have ended three months earlier. Fuller comments:

'If the war had ended in May, 1945, and but for the political and strategical lunacy induced by the policy of unconditional surrender it might well have done so, Russia – whatever she might eventually have done – would not have been given a free and cordial hand to expand her influence over the Far East. Equally important, the atomic bomb would not have been dropped by Americans. "My own feeling was," writes Fleet Admiral William D. Leahy, Chief of Staff to Presidents Roosevelt and Truman, "that in being the first to use it, we had adopted an ethical standard common to the barbarians of the Dark Ages. . . . There is a practical certainty that potential enemies will have it in the future and that the atomic bomb will sometime be used against us. . . . Employment of the atomic bomb in war will take us back in cruelty towards noncombatants to the days of Genghis Khan. . . . These new and terrible instruments of uncivilized warfare represent a modern type of barbarism not worthy of Christian man."[1] '

---

[1] *I Was There* (1950), pp. 441-442. Words very similar were voiced by the Vatican in the *Osservatore Romano* of August 7, 1945. "This war," we read, "provides a catastrophic conclusion. Incredibly this destructive weapon remains a temptation for posterity, which, we know by bitter experience, learns so little from history."

The Second World War in retrospect and prospect

The second American crusade ended even more disastrously than the first, and this time the *agent provocateur* was not the German Kaiser but the American President, whose abhorrence of National Socialism and craving for power precipitated his people into the European conflict and so again made it worldwide. From the captured German archives there is no evidence to support the President's claims that Hitler contemplated an offensive against the western hemisphere, and until America entered the war there is abundant evidence that this was the one thing he wished to avert.

One of the first to warn his fellow countrymen against involvement in the European quarrel was Roosevelt's predecessor, the former President, Mr. Herbert Hoover. "I opposed and protested every step in the policies which led us into the Second World War," he said in a broadcast on August 10, 1954. "Especially in June, 1941, when Britain was safe from German invasion due to Hitler's diversion to attack on Stalin, I urged that the gargantuan jest of all history would be our giving aid to the Soviet government. I urged we should allow those two dictators to exhaust each other. I stated that the result of our assistance would be to spread Communism over the whole world. I urged that if we stood aside the time would come when we could bring lasting peace to the world. I have no regrets. The consequences have proved that I was right."

Soon after the United States entered the war, there appeared a book by a Yale professor[1] in which he pointed out that, "If the foreign policy of a state is to be practical, it should be designed not in terms of some dream world but in terms of the realities of international relations in terms of power politics." He urged that the two objectives of United States policy should be predominance in the New World, and a balance of power in the Old, and because

---

[1] *America's Strategy in World Politics: The United States and the Balance of Power*, Nicholas J. Spykman (1942), pp. 446, 460.

this balance had been upset on the opposite shores of the Atlantic and Pacific, the war aim of the United States should be to restore it. This, he wrote, did not demand the annihilation of Germany and Japan, lest Europe and the Far East be opened to domination by Russia. "A Russian state from the Urals to the North Sea," he said, "can be no great improvement over a German state from the North Sea to the Urals." The same reasoning applied to the Far East and he wrote: "The danger of another Japanese conquest of Asia must be removed, but does not inevitably mean the elimination of the military strength of Japan and the surrender of the Western Pacific to China or Russia."

This policy, which was to be adopted after the war,[1] applied equally to Great Britain, for her position was analogous to that of the United States. Her objectives should have been the security of her empire and the maintenance of the balance of power in Europe and Asia, and for the identical reason given by Spykman, neither objective demanded the annihilation of her enemies. When the two great western powers were united in arms, Russia became the crux of their war problem. That they had to support Russia in her fight against the common enemy was obvious, but it should have been equally obvious that support should not lead to her dominance; for were it to do so, then their problem would remain unsolved.

As we have seen, Roosevelt's policy was diametrically opposed to Spykman's; "Unconditional Surrender" had nothing to do with the balance of power, and everything to do with its negation. Nor had Churchill's policy which, three days after his advent to power in 1940, he proclaimed to be: "Victory – victory at all costs."[2] These policies were the obverse and reverse of the same idea – annihilation; and that Churchill, a man of incomparably greater military insight than the President, should have fixed on such an aim is bewildering when it is compared with his epitaph on the First World War:

"Governments and individuals," he wrote, "conformed to this

[1] Some years after the war, a French historian pointed out: "The goal that Western strategy has [now] set itself in Japan as well as in Germany is not very different from the situation that would have arisen of its own accord if peace had been concluded before the entry of Soviet troops into the Reich and Manchuria, and before complete destruction of both armies and countries. We are trying to efface the consequences of a too complete victory, and get back to a victory compatible with the resurrection of the vanquished" (*The Century of Total War*, Raymond Aron, English edit., 1954, p. 194).
[2] *The Second World War*, vol. II, p. 24.

rhythm of the tragedy and swayed and staggered forward in helpless violence, slaughtering and squandering on ever-increasing scales, till injuries were wrought to the structure of human society which a century will not efface, and which may conceivably prove fatal to the present civilization. . . . Victory was to be bought so dear as to be almost indistinguishable from defeat. It was not to give even security to the victors. . . . The most complete victory ever gained in arms has failed to solve the European problem or to remove the dangers which produced the war."[1]

His choice of "Victory at all costs" becomes even stranger when we read his epitaph on the Second World War:

"The human tragedy," he writes, "reaches its climax in the fact that after all the exertions and sacrifices of hundreds of millions of people and the victories of the Righteous Cause, we have still not found Peace and Security, and that we lie in the grip of even worse perils than those we have surmounted."[2]

What a confession of failure.

When we remember that both Roosevelt and Churchill are to be reckoned among the most prominent of the presidents and prime ministers of the United States and Great Britain, it is perplexing to have to record this. What persuaded them to adopt so fatal a policy? We hazard to reply – blind hatred! Their hearts ran away with their heads and their emotions befogged their reason. For them the war was not a political conflict in the normal meaning of the words, it was a Manichean contest between Good and Evil, and to carry their people along with them they unleashed a vitriolic propaganda against the devil they had invoked. As this was the identical process adopted by Hitler, it is in no way strange to read in *The Economist* of August 11, 1945: "At the end of a mighty war fought to defeat Hitlerism, the Allies are making a Hitlerian peace. This is the real measure of their failure."

After Stalingrad, when it was obvious that Hitler's star was sinking and Stalin's rising, it is astonishing to look back on the views then held on Russia by allied statesmen, such as those of Sir Samuel Hoare;[3] and it is even more astonishing to believe that it was possible at the First Quebec Conference for the policy toward Russia, as set forth in the Hopkins document,[4] to have been discussed and adopted.

---

[1] *The World Crisis, 1915* (1923), pp. 17–18.
[2] *The Second World War*, vol. I, p. viii.
[3] See *supra*, pp. 528–530. [4] See *supra*, pp. 534–535.

This blind trust in Russia's motives can only be explained by Roosevelt's and Churchill's ignorance of her history, or by the trance into which they had been induced by their pro-Soviet propaganda. For 200 years Russia had knocked at the eastern door of Europe, and for well over a century European statesmen and historians of note had warned the peoples of Europe against her designs. It is more than a matter of interest to refer to what they said, not only because the results of the war reveal how profoundly right they were, but because the future is rooted in the present.

What these men recognized was that Russia has never belonged to Europe; her civilization owes nothing to Latin culture; she never took part in the Crusades, the Renaissance, the Reformation and the Thirty Years War, and was unaffected by the discovery of the New World and the French Revolution. Since the battle of Poltava the Muscovites have been to Europeans "the Turks of the North" – the spearhead of the Asiatic threat to Europe.

Châteaubriand realized this and he longed to visit Russia because he believed that she threatened to overwhelm the world.[1] Custine visited Russia in 1839 and he wrote: "They wished to rule the world by conquest; they mean to seize by armed force the countries accessible to them, and thence to oppress the rest of the world by terror";[2] and De Tocqueville pictured a disunited Europe conquered by a Russian Philip.[3] In 1823 the Abbé de Pradt, at one time Napoleon I's ambassador at Warsaw, wrote: "On the other side of the Vistula falls a curtain behind which it is most difficult to see clearly what is happening within the Russian empire. In the manner of the Orient, from which it has derived its character, the Russian government is concentrated in the court of the prince: he alone speaks, writes little and publishes nothing. In a country constituted to hide everything from public knowledge, one is more or less limited to guesswork, and this limitation also applies to the Russian army. . . . Since the days of Peter the Great, the policy of Russia has never ceased to be one of conquest; one might say that for a whole century her government has consisted in one and the same man, with one and the same idea – methodical aggrandizement."[4] And in 1850 Donoso

[1] See *Liberty or Equality: The Challenge of our Time*, Erik von Kuehnelt-Leddihn (1952), p. 75.
[2] *Journey for our Time: The Journals of the Marquis de Custine*, trans. Phyllis Penn Kohler (1953), p. 164.
[3] See *Liberty or Equality*, p. 77.
[4] *Parallèle de la puissance anglaise et russe relativement à l'Europe* (1823), pp. 154, 156.

Cortés was as prophetic: ". . . when nothing is left in the West," he said, "but two camps, that of the despoilers and that of the despoiled – then, gentlemen, the hour of Russia in the clock of time will have struck. Then Russia will be able to march peacefully, arms shouldered, into our lands; then, also, gentlemen, the world will witness the greatest chastisement in all history; this tremendous chastisement, gentlemen, will be the chastisement of England. Her ships will be useless against the colossal empire which grips Europe with one hand and India with the other. . . . Russia will fight in order to inflict defeats . . . in order to protect the defeated country. And in the moment the defeated nation considers itself an ally it becomes Russia's victim and prey. The victories of Russia lead to 'protection' – her protection to death."[1]

Later historians have been no less prophetic. In 1878, Constantin Frantz, writes Keuhnelt-Leddihn, ". . . was convinced that Russia would invade Western Europe and that in the coming war between Britain and Russia the United States would play a decisive role," and that "the future belonged to the United States and Russia."[2] And shortly before the First World War, Richard von Kralik, an Austrian historian, in connexion with the invasions of Asiatic hordes on the European continent, wrote: "Europe has even now to fear the Russian Empire and Eastern Asia which represents elements half or fully Mongol. This issue marks the most decisive struggle in world history which is the antagonism between East and West. . . . Here the future will by no means spare us disagreeable surprises. It is possible that Asiatics penetrate France and Spain, as it happened in the 8th century, or that they get to Germany, as in the 13th century the Mongols, or that they appear before Vienna, as the Turks in the 16th and 17th centuries. . . . Nor is it unthinkable that it will, perhaps, be America which pushes back the Asiatic East on European soil."[3]

Surely, before the Second World War engulfed Europe, western statesmen should have been aware of these predictions, and although no one would suggest that presidents and prime ministers can find the time to delve into dusty history, at least one would expect that their foreign offices and intelligence staffs would do so, for "to know your enemy" – potential as well as actual – is every bit as important as knowledge of his country, resources, and

---

[1] Quoted in *Liberty or Equality*, pp. 78, 79.
[2] *Ibid.*, p. 76.   [3] *Ibid.*, p. 302.

armed forces. At least they might have borne in mind Lenin's prediction of the inevitable clash between the bourgeois states and the Soviet Union. Instead they bandied witticisms between each other on Uncle Joe!

The Asiatic hordes are back in Germany, and this time they penetrated within the walls of Vienna. The wheel of history has turned full circle, and the threat which faces Europe to-day is not far removed from the threat which faced her in the days of Xerxes and Darius. Added to this, Japan, the counterpoise to Russia in the Far East, was eliminated, and thereby the sluice-gate opened for Communism to inundate China. Such were the political consequences of the war.

The military consequences were no less remarkable. At Hiroshima the nuclear theory of the atom and the ability of man artificially to transmute one element into another, which had revolutionized physics, became a demonstrable fact to the most ignorant and illiterate of human beings. It inspired a universal terror, not because 70,000 to 80,000 people had perished, but because one bomb, manipulated by a single man, had slaughtered this multitude.

The repercussions of August 6, 1945, shook the accepted theory of war to its foundations. If one bomb could wreck a great city, what would hundreds effect in another war? It bereft organized international warfare of its political significance; for it reduced this type of war to an absurdity. It knocked the bottom out of the theory that armed conflicts are the instruments of policy, by transforming their threat into a deterrent of war between armed men.

Does this mean that war is approaching its end? Assuredly no, because in an ideological age the fundamental causes of war are profoundly psychological; they cannot be eliminated either by a negation, or a surplus, of physical force. All it means is that one form of war has become obsolete, and that another will replace it. For lack of a better name, the new form in this age of man in the mass is called "cold war." It is a combination of psychological war, the weapons of which are the emotions; of economic war aimed at destroying financial stability; of guerrilla war, the most primitive form of war; and civil war, its most brutal form. M. Aron points out that cold war is a limited war, limited "not as to the stakes, but as to the means employed";[1] it may be compared

[1] *The Century of Total War*, p. 171.

with the limited methodical wars which for a century and a half followed the Thirty Years War. But there is this profound difference: it is the readiness to wage nuclear war which, by deterring an opponent from resorting to physical war, makes cold war so deadly.

Russia is the leading exponent of this form of conflict, and by waging it on methodical lines, immediately after the shooting war ended she established her dominion over a third of Europe without firing a shot, since when she has waged it by propaganda, sabotage and subversion in every non-Communist country in the world; for all countries which have not accepted Soviet Communism are held to be active enemies of Russia. Further, as Aron observes: Western military experts are not sufficiently freed from traditional conceptions to realize that the cold war is the real war which is raging all the time and that the battle against propaganda and subversion must be waged indefatigably; "the elimination by trade unions of Stalinist ringleaders," he writes, "often signalizes a victory comparable with the formation of an additional army division."[1]

Another limitation of the means to wage physical war is the enormous cost of nuclear and supersonic weapons. No longer is it possible for even medium sized nations to equip themselves with the full panoply of war, and even were they wealthy enough to do so, most could neither obtain the requisite raw materials with which to fashion nuclear weapons nor find the necessary uninhabited territory in which to test them.

These limitations have led to the strategical division of the world between two super-States, the United States of America and the Soviet Union, each possessed of an ideology which neither will abandon. As in the days of Abraham Lincoln, "a house divided against itself cannot stand." It "cannot endure half slave and half free . . . it will become all one thing or the other." Coexistence of incompatibles is the father of war.

In 1823, faced with the outcome of the Napoleonic wars, on the opening page of his essay on a comparison between the power of England and Russia, the Abbé de Pradt wrote these words: "Two flags are now raised at the two extremities of Europe; one over the land and the other over the sea"; and in his concluding pages he observed: "England and Russia are the two preponderant powers in Europe. . . . The political aim of England is to

[1] *Ibid.*, p. 233.

oppose whosoever would dominate the continent; she watches over the political liberties of Europe. Russia is this dominant power and through necessity the born enemy of the liberties of Europe."[1]

The Union Jack, the banner of the *Pax Britannica*, has now been furled, and to-day in its stead floats the Stars and Stripes to face the Hammer and Sickle. The supreme question set by the Second World War is: Which will be hauled down? Is the future to see a *Pax Americana* or a *Pax Tartarica*? We hazard to suggest that the answer will be found, not in the contending military strengths of the United States and the Soviet Union, but in their antagonistic political, social, economic and cultural systems. Which of the two is the more fitted to solve the crucial problem set to mankind by the Industrial Revolution – the status of man, his government and way of life in a fully mechanized world?

[1] *Parallèle de la puissance anglaise et russe, etc.*, pp. 1 and 168–9.